Who's Who
IN TWENTIETH-CENTURY WORLD POETRY

THE ROUTLEDGE WHO'S WHO SERIES

Accessible, authoritative and enlightening, these are the definitive biographical guides to a diverse range of subjects drawn from literature and the arts, history and politics, religion and mythology.

Who's Who in Ancient Egypt
Michael Rice

Who's Who in the Ancient Near East
Gwendolyn Leick

Who's Who in Christianity
Lavinia Cohn-Sherbok

Who's Who in Classical Mythology
Michael Grant and John Hazel

Who's Who in Contemporary Gay and Lesbian History
Edited by Robert Aldrich and Garry Wotherspoon

Who's Who in Contemporary Women's Writing
Edited by Jane Eldridge Miller

Who's Who in Contemporary World Theatre
Edited by Daniel Meyer-Dinkegräfe

Who's Who in Dickens
Donald Hawes

Who's Who in Europe 1450–1750
Henry Kamen

Who's Who in Gay and Lesbian History
Edited by Robert Aldrich and Garry Wotherspoon

Who's Who in the Greek World
John Hazel

Who's Who in Jewish History
Joan Comay, new edition revised by Lavinia Cohn-Sherbok

Who's Who in Lesbian and Gay Writing
Gabriele Griffin

Who's Who in Military History
John Keegan and Andrew Wheatcroft

Who's Who in Modern History
Alan Palmer

Who's Who in Nazi Germany
Robert S. Wistrich

Who's Who in the New Testament
Ronald Brownrigg

Who's Who in Non-Classical Mythology
Egerton Sykes, new edition revised by Alan Kendall

Who's Who in the Old Testament
Joan Comay

Who's Who in the Roman World
John Hazel

Who's Who in Russia since 1900
Martin McCauley

Who's Who in Shakespeare
Peter Quennell and Hamish Johnson

Who's Who of Twentieth-Century Novelists
Tim Woods

Who's Who in Twentieth-Century World Poetry
Edited by Mark Willhardt and Alan Michael Parker

Who's Who in Twentieth-Century Warfare
Spencer Tucker

Who's Who in World War One
John Bourne

Who's Who in World War Two
Edited by John Keegan

Who's Who IN TWENTIETH-CENTURY WORLD POETRY

Edited by Mark Willhardt
and Alan Michael Parker
(North American editor)

with a Foreword by
Andrew Motion, Poet Laureate

ROUTLEDGE
Taylor & Francis Group

London and New York

First published 2000
by Routledge
11 New Fetter Lane, London EC4P 4EE

Simultaneously published in the USA and Canada
by Routledge
29 West 35th Street, New York, NY 10001

Second edition first published 2002

Routledge is an imprint of the Taylor & Francis Group

Typeset in Sabon by RefineCatch Limited, Bungay, Suffolk
Printed and bound in Great Britain by
TJ International Ltd, Padstow, Cornwall

British Library Cataloguing in Publication Data
A catalogue record for this book is available from the British Library

Library of Congress Cataloging in Publication Data
A catalog record for this book has been requested

ISBN 0–415–16356–0

Contents

List of contributors vi
Foreword by Andrew Motion, Poet Laureate ix
Editors' Preface xi

WHO'S WHO IN TWENTIETH-CENTURY WORLD POETRY 1

Contributors

Barbara Becker, University of St Thomas [BB]

Nicholas Birns, The New School [NB]

Yomi Braester, University of Washington [YB]

R. Victor Brand, Davidson College [VB]

Bethany R. Brown, University of St Thomas [BRB]

Brian C. Brown, University of St Thomas [BCB]

Alan S. Bruflat, Wayne State College [AB]

Avery D. Cahill, University of Wisconsin, Madison [AC]

Kevin Anthony Carollo, University of Illinois [KAC]

Robin Clarke, Pennsylvania State University-Erie, The Behrend College [RC]

David Clippinger, Pennsylvania State University, Beaver [DC]

Debbie Comerford, University of South Queensland [DCO]

Katherine Conley, Dartmouth College [KC]

Constantine Contogenis, Columbia University [CC]

Robin Davidson, University of Houston [RD]

Fleur Diamond, Monash University [FD]

Alison Dolph, Davidson College [AD]

Heather Elko, Florida Institute of Technology [HE]

Andrew Epstein, Columbia University [AE]

Heid E. Erdrich, University of St Thomas [HEE]

Georgiana Fornoaga, University of California, Los Angeles [GF]

Margaret Franklin, University of Houston [MF]

Lilias Fraser, St Andrews University [LKMF]

Laura Fyfe, University of Illinois [LF]

Susan M.E. Glen, George Mason University [SG]

Charles E. Gribble, Ohio State University [CG]

Lyubomira Parpulova Gribble, Ohio State University [LPG]

Waïl Hassan, Western Illinois University [WH]

Stephanie Mathilde Hilger, University of Illinois [SH]

Felicity Holland, University of New England [FH]

Steven Jaron, Columbia University [SJ]

Dubravka Juraga, University of Arkansas [DJ]

Leisa Kauffmann, University of Illinois [LKA]

Monique Maier Keffer, University of Wisconsin, Milwaukee [MK]

Bert-Jaap Koops, Tilburg University [BK]

LeeAnn Kriegh, Hamline University [LK]

Lee Yu-Lin, University of Georgia [LY]

Johann K. Leida, University of St Thomas [JL]

Michael F. Leruth, College of William and Mary [ML]

Li Guicang, Indiana University of Pennsylvania [LG]

Mark L. Lilleleht, University of Wisconsin, Madison [MLL]

Silvia L. Lopez, Carleton College [SL]

Andrew Lynch, University of Western Australia [AL]

David McCooey, Deakin University [DM]

Andrew McCord, Alef books [AM]

Lyn McCreddon, Deakin University [LM]

Kristi McKim, Emory University [KM]

Eric Matas, University of St Thomas [EM]

Joe Moffat, West Virginia University [JM]

Rosina Neginsky, University of Wisconsin, Oshkosh [RN]

Maria Negroni, Universidad de Buenos Aires [MN]

Nguyen Ngoc Bich, Radio Free Asia [BN]

Matthew T. Otremba, University of Houston [MO]

Seija Paddon, Centennial College [SP]

Anne Pender, Australian National University [AP]

Robert Phillips, University of Houston [RP]

Mathew W. Piasecki, University of St Thomas [MP]

Cintra Pollack, Davidson College [CP]

Esther Raizen, University of Texas at Austin [ER]

Robert Ross, University of Texas at Austin [RR]

Benjamin David Saunders, University of Oregon [BS]

Ronald R. St Onge, College of William and Mary [RSO]

Martine Sauret, Western Michigan University [MS]

Jennifer Solberg, University of St Thomas [JS]

Sarah E. Spencer, University of St Thomas [SS]

Kristina A. Stanley, University of Illinois [KS]

Robin L. Stewart, University of Wisconsin, Madison [RS]

Ingo R. Stoehr, *Dimension*[2] (editor), Kilgore College [IRS]

Jennifer Strauss, Monash University [JST]

Giuseppe Strazzeri, Mondadori Publishing House [GS]

James D. Stuntz, Davidson College [JDS]

George Syrimis, Harvard University [GSY]

Imre Szeman, McMaster University [IS]

Carol Tell, *Educational Leadership Magazine* [CT]

Mike Theune, University of Houston [MT]

Katrina Daly Thompson, University of Wisconsin, Madison [KT]

Jennifer Tonge, University of Wisconsin, Madison [JT]

Terri L. Topness, University of St Thomas [TT]

Thomas Vaessens, Institut Nederlands Universiteit Utrecht [TV]

Connie Voisine, University of Hartford [CV]

Valerie M. Wilhite, University of Illinois [VW]

Troy Williams, Davidson College [TW]

Foreword

Reference works such as *Who's Who in Twentieth-Century World Poetry* exist to provoke argument, as well as to offer panoramic views. Some entries will be questioned; some omissions will be lamented; some judgements will be doubted. But these responses only serve to endorse the premise of this book, which is to illustrate the extraordinary range and vitality of poetry written round the world during the last hundred years. From the satirical to the sensational, from the public to the personal, from the conservative to the experimental, from the softly spoken to the stentorian: every kind and category of poetry that one can imagine is included.

Turning the pages, it is difficult not to look for things-in-common, as well as for differences. Difficult, too, not to think that what holds everything together is the primitive appeal of poetry – its unique ability to connect with our deepest feelings. Many of the writers represented have lived some of their lives in academies of one kind or another. Many have seen their work discussed by critics and students. Many have themselves learned the language of exegesis and analysis. But what keeps their work alive is its contact with experience that is essentially human; what keeps drawing back their readers is the fact that it speaks to something fundamental.

To ponder this reciprocity in work emanating from any one country is stimulating enough. To consider its operation on a global scale is truly heartening. This book offers nothing less than proof of the spirit endlessly renewing itself, defining itself by a continuous effort of exploration, and pursuing its manifold kinds of truth with mingled awe, determination, and humility.

Andrew Motion

Editors' Preface

To compile a volume such as this may seem absurd; to do so successfully may be impossible. Yet the Routledge *Who's Who in Twentieth-Century World Poetry* can be seen as an argument for the finest period of invention, lyricism, and social engagement that poetry has known. There are certainly absurd moments in the poetic history encapsulated here, but there is also a generous complement of the sublime: for every Breton there is a Rich, for every 'Ern Malley' hoax there is a *La Jeune Parque*. Representative, if not inclusive, the volume presents what we hope will be a primer to world poetry during the twentieth century.

As editors, we have made our requirements for inclusion in the volume clear: we have selected poets whose national or international reputations have drawn readers, and kept readers coming back. This means that canonical poets are represented, but so are popular poets and less-established poets whose work has recently begun to garner praise. Of course, thousands of poets could easily have been included here, just as the definitions of both 'poet' and 'poetry' could easily have been expanded. However, for the purposes of this volume, we have consciously avoided the sort of loose definitions that might be applied, for instance, to songwriters; neither Bob Dylan nor the Mighty Sparrow is included here, but because they have attained significant, purely textual accomplishment, both Leonard Cohen and Linton Kwesi Johnson are. Though acknowledging the fundamental importance of music to poetry, we also assume that music and poetry are fundamentally different, and require fundamentally different Who's Whos.

This volume lists poets by their most common names and by the country most commonly associated with them. A poet's birth-country may have little to do with her or his written concerns; thus to identify Czeslaw Milosz as 'Lithuanian' simply because he was born there seemed a fundamental mistake, given his poetry's overwhelming importance in and to Poland.

Entry lengths were determined by following a poet's reputation: internationally recognized poets were given the longest entries, important national figures the medium entries, and young or more local poets the shortest. Cases can always be made that this poet or that should have been moved up or down; in fact, you may well be making such cases now, based on a cursory glance at the book. As editors and scholars, we are deeply pleased with the prospect of resistance to our efforts, for resistance presents one measure of the book's success: if those most engaged with poetry contribute to the conversations begun here then such a colloquy (one of our highest aspirations) can only further understanding of poetry itself.

If our research in crafting this book has shown us nothing else, it is that the Routledge *Who's Who in Twentieth-Century World Poetry* is needed. Though the volume presents but one way of many to organize and recommend that century's poets, it is nonetheless a necessary book, useful for poets, scholars, and general readers alike.

MW and AMP

Acknowledgments

No book this substantial comes without substantial debts of gratitude. First of all, I would like to thank my contributors, who have done excellent work and been patient in the face of their editors' questions and demands. Likewise, for helping to craft the volume and for their generous support of this project, I would like to thank Susan Lever, Ross Sutherland, Jacqueline Osherow, Felicia van Bork, and William Wadsworth.

Colleagues at the University of St. Thomas, Ohio Northern University, Pennsylvania State University, Erie-The Behrend College and Davidson College have been steadfast in their support of this work. Ann Douglas, Arnie Hoersten, Eric Kistler, and Nancy Mitchell, with their technical assistance, made our computer and organizational conundra manageable. The three interns on this project, Matthew Otremba, Bethany Brown, and Maureen Gallagher, deserve even greater thanks: Matthew's incisive understanding of poetry helped launch the lists and searches; Bethany's dedication to the work kept us rolling in the last year of the project; Maureen's intrepid research was always produced cheerfully. Each made this volume possible in a very real sense. And to our editors at Routledge, Kieron Corless and Roger Thorp, who gave all the time and support needed as this project grew in complexity and scale, I offer profound gratitude.

Finally, I wish to thank my wife, Ronda. Her good humor is bountiful and her patience endless. For three years, at every step, she helped me through this project – without her, more than anyone else, there would be no book.

MW (and AMP)

A

'Aql, Sa'id (Lebanon, b. 1912) 'Aql was born in Zahla, educated in Baalbek, and now lives in Beirut. As a child and young man he read the Bible, the Qur'an, Phoenician legends, and much classical and neoclassical Arabic poetry.

'Aql became the major proponent of Symbolism in Arabic poetry. Derived mainly from the French Symbolists, 'Aql's controversial ideas on poetry as a purely aesthetic activity gained popularity in the late 1930s and 1940s, but lost much of their influence after World War II. His experiment, however, was instrumental to the development of the avant-garde of the 1950s, which used Symbolist techniques while embracing social and political causes.

Selected works: *Al-Majdaliyya* (1937); *Qadmus* (1944); *Rindala* (1950); *More Beautiful than You? No!* (1960).

[WH]

al-Bayyati, Abdel-wahab (Iraq, b. 1926) Al-Bayyati graduated from the Teachers' Training College in Baghdad and taught Arabic literature. He was exiled because of his involvement in politics and his Communist beliefs. In 1972 he returned to Baghdad to be officially honored and appointed cultural attaché in Madrid.

Deep political commitment to Arab revolutions and nationalism marks al-Bayyati's poetry. A prominent and prolific avant-garde figure, in his early work he portrayed both village and city life without the romanticism of the earlier generation. His later work betrays the strong influence of Symbolism, Surrealism, Futurism, and ADUNIS.

Selected works: *The Complete Works* (1971).

[WH]

al-Jabal, Badawi (Muhammad Sulaiman al-Ahmad; Syria, 1907–81) Al-Jabal was educated and trained in Arabic classics and the Qur'an by his father, a learned Shiite Imam of the Alawites of northern Syria. Al-Jabal later went to Damascus, publishing his first collection in 1925, and entering politics.

Badawi al-Jabal's education and mystical background mark his poetry. Like other neoclassicists, he saw the poet as a spokesman for society who wrote poems of occasion and elegies on the death of public figures. Yet he was not simply an imitator who used stock images and expressions; his poetry has an immediacy which reveals a modern sensibility.

His poetry is collected in *Diwan Badawi al-Jabal* (1978).

[WH]

al-Jawahiri, Muhammad Mahdi (Iraq, 1900–97) Born in al-Najaf to an Iranian family, al-Jawahiri took Iraqi citizenship after World War II. As a member of the

Iraqi Communist Party, his revolutionary involvement in turbulent politics at the time brought him both persecution by and honors from successive governments. Profoundly influenced by classical Arabic poetry, he shared much with other neoclassicists, but was among the few whose mastery of the tradition reinforced their originality. The rhythmic power, intensity, and emotional force of his poetry were influential on younger poets who used those qualities to break away from the classical form.

Selected works: *Diwan al-Jawahiri* (*Collected Works*, 1949, 1950, 1953); *Mail from Exile* (1965); *Return Mail* (1969); *To Sleeplessness* (1971).

[WH]

al-Mala'ika, Nazik (Iraq, b. 1923) Born in Baghdad, al-Mala'ika attended the Teachers' Training College there before going to Princeton University to study English. She has taught at various universities in Iraq and Kuwait.

Initially writing traditional poetry in the Romantic vein, al-Mala'ika became a major advocate, as a poet and critic, of the free verse movement in Arabic poetry in the late 1940s and 1950s. Technical and thematic innovation mark her poetry, which has increasingly displayed a religious sensibility since the 1970s.

Selected works: *Splinters and Ashes* (1949); *The Bottom of the Wave* (1957); *The Moon Tree* (1968); *Issues in Contemporary Poetry* (1962).

[WH]

al-Sayyab, Badr Shakir (Iraq, 1926–64) Al-Sayyab graduated from the Teachers' Training College in Baghdad. A Marxist with a deep commitment to Arab nationalism, his political activities brought him persecution and exile. He died young of a degenerative nervous disorder.

A pioneer of the free verse movement, al-Sayyab's first collection, *Withered Flowers* (1947), coincided with the publication of NAZIK AL-MALA'IKA's first free verse poems. Both poets initiated a revolution in modern Arabic poetry, which until then used the traditional two-hemistich line and monorhymed verse form. Although he started as a Romantic, al-Sayyab broke those conventions under the influence mainly of ELIOT and LORCA. In the preface to his second collection, *Myths* (1950), al-Sayyab points out the main features of the new poetry, such as irregular meter, unconventional rhythms, and free association of ideas, although as a Marxist he stresses the sociopolitical function of poetry. Such commitment becomes the overriding concern of his gloomy third collection, *The Rain Song* (1960), in which the public and the private merge. He also made heavy use of symbolism and mythology, especially the Tammuz myth of death and rebirth, as a vehicle for veiled political satire. With his death approaching, al-Sayyab's later poetry became increasingly introspective and preoccupied with mortality.

Selected works: *The Sunken Temple* (1962); *Iqbal* (1965).

[WH]

al-Shabbi, Abul-qasim (Tunisia, 1909–34) Al-Shabbi received a traditional education at home, then at al-Zaytuna Mosque and the Law College in Tunis.

Indisputably Tunisia's major poet of the twentieth century, he was influenced by the Mahjar school and by French Romantics, whom he read in Arabic translation. In a lecture on 'Arab Poetic Imagination' delivered when he was twenty, he rejected all of Arabic literature, mythology, and poetic conventions and themes, an act that made him the most extreme of the Arab Romantics. Although in his poetry he retained the classical form, he jettisoned its emphasis on intellect, instead championing feelings and imagination. His poetry displays an overall tension between classical and Romantic sensibilities.

Selected works: *Songs of Life* (1955); *The Arab Poetic Imagination* (1929).

[WH]

al-Tijani, Yusuf Bashir (Sudan, 1912–37) Al-Tijani came from a religious, Sufi family. He studied at a traditional Qur'anic school and later read classical literature at a college in Umdurman.

Al-Tijani was the leading Sudanese Romantic in the 1930s. Blending classical style and diction with Romantic sensibility and Sufi pantheism, his sometimes uneven poetry reflects the diverse forces at work in Sudanese culture at the time and adds a fresh, mystical dimension to Arabic Romanticism. Metaphysical depth and complexity of vision, in volumes such as *Illumination* (1942), mark his treatment of love, beauty, time, religious doubt, and faith. His untimely death of tuberculosis halted the development of a great poet.

[WH]

Abdel-Sabur, Salah (Egypt, 1931–81) Abdel-Sabur graduated from the College of Arts at Cairo University in 1951. He worked in journalism and held a number of important government positions, including a post as cultural attaché in India (1977–8), and headed the General Egyptian Book Organization (1978–81).

A pioneer of free verse in Egypt, Abdel-Sabur adopted a subdued tone, simple diction, and an unadorned style that was close to ordinary prose. He believed that, unlike the stylized, oratorical, monorhymed classical poem, free verse better suited the spirit of the modern age. His poetry also abandoned the escapism of the Romantics in the 1920s–1940s. A moral and spiritual sense pervades his poetry and poetic dramas as they are committed to advocating freedom, justice, and truth. His early poetry blends uncompromising social critique with a humane, almost mystical, vision of human imperfection. This gives way, however, to a growing sense of disappointment and despair, and his verse plays, beginning with *Night Traveler* (1969), reveal a strong influence of the Theater of the Absurd.

Selected works: *People in My Country* (1957); *I Say to You* (1961); *Dreams of the Old Knight* (1964); *Meditations on a Wounded Age* (1969); *Layla and the Madman* (1969); *The Princess Waits* (1970); *After the King Dies* (1973); *Sailing into Memory* (1979).

[WH]

Abse, Dannie (Wales, b. 1923) Abse was born into a Jewish household in Cardiff. He studied medicine at Cardiff, King's College, London, and Westminster Hospital, followed by many years practicing in a London chest clinic. Writing even during his studies, Abse published *After Every Green Thing* in 1948, the first of his eleven volumes of poetry, including a *Collected Poems* (1977). His poems frequently draw upon his Welsh-Jewish background for their inspiration, as does his first novel, *Ash on a Young Man's Sleeve* (1954). He has served as the head of the Poetry Society, and has edited several anthologies, the most recent being *Twentieth Century Anglo-Welsh Poetry* (1997). In addition to poems and novels, Abse has published several plays, autobiographical writings, short stories, and other occasional works.

[BS]

Abu-Madi, Ilya (Lebanon, 1890–1957) Born in Lebanon, Abu-Madi grew up in Egypt and emigrated to the United States in 1911. He was the most famous of the Mahjar (immigrant) poets who adopted many attitudes of the European Romantics and American Transcendentalists. In 1920 in New York Abu-Madi co-founded the Arabic literary society, Al-Rabita al-Qalamiyya, and with other Mahjar poets, helped launch the Romantic movement of the 1920s–1940s in Arabic poetry.

Abu-Madi's first collection, *Remember the Past* (1911), is rooted in the classical tradition which had formed his poetic education. By the time his second collection appeared in 1919, he had come under the influence of NU'AIMA and GIBRAN, and undergone a change in poetic sensibility. However, his early classical formation remained important, often blending harmoniously with his acquired tastes, and was increasingly dominant again in his later poetry. The idealization of nature and love in his Romantic phase also gave way later on to an ascetic detachment from the world and its ills. His popularity in the Arab world was due to his skill in composing epigrams and wise sayings in the manner of classical poets, but also to his ability as a Romantic to create symbols out of everyday objects and experiences.

Selected works: *Diwan Ilya Abu-Madi* (*Collected Works*, 1919); *The Streams* (1927); *Gold and Dust* (1960).

[WH]

Achterberg, Gerrit (The Netherlands, 1905-62) Outstanding for his originality and for his poetry's unity-in-variety, Achterberg is one of the most important Dutch poets of the century. Born in Langbroek to a family of farmers and trained as a teacher, he occupied several posts as a schoolmaster and as a civil servant. In his early period, his writing was influenced by the verse of J.H. Leopold and A. Roland Holst, yet asserted a distinct voice of his own. His first volume, *Afvaart* (*Departure*, 1931) was followed by a period of mental turmoil in which he wrote many poems but published only a few.

Having been hospitalized in psychiatric clinics for brief periods in 1932 and 1933, he eventually landed a position as civil servant at the Agriculture Crisis Organization in Utrecht. Then in December, 1937 an act occurred that, as he saw it, was fated to happen: he killed his landlady and wounded her sixteen-year-old daughter. At trial he was found unsound and discharged, being sentenced to detention or supervision at Her Majesty's discretion. In the following years, he was held in several mental homes, where he devoted himself to writing poetry. His bitter experience in mental hospitals is expressed in the posthumously published volume *Blauwzuur* (*Prussic Acid*, 1969). He was allowed more freedom after 1943; he married Cathrien van Baak in 1946. His period of supervision was abolished officially in 1955. By then, he was widely regarded as the major Dutch poet then living. Only a few years later, in January 1962, he died of a heart attack.

During his legal supervision, he published prolifically. As his life was marked by mental problems and the 1937 tragedy, so his poetry is marked by a central theme: an 'I' who endeavors to reach a 'Thou' (or 'You') by means of the poem. Much of the discussion about Achterberg's poetry centers on the question of the degree to which this central theme reflects his life. The 'Thou' in many poems seems to be a dead beloved, whom the 'I' wants to resurrect through the magic of his poetry. But the central theme is more complex: in various poems, the 'Thou' can be interpreted as Christ or as poetry itself. Moreover, the theme of a beloved the poetic 'I' has killed occurs long before 1937.

Achterberg draws from an infinite well of metaphors to express his theme. Most strikingly, he uses contexts usually considered unpoetic, such as in the *Ballade van de gasfitter* (*Ballad of the Gas Fitter*, 1953) and in the volumes *Limiet*, *Energie*, and *Existentie* (*Limit*, *Energy*, *Existence*, all 1946), which are steeped in physics, chemistry, and mathematics. Religion also plays an important part, as in *En Jezus schreef in 't zand* (*And Jesus Wrote in the Sand*, 1947).

Many of these poems have a magic quality, through the force of the poem that seeks to reunite 'I' and 'Thou', usually unsuccessfully, but sometimes succeeding, e.g., through the chemical process of *Osmose* (*Osmosis*, 1941). For Achterberg, there was no absolute borderline between poetry and life, between waking and dreaming, or between life and death. This magic has remained popular with readers; his *Verzamelde Gedichten* (*Collected Poems*, 1963) has sold over 60,000 copies.

[BK]

Adcock, Fleur (England, b. 1934) Even

though she was born in New Zealand, Adcock spent much of her childhood in Britain. In 1947, she returned to New Zealand and later earned an M.A. in Classics at the Victoria University of Wellington. In 1963 she emigrated to Britain, worked as a librarian, and became a freelance writer in 1979.

Adcock's poetry is imbued with an awareness of her ambivalent status as an émigré. Her poems present sharp physical and psychological observations, which have sometimes been read as depicting human relationships in an unsentimental manner. This detachment also controls her precise poetic style.

Selected works: *The Eye of the Hurricane* (1964); *Tigers* (1967); *High Tide in the Garden* (1971); *The Inner Harbour* (1979); *The Incident Book* (1986); *Time-Zones* (1991).

[SH]

Adunis (Ali Ahmad Sa'id; Syria, b. 1930) Born in a small village in the Alawite mountains of northern Syria, Adunis attended school at Tartus, then studied philosophy at the Syrian University, graduating in 1954. His involvement with the Syrian Nationalist Party led to his imprisonment. In 1956 he moved to Beirut where he attended St Joseph's University, earning a doctorate and eventually Lebanese citizenship. He has lived in Paris since 1986.

Adunis is the most distinguished champion of New Poetry and a prolific poet and critic. His early pronouncements on poetry reveal the influence of Baudelaire, Rimbaud, André Malraux, and RENÉ CHAR, whom he enlisted in support of his revolutionary conception of poetry as 'vision' and as 'a rebellion against the forms and methods of old poetry'. The New Poetry, he argued, was a 'metaphysics of human existence' and an attempt to revolutionize society by creating a new language. This was a rejection of both the classical and neoclassical stance of the poet as a public spokesman using ready-made forms, and of the Romantic conception of poetry as an exploration of inner life. Yet while relying on Symbolist techniques of defamiliarization and obscurity, it is a committed poetry seeking social and political regeneration.

Adunis' earliest poetry of direct social protest, written in the classical form, quickly gave way to Symbolist verse employed in satirizing Arab society. In the collection *Songs of Mihyar the Damascene* (1961), he evokes a medieval Arab poet who takes on the mythological attributes of Noah, Adonis, Shaddad Ibn 'Ad, and Odysseus. Mihyar travels through time and regions of consciousness exploring the meaning of good and evil. Though always optimistically prophesying regeneration after defeat and death, Adunis's poetry of the late 1960s and early 1970s bitterly laments Arab weakness, satirizes capitalism and American foreign policy in the Middle East and Vietnam, and asserts the poet's freedom from all rules. Adunis's mysticism grows in depth in his successive collections, his use of prose poetry becomes more frequent, and his language more obscure. In *Theater and Mirrors* (1968), poetry is mixed with dramatic scenes; in *The Book of Siege* (1985), with prose poetry and discursive prose; and, in *A Celebration of Mysterious, Obvious Things* (1988), with all that plus aphorisms.

Selected works: *The Book of Changes and Migration to the Regions of Day and Night* (1965); *A Time between Ashes and Roses* (1970); *A Tomb for New York* (1971); *Singular in the Form of Plural* (1974); *Further Songs of Mihyar the Damascene* (1975); *The Book of Five Poems* (1980); *Introduction to Arab Poetics* (1985, in French).

[WH]

Ady, Endre (Hungary, 1877–1919) The father of modern Hungarian poetry, Ady was born in Erdmindszent and studied law, before giving it up to become a journalist. Although he published two earlier volumes, it was his *Új versek* (*New Poems*, 1906) which took the Hungarian literary world by surprise; in its repetitions and combinative symbolism, it marked a new venture in Hungarian poetry. A contributor to the pre-eminent journal *Nyugat* (see JÓZSEF and ILLYÉS), Ady's poems ranged from the bitter, as in *Vér és arany* (*Blood and Gold*, 1908), to the spiritual, expressing agape and concupiscence alike in *Ifal Az Illés szekerén* (*In the Chariot of Elijah*, 1909) and *Szeretném, ha szeretnének*(*I Wish to Be Loved*, 1910). Although not a writer of propagandistic verse, Ady crafted poetry which struck a chord in his nation; alongside his poetic innovations, this helped carry Hungary into the twentieth century.

[MW]

Æ (George William Russell; Ireland, 1867–1935) A poet, painter, mystic, and socialist, Æ is more distinguished for his influence on other poets than for his own poetry. With such writers as WILLIAM BUTLER YEATS, Lady Gregory, and OLIVER ST JOHN GOGARTY, Æ played a central role in the Irish Literary Renaissance.

After his birth in Lurgan, County Armagh, Northern Ireland, Æ's family moved in 1878 to Dublin, where Æ pursued an early career in painting. In art class he became acquainted with W.B. Yeats and went on to become a mainstay of Dublin's growing intellectual and artistic community. His pseudonym was the shortened pen name of 'Aeon', which he changed to Æ because he thought it less likely to be misspelled.

Æ's interest in spirituality led him to support the establishment of the Dublin Lodge of the Theosophical Society in 1891 and, a few years later, the Hermetic Society. His passion for the occult found expression in many volumes of his poetry: *Homeward: Songs by the Way* (1894); *The Earth Breath* (1897); and *The Divine and Other Poems* (1904). Although Yeats championed his work, much of Æ's early poetry is considered thematically and technically immature.

Along with a commitment to spirituality, Æ was also an ardent socialist, devoted especially to the agricultural cooperative movement. In 1905 he became editor of the *Irish Homestead*, an independent weekly, and in 1923–30 was editor of *The Irish Statesman*.

Although his later works, including *Collected Poems* (1913), *Voices of the Stones* (1925), *Vale and Other Poems* (1931), and *Selected Poems* (1935), received critical acclaim, Æ never achieved the stature he felt he deserved. He continued to encourage, throughout his life, writers such as James Stephens, PADRAIC COLUM, and PATRICK KAVANAGH.

[CT]

Agard, John (Guyana, b. 1949) Agard was born in Guyana and moved to England in 1977. During the 1980s, as a Commonwealth Institute speaker he traveled to almost 2,000 schools educating the public about Caribbean poetry and culture. In 1993 Agard became the first Writer-in-Residence at London's South Bank Centre, a position resulting not only from his poetry but also from his publication of children's literature and plays and recognizing his positions as storyteller, performer, and anthologist. He now lives with poet GRACE NICHOLS and their family in Sussex.

Offering the reader a uniquely Caribbean voice – akin in its performative quality to the works of LINTON KWESI JOHNSON, BENJAMIN ZEPHANIAH, and MERLE COLLINS – Agard's poetry speaks with lively language, exploring the sensuality and pleasure around and within the love between man and woman.

Selected works: *Man to Pan* (1982), winner of the Casa de las Americas Prize; *Mangoes and Bullets: Selected Poems 1972–84* (1985); *Lovelines for a Goat-Born Lady* (1990); *From the Devil's Pulpit* (1997).

[MK]

Agustini, Delmira (Uruguay, 1886–1914) Born into a wealthy family which supported her writing, Agustini became famous for her extremely sensual poetry in which opposites such as love and death, pain and pleasure become confused. Rich with typically Modernist symbolism, such as the exoticized orient, animals, the night, vases, and the abyss, Agustini's verse also tends toward the Romantic with its use of a highly personal voice and its openly sexual content. Agustini was tragically killed by her husband, whom she was in the process of divorcing.

Selected works: *El libro blanco* (*The White Book*, 1907); *Cantos de la mañana* (*Morning Songs*, 1910); *Los cálices vacíos* (*Empty Chalices*, 1913); *El rosario del Eros* (*Eros' Rosary*, 1924).

[LK]

Ai (Florence Anthony; United States, b. 1947) Born in Albany, Texas of Japanese, Choctaw, Black, and Irish descent, Ai was raised and educated as a Catholic before attending the University of Arizona and the University of California, Irvine.

Many of Ai's poems are dramatic monologues. Though some of her characters are famous, like Trotsky and Marilyn Monroe, most are common people with lyrically large concerns, who manage to break out of their social roles for the moment of the poem. The poems, which began as brief, intensely rendered pieces of experience, have steadily grown longer and broader in scope. Though sometimes criticized for the sameness of her verse, her evenness is the key to her universal appeal.

Selected works: *Cruelty* (1973); *The Killing Floor* (1979); *Sin* (1986); *Fate* (1991); *Greed* (1993); *Vice* (1999).

[JT/RP]

Ai Qing (also known as Jiang Haicheng; China, 1910–96) A native of Jinhua, Zhejiang, the son of a wealthy landowner, Ai Qing displayed his talent in poetry at an early age and has maintained a great interest and literacy in Western languages all his life. Ai went to France to study in 1928 and was influenced by both French poetry and Western democratic ideas. Upon his return from France in 1932, Ai was imprisoned for three years for these 'dangerous ideas'. A year after his release from prison, he published his first collection of poetry, *Dayanhe* (*The Dayan River*). The book was warmly received and widely circulated, and established his position as one of the leading modern Chinese poets. His great concern and unbridled sympathy for the underprivileged, and his artistic articulation of the tragic life of the poor, turned out to be similar to the literary teachings of Mao. This helped him secure a job as an editor of *The People's Literature* from 1949 to 1953, an official literary magazine serving as a guiding voice for the development of literature in the People's Republic of China.

A leading exponent of free verse, and an advocate of free expression, Ai was denounced as a rightist in 1957, and as a result of his criticism of the Party, was sent to work in the labor camps in Xinjiang and Helongjiang. The charge was removed in 1961; nevertheless, Ai did not begin writing again until 1978. The aftermath of the charge remained with him: his poignant criticism of social injustice was gone. Though a socially oriented poet all his life, his later works were characterized by deliberate avoidance of serious social issues. Because of this, the majority of his later poems have been ignored.

[LG]

Akhmadulina, Bella (Russia, b. 1937) Of Tatar and Italian ancestry, Izabella Akhatovna Akhmadulina was born and raised in Moscow at the height of Stalin's reign. Her first work, *Family Tree*, was published in 1955, and her first collection, *The String*, in 1962. In 1960 Akhmadulina graduated from the Gorky Literary Institute. In the 1950s, she was married to poet YEVGENY YEVTUSHENKO, and later to prose writer Yury Nagibin. A lyric poet, Akhmadulina frequently addresses life in a large city and the status of women and motherhood in the Soviet state. The mundane world and inanimate objects are given fresh voices and emotions in Akhmadulina's work. Akhmadulina has been rarely published since *The Chills* (1968), though she also published *Dreams of Georgia* in 1977.

[TW]

Akhmatova, Anna Andreevna (Anna Gorenko; Russia, 1889–1965) Akhmatova spent her childhood near St Petersburg, in Tsarskoe Selo, studying there, and in Sebastopol and Kiev. She entered law school at Kiev's College for Women in 1908, but withdrew in 1910 to study literature in St Petersburg. That spring she also married the poet NIKOLAI GUMILIEV, whom she had first met in 1903; they spent their honeymoon in the artistic hub of Paris.

Upon their return to Russia, Gumiliev founded the Guild of Poets, with Akhmatova as its secretary. The Guild was an outlet for Acmeism, which believed in clarity and precision, in direct expression through images, not intimations through symbols. By 1912, Akhmatova was coming into her own, poetically. Her first volume, *Vecher* (*Evening*, 1912), focused on love, but her second book, *Chyotki* (*Rosary*, 1914), which added elements of religion, brought her fame: one Soviet critic discussed her non-Social Realist ideas as those of a 'half-nun, half-whore'.

Between the publication of these two volumes, Akhmatova's personal life had changed radically. Her son Lev was born in the fall of 1912; she and Gumiliev divorced less than a year later.

Akhmatova's third volume, *Belaia Staia* (*White Flock*, 1917) addressed war's effect on human destiny and included her celebrated poem about World War I, 'In Memoriam, July 19, 1914'. After the October Revolution, she published a number of collections. *Podorozhnik* (*The Plantain*, 1921) discusses her refusal to emigrate, as many of her friends and artistic colleagues did when they established themselves in Paris after the revolution. Poems in *Anno Domini MCMXXI* (1921) addressed the Soviet terror and Gumiliev's execution by the Soviet Secret Service (CHEKA). One Marxist critic denounced her poetry as not suitable for the new Soviet society. As a result, *Anno Domini MCMXXI* was Akhmatova's last volume for nearly twenty years.

Iz shesti knig (*From Six Books*, 1940) collects the poems written in 1921–40, and shows that Akhmatova's verse was still charged: a few months after its publication the book was withdrawn from sale and from libraries. When she returned to Leningrad after World War II, her poetry once again was lambasted, this time by the Central Committee of the Communist Party, and she was expelled from the Union of Soviet Writers. In 1950, as an attempt to save her son, Lev, arrested and exiled to Siberia in 1949, Akhmatova published a number of poems eulogizing Stalin and Soviet Communism. The spirit of these poems is completely different from the universal beauty of her lyrical cycle 'Rekviem' ('Requiem'), written between 1935 and 1940, and occasioned by her pain over an earlier arrest of her son in 1937.

After Stalin's death, Akhmatova was rehabilitated, publishing some lyrics in 1958 and the poem *Beg vremeni* (*The Course of Time*) in 1965. Yet the pace of rehabilitation was slow: her greatest (and longest) philosophic meditation on her life and poetry, 'Poema bez geroia' ('Poem Without a Hero'), was not published in the Soviet Union until 1976. By then her international standing was firm, and she had received the Etna-Taormina Prize (Italy, 1964) and an honorary doctorate from Oxford (1965). Her multi-volume *Complete Works* appeared in 1986 and 1990.

With her images of 'beautiful clarity' and powerful yet everyday phrasing, Akhmatova secured herself a position as one of twentieth-century Russia's greatest poets.

[RN]

Alberti, Rafael (Spain, b. 1902) This member of the Generation of 1927 was born on the southern coast of Spain near Cádiz. (The Generation of 1927 lauded the Baroque poet Luis de Góngora and was also influenced by Ortega y Gasset's *The Dehumanization of Art*. As a result, these poets did not view aesthetic ideals as dependent upon ordinary reality, but instead sought to create artistic worlds that were more profound and real than the world around them. Styles ranged from GUILLEN's Symbolism to LORCA and ALEIXANDRE's Surrealism.) Alberti's skillful use of color and visual imagery in his poetry comes from his youthful love of painting. His family moved to Madrid in 1917, and Alberti began publishing poetry in the early 1920s. His first period, characterized by *A Sailor on Land* (1924), is of childhood remembrances by the sea.

However, Alberti soon adopted the vanguardist tendencies of his contemporaries; *On Angels* (1929) approaches the Surrealist mode, but with moral and social undertones. A Communist, Alberti emigrated after the Civil War but continued to write and produced several volumes of poetry. He returned to Spain in 1977.

Selected works: *Quicklime and Song* (1927); *Sermons and Sojourns* (1929–30); *Between Sword and Carnation* (1941); *Homage to Painting* (1948); *Returns of the Distant and Living*(1952).

[AB]

Albiston, Jordie (Australia, b. 1961) Albiston completed her Ph.D. in literature in 1995. Her first poetry collection, *Nervous Arcs* (1995) was awarded first prize in the Mary Gilmore Award, and second prize in the Anne Elder Award, as well as being shortlisted for the New South Wales Premier's Kenneth Slessor Prize. Albiston's second collection, *Botany Bay Document: A Poetic History of the Women of Botany Bay* (1996), is a poetic recreation of the life of female convicts in Botany Bay and Port Jackson which utilizes historical sources such as newspapers, ship log books, maps, and diaries. Her third collection, *The Hanging of Jean Lee* (1998), gives voice to the last woman hanged in Australia. These latter collections have an intellectual and educational focus, while simultaneously reconfiguring the male domain of the traditional Australian ballad and reconfiguring Australian history to give voice to 'herstory'.

[DCO]

Aldington, Richard (England, 1892–1962) Richard Edward Godfree Aldington was educated at Dover College and University College London. In 1914–17, he edited *The Egoist* with his then wife, fellow Imagist HILDA DOOLITTLE (H.D.), whom he had met in 1911 and married two years later. Aldington's first book of poetry, *Images Old and New* (1915), consists of Imagist poetry; as such, simplicity and brevity characterize the volume's work. Although *A Fool i' the Forest* (1925) displays the influence of T.S. ELIOT, it is arguably Aldington's finest poetry, displaying a more narrative style than his previous verse.

Despite his published poetry, Aldington's most popular works were novels, particularly *Death of a Hero* (1929); biographies, such as his life of D.H. LAWRENCE, *Portrait of a Genius, But . . .* (1950); and translations.

Selected works: *War and Love* (1918); *Images of War* (1919); *Images of Desire* (1920); *Exile and Other Poems* (1923); *Collected Poems* (1928).

[MK]

Alečković, Mira (Yugoslavia, b. 1921) Recipient of many Yugoslav literary awards, the well-known poet, cultural and political activist Alečković was born in Novi Sad, Vojvodina. She studied Slavic and comparative literature in Belgrade and in Paris at the Sorbonne. A pre-war Communist, during World War II she actively fought in the Yugoslav resistance movement. She has founded and edited numerous Yugoslav journals and magazines. Though still writing, her focus has shifted from the literary to the political.

Alečković's poems are characterized by openness and immediacy; they often address the possibility of love and happiness in an everyday context. Her poems are written from an overtly feminine perspective. Many are nostalgic laments for the lost innocence of childhood. Often, her poems are permeated with reminiscences of war and its horrors.

Selected works: *Podzemni heroji* (*Underground Heroes*, 1947); *Tri proleća* (*Three Springs*, 1949); *Ljubavi je malo* (*There Is Not Enough Love*, 1959); *Da život bude ljubav* (*Let Life be Love*, 1970); *Zatečena u ljubavi* (*Caught in Love*, 1981).

[DJ]

Alegria, Claribel (El Salvador, b. 1924) Although born in Nicaragua, Alegria is considered a poet of the Salvadoran canon since she spent all her formative years in El Salvador and considers it her native home. With her husband Darwin J. Flakoll, Alegria introduced testimonials about the political events of El Salvador at a time when few dared to tell of the country's atrocious past. Their book *Ashes of Izalco* (1966),which tells the story of the massacre of thousands of peasants during the insurgency uprising of 1932, catapulted them into the international limelight.

Alegria's poetic work is vast and ranges from the early experiential poetry of her youth to the more political poetry of the 1980s. Her introspective yet politically charged volume *Sobrevivo* (*I Survive*, 1978) won the prestigious Casa de las Americas Prize. In her later years, and especially after the death of her husband and translator, Alegria has returned to an intimate poetry that speaks of love, life, and loss. Her enormous influence on the younger generations has guaranteed her a place in the canon of Salvadoran writers.

Selected works: *Anillo de silencio* (*Ring of Silence*, 1948); *Acuario* (*Aquarium*, 1955); *Huésped de mi tiempo* (*Guest of My Time*, 1961); *Aprendizaje* (*Apprenticeship*, 1970); *Flores del volcano* (*Flowers from a Volcano*, 1982); *Fuga de canto grande* (*Fugue to Canto Grande*, 1992); *Umbrales* (*Thresholds: Poems*, 1997).

[LK]

Aleixandre, Vicente (Spain, 1898–1984) Winner of the Nobel Prize for Literature in 1977, Aleixandre's work bridges the changing styles and themes of twentieth-century poetry. He was born in Seville but spent most of his life in Madrid. Although he belonged to the literary renaissance of the Generation of 1927 (see ALBERTI, GUILLÉN, HERNÁNDEZ and LORCA), his poor health often left him isolated. Nevertheless, he began publishing in the late 1920s with *Ambit* (1928), which was in the avant-garde style of the period. By 1932 he became firmly established as a leading poet of the generation and demonstrated his Surrealist tendencies with *Swords Like Lips* (1932). He was to continue on this path with *Destruction or Love* (1935), considered by many to be his master work.

At the close of the Civil War Aleixandre remained in Spain and influenced generations of poets. *Shadow of Paradise* (1944) treats the fall of humankind but places it in a more personal and social context by recalling the tragedy that befell the poet's homeland. This work heralds a change in Aleixandre's poetry toward social and human concerns, but symbol and metaphor continue to predominate. Love poetry is also important to this period and exhibits neo-Romantic tendencies. *History of the Heart* (1954) exemplifies this shift.

Aleixandre continued writing into the 1960s and 1970s, with *In a Vast Domain* (1962) and *Dialogue of Knowledge* (1974). Overall, Aleixandre had one of the fullest and most dynamic poetic careers of his generation.

[AB]

Allen, Paula Gunn (United States, b. 1939) Allen was born in Albuquerque, New Mexico, and she grew up near Laguna Pueblo, her tribal community. In her work she describes herself as 'a confluence' due to her mixed ancestry: her mother was Laguna Pueblo and Sioux Indian and her father was Lebanese-American.

Educated in Catholic schools, at Colorado Women's College, the University of New Mexico, and the University of Oregon (B.A., M.F.A.) she eventually earned her Ph.D. from the University of New Mexico in 1975. She is a professor of English at UCLA.

Allen has published seven volumes of poetry along with numerous works of criticism and one novel. Recognition of her critical work includes a National Endowment for the Arts fellowship and a Ford Foundation grant. She earned an American Book Award for editing the prose anthology *Spider Women's Granddaughters*.

Her poems find balance between the land-centered world of Native Americans and the material concerns of contemporary culture. Deeply female and spiritual in subject, her poems speak of the continuance of Native cultures in the wake of colonization and despair.

Selected works: *The Blind Lion* (1974); *Coyote's Daylight Trip* (1978); *A Cannon between My Knees* (1981); *Star Child* (1981); *Shadow Country* (1982); *Wryds* (1987); *Skins and Bone: Collected Poems* (1988).

[HEE]

Allott, Kenneth (England, 1912–73) Born in Glamorgan in Wales, but having spent a great part of his childhood in Cumberland, Allott was educated at the Universities of Durham and Oxford. Most of his adult life was spent teaching, first in adult education, then at Liverpool University where he was an English literature professor until his death.

Best known for critical work on Matthew Arnold and as editor of the *Penguin Book of Contemporary Verse*, Allott also worked as the assistant editor for *New Verse* and as a journalist. His early poetry has been criticized for its wordplay and phrasing, which make it difficult to discern his meaning. Having rejected the Catholic tradition in which he was raised, Allott expressed in his poetry despair and hopelessness at the Holocaust and the human condition in general.

Selected works: *Poems* (1938); *The Ventriloquist's Doll* (1943); *Collected Poems* (1975).

[BRB]

Alterman, Nathan (Israel, 1910–70) Alterman was born in Warsaw, Poland, in 1910; his family emigrated to the Land of Israel in 1925, settling in Tel Aviv. Through his regular weekend column in the Labor daily *Davar*, he gave poignant expression in verse to the struggle for independence and the predicament of the Jewish people at the time. Alterman's poetry was characterized by strong emphasis on urban reality and the search for self, rich imagery, formal rhythm, and rhyme. A leader of the Modernist movement in Israel, Alterman eventually became the target of the younger generation of poets, who decried his excessive stylistic formality and reliance on imagery and alliteration, and what they viewed as emphasis on political themes at the expense of the highest standards of lyrical expression. Alterman was also known as a playwright and essayist, and translated works from Yiddish, Russian, French, and English. His first collection *Stars Outside* was published in 1938, and a series of his collected works were brought out posthumously in the 1970s.

[ER]

Amichai, Yehuda (Israel, b. 1924) Amichai, Israel's most widely known poet of the twentieth century, was born in Würzburg, Germany, in 1924. At the age of twelve he came to the Land of Israel and settled with his family in Jerusalem, where, like many of his contemporaries, he would later achieve greatness in a language which was not his mother tongue. During World War II he served in the Jewish Brigade of the British army, and later fought in the Israeli War of Independence. War would become a constant theme in his poems, as would the free human spirit, going through a roller-coaster of despair and love, pain and joy, yet prevailing in spite of all obstacles. This emphasis on simple, basic humanity, combined with sophisticated humor and sharpness of expression, gained Amichai wide recognition, but, more than that, the love and respect of readers of all ages in Israel and outside of it. More than any other poet of his generation, Amichai manages to depict in his poetry the multifaceted conflicts inherent in modern Israeli society, and the struggle of its young generations, each in its turn, for identity, acceptance, and genuine expression. His love poems are soft and flowing, his despair and irony deep. His words, which often allude to both traditional Jewish and European sources, are devoid of pathos and excessive alliteration. Amichai's first collection, *Now and in the Other Days*, was published in 1955. It was followed by many other poetry volumes, two novels, and a book of short stories. His style, which is highly dependent on the spoken language, has influenced both his contemporaries and the younger generation of Israeli poets. Amichai was awarded the Israel Prize in 1982 and is often mentioned in one breath with Nobel laureates. His poems, such as 'God Has Mercy on School Children', 'Of Three or Four in a Room', or 'Tourists', are frequently taught at academic institutions all over the world. Amichai's work has appeared in translation in over thirty languages.

Selected works: *Poems* (1969); *Songs of Jerusalem and Myself* (1973); *Amen* (1977); *Time* (1979); *Love Poems* (1981); *Great Tranquillity: Questions and Answers* (1983); *Poems of Jerusalem* (1988); *Even a Fist Was Once an Open Palm with Fingers* (1989); *The Selected Poetry of Yehuda Amichai: Newly Revised and Expanded Edition* (1996).

[ER]

Amis, Kingsley (England, 1922–95) Born the same year as his lifelong friend PHILIP LARKIN, whom he met at Oxford, Amis was a diverse author, publishing everything from literary novels to science and detective fiction as well as poetry.

Although also identified with the 'Angry Young Men', Amis is better understood as a member of The Movement, which favored realism and empiricism over the romanticism of the 1940s. These values shine through in Amis' poems, which bemoaned the use of fantasy as a shield against reality, although romantic undercurrents crept in as he explored emotionally charged subjects such as death and sex. One of his best pieces was 'In Memoriam W. R. A.' about his father.

Amis also typified Movement values in his teaching efforts at Swansea, Princeton, and later Cambridge, where, as in his writing and editing, he emphasized lucidity and discouraged literary and political snobbery.

Besides his teaching and poetic efforts, Amis was an acclaimed novelist; *Lucky Jim* (1954) won the 1955 Somerset Maugham Award, and *The Old Devils* (1986) won the Booker Prize. He was made Commander of the British Empire in 1981, and knighted in 1990, five years before his death from injuries sustained in a fall.

Selected works: *Bright November* (1947); *A Frame of Mind* (1953); *Kingsley Amis: No. 22. The Fantasy Poets* (1954); *A Case of Samples* (1956); *The Evans Country* (1962); *A Look around the Estate* (1967); *Collected Poems 1944–79* (1979).

[JL]

Ammons, A. R. (United States, 1926–2001) Born in Whiteville, North Carolina, Archie Randolph Ammons began work as an elementary school principal and then worked as an executive of a glassware company before ultimately becoming a creative writing professor in 1964 at Cornell University, where he still teaches. He published his first work of poetry, *Ommateum with Doxology*, in 1955, but his career did not gather momentum until 1964, with the publication of his second collection, *Expressions of Sea Level*. Although Ammons once imagined himself as merely an 'amateur' poet, he has had a prolific and highly successful career – publishing over twenty-six works of poetry and earning two National Book awards, for his *Collected Poems* (1973), and for his book-length poem *Garbage* (1993), which was also awarded the Bollingen Prize in 1994.

Ammons' poetry is often regarded as distinctively American in its diction and lineation, and he is frequently linked with the American Transcendentalists as well as with ROBERT FROST, WALLACE STEVENS, and WILLIAM CARLOS WILLIAMS. Explicitly concerned with the relationships between nature and humanity, Ammons' poems often strive to achieve a moment of pause and place in the world. These ambitions have prompted many to regard Ammons as one of the more imporant Eco-Poets or environmental poets. And Ammons' critically acclaimed poem *Garbage* is considered a testament to the processes of birth, death, and decay.

Ammons continues to be a significant and influential voice in the American poetic landscape, gaining the respect and praise of such prominent literary critics as Harold Bloom and Helen Vendler.

[DC]

Andreu, Blanca (Spain, b. 1959) Andreu was born in La Coruña (Galicia); her provincial background plays a prominent role in her early work. Her intimate style and personal themes place her with the *post-novísimos*, a group of poets who began writing in the 1970s, reacting to the depersonalized, stylized verse of the previous generation (see CARNERO), often by incorporating autobiographical elements into their verse. Andreu's poetry exhibits a wide range of themes and influences. Her first book, *About a Girl from the Provinces Who Went to Live in Chaguall* (1981) reaches beyond the autobiographical to explore the pressures of the adolescent environment. It also hints at escaping the chaos of reality through poetry, a theme further explored in *Staff of Babel* (1983), a collection of prose poems influenced by Rimbaud. *Elphistone* (1988) fashions a pirate-hero à la Espronceda, but with poetry's illuminating power as its theme.

[AB]

Angelou, Maya (United States, b. 1928) Pulitzer-nominee Angelou was born Marguerite Johnson in St Louis, Missouri. Following a stage career in which she toured internationally and appeared Off-Broadway, she worked in Egypt and Ghana. She was the Inaugural Poet for President Bill Clinton in 1993.

Angelou's poetry is strongly formal and performance-based, utilizing rhyme, meter, repetition, and refrain. Drawing on blues and gospel, her poems focus on the intricacies of human relationships. She enjoys considerable commercial popularity.

Selected works: *Just Give Me a Cool Drink of Water 'Fore I Die* (1971); *Oh Pray My Wings Are Gonna Fit Me Well* (1975); *And Still I Rise* (1978); *Shaker, Why Don't You Sing* (1983); *I Shall Not Be Moved* (1990).

[JT]

Angus, Marion (Scotland, 1866–1946) The daughter of a Church of Scotland minister, Angus was born in Aberdeenshire, living there for much of her life. After her sister suffered a breakdown in 1931, Angus moved around Scotland (including Helensburgh, where the relatively unknown AUDEN read her his poems) until her death in Arbroath. A member of Scottish PEN and an avid explorer of traditional Scots form and language, she nonetheless had little enthusiasm for Scottish nationalism and chose not to emulate MACDIARMID's approach to Scots. Now best known for the frequently anthologized 'Alas! Poor Queen', her poems often contrast women's age and youth in subtle treatments of loss and unexplained incident.

Selected works: *The Lilt and Other Poems* (1922); *The Tinker's Road* (1924); *The Singin' Lass* (1929); *Lost Country* (1937); *Selected Poems* (1950).

[LKMF]

Annensky, Innokenty Fyodorovich (Russia, 1856–1909) Born in Siberia, Annensky spent most of his life in St Petersburg. He graduated from university there in 1879 with a degree in comparative linguistics. Annensky taught Greek, Latin, and Russian literatures at secondary school. From 1896 to 1906 he was the headmaster of a *gymnasium* in Tsarskoe Selo. A literary critic, playwright, and translator of classical Greek, Annensky anonymously published *Tihie Pesni (Quiet Songs)*, his first book of poems, just five years before his death. His verse is in the psychological tradition of French Symbolism and avoids the mysticism common to Russian Symbolism. Annensky typically places images of decay or ennui on a background of vibrant landscapes. Annensky was neither a verbose nor a prolific writer. His posthumous collection, *Cypress Box* (1904) was a prototype for the Acmeists, lead by Annensky's former student, GUMILIEV. In his brief poetic career, Annensky encouraged the young Petersburg poets and was briefly affiliated with the journal *Apollon*.

[TW]

Apollinaire, Guillaume (Wilhelm Albert Wladimir Alexandre Apollinaris de Kostrowitzky; France, 1880–1918) Born illegitimate in Rome, de Kostrowitzky took the pseudonym Apollinaire in 1902. While working as a journalist in 1904 in Paris, he met some of the principal personalities of the avant-garde, including painters André Derain and Picasso, and poet MAX JACOB.

Though dismissed by Picasso, Apollinaire's articles on the development of Cubism, collected in *Les Peintres cubistes* (*The Cubist Painters*, 1913), were important pieces in support of Modernist art. He further supported the Futurist poets, including MAYAKOVSKY, the Fauve and Orphist painters, and was one of the first to champion African and Oceanic art. His neologism, 'Surrealism', came to designate ANDRÉ BRETON's literary and visual experimentation – and named a whole generation of artists as well.

Apollinaire's first important book of poetry, *Le Bestiaire ou Cortège d'Orphée* (*The Bestiary, or Procession of Orpheus*, 1911), illustrated with woodcuts by Raoul Dufy, was published the year he was arrested for stealing the Mona Lisa from the Louvre. He was imprisoned, but not before his innocence could be proved. The composer Francis Poulenc set his play, *Les Mamelles de Tirésias* (*The Teats of Tiresias*, 1903), to music in 1944. *Alcools* (*Spirits*, 1913) breaks with many of the conventions of lyric poetry of the time; in 'Le Pont Mirabeau' ('Mirabeau Bridge'), for example, the poet has done away with all punctuation marks in favor of verbal markers. Apollinaire's most distinctive work, in *Calligrammes* (*Beautiful Writing*, 1918), appeared several months before his death from influenza and complications from a head injury sustained in battle in 1916. In addition to documenting his war experience, *Calligrammes* demonstrates his belief that poetry, more than a verbal art, should also be visually accessible. While not exactly true, he earned for himself the posthumous title of 'le poète assassiné' ('the poet dropped dead') in reference to his partially autobiographical prose work of 1916 by that name.

[SJ]

Aragon, Louis (Louis Andrieux; France, 1897–1982) A writer whose legacy is still contested, Aragon was a prolific poet and novelist. Born the illegitimate son of an innkeeper (a fact about which he talked little), he studied medicine at the University of Paris. It was there he met ANDRÉ BRETON in 1917; the two immediately began to share their love of literature and their dissatisfaction with the literary establishment. After brief service in World War I, Aragon returned to France where, with Breton and PHILIPPE SOUPAULT (and following the lead of TRISTAN TZARA), he founded the Dadaist mouthpiece, *Littérature*. Early volumes of poetry, such as *Feu de joie* (*Bonfire*, 1920) and *Le mouvement perpétuel* (*Perpetual Motion*, 1925), evince Aragon's able handling of the expressiveness and immediacy that came from Dada itself.

As Breton was beginning to define Surrealism, the more serious artistic successor to Dadaism, Aragon took a different path, joining the Communist Party in 1930. He traveled to the Soviet Union the same year and was thoroughly converted. Denouncing his Dadaist experiments as juvenilia, Aragon would go on to become a conventional socialist realist for much of the rest of his life, something particularly expressed in his many novels. Poetically, he is best remembered for his World War II verse, such as *France, écoute* (*France, Listen*, 1944), which fired the citizens of France with patriotic zeal throughout the war. Aragon was also a gifted love poet, writing a number of volumes to and about his wife Elsa. Despite being important as a Dadaist innovator and a passionate political poet, Aragon continues to be met with critical ambivalence today due to his unyielding identification with Soviet policies.

Selected works: *The Red Front* (1933); *Le crève-coeur* (*The Heartbreak*, 1941); *Les yeux et la mémoire* (*The Eyes and the Memory*, 1954); *Le Fou d'Elsa* (*Elsa's Madman*, 1963); *Elegie à Pablo Neruda* (*Elegy to Pablo Neruda*, 1966); *L'oeuvre poétique* (*Poetic Works*, 1974–81).

[MW]

Arghezi, Tudor (Romania, 1880–1967) Arghezi was born in Bucharest but his family came from Cărbuneştii Gorjului, a village in south-western Romania. After a serious argument with his father when he was twelve, Arghezi started working to keep himself in school; by nineteen he had become a monk. In 1905 he went to study theology at the Catholic University of Fribourg, Switzerland, but left very soon, alienated by the locals' attempts at converting him to Catholicism. From 1906 to 1910 he worked as an apprentice watchmaker in Geneva, audited university courses, read French literature, and traveled to France and Italy.

Back in Bucharest, Arghezi wrote prodigiously – poetry, political and polemical articles, novels – and founded and edited several magazines. During World War I he foolishly contributed to two German occupation papers, for which he was imprisoned in 1918–19. In 1943 he was imprisoned again, this time for publishing a lampoon against Germany's Nazi ambassador to Bucharest (*Baron!*). In 1948 Arghezi was declared a poet of 'putrefaction' by Communist proletcult critics and had to withdraw from the literary scene. After the removal of the publication ban in 1953, Arghezi was elected to the Romanian Academy (1955) and received the National Prize for Literature (1957). He died in 1967, one year after his wife, at the end of a literary career spanning seven decades, internationally recognized (he received the Herder Prize in 1965) and Romania's greatest modern poet, second only to the nineteenth-century romantic Mihai Eminescu (1850–89).

Arghezi engaged most of the themes of twentieth-century poetry. In *Fitting Words* (1927) he included a series of Psalms which detail his agonizing search for a supreme being: 'You have let me alone to attain my end; /I torment myself at the root, and I bleed' (Psalm 3). Arghezi revolts against God, asks for a dialogue with the Divinity, acknowledges his own insignificance, and displays his humility. In *Flowers of Mildew* (1931) Arghezi describes the prison underworld, a theme never before approached in Romanian poetry. With compassion and sensitivity, while using unorthodox language, he portrays nature's miscreants, thieves, murderers, rebels. By introducing unconventional images of moral and physical decay – mildew, dirt, pus, boils, warts, rats, lice, bedbugs – into his repertoire, Arghezi creates an aesthetics of ugliness, enriching and extending the scope of poetry and poetic language. *Evening Verses* (1935) and *Horas* (1939) are an incursion into the family haven replete with children, small animals, plants, and insects. These volumes chart a miniature world of play and wonder at creation, seen through the innocent eyes of the child.

Throughout his work, Arghezi was preoccupied with the essence of the creative act, seeing poetry as the 'transformation of mythic experience – the psychic patrimony of an entire community – into the individual and creative experience of dream' (M. Impey).

Selected works: *One Hundred and One Poems* (1947–55); *Song to Man* (1956); *Pages from the Past* (1956); *Motley Verse* (1957); *Leaves* (1961); *New Poems* (1963); *Syllables* (1965); *Cadences* (1965); *Rhythms* (1966); *Night* (1966); *Litanies* (1967).

[GF]

Armitage, Simon (England, b. 1963) Born in Huddersfield, West Yorkshire, Armitage was educated at Portsmouth Polytechnic and Victoria University of Manchester. Like his father, Armitage works as a probation officer in Manchester.

Well-versed in formal poetics, Armitage is widely considered one of the most promising young poets in England, having won the Society of Authors' Eric Gregory Award (1988) and the *Sunday Times* Young Writer of the Year Award (1993). His work is decidedly working-class, and specifically non-academic. He writes from the position of the careless observer on the street, using vulgarity and deadpan vernacular to astute and energetic effect. Armitage is passionate about the ordinary, creating one seamless human experience.

Selected works: *Zoom!* (1989); *Around Robinson* (1991); *Kid* (1992); *Xanadu* (1992); *Book of Matches* (1993); *Dead Sea Poems* (1995); *Moon Country* (1996).

[SG]

Artaud, Antonin (France, 1896–1948) Known primarily for his theoretical work on theater, *Le Théâtre et son double* (*The Theater and Its Double*, 1938), Artaud was a member of the Surrealist group as early as 1924, and composed books of poetry that exhibit themes of sexuality and violence. In addition to his work in the theater, he acted in film, notably in Abel Gance's *Napoléon* (1928–34). His visit to the Tarahumara Indians in Mexico produced a study on magic and shamanism, *D'un voyage au pays des Tarahumaras* (*On a Voyage to the Land of the Tarahumaras*, 1945).

Addicted to drugs and debilitated by mental illness, Artaud spent his last years in the psychiatric hospital of Rodez, where he received shock treatments. His poetry during this period is increasingly violent, and verges on the incomprehensible. Throughout his diverse writings there emerges an anguished, often disheartening picture of the individual as one who is frequently, as he said of his kindred avant-garde spirit Van Gogh, 'suicided by society'.

Selected works: *L'Ombilic des limbes* (*The Umbilicus of Limbo*, 1925); *Le Pèse-nerfs* (*The Nerve Meter*, 1927).

[SJ]

Artmann, H.C. (Austria, 1921–2000) Raised in Austria, where he again lived since 1972, Hans Carl Artmann was drafted into the German military, was wounded, and was subsequently a prisoner of war. In the years after the war, he lived in Sweden, Austria, and Germany. Primarily noted as a writer of fantastic realism, Artmann quickly incorporated avant-garde aspects after early nature poems. Collaborating with concrete poets and Avant-gardists of the 'Vienna Group' during the 1950s, Artmann delineated and proclaimed his concept of the 'poetic act', including the belief that one can be a poet without ever writing or publishing a word. Artmann afterward followed this anarchic principle both in his texts and in his life.

His first book publication, *With Black Ink* (1958), presented black humor in Viennese dialect. The combination of various elements, such as surrealism, antimilitarism, and escapism (via a vampire motif), may be found in *a lilly-white letter from lincolnshire* (1969), a typical representation of his verse.

Selected works: *Poems about Love and Vice* (1975); *61 Austrian Haiku* (1984).

[IRS]

Ash, John (England, b. 1948) Born in Manchester and educated at Birmingham University, Ash spent a year teaching in Cyprus and traveling in the Middle East before settling down once again in Manchester. He moved to the United States in the 1980s.

His collections before *Casino* (1978), a successful long poem, are not very notable and he himself has commented on their unworthiness. In 1981, *The Bed and Other Poems* appeared and was an instant success, containing elements of romanticism alongside absurdity and humor, often in short fragmentary episodes. Although the following collection, *The Goodbyes* (1982), contained some acclaimed poems, it showed a decrease in creativity as a whole and resembled too much the poems of JOHN ASHBERY and Lee Harwood. *The Branching Stairs* (1984), which differs from his previous poetry, has been a lauded piece of postmodern writing. *Disbelief* (1987) and *The Burnt Pages* (1991) show clearly the influence of Ash's move to New York and his increasing poetic maturity which reveals itself through precise images and clarity of meaning.

[BRB]

Ashbery, John (United States, b. 1927) The poetry of John Ashbery has come to dominate the American literary world. Since 1956, when *Some Trees* was awarded the Yale Series of Younger Poets Prize, Ashbery's place in the American canon has been firmly established. His best-known volume, *Self-Portrait in a Convex Mirror* (1975), is a classic in American poetry and is often regarded as the most astute reflection of postmodernity in the United States.

Born in Rochester, New York, and educated at Harvard University (B.A., 1949), Columbia University (M.A., 1951), and with some graduate study at New York University (1957), Ashbery's life has revolved around two forces: poetry and the visual arts. His early career as an art critic for the *New York Herald Tribune* (1960–65) and *Art News* (1964–72) placed him within the dynamic New York art scene of the 1950s and early 1960s. Usually identified with the New York School of poetry that included BARBARA GUEST, FRANK O'HARA, and KENNETH KOCH, art was and continues to be an important influence upon his poetry.

Influenced by the abstract expressionist painters such as Mark Rothko and Jackson Pollock, Ashbery's poetry echoes in language the fluid yet sublime element in these painters' work. Their techniques profoundly influenced Ashbery's style, which has been referred to as the verbal equivalent of modern painting.

In addition to these painterly techniques, the arts impact the content of Ashbery's poetry in other ways. For example, 'Self Portrait in a Convex Mirror', his masterpiece, is a sustained rumination upon Francesco Parmigianino's painting of the same title. Moreover, in addition to his more than thirty volumes of poetry, Ashbery has also edited or written eleven books on the arts including *Reported Sightings: Art Chronicles 1957–1987* (1989). The body of his writing to date also includes three plays and numerous translations of French poets.

With the championing of Ashbery by such prominent critics as Helen Vendler, Marjorie Perloff, and Harold Bloom, Ashbery has certainly been the most critically acclaimed and honored poet of his generation. Such acclaim is not without merit: he has been awarded Fulbright Fellowships, Guggenheim Awards and National Endowment for the Arts grants. His poetry has also won more than thirty awards, including such prestigious prizes as the Pulitzer Prize, National Book Award, and National Book Critics Award (all in 1976 for *Self Portrait in a Convex Mirror*), as well as the Lenore Marshall Award in 1986. Ashbery's honors also include holding prestigious academic positions including the Charles Eliot Norton Professorship of Poetry at Harvard University. Since 1991, Ashbery has been the Charles P. Stevenson, Jr. Professor of Languages and Literature at Bard College.

[DC]

Atwood, Margaret (Canada, b. 1939) Poet, novelist, critic, short-story writer and essayist, Atwood has established herself as one of the finest Canadian writers of the century. Although in recent years she has become best-known for her novels, especially *The Handmaid's Tale* (1985) and *Cat's Eye* (1988) (both of which were shortlisted for the Booker Prize), Atwood initially established her reputation as a poet, and has continued to write poetry. *Morning in the Burned House* (1995), her first original volume in a decade, is the fourteenth volume of poetry that has appeared in her acclaimed career.

Atwood was born in Ottawa. Up to the age of twelve, she spent part of each year living in the wilderness of northern Québec and Ontario with her family. Her early experience of the Canadian bush has had an impact on both her poetry and prose, in terms of her choice of subject matter. Her first book of poetry, *Double Persephone* (1961), appeared in the year she completed her B.A. at the University of Toronto. Atwood completed her M.A. in English at Harvard University in 1962, and pursued further graduate work at Harvard in 1962–63 and 1965–67.

Atwood's second book of poetry, *The Circle Game* (1966), which won the Governor General's Award, introduces what was to become one of the constant themes of her work: the opposition of nature and civilization. Nature is identified with women, whereas the civilizing impulse is seen as a male desire to tame and control. Atwood's attention to sexual politics, the politics of nationalism, and the search for authentic individual and communal identities, are features of virtually all of her work, including *The Animals in That Country* (1968), *Procedures for Underground* (1970) and especially *The Journals of Susanna Moodie* (1970). Atwood has Moodie, the author of the classic account of settling Canada in the 1830s, *Roughing it in the Bush*, reflect on the spiritual and environmental devastation that has been the unfortunate result of her early, difficult life in the New World.

Power Politics (1971) initiates a period of explicit attention to the relationships between men and women. *You Are Happy* (1974) reworks *The Odyssey* from the perspective of Circe, the first of a number of revisionist myths in Atwood's oeuvre. *Two-Headed Poems* (1978) explores the duplicity of language in the particular context of the gap between English Canada and Québec. Consistent with her involvement in the 1980s with P.E.N. and Amnesty International, Atwood's poetry has turned to a consideration of political violence and torture, and to the difficulty of adequately capturing the traumas of the contemporary world in the language of poetry.

Atwood has received numerous awards and honorary degrees for her work. Her writing has been translated into over twenty languages. She remains one of the best-known and most popular contemporary Canadian writers.

Selected works: (fiction) *The Edible Woman* (1969); *Surfacing* (1972); *Alias Grace* (1997); (non-fiction) *Survival* (1972); (poetry) *Selected Poems* (1990).

[IS]

Auden, W. H. (England, 1907–73) Despite arguments over the lasting quality of his late poetry, Wystan Hugh Auden was undeniably one of the twentieth century's most powerful voices in English poetry. With YEATS' control of form and ELIOT's dry wit and eye for detail, Auden moved English poetry beyond Modernism through social and, finally, Christian commitment.

Born in York to a city medical officer and his devout wife, Auden lost confidence in traditional Christianity at fifteen; this crisis of faith was to leave a void that would be filled with the secular religion of poetry and the guiding principles of Socialist politics when he went to Oxford in 1925. Although he graduated in 1928 without much distinction, his ties to fellow writers Christopher Isherwood, C. DAY LEWIS, STEPHEN SPENDER and LOUIS MACNEICE – collectively known as the Oxford Group or the Thirties Poets – were firmly established during his time at Oxford. After graduation, Auden spent eighteen months in Berlin, an important sojourn because it granted him a greater comfort in his homosexuality and in his emerging powers as a poet.

Auden's return to England in 1929 begins the first of three periods in his artistic life. *Poems* (1930) and *The Orators* (1932) include stark, startling, and often opaque poems. The personal images of these volumes became more and more imbued with Socialist politics and psychoanalytical motifs in *Look, Stranger!* (1936) and, particularly, *Spain* (1937), which grew out of Auden's experiences as a stretcher bearer in the Spanish Civil War and which includes his most powerful political poem, 'Spain, 1937.' He won the King's Poetry Medal in that year.

Auden's middle period began when he moved to the United States in 1939. The clear, commonplace diction of 'Musée des Beaux Arts' and 'In Memory of W.B. Yeats' marks a change from the often dense imagery of the earlier work. The move to New York was accompanied by a more fundamental shift in his world view, also, his return to the church. In volumes such as *Another Time* (1940) and *New Year Letter* (1941) Auden crafted a new vision of the communal; rather than being politically directed via Socialism, this communal spirit sprang from the need to embrace agape at the most basic, personal level. This personal and political philosophy is made most palpable in the long poem *The Age of Anxiety* (1947), a four-character examination of the war and its human legacy, for which Auden won the Pulitzer Prize in 1948.

Partnered with writer Chester Kallman since the early 1940s, Auden's life after about 1950 – general domestic harmony, pre-eminent poetic status – is his last period. He wrote some of the century's most respected literary criticism. In 1956, he was elected to the prestigious position of Professor of Poetry at Oxford and, after winning the well-endowed Feltrinelli Prize (1957), he and Kallman bought a small cottage in Austria; they spent half of each year there. Poetic volumes such as the genteel *About This House* (1965) showed a new quietude. Though he was always a technically adventurous and meticulous craftsman, Auden's late writings were frequently attacked, by RANDALL JARRELL, PHILIP LARKIN, and others; Roger Kimball summarizes their argument succinctly: 'technique, uncatalyzed by sensibility and subject matter, can be the enemy of poetic achievement'.

Despite these claims, however, Auden left behind a corpus that is adroit public poetry, engaged with its times no matter what those times were: tense pre-war anticipation, war-years dissipation, or post-war reclamation.

[MW]

Awoonor, Kofi (George Awoonor-Williams; Ghana, b. 1934) A multi-talented writer, Awoonor is best known for his poetry. His literary career spans four decades, beginning with the publication of his first book of poetry in 1964, *Rediscovery, and Other Poems*. His work has incorporated the Ewe dirge and halo traditions (he has also translated Ewe poetry into English), but his poetry is more than simply traditional; it illustrates how notions of tradition are deeply embedded in modern articulations of identity. His lamentations reflect the loss of certain African communities due to European colonization, as well as the strength of cultural roots to sustain him. Awoonor is among the finest and most provocative poets of the twentieth century, one with an acute sense of the poetics of loss and justice.

This sensibility is reflected in the poet's reflections on the area where he grew up. As a child, Awoonor lived six miles from the sea, in a region defined by a lush forest with diverse animal life. In *Until the Morning After: Collected Poems* (1987), he writes that a government-sponsored rice farm project (with aid from China) has since desecrated the land to the extent that only a reduced number of water fowls return to the area.

Awoonor attended various mission schools, but he also asserts that he grew up 'on the lap of my grandmother', a great singer of dirge songs. He later earned a B.A. in English in Legon, Ghana, an M.A. in English in London, and completed a Ph.D. in comparative literature at the University of New York–Stony Brook in 1972, while teaching as an assistant professor. During this time, Awoonor edited an anthology of Ghanaian poetry, *Messages: Poems from Ghana* (1970), and published *Night of My Blood* (1971), perhaps his most widely acclaimed book of poetry, and a well-received novel, *This Earth, My Brother* (1972). Two books of poetry followed among other writings, before Awoonor returned to Ghana in 1975.

Awoonor became less prolific at this time, perhaps a reaction to the contemporary political upheaval in Ghana. He was arrested on New Year's Eve 1975 for suspected subversion, and detained without trial. The collection *The House by the Sea* (1978) depicts the ironies of coming home to incarceration. The title itself refers to Ussher Fort Prison in Accra. Awoonor's own ambivalent homecoming connects with the hostile realities faced by other artists and peoples, both within and outside Africa.

The following years saw the publication of *The Ghana Revolution: A Background Account from a Personal Perspective* (1984), *Ghana: A Political History from pre-European to Modern Times* (1990), and a second novel, *Comes the Voyager at Last* (1992), which involves an African-American's journey to Ghana. Years of traveling abroad, political activism, and a diverse array of writing reflect Awoonor's search for a just homeland.

[KAC]

Azofeifa, Isaac Felipe (Costa Rica, 1912–98) Azofeifa was a philologist, professor, literary historian, and a renowned advocate and reformer of Costa Rica's secondary schools. He was also a founder of the Centro de Estudios para los Problemas Nacionales (Center for the Study of National Problems) and a key intellectual figure in modern Costa Rican life. His poetry is both intimate and national in tone, touching on Costa Rican reality in its physical, social, and democratic expression. In his later works more autobiographical reflections, of nostalgic and solitary moods, dominate. His death in 1998 was observed as a major national event.

Selected works: *Trunca unidad* (*Truncated Unity*, 1958); *Vigilia en pie de muerte* (*Death Vigil*, 1962); *Canción* (*Song*, 1964); *Días y territorios* (*Days and Territories*, 1969); *El viejo liceo* (*The Old School*, 1973); *Poesía reunida* (*Collected Poems*, 1995).

[SL]

B

Bachmann, Ingeborg [Austria, 1926–73] Bachmann is one of the greatest poets of her generation. In 1950 she finished her university studies with a dissertation on Heidegger's philosophy. At first she worked for the radio and, in the mid-1950s and then again since 1965, lived in Rome. She had complex personal and professional relationships with writer Max Frisch and composer Hans Werner Henze. She died at her home in Rome in a fire, probably caused by her burning cigarette.

Bachmann's main themes were love, loss, and death; her tone was often hymnal. However, especially important were her works' dark aspects. Her prose is radically feminist, equating male-dominated society with Fascism. Her early poetry is equally radical in evoking the precariousness of impending change and in probing unknown regions of subjectivity in an increasingly meaningless world; it addresses the human condition in general.

Her lyrical debut, *Installments of Time* (1953), and her second volume, *Invocation of the Great Bear* (1956), established Bachmann as a great poet with a new and powerful voice. As symbols of precariousness, metaphors from mythology and nature reveal the damage done by humankind, specifically tied to the concrete experience of Fascism during Bachmann's youth. Doubting the 'beautiful' poetic word, Bachmann did not write much poetry after 1956; see *Love: The Dark Continent* (1984).

[IRS]

Bacovia, George (Romania, 1881–1957) Born into a middle-class family in the town of Bacău in north-eastern Romania, Bacovia studied law at the Universities of Bucharest and Iassy but never practiced. Due to a feeble constitution and frequent bouts of depression, he held a succession of temporary jobs, yet he sublimated his obsessions into his work, turning them into effective lyrical motifs: void, solitude, illness, agony, death.

Initially a Symbolist, Bacovia created an anti-symbolist poetry by reducing language to the most prosaic and commonplace and by exacerbating poetic conventions. His poetic effects are achieved by the recurrence of motifs, individual words or entire lines, by the use of strong colors, dissonant sounds, repugnant smells. Indeed, the poet's physical and poetic universe is circumscribed by the cemetery, the slaughter house, and the cancerous park. His world is imbued with the colors of death and decay – black, white, grey, violet, and yellow – (*Lead*, 1916; *Yellow Sparks*, 1926). Even love and the traditional symbols of rebirth, the seasons, are touched by the specter of extinction. Alienated from himself and his environment, Bacovia expressed his tragic desolation in forms 'anticipating expressionism and futurism' (Gh. Crăcium). 'The first anti-poet in Romanian literature, Bacovia has been rediscovered and emulated by poets of the last three decades.

Selected works: *Bits of Nights* (1926); *With You* (1934); *Bourgeois Stanzas* (1946); *Poems* (1956); *Poems* (1957).

[GF]

Bagryana, Elisaveta (Elisaveta Belcheva; Bulgaria, 1893–1991) 'The best woman poet Bulgarian literature has yet produced' (Charles Moser) graduated from the University of Sofia, and worked as a teacher (1915–19) and an editor of literary periodicals and in publishing houses. When her first book of poetry, *Vechnata i svyatata* (*The Eternal and Holy*, 1927), appeared she was already a celebrated poet and an active member of P.E.N. Collections of her poems were published in France, Russia, Poland, Czechoslovakia, Italy, and Romania. She received several prestigious Bulgarian awards and the Gold Medal of the International Poetry Association (Rome, 1966).

Bagryana constantly reflects on woman's place in life. Her 'eternal and holy,' 'first and last woman' ('Penelope of the Twentieth Century') hovers over the boundary between life and death. Bagryana perceives the world from a distinct feminine point of view, fusing together personal experience, literary allusions, and history. Her lyrics evoke images of the sea, wind, and journeys to unknown lands as they celebrate youth, beauty, the elemental forces of nature, and, above all, freedom. Love as both sexual attraction and maternal devotion is seen as inseparable from destiny, self-fulfillment and self-restriction, death and immortality. Acutely aware of the delicate balance between human society and nature, Bagryana is at once attracted to and weary of modernity, especially of the human toll of industrialization.

Selected works: *Zvezda na moryaka (Sailor's Star*, 1932); *Sŭrtse choveshko* (*Human Heart*, 1936); *Kontrapunkti* (*Counterpoints*, 1972); *Na brega na vremeto* (*On the Banks of Time*, 1983).

[CG/LPG]

Baraka, Amiri (United States, b. 1934) Born Everett LeRoi Jones in Newark, New Jersey, Amiri Baraka attended Howard University, served in the Air Force, and then moved to New York. He received graduate degrees from Columbia and the New School, and quickly became a central figure in avant-garde literary circles. Baraka edited several influential journals, and became a close friend and affiliate of important Beat, Black Mountain, and New York School poets. With the success of his 1964 play exploring racial tension and hatred, *Dutchman*, Baraka's national reputation was established By the mid-1960s, he had grown disillusioned with the bohemian world, and increasingly angered by racial prejudice and injustice; in 1965, he left his white wife and their children, cut ties with his white Village friends, changed his name, and moved to Harlem, eventually returning to Newark – where he became a central writer of the Black Arts movement, and a controversial political activist for black nationalism and separatism. By 1974, Baraka's ideology and poetry had changed again; he rejected his earlier black nationalism and began to espouse Marxism.

Throughout the different phases of Baraka's widely ranging career, one finds a restless, incisive mind and keen verbal imagination. His earlier poems are elliptical, painful and personal lyrics that employ visceral images and fragmented syntax to convey the agonized self-consciousness of a soul tormented by self and society. His later, often polemical poetry more frequently uses dialect; it often draws on blues and jazz forms, and tends to be more direct and performance-oriented.

Selected works: *Preface to a Twenty Volume Suicide Note* (1961); *The Dead Lecturer* (1964);

Black Magic (1969); *Transbluesency: Selected Poems 1961–1995* (1995).

[AE]

Baranczak, Stanislaw (Poland, b. 1946) Born in Poznan, Baranczak graduated with a degree in literature from Poznan University and eventually taught there until 1977, when he was fired for political reasons. In 1981, after a prolonged attempt obtain a passport, Baranczak emigrated to the United States and accepted the position of Alfred Jurzykowski Professor of Polish Language and Literature at Harvard University, a position he still holds.

Baranczak belongs to a generation of Polish poets that came to life in the late 1960s. These poets, refusing to limit themselves to the Surrealism or Neoclassicism characteristic of their predecessors (such as ADAM WAZYK and ZBIGNIEW HERBERT), sought a linguistic mechanism with which they could retaliate against the abuses of their totalitarian surroundings. What they developed was a simpler, unmasked language which remained both potent and vital. Baranczak's recent work, though never divorcing itself from its political roots, has taken on the difficulty of being an exile living in the United States.

Baranczak is also an accomplished essayist, critic, literary historian, and translator into Polish of works of Shakespeare, John Donne, G.M. Hopkins, JAMES MERRILL, OSIP MANDELSHTAM, JOSEPH BRODSKY, and other poets. His books in English include *Selected Poems: The Weight of the Body* (1989) and a study of Herbert's poetry entitled *A Fugitive from Utopia* (1987). He has also collaborated with Clare Cavanagh in translating into English two collections of Nobel Laureate WISLAWA SZYMBORSKA's poetry: *View with a Grain of Sand* (1995) and *Poems New and Collected* 1937–97 (1997).

[MO]

Barbu, Ion (Romania, 1895–1961) Born in Câmpulung Muscel, Barbu studied mathematics at the Universities of Bucharest, Göttingen, and Tübingen. He was appointed professor of algebra at the University of Bucharest in 1942. He published important studies and treatises in geometry and algebra.

A major Romanian poet, Barbu was a model for the poets of both the 1930s and the 1960s through his programmatic attempt to reach the essence of poetry, his cryptic language, and the richness of his 'Balkanic' scenes and language. Barbu's poetry, a selection of which was contained in *Second Play* (1930), shows him a classicist in form and vision, and a gnomic romantic in temperament and inspiration. Barbu tried to return poetry to its initiatic function, using archetypal symbols to teach about the unity of the universe. The duality of the Apollonian and the Dionysiac drives, the masculine and feminine principles, as well as the unifying role of marriage are recurrent motifs in his poems (e.g. 'Rhythms for the Necessary Marriages'). In *The Dogmatic Egg*, Barbu 'addresses the potentialities and mystery of an uncreated world' (N. Manolescu), while the atemporal city of Isarlak, in his ideal 'Other Greece', embodies his belief in an ahistorical Hellenism. The ambiguity of the two drives and principles is united by marriage, though Barbu sees mystery as necessary, so it becomes a hidden, secondary aspect of his world.

[GF]

Barker, George (England, 1913–91) Born in Loughton, Essex, to a working-class family, George Granville Barker dropped out of school at age fourteen, eventually going on to publish over thirty books. Although he spent his adult life moving between England, America, Japan, and Italy, his poetry remained firmly embedded in his English roots.

Barker was preoccupied with suicide and death, and macabre themes run through virtually all of his early work. *Thirty Preliminary Poems* (1933), Barker's first collection, touches on despair, sexuality and eroticism, frustration, suffering, guilt, and death, introducing the themes with which Barker was to remain obsessed throughout his career. In many ways, his attitude was typical of the time, although Barker remained fascinated by despair long after influential contemporaries such as LOUIS MACNEICE moved on.

A highly romantic poet, Barker toyed with French Symbolism, a move that earned him the respect of most literary critics by the late 1930s. The title poem of *Elegy on Spain* (1939) was widely hailed as one of the best poems written on the Spanish Civil War. During the 1960s, his work was well-lauded, garnering him the Guinness Prize (1962), *Poetry* magazine's Levinson Prize (1965), and the Boreston Mountain Poetry Prize (1967). However, Barker was to earn mixed critical reviews throughout the rest of his career, receiving particularly hostile reviews of his work in the late 1970s, which was considered hollow, redundant, and littered with clichés.

Selected works: *Poems* (1935); *Calamiterror* (1937); *Lament and Triumph* (1940); *Eros in Dogma* (1944); *The True Confessions of George Barker* (1950); *Seven Poems* (1977).

[SG]

Baughan, Blanche (New Zealand, 1870–1958) Born in London, Baughan graduated from the University of London with a B.A. in Classics. She worked for the poor in the capital's East End and supported suffrage. In 1900, Baughan emigrated to New Zealand and continued social work as a proponent of prison reform. In 1930, she retired to Akaroa, on Banks Peninsula, where she was active as a town councilor and co-wrote a compilation of case studies, published as *People in Prison* (1936).

Her poetry resonates with a variety of pioneer voices which express the colonial experience. Her poems recount everyday life set within an exotic landscape. Baughan's dramatic monologues reflect the New Zealand (immigrant) experience in an energetic way.

Selected works: *Reuben and Other Poems* (1903); *Shingle-Short and Other Verses* (1908); *Brown Bread from a Colonial Oven* (1912); *Poems from the Port Hills* (1923).

[SH]

Baxter, James Keir (New Zealand, 1926–72) Born in Dunedin, New Zealand, Baxter was educated at Quaker schools in England and New Zealand, then attended Otago University, Dunedin, and Victoria University, Wellington. After his conversion to Roman Catholicism in the late 1950s and his effort to end his alcoholism, Baxter founded a religious community in Jerusalem on the Wanaganui River and was active in social and community work, often among young Maori people. Poetically, he was associated with the Wellington magazine *Numbers* and held a writer's fellowship during the years 1966–69.

In Baxter's view, the poet was charged with enormous responsibilities and his poetry publicly challenged insincerity, hypocrisy, and what he considered New Zealand's lack of spirituality. Baxter was associated with other socially concerned poets in the 'Wellington group' (see LOUIS JOHNSON). Although Baxter's early post-war writing can be characterized as romantic, his poetry from the 1960s onwards is openly polemical, reworking such personal experiences as his active protest against New Zealand's participation in the Vietnam War. His *Jerusalem Sonnets: Poems for Colin Durning* (1970) and *Jerusalem Daybook* (1971) criticize the subject's alienation by urban life and relate the powers of everyday activities in the commune.

Selected works: *Beyond the Palisade* (1944); *Blow, Wind of Fruitfulness* (1948); *In Fires of No Return* (1958); *Pig Island Letters* (1966); *The Bone Chanter: Unpublished Poems 1945–72* (1976).

[SH]

Beaver, Bruce (Australia, b. 1928) Born in Manly, Sydney, Beaver lived and worked in New South Wales and New Zealand before returning in the early 1960s to Manly, where he has remained. Beaver has worked as a chainman for a surveyor, radio programmer, clerk, and proofreader. His first collection, *Under the Bridge*, appeared in 1961, but his fourth, *Letters to Live Poets* (1969), established his reputation. He has won various literary awards, and in 1991 was awarded the Order of Australia in recognition of his contribution to Australian literature. He has published a novel, *You Can't Come Back* (1966), and was a contributing editor to *Poetry Australia*.

In its attraction to American poets (such as WILLIAMS and O'HARA), its freeing up of prosody, and its confessional turn, *Letters to Live Poets* was quickly seen as having prefigured the stylistic changes espoused by the 'Generation of '68' (see DUGGAN, FORBES, MAIDEN). Beaver's status as 'Godfather' of that group is supported by his inclusion in JOHN TRANTER's *The New Australian Poetry* (1979).

Beaver's long-standing biographical interests are seen in *As it Was . . .* (1979), a discontinuous verse autobiography detailing the poet's unhappy childhood and onset of manic depression. *Charmed Lives* (1988) includes a verse biography of RILKE; the eponymous poem of *Anima* (1994) is a tribute to the poet's wife. *Poets and Others* (1999) continues Beaver's auto/biographical interests. Attracted to both the quotidian and the metaphysical, Beaver writes loose, long, free verse lines (though recently he has written stanzaically). While criticized for prosodic slackness, Beaver has long been recognized as an important, progressive force in contemporary Australian poetry.

Selected works: *New and Selected Poems: 1960–1990* (1991).

[DM]

Beckett, Samuel (Ireland, 1906–89) Although Beckett is better known for his plays and novels than for his poetry, all his writings share a similarly distanced aesthetic style, as his speakers search for, struggle, and usually fail to find a language adequate to their experience. Frequently called an existentialist or an absurdist, Beckett's watermark style cannot be easily labeled.

Born in Dublin to an Anglo-Irish, middle-class Protestant family, Beckett graduated from Trinity College, Dublin, in 1927, and went on scholarship to Paris in 1928. He fell in love with the city and while there formed strong attachments to Thomas MacGreevy and James Joyce. He completed the poem *Whoroscope* (1930) in one night, and it won the Hours Press competition. His second volume of poetry, *Echo's Bone* (1935), was influenced by French Symbolist poets.

After returning to Ireland in the 1930s, Beckett suffered from bouts of depression, anxiety, and emotional breakdowns. In 1938 he returned to Paris permanently, preferring, as he later acknowledged, Paris at war to Ireland at peace. He met Suzanne Deschevaux-Dumesnil, a French pianist, at the end of the 1930s, and although he lived with her most of his life, they did not marry until 1961. During World War II, Beckett joined the French Resistance, and in 1945 he received the Croix de Guerre and the Médaille de la Résistance.

Although critics praise his novels, particularly the trilogy *Molloy, Malone Dies*, and *The Unnameable* (1947–57), Beckett is most noted for his plays, notably *Waiting for Godot* (1952), *Endgame* (1957), and *Happy Days* (1961). In 1969 he was awarded the Nobel Prize for Literature. His *Collected Poems in English and French* was published in 1977 and his *Collected Poems 1930–78* in 1984.

[CT]

Beer, Patricia (England, b. 1924) Beer was born in Exmouth, Devon, the setting that influences many of her poems. Her poetry is deceptively simple and understated, with an economy of phrasing and straightforward narrative that frequently contrasts with the preoccupation with death that is often at the center of her poems.

In her first book, *Loss of the Magyar and Other Poems* (1959), Beer ruminates on death and uses the title poem to consider her great-grandfather's death at sea. Her second book, *The Survivors* (1963), continues her focus on death, using traditional forms and meters, as well as literary characters such as Ophelia and Desdemona. After writing her autobiography, *Mrs Beer's House* (1968), Beer began to include more autobiographical material in her poetry. *The Estuary* (1971), a critically unsuccessful book, focuses on Beer herself and her childhood memories.

Later works were more successful, including *Driving West* (1975) and *The Lie of the Land* (1983), which reflect on country life. The books contain Beer's customarily rich imagery, blended with the quiet understatement that she continues to master in her later works. Although it has become more autobiographical, Beer's poetry is not confessional; rather, she uses her own experiences as a bridge of understanding between herself and her readers.

Selected works: *Loss of the Magyar and Other Poems* (1959); *The Survivors* (1963); *Just Like the Resurrection* (1967); *Driving West* (1975); *Selected Poems* (1979); *The Lie of the Land* (1983); *Collected Poems* (1988); *Friend of Heraclitus* (1993).

[LK]

Bei Dao (Zhao Zhenkai; China, b. 1949) Leading contemporary poet Bei was born and grew up in Beijing. After graduation from the Fourth High School in Beijing in 1969, Bei was unable to continue his formal education due to the tremendous social turbulence resulting from the Great Cultural Revolution (1966–76); he became a construction worker and, later, an editor and journalist. By chance Bei was in East Germany when the Student Democratic Movement broke out in 1989. Subsequent censorship of his works in China, however, has less to do with any involvement in the Movement, than with his previous writings and the ideas expressed in them. Since the Democratic Movement, Bei has traveled constantly in Europe and the United States. His works translated into a dozen languages, Bei now teaches at the University of California at Davis.

Bei first came to public attention in China not as a prominent poet or a fiction writer – he wrote a novella (*The Waves*) before he tried his hand at poetry – but as a founder and a co-editor (with Mang Ke) of the Vanguard underground literary magazine *Today* (1978–79), which was revived in the U.S. in 1990. Having read modernist Western writings extensively, especially the poems of the British and American imagists, Bei modernized his own work. His first poem, 'The Answer', appearing in the sole official poetry magazine *Poetry* in 1979, immediately brought him great fame as an original poet, one who expressed for his whole generation a long-denied and deep-buried desire for freedom, love, understanding, and an ability to better control one's life and fate in a society such as China's. After 'The Answer', Bei, along with GU CHENG, SHU TING, JIAN HE, and others, flooded Chinese literary magazines with a distinctively new and truly modern poetry in the early 1980s, 'Obscure Poetry'. The Obscure Poetry embarrassed many readers and critics as well, because it was no longer devoted to direct praise of the remarkable achievements made under the leadership of the Communist Party, or simple, indirect complaints about minor social wrongs at the time. Rather, it is a poetry about unfulfilled dreams, frustrations, illusions, personal disintegration, uncertainty, and the perseverance in the search for meaning. It is a poetry about despairing desire for love, understanding, and healthy human relationships. It is also a poetry with a subtle but effective criticism of the society as a whole. Critics also chided the Obscure Poetry's technique, as sometimes private images speak for themselves without bothering to have much connection built between them.

Bei is essentially a political poet with a strong conscience for public duty and a Confucianist sense of morality. His belief in the critical social role of the poet may be responsible for his sometimes difficult verse; he has taxed to the utmost his talent to use a unique palimpsest of images, a bold laconism and highly westernized syntax in order to suggest a political effect and the terror of history. A good example of this kind is in his magnificent *Daydreams* (1986), a long poem sequence featuring strange and even morbid images tumbling upon each other, fragmented syntax, harsh language, and broken rhythm. For Bei, the more obscure the poem, the harder political and social pressures he senses. Still, not every poem by Bei is hard: the majority of his poetry is comprehensible and hauntingly beautiful. Bei's later poems are quite lucid, perhaps because he experiences a much more relaxed life abroad.

Selected works: *Collected Poems* (1986); *Poems* (1988); *Old Snow* (1992); *The Midnight Singer* (1995); *Landscape Over Zero Degree* (1996).

[LG]

Bejerano, Maya (Israel, b. 1949) Bejerano was born in Haifa, Israel, in 1949. She holds a Bachelor of Arts in literature and philosophy and works as a librarian. Bejerano has been actively involved in photography and music, and has published both poetry and prose. Her poetry, which is characterized by strong sensuality and sharp transitions, won her the Prime Minister's Prize (1989, 1996). Her imagery is intensive and wide, often merging the self and its surroundings. Her style is characterized by unexpected and at times absurd juxtapositions of themes and language formats. Bejerano's first book was *Ostrich* (1978) and her most recent book is *I Will Try to Touch my Navel* (1997).

[ER]

Bell, Julian (England, 1908–37) Born in London, Bell was the son of Clive and Vanessa Bell and nephew of Virginia Woolf. He was educated at King's College, Cambridge, where he contributed to *The Venture*, a literary magazine, and was elected to the prestigious Apostles Society. In 1935 he accepted a position as professor of English at Wuhan University in China. He did not hold the position long, however, and soon moved to Spain during the Spanish Civil War, where he served as an ambulance driver for the Republicans. He was killed there in 1937. Bell's poetry is distinguished by its experimental form and its detailed exploration of the English countryside. His later poetry often focused on personal and political themes.

Selected works: *Winter Movement and Other Poems* (1930); *We Did Not Fight: 1914–18, Experiences of War Resisters* (ed., 1935); *Work for the Winter and Other Poems* (1936).

[TT]

Bell, Martin (England, 1918–78) Born in Southampton and educated at Taunton's School and the University of Southampton, Bell was a follower of W.H. AUDEN and a member of the Communist Party. He served in the Royal Engineers in Italy and worked as a schoolteacher in London. During the decade 1955–65, he was a member of an exclusive poets' workshop, The Group, and produced a great deal of work during this time which was influenced by fellow poets Philip Hobsbaum, PETER REDGROVE, and ALAN BROWNJOHN. Later in his life he produced translations of French Surrealist poets. He completed one book of poetry during his lifetime, *Collected Poems* (1967), although the posthumously published *Complete Poems* (1988) collects some of his later works. He died in poverty in Leeds in 1978.

[TT]

Belli, Gioconda (Nicaragua, b. 1948) Winner of the prestigious *Casa de las Americas* prize for her book *Línea de Fuego*

(*Line of Fire*, 1978), Managua-born Belli has become one of the leading poetic voices of her generation. Her poetry is intensely personal as love, eroticism, and feminism find themselves woven into unique configurations. Like the work of many female poets of her generation, such as Daisy Zamora, Michelle Najlis, and Vidalus Meneses, Belli's verse celebrates the human body, protest, and revolution, irreversibly connecting the private and the public. Since the late 1980s she has devoted herself to the writing of prose and has become a celebrated novelist.

Selected works: *Sobre la grama* (*On the Grass*, 1974); *Truenos y arcoiris* (*Thunder and Rainbow*, 1982); *Amor Insurrecto* (*Insurgent Love*, 1984); *De la costilla de Eva* (*From Eve's Rib*,1986); *El ojo de la mujer* (*Through a Woman's Eye*, 1991).

[SL]

Belloc, Hilaire (England, 1870–1953) Hilaire Pierre René Belloc was born near Paris to a French lawyer and his English wife; the family moved to England during his infancy. Educated at Oxford, Belloc became a British citizen in 1902, and was a Liberal MP from 1906 to 1910. During these years he was also editor of *The Morning Post* and, after disillusionment with the party system led him out of politics, he turned to writing and founded the journal *The Eye Witness*.

Belloc's verse falls into two categories, serious and light. The light verse comes in such delightful and mock-solemn children's books as *The Bad Child's Book of Beasts* (1896) and *Cautionary Tales* (1907). Serious works are collected in *Verses and Sonnets* (1896) and *Sonnets and Verses* (1923); two well-known poems are 'Tarantella' and 'Ha'nacker Mill', which illustrate the musical, metrical nature of Belloc's best verse.

Ferocious polemics in advocating Roman Catholicism offset the popularity garnered by Belloc's poetry, novels, biographies, histories, and travel books, and although he was once ranked in the 'big four' along with H.G. Wells, George Bernard Shaw, and his friend G. K. Chesterton, his fame, along with his skill, gradually waned. The untimely death of his wife Elodie Hogan in 1914 compounded his troubles; Belloc mourned her until his death.

Selected works: *The Modern Traveller* (1898); *Verses* (1910); *Sonnets and Verses* (1923, 1938).

[JL]

Benn, Gottfried (Germany, 1886–1956) Benn was a doctor, both in the army during the First World War and then in private practice. Attempting to overcome nihilism, he welcomed National Socialism in 1933; when he later realized his error, he re-enlisted as an army doctor in 1935, hoping the military enclave (which was independent of, though working for, the Nazis) would protect him from Nazism itself. In 1938 he was expelled by the Nazis from both medical and literary professional associations and banned from writing. From 1945 to 1948, the Allies also prohibited him from publishing in Germany; he turned to Swiss presses then. Amid controversy, his literary reputation grew.

Benn's poetry and prose achieved continuity by expressing his absolute subjectivity but went through major changes in tone and form during his career. He reached an early climax between 1912 and 1920, becoming the most radical practitioner of an aesthetics of negativity and the Expressionist destruction of the bourgeois language and world. In the poems in *Morgue* (1912), *Sons* (1913), and *Flesh* (1917), death and disease, surreal and visionary imagery, and a new language demolished reality and were received as brutal and shocking.

Between 1922 and 1931 his poems, such as those in *Collected Poems* (1927), became more formally structured while celebrating a metaphysical intoxication with individual consciousness that added a more lyrical tone to his earlier poems' criticism. Between 1933 and 1947, Benn achieved classicist perfection in his *Static Poems* (1946, 1948), which are considered his verses' pinnacle. The poems after 1949 returned to his earlier aggressiveness yet were still unhurried to the point of melancholy and resignation.

Selected works: *Fragments* (1951); *Distillations* (1953); *Aprèslude* (1955).

[IRS]

Bennett, Louise (Jamaica, b. 1919) Born in Kingston, Jamaica, Bennett began writing poetry in the 1930s. She is one of the first poets to write in the language and rhythm of creole, the vernacular English of everyday Jamaican life. Through her poetry column in *The Daily Gleaner*, begun in 1943, and as the radio personality 'Miss Lou', Bennett has become a popular and much-beloved cultural icon. Her poetry, often written in the first person, criticizes and comments on the pretensions and prejudices of Jamaican society with characteristic wit and insight, while also celebrating the unique strengths and traditions of Jamaican culture.

Bennett's poetry is best experienced when it is performed live, which enables her to show fully her skillful use of the textures and rhythms of Jamaican creole. She has thus unsurprisingly been cited as a formative influence by contemporary 'dub' poets, and has released several of her own recordings. As with the verse of other 'performance' poets, such as Mutabaruka, LINTON KWESI JOHNSON, Bob Marley, and the Mighty Sparrow, Bennett's work has not always been critically well received. *JamaicaLabrish* (1966), an early anthology of her work, began the more serious study of Bennett's poetry; the collection edited by MERVYN MORRIS, *Selected Poems* (1982), has helped to further ensure her place as one of the Caribbean's most respected and original voices.

[IS]

Berggol'ts, Olga Federovna (Russia, 1910–75) A 1930 graduate of the Philosophy Department of Leningrad University, Berggol'ts had published three volumes of poetry by 1938. Her poetic reputation, however, rests on her descriptions of her experience in Leningrad during World War II. She survived the three-year siege and, during that time, worked at a Leningrad radio station. She 'registered' this experience as lyric poetry, under the titles *Leningradskaia tretrad'* (*Leningrad Notebook*, 1942), *Leningrad* (1944), and *Tvoi put'* (*Your Road*, 1945). In 1951 she was awarded a Stalin Prize for her poem 'Pervorossiisk', which narrates the story of the workers' commune of 1918.

Although Berggol'ts can be characterized as a typical Soviet state poet, she was aware of the complexity of Soviet rule, as hinted at in a number of her poems. She endeavored to escape into lyric poetry or emotional prose to avoid touching these delicate and dangerous issues. Berggol'ts' poetry is a description and representation of problems and issues that concerned the Soviet people of her generation.

Selected works: *Stikhotvoreniia* (*Poems*, 1934); *Kniga pesen* (*Book of Songs*, 1935); *Listopad* (*Leaves Fall*, 1938).

[RN]

Bernstein, Charles (United States, b. 1950) Charles Bernstein, one of the leading 'language' poets, was born in New York and attended Harvard. A prolific poet and theorist/critic, Bernstein co-edited the influential journal *L=A=N=G=U=A=G=E*, and is currently a professor at the State University of New York, Buffalo.

A tireless promoter of experimental poetry, Bernstein has long crusaded against what he calls 'official verse culture' – any bland traditional poetry devoted to naive self-expression. Bernstein's difficult, innovative writing highlights the artifice of linguistic conventions and the indeterminacy of meaning. His poems, often collages that juxtapose discontinuous statements and feature exuberant wordplay, self-consciously probe the constructed, ideological nature of language itself.

Selected works: *Islets/Irritations* (1983); *A Poetics* (1992); *Dark City* (1994).

[AE]

Berry, James (Jamaica, b. 1925) Berry emigrated to England in 1948 and, alongside EDWARD KAMAU BRATHWAITE, became a seminal member of the first generation of Caribbean writers to make their impact felt in post-war Britain. Writing both poetry and fiction, and working as a teacher and broadcaster, Berry has connected his Jamaican heritage to the present state of England, particularly the London he calls home. Wide recognition came after publication of the collection of Jamaica-based children's stories, *A Thief in the Village and Other Stories* (1987), which won both the Smarties Prize for Children's Books (1987) and a Coretta Scott King honor (1988). However, his poetry has also been recognized, with both a British Poetry Society prize (1981) and the *Signal* Poetry Award for *When I Dance* (1989). Other volumes of poetry include *Fractured Circles* (1979) and *Hot Earth, Cold Earth* (1995). Berry is also important for his stewardship of British-Jamaican poetry, editing both *Bluefoot Traveller: An Anthology of Westindian Poets in Britain* (1976; 1981) and *News for Babylon: The Chatto Book of West Indian-British Poetry* (1984).

[MW]

Berry, Wendell (United States, b. 1934) Wendell Berry was born and raised on a farm in Henry County, Kentucky. After studying at the University of Kentucky, Lexington and at Stanford University and teaching for several years, he returned to Henry County and has farmed there since.

Berry's meditative, often psalm-like poems are informed by his close relationship to the land of his ancestors and to religious ideas. Common themes include family, community, and the natural world, with its cycles of death and regeneration. A long-standing environmentalist, Berry has written a number of poems on misuse of the land, and is often considered part of the Eco-Poetry movement.

Selected works: *Openings* (1968); *The Country of Marriage* (1973); *Clearing* (1977); *A Timbered Choir: The Sabbath Poems, 1979–1997* (1999).

[JT]

Berryman, John (United States, 1914–72) Berryman, a major figure of the 'middle generation' that included ROBERT LOWELL, ELIZABETH BISHOP and THEODORE ROETHKE, was born John Smith in McAlester, Oklahoma in 1914. From the start, Berryman's life was marked by turmoil: the marriage between his father, a banker, and his mother, a schoolteacher, was extremely unhappy. Financial problems drove Berryman's father to move the family to Florida, where he committed suicide by shooting himself outside his twelve-year-old son's window. The father's death cast a long, terrible shadow across Berryman's entire life and poetry ('that mad drive wiped out my childhood', he would later write), and sadly prefigured his own fate. When his mother remarried, he took his stepfather's name and became John Berryman.

Berryman received degrees from Columbia College, and Clare College, Cambridge. A professor at various universities, including Wayne State, Harvard (1940–3), Princeton (intermittently for ten years), Berryman ultimately settled at the University of Minnesota, where he was to remain from 1955 until his death. Berryman's life was volatile, marked by struggles with alcoholism, three marriages, affairs, breakdowns, and hospitalizations. On January 7, 1972, he committed suicide by jumping off a bridge in Minneapolis.

Deeply influenced by poets such as W. B. YEATS, W. H. AUDEN, and Gerard Manley

Hopkins, Berryman began his career by writing in the rigid academic style of the late 1940s, as evidenced by the carefully crafted poems in *The Dispossessed* (1948). After years of research and writing, Berryman finished his first major work, *Homage to Mistress Bradstreet*, an eccentric long poem in which he impersonated the voice of the early American poet Anne Bradstreet. But Berryman's posthumous fame rests almost solely upon the series of *Dream Songs* that he would write over the course of a dozen years. The first installment of these poems, *77 Dream Songs*, was published in 1964 and won the Pulitzer Prize; a collection of all 385, *His Toy, His Dream, His Rest*, won the National Book Award in 1969.

Berryman conceived of his major project as a long, fluid poem in the tradition of Walt Whitman's 'Song of Myself'. A sequence of poems each consisting of three six-line stanzas, it relates the antics and tribulations of Berryman's alter ego. A troubled figure most often called Henry, the starring persona in this psychological drama is frequently spoken to by an unnamed sidekick who addresses him as Mr Bones. Occasionally appearing – controversially and somewhat inexplicably – in blackface, Henry chronicles his fantasies and nightmares, desires and anxieties, memories and sorrows, in tones that swing rapidly from spiritual elation to suicidal angst, wicked irony to elegiac pathos. The poem is notable for its enormously varied and imaginative diction (ranging from high poetic speech to minstrelsy to contemporary slang); its punning wordplay, twisted syntax, intentional misspellings, and ambiguous pronouns; as well as for its mixture of unrelenting self-pity, self-mockery, 'confessional' despair and wild comedy. Some of the most fully realized and memorable of the *Dream Songs* include numbers 1 ('Huffy Henry hid the day'), 14 ('Life, friends, is boring'), 29 ('There sat down, once, a thing on Henry's heart'), 76 ('Nothin' very bad happen to me lately'), and 384 ('The marker slants, flowerless').

Finding himself renowned for his long poem, Berryman wrote two more volumes of poetry (*Love and Fame*, 1970, and *Delusions, etc.*, 1972), in which he pondered his fame, his alcoholism, death, and Catholicism. These poems turn toward a more autobiographical style, but lack the manic wit and imagination that energize the best of his *Dream Songs*. Berryman's work, other than *Dream Songs*, is collected in *John Berryman: Collected Poems, 1937–71* (1990).

[AE]

Bertolucci, Attilio (Italy, b. 1911) Since his early collections, the Parma-born Bertolucci found his main source of inspiration in the delicate palette of colors offered by his native region, which he depicted with a plain language and a measured style. Regarded by some critics as a consciously provincial writer relying on a strong thematic consistency (the land, family roots), Bertolucci soon proved, especially through his refined technique, to be anything but a naive poet. In his collection *La camera da letto* (*The Bedroom*, 1984–8), his usual themes expanded to the point of reaching the ambitious structure of a 'novel in verse'.

Selected works: *Sirio* (*Sirius*, 1929); *La capanna indiana* (*The Indian Hut*, 1955); *Viaggio d'inverno* (*Winter Travel*, 1971); *La lucertola di Casarola* (*The Lizard of Casarola*, 1997).

[GS]

Bethell, Ursula (Evelyn Hayes; New Zealand, 1874–1945) Born in England, Bethell emigrated to New Zealand in 1881. After completing her education in Oxford and Geneva and moving back and forth between Britain and New Zealand, Bethell finally settled in Christchurch in 1924. She had worked for the poor in a London Anglican community and established a grouping of women of the Church of England when she came to Christchurch.

Bethell started writing poetry in her fifties. Her domestic cottage life and her interest in gardening permeate her writing, and inform her vision of life. The style and language of her *From a Garden in the Antipodes* (1929) are straightforward, which sets her poetry apart from the more exotic imagery of her contemporaries. This aspect of her work makes her one of the first modern poets in New Zealand. Bethell's later poems are stylistically more complex and reflect her preoccupation with religious belief. Words almost assume a graspable presence in Bethell's poetry, reflecting her fascination with their sound, semantics, and etymology. The meditative tone of her later poetry influenced younger poets such as JAMES K. BAXTER and ALLEN CURNOW, and has drawn attention from other women poets such as FLEUR ADCOCK and BLANCHE BAUGHAN.

Selected works: *Time and Place* (1936); *Day and Night, Poems 1924–35* (1939); *Collected Poems* (1950).

[SH]

Betjeman, John (England, 1906–84) Betjeman was born in London and privately educated (T.S. ELIOT was one of his teachers). In 1925, Betjeman matriculated to Magdalen College, Oxford, though he left in 1928 before taking his degree. His first important job was as an assistant editor at *Architectural Review* in 1930–33.

That Betjeman's first poetry, *Mount Zion* (1931), and architectural writings, *Ghastly Good Taste* (1933), appear at the same moment is no accident. His poetic career was marked by what AUDEN, LARKIN, and others have recognized as poetry rooted in the particular landmarks of a given spot. Unlike some of his Modernist contemporaries, Betjeman was content to document this particular place, with an eye toward buildings, in particular, as markers of human connection or history. His championing of the Victorian Gothic revival in architecture and avowed use of Victorian models, especially Tennyson, for his predominantly formalist verse has been held against him in recent criticism.

Although often still known for early light verse such as 'Slough', Betjeman's mature career began with *Old Lights for New Chancels* (1940). Here, his control of the formal verse which he was never to eschew was masterful and the sometime comic overtones tempered with more serious considerations of childhood memories and lyric expression. These themes, along with Betjeman's use of the sea and the stalwart, athletic woman were to build through *New Bats in Old Belfries* (1945), *Selected Poems* (1948), and *A Few Late Chrysanthemums* (1954), until they culminated in *Collected Poems* (1958). This volume is remarkable not only for the breadth of the poetry but for its popularity. Having reported sales of over 100,000 copies, it cemented Betjeman's public reputation. This reputation was no doubt helped by his frequent appearances on the fledgling medium, television, during the 1950s, discussing architecture and poetry alike.

In recognition of a long poetic and public career, he was granted the OBE in 1960 and knighted in 1969; he succeeded C. DAY LEWIS as Britain's Poet Laureate from 1972, serving until his death from Parkinson's Disease in 1984.

[MW]

Bialik, Hayim Nahman (Israel, 1873–1934) Born in Radi, Russia, in 1873, Bialik received a traditional Jewish education. He studied at a *yeshiva* in Lithuania, yet was strongly attracted to the Enlightenment movement and to political and cultural Zionist circles. He left for Odessa, a center of Jewish literary activity, in 1891, and in the same year published his poem 'To the Bird', which earned him immediate recognition and is still widely recited. He worked in Odessa and eventually became the literary editor of the weekly *Hashiloah*; in 1921 he moved to Berlin and there founded the Dvir publishing house. Three years later Bialik emigrated to the Land of Israel and settled in Tel Aviv, where he lived until his death. He continued writing poetry cast in the (primarily East European) Ashkenazic accent, which alienated him somewhat from the vibrant local culture, but he was generally regarded as *the* poet of national Jewish renaissance, a title which is still firmly attached to his name. Bialik wrote both national and personal poetry, essays, short stories and children's poems, and was also active in collecting and re-writing Jewish folk-tales. His national poetry, calling for rejuvenation and strength, and criticizing Jews for passivity and indifference to the predicament of exile, was widely read in Zionist circles. His personal poems, in particular passionate love poems, gave expression to a longing for warmth and comfort in a world he found often cold and uncompromising. Bialik brought back into the language of Hebrew poetry strong reliance on Biblical and other traditional modes of expression often shunned by writers of the Enlightenment period, and molded it into an ever-flexible language. His first collection of poems was published in Warsaw in 1901, and comprehensive poetry volumes were published in 1938, 1983, and 1990. His work was translated into many languages, among them Yiddish, French, German, Russian, Italian, and Spanish. Collections in English were published in 1981 and 1987, and poems of his were included in numerous anthologies of Jewish literature.

[ER]

Bialoszewski, Miron (Poland, 1922–83) Bialoszewski was born in Warsaw. During the war he studied Polish philology at an underground university, witnessed the uprising of 1944, and was later sent to a labor camp in Germany. Bialoszewski eventually returned to Warsaw, and in 1955 he became one of the cofounders of the vanguard theater called the Separate Theatre. In 1956 his first collection of poems, *The Evolution of Things*, received a great deal of critical attention. His English-language *The Revolution of Things: Selected Poems* was published in 1974.

In poetry his interests have always been in linguistic experimentation, specifically the possibilities of colloquial language. He often takes for his subject matter objects that seem to find themselves on 'the periphery' of everyday life.

Bialoszewski also wrote the successful *A Memoir of the Warsaw Uprising* (1977, 1991), which has been translated into English and reprinted.

[MO]

Bian Zhilin (China, b. 1910) Poet, translator, and critic, Bian was a native of Haimen, Zhejiang. His engagement with poetry ran deep: before he entered Beijing University to study English, he had a very solid foundation in classical Chinese literature. It was during his college years that Bian was first introduced to the British Romanticists and the French Symbolists, and began to write poems. His early collections, *Grass of the Three Autumns* (1933), *Eyes of the Fish* (1935), and *The Han Garden* (1936) – the last was a collaboration with LI GUANGTIAN and He Qifang – show apparent influence by the French Symbolists. The majority of his World War II poetry is characterized by a technically refined synthesis of Chinese and Western elements, a highly meditative quality, and a subtle irony against social injustice. His best lyrics are those that combine ideas and sentiments in a well-balanced syntax and a very polished language.

During the Sino-Japanese War, Bian first taught in Sichuan University, and later at Southwestern United University. Meanwhile, he wrote a large number of patriotic poems which are now ignored. A professor of English, Bian has made a number of valuable translations, including a widely acclaimed verse translation of *Hamlet* (1957), since the founding of the People's Republic. He has been a guest editor of such prestigious literary magazines as *Literary Review*, *World Literature*, *Foreign Literature Review*, and *Poetry*.

Bian has been a Research Fellow of the Chinese Academy of Social Sciences since 1953. His latest book of poetry, *Selected Poems: Pilgrimage of Linguistic Sculpture from 1930 to 1958*, was published in 1979.

[LG]

Bidart, Frank (United States, b. 1939) A National Book Award nominee, Frank Bidart was born in the west California town of Bakersfield, and attended Harvard. There he studied and became friends with ELIZABETH BISHOP and ROBERT LOWELL. Bidart's early work was influenced by these associations, depending on a similar directness and on local detail. His poetry is heavily voiced and confessional; his strongest poems use these techniques dramatically, as in the voices of Nijinsky, an anorexic woman, and a serial killer. His characters debate intensely spiritual themes – about guilt, the burden of life and the connection between the noumenal and the phenomenological.

Selected works: *In the Western Night, Poems 1965–1990* (1990); *Desire* (1997).

[CV]

Bidgood, Ruth (Wales, b. 1922) Born near Neath and raised as a vicar's daughter in Port Talbot, Bidgood studied English at Oxford, and subsequently served in the Women's Royal Naval Service as a coder. After leaving the Navy, Bidgood worked in London for *Chambers's Encyclopedia* before returning to Wales in the 1960s, eventually making her home in Abergwesyn, Breconshire. The natural beauty, traditions, and people of the Breconshire region comprise the primary source of inspiration for her poetry. She has published seven well-received collections, beginning with *The Given Time* (1972), and including a *Selected Poems* (1992). She has also published several articles on the history of the area, and her best poems are enhanced by a historian's sense of place and detail.

[BS]

Biermann, Wolf (Germany, b. 1936) Karl-Wolf Biermann is important both as writer and as catalyst of political events. In 1953 he moved to Communist East Germany, where by 1963 he was not permitted to publish or perform because of his criticism of the government. During his 1976 concert tour in West Germany, Biermann was expatriated by East Germany. Wide-scale protest against this action led to many dissidents leaving East Germany.

Even Biermann's private poems are political. Performed in his unique manner as songs, the poem's text and the music counterbalance each other. His political criticism grew over time from constructive to openly negative. Since German unification, Biermann seems to have come closer to the mainstream.

Selected works: *The Wire Harp* (1965); *With Marx and Engels' Tongues* (1968); *Germany: A Winter Tale* (1972); *Prussian Icarus* (1978); *World Turned Upside Down* (1982).

[IRS]

Binyon, Laurence (England, 1869–1943) Best known for the World War I poem, 'For the Fallen', Binyon was born in Lancaster, educated at St Paul's School and Trinity College, Oxford, and spent his long career at the British Museum.

Binyon was active throughout his life in advocating an appreciation for both art and literature and his work reflects a shift between poetry, art catalogues, and interpretative essays about the visual arts. His poetic subjects were often classical, and frequently focused on the late Victorian period. He was also involved in movements to encourage the speaking of verse as well as experimental versification.

Selected works: *Lyric Poems* (1894); *London Visions* (1896); *Painting in the Far East* (1908); *The Winnowing Fan: Poems of the Great War* (1914); *The Sirens: An Ode* (1924); *The Idols* (1928).

[SS]

Birney, Earle (Canada, 1904–95) Birney is considered to have been one of Canada's finest poets. He has been seen first and foremost as a spokesperson for the nation, both to a native audience and as a representative of Canada on his many journeys abroad. Birney's poetry exhibits perhaps the greatest variety of technique in Canadian poetry, moving from an imitative British Modernism early in his work, to poetry influenced by the experimentation of the Black Mountain School, to the confident use of his own, mature style. Throughout his career, Birney was known as a satirist of great skill and idiosyncratic humor.

Birney was born in Calgary, Alberta. He studied at the University of British Columbia, Berkeley, and the University of Toronto. Although he wrote poetry throughout the 1930s, his first book, *David and Other Poems* was only published in 1942. The title poem, which recounts a failed climbing expedition in the Canadian Rockies, remains an enduring classic of Canadian verse. *David* and Birney's second collection, *Now is the Time* (1945) were both awarded Governor General's Awards. In 1946, Birney accepted an academic position at the University of British Columbia, where he remained for two decades. In 1963, he founded the Creative Writing Department at UBC, a program in which many West Coast Canadian poets would learn their craft.

The polished modernism of Birney's earliest works, which include *The Strait of Anian* (1948) and *Trial of a City and Other Verse* (1952), came to an end in the 1960s as Birney turned to a more experimental style that has not always been critically well received. *Near False Creek Mouth* (1964), *Phomes, Jukollages and Other Stories* (1969; edited by B.P. NICHOL) and other collections from this period, experiment with print, spacing, type size, and an absence of punctuation. Birney's later poetry shows evidence of the influence of his frequent travels in the 1950s and 1960s to Europe, Asia, and Latin America, in terms of both content and form. In the last decade of his life, Birney produced very little work, slowed in 1987 first by a heart attack and then silenced by a stroke. Birney's final volume of new and selected poems, *Last Markings*, appeared in 1991.

[IS]

Bishop, Elizabeth (United States, 1911–79) Effectively orphaned at an early age (her mother institutionalized and her father dead), Bishop always felt the isolation and precariousness of her position in the world. Cared for by relatives and at boarding schools, the young Bishop moved between eastern Canada and Massachusetts, finally settling at Vassar College. It was in college that she fell in love with literature and the metaphysical poets. She was attracted to the simplicity of metaphysical poetry, especially to that of George Herbert. In all her work we can see the influence of Herbert's plain-spokenness, and of his reluctance to write poetry that is decorative or too personal. Through Herbert, Bishop learned a sleekness of line and a relationship to language marked by humility.

Bishop's life and work are marked also by a longing for roots; her poems re-create many of the places she tried to call home, Canada, Key West and Brazil. In her famous villanelle she writes, 'the art of losing isn't hard to master,' in reference to these three homes. Her personal relationships, especially her friendship with ROBERT LOWELL, often struggled from the burden of her low self-esteem and her never-ending battle with alcoholism. These struggles may have affected her output; on the one hand, in her lifetime she published only four collections and some translations from French, Spanish and Portuguese. On the other hand, her poetry grew with each collection, with hardly a misstep. From the terse abstractions of her first book, *North and South*, Bishop developed a looser line, one managed more by a natural rhythm of speech – and the speaker of these later poems allows the reader to witness the development of her ideas, as evidenced by her constant self-correction and playful self-exhortations. Her work also became more autobiographical but never crossed into the confessional. In fact, Bishop urged LOWELL to abandon his most confessional project, *The Dolphin*, because it told too much to be 'art'. Indeed, in Bishop's masterpieces of autobiography, 'Sestina' and 'In the Waiting Room', the reader is overwhelmed more by what is buried than by what is exposed.

Another early, and lesser known, influence on Bishop's poetry is the work of Mallarmé. One can see his fondness for the surreal in the way in which natural subjects in her poems have an almost supernatural power. The Florida Everglades become a self-creating world, where vegetation, the skies and the animals are the agents of progression for the poem. The transformations themselves are not the speaker's responsibility, hers is only to record them faithfully. In her appropriation of these surrealist techniques, readers can appreciate how it was not, for Bishop, such a contradiction to be influenced by both Mallarmé and Herbert.

Critics have often tried to read her lesbianism into these works, into all of her poetry, but Bishop herself would have abhorred these efforts. Like MARIANNE MOORE, an early mentor, Bishop always remained intensely private and much more of a humanist than a feminist. While not receiving as many public honors as many of her contemporaries, she was always well respected by her fellow poets; she held a poetry consultantship at the Library of Congress and was teaching at Harvard when she died at the age of 68 in 1979.

[CV]

bissett, bill (Canada, b. 1939) William Frederick bissett was born in Halifax, Nova Scotia. After briefly attending Dalhousie University in Halifax, bissett moved to Vancouver in the early 1960s to attend the University of British Columbia, where he studied with EARLE BIRNEY and became closely associated with the city's vibrant poetry scene.

bissett has written over fifty volumes of poetry, most published by bleiwointmentpress, which he founded in 1963. Influenced by Gertrude Stein, bissett's poetry is characterized by experiments with syntax and typography, phonetic spellings of words, and the frequent use of colloquialisms, all with the aim of producing a poetic vernacular that works against the rigid conventions and assumptions governing the usual 'élite' production of poetry.

Selected works: *nobody owns the earth* (1971); *MEDICINE my mouths on fire* (1974); *canada gees mate for life* (1985); *what we have* (1989).

[IS]

Biton, Erez (Israel, b. 1942) Born in Algeria in 1942, Biton emigrated to Israel as a child in 1948. Blind since early childhood and trained as a social worker, Biton holds a Master's degree in psychology, and has held various editorial and administrative positions, among them chairmanship of the Hebrew Writers' Association. Biton's poetry, which earned him the Prime Minister's Prize, often turns inward, drawing on the rich, sensual experience of the North African Jewish communities as well as his own struggle for expression and acceptance. The work is strongly influenced by folk ballads and exhibits longing for the mysterious, a joining with nature and the entire cosmos. Biton's first collection, *Moroccan Mint*, was published in 1976.

[ER]

Bjørnvig, Thorkild (Denmark, b. 1918) Author of sixteen poetry collections to date, Bjørnvig is among the best representatives of post-World War II Danish poetry, starting with his first collection, *Stjrnen bag gavlen* (*The Star Behind the*

Gable, 1947). While this volume is heavily indebted to RILKE and ELIOT, Bjørnvig's second collection, *Anubis* (1955) already demonstrated greater originality and made TOM KRISTENSEN declare the author to be the most significant poet of that decade. Bjørnvig also co-founded and co-edited the literary magazine *Heretica* (1948–50), and in 1960 was appointed Member of the Danish Academy.

[VB]

Blaga, Lucian (Romania, 1895–1961) Born in Lancrăm southern Transylvania to a Romanian Orthodox priest and his devout wife, Blaga attended high school in Braşcov, where he voraciously read literature and philosophy. After attending seminary, Blaga moved to Vienna in 1917; he took his doctorate in philosophy in 1920, after winning the Prize of the Romanian Academy the year before.

In 1921, Blaga co-founded the magazine *Gândirea* (*Thought*), in which he published poetry, philosophical essays, and plays; he dissociated himself from the magazine in 1942 because of its pro-Fascist orientation. During the 1920s and 1930s Blaga served in a number of Romanian legations and embassies, and in 1939–49 taught cultural philosophy at the University of Cluj. In 1949 when the Communist regime removed him from the Romanian Academy and banned his work, Blaga was forced to work as a researcher and librarian. He was 'rehabilitated' in 1960, one year before his death.

Transylvania's greatest lyrical voice and one of the major Romanian poets, a Nobel Prize nominee in the mid-1940s, Blaga was also a prominent philosopher (*Trilogy of Knowledge*, *Trilogy of Culture*, *Trilogy of Values*), his poetic and philosophical writings being closely interrelated. Blaga's main theme was Mystery, going from metaphysical anxiety to peace and reconciliation. Along this thematic continuum, his forms changed from expressionist free verse to the equilibrium of classical prosody. In the process, he created a number of significant metaphors – light, sleep, ashes, fire, seeds – which made him a leading creator of images in Romanian poetry.

In *Poems of Light* (1919), light both reveals and hides Mystery, as the poet ecstatically declares the cosmic unity of man, nature, and divinity. *The Great Passage* (1924) and *In Praise of Sleep* (1929) are imbued with metaphysical sadness, opposing the village, as repository of archaic magic rituals and eternal prehistory, to the modern city. In later volumes (*On the Great Water Divide*, 1933; *At the Court of Yearning*, 1938; *The Unsuspected Stair*, 1943) and in works published posthumously, Blaga acknowledges the germinative wonders of nature, love, mystery, and literary creation.

[GF]

Blandiana, Ana (Romania, b. 1942) Internationally recognized (she won the Herder Prize in 1982) and popular for her literary acts of revolt against totalitarianism, Blandiana has been constantly preoccupied with the poet's ethical responsibility. Born in the city of Timişoara in south-western Romania, she studied philology at the University of Cluj, then worked as an editor and columnist for national student and literary magazines. If her first volume, *First Person Plural* (1964), was an explosion of vitality within standard social topics, *Achilles Heel* (1966) voiced – in impersonal, sententious discourse – the tension between an 'irresponsible' universe and the 'naive austerity' dictated by the poet's conscience. In *Third Mystery* (1969), with the poet's 'weariness in the quest for the absolute', the tone becomes lyrical, melancholic, and elegiac: 'angels fall not from sin but from tiredness'. In later volumes (*October, November, December*, 1972; *Sleep from Sleep*, 1977; *The Cricket's Eye*, 1981; *The Hour of Sand*, 1983), the poet tries to liberate herself from the burden of knowledge by reconciliation with the eternal rhythms of nature.

[GF]

Blight, John (Australia, 1913–95) Born in Unley, South Australia, Blight was a lifelong resident of Australia. His first collection of verse, *The Old Pianist*, was published in 1945, but it was not until he was named Senior Fellow by the Australia Council Literature Board in 1973 that Blight declared himself a full-time writer. Before this, Blight was employed as, among other things, a miner, an accountant, and a Commonwealth Government costing officer before he became the part-owner of several sawmills.

Blight received the Myer Award in 1964 for his third volume of poetry, *A Beachcomber's Diary*, a collection of sea sonnets. In 1976, he was presented with the Patrick White Literary Award for under-recognized, but highly creative work.

[MP]

Blok, Alexandr Aleksandrovich (Russia, 1880–1921) Block's father was a lawyer and a professor at the University of Warsaw. Blok spent his early childhood in the intellectual, highly cultured family of his maternal grandfather, A.N. Beketov; he already manifested literary inclinations during these years, writing poetry at the age of five. While in his teens, Blok published *Vestnik* (*The Herald*), including his poetry, prose, and translations.

From the start, his romantic relationships played an important role in his creativity. His first love was K.M. Sadovskaia, who inspired him to write the powerful love lyrics collected in the cycle 'The Poetry of Youth', published posthumously in 1922. Likewise, his wife, Liubov' Dmietrievna Mendeleeva (the daughter of scientist D.I. Mendeleev), inspired his writing; the complexities of Blok's relationship with Mendeleeva are expressed in some eight hundred poems.

Blok's first attempts to publish his poetry publicly, made while he was studying at the law school of the University of St Petersburg (1898–1901), were not successful, though in the 'Argonauts', Bely's Moscow literary circle, Blok's poetry became very popular. In 1902, he met the prominent Symbolist poets ZINAIDA HIPPIUS and her husband Dimitri Merezhkovski, who immediately appreciated him and published ten of his poems in their journal *The New Path* (1903). After placing poems in several other journals as well, Blok published his first collection of poetry, *Poems about a Beautiful Lady* (1905), a volume praised for its beauty, depth, and originality. The book's main theme is the admiration of mystical, eternal femininity which saves by beauty, and is expressed through passionate and romantic love.

During the revolution of 1905, Blok's views of Symbolism changed. In 1907 he published the collection *The Accidental Joy*, which expressed his new views of life, including his rejection of the idea that the world could be saved by beauty and his emerging interest in radical politics. The same year he published the collection *The Snow Mask*, and in 1908 the cycle 'Faina', both the result of his romantic relations with the actress N.N. Bolokhova. Two more collections appeared within the next three years, *The Earth in Snow* (1908) and *The Night Clock* (1911), and marked the beginning of Blok's finest work. Between 1909 and 1919 he published the cycles 'The Terrifying World' (1909–16), 'Retribution' (1908–13), 'Harps and Violins' (1908–16), 'Different Poems' (1908–16), and 'Iambus' (1919), in addition to three books of his first collection of poetry (1911).

Although his romantic attachment to singer L.A. Andreeva-Del'mas is reflected in his poem 'Nightingale Garden' and his cycles 'Harps and Violins' and 'Carmen', written during World War I, the wider context of the war did not have any effect on Blok's inner world. With the inspiration he gained from the October Revolution, however, he wrote the powerful 'Twelve' and 'Scythians' (1918) and began to participate in various Soviet cultural organizations. Unfortunately, in 1920–21 he fell into a deep depression, became physically ill in April, and died in August.

Blok saw his work as a united lyrical trilogy charting the movement of the individual from harmony through chaos and despair, then through a struggle to liberate beauty, and finally to the creation of a new life in Russia. For subsequent generations of Russian writers, his legacy as a poet has been profound.

[RN]

Blunden, Edmund (England, 1896–1974) Blunden grew up in Yalding, Kent, and eventually won a scholarship to Queen's College, Oxford. He soon withdrew from the university, however, in order to serve in the army. Upon his return to England in 1918, he unsuccessfully attempted to resume his studies at Oxford. Blunden went on to spend his adult life continually moving between England and Japan, serving as Professor of English at Oxford (eventually serving as the English Department chair), the Imperial University of Tokyo, and the University of Hong Kong.

Though he produced several important works while in Japan, his distance from the English literary community is widely thought to be responsible for the declining quality of his poetry; Blunden is generally considered a potentially brilliant poet who, because of his stubborn refusal to experiment with the poetic forms of his time, never really achieved his potential. His early works, such as the Hawthornden Prize-winning *The Shepherd, and Other Poems of Peace and War* (1922), were widely praised for their objective examination of rural culture and nature. He was considered a master of stanzaic art whose distaste for free verse served to reinstate traditional poetic forms. But it was not long before he was criticized for having too little substance behind his keen detail, and his lack of artistic development was often noted. The sporadic, deliberate, and impersonal nature of Blunden's later works defines a legacy of untapped literary potential, though one whose early significance, at least, was rewarded with membership of the Order of the British Empire (1951) and the Queen's Gold Medal for Poetry (1956).

Selected works: *Masks of Time* (1925); *English Poems* (1926); *Undertones of War* (1928); *Shelley: A Life Story* (1940); *After the Bombing and Other Short Poems* (1949); *A Hong Kong House: Poems 1951–61* (1962).

[SG]

Bly, Robert (United States, b. 1926) A prolific writer, editor and translator, Bly's first book of poetry, *Silence in the Snowy Fields*, was published in 1962; with the publication of his second book, *The Light Around the Body*, which received the National Book Award in 1968, Bly's literary reputation was firmly established as a poet who plumbs the unconscious for poetic inspiration.

Bly's poetry generally falls into three distinctive chronological categories: 'deep image' poetry; public/political poetry; and public/interpersonal poetry. These periods can be attributed loosely to his influences, which included – throughout the 1950s and early 1960s – the poems of FEDERICO GARCIA LORCA and PABLO NERUDA. During the 1960s, Bly embarked upon a mode of public and political poetry in a response to the Vietnam War, a way of writing that included the prose poem as a public act. He also co-founded 'American Poets Against the Vietnam War' and frequently participated in protests.

From 1985 onward, the public/political dimension of Bly's work shifted to the public/interpersonal, which may have been related to his marriage in 1980. His poetry sought to bring into relief the cruelty and injustice present in everyday lives. During this period, Bly became a spokesman for family values while simultaneously enjoying the success of his book *Iron John: A Book About Men* (1990), which has brought him fame as the leader of the Men's Movement. Bly continues to live and write in his home in Minnesota.

[DC]

Bogan, Louise (United States, 1897–1970) Bogan was a miniaturist. Her first book consisted of more than twenty poems, only two of which are longer than a page (*Body of This Death*, 1923). In her formalism and melancholy she has been compared to W.B. YEATS – but she lacks his fire.

Bogan was born in Livermore Falls, Maine. She received her education at The Girls' Latin School in Boston and Boston University. She spent a year in Vienna and another in Santa Fe, New Mexico. In 1917 she married Curt Alexander and, as an army wife, moved with him to Panama. They had one daughter, Mathilde (Maidie). She left Alexander in 1919 and moved to New York City, where she lived for the rest of her life – writing poetry reviews for *The New Yorker*. In 1925 she married poet Raymond Holden, but was divorced in 1937.

Bogan never received the National Book Award or the Pulitzer Prize, but in 1954 she shared the Bollingen Prize with Léonie Adams. She published six books of poetry, the last two being collected editions. She died alone in her Manhattan apartment, of a coronary occlusion, in February 1970. Her reputation has grown since her death.

Selected works: *The Blue Estuaries: Poems 1923–1968*; *Achievement in American Poetry 1900–1950* (prose, 1950); *A Poet's Alphabet: Reflections on the Literary Art Vocation* (1970).

[RP]

Boland, Eavan (Ireland, b. 1944) Boland is one of the most celebrated women poets in Ireland today. Born in Dublin, she spent much of her childhood in England and in the United States because her father was a diplomat. She graduated from Trinity College, Dublin in 1966.

In her poetry and prose, Boland describes the precarious position of the female Irish poet, writing both within and outside the English literary tradition. In her prose works, *A Kind of Scar* (1989) and *Object Lessons: The Life of the Woman and the Poet in Our Time* (1995), Boland examines the tradition in which women were objects within poems rather than subjects and authors. In particular, Irish women have been objectified into heroic, patriotic symbols. Boland's work attempts to repossess women into flesh-and-blood subjects and voices rather than symbolic objects.

Influenced by such feminist poets as ADRIENNE RICH, Boland's poetry explores themes of suburbia, motherhood, domesticity, and the female body. Not only does she infuse these everyday details and experiences with aesthetic richness and power, but she also gives a public voice to what had been traditionally private or distorted when viewed from a male perspective. The title poem from *The Journey and Other Poems* (1986) transforms conventional male mythology to encorporate the experiences of motherhood and loss. Later volumes include *Outside History* (1990); *In a Time of Violence* (1994); *An Origin Like Water: Poems 1967–87* (1996); and *The Lost Land: Poems* (1998).

Boland is currently the director of the creative writing program at Stanford University in the United States, and lives part of the year in Dublin.

[CT]

Bonnefoy, Yves (France, b. 1923) Born in Tours, where he spent a conventional youth, Bonnefoy sought greater creative vitality in the French capital during his early twenties. His initiation occurred during the Occupation of France, at which time he founded the review *La Révolution la nuit (The Revolution, the Night)* to announce his affiliation with the Surrealist movement. He did not, however, remain a proponent of Surrealism for long, finding in the surreality of the image an unsettling disjunction not only with historical reality but with the affective life of his imagination.

Bonnefoy's first important book of verse was *Du mouvement et de l'immobilité de Douve* (*On the Motion and Immobility of Douve*, 1953), at the center of which is the mysterious presence of Douve. At once corporeal and disembodied, she appears to be a figure of the process of poetic creation itself. The specter of death and loss, which is intimately connected with creation, is also present in this book, which was followed by *Hier régant désert* (*In Yesterday's Desert Realm*, 1958) and *Pierre écrite* (*Pierre écrite – Words in Stone*, 1965).

The spirituality of Bonnefoy's verse should not dissuade readers from approaching his learned essays on classical antiquity, poetry, and painting, since they further inform his verse; he is, for instance, one of the foremost commentators on Rimbaud. Bonnefoy has also translated YEATS into French, as well as Shakespeare's sonnets and several of his plays, including *The Winter's Tale*, *Hamlet*, and *King Lear*. In 1981, following the death of Roland Barthes, he was elected to a chair at the Collège de France. In 1987 he was awarded the Prix Goncourt.

Selected works: *Rome 1630: l'horizon du premier baroque* (*Rome 1630: Early Baroque and its Context*, 1970); *Dans le leurre du seuil* (*In the Lure of the Threshold*, 1975); *La Vérité de parole* (*The Truth of Speech*, 1988); *Début et fin de la neige* (*Beginning and End of the Snow*, 1991); *Alberto Giacometti* (1991).

[SJ]

Borges, Jorge Luis (Argentina, 1899–1986) Born in Buenos Aires, in 1914 Borges traveled with his family to Europe and lived in Geneva, where he finished his schooling. In 1919–21 he lived in Spain, where he came into contact with the literary movement Ultraismo and with Rafael Cansinos-Assens. Back in Buenos Aires in 1921 he founded *Proa*, an avant-garde poetry magazine. From then on he published continuously, producing short stories, poetry, and essays. He is considered to be the major figure in Argentine literature, with his books translated into more than twenty languages. His collections of poems include *Fervor de Buenos Aires* (*Buenos Aires Fever*, 1923), *Luna de enfrente* (*Moon across the Way*, 1925), *Cuaderno San Martín* (*San Martin Notebook*, 1925), and *El oro de los tigres* (*The Gold of the Tigers*, 1972). He is perhaps better known as a fiction writer, with his *Ficciones* (*Fictions*, 1944) being awarded the Gran Premio de Honor de la Sociedad Argentina de Escritores.

In 1955 he was made Director of the National Library where he stayed until 1973, a period of increasing fame. In 1955 also he was awarded the first Premio Nacional de la Literatura. Columbia University, the University of Michigan, and Oxford all awarded him honorary doctorates. In 1961, jointly with SAMUEL BECKETT, he received an Internacional Congress Reyers Prize in Mexico. He died in Buenos Aires in 1986 but, according to his wishes, he was buried in a cemetery in Geneva.

Whether as poet, fiction writer or essayist, Borges created a very idiosyncratic universe. He took his inspiration from the entire corpus of universal literature, from Hindu texts to medieval poetry, from Arabic mystics to English idealist philosophers, from Dante to Martin Fierro, but particularly from Anglo-Saxon literature, including epic texts such as *Beowulf*. He was also very interested in Icelandic sagas and even studied these languages. Like ELIOT and POUND he liked to borrow from obscure or marginal texts and use quotations from them in his own writings, playing with erudite footnotes and making it difficult for the reader to ascertain where quotation ends and invention begins. His short fiction is often in the form of pseudo-essays, simulacra of serious pieces, and he also liked playing with the structure of an encyclopedia. He was deeply interested in philosophical questions such as the nature of time, the self and the other, reality and dreams, the infinite representations of God, the world as text, as library, as labyrinth, and a sense of metaphysical vertigo. In his poetry, all of these themes recur, confirming this very personal imaginary world. Apart from his very early poetry, which was more avant-garde, his poetry is largely based on classical forms and rhythms, on the elements of heroic sagas which include the themes of bravery, honor, treason, and family history. Paradoxically, it is the very universality of his inspiration that makes Borges an archetypal Argentine writer, able to draw on an infinity of texts to create a corpus which is both local and unique in world literature.

[MN]

Bowering, George (Canada, b. 1936) Born in Keremos, British Columbia, educated at the University of British Columbia, and currently a professor at Simon Fraser University in Vancouver, Bowering is a prolific poet, novelist, short story writer, editor and critic. As the poetry of eastern Canada has been influenced by the 'Montréal Group', and later by the trio of LOUIS DUDEK, IRVING LAYTON and Raymond Souster, Bowering has had much to do with the flowering of poetry in western Canada in the 1960s. It was Bowering who, along with Frank Davey and Fred Wah, founded *Tish* (1961–63), the influential poetry journal that introduced the open form poetics of CHARLES OLSON and the Black Mountain group into a Canadian poetry largely dominated by modernism, a journal that had an enormous impact on contemporary Canadian poetry.

Bowering's first three collections, *Sticks and Stones* (1962), *Points on the Grid* (1964) and *The Man in Yellow Boots* (1965) exhibit Olson's strong influence on the young poet. *Rocky Mountain Foot* and *The Gangs of Kosmos*, which together earned Bowering a Governor General's award for poetry for 1969, first showed evidence of what became a characteristic emphasis on the life and landscape of the West, deliberating eschewing the nationalist concerns that dominated Canadian literature. Beginning with *Baseball* (1967), Bowering experimented with the production of 'serial' texts – immediate compositions produced within a previously established set of rules. One of these texts, *Autobiology* (1972) is perhaps Bowering's best work of poetry. More recently, Bowering has written three novels that share some characteristics with these earlier, serial poems. *Burning Water* (1980, winner of the Governor General's award for fiction), *Caprice* (1987) and *Harry's Fragments* (1990) are self-reflexive, postmodern texts, that show the poet at both his best (in *Burning Water)* and his worst (with *Caprice).*

Of the major Canadian poets writing after World War II, the quality of Bowering's output has been the most uneven. Nevertheless, his continued willingness to experiment and his engagement in all of the major literary debates of the day have assured him of a place among the most important poets of the century.

[IS]

Brackenbury, Alison (England, b. 1953) Brackenbury was born in Lincolnshire, and graduated with honors in English from St Hugh's College, Oxford, in 1975. In 1981, Brackenbury published her first book, *Dreams of Power and Other Poems*, which earned her a Poetry Book Society recommendation.

Brackenbury's poems engage historical and biographical themes, and her strong local focus merges with dreams and myths to challenge the boundary between historical fact and imagination. The title poem in *Breaking Ground and Other Poems* (1984) is a long dialogue between a patient and his female therapist. The poem recounts episodes from the life of poet John Clare and demonstrates Brackenbury's exploitation of iambic pentameter.

More recent works include *Christmas Roses and Other Poems* (1988), *Selected Poems* (1991), and *1829 and Other Poems* (1995).

[LK]

Brathwaite, Edward Kamau (Jamaica, b. 1930) Though he has perhaps not gained the same measure of international recognition as his contemporary DEREK WALCOTT, Brathwaite is without question one of the major figures in all of Caribbean literature. He has done important work not only as a poet, but as a writer of numerous and diverse texts on Caribbean literature, culture, music, and history. As one of the founding members of the Caribbean Artists' Movement and founder (with critic Kenneth Ramchand) of the publishing house and journal *Savaou*, Brathwaite has been an influential figure in the establishment of a vibrant and self-assured Caribbean culture. Since 1991, he has been a member of the Comparative Literature department at New York University, after a long tenure as a professor of Social and Cultural History at the University of the West Indies.

Brathwaite was born in Bridgetown, Barbados. He studied history at Cambridge University, receiving his B.A. in 1953; he would later earn a Ph.D. from Sussex University for his study of *The Development of Creole Society in Jamaica, 1770–1820* (1971). For seven years, in 1955–62, Brathwaite taught in Ghana. The opportunity to live in Africa and to learn in detail African customs, traditions, and literary forms had an enormous impact on his intellectual development and subsequent poetic output. Brathwaite believes that the cultural and spiritual dispossession of the Caribbean can only be overcome by a reconnection to its African roots; this belief is reflected in the thematic and formal preoccupations of all his poetry, particularly the earlier work for which he is best known.

The Arrivants trilogy (1970), which comprises his first three volumes of poems, remains Brathwaite's most important work. By any standard, this is one of the great poetic works of the New World, an epic exploration of the Black Diaspora written in an impressively diverse variety of poetic forms and languages. *Rights of Passage* (1967) traces the journey of Africans to the Americas, and explores the continuities in their responses to the New World from North America to the West Indies. *Masks* (1968) makes the reverse journey from the West Indies to Africa, examining African spirituality and its possibilities for the Caribbean. The final volume, *Islands* (1969), marks a return home to the West Indies, and celebrates the power of the islands' folk culture and the emergence of a genuine national consciousness. A second trilogy, consisting of *Mother Poem* (1977), *Sun Poem* (1982), and *X/Self* (1987), repeats many of the themes of *The Arrivants* in the specific context of Barbados, while also exploring gender in the Caribbean, the persistence of imperialism, and the role of the artist in an indifferent world.

Brathwaite has continued to produce significant collections of poetry. *Visibility Trigger* (1986) and *Jah Music* (1986) contain poems dedicated to murdered artists and activists as well as poems that deal with the difficulties faced by the poet in his own life. The poems of *The Zea/Mexican Diary* (1993) mourn the death of Brathwaite's wife. There is a noticeable darkening of mood in these later works and a growing despair about the possibilities of poetry in the modern world.

[IS]

Brault, Jacques (Canada, b. 1933) Poet, essayist, playwright, novelist, Brault was born in Montréal, studied philosophy there and in France, and has been a professor at the Université de Montréal for most of his adult life. In addition to several books of poetry, Brault has also written important works of criticism, including articles and books on the work of Alain Grandbois, Émile Nelligan, HECTOR DE SAINT-DENYS GARNEAU, and GASTON MIRON.

Like Miron, Brault's poetry expresses both the painful state of existing in a colonized society and the desire for the liberation of Québec. These themes are most pronounced in *Mémoire* (*Memoir*, 1965) and *La poésie ce matin* (*The Poetry of This Morning*, 1971). In *Poèmes de quatre côtés* (*Poems of Four Dimensions*, 1975), Brault freely transforms/translates the work of the American poets E. E. CUMMINGS and John Haines, and of the Canadian poets MARGARET ATWOOD and GWENDOLYN MACEWEN. *L'en dessous l'admirable* (*Below the Admirable*, 1975) finds the poet turning inward to examine the question of identity, an exploration which continues in *Trois fois passera* (*Three Times Will Pass*, 1981), a collection of prose and poetry that deals with the difficulties and joys of the writing life.

[IS]

Brecht, Bertolt (Germany, 1898–1956) A major innovator of world literature with his 'epic theater', Brecht was also a great lyrical poet. Born into a wealthy family as Berthold Eugen Friedrich Brecht, he became interested in theater and Marxism, and he combined the two. In 1933 he fled from Nazi Germany, exiled in Denmark, the Soviet Union, and finally the United States. After his appearance before Senator McCarthy's Committee for Unamerican Activities in 1947, Brecht returned to Europe and eventually settled in East Berlin, where he founded his own theater, the 'Berlin Ensemble', in 1949. Four days after attending a rehearsal for his *Galileo* there in 1956, Brecht suffered a fatal heart attack.

Brecht's early poems, such as those collected in *B. B.'s House Courier* (1927), show his disdain for the bourgeois life style and his support of the outsider, which became increasingly identified with the proletariat or its representatives after 1926, when Brecht became an idiosyncratic Marxist. Brecht used the correspondence between his poems and plays by integrating many poems as songs in his plays, where the songs interrupted and commented on the dramatic action in keeping with his epic theater. *The Songs of the Three Penny's Opera* (1929), especially 'Mack the Knife', are known worldwide.

The *Svendborg Poems* (1939) represent a poetic high point with narrative and politically didactic poems questioning, for instance, why the little people who do all the work are never mentioned in history books. The *Buckow Elegies* (1964) express Brecht's fundamental humanism and feelings of resignation concerning politics.

[IRS]

Brennan, Christopher (Australia, 1870–1932) Brennan was born in Sydney, of Irish Catholic background, though his ethnicity never figured largely in his poetry. He studied at the University of Sydney and in 1892 visited Berlin on scholarship. Here, he became apprized of the latest trends of European poetry. He also met and eventually married Anna Werth, a marriage that proved troublesome when the couple (accompanied by Brennan's mother-in-law) returned to Australia.

Brennan's work, as seen in *Towards The Source* (1897) was occult, opaque, refined – the total opposite of the tough, rousing, nationalist verse favored by Australian culture in the 1890s. Most of Brennan's poetry appears in *Poems* (1913), actually published in 1914. This volume is dominated by the section called 'The Forest of Night' in which Brennan powerfully evoked the figure of Lilith, Adam's apocryphal first wife, as a symbol of all that is both alluring and destructive about womankind. *A Chant of Doom and Other Verses* (1918) was largely war-inspired poetry, emphatically anti-German in tone.

Brennan corresponded with Mallarmé, and was thoroughly affected by Mallarmé's Symbolist theories of poetry. Although Brennan's type of intellectuality was a rare phenomenon in the Australia of his day, he was nonetheless widely celebrated and recognized. Still, the University of Sydney barely kept him on in part-time positions and only grudgingly granted him a full-time appointment as Associate Professor of German in 1920. Increasing alcoholism and despair inhibited his later productivity and, combined with a personal scandal stemming from a liaison with a younger woman, led to Brennan's dismissal from his university post in 1925. His last years, though, were a period of comparative tranquility, even if most of his memorable poetry had been composed before he reached forty.

[NB]

Breton, André (France, 1896–1966) From a global perspective, the Surrealist movement, which Breton founded in Paris in 1919 with LOUIS ARAGON and PHILIPPE SOUPAULT, is among the most influential literary and artistic movements of the twentieth century. Like the Dada movement from which it evolved, Surrealism (a term adopted from APOLLINAIRE, who coined it in 1917) was first and foremost a call to shared revolt against dominant bourgeois values and systems of thought, perception, and expression. The Surrealist project, conceived as a cultural movement, attracted some of the most imaginatively original writers, painters, and film makers in France, and as its influence spread, in countries as far from the Hexagone as Mexico, Egypt, Japan, and China.

As the head (or 'pope' as he was sometimes derisively called) of the Surrealists from the inception of the movement until his death, Breton combined in his personality the libertarian spirit of the anarchist with the strong hand of a master, the result being a movement which was in flux from its beginnings. He registered his opinions of his peers in the *Manifestes du surréalisme* (*Surrealism Manifestoes*, 1924 and 1930) and elsewhere. The ever-changing shape of the Surrealist group mirrored the unconscious, which Surrealists sought to liberate from the debilitating effects (insofar as it hampered creative expression) of logical positivism. With his fellow Surrealists, Breton initiated several innovative directions in composition, among them automatic writing – *Les Champs magnétiques* (*The Magnetic Fields*, 1920), co-written with Soupault, being the earliest specimen – and the exquisite corpse. He demonstrated the astounding effect of the Surrealist image in verse collections such as *Clair de terre* (1923, revised in 1966) and *Le Revolver à cheveux blancs* (*Revolver with White Hair*, 1932).

Selected works: *Poisson soluble* (*Soluble Fish*, 1924); *Nadja* (1928); *L'Amour fou* (*Mad Love*, 1937); *Arcane 17* (1944); *La Clé des champs* (*Free Rein*, 1957).

[SJ]

Breytenbach, Breyten (South Africa, b. 1939) One of the best-known Afrikaans-language writers of his generation, Breytenbach was born in the Western Cape and studied in Cape Town. He moved to Paris in 1962 and returned in disguise in 1975 to South Africa, where he was arrested and sentenced to nine years in prison for terrorism. Since his release in 1982, he has published in Afrikaans in South Africa and translated his own English versions elsewhere. In his earlier works he fluctuates between intense outrage at apartheid's racist structures and the love for his homeland and the people of South Africa. This love–hate relationship informs most of his work, including a sharp critique of governmental policy and the penal system, *The True Confessions of an Albino Terrorist* (1985). His poetry is often described as surrealist, full of dreamlike fragments and images of isolation.

Selected works: *Sinking Ship Blues* (1977); *And Death White as Words* (1978); *In Africa Even the Flies are Happy* (1978); *Judas Eye* (1988).

[KS]

Bridges, Robert (England, 1844–1930) Poet Laureate for seventeen years, Bridges was born in Walmer, Kent, and educated at Corpus Christi College, Oxford, and St Bartholomew's Hospital, London. He retired early from medicine in 1881, relying on an inheritance he received from his father; that financial stability allowed him to spend the rest of his life writing poetry. He lived most of his adult life near Oxford with his wife Monica Waterhouse and their three children.

A traditional, formalist lyric poet, Bridges also experimented with 'stress prosody' and, later, 'neo-Miltonic syllabics'. The dominant theme of Bridges' career was beauty, both spiritual (heaven, art) and earthly (nature, woman). He also wrote extensively on love and grief, while mastering both English and Italian sonnet forms. Although many of Bridges' poems have tragic subject matter, and although he did write some particularly somber poetry in light of World War I, his work maintains subtle hints of optimism. To truly experience beauty in all its forms was, for Bridges, the highest goal of humankind.

Bridges was also an editor, a playwright, and a literary critic, as well as founder of the Society for Pure English, an organization dedicated to preserving the integrity and authenticity of the English language. His work was rewarded with the Order of Merit (1924) and his tenure as Poet Laureate in 1913–30.

Selected works: *Nero Part 1* (1885); *Eros and Psyche* (1885); *The Shorter Poems* (1890); *Nero Part 2* (1894); *The Spirit of Man* (1916); *The Testament of Beauty* (1929); *Collected Essays* (10 volumes, 1927–36).

[SG]

Brinkmann, Rolf Dieter (Germany, 1940–75) Coming of age in the 1960s, Brinkmann was fascinated by American pop art as an expression of a new sensitivity. He was a prototypically rebellious and struggling artist and established himself as Germany's leading representative of pop and underground literature, as shown in *The Pilots* (1968).

Frustrated with his personal life and with failed liberation through pop art, he explored new expressive forms in longer poems, as in *Go West 1 and 2* (1975), and in a more radical collage technique that integrated visual elements, from as early as *Godzilla* (1968) to *Ice Water on Guadalupe St.* (1985). Brinkmann was killed in a car accident in London.

[IRS]

Briusov, Valerii Iakovlevich (Russia, 1873–1924) Briusov's three-volume *Russian Symbolists* (1894–5), published while he was a student at Moscow University (and containing mainly his own poetry), marked the first appearance of Symbolism in Russia. However, it was not until the publication of *Tertia Vigilia* (1900) in the Symbolist outlet *Skorpion* that he established his reputation as a new poet of consequence. In 1904, Briusov assumed the editorship of the Symbolist critical journal *Vesy*, a magazine created partly by his own efforts and published by *Skorpion*'s house.

By 1910 Briusov was poetically prolific: both *The Mirror of Shadows* (1912) and *Seven Colors of Rainbow* (1916), which included poems about World War I, departed from Symbolism's abstraction. His last works were inspired by the Bolshevik Revolution, which he not only accepted, but also actively supported. Despite this late political enthusiasm, expressed in *Last Hopes* (1920), *In Such Days: Poems 1919–20* (1921), and *Moment: Poems 1920–1* (1922), Briusov is best remembered as one of the most important figures of Russian Symbolism, a writer influenced by the French Decadence of Rimbaud, Verlaine, and Mallarmé.

Selected works: *Urbi et Orbi* (1903); *Mea* (1924).

[RN]

Brodsky, Joseph (Russia, 1940–96) Iosif Brodsky Aleksandrovich began writing poetry in 1958. Soon afterwards he became friends with ANNA AKHMATOVA, who called him 'the most talented poet of his generation'. In early 1960, Soviet authorities claimed his poetry to be pornographic and anti-Soviet. His first collection of poetry, *Stikhotvoreniia i poemy* (*Poems and Narrative Verse*, 1965), appeared in the West one year after he was sentenced to hard labor in Arkhanglesk; soon after its publication, thanks to the pressures of public opinion, he was released and authorized to return to Leningrad. Yet in 1972, only two years after the publication of his second volume, *Ostanovka v pustyne*(*A Halt in the Wilderness*), Brodsky was forced by the Soviet government to leave Russia; he emigrated to the United States, where he taught at various universities. After his emigration, Brodsky published two important collections of poetry, *Konets prekrasnoi epokhi* (*The End of a Beautiful Epoch*, 1977) and *Chast' rechi* (*A Part of Speech*, 1977), both reflecting his perception that the poetic word is a salvation, a way to overcome the condition of exile, of separation from the essential. His poetry passes from certain warmth and hope to coldness and a state of anaesthesia, when nothing is felt, though things are observed and understood.

A major international poet – he received a Nobel Prize for Literature in 1987 and was named the United States Poet Laureate in 1991 – Brodsky is very much admired by the Russian intelligentsia. Still, given the relative newness of his esteemed position, it is too early to say what is or will be his effect on Russian literature. However, revered for his monologic teaching style, his essays in English, and his love for the work of poets such as ROBERT FROST and W.H. AUDEN, Brodsky remains a powerful figure to many contemporary poets.

Selected works: *Rimskie elegii* (*Roman Elegies*, 1982); *Urania: Novaia kniga stikhov* (*Urania: A New Book of Poetry*, 1987).

[RN]

Bronk, William (United States, 1918–99) Born in 1918 in upstate New York, Bronk attended Dartmouth College, served in the army during World War II, and lived his whole life in the small town of Hudson Falls, New York, where he ran the family coal and lumber business. A highly regarded author of nearly twenty books, Bronk won the American Book Award for *Life Supports* in 1982.

In stripped-down poems of blunt statement, crisp, clear imagery, and dark, mordant wit, Bronk grapples with philosophical themes. His spare, moving poetry is thoroughly skeptical of our ability to understand the world. Like WALLACE STEVENS, to whom he is often compared, Bronk explores the fictions we create in order to survive in such an uncertain universe.

Selected works: *The World, the Worldless* (1964); *Life Supports: New and Collected Poems* (1982); *Selected Poems* (1995).

[AE]

Brooke, Rupert (England, 1887–1915) Brooke was born in Rugby, Warwickshire, where his father served as a headmaster at Rugby School. Educated there, Brooke began writing poetry at age nine, and had two of his poems, 'The Pyramids' (1904) and 'The Bastille' (1905), published by the school. As a young boy he not only excelled in writing and scholarship, but was also a first-rate footballer.

His outstanding academic work at Rugby earned him a fellowship at King's College, Cambridge, and eventually led to the publication of his *Poems* in 1911, the only book of his poetry to be published during his lifetime. While at university, Brooke was both an active member of the exclusive, by-invitation-only discussion club, the Cambridge Apostles, and president of the Socialist Fabian Society. His studies at Cambridge coincided with these of several members of the famed Bloomsbury Group.

Influenced by such poets as Baudelaire,

Wilde, Shelley, and Keats, Brooke continued to write poetry and to lecture after leaving Cambridge. Soon after World War I began, Brooke enlisted in the Royal Naval Division as a volunteer reservist. Upon the completion of his training and service in Belgium, he became a commissioned officer. In 1915, while en route to the Dardanelles, Brooke was unexpectedly stricken with an infection as a result of sunstroke. Shortly thereafter, he incurred an insect bite on his lip that gave him blood poisoning. The young officer never recovered and died on board his ship. He was buried in an olive grove upon the ship's arrival in the Dardanelles. His well-known poem, 'The Soldier', was written only months before his death.

Brooke's war poems, most of them sonnets, were uncommonly grounded in reality. His youthful enthusiasm and uncompromising patriotism not only gained him wide recognition from such people as Winston Churchill and Virginia Woolf, but also helped establish his reputation among Britain's youth as a poetic and political model.

[BCB]

Brooks, Gwendolyn (United States, 1917–2000) Brooks' work can most easily be divided into two periods: before and after the Second Black Writers Conference of 1967. There, she was exposed to the newer, freer and angrier styles of such writers as AMIRI BARAKA, Ron Milner and others. Up until that point, Brooks had received much attention for her poetry, winning a Guggenheim Fellowship at age twenty-nine and the Pulitzer Prize at thirty-three. Her early verse is still deeply relevant, combining the formal diction of classic English poetry with street English. Her pleasure in 'roughening up' traditional verse is obvious: the new combinations of words and the originality of her subjects and descriptions make her early poems among the most anthologized of their time. Her love of abstractions invites comparisons with Emily Dickinson, Gerard Manley Hopkins and WALLACE STEVENS.

Since 1967, Brooks has written poetry that is looser in style, more connected to black vernacular English. These poems still use formal structures, but ones more common to song, such as repetition, or common to preaching, moving in a series of urgent commands or using a pastiche of biblical and popular texts. While her critical reputation has dulled somewhat, Brooks' social role as an activist has only grown over the years since the Second Black Writers Conference. She has taught extensively throughout the United States, appeared on television numerous times, and remains the Poet Laureate of Illinois. There are anthologies of her later work easily available, but a consideration of her work must include her first two books, *A Street in Bronzeville* (1945) and *Annie Allen* (1949).

[CV]

Brossard, Nicole (Canada, b. 1943) Brossard is one of the most constantly inventive and theoretically sophisticated of contemporary Canadian writers. In both her poetry and prose, she has continually conducted radical experiments with genre, form and style. As well as being an influential figure as an organizer of literary conferences and events, and as an editor of literary journals (most notably *La Barre du Jour*) and presses, Brossard has continued to produce significant works of poetry and prose at a breathtaking pace; she has written over twenty volumes of poetry since 1965.

Brossard was born in Montréal. *Aube à la saison* (*Dawn of the Season*, 1965) was her first collection, and her only collection of relatively traditional verse. As in the poetry of GASTON MIRON and PAUL CHAMBERLAND, these poems explore the landscape of Québec in an effort to define the essence of the Québécois nation. Her second book, *Mordre en sa chair* (*To Bite in the Flesh*, 1966) inaugurates Brossard's bold and ceaseless experiments with form. Brossard's subversion of dominant forms of poetic spacing and punctuation were in the mid-1970s connected to a growing thematic interest in feminism and lesbianism. It was also at this time that she became influenced by French post-structuralism, which she has employed in her own highly original theoretical works on poetics and language. The connections between sexuality, textuality and the politics of sexual difference have become the central concern of her most recent poetry and prose.

Selected works: *L'écho bouge beau* (*Echo of a Beautiful Slum*, 1968); *Suite logique* (*Suite Logic*, 1970); *Le centre blanc* (*The White Center*, 1978); *Daydream Mechanics* (1980); *Amantes* (*Betrothals*, 1980); *Double Impression: Poèmes et textes 1967–84* (*Double Impression: Poems and Texts, 1967–84*,1985); *Langage obscure* (*Obscure Language*, 1992).

[IS]

Brown, George Mackay (Scotland, 1921–96) Brown's poetry and fiction is largely set in 'Hamnavoe', based on Stromness, Orkney, where he was born and educated. Tuberculosis prevented him from working after leaving school, and in 1951–2 he studied at Newbattle Abbey College where EDWIN MUIR encouraged his writing of poetry. Two collections, *The Storm* (1954) and *Loaves and Fishes* (1959) were published before he graduated from Edinburgh University in 1960, where he did postgraduate work on Manley Hopkins in 1963–64. He returned to Stromness in 1964, rarely leaving Orkney until his death; he used his Society of Authors travel award (1968) to travel round Ireland. He was the recipient of a number of honorary degrees and awards, including the Order of the British Empire in 1975.

In 1961 he converted to Catholicism which became central to his imagery. Throughout his work, Orkney is used as a sampler of human life and history; the traditional ways of life in the islands furnish symbols of cyclical renewal in a pared-down language which owes much to Norse sagas. His best-known novels are probably *Beside the Ocean of Time* (1994), shortlisted for the Booker Prize, and *Greenvoe* (1972). He also collaborated with the composer Sir Peter Maxwell Davies on settings of his poems and opera libretti.

Selected works: *The Year of the Whale* (1965); *Fishermen with Ploughs* (1971); *Winterfold* (1976); *Voyages* (1983); *The Wreck of the Archangel* (1989); *Selected Poems 1954–83* (1991); *Following a Lark* (1996); *Selected Poems 1954–92* (1996).

[LKMF]

Brown, Sterling A. (United States, 1901–89) Sterling Brown was born in Washington, D.C., the son of a professor of religion at Howard University who had once been a slave. He received a B.A. from Williams College, an M.A. from Harvard, and became an influential professor at Howard. Brown became associated with the Harlem Renaissance, and with such writers as LANGSTON HUGHES, though he never lived in New York and resisted the 'Harlem' label. His first volume of poems, *Southern Road*, was widely hailed by critics when published in 1932, but the Depression effectively ended the African-American creative renaissance, and Brown could not find a publisher for his second volume. Turning his attention to writing literary and cultural criticism, and to editing several important anthologies of African-American literature, Brown did not publish his next volume of poems until 1975. By then, young writers had reawakened the interest in Brown's work which continues today.

Brown's poetry, like Hughes's, draws on various elements of African-American folk idiom – spirituals, ballads, work songs, folk tales, blues and jazz – and fuses them into a lyrical, expressive style. His best poems use dialect to great effect, and transform vernacular materials into moving poems of social protest. Brown's work both conveys the tragedy and drama of the struggles endured by African-Americans, and decries the history and persistence of racial injustice in America.

Selected works: *Southern Road* (1932); *The Collected Poems of Sterling Brown* (1980).

[AE]

Brown, Wayne (Trinidad, b. 1944) Born in Woodbrook, Trinidad, Brown is commonly associated with the new generation of Caribbean poets who first came to prominence in the early 1970s, including such writers as Anthony McNeill, MERVYN MORRIS, and DENNIS SCOTT. Of these poets, Brown has attracted the least critical and public attention, which is due no doubt to his relatively limited literary output.

Brown's first book of poetry, *On the Coast* (1972), was awarded the Commonwealth Prize for Poetry. A second volume of poetry did not appear until *Voyages* (1989), although in the intervening years Brown wrote a well-received biography, *Edna Manley: The Private Years: 1900–38* (1976) and edited *Derek Walcott: Selected Poetry* (1981). Brown is a lyrical poet, whose influences include WALCOTT and TED HUGHES. Thematically, his poems explore the psychological complexity of self-identity as a means of addressing larger questions of national and cultural identity.

As he has for many years, Brown continues to teach at the University of West Indies, Trinidad, and to write a column for the *Trinidad Express*.

[IS]

Brownjohn, Alan (England, b. 1931) Born in south-east London and educated at Oxford, Brownjohn has worked as a broadcaster and freelance writer, reviewed for *The Times Literary Supplement*, served as a borough councillor, and been a parliamentary candidate. As a poet, Brownjohn came to distinction as a member of The Group, the exclusive poets' workshop founded by Philip Hobsbaum which ran from 1955 to 1965 and included members such as PETER REDGROVE, PETER PORTER, Edward MacKenzie, George Lucie-Smith, FLEUR ADCOCK, and B.S. Johnson. In 1965 he accepted a position as a lecturer at Battersea College of Education. Brownjohn also wrote as a poetry critic for the *New Statesman* (1968–76), served as a member of the Arts Council Literature Panel (1967–72), chaired the Greater London Arts Association Literature Panel (1973–77), and was Deputy President of the Poetry Society. He has been a full-time writer since 1978, and in 1979 received the Cholmondeley Award. Brownjohn is considered by many to be one of Britain's best social poets. His subject matter covers the traditional themes of childhood and love, but it is his concern with and awareness of social issues that sets his poetry apart. He often informs his work with images of disillusionment and with satires of progress in post-war England.

Selected works: *Collected Poems 1952–83* (1983); *The Old Flea-Pit* (1987); *The Observation Car* (1990).

[TT]

Brutus, Dennis (South Africa, b. 1924) Born in Harare (then Salisbury, Rhodesia), Brutus was educated at Fort Hare and the University of Witwatersrand. He taught for fourteen years in South African high schools. His political campaigns led to his being banned from all social and political meetings and activities. He was arrested in 1963 for his active protest against apartheid. Shot in the back for trying to escape while on bail, he was rearrested and sentenced to eighteen months of hard labor. He left South Africa in 1966 after serving time on Robben Island and a year under house arrest. He has served as president of the South African Non-Racial Olympic Committee, acting chairman of the International Campaign against Racism in Sport, and United Nations Representative for International Defense and Aid. He has also been Visiting Professor at the University of Denver and a Professor of English at Northwestern University.

First coming to prominence in the 1950s, Brutus rapidly established himself as one of South Africa's leading poets. He offered a liberal humanism approach in a post-war climate, straddling an African and Western philosophical and literary mode. The simple and elegant verse in one of his best collections, *Letters to Martha* (1968), also presents his view of life in prison on Robben Island.

Selected works: *Sirens, Knuckles, Boots* (1963); *Poems from Algiers* (1970); *Thoughts Abroad* (1970); *A Simple Lust: Collected Poems of South African Jail and Exile* (1973); *Strains* (1975); *Stubborn Hope* (1978); *Airs and Tributes* (1989).

[KS]

Buckley, Vincent (Australia, 1925–88) Buckley grew up in Melbourne, where he became involved in politics and publishing. After serving in World War II, Buckley published formally inclined verse, as in *The World's Flesh* (1954), and nonfiction books, such as *Poetry and Morality* (1959), which reflected Buckley's lifelong interest in religion. *Arcady and Other Poems* (1966) was more personal, including a sequence devoted to the poet's relationship with his father. Buckley came more and more to identify with his Irish Catholic origins, and he spent increasing amounts of time in Ireland, adopting a fiercely nationalist position in Irish politics, a preoccupation reflected in *The Pattern* (1979). He continued teaching, though, at the University of Melbourne and was a mentor to younger poets such as KEVIN HART. Buckley died of cancer, and his illness was a subject of the posthumously collected *Last Poems* (1991).

[NB]

Bukowski, Charles (United States, 1920–94) Charles Henry Bukowski disdained poetic tradition and taste. His poems, though, make clear that he valued compression and linearity as well as the truthfulness he finds in narratives of sexual frankness and seamy, often violent, realism.

Born in Andernach, Germany and raised in Los Angeles, California, Bukowski attended Los Angeles City College in 1939–40. Often beaten as a child, he became and remained a brawling, heavy drinker. His life spanned the full range of social condition – from destitution to wealth and international celebrity.

Bukowski's first book of poems, *Flower, Fist and Bestial Wail*, appeared in 1960. His early work has been compared with that of ROBINSON JEFFERS. Bukowski published twenty-seven more books of poems in addition to more than thirty books of prose. His screenplay, *Barfly* (1987), was the basis of a notable motion picture.

[CC]

Bull, Olaf (Norway, 1883–1933) One of the prominent Norwegian poets of the early twentieth century, Bull won immediate recognition with his first collection, *Digte* (*Poems*, 1909). After studying philology, Bull made his living as a journalist, writing while publishing his poetry. He lived alternately in Oslo, Rome, Copenhagen, and Paris, and his stay in the French capital is reflected in French Symbolism's strong influence on his poetry. Known for his rich imagery and crystalline form, Bull has arguably contributed more than any other writer to the formation of modern Norwegian poetry. *Digte* was followed by *Ny digte* (*New Poems*, 1913), *Digte og noveller* (*Poems and Short Stories*, 1916), *Samlede digte* (*Collected Poems*, 1919), *Stjernerne* (*The Stars*, 1924), and *Metope* (1927). It was not until the late 1920s, however, that Bull found a less esoteric and more socially involved voice. The new development is evident in his last works, *De hundreder* (*The Hundred Years*, 1928), *Ignis* (*Arden*, 1929) and *Oinos og Eros* (*Oinos and Eros*, 1930). His *Collected Poems* was published in 1942.

[YB]

Bunting, Basil (England, 1900–85) Bunting was born in Northumberland and educated at a Quaker boarding school in Yorkshire. He served six months in prison during 1918 as a conscientious objector to World War I. In 1923 he worked in Paris for Ford Madox Ford on the *Transatlantic Review*. During his time there he also met EZRA POUND and their friendship solidified when they met again in Rapallo, Italy. His early work, such as *Redimiculum Matellarum* (1930), went virtually unnoticed and Bunting continued working and traveling, eventually joining the Royal Air Force following the outbreak of World War II; he received a posting to Persia, becoming Vice-Consul in Isfahan after the war. He also worked as a correspondent for *The Times* and as subeditor of the *Newcastle Morning Chronicle* throughout the 1950s and 1960s. In 1963, with the encouragement of Newcastle poet Tom Pickard, he began to write again after a period of inactivity. The publication of his collection *Briggflatts* in 1966 brought him considerable critical acclaim and established his name as a respected poet, particularly in the United States. He spent the latter part of his life as a visiting poet at various American and British universities, particularly Newcastle University, which awarded him a D. Litt in 1971. Bunting's poetic themes vary from childhood to odes based on his many travels, especially in Persia. Many critics consider Bunting's unique adaptation of the sonata form to poetic structure to be his most significant contribution to the genre.

Selected works: *Poems 1950* (1950); *First Book of Odes* (1965); *The Spoils* (1965).

[TT]

Burnside, John (Scotland, b. 1955) Burnside was born in Dunfermline, Fife, and uprooted to England at the age of ten. He was educated at Catholic schools in Scotland and England and at technical college in Cambridge. He held a variety of jobs, including computing systems designer, and after returning to Fife in 1995 he was creative writer-in-residence at Dundee University. His poems often have a spiritual perspective: his first collection, *The Hoop* (1988), uses Celtic myth and symbolism. Subsequent collections use Christian and Catholic iconography in an unobtrusive portrayal of silence and the natural world. His second collection, *Feast Days* (1992), won the 1994 Faber Memorial Prize.

Selected works: *Common Knowledge* (1991); *The Myth of the Twin* (1994); *Swimming in the Flood* (1995); *A Normal Skin* (1997).

[LKMF]

Butler, Guy (South Africa, b. 1918) Butler was born in Cradock and educated at Rhodes and Oxford Universities. During World War II, he was stationed in the Middle East, Italy, and the United Kingdom. He lectured at the University of Witwatersrand for two years before taking a position at Rhodes University in Grahamstown. There he served as Head of the English Department until his retirement in 1983 while also working as a playwright, autobiographer, and poet. An outspoken critic for humanist and liberal values, his influential *Stranger to Europe* (1952) set much of the standard and tone for post-World War II English-language verse in South Africa. In 1975 he won the C.N.A. Prize for his *Selected Poems*. He also edited several highly influential publications: *A Book of South African Verse*, first published in 1959 (with Chris Mann), the Afrikaans journal, *Standpunte*, and *New Coin* poetry magazine in 1965.

Selected works: *South of the Zambezi* (1966); *Take Root or Die* (1966); *On First Seeing Florence* (1968); *Songs and Ballads* (1978).

[KS]

C

Campbell, David (Australia, 1915–79) Born near Adelong in New South Wales, Campbell was educated at Kings School, Parramatta (Australia's oldest school) and Cambridge University. During World War II he served with distinction as a fighter pilot in the RAAF. Returning to Australia, he farmed properties in the Canberra region and wrote poetry. He also edited two anthologies, wrote two volumes of short stories, and translated two volumes of Russian poetry with ROSEMARY DOBSON. He was poetry editor of *The Australian* in 1964–67.

Campbell's early poems were formal and pastoral in character, with an interest in balladry influenced by John Manifold. *The Branch of Dodona* (1970) evinced a new interest in technique and topical themes, such as the Vietnam War. Campbell continued to show an openness to new forms (such as the 'life-studies' work of 'Starting from Central Station'), and encouraged younger poets, without abandoning his pastoral subject matter. His *Collected Poems* was published in 1989.

[DM]

Campbell, Roy Dunnachie (South Africa, 1901–57) Ignatius Royston Dunnachie Campbell was born in Durban and moved to England in 1918. He spent one year at Merton College, Oxford, then returned to South Africa in 1926 to become one of its best-known men-of-letters. In 1926 he edited, with Laurens van der Post and William Plomer, the literary and cultural periodical, *Voorslag* (*Whiplash*). He lived in Spain, France, Portugal, and England, translating and publishing poets from all these countries. During World War II he worked for the British Intelligence Corps in Britain, East Africa, and the Western Desert. After the war he was awarded the Foyle Prize for Poetry (1951) and, in 1954, an honorary doctorate from the University of Natal. He died in a car accident in Portugal in 1957. He is renowned both for his satirical work attacking South African life (particularly the Afrikaner) and for his translations, including *The Poems of St John of the Cross* (1951) and Baudelaire's *Les Fleurs du Mal* (1952).

Selected works: *The Flaming Terrapin* (1924); *The Wayzgoose* (1928); *The Georgiad* (1931); *Flowering Reeds* (1933); *Flowering Rifle* (1939); *Song of the Mistral* (1941); *Collected Poems* (3 volumes, 1949, 1957, 1960); *Light on a Dark Horse* (1951); *Selected Poems* (1982).

[KS]

Caproni, Giorgio (Italy, 1912–90) Born in Livorno and raised in Genoa, Caproni moved to Rome in 1938, where he worked as an elementary school teacher and founded, with MARIA LUISA SPAZIANI and Danilo Dolci, the Eugenio Montale International Center of Poetry. The apparent facility of his poetry, combined with the themes of alienation and death often hidden under the metaphor of travel, results in an uncanny mixture of verbal expressionism and melodious rhymes, folk-like versification and metrical experimentation. Caproni was also an extremely refined translator of French authors such as Frenaud and APOLLINAIRE.

Selected works: *Il passaggio di Enea* (*The Passages of Aeneas*, 1956); *Congedo del viaggiatore cerimonioso e altre prosopopee* (*The Farewell of the Ceremonious Traveler and Other Prosopeias*, 1966); *Il muro della Terra* (*The Wall of the Earth*, 1975); *Il franco cacciatore* (*The Franc-Hunter*, 1982); *Res amissa* (*Lost Things*, 1991).

[GS]

Cardenal, Ernesto (Nicaragua, b. 1925) Born in Granada, Nicaragua, this poet, critic, and political figure of the Nicaraguan revolution has gained world-wide acclaim as a Central American writer. As a young man, Cardenal studied in Mexico and the United States, taking a doctorate from Columbia University.

Upon his return to Nicaragua he became involved in the first attempt to overthrow the dictator Anastasio Somoza. That failed attempt, among other things, pushed him into spiritual pursuits and led him to a life as a Trappist monk for a period. He became known world-wide for the experimental Catholic community he founded on the isle of Macarron in Lake Nicaragua where he experimented with the teaching of poetry and created popular poetry workshops. He was also an important member of the Sandinista Popular Liberation Front (FSLN) and, upon the triumph of the revolution in 1979, he became Minister of Culture. From this post he supported and disseminated the popular poetry experiments of his Solentiname years. During the mid-1990s, however, he resigned his membership of the FSLN due to internal disagreements with its directorate.

His poetry is often divided into two periods, one preceding his spiritual conversion in 1956 and one following that sea change. Typical of the first is the long poem 'La Ciudad Desheredada'('The Disinherited City'), a passionate poem about Granada and about the bitter frustration of love. His early Surrealism gives way to a more testimonial and political poetry in his second period as he writes an outspoken commitment to social justice and to a new form of Latin American Catholicism.

Selected works: *Gethsemani, Ky* (1960); *Epigramas: poemas* (*Epigrams: Poems*, 1961); *Salmos* (*Psalms*, 1967); *Vide en el amor* (*To Live is to Love*, 1971); *Canto cosmico* (*Cosmic Song*, 1993); *El estrecho dudoso*(*The Doubtful Street*, 1995).

[SL]

Carnero, Guillermo (Spain, b. 1947) Carnero belongs to the Generation of 1970, or *novísimos* ('very new poets'). Taking Ortega y Gasset's *The Dehumanization of Art* to an extreme, they focus primarily on the intellectual character of poetry. The poem creates its own reality and is not beholden to any external referent. Hermeticism and frequent allusions to other art forms characterize this period.

For Carnero, the poem does not reflect reality but creates its own, and the text becomes, in postmodern fashion, a linguistic construct. *A Drawing of Death* (1967) shows how reality (life) becomes lost or distanced through artistic expression. *Scipio's Dream* (1971) further develops this theme and weaves countless intertextual references into the poems. With *Essay on a Theory of Vision* (1977) and *Indefinite Divisibility* (1990) Carnero's work turns metapoetic, with its own act of creation as theme. Carnero writes, teaches, and edits a literary journal (*Anales de la literatura española contemporánea)* in Alicante.

[AB]

Carpelan, Bo (Finland, b. 1926) Carpelan is a leading Finnish-Swedish poet, internationally acknowledged novelist, author of prose for children, of plays for radio and television, and an acclaimed translator. Carpelan first worked as a literary critic, then subsequently as an assistant director of Helsinki's city library. He held the prestigious national Professor of Arts position in Helsinki in 1980–85.

Carpelan was twenty years old when he published his first collection of poetry, *Som en dunkel värme* (*Like a Mysterious Warmth*, 1946), followed by another collection the year after; both were surprisingly mature, and rich in symbolism. This early lyricism was suggestive of the main themes to come, among them the insistent presence of what has been called the 'chance factor' in life, whether concerning one's birth, growing up, or the inevitability of death. The collection *Variationer* (*Variations*, 1950) is expressive of mature lyric independence. The subsequent collection *Minus sju* (*Minus Seven*, 1951) gives shape to poetry's link with transience; in it he is playfully allegorical while crossing the border into the world of the absurd.

Carpelan is seen as having renewed the traditions of Finnish-Swedish modernism. In his poems of the 1960s he employs abrupt image shifts reflecting on the ways one experiences nature and history. In the recent poems his world view has become more concrete. In *I de mörka rummen, i de ljusa* (*In Dark Rooms, In Light Ones*, 1976) he reflects – in metapoetic terms – on the same scenery under varying light, thus examining the limits of lyric expression. His 1980s collections have received the highest critical acclaim.

Carpelan is not only considered among the most talented lyricists in Finland and Sweden, but his position as the leading Finnish-Swedish classic modernist remains unchallenged. Among Carpelan's numerous honors are six State Awards for Literature (1951, 1967, 1970, 1972, 1987, 1989), the Finlandia Prize (1993), and the Swedish Academy's Prize (1997).

[SP]

Carruth, Hayden (United States, b. 1921) Carruth draws directly upon his experience and his immediate environment, which he blends with a mix of Eastern philosophy and a keen sense of observation. Born in 1921 in Waterbury, Connecticut, Carruth received his B.A. from the University of North Carolina, and his M.A. from the University of Chicago.

From 1949 to 1950 Carruth was the editor-in-chief of *Poetry*; he then became an associate editor for the University of Chicago Press (1951–2), and later became the poetry editor for *Harper's* from 1977 to the present. Since 1972 Carruth has served as professor of English at five universities, until his recent retirement from Syracuse University.

A prolific poet, essayist and anthologist, Carruth has published over forty-three books, and he has won over twenty-nine awards, fellowships, and honorary degrees including National Endowment for the Humanities fellowships, National Book Critic Awards for *Collected Shorter Poems* (1993), and the National Book Award for *Scrambled Eggs and Whiskey* (1996). While Carruth's later writing has waned in intellectual intensity, he continues to be one of America's poetic legends.

[DC]

Carson, Ciaran (Ireland, b. 1948) Born in Belfast and educated at Queen's University, Belfast, Carson depicts the urban violence and paradoxes of gritty Belfast life with poignancy, savagery, and humor. Frequently called a postmodernist, Carson is concerned with the politics of language. Many of his volumes, from *The Irish for No* (1987) through *Letters from the Alphabet* (1995), address Carson's first language – Irish – but more generally they deal with the relationship of language to culture and history. His poems, which often make use of the long poetic line, also possess a dark humor in response to violence, as in *First Language (*1994), when he welcomes a visitor to Belfast, 'home of the best knee surgeons in the world'.

Selected works: *The New Estate* (1976); *The New Estate and Other Poems* (1988); *Belfast Confetti* (1993).

[CT]

Cărtărescu, Mircea (Romania, b. 1956) A native of Bucharest, Cărtărescu studied at the University of Bucharest. A middle school teacher, then editor of the *Contrapunct* literary journal, Cărtărescu is now associate professor of Romanian literature at the University of Bucharest.

Cărtărescu entered the literary scene tempestuously, superposing autobiographical youth angst and city street life over sacred monsters' themes and clichés. The merge between the poet's readings of Romanian and world literature and his postmodernist use of the 'inexhaustible lyrical reserves of everyday life' (E. Simion) has led to a poetry brimming with ironic trivia and romantic symbolism, with solemn and parodic tones, scholarly and trite phraseology.

Cărtărescu's literary achievements have been recognized both nationally and internationally. In 1980, *Lighthouses, Shopwindows, Photographs* earned him the Romanian Writers' Union prize for a literary debut, while his short prose volume *Le rêve* (*The Dream*, 1992) was nominated for the best foreign book prize.

Selected works: *Love Poems* (1983); *Everything*, (1985); *The Levant*, (1990).

[GF]

Carter, Martin (Guyana, 1927–97) Carter is known as the English Caribbean's most politically radical writer. Born in Georgetown, Guyana, he was an active participant in the Guyanese independence movement. His poems almost always deal with politics, revolution, and the struggle to overcome colonial oppression.

The anti-colonial themes of Carter's earliest poetry in the collections *The Hill of Fire Glows Red* (1951) and *The Kind Eagle* (1952), and his prominence as a voice of the revolutionary movement, led him to be arrested and imprisoned by the British in 1953. While in prison, he wrote *Poems of Resistance* (1954), which contains the poems for which he has become best-known. After his release from prison, he continued his involvement with the independence movement in varying capacities. He was an independent Guyana delegate to the United Nations in 1966–67; in 1967–70, he served as the Minister for Information and Culture. Since the early 1970s, Carter has spent his life teaching at various universities, and has continued to write poems that have become less polemical and more philosophical, as in the collections *Poems of Succession* (1977) and *Poems of Affinity* (1980).

[IS]

Castellanos, Rosario (Mexico, 1925–74) A feminist whose life dedicated to promoting Mexican art and culture was marked by sorrow, Castellanos began writing poetry as an adolescent. Her early poetry, influenced by her vanguardist contemporaries, is metaphysical and imagistic, while later poems are personal, often constructed as first-person dramatic monologues. Major themes include women's lives in patriarchal society, the notion of 'otherness', death, solitude, and the nature of poetry itself. Castellanos also wrote award-winning novels, a play, short stories, and essays. Her collected poems can be found in *Poesía no eres tú: obra poética 1948 – 1971* (*You are not Poetry*, 1975).

Selected works: *Meditation on the Threshold* (1988); *The Selected Poems of Rosario Castellanos* (1988); *Another Way to Be: Selected Works of Rosario Castellanos* (1990).

[LKA]

Castillo, Otto Rene (Guatemala, 1936–67) A poet and guerrilla, Castillo was burnt alive by his captors of the Guatemalan army. Castillo was exiled to El Salvador in 1953 for his political work and, like other poets of his generation in Central America, ended up studying behind the Iron Curtain. While in Budapest he won the World Federation of Democratic Youths international poetry prize (1957), which marked the beginning of his recognition as a poet. He returned to Guatemala as part of a film team to document the struggle against the regime of Méndez Montenegro and eventually joined the ranks of the FAR (Revolutionary Armed Front) before his martyrdom.

Selected works: *Vámonos Patria a Caminar* (*Let's Go Walking, Homeland*, 1967); *Informe de una Injusticia: antología poética* (*Report of an Injustice: A Poetic Anthology*, 1975).

[SL]

Causley, Charles (England, b. 1917) Causley was born in Launceston in Cornwall and made his name first as a playwright in the 1930s. He served in the Royal Navy during World War II. After the war he began work as a teacher, until resigning in the late 1960s to become a full-time author. Since then, he has taken up literary appointments around the world. He received the Society of Authors travel scholarship (1954, 1966), the Queen's Gold Medal for Poetry (1967), the Cholmondeley Award (1971), the *Signal* Award (1987), and the Maschler Award (1987). As a poet, his themes center on the Cornish landscape and people; however, his poetry is also inspired by his naval war experiences. He is renowned for employing a traditional ballad form in his poetry, which is popular with a wide audience of children and adults. Causley's lyrical musicality and humor have made him one of those modern poets who is both admired by critics and read by the general public.

Selected works: *Farewell, Aggie Weston* (1951); *Union Street* (1957); *Underneath the Water* (1967); *Figure of Eight* (1969); *Figgie Hobbin* (1970); *Collected Poems 1951–75* (1975): *A Field of Vision* (1988).

[TT]

Cavafy, Constantine (Greece, 1863–1933) Born in Alexandria, Cavafy lived as a child in England, where his family had business ventures, but spent most of his life in Alexandria, the mythical locus of his poetry. An impoverished bourgeois, he worked as a civil servant in the Department of Irrigation in colonized Egypt and visited Greece briefly in 1901. There he met the already established novelist Gregorios Xenopoulos, who has the distinction of being the first to have introduced Cavafy to the Greek literary public. In 1927 he was honored by the Greek state with the Medal of the Phoenix. Shortly before his death, he returned to Greece for medical reasons. He died on his birthday at age 70.

No poet in the Greek tradition has written so little and influenced so many. Cavafy began writing relatively late in his life and wrote sparingly until the year of his death. His surviving work consists of fewer than 280 lyrics, of which only a handful were published in literary journals during his lifetime. Instead he circulated his work in broadsheets which he distributed to chosen friends. In 1914 he met E. M. Forster who was visiting Alexandria. The latter introduced his work to the British public including T. S. ELIOT, T. E. Lawrence, and later W. H. AUDEN and LAWRENCE DURRELL, both of whom were heavily influenced by Cavafy.

The first phase of his writing (1894–1910) is predominantly allegorical and symbolic, betraying the influence of the French Symbolism which Cavafy later abandoned as he came to terms with his homosexuality and poetic persona. In such early poems as 'Walls', 'Ithaca', and 'Waiting for the Barbarians', he adopts an existential attitude toward the fickleness of human affairs. His style became subsequently more direct, dramatic and prosaic, with a restrained abstention from adjectival adornment and rhetorical flair. His language is an idiosyncratic blend of primarily colloquial forms and formal, classical, Hellenistic or Byzantine expressions. An erudite poet and a master of irony, he found inspiration in minor historical figures and moments of cultural decline, emphasizing human vanity and frailty, the threat of oblivion and the futility of lofty ideals and trite patriotism; his themes favored periods of cultural transition, hybridity, and diversity but always through the prism of Hellenic culture and language.

After 1910, his erotic poems became increasingly more daring and openly homosexual though never sexually explicit. He frames these poems within the poetics of aestheticism and decadence by affirming what he calls the 'brave' and 'eclectic excesses' of homosexuality (see 'I Went', 'Chandelier', 'Temethos, Antiochian, A.D. 400', 'Theater of Sidon (400 A.D.)'). Some of the recurrent themes of his erotic poems are past sexual encounters, a fascination with youthful male bodies, and a haunting preoccupation with premature death.

His poetry has been translated into numerous languages. Two of the English translations are the bilingual *Collected Poems* (1975) and *The Complete Poems of Cavafy* (1976).

[GSY]

Celan, Paul (Germany, 1920–70) Born Paul Anczel into the Jewish minority within the German-speaking minority within the multicultural environment of Romania, Celan was strongly influenced by the cultural and linguistic experience of growing up in this south-east European region. More important, however, was his traumatic experience when the Nazi military occupied Romania in 1941. His parents were deported and murdered, and Celan himself was a prisoner in a forced labor camp. After his release he went to Vienna in 1947 and then to Paris a year later to study German literature and linguistics. In Paris, Celan worked as translator and then as lecturer at the Ecole Normale Supérieur; he became a French citizen, but he continued to write in German.

Often considered a high point of European Late Modernism, Celan's intensely personal and political poetry is a major contribution to world literature, not just because the Holocaust was its thematic focus but also because Celan's poetic treatment of the Holocaust acknowledged the Chassidic teaching that authentic suffering cannot be expressed in words. Expressing the suffering of the victims and the sorrow of the survivors, Celan questioned human existence and criticized a language that had become corrupted through political abuse. His poems increasingly presented a sense of community that can only be shared in silence but that needs to be evoked by language. In his own life, Celan crossed over to silence: in 1970, he committed suicide.

Celan's mature poems (since the early 1950s) are stunning in their precision and associative power. Over the years, he condensed and intensified his metaphoric language, making his poems paradoxical, enigmatic, and evocative, as in the oxymoron 'black milk' from his most famous poem, 'Death Fugue'. *Poppies and Memory* (1952) presents poems, including 'Death Fugue', with often hymnic rhythm and complex, hermetic metaphors. The poems clearly yet only indirectly address the Holocaust, pointing to the insufficiency of language to express suffering authentically. Despite their powerful metaphors, Celan himself considered these poems too aesthetic.

In *From Threshold to Threshold* (1955), he tried to write more laconically, referring to words as 'corpses', to evoke the silence in which suffering can be expressed. *Language Grid* (1959) and *The No-One's-Rose* (1963) continued this endeavor; the poem 'Engführung' ('Stretto') refers to and sums up Celan's work and its motifs, including his montage technique of combining quotations from and allusions to other poets such as RILKE, TRAKL, and the French Modernists. *Breath Change* (1967), including the poems from *Breath Crystal* (1965), is considered the climax of Celan's poetry. Its irony, ellipsis, and fragmentation document Celan's belief that authentic poetry encompasses a new tone and silence – the change in breath. His last poems were published in *Compulsory Light* (1970) and posthumously in *Snowpart* (1971) and *Time Farm* (1976).

[IRS]

Cendrars, Blaise (Frédéric Sauser; France, 1887–1961) Though he worked in publishing, film, ballet, and journalism, Swiss-born Cendrars' greatest creation was his own legend, as expressed in his literary works, including the narrative poems for which he is best known: *Les Pâques à New York* (*Easter in New York*, 1912), *La Prose du Transsibérien et de la petite Jehanne de France* (*The Trans-Siberian Express*, 1913), and *Le Panama: Ou, Les Aventures de mes sept oncles* (*Panama: Or, The Adventures of My Seven Uncles*, 1918). Cendrars may not have been the diamond smuggler he claimed, but he did join the French Foreign Legion and lost his right arm in World War I – an experience that came to symbolize mankind's spiritual mutilation. An emblematic Modernist, Cendrars wrote verse infused with the restless rhythm and latent solitude of modern life, offering heterogenous imagery with all the immediacy of telegraph dispatches and advertising posters.

Selected works: *Dix-neuf poèmes élastiques* (*Nineteen Elastic Poems*, 1919); *Kodak* (1924).

[ML]

Cernuda, Luis (Spain, 1902–63) Cernuda belongs to the Generation of 1927 (see GUILLÉN, HERNÁNDEZ and LORCA). Like PEDRO SALINAS and JORGE GUILLÉN, Cernuda seeks the essence of life through poetry. Born in Seville, he lived and taught in England, the United States, and Mexico after the Spanish Civil War. Cernuda's work frequently involves presenting, in clear, precise language, tensions between opposing forces. Cernuda also explores the alienated poet in *Invocations* (1935) and *Like Someone Waiting for the Dawn* (1947). *The Clouds* (1940), written in the aftermath of the war, is a meditation on death. Later in his career Cernuda wrote love poetry (*With Time Running Out*, 1956) and published an important study of contemporary Spanish verse. His collected works were published as *Reality and Desire* (1965).

[AB]

Cervantes, Lorna Dee (United States, b. 1954) Born into a Chicano and Native American family in California, Cervantes writes of a multi-lingual, multi-cultural, *mestizo* world. Not prolific, Cervantes composes with precision, creating many-layered, highly imagistic poems. In them, Cervantes discusses issues such as women's rights and poverty by a densely woven set of associations. Her lyric connections highlight the intellectual aspects of *mestizo* ethnicity, along with the emotional and political. She is considered one of the best poets writing about Latino/a life in the United States.

Selected works: *Emplumada* (1981); *From the Cables of Genocide: Poems on Love and Hunger* (1990).

[CV]

Césaire, Aimé (Martinique, b. 1913) Césaire is considered by many to be one of the century's greatest French poets. Born in Basse-Point, Martinique, Césaire moved to Fort-de-France when he was eleven, which gave him the opportunity to attend the only secondary school that existed in the French Antilles at the time. At the age of 18, Césaire left Martinique to study in Paris. There he was influenced by the revolutionary politics of Marxism and aesthetics of Surrealism. With Léon-Gontran Damas and LEOPOLD SEDAR SENGHOR, who was later to become president of Senegal and a famous poet in his own right, Césaire founded the magazine *L'étudiant noir* (*The Black Student*) in 1934. It was here that the concept of 'Negritude', which has since become synonymous with Césaire's name, was first articulated, even though the actual word did not appear until the publication of *Cahier d'un retour au pays natal* (*Return to My Native Land*, 1939), Césaire's greatest and most influential work.

Cahier d'un retour au pays natal was written as Césaire prepared to return from Paris to Martinique. An astonishingly powerful poem, exhibiting a Surrealist's pleasure in difficult metaphors, an uncontrollable profusion of images and phrases, and language pushed to the edge of intelligibility, the journey back to Césaire's native land is a movement into the future rather than back into his past. The poem is an act of individual and collective self-assertion, a thorough-going cleansing of colonial attitudes of self-hatred and abjection, and, simultaneously, a powerful expression of the culture that connects peoples of African ancestry around the world. The poem's struggle against black oppression and alienation, and its revolutionary expression of the authenticity of African culture has made it an enormously influential text in the Third World.

In his later work, Césaire has turned away from Surrealism and has written in simpler, more realistic language in order to make his work available to a wider audience. In addition to several books of poetry, collected in English in *Aimé Césaire: The Collected Poetry* (1983), he has written plays (most notably *La tragedie du roi Christophe* (*The Tragedy of King Christopher*)and *Une saison au Congo* (*A Season in the Congo*)) and several important non-fiction books, including *Discours sur le colonialisme* (*Discourse on Colonialism*, 1950) and *Touissaint L'Ouverture* (1960). Césaire is also an important political figure in Martinique. He has been the mayor of Fort-de-France and a member of the French National Assembly since 1945, and was instrumental in establishing Martinique as an overseas department of France. This might seem to be a contradiction for a figure who has been seen as an advocate of national liberation, as is his use of typically European Modernist strategies to explore black nationalism in the *Cahiers*. It is, however, precisely these tensions in his literary and political views that have made Césaire an enduring and relevant figure in the West and the Third World.

[IS]

Chacel, Rosa (Spain, 1898–1994) Chacel is known primarily as a novelist and essayist, but her poetry is instrumental to understanding her life and career. Born in Valladolid, she was of the Generation of 1927 (see GUILLÉN, HERNÁNDEZ and LORCA) and a friend of JUAN RAMÓN JIMÉNEZ. She studied drawing and sculpture. Like many writers, Chacel fled from Spain in the late 1930s and lived in Argentina for many years, where she worked as a novelist, critic, and translator before returning to Spain in 1977. Chacel published two major volumes of poetry, *At the Edge of the Well* (1936), in the neogongorine style, and *Forbidden Poetry* (1978), a collection of works written since the Civil War. Chacel's poetry is both autobiographical and topical and shows her love for the arts.

[AB]

Chamberland, Paul (Canada, b. 1939) Born in Longueuil, Québec, Chamberland studied philosophy at the Université de Montréal, and is infamous for destroying the completed version of his doctoral thesis, written under the supervision of Roland Barthes at the Sorbonne, during the May 1968 student uprising in Paris.

Chamberland has long been one of Québec's most powerful political poets. Poetry is for him necessarily subversive, both politically and aesthetically. Politically, he has supported the cause of Québec nationalism in the virulent, strident poetry of *L'afficheur hurle* (*The Shouting Sign Painters*, 1964) and *L'inavouable* (*The Unavowable*, 1968); aesthetically, Chamberland has challenged bourgeois poetic taste by deliberately writing 'badly' and in *joual* – the form of the French language spoken in Québec. The title of Chamberland's early book, 'The Shouting Sign Painters', has become a descriptive term for the Québécois poets of this generation, via critic Malcolm Reid's study of the revolutionary Québécois poetry of the 1960s.

Following the culmination of revolutionary energies in FLQ Crisis and the outrage at the declaration of the War Measures Act, Chamberland's politics took a turn similar to that of his poetic contemporaries. Though not forgetting the situation of Québec, Chamberland's poems in the 1970s and 1980s, from *Éclats de la pierre noire d'où jaillit ma vie* (*Glimmers of the Black Stone My Life Flows From*, 1972) to *Terre souveraine* (*Sovereign Ground*, 1980), show his concern with the deteriorating political and ecological condition of the Earth as a whole. His effort to make sense out of a coming apocalypse appears in his use of poetic collages that produce poetry out of the detritus of modern culture.

[IS]

Char, René (France, 1907–88) René-Emile Char was born in l'Isle-sur-Sorgue and received his Baccalaureate degree from Lycée d'Avignon. Upon meeting BRETON and ELUARD, with whom he collaborated on *Ralentir Travaux* (*Stopping Work*, 1930), Char became interested in the Surrealists. Although he later broke with them, his home was searched by the Vichy police in 1940 and he was condemned as a Communist because of his earlier affiliation with the group.

The lasting impact of the Surrealists can be seen in Char's startling imagery and his attempts to make contradictory ideas harmonious. His poetry ranges from aphorisms to free verse to prose poems, and is often criticized for its obscurity of meaning. Quite prolific, Char continued to write until his death in 1988.

Selected works: *Arsenal* (1929); *Seuls demeurent* (*Half-Witted People*, 1945); *Feuillets d'Hypnos* (*Hypnos Waking*, 1946); *Poèmes et prose choisies* (*Selected Poetry and Prose*, 1957); *La Parole en archipel* (*The Archipelago Language*, 1962); *Oeuvres complètes* (*Complete Works*, 1983).

[BRB]

Chase, Alfonso (Costa Rica, b. 1945) A journalist and university professor, Chase's lyric poetry is characterized by an intimate search for identity and by the processing of his personal experience, especially in his early poetry books, *El reino de mi mundo* (*The Kingdom of My World*, 1966) and *El árbol del tiempo* (*The Tree of Time*, 1967). After 1970 he became preoccupied with the social problems of urban youth culture in Costa Rica in books such as *Las puertas de la noche* (*The Doors of the Night*, 1974) and *Mirar con inocencia* (*To Look with Innocence*, 1975). His preoccupation with the life of Costa Rican youth is also a theme treated in his prose. Chase is an important cultural and public figure and has served as director of publications for the Ministry of Culture and as president of the Society of Costa Rican authors.

Selected works: *Cuerpos* (*Bodies*, 1974); *Días y Territorios* (*Days and Territories*, 1980).

[SL]

Chédid, Andrée (Lebanon, b. 1920) Born in Cairo, Chédid was raised and educated in Lebanon and has lived in Paris since 1946. Her considerable works include poetry, essays, plays, novels, and short stories. Her first novel, *Le Sommeil délivré* (*From Sleep Unbound*, 1952), was immediately a success and has been followed by many others. *Visage premier* (*First*

Face, 1971), originally titled *Textes pour un poème* (*Texts for a Poem*), narrates her life and experience in Lebanon and France. Two years later, *Fêtes et Lubies* (*Holidays and Whims*, 1973), established her poetic reputation. Turning *Fraternité de la parole* (*Brotherhood of Language*, 1976) and the same year *Cérémonie de la violence* (*Ceremony of Violence*, 1976) into wildly imaginative poetry, she indulged both image and metaphor.

By *Cavernes et Soleils* (*Caves and Suns*, 1979) she passionately described the happy life before war. *Textes pour un poème* (1986) regrouped her earlier poetry. She used this title again many years later to show that over time, her goal remained the same; she wanted to keep tapping the same inspiration inside of her. In her work, private, pure poetry echoes her joy in everyday life, mixed with questions about herself and mankind. Andrée Chédid claims that each poem is only a stone in a forest but is nonetheless directly connected to the cosmos. Since 1986 she has been copiously writing, editing and publishing. Her most recent work has included themes of joy in language and love of life.

[MS]

Cheney-Coker, Syl (Sierra Leone, b. 1945) Born to Christian Creole parents in Freetown, Cheney-Coker's family was thus part of the Sierra Leonean social and cultural elite of the country. He was educated in Sierra Leone prior to leaving for the United States in 1966 to pursue post-secondary studies. Cheney-Coker has since worked as a journalist, professor and, for a time in the late 1980s – early 1990s, as the publisher of the only independent newspaper in his native Sierra Leone.

An intensely personal and self-reflective work, Cheney-Coker's first published collection of poetry, *Concerto for an Exile* (1973), also reflects what might most charitably be called an ambivalence about his background: at once a celebration of an African essence which Cheney-Coker sees in the downtrodden of his homeland (and which owes much to the poetry of Négritude) it is also angry and despairing about the colonial and Christian legacy which is part of his personal heritage and which is reflected in his poetic imagery.

Cheney-Coker's second collection, *The Graveyard Also Has Teeth* (1980), continues in the same vein although it focuses more on Cheney-Coker's feelings for Sierra Leone and the role of the artist in a developing country. It also anticipates the growing maturity of vision and outward looking poetic gaze that is evident in his third volume, *The Blood in the Desert's Eyes* (1990). While the subject matter of his poetry has increasingly concerned more general social and political issues, the form has remained constant: a loose metrical structure which relies more on images piled one on top of another than the focused poetic explication of a single motif.

[MLL]

Chimombo, Steve (Malawi, b. 1945) Chimombo is from the Zomba Mountain region of Malawi and studied at a Catholic secondary school before attending the University of Malawi. He has also studied linguistics and literature at the University of Wales, the University of Leeds, and Columbia University. He is currently a professor in the English department of the University of Malawi and has been at the forefront of the literary scene in Malawi. His recent journal, *Wasi Writer*, is a resource for aspiring and practicing authors in Malawi. In addition to his contributions to the Writer's Workshop of Malawi and to international journals and anthologies, Chimombo published *Napolo Poems* in 1987. The poems of this collection are based on the Chewa mythic hero, Napolo. As both a poet and a well-known playwright, Chimombo often draws from oral traditions to interpret modern Malawi in his literary works.

[RS]

Chipasula, Frank Mkalawile (Malawi, b. 1949) Chipasula is from Likoma Island in Lake Malawi. He attended Malosa Secondary School before pursuing an English degree at Chancellor College of the University of Malawi. In 1970, he was a founder and participant in the Writers' Workshop of Malawi and in 1971 one of his poems was published in *Mau: 39 Poems from Malawi*. The following year *Visions and Reflections* was published; it was the first published collection by a Malawian poet. After dictator Kamuzu Hastings Banda's accession to power, he went into exile in Zambia and in 1978 moved to the United States where he has received an M.A. in creative writing from Brown University, an M.A. in African American literature from Yale University, and a Ph.D. in English literature from Brown University.

Since his exile he has published *O Earth, Wait for Me* (1984) and edited a collection of regional poetry, *When My Brothers Come Home: Poems from Central and Southern Africa* (1985). In 1986, *Nightwatcher, Nightsong* appeared in the Dangerous Writers series. Chipasula's poetry has appeared in journals and anthologies internationally. His poetry focuses on the devastating effect of the Banda regime on Malawi and the predominant imagery is dark and bloody. His work also addresses the state of exile from one's homeland and the role of poetry as a weapon or tool for political and personal growth. Chipasula is currently a professor of literature at University of Nebraska at Omaha and his latest and most acclaimed collection of poetry is *Whispers in the Wings* (1991).

[RS]

Chuilleanáin, Eiléan Ní (Ireland, b. 1942) Born in Cork and educated at University College, Cork, and Oxford University, Ní Chuilleanáin launched her literary career in 1966 when she won the *Irish Times* Prize for poetry. Since then, her writing has blended history, legend, and mythology with contemporary voices and social themes. Like EAVAN BOLAND, she portrays domestic objects and scenes with clarity and insight, though her work is less self-consciously feminist or political. Her themes are personal, often lonely, epiphanic moments, frequently followed by visual descriptions. Many of her poems deal with voyages and voyagers, as does the sequence *Cork*, which mythologizes her native city. Her work has been influenced by the Elizabethan poets, whom she studied at Oxford University. Ní Chuilleanáin lectures at Trinity College, Dublin, and is an editor of *Cyphers*, a poetry magazine.

Selected works: *Acts and Monuments* (1972); *Site of Ambush* (1975); *The Second Voyage* (1977); *The Rose-Geranium* (1981); *The Magdalene Sermon* (1990); *The Brazen Serpent* (1995).

[CT]

Ciardi, John (United States, 1916–86) Author of more than forty volumes of poetry and literary criticism, Ciardi is best known for *How Does a Poem Mean?* (1959), which became a standard text for college and high school poetry courses. He was also the author of an influential translation of Dante's *Divine Comedy*, a regular commentator on National Public Radio, and the poetry editor of *Saturday Review* for many years.

Ciardi's complex, formally intricate poetry explores everyday subjects such as money concerns, family and community, and avoids 'elevated' themes he associated with sentimental and romantic sensibilities. Kinship and marriage are the subjects of some of his best poems, such as 'Men Marry What They Need' and 'Most Like an Arch This Marriage'.

Selected works: *Person to Person* (1964); *Selected Poems* (1984); *The Birds of Pompeii* (1985).

[JDS]

Çirak, Zehra (Germany, b. 1960) Three years after her birth in Istanbul, Çirak moved with her family to West Germany. On her own in 1982 she moved to Berlin, where she still lives. Similar to other writers who have made Germany their home despite an at-times uneasy relation between Germans and those of other ethnic backgrounds, Çirak focuses her poems on cultural, linguistic, and personal identity in all areas of life.

In her poetry's images and word plays, which range from subtle to grotesque, Çirak has already established her own linguistic identity with which she proclaims her right to a cultural identity which is neither Turkish nor German. During the 1990s, she became one of the most visible minority authors with collections such as *Bird on an Elephant's Back* (1991) and *Strange Wings on One's Shoulders* (1994).

[IRS]

Clampitt, Amy (United States, 1915–94) Clampitt worked as an editor at Oxford University Press and the National Audubon Society before beginning to write poetry in earnest in the 1960s, and did not publish her first major collection *The Kingfisher* until 1983. Upon its heralded arrival, with the help of *The New Yorker* magazine, she become a prominent figure, and later taught at the College of William and Mary and at Amherst College.

Clampitt's poetry is concerned chiefly with nature, death and art, and involves rich, often difficult vocabulary and allusions. She described herself as both 'a poet of place' and 'a poet of displacement'. Her themes often recall the work of Gerard Manley Hopkins, whom she cited as her earliest poetic influence. Her accolades included a Guggenheim Fellowship and an award from the American Academy and Institute of Arts and Letters.

Selected works: *What the Light Was Like* (1985); *Archaic Figure* (1987); *Westward* (1990).

[JDS]

Clark, John Pepper (Nigeria, b. 1935) Perhaps better-known internationally as a playwright than as a poet, John Pepper Clark-Bekederemo is one of the most dominant voices in Nigerian literature. Like his compatriots WOLE SOYINKA and CHRISTOPHER OKIGBO, Clark's writings embrace the specifically Nigerian via English, a language capable of crossing both domestic dialects and national barriers.

Born to the Ijaw people of the Niger Delta and educated at Ibadan University, Clark founded the influential journal *The Horn* while an undergraduate. After graduation, he took up a career in journalism, though he eventually turned to teaching. His first play, *Song of a Goat*, appeared in 1961, followed the next year by *Poems*. Though his plays drew on classical and Ijaw models, his poetry was more influenced by the prosody of Gerard Manley Hopkins. By the time of *A Reed in the Tide* (1965), however, this tendency toward florid language gave way to a sparser verse. *Casualties: Poems 1966–8* (1970) was a reporting of the Nigerian civil war; moving and direct, its verse was an attempt both to account for the horror of Biafra's regime and to heal its damage. Clark is a professor of English at Lagos University.

Selected works: *A Decade of Tongues: Selected Poems 1958–68* (1981); *State of the Union* (1985); *Mandela and Other Poems* (1988); *Collected Plays and Poems 1958–88* (1991).

[MW]

Clarke, George Elliot (Canada, b. 1960) Born in Windsor, Nova Scotia, Clarke has been instrumental in bringing greater attention to the achievements of African-Canadian poets. His poetry has examined the lives and histories of the 'Africadian' community of escaped American slaves living in the Maritimes, in lyrical works such as *Saltwater Spirituals and Deeper Blues* (1983), *Lush Dreams, Blue Exile:*

Fugitive Poems (1994), and especially *Whylah Falls* (1990). He is the editor of *Other Voices: Writings by Blacks in Canada* (1985) and the two volume *Fire on Water: An Anthology of Black Nova Scotian Writing* (1991–92), and is presently a professor of Canadian Studies and English at Duke University.

[IS]

Clarke, Gillian (Wales, b. 1937) Clarke was born in Cardiff and received her B.A. in English from the University of Wales. A broadcaster, freelance writer, and teacher, her first poems appeared in *Poetry Wales* in 1970, and her first full-length collection, *The Sundial*, was published in 1978. Her *Selected Poems* (1985), which contained several new works, became one of the most successful volumes in recent years by a contemporary Anglo-Welsh poet. Clarke's third collection, *Letting in the Rumour* (1989), was a Poetry Book Society recommendation. Her meditative, observational style encompasses a wide range of subjects – pastoral, domestic, and aesthetic. Generally a writer of short lyrics, she has also written longer, formally disjunctive pieces of considerable ambition (such as *Letting in the Rumour*'s 'Cofiant'). Her *Collected Poems* was published by Carcanet in 1997.

[BS]

Claudel, Paul (France, 1868–1955) Along with JAMMES, Claudel is a predominant figure in the pre-World War II Catholic revival in French writing. His reading of Arthur Rimbaud in 1886, the year he also converted to Catholicism, marks a turning point in his thinking about poetry. For Claudel, lyric poetry, as demonstrated in the *Cinq Grandes Odes* (*Five Great Odes*, 1910), is inseparable from a religious conception of the world. Biblical and liturgical imagery meets Greek tragedy in this work, as the individual seeks to define his relationship with the divine spirit.

Born north-east of Paris, he later studied at the Lycée Louis-le-Grand before taking examinations leading to a diplomatic career. His diplomatic duties, which occupied most of his professional life, took him to Shanghai (1898), Prague (1910–11), and Germany (1911–14), and he served as ambassador of France in Tokyo (1921–27), Washington (1927–33), and Brussels (1933–35). In 1946 he was elected to the Académie Française.

Selected works: *Partage de midi* (*Break of Noon*, 1906, 1946); *L'Annonce faite à Marie* (*The Tidings Brought to Mary*, 1912); *Le Soulier de satin* (*The Satin Slipper*, 1929).

[SJ]

Clemo, Jack (England, 1916–94) From birth, Reginald John Clemo suffered hardship. Suffering from tremendous physical ailments that caused him periods of deafness and blindness, which became permanent in later life, Clemo is often credited for what he has overcome to write poetry, rather than simply for the poetry itself.

Influenced by a strictly religious mother, Clemo always felt his role as a poet to be evangelical and his poetry deals with the struggle to reconcile religion and sexuality. His first two brief collections of poetry *The Clay Verge* (1951) and *The Wintry Priesthood* (1951) were combined with newer poems in his 1961 volume *The Map of Clay*. To recognize his consistent contributions to the English literary scene and its journals, Clemo received a Civil List pension, also in 1961. In addition to poetry, Clemo published one novel and several autobiographical volumes.

Selected works: *Cactus on Carmel* (1967); *Broad Autumn* (1975); *The Marriage of a Rebel* (1980).

[BRB]

Clifton, Lucille (United States, b. 1936) Pulitzer Prize finalist Thelma Lucille Sayles Clifton was born in New York, educated at Howard University and Fredonia State Teachers College, and is now a professor at St Mary's College, Maryland.

Clifton's poetry finds the extraordinary in the ordinary. Her early work reflected ghetto life and her experiences as a black woman, a wife, and a mother of six. Echoing the gospel tradition and eschewing academic forms, her concentrated verse sings an international lyric of endurance and hope (themes also explored in her many children's books).

Selected works: *Good Times* (1969); *An Ordinary Woman* (1974); *Two-Headed Woman* (1980); *A Good Woman* (1987); *Next* (1987); *Quilting* (1991); *The Book of Light* (1993); *The Terrible Stories* (1996).

[MW]

Cohen, Leonard (Canada, b. 1934) Born in Montréal and educated at McGill and Columbia Universities, Cohen currently divides his time between Montréal, Los Angeles, and Greece.

Cohen burst onto the Canadian poetry scene with the publication of three books of poetry and a novel while still in his twenties. Winner of a Governor General's award for poetry for *Selected Poems, 1956–68*, Cohen's lyrical and romantic verse has since found its primary outlet in a series of Dylanesque recordings, beginning with *Songs of Leonard Cohen* (1968) and *Songs from a Room* (1969). While Cohen's enduring popularity is due more to the popular and critical success of his albums than to the lasting influence of his poetry, he remains an important literary figure in Canada, receiving the Order of Canada in 1991.

Selected works: *Let Us Compare Mythologies* (1956); *Spice Box of the Earth* (1961); *The Favorite Game* (1963); *Flowers for Hitler* (1964); *Beautiful Losers* (1966).

[IS]

Collins, Merle (Grenada, b. 1950) Poet and novelist Collins was born in Aruba, but was raised in Grenada. Her reputation as a poet developed during her involvement with Maurice Bishop's People's Revolutionary Government in Grenada. This experience had a formative influence on her poetry, which is characterized above all by the degree of its political commitment. After the assassination of Bishop, Collins moved to England, where she has continued to write both about Grenada and about the experience of living in Britain. As a member of the group African Dawn, she performs her poetry to African music. Collins has published two collections of her own poems, *Because the Dawn Breaks!: Poems Dedicated to the Grenadian People* (1985), and *Rotten Pomerack* (1992); her early poems, many of which are written as performance pieces, are collected in *Callaloo: Four Writers from Grenada* (1984).

[IS]

Colum, Padraic (Ireland, 1881–1972) An Irish poet and dramatist, Colum was one of the first playwrights of the Abbey Theatre, which produced his *Broken Soul* (1903) and *Thomas Muskerry* (1910). However, he received greater acclaim for his poems, which typically depict the rural Irish landscape and its people. His most famous poems, 'The Old Woman of the Road' and 'She Moved through the Fair', were set to music. In 1914, he and his wife Mary, also a writer, journeyed to the United States ostensibly for a short honeymoon. But they remained – mainly for financial reasons. Colum lectured, gave poetry readings, and taught in several U.S. universities.

Selected works: *Collected Poems* (1932); *The Story of Lowry Maen* (1937); *The Poet's Circus* (1960); *Images of Departure* (1968).

[CT]

Comfort, Alexander (England, 1920–2000) Born in London and educated at Cambridge University, London Hospital, and the University of London, Comfort is the sum of rather extraordinary parts: he is a poet, playwright, novelist, physician, medical researcher, critic, and sex therapist.

Recognizing the compatibility of art

and science, Comfort's poetry is heavily influenced by both his medical research and his own political and social philosophies. Comfort advocates both anarchy and pacifism in his poetry, and his poems frequently confront death, a preoccupation that undoubtedly stems from his scientific work on aging.

Selected works: *A Wreath for the Living* (1942); *On This Side of Nothing* (1948); *And All but He Departed* (1951); *All but a Rib: Poems Chiefly of Women* (1973); *The Joy of Sex* (1991); *Mikrokosmos* (1994).

[SG]

Conde, Carmen (Spain, 1907–94) Conde's election to the Spanish Royal Academy in 1978 gave her long-overdue recognition for a distinguished career as poet and literary critic. She was born in Cartagena and lived in Morocco as a child. Above all, Conde's poetry is a reflection, through language, of her life experiences. *The Well-Stone* (1929) and *Rejoicings* (1934) recall her youth by the sea. After the Civil War she remained in Spain, and her poetry took a pessimistic turn with *Deep Remembrance of Myself* (1944) and *Women without Eden* (1947); the latter portrays the historical oppression of women. Conde's preoccupation with the themes of life and death continue in *Defeated Archangel* (1960) and *Corrosion* (1975), while *Crater* (1988) is influenced by Greek mythology. Conde also wrote biographies for children and compiled anthologies of women's poetry.

[AB]

Conquest, Robert (England, b. 1917) Equally respected for his poetry and for his writing on current affairs, George Robert Ackworth Conquest was born in Great Malvern and educated at Oxford. He served in the army for seven years (1939–46) and his time in the Balkans with the Soviet Army Group (1944–5) proved to influence much of his writing throughout his life. The first secretary of the United Kingdom's delegation to the United Nations, Conquest was awarded the Order of the British Empire in 1955.

In that same year, he would publish *Poems*. He would also help to compile the seminal volume of English World War II poetry, *New Lines* (1956), which included works by THOM GUNN, PHILIP LARKIN, and KINGSLEY AMIS and was meant to emphasize a control of language and to reestablish a formal sense of poetry. Conquest published a second collection of poetry, *Between Mars and Venus* (1962), which was followed by *Arias from a Love Opera* (1969). He is currently a senior research fellow at the Russian and Commonwealth of Independent States Collection at the Hoover Institution.

[BCB]

Coolidge, Clark (United States, b. 1939) Coolidge was born in Providence, Rhode Island, the son of a professor of music at Brown University, where Coolidge himself later studied. His own musical background may have some influence in the lyrical quality of Coolidge's poetry, and in some of his career choices. Like his output, his life seems divided between the aural quality of the spoken word and the effects of words in juxtaposition on the printed page. Coolidge has worked as disc jockey, musician, and also as researcher and magazine editor. His work in some ways anticipates Language poetry (see CHARLES BERNSTEIN, RON SILLIMAN, SUSAN HOWE) and the performance poetry of the 1970s and 1980s, and can be found in *Solution Passage: Poems, 1978–1981* (1986), *Mesh* (1988), *At Egypt* (1988), *Maintains* (1988), and *Heart of the Breath: Poems, 1979–1992* (1996)

[VB]

Cope, Wendy (England, b. 1945) Cope was born in Erith, Kent, and earned her B.A. from St Hilda's College, Oxford, in 1966. From 1967 to 1981, Cope taught at junior schools, before she began writing for newspapers.

Cope's poems are full of parodies and literary jokes, although her 'light verse' often contains deeply emotional themes. In 1986, Cope published her first book of poems, *Making Cocoa for Kingsley Amis*, in which she uses her fictional character Jason Strugnell to parody Modernist poetry. Strugnell is an ambitious but inferior poet who imitates poets such as T.S. ELIOT and TED HUGHES.

In *The River Girl* (1990), Cope's poetry is very different. The book is a long narrative poem exploring a love affair between a mortal and an immortal. In *Serious Concerns* (1992), the poetry has again changed, and while Cope's humor remains, the book is perhaps her darkest.

[LK]

Corn, Charles (Lebanon, 1894–1963) Writing in Beirut between the two World Wars, Corn represents a second generation of Lebanese poets writing in French. Dedicated to the national lifestyle and ready to fight for it, he created an ambitious, prestigious, but short-lived review, *La revue phénicienne* (*The Phoenician Review*, 1920), where he demonstrated the link of modern Lebanon with its important Phoenician roots. Throughout his life, Corn worked hard to defend his concepts of freedom and traditional Lebanese values. His most famous patriotic work, *la Montagne inspirée* (*The Inspired Mountain*, 1934), is divided into three parts, 'le Dit de l'enthousiasme'('the Word of Enthusiasm'), 'le Dit de l'agonie' ('the Word of Agony'), and 'le Dit du souvenir' ('the Word of Memory'). Written for the glory of Lebanon, this book was considered by many Lebanese people as their national saga. In this ambitious work, Corn showed the continuation of the Lebanese life, his cultural identity as well as links and roots in his past. His importance rests too in the power of his lyricism, insight, and specific use of linguistic inventions. It established Corn's reputation and influenced other fervent and optimistic contemporary poets, Hector Klat, Elie Tyand, Michel Chiha, and later GEORGES SHÉHADÉ. Corn is still considered by many Lebanese people as the one man who perfectly understood Lebanon.

[MS]

Coronel Urtecho, José (Nicaragua, 1906–94) Coronel Urtecho was a key figure in the formation of the Nicaraguan Vanguard movement. His 'Oda a Rubén Darío' was the generational turning point in the reinvention of a poetic tradition that lived with the heavy influence of Nicaraguan 'modernismo' while simultaneously rejecting it. Coronel Urtecho founded several important literary magazines, including *Rincón de Vanguardia* (*Corner of the Avant-garde*, 1931), which became the organ of publication for most of the vanguard movement. A great experimenter with form and irony, Coronel Urtecho opened the way for most of the modern poets of Nicaragua in the twentieth century. His poetry was first collected in volume form in 1970.

Selected works: *Pól-la d'anánta katánta paránta. Imitaciones y traducciones* (*Imitations and Translations*, 1970).

[SL]

Corso, Gregory (United States, 1930–2001) Born in New York City into a poor family, Corso began his career as a thief – and was sentenced to three years in jail when he was sixteen. While incarcerated he read extensively, especially the works of one of his favorite poets and most profound influences, Percy Bysshe Shelley. Corso published his first book, *The Vestal Lady on Brattle and Other Poems* (1955) soon after his release. ALLEN GINSBERG admired these first poems and informally inducted Corso into the Beat literary movement. Corso's work incorporates more humor than that of the other Beats, is more unschooled, and may be considered more naive.

Selected works: *Gasoline* (1958); *Bomb* (1958); *The Happy Birthday of Death* (1960); *Elegiac Feelings American* (1970).

[CP]

Crane, Hart (United States, 1899–1933) Crane was born in Ohio, the son of a candy manufacturer. His childhood was deeply marked by his parents' incessant arguments and difficult divorce. Crane moved to New York City in 1917, before finishing high school, to become a writer, eventually entering the bohemian Greenwich Village world of artists and poets. While his reputation as a poet grew, Crane's personal life was marked by turmoil, caused by ongoing bouts of poverty, alcoholism, and self-doubt, volatile love affairs, and the social strain brought about by his homosexuality. A grant from a banker enabled Crane to complete, with much difficulty, his ambitious epic poem, *The Bridge*. Unhappy with its lukewarm reception, Crane left for an unproductive stay in Mexico on a Guggenheim grant; on the return voyage, Crane jumped overboard to his death at 33.

Despite his tragically short life, Crane has come to be seen as a major American poet. Filled with verbal and intellectual excitement, his poems contain highly unusual diction and imagery, complex and ambiguous syntax, and multi-layered metaphors. These densely textured poems often combine ecstatic visions with a conversational American idiom. In his major work, *The Bridge*, Crane deliberately responds to the pessimism of T. S. ELIOT's *The Waste Land*, as he uses modernist techniques to build an affirmative ode to America. Taking the Brooklyn Bridge as its central symbol, Crane's visionary epic explores connections between the modern world and America's past.

Selected works: *White Buildings* (1926); *The Bridge* (1930); *Collected Poems* (1933).

[AE]

Crawford, Robert (Scotland, b. 1959) Born in Bellshill near Glasgow, Crawford studied English at Glasgow University and at Oxford where he wrote a doctoral thesis on T.S. ELIOT. An academic and poet, he returned to Scotland in 1987 and received an Eric Gregory Award for poetry in 1988. He is currently Professor of Modern Scottish Literature at St Andrews University, and was co-editor of the poetry magazine *Verse* for eleven years (1984–95). His poetry and criticism often deal with Scottish cultural and social issues. The poetry particularly plays on the idiosyncrasies of Scots language, and a vivid awareness of the Scottish condition placed in an international context.

Selected works: *A Scottish Assembly* (1990); *Sharawaggi* (with W.N. Herbert; 1990); *Talkies* (1992); *Masculinity* (1996); *Spirit Machines* (1999).

[LKMF]

Creeley, Robert (United States, b. 1926) Creeley was born in Massachusetts. His father died when Creeley was four and he lost one of his eyes in a childhood accident. He attended Harvard, left without a degree, and moved eventually to Mallorca, Spain, where he founded the Divers Press. Creeley soon began a voluminous correspondence with CHARLES OLSON, an encounter which proved to be a life-changing experience for both poets. With Olson's encouragement, Creeley developed his idiosyncratic style, taught at Black Mountain College, edited its influential review, and became a leading figure in Black Mountain poetry. Though his restlessness led him to move frequently (to places like New Mexico, Guatemala, and San Francisco, where he befriended the Beat poets), he eventually settled at the State University of New York, Buffalo, where he has taught for thirty years.

Creeley uses short lines and jagged syntax to convey minute shifts of emotion and thought in compressed, stumbling language. His minimalist poems avoid grand subjects and conventional descriptions, choosing instead to struggle with the pain of a mind intensely aware of its own efforts at self-expression; the poems haltingly probe the paradoxes of self-consciousness and of love. Though

Creeley's more recent poetry continues to wrestle with the difficulties of language and communication, it has grown increasingly concerned with aging and the effects of time.

Selected works: *For Love* (1962); *Words* (1967); *The Collected Poems of Robert Creeley (1945–75)* (1982); *Selected Poems* (1991).

[AE]

Croggon, Alison (Australia, b. 1962) Born in South Africa, Croggon has lived in Australia since age seven. She has been awarded four Australian Council Fellowships and has won various awards for her collections of poetry, *This is the Stone* (1991) and *The Blue Gate* (1997), and her novella, *Navigatio* (1996). Croggon has worked as a theatre critic with the *Bulletin*, poetry editor of *Overland Extra* (1989), *Modern Writing* (1991), *Voices* (1996), and is now the founding editor of *Masthead*. One aspect of Croggon's poetics is voiced by the narrator of *Navigatio* who reminds us that 'poetry is a making of love'. Being a mother of three children plays a vital role in Croggon's poetry and hence there are poems which focus on 'traditional' women's experiences such as pregnancy, miscarriage, and childbirth. However, what Croggon does with these traditional themes, such as shifting from the neo-romantic sequence to the post-modern series (as in 'Divinations'), has more in common with postmodern forms of poetry than with conventional ones.

[DCO]

Cronin, Jeremy (South Africa, b. 1949) The son of a South African naval officer, Cronin grew up in Simonstown. He studied at the University of Cape Town, where he became a Marxist, and at the Sorbonne in Paris, where he took his M.A. in philosophy. Returning to South Africa in 1974, he lectured in philosophy and political science at the University of Cape Town until he was arrested and convicted in 1976 under the Terrorism Act. He was charged for his work with the African National Congress and served a seven-year sentence in maximum security prisons. While he was serving his sentence his wife died unexpectedly, and this inevitably colored his life and work. A few months after his release he received the Ingrid Jonker Prize for Poetry for his volume, *Inside* (1983). In 1990 he returned to South Africa after spending three years in exile in London and Lusaka, and has served as Education and Training Officer for the United Democratic Front and is currently on the executive committee of the South African Communist Party.

Heavily influenced by black poets who were writing in the 1970s (such as SEROTE, Medingoane, and Mafika Gwala), Cronin places strong emphasis on sound, parallelism, and repetition. His autobiographical work reflects the time spent in prison, using visual imagery and drawing on intensely personal experiences. In the mid-1980s he became involved with agit-prop theatre and oral performance, combining poetry recital with gesture and mime.

[KS]

Cullen, Countee (United States, 1903–46) Once known as the poet laureate of the Harlem Renaissance, Cullen is now considered a minor poet. The reasons for this demotion were evident and remarked upon in his own lifetime, as were his unusual gifts. A lyric poet of great technical skill, Cullen was a reverent follower of Keats and other members of the English canon, and this reverence often restricted his own verse to the level of imitation.

Cullen grew up in Harlem as the adopted son of a Methodist minister. He attended the prestigious and predominantly white De Witt-Clinton High School before going on to New York University and Harvard. During this period he was published widely and received a number of awards. He then worked as an editor and columnist, becoming an active contributor to the Harlem literary scene. A Guggenheim Fellowship allowed him to spend two years in Paris, which he continued to visit regularly until the advent of World War II.

While his language and prosody clung to the templates of the English Romantics, Cullen's poetry dealt frequently with racial themes. This is true of his strongest poems, including the striking and much-anthologized sonnet 'Yet Do I Marvel'.

Selected works: *Color* (1925); *Ballad of the Brown Girl* (1927); *Copper Sun* (1927); *Caroling Dusk* (ed., 1927); *The Black Christ* (1929); *The Medea and Some Poems* (1935).

[JT]

Cullinan, Patrick (Patrick Rolland; South Africa, b. 1932) Born in Pretoria, Cullinan studied at Charterhouse and Magdalen College, Oxford. He traveled in Europe and Africa and has worked as a sawmiller, farmer, teacher, and publisher. He has taught in the English department at the University of the Western Cape and co-founded Bateleur Press. From September 1980 to December 1981 he was editor of *The Bloody Horse*. He was awarded the Olive Schreiner Prize in 1980 and the Pringle Award in 1983.

Selected works: *The Horizon Forty Miles Away* (1973); *Today is not Different* (1978); *The White Hail in the Orchard* (1984); *Selected Poems* (1992).

[KS]

cummings, e. e. (United States, 1894–1962) edward estlin cummings was born in Cambridge, Massachusetts, where his father was a minister and a Harvard professor. cummings himself attended Harvard, and then served as an ambulance driver in World War I. After being wrongly imprisoned in a French detention camp, cummings recorded the experience in his well-regarded novel, *The Enormous Room* (1922). He studied art in Paris, and eventually settled in New York, where he became a leading bohemian artist and important force in American modernism.

As part of his lifelong crusade against middle-class conformity, repression and lifeless rationality, cummings cultivated a deliberately idiosyncratic style. He playfully deployed unusual syntax, unconventional spelling, and puns, while experimenting with the visual arrangement of the poem on the page. His quirky poems celebrate the simple, the eccentric, the spontaneous and vital and denounce all that is collective, rigid and uninspired. Not surprisingly, many of his best works are love poems filled with childlike exuberance and frank sensuality, or sharp satires aimed at a complacent culture. Though many critics feel his linguistic play tends to mask rather traditional and even didactic concerns, and others complain that his poetry lacks the ambition of his modernist peers, cummings' wit, buoyancy, and formal innovations create an exuberant, important body of work which continues to enjoy widespread popularity, particularly among children and teenagers.

Selected works: *Tulips and Chimneys* (1923); *is 5* (1925); *Complete Poems 1913–62* (1973).

[AE]

Curnow, Allen (New Zealand, 1911–2001) Curnow is widely recognized as the central figure in New Zealand poetry. Born in Timaru, Curnow worked as a journalist in New Zealand and Britain, then studied for the Anglican ministry at St John's College, Auckland. Before ordination, he went back to journalism and later studied at Auckland University, writing light verse under the pseudonym 'Whim-Wham'. In 1950, he became a faculty member in the English Department at Auckland University, a post which he held until his retirement in 1976.

Besides being a poet, Curnow is also a playwright, critic, and editor. His editions of, and introductions to, two influential and controversial anthologies, *A Book of*

New Zealand Verse 1923–45 (1945) and *The Penguin Book of New Zealand Verse* (1960), have been central in shaping the perception and the critique of a New Zealandian canon to this day.

His early poetry, especially that of the late 1930s and early 1940s, strives to link New Zealand to its colonial past. Curnow's concerns for history and the idea of New Zealand as a nation are most forcefully represented in *Not in Narrow Seas* (1939), *Island and Time* (1941), and *Sailing or Drowning* (1944). Curnow's critics have sometimes interpreted this focus on national issues and on questions of cultural identity as overly nationalistic or patriotic.

Curnow was one of the first New Zealand poets to write Modernist poetry, especially from the mid-1940s onwards. This Modernist poetry stood in contrast to the pervasiveness of Romantic poetry in postwar New Zealand. *Jack Without Magic* (1946), *At Dead Low Water and Sonnets* (1949), and *Poems, 1949–57* (1957) show Curnow gradually shifting focus away from the national to the personal. These poems deal with his travels to England and the United States and express a Modernist poet's epistemological quest.

Curnow's later work includes *Trees, Effigies, Moving Objects* (1972), which intensifies his questioning of the relationship between language and reality. Apocalyptic visions make 'reality' appear threatening, a theme which links his late poetry to his earlier concern with New Zealand history. *An Incorrigible Music* (1979), *You Will Know When You Get There* (1982), and *The Loop in Lone Kauri Road* (1986) continue this focus on violence and death. Curnow has also published both *Collected Poems* (1974, 1988) and *Selected Poems* (1982, 1990).

Throughout his fifty years as a writer of 'high' poetry, Curnow has never been very popular with the general public. Allusive in both senses, his poetry is rich in myth and biblical imagery; Curnow's fascination with and doubt concerning religion imbues his work. His style, like his subject matter, is highly complex and infused with both American Modernist influences and variations on traditional forms, which opposes his poetry to the stylistic conservatism of such neo-Romantic New Zealand poets as JAMES K. BAXTER.

[SH]

Cynan (Albert Evans-Jones; Wales, 1895–1970) Evans-Jones, born at Pwllheli, served during World War I as a soldier and later as a chaplain. He became a Methodist minister, and eventually joined the University College of North Wales, Bangor (his *alma mater*) as a tutor. As Cynan he took the Crown at the National Eisteddfod in 1921 for 'Mab y Bwthyn' ('Son of the Cottage'), perhaps the most famous Welsh language poem of the war. Cynan enjoyed great popular success, winning the Crown twice more, but academic audiences were more critical, finding him too sentimental. He wrote plays and pageants as well as verse, and was also an influential administrator of the Eisteddfod, serving as Archdruid in 1950–53. His collected poems, *Cerddi Cynan*, appeared in 1959; he was knighted in 1969.

[BS]

D

D'Aguiar, Fred (England, b. 1960) Born in London but raised in Guyana until the age of twelve, D'Aguiar is a leading name among the black poets who made their undeniable mark on British literature, art, and music during the past two decades. Like his upbringing, D'Aguiar's poetry synthesizes cross-cultural traditions – the mainstream written literary English tradition and the oral roots of the Caribbean.

D'Aguiar's first book, *Mama Dot* (1985), sets this trans-Atlantic conversation in motion. Mama Dot, a composite of D'Aguiar's two grandmothers in Guyana, represents a metaphor of mother, grandmother, and woman. He blends an archetype of past, future, and Guyana herself, embedded in indigenous folklore. Structured in three sections, Mama Dot accentuates D'Aguiar's poetic strength of creating a compelling image in a few lines as well as sustaining a long poem.

Airy Hall (1989), D'Aguiar's second book, continues the poet's recollection of his Caribbean childhood. As in *Mama Dot*, Guyanese culture flows through the first two sections, exploring the black British poet's sense of being the 'other', although it has a more magical-realist quality to it than his first book. The most notable section is Part Three, an extended poem called 'The Kitchen Bitch'. This poem, named after a tin kerosene lamp used by Jamaican peasants, puzzled reviewers with its complex, interweaving imagery and dislocation of narrative.

After the publication of *Airy Hall*, D'Aguiar spent time working in radio, stage, and film. He wrote and produced *1492* (1992), a long, dramatic poem aired on BBC Radio 3. The poem is structured in twenty-three sections and has two parts, a narrator and Columbus. His third book of poems, *British Subjects* (1993), returns to England to root itself firmly in British culture and immigrants' experience of it.

Selected works: *The New British Poetry* (1988); *The Longest Memory* (ed., 1994); *A Jamaican Airman Foresees His Death* (1995).

[SS]

D'Annunzio, Gabriele (Italy, 1863–1938) Probably the only Italian author to embody the spirit of European Decadence in its endeavor to combine art and life, D'Annunzio was an extremely prolific poet, whose work represents, both chronologically and aesthetically, a link between the nineteenth and twentieth centuries. His poetry combines the cult of the poet as a prophetic and heroic figure with dense mythological references and a complex use of synesthesia and metrical innovations. His most influential poems are collected in the first three books of *Laudi* (1903), among which *Alcyone* clearly anticipates the poetics of Ermetismo (see UNGARETTI, QUASIMODO), offering a few of the earliest and finest examples of free verse in contemporary Italian poetry.

Selected works: *Poema Paradisiaco* (1893); *Intermezzo* (1894); *Canto novo* (1896).

[GS]

Dabydeen, David (England, b. 1955) Born in British Guiana (now Guyana), Dabydeen emigrated to England at age fourteen. He was educated at Cambridge and also held fellowships at Yale and Oxford. Since 1984 Dabydeen has served as lecturer in Caribbean Studies at Warwick University. He has also acted as president of the Association for the Teaching of Caribbean, African, and Asian Literature (1985–87), received the Cambridge University Quiller-Couch Prize in 1978, a Yale University Centre for British Art resident fellowship in 1982, and the Commonwealth Poetry Prize in 1984 for his collection *Slave Song* (1984). Dabydeen's poems are distinguished by their innovative use of Guyanese-Creole and their themes concerning the complications of the Caribbean experience. His poetry addresses issues such as enslavement, exploitation, emigration, and various modern problems of the Caribbean people, using the voices of those people as well as his own voice and experiences. His work, especially *Slave Song*, has been widely praised not only for its strong lyrical writing style but also for the political and social power of the poetry.

Selected works: *Coolie Odyssey* (1988); *Hogarth's Blacks* (1987); *Hogarth, Walpole and Commercial Britain* (1987); *The Intended* (novel, 1991).

[TT]

Dadi, Bernard Binlin (Ivory Coast, b. 1916) Dadi has published poetry, plays, novels, collections of oral tales, and chronicles rewritten in novel form. He has always been a prolific writer, even while holding various governmental positions (since 1957). He spent much of his childhood living with his uncle, attended a Catholic school in Grand Bassam, and then studied at the William Ponty School on the island of Gore (in Senegal).

His first book of poems, *Afrique debout* (*Africa Upright*, 1950), inaugurated Dadi's diverse literary career. They were released shortly after a sixteen-month detention for participating in a national demonstration. Two other volumes of poetry have followed: *Ronde des jours* (*Daily Rounds*, 1956), and *Homme de tous les continents* (*Man of All the Continents*, 1967). His work clearly illustrates a pan-African sensibility, one that is bolstered by the influence of African legends and folk tales.

[KAC]

Dai Wangshu (Dai Meng'ou; China, 1905–50) Upon graduation from Zhendan University, where he took his major in French, Dai went to France to study literature. Dai is considered the most eminent Chinese Symbolist poet. 'Alley in the Rain' (1928), his first published poem, immediately brought him fame as one of the best poets writing in vernacular Chinese. Most of his poems were published in *The Modern* and *Poetry*; he was the editor of the latter. Highly influenced by the French Symbolists and classic Chinese poetry, Dai worked out his own symbolism. Images hit upon perhaps accidentally began to recur with double meaning. At first these were common ones, such as sunset, twilight, dusk, drizzle, dead leaves, etc., but gradually uncommon images were added, such as the old tree, and the broken hand's palm. His common images expressed in a haunting melody his unbearable loneliness and acute sense of loss; his uncommon images articulated his burning patriotism, lofty sentiments, aspiration, and heroic spirit during the Sino-Japanese War.

'Alley in the Rain' is to his early poetry what 'With My Broken Palm' is to his later work. Both poems have remained tremendously popular. After Hong Kong fell in 1942 during the Pacific War, Dai was put in jail there by Japanese invaders. Brutal torture in jail severely harmed his health.

He came out with chronic asthma, of which he died in Beijing on February 28, 1950.

Dai was not only an eminent modern poet, but also a great translator, with his translations from French and Spanish still being published. The books to his credit include *What I Remember*, *Wangshu's Grass* (reprinted 1997), *The Best French Short Stories*, and *The Anthology of Belgian Short Stories*.

[LG]

Dallas, Ruth (Ruth Mumford; New Zealand, b. 1919) Born in Invercargill, Dallas began publishing at the age of twelve, the start of a long and distinguished poetic career. She won the 1977 New Zealand Book Award for Poetry for *Walking on the Snow* (1976). Dallas has lived in Dunedin most of her life.

Her poetry is influenced by Wordsworth. Nature and its objects, especially those of the southern New Zealand landscape, are central to her poems. Her style is notably economical and clear in her later verse, which is further influenced by Chinese, Indian, and Japanese art.

Selected works: *Country Road and Other Poems, 1947–52* (1953); *The Turning Wheel* (1961); *Day Book: Poems of a Year* (1966); *Song for a Guitar and Other Songs* (1976); *Collected Poems* (1987).

[SH]

Dalton, Roque (El Salvador, 1935–75) Dalton achieved immediate mythic status all over Latin America as a guerrilla poet after his assassination at the hands of his own comrades of the Revolutionary Army of the People (ERP). His poetic career, however, dates to the mid-1950s when he founded the *Circulo Literario* at the University of El Salvador. Major poetic works, including *Taberna y otros lugares* (*Taverns and Other Places*), winner of the Casa de las Americas Prize (1969), also date back to his pre-military days.

Prior to joining the guerrilla movement in El Salvador he lived in Mexico, Cuba, and Czechoslovakia where he was deeply influenced by some of the great Latin American writers of the time. His poetry shows the influence of many poetic traditions that range from SAINT-JOHN PERSE to BERTOLT BRECHT. Very familiar with the Marxist debates on the function of literature, he sided against socialist realism and was enormously influenced by the Marxist European avant-garde, particularly NAZIM HIKMET. Though his legacy is greatly contested, Dalton is generally considered El Salvador's most important post-World War II poet, even having been granted the posthumous title of National Poet of El Salvador (1997).

Selected works: *La ventana en el rostro* (*The Window in the Semblance*, 1961); *El turno del ofendido* (*The Offended's Turn*, 1962); *Los pequeños infiernos* (*Little Hells*, 1970); *Poemas clandestinos* (*Clandestine Poems*, 1980); *Las historias prohibidas del Pulgarcito* (*Forbidden Stories of Tom Thumb*, 1988); *Un libro levemente odioso* (*A Slightly Odious Book*, 1989).

[SL]

Darío, Rubén (Nicaragua, 1867–1916) One of the most influential poets of Latin America, Darío revolutionized Spanish verse and is regarded as the founder and instigator of Latin American Modernism. Born Félix Rubén García Sarmiento in Metapa, Nicaragua, Darío was a child prodigy. Due to economic constraints, however, his education was limited to secondary school at the Instituto de Occidente in León, paid for by the great aunt and uncle who raised him. Throughout his life, Darío wrote extensively for various newspapers in Europe and Central and South America, where he first published his prolific and masterful body of prose and poetry.

Numerous diplomatic and editorial positions enabled Darío to meet and correspond with some of the most important poets of his day: Paul Verlaine, Julián del Casal, Leopoldo Lugones, José Martí, and

JUAN RAMÓN JIMÉNEZ, the latter of whom regarded him as a mentor. His first significant experience outside Nicaragua was a three-year stay in Chile, where he was exposed to the French Symbolist and Parnassian poets, and to a cultural cosmopolitanism that transformed his verse. Here, he published *Azul* (*Blue*, 1888), a volume containing poetic prose and poetry, considered by critics to be the defining book of Spanish American Modernism in its prioritization of form, its symbolic use of nature and classical themes and imagery, and search for totality, balance, and harmony.

From 1893 to 1896, while living in Buenos Aires, Darío founded a literary magazine, *Revista de América* (*Magazine of America*, 1894) with Ricardo James Freyre, published a book of literary criticism entitled *Los raros* (*The Exceptional Ones*, 1896) and brought out his second major book of poetry, *Prosas profanas y otros poemas* (*Profane Hymns and Other Poems*, 1896). The latter is stylistically and thematically a continuation of *Azul*. *Cantos de vida y esperanza* (*Songs of Life and Hope*, 1905), Darío's last major collection of poems, was published during the last third of his life, when he lived variously in Spain, France, and Latin America, writing poetry but also publishing an autobiography (*Vida de Rubén Darío, escrita por el mismo* (*The Life of Rubén Darío, Written by Himself*, 1916) and many other volumes of non-fiction on diverse subjects. *Cantos de vida y esperanza* departs from the previous two collections in that it is more personal and engages social-political issues, such as North American expansionism.

The inevitability of death, tempered by poems celebrating sensuous love, is a persistent poetic subject and personal obsession of Darío, known for his effusive, often depressed temperament and an indulgence in alcohol. Throughout the poetry, Darío's lyric – the fluid, poignant, and musical product of a brilliant versifier – stands out. Later books of poetry include *El Canto errante* (*The W*, 1907); *Poema del otoño y otros poemas* (*Poem of Autumn and Other Poems*, 1910); *Canto a la Argentina y otros poemas* (*Song for Argentina and Other Poems*, 1914). Translations of Darío's poetry into English are scarce, but include *Eleven Poems of Rubén Darío* (1916) and *Selected Poems* (1965). Darío died in Léon, Nicaragua after contracting pneumonia during a tour of the United States.

[LKA]

Darwish, Mahmoud (Palestine, b. 1942) Darwish was born in al-Birweh, a village in the district of Acre which was razed by the Israelis in 1948. As a refugee, he participated in the political struggle of Palestinians, joining Rakah, the Israeli Communist Party, and editing its newspaper, *Al-Ittihad* (*Unity*). Like other poets such as Fawzi al-Asmar and Samih al-Qasum, Darwish was subjected to harassment, imprisonment, torture, and house arrest by the Israeli authorities, until he left for the Soviet Union in 1971. In 1972 he became a member of the Palestine National Council, and lived in Beirut until 1982, where he edited the Arabic monthly, *Palestinian Affairs*. Later he moved to Paris, where he has edited the Palestinian literary magazine, *Al-Karmal*.

Among those who influenced him, Darwish lists ARAGON, ELUARD, HIKMET, LORCA, and NERUDA. One of the most distinguished contemporary Arab poets and the leading figure in Arabic 'Resistance Literature', Darwish's early poetry was simple, direct, and employed emotional appeal in depicting the plight of Palestinian refugees. Later on, his poetry gained metaphorical depth, technical sophistication, and musicality. His imagery is vivid and his diction free of conventional usage. The mood of his poetry has consistently been one of resolve and hope.

Selected works: *Birds Without Wings* (1960); *Olive Leaves* (1964); *A Lover from Palestine* (1966); *Birds Die in Galilee* (1970); *Attempt No. 7* (1974); *The Music of Human Flesh* (1980);

It's a Song, It's a Song (1986); *Fewer Roses* (1986); *Eleven Planets* (1993).

[WH]

Daryush, Elizabeth (England, 1887–1977) Born the daughter of Poet Laureate ROBERT BRIDGES in Chilswell on Boar's Hill overlooking Oxford, Daryush was acquainted at an early age with JOHN MASEFIELD, ROBERT GRAVES, and THOMAS HARDY. Daryush's family was part of the privileged upper class, which she later rebelled against and criticized in her poetry, especially in *The Last Man and Other Verses* (1936) and *Verses: Sixth Book* (1938). In 1923, Daryush married and moved to Persia, returning with her husband four years later to Boar's Hill where they spent the rest of their lives. Since her death in 1977, Daryush has gained popularity and won the admiration of DONALD DAVIE and ROY FULLER who have promoted her work.

Much of Daryush's poetry warned against the danger of using imagination to override the harsh realities of life. Her poetry is often criticized for its traditional forms and antiquated diction and phrasing. Despite her strong traditional tendencies, Daryush continued the experimentation with syllabics that her father had started. AUDEN acknowledged her in his lecture at Oxford for her great contributions in this area.

Selected works: *Charitessi* (1912); *Selected Poems* (1948, 1972); *Collected Poems* (1976).

[BRB]

Daumal, René (France, 1908–44). Daumal temporarily allied himself with Surrealism when he co-founded the review *Le Grand Jeu* (*The Big Game*, 1928), in which he published his first poems. Beyond Surrealism, the poetry of Daumal reveals an ongoing quest for originality, self-knowledge, and the Absolute. He seeks to reclaim an authentic sense of spiritual faith for the reason-centered West. His major influences include occultism, mysticism, and Hinduism. These influences manifest themselves both in Daumal's translation of Sanscrit texts and in his use of narcotics. He died following several long stays in sanatoria. Only two of Daumal's works, *Contre-ciel* (*The Anti-Heaven*, 1935) and *La Grande Beuverie* (*The Great Drinking Binge*, 1938), were published during his short lifetime.

Selected works: *Le Mont analogue* (*Mount Analogue*, 1952), *Chaque fois que l'aube paraît* (*Each Time Dawn Appears*, 1953), *Poésie noir, poésie blanche* (*Black Poetry, White Poetry*, 1954), *Lettres à ses amis* (*Letters to His Friends*, 1958).

[AD]

Davičo, Oskar (Yugoslavia, 1909–89) Davičo was one of the most dynamic, active, and controversial Yugoslav writers. His poetic oeuvre incorporates several phases which parallel larger social developments in Yugoslav society, while his novels are important literary documents of the history of Yugoslavia in the twentieth century.

Born in Šabac, Davičo was educated at the University of Belgrade where he graduated from the Faculty of Philosophy in 1930. He began his literary career as an exceptionally talented Surrealist poet. Soon afterward, he became a Communist and fundamentally modified his poetics. He abandoned Surrealism and espoused the idea of committed art, i.e., art that participated in the struggle for political and social justice. After 1934, Davičo became one of the main representatives of the Yugoslav 'Socialist literature' movement, which advocated active political and social responsibility of writers, and active artistic engagement in the struggle for the creation of a more just society.

During World War II, after a period of incarceration in a concentration camp, Davičo joined the Yugoslav partisan liberation movement in 1943. After the war, he devoted himself to writing poetry. His active social and political engagement is discernible in poems such as 'Balada o robu'

('Ballad about a Slave') and 'Dva soneta sa Banjičkog groblja' ('Two Sonnets from Banjica Cemetery') and many others, as well as in collections of poetry such as *Zrenjanin* (1949), *Višnja za zidom* (*A Cherry Tree behind a Wall*, 1950), and *Čovekov čovek* (1953).

His poetic style underwent another change soon after the publication of these collections, when he was again attracted to Surrealism. His post-war poetry is an impressive endeavor in which he combines the two contradictory aspects of his poetry, social commitment and experimental technique. *Hana* (1951), *Flora* (1955), *Kairos* (1959), and *Trg M* (1969) are some of Davičo's works which successfully merge different aspects of his creative personality.

Davičo's language is exuberant and creative, characterized by a wealth of unconventional imagery and sound. His poetry is robust and sensual, full of extraordinary stylistic and linguistic effects. His language is simple yet powerful, and he uses it to create a true testimonial to his comrades who sacrificed their lives for the belief in social justice. But his poetry also exudes optimism that the deaths and suffering were not in vain, and that they will bring a better future to the generations to come. Many of his poems are monuments to the heroic struggle of Yugoslav partisans and Communists before and during World War II. His poetry is revolutionary, both in its social engagement and in its efforts to find effective ways of expressing this engagement.

Selected works: *Gladi* (*Hungers*, 1963); *Tajne* (*Secrets*, 1964); *Telo–telu* (1975); *Dvojezicna noc* (*A Bilingual Night*, 1987).

[DJ]

Davie, Donald (England, 1922–95) Born in Barnsley, Yorkshire, Davie was educated at Cambridge University, taking a Ph.D. in 1951. While he traveled and taught widely, he spent much of his time after the 1960s in the United States, where he lived with his wife Doreen John, with whom he had three children. Davie was as well known for his literary criticism as for his scholarly, formalist poetry.

Concerned with the technical elements of poetry, Davie advocated the responsible use of diction and syntax; he believed that certain words and subjects simply are not poetic. Along with LARKIN and JENNINGS, he was one of the founders of The Movement, a group of 1950s poets who generally disdained symbolism and imagery, preferring instead to examine a poem in light of its social implications and morality. While he finally softened his harsh critiques of the game-playing poetics of POUND and ELIOT, he nonetheless believed that poetry should ultimately be valued for its rationality and lucidity. Davie's Baptist upbringing greatly influenced his own work, which concerns itself with traditions of dissent, various religious subjects, and social losses.

Selected works: *Purity of Diction in English Verse* (1952); *Brides of Reason* (1955); *A Winter Talent and Other Poems* (1957); *Events and Wisdoms: Poems 1957–1963* (1964); *Collected Poems 1970–1983* (1983).

[SG]

Davies, Idris (Wales, 1905–53) Davies was born in the Rhymney Valley, and worked in the coal mines from the age of fourteen until the General Strike of 1926. He educated himself by correspondence course, eventually studying at the University of Nottingham and becoming a schoolmaster. His first volumes, *Gwalia Deserta* (1938) and *The Angry Summer* (1943), are 'industrial' sequences detailing social injustice; his last, *Tonypandy* (1945), offered a more generically varied selection. To contemporary ears, Davies' sincere tone risks the mawkish, but it also makes for a powerful directness (as protest singer Pete Seeger recognized when he recorded 'O what can you give me?'), and his poetic character sketches display a bitter wit. Davies died in middle age, from cancer.

The Complete Poems of Idris Davies appeared in 1994.

[BS]

Davies, W. H. (Wales, 1871–1940) William Henry Davies is most famous for *The Autobiography of a Supertramp* (1908), a memoir of the Newport, Monmouthshire-born author's experiences as a hobo in North America. This volume describes, *inter alia*, the 1889 accident in which Davies lost his right leg, curtailing his wanderings, but also prompting his literary career. After some years of struggle, Davies was sponsored by George Bernard Shaw and EDWARD THOMAS, and by 1913 his reputation among the Georgian poets was well established. His work is deliberately simple, even naive, generally celebrating the delights of nature and the pleasure of human companionship. Davies was prolific, publishing over twenty books of poetry, of which *Songs of Joy* (1911) is numbered among the finest. His *Complete Poems* appeared in 1963.

[BS]

Davis, Jack (Australia, b. 1917) A tireless worker for Aboriginal rights in his native country, Davis' work has addressed race relations worldwide. Born in Perth, he was raised in a working-class household in Western Australia, returning to Perth to work as a manual laborer and, later, as editor of the Aboriginal Publications Foundation (1942–79). His first volume, *The First Born*, appeared in 1970 and was followed by *Poems from Aboriginal Australia* eight years later. Also noted for his plays, Davis was awarded the British Empire Medal in 1977 and the Order of Australia.

Selected works: *John Pat and Other Poems* (1988); *Black Life* (1992).

[MW]

Dawe, Bruce (Australia, b. 1930) An indifferent student, Dawe left school at sixteen. He then held a variety of jobs, attended night school, and in 1954 entered the University of Melbourne, where he developed his interest in writing fiction and poetry. Leaving the university before graduating, Dawe moved to Sydney where he was a postman and factory worker. He served in the Australian Air Force for nine years, then completed his bachelor's degree at the University of Queensland and eventually earned a Ph.D. In addition to teaching at various Australian colleges, he has written fiction, edited anthologies, and published several volumes of poetry, his first in 1962. He has received numerous awards for his work, including the Patrick White Literary Award in 1980.

Dawe criticized Australian poetry for its lack of social awareness, and set out in his own poetry to fill that gap. He censures government and its institutions, denounces social structures that hamper individual freedom, and ridicules Australia's insularity and nationalistic stance. But it is the oppressiveness of modern life that receives the poet's harshest reproach. In spite of this pessimistic posture, Dawe's poetry is neither gloomy nor fatalistic. He lightens the darkness through humor and an informal style. The whimsical and the droll soften but do not alleviate the serious and somber elements. Technically, he balances Australian colloquial speech with lyrical qualities. Dawe is considered Australia's most popular and best-selling poet.

Selected work: *Sometimes Gladness, Collected Poems–1954 to 1997* (1997).

[RR]

Day Lewis, C. (England, 1904–72) Cecil Day Lewis was born in Ballintubbert, Ireland to Reverend Frank Cecil and Kathleen Blake Squires Day Lewis. He was educated at home for several years, and it was assumed that he would follow in his father's footsteps as a clergyman. The literary held more interest than the religious, however, so Day Lewis financed the publication of his first volume of poetry, *Beechen Virgil and Other Poems* (1925), which reveals his tendency toward Georgian nature verse. *Transitional Poem*, a lyric sequence published in 1929, blends the ideas and manners of AUDEN and ELIOT with his own traditional, romantic sensibility into the theme of a journey toward wholeness.

Unable to depend solely on poetry as a career, Day Lewis reluctantly taught in 1927–35. He continued to view himself as a poet, however, and in 1931, inspired by the birth of his son, he wrote the personal and meditative *From Feathers to Iron*, which invokes imagery of journey, exploration, and rebirth. Day Lewis' growing political commitment can be read as a part of the poem's background (some critics even viewed it as political allegory), but emerges much more clearly in his next volume, *The Magnetic Mountain* (1933), which celebrates the new (socialist) world to come.

In 1934, Day Lewis published his first book of critical prose, *A Hope for Poetry*, in which he appropriates the political base of Communism as it serves the poet, who, he argues, needs to be part of a close society in order to function. While his revolutionary writing of the 1930s was heavily influenced by his left-wing contemporaries Auden, SPENDER, and MACNEICE (the Oxford Group), Day Lewis was the most politically active of the group. In 1935, he joined the Communist Party and took responsibility for the political education of his local party group.

Upon joining the party, Day Lewis resigned from his teaching position at Cheltenham College and became a full-time, freelance writer. During this time, he produced over twenty popular detective novels under the pseudonym Nicholas Blake. *A Time to Dance and Other Poems* (1935), which was viewed by some as balancing his bourgeois romanticism with his proletarian politics, presents a developed self-awareness and returns to familiar journey, warfare, and heroism images.

He felt, however, that his poetry was suffering because of his political commitment and he left the Communist Party in 1938. In 1946, he returned to teaching and delivered the Clark Lectures at Cambridge (published the next year as *The Poetic Image*), served as Professor of Poetry at Oxford from 1951 to 56, and gave the Charles Eliot Norton lectures at Harvard from 1964 to 65 (published as *The Lyric Impulse*). While there were those who believed that his political beliefs and practices inspired his best verse, giving it an energy and complexity that made it superior to his later work, others favored his ensuing meditative, memory-filled writings (*Selected Poems*, 1967; *The Whispering Roots*, 1970; and his autobiography, *The Buried Day*, 1960).

Day Lewis was made Commander, Order of the British Empire (1950); Fellow and Vice President, Royal Society of Literature; Fellow, Royal Society of Arts; and Member, American Academy of Arts and Letters. He was Poet Laureate of Britain from 1968 until his death. Yet, despite his prominence, Day Lewis' work has received little independent critical attention and is generally discussed as a part of the Oxford Poets, or of the 1930s as a period of combined politics and poetry.

[JS]

De la Mare, Walter (England, 1873–1956) De la Mare, who also published under the name Walter Ramal, was born in Charlton, Kent, and received little formal education. In 1899, he married Constance Elfrida Ingpen, with whom he had four children. An extremely prolific writer, de la Mare is known for his poetry (over forty titles), fiction (close to twenty works), and children's books (over thirty collections).

De la Mare enjoyed primarily favorable reviews during his lifetime, particularly for his children's poems, which were considered among the very best at the century's start. And while he wrote on all the traditional romantic subjects (death, dreams, intense emotion), he is best known for his childlike, playful tone and diction. Not a simple poet, de la Mare managed to write with and complicate a youthful imagination that stressed his belief in childhood as a time of intense intuition and spiritual insight. Eventually, critics somewhat tired of his naive approach to life, and he was frequently referred to as an escapist by those who both praised and panned his work. Still, late tributes were heaped upon him: he was awarded the Order of Merit in 1953 and the Foyle Poetry Prize in 1954. De la Mare's work strives toward a transcendent understanding of life that is recovered from childhood.

Selected works: *Songs of Childhood* (1902); *Poems* (1906); *The Listener and Other Poems* (1912); *A Child's Day* (1912); *Peacock Pie* (1913); *The Sunken Garden and Other Poems* (1917); *The Veil and Other Poems* (1921); *The Burning-Glass* (1945).

[SG]

De Sousa, Nomia (Mozambique, b. 1927) De Sousa did much of her writing between 1951 and 1964, when she worked on various Angolan and Mozambiquan journals. From the 1940s, she was a figurehead for the Mozambiquan cultural renaissance, actively linking artistic endeavors to protest movements. Considered an artist of the Negritude movement, she was the first African woman to gain international attention for her poetry.

De Sousa adds an important feminist dimension to Negritude poetics. The poem 'Call' (or 'Appeal') asks that Africa not abandon her heroic sister. In a different vein, 'The Poem of Joao' insists that Joao, a man taken by colonial authorities, is father, mother, and brother – us all.

English translations of her work are found in *Poems of Black Africa* (1975) and, more recently, in the Penguin (1984) and Heinemann (1995) anthologies of African verse.

[KAC]

Deane, Seamus (Ireland, b. 1940) Born in Derry, Northern Ireland, Deane was educated at Queen's University, Belfast, and Cambridge University. After lecturing at Reed College and the University of California at Berkeley, Deane was appointed Professor of Modern English and American Literature at University College, Dublin. He remained there until 1994, when he was appointed Keough Professor of Irish Studies at Notre Dame University. His first volume, *Gradual Wars* (1972), won the Æ Memorial Award in 1973. However, Deane is perhaps better known for his literary criticism and for his role as a director of the Field Day movement than for his verse. He was the general editor of *The Field Day Anthology of Irish Writing* (1991). His first novel, the semi-autobiographical *Reading in the Dark* (1996), depicts a young Catholic boy growing up in Derry. It won the *Guardian* Fiction Prize, the *Irish Times* Fiction Award and International Award, and was a Booker Prize finalist.

Selected works: *Rumours* (1977); *History Lessons* (1983); *Selected Poems* (1988).

[CT]

Deguy, Michel (France, b. 1930) As well as a translator and reader in a publishing house, Deguy is a poet, professor, and philosopher. The poet's first collections encompass what Deguy describes as an 'examination of space': *les Meurtières* (*The Loopholes*, 1959), *Fragments du cadastre* (*Fragments of the Land Register*, 1960), *Poèmes de la presqu'île* (*Poems of the Peninsula*, 1962), *Biefs* (*Reaches*, 1964). Language and metaphor are the primary focus of *Ouï-dire* (*Hearsay*, 1966) and *Actes* (*Acts*, 1966). Deguy's more modern works include *Figurations* (*Figurations*, 1969), *Tombeau de Du Bellay* (*The Tomb of Du Bellay*, 1973), *Jumelages suivi de Made in USA* (*Twinnings followed by Made in USA*, 1978), and *Gisants* (*Recumbent Effigies*, 1985). Deguy compares his poetic work to walking; he listens to the 'spirit of the earth' to compose his poems, which become 'the ceremonial banner of perception in the wind of the lungs'. For Deguy, the true poet reveals the powers of language to language itself.

[AD]

Depestre, René (Haiti, b. 1926) Born in Jacmel, Depestre studied at the Sorbonne and at the Musée de l'Homme in Paris before returning to Haiti in 1945. In a century in which exile has guaranteed many writers an international audience, Depestre's subsequent exile from Haiti in 1946 has left him virtually unknown in the English-speaking world. Much of this has to do with Depestre's revolutionary, Marxist politics, and the fact that he has lived in Cuba since 1958. Only two collections of his poetry have been translated into English: *A Rainbow for the Christian West* (1972) and *Vegetations of Splendor* (1981). Depestre's work is much more widely available in French and Spanish, and while he may be relatively obscure to English-speaking audiences, he has long been recognized as one of the most articulate and important radical voices in the Third World.

From his very first book of poetry, *Etincelles* (*Sparks*, 1945), Depestre has written radical, revolutionary verse that expresses a deep sympathy for the masses and articulates the need to think things anew. Yet emphases on Depestre's politics can all too easily obscure his considerable skill as a poet. Far from being a didactic, dogmatic writer, the underlying politics of Depestre's poetry find expression in verse that is lyrical, marked by the use of intense and powerful imagery, and characterized by an exploration of the full range of human emotion and experience, including the desire for peace, tenderness, and love.

Selected works: *Gerbes de sang* (*Showers of Blood*, 1946); *Traduit du grand large* (*The High Seas Translated*, 1952); *Journal d'un animal marin* (*Journal of a Marine Animal*, 1964); *Poeta a Cuba* (*Poet in Cuba*, 1973); *Ela palo ensebado/Le Mât de cocagne* (*Greasy Pole*, 1974); *Bonjour et adieu à la negritude* (*Hello and Goodbye to Negritude*, 1980); *Hadriana dans tous mes rêves* (*Hadriana in All My Dreams*, 1988).

[IS]

Desnos, Robert (France, 1900–45) Paris-born Desnos was at the center of the Surrealist movement, particularly during his star turn in the period of Surrealist experiments with automatism known as the 'hypnotic sleeps' (1922–3). He published word-game poems, lyric love poems, dreams, poetic prose, and a novel, *La Liberté ou l'amour! (Liberty or Love!*, 1927). He broke with the Surrealist group in 1930, the year he published his most famous collection of poems, *Corps et Biens* (*Bodies and Goods*), though he continued to produce Surrealistic work for the rest of his life.

Desnos worked in journalism and, starting in 1930, in radio. He wrote poetry, popular songs, librettos for cantatas, advertising jingles and dramas for radio, film scenarios, and children's verse – the *Chantefables* (*Songfables*) and *Chantefleurs* (*Songflowers*), which are still very popular in France. Most of the 1920s love poetry was dedicated to his 'star', the music- hall singer Yvonne George; in the 1930s it was dedicated to his 'mermaid', his companion Youki. He worked for the Resistance during the German Occupation, when he wrote both legal and illegal political poems. In 1944, Desnos was arrested and deported to Auschwitz, Buchenwald, Flossenbürg, and Flöha. He died at Terezin of exhaustion, in June 1945, one month after his arrival and the camp's liberation.

Selected works: *Fortunes* (*Fortune*, 1942); *Etat de Veille* (*Waking State*, 1943); *Trente Chantefables pour les enfants sages* (*Thirty Songfables for Good Children*, 1944); *Contrée* (*Country*, 1944).

[KC]

Devlin, Denis (Ireland, 1908–59) An international Modernist poet, Devlin spent most of his life outside Ireland. Born in Scotland and educated at University College, Dublin, Munich University, and the Sorbonne, he joined the Irish foreign service in 1935 and thereafter resided in Europe and in the United States. Although his work has been praised by SAMUEL BECKETT and ROBERT PENN WARREN and has influenced such poets as JOHN MONTAGUE and THOMAS KINSELLA, Devlin has not received the same widespread critical acclaim as many of his Irish contemporaries – perhaps because his poems, which introduce Irish themes in broad, nontraditional contexts, are allusive and sometimes difficult to interpret. Influenced by European poetry, his work is marked by a probing spirituality and rich ambiguity.

Selected works: *Intercessions* (1937); *Lough Derg* (1964); *Collected Poems* (1964); *The Heavenly Foreigner* (1967); *Collected Poems of Denis Devlin* (1989).

[CT]

Dhomhnaill, Nuala Ní (Ireland, b. 1952) Born in England but raised in Kerry, Ireland, in an Irish-speaking region (Gaeltacht), Ní Dhomhnaill is today one of the most widely read poets writing in the Irish language. Able to reach a broad audience of non-Irish readers in part because her work has been translated by notable contemporary Irish poets, her volumes often have a dual-language format, such as *Selected Poems (*1988), translated by MICHAEL HARTNETT; *Pharaoh's Daughter* (1990), translated by 13 well-known Irish poets; and *The Astrakhan Cloak* (1992), translated by PAUL MULDOON. Her poems often fuse contemporary images of Irish women and social themes with the traditional mythic heroines of Irish literature and legend, creating a distinct voice that is powerful, sexual, ironic, and playful. Despite many excellent translations, Ní Dhomhnaill insists that her poems be read in Irish to be fully appreciated.

Selected works: *Selected Poems: Rogha Dánta* (trans. Hartnett, 1997); *Cead Aighnis* (1998).

[CT]

Dickey, James (United States, 1923–97) If one-half of a career can make a reputation, then James Dickey is an important American poet, especially for his lyrical first four books. The fourth, *Buckdancer's Choice* (1965) won the National Book Award. In his later work he abandoned formalism and wrote long-line and split-line poems, with an emphasis on rhetoric and narrative. Some of his later works, including a book of love poems, *Puella* (1982), were judged obscure failures – as Dickey's alcoholism and psychological disabilities overwhelmed his accomplishments. But he remains admired for his poetic energy and the audacity of his subject matter, as in poems like 'The Sheep Child' and 'Falling'.

Dickey was also author of three novels: *Deliverance* (1970), *Alnilam* (1987), and *To the White Sea* (1993). He published two volumes of autobiographical essays.

He was born in Atlanta, Georgia, earned degrees from Vanderbilt University, and served in the U.S. Army Air Corps in the early 1940s and again in the 1950s. He worked as an advertising copywriter in Atlanta until he began an academic career. At the time of his death he taught at the University of South Carolina.

Selected works: *The Whole Motion: Collected Poems 1945–92* (1992); *Poems 1957–67* (1967); *Babel to Byzantium* (prose, 1968); *Night Hurdling* (prose, 1983).

[RP]

Dickinson, Patric (England, 1913–94) Although he has produced a significant amount of poetry, Dickinson (born in India) was best known for his BBC radio broadcasts and his translations of Virgil and Aristophanes.

After teaching school and serving a brief stint in World War II, Dickinson published his first book, *The Seven Days of Jericho* (1944), a verse play. This and other early, stridently symbolic works focus on nature and man's destruction, as well as the ability of poetry and love to overcome.

Shortly after his mother died in the 1950s, Dickinson began to write obsessively about death and war, remembering his father's death in World War I and his brother's in World War II. His poetry took a major step in 1973 with *A Wintering Tree* which won the Cholmondeley Award. This volume and those that followed changed dramatically from the fearful view of the harsh world to a more meditative perspective.

Selected works: *Theseus and the Minotaur, and Poems* (1946); *The Sailing Race, and Other Poems* (1952); *The World I See* (1960); *This Cold Universe* (1964); *The Bearing Beast* (1976); *Our Living John* (1979); *A Rift in Time* (1982).

[BRB]

Dimitrova, Blaga (Bulgaria, b. 1922) Author of twenty-seven books of poetry, six novels, two plays, several collections of essays, travelogues, and memoirs, Dimitrova is also an accomplished translator of Classical (the *Iliad*) and modern European poetry (Russian, Polish, Swedish). She is widely regarded as the best living Bulgarian woman writer. According to Julia Kristeva, seldom has a woman's writing been at once more cerebral and more sensual. One might also add that seldom has a woman's writing been at once more intimate and more politically engaged. Dimitrova was awarded the Herder Prize for Poetry (Vienna, 1992), the Lundkvist Prize (Stockholm, 1984), and the Polish P.E.N.-Club Award (Warsaw, 1977) for her contributions to Bulgarian and world literature.

Born in Byala Slatina, Dimitrova earned a B.A. in Slavic philology from the University of Sofia (1945) and a Ph.D. in Russian literature from the Maxim Gorky Literary Institute (Moscow, 1951). Between 1950 and 1982 she worked as editor of several literary magazines and in major publishing houses. In the 1960s, the harsh reality of life in a totalitarian state gradually extinguished her earlier enthusiasm for Communist ideals. A prominent political dissident during the 1970s and 1980s, Dimitrova became one of the leaders of the democratic forces in her native country. Soon after the demise of the totalitarian regime (1989) she was elected vice-president of Bulgaria (1992–3). Today, she continues to be both a major literary and political figure.

Dimitrova's poems are emotionally and intellectually honest, innovative in terms of form, and non-conformist in terms of ideology. Her works of the 1950s, whose themes focus on the anti-Fascist resistance, World War II, and the Communist-led effort to rebuild and modernize the country, bear the signs of poetic apprenticeship. Her poetry and prose (*Pŭtuvane kum sebe si* (*Journey to Oneself*), *Otklonenie* (*Detour*)) of the 1960s, however, compellingly display her original literary style and intellectual independence. Dimitrova's vintage poetry, especially the works created after her battle with cancer in the 1970s, addresses issues such as life and death, love, motherhood, nature, truth, meaning, and the power of the word with artistic brilliancy and philosophical sophistication.

Like her poetry, Dimitrova's fiction and plays have been enthusiastically received by readers both in Bulgaria and abroad. These excellent pieces of what one may call poet's prose are characterized by oblique parallels with her poetry, female agency, and a fusion of psychological insights and political and ethical issues. All of her works are informed by an unambiguously female voice which speaks with confidence and fortitude.

Selected works: *Ekspeditsiya kŭm idniya den* (*An Expedition Toward the Coming Day*, 1964); *Osŭdeni na lyubov* (*Sentenced to Love*, 1967); *Ime* (*Name*, 1971); *Kak* (*How*, 1974); *Zabraneno more* (*Forbidden Sea*, 1976); *Prostranstva* (*Spaces*, 1980); *Glas* (*Voice*, 1985); *Labirint* (*Labyrinth*, 1987); *Mezhdu* (*Between*, 1990); *Noshten dnevnik* (*Night Diary*, 1992); *Belezi* (*Scars*, 1997).

[CG/LPG]

Diop, Birago (also known as Max and d'Alain Provist; Senegal, 1906–89) Veterinarian, diplomat, playwright, author, and poet, Ismael Birago Diop contributed to the works collected by LEOPOLD SENGHOR and AIMÉ CÉSAIRE in the 1930s Negritude movement. Found in Senghor's 1948 *Anthology* and other collections, and his own 1960 collection, Diop's poetry musically treats the misery and joys of life and death, while integrating influences of classic French form and themes of the Harlem Renaissance and Negritude. Best known for his award-winning folktales *Tales of Amadou Koumba* (1947, 1958), Diop brought African oral tales into a written form in French.

Selected works: *Leurres et lueurs* (*Lures and Lights*, 1960); *Mémoires* (3-volume memoirs) (1978–85); *The New Tales of Amadou Koumba* (1958).

[LF]

Diop, David Mandessi (Senegal, 1927–60) Born in France to a Senegalese father and Cameroonian mother, Diop wrote some thirty poems harshly criticizing oppression and colonialism in Africa. His 1956 collection and 13 poems published elsewhere condemn problems of slavery and the colonial legacy during his generation's struggle for African independence. His most famous poem 'Afrique' ('Africa') optimistically predicts freedom for his then distant Africa. 'Rama Kam', and 'A une danseuse noire' ('To a Black Female Dancer') sensually repeat the themes of memories, roots, and illness. He and his family died in a plane crash near Dakar; his unpublished manuscripts were found with him.

Selected works: *Coups de Pilon: poèmes* (*Hammer Blows and Other Writings*, 1956; trans. and updated, 1973); *Anthologie de la nouvelle poésie nègre et malgache* (*Anthology of New Black and Malgachey Poetry in French*, 5 poems, 1947).

[LF]

Dobson, Rosemary (Australia, b. 1920) Dobson was born in Sydney and has lived in Canberra since 1972. During World War II she joined publishers Angus and Robertson, and worked with DOUGLAS STEWART, Beatrice Davis, and Nan McDonald. From 1966 until 1971 she and her husband lived in London. Dobson's first collection of poems, *In a Convex Mirror*, was published in 1944. While living in England she traveled in Europe, studying the art that was to have a significant influence on her poetry.

Dobson's early poetry reflects on time and impermanence as well as on her interest in Renaissance art. In *Child with a Cockatoo* (1955) Dobson writes, with elegance and restraint, about her own life as a poet, wife, and mother. Her belief in the power of art, her calm erudition, the breadth of her material, and the discipline of her verse distinguish her poetry. Rosemary Dobson has established her reputation as one of Australia's foremost poets.

Selected works: *The Ship of Ice* (1948); *Cock Crow* (1965); *Three Poems on Water Springs* (1973); *Greek Coins: A Sequence of Poems* (1977); *Over the Frontier: Poems* (1978); *Twelve Poems for David Campbell* (1981); *The Three Fates and Other Poems* (1984); *Seeing and Believing* (1990); *Directions* (1991); *Collected Poems* (1992).

[AP]

Dorn, Edward (United States, 1929–99) Dorn was born in rural Illinois, attended the University of Illinois and graduated from Black Mountain College, where he became associated with his teacher, CHARLES OLSON, and other Black Mountain poets. He taught at numerous schools, including the University of Colorado.

By turns lyrical, sarcastic, and comic, Dorn's poetry often focuses on the significance of place in shaping identity and meaning. *Gunslinger*, Dorn's major work, is an ambitious mock-epic of the American West, a fractured, fantastic narrative that critiques and dismantles cultural myths. The work contains sharp satire, antic humor and wildly shifting voices, in which 1960s drug slang, cowboy dialect and lyricism collide.

Selected works: *Gunslinger* (1975); *Collected Poems* (1983).

[AE]

Doty, Mark (United States, b. 1953) Through a traditional lyricism, Doty dramatizes sensuality and sexual identity. His untraditional topics, such as drag queens and the gay bar scene, are balanced by romantic and mellifluous language. While the scale of his poems might be criticized as over-reaching, Doty asks that his human scenery be considered large – a metaphysics of the ordinary – as the speaker in most of his poems remains open to the melancholia of the everyday. Doty teaches at the University of Houston Creative Writing Program and lives in Provincetown, Massachusetts.

Selected works: *My Alexandria* (1993); *Atlantis* (1995).

[CV]

Douglas, Keith (England, 1920–44) Keith Castellain Douglas was born into a middle-class family in Tunbridge Wells, Kent, and was educated at Christ's Hospital and Merton College, Oxford. Douglas wrote accomplished poetry by the age of 14, and went on to work closely with EDMUND BLUNDEN and T. S. ELIOT. He died in France, at the age of 24, while serving in World War II.

Douglas wrote in fluent metric forms and mastered sonnets early in his career, although he later came to view rhythm as a means to an end, allowing the reader fully to engage the purposeful speech of his poetry. He is known primarily for his war poetry, which is overwhelmed not just by his foreshadowing of his own death as a result of war, but by his understanding of soldiers as trained killers. In light of his edified understanding of the brutality of war, he began to view sentimentality – and apparently his distinctive six-line stanza – as counterproductive, and saw his purpose as a poet as conveying 'true' reality, as he saw it. The poetry he wrote in the year before his death is considered his best, and Douglas himself, sensing that he would not survive the war, prepared most of his work for publication in 1943 and 1944. While very little of Douglas' work was published during his lifetime, it has since been actively championed by TED HUGHES, among others.

Selected works: *Selected Poems* (1943); *Alamein to Zem Zem* (1946); *The Complete Poems of Keith Douglas* (1978).

[SG]

Dove, Rita (United States, b. 1952) Pulitzer Prize-winner and former U.S. Poet Laureate, Dove was born in Akron, Ohio and educated at Miami University in Ohio, the University of Tübingen in West Germany, and the University of Iowa. She is Commonwealth Professor of English at the University of Virginia.

Dove's finest lyrics delve into history, both personal and cultural, mythology and domestic experience. Drawing on a lifetime of passionate study and a deep affinity for the oral tradition, her poems manage to be both cerebral and emotionally affecting, as they explore directly the emotional truths of dailiness and personal relationships.

Selected works: *The Yellow House on the Corner* (1980); *Museum* (1983); *Thomas and Beulah* (1986); *Grace Notes* (1989); *Mother Love* (1995).

[JT]

Dransfield, Michael (Australia, 1948–73) Born in Sydney, Dransfield was educated at Sydney Grammar School and the University of Sydney. He discontinued his university studies to write poetry, working as a journalist and a clerk. Dransfield's first publications were in the new underground magazines which sprang up in the late 1960s, and which, in retrospect, were seen as enabling the revitalization of Australian poetry. This movement, the New Australian poetry, or the Generation of '68 (see TRANTER, DUGGAN, FORBES, MAIDEN), experimented with form, and protested against conventional society. Dransfield himself sought an alternative to the regimentation of ordinary life, and spent itinerant years mainly in rural New South Wales, traveling and writing. He is perhaps most famous for writing about drug-taking and addiction, and his poetry contains an ambivalent mixture or tension between an almost primitivist romantic nostalgia, and a protest against the forces of conservatism. He died in 1973, on Good Friday. Dransfield published three volumes of poetry during his life, *Streets of the Long Voyage* (1970), *The Inspector of Tides* (1972), and *Drug Poems* (1972). *Memoirs of a Velvet Urinal* and *The Second Month of Spring* were published posthumously in 1975 and 1980 respectively, and Rodney Hall edited a *Collected Poems* (1987).

[FH]

Drosinis, Georgios (Greece, 1859–1951) Drosinis is considered, along with KOSTIS PALAMAS, the founder of the 'New Athenian' school of literature. The offspring of a distinguished family from Messolongi, he was born in Athens where he received his degree from the Faculty of Letters and Philosophy. After three years in Europe he returned to Greece where he became the editor of literary journals, including the most influential *Estia*. His poetry, prominently influenced by the Greek folk tradition, is characterized by its lyrical adoration of the Greek countryside and its romantic nostalgia.

Selected works: *Idylls* (1885); *Unwilting Flowers* (1890); *Closed Eyelids* (1914); *Illuminated Darkness* (1918); *Night Will Be Falling* (1922).

[GSY]

Du Bouchet, André (France, 1924–2001) With the publication of his first major work, *Dans la chaleur vacante (In the Vacant Heat*, 1961), Du Bouchet revealed what would become a lifelong fascination with blank space, void, and various types of emptiness. In the tradition of Baudelaire and Mallarmé, he constantly struggles in search of what lies beyond, of a place that always eludes him. For Du Bouchet, however, the arduous quest for the unknown, whose lack he senses acutely, allows him to become increasingly conscious of his own being as it exists both *here* and *there*. The poetic adventure becomes a way of reconciling, through his consciousness, the universe that he ardently desires with the one in which he is firmly rooted.

What immediately strikes the reader who takes up any of Du Bouchet's poetry is the printed page itself. Everywhere, on each sheet of unpaginated text, gaps separate words, lines, and even letters. Words are of no greater importance than the silence and emptiness that surround them. Thematically, we are dealing with a concrete world, made up of brute matter, the elements and, especially, the words that designate these essential components. Words cease to be mere symbols and become themselves objects of discovery in a poetic corpus that is the antithesis of spontaneous, free release of imagery.

Selected works: *Laisses* (1979); *Ici en deux* (*Here in Two*, 1986); *Des Hauts-de-Buhl* (1990); *Axiales* (1992).

[RSO]

Dudek, Louis (Canada, b. 1918) Dudek was born in Montréal, and with the exception of his graduate studies at Columbia University, the city has been his home for his entire life. As in the case of numerous Canadian writers, Dudek has combined a literary career with a successful academic career, having spent almost four decades as a professor at McGill University.

As both a poet and a critic, Dudek has

been a consistent practitioner and defender of Modernism. Profoundly influenced by EZRA POUND, Dudek's poetry is difficult, philosophical and erudite. His early poetry, as exhibited in his first collection, *East of the City* (1946), is forcefully Imagist. Dudek's work in the 1950s and 1960s, his most productive period, consists of long, non-narrative, meditative poems; work in this vein includes *Europe* (1954), *En Mexico* (1958), and *Atlantis* (1967). Along with his friend Raymond Souster and the poet IRVING LAYTON, Dudek has also been influential as a publisher and editor of poetry. Dudek's work is best sampled in the selections included in *Infinite Worlds* (1988). He received the Order of Canada in 1984.

[IS]

Duffy, Carol Ann (Scotland, b. 1955) Duffy was born in Glasgow, and educated at St Joseph's Convent, Stafford and Stafford Girls' High School. She read Philosophy at Liverpool University in 1974–7, and from 1983 was poetry editor for *Ambit* magazine. Her work first came to public notice with two plays produced in Liverpool; the playwright's observation of dialogue and character is instantly recognizable in her wide-ranging poems, some of which are subversive monologues written for undernoticed historical or fictional characters. She is the recipient of a number of awards such as the C. Day Lewis Fellowship (1982–4) and the Whitbread Award for Poetry (1993).

Selected works: *Standing Female Nude* (1985); *Selling Manhattan* (1987); *The Other Country* (1990); *Mean Time* (1993); *Selected Poems* (1994).

[LKMF]

Dugan, Alan (United States, b. 1923) Dugan, who has lived throughout New England, was a member of the Air Force during World War II, and graduated from Mexico City College. He has won the Yale Younger Poets Prize (1961), a Pulitzer Prize, a National Book Award, and a Prix de Rome. RICHARD HOWARD has commented that Dugan 'writes to save himself'; indeed, Dugan's poetry is marked by a comic, dark consideration of the quotidian – of marriage, health, and newspaper stories – that mixes formal phrasing and diction with fricative American slang. He is a Staff Member for Poetry at the Fine Arts Work Center in Provincetown, Massachusetts.

Selected works: *New and Collected Poems 1961–83* (1983); *Poems* (1989).

[CV]

Duggan, Eileen (New Zealand, 1894–1972) Born of Irish Catholic immigrant parents, Duggan was educated at Victoria University. She later lectured there and regularly wrote for *The New Zealand Tablet*.

Her poems are infused with her Roman Catholicism and her celebration of the New Zealand landscape and the Maori language and legends. Still, Duggan's verse has been attacked by ALLEN CURNOW and JAMES K. BAXTER, among others, for its clichés, its conservatism, its romantic phrases, and its Georgian conventionality.

She gained an international reputation as her work was widely read and praised in the United States and Britain during the 1930s and 1940s. In the 1950s, in the context of the increasing influence of modernism on New Zealand poetry, Duggan's fame declined. Her last collection, *More Poems* (1951), is often considered her most austere and complex.

Selected works: *Poems* (1922); *New Zealand Bird Songs* (1929); *Poems* (1937); *New Zealand Poems* (1940).

[SH]

Duggan, Laurie (Australia, b. 1949) Born in Melbourne, Duggan attended Monash University and was involved in the important poetry readings there. He has taught creative writing, been an art critic, a script writer, and poetry editor of *Meanjin*

(1994–97). His literary awards include a Victorian Premier's Award for *The Ash Range* (1987), a poetic history of the Gippsland, home of his ancestors. His *New and Selected Poems* appeared in 1996.

Duggan characteristically employs found texts, bricolage, and ironic juxtaposition. His lightness does not produce light verse, though Duggan is among the best parodists of Australian poetry. While not a metrical poet, Duggan's formal interests range from epigram (seen in his brilliant translations of Martial) to epic. His many autobiographical poems are documentary, rather than confessional, projects. He is one of Australia's most amusing serious poets.

Duggan recently gained a Fine Arts Ph.D. from Melbourne University.

[DM]

Duncan, Robert (United States, 1919–88) Duncan was a prolific writer who synthesized Gnostic mysticism, romanticism, politics, as well as his homosexuality into his more than thirty volumes of writings. Committed to its Romantic legacy, Duncan's poetry explores the relation of childhood, the unconscious and the world, which he perceives as the field for spiritual encounters. Duncan is best known for his affiliation with the San Francisco Renaissance of the 1950s, and may be the movement's greatest writer.

Duncan taught at the legendary Black Mountain College in North Carolina along with CHARLES OLSON and ROBERT CREELEY as well as painters such as Joseph Albers and Robert Rauschenberg, Duncan's longtime partner was the American painter, Jess Collins, and they often collaborated on poetry/painting projects.

Duncan was the first recipient of the National Poetry award. He died of a heart attack in San Francisco.

Selected works: *Selected Poems* (1993); *A Selected Prose* (1995).

[DC]

Dunn, Douglas (Scotland, b. 1942) Douglas Eaglesham Dunn was born in Inchinnan, Renfrewshire, and educated at Renfrew High School and at Camphill School, Paisley. After leaving school, he worked at Renfrew Public Library and studied at the Scottish School of Librarianship. He was a librarian at the University of Strathclyde in Glasgow in 1962–4 and then in the United States in 1964–6. He returned to Britain in 1966 and read English at the University of Hull in 1966–9, subsequently working at the university library with PHILIP LARKIN for two years. His first collection was *Terry Street* (1969) about a poor Hull backstreet. Alongside *Elegies* (1985), which won the Whitbread Book of the Year Award in 1986, *Terry Street* is probably his best-known work: it won the Somerset Maugham Award, a Scottish Arts Council award and was selected as a Poetry Book Society choice. His next collection, *Love or Nothing* (1974) won the Geoffrey Faber Memorial Prize. He became a freelance writer and critic, holding writer-in-residence posts in Hull and later at Dundee and St Andrews, and also writing for radio and television. In 1991 he became Professor of English at St Andrews University, where he is also Director of the Scottish Studies Institute. He has published two collections of short stories and in 1992 edited the *Faber Book of Twentieth-Century Scottish Poetry* (1992).

Selected works: *The Happier Life* (1972); *Barbarians* (1979); *St Kilda's Parliament* (1981); *Europa's Lover* (1982); *Selected Poems 1964–83* (1986); *Northlight* (1988); *Dante's Drum-kit* (1993).

[LKMF]

Dupin, Jacques (France, b. 1927) Dupin's poetry reflects the poet's roots in the mountainous region of Ardèche. He is attentive to landscapes, and what populates them. Like his friend RENÉ CHAR, Dupin's work – exemplified in volumes such as *Cendrier du voyage (The Ashtray of the Journey*, 1950), *L'embrasure (The*

Opening, 1969), *Gravir (To Climb: Poems from Gravir*, 1970), *Dehors (Outside*, 1975), *Une apparence de soupirail (Appearance at the Cellar Window*, 1982), *Chansons troglodytes (Troglodyte Songs*, 1989) – departs from poetic conventions in favor of a fragmented, even brusque style. Dupin moved to Paris at the end of the war, and became one of the premier French poets of the late 1950s, alongside JACCOTTET, BONNEFOY, and DU BOUCHET. Like many of these poets, Dupin is fascinated by language. Yet visual art also influences his work: Dupin worked as an art editor, and artists including Braque, Masson, Tapies, and Adami illustrated his texts.

[AD]

Durcan, Paul (Ireland, b. 1944) Durcan, a poet of unique wit, dark humor, and at times painful self-scrutiny, was born in Dublin and educated at University College, Cork. He has traveled widely, and his poems often reflect a refracted, wandering existence. Many poems are Surrealistic monologues; others are almost reminiscent of PHILIP LARKIN in their juxtaposition of mundane and metaphoric language. A prolific writer and a popular reader of his poems, Durcan has published extensively. His poetry has won numerous prizes, including the Patrick Kavanagh Award in 1975 and the Whitbread Award for Poetry in 1990.

Selected works: *Teresa's Bar* (1976); *The Selected Paul Durcan* (1982); *The Berlin Wall Cafe* (1985); *Daddy, Daddy* (1990); *Crazy about Women* (1991); *A Snail in My Prime* (1994); *Christmas Day: With a Goose in the Frost* (1996); *Greetings to Our Friends in Brazil: 100 Poems* (1999).

[CT]

Durrell, Lawrence (England, 1912–90) Durrell, a novelist, poet, editor, and critic, is known primarily as the author of *The Alexandria Quartet*, a tetralogy of novels. Within his poetry, he experiments with structure while probing the human psyche. His observations on the nature of reality show the influence of both Einstein's and Freud's theories.

Born in Jullundur, India, to Anglo-Irish parents, Durrell was sent to England for schooling in his early teens. After failing to pass his university exams – a symptom of his general lack of ease with England – he married; in what proved an artistically astute occurrence, he moved his family to Corfu in 1935. He would live on and off in Greece and the Middle East for most of his life (marrying three more times in the process), teaching and working for the British government.

In his poetry, the sensual Mediterranean world blends with traditional lyric forms of the West. He explores the relationship of Eastern and Western religions and philosophies, as well as the nature of sexuality. Durrell skillfully displays a range of poetic styles, including satires, dramatic monologues, love lyrics, translations, and lustful ballads.

Selected works: *Quaint Fragment* (1931); *Ten Poems* (1932); *A Private Country* (1943); *Cities, Plains, and People* (1946); *Selected Poems, 1935–63* (1964); *Collected Poems* (1968); *Selected Poems* (1977).

[EM]

Dzhagarov, Georgi (Bulgaria, b. 1925) Recipient of the Special Prize for World Poetry of the French Academy (1982), Georgi Georgiev Dzhagarov was born in the village of Byala, Sliven area. Imprisoned during World War II as a member of the Antifascist Resistance, he graduated from the Maxim Gorky Literary Institute (Moscow) and became a prominent literary and political figure, holding positions as Chairman of the Union of Writers (1966–72) and Vice-President of the State Council (1971–89).

Dzhagarov struggles to accommodate his personal vision of the world with the stereotypes of Social Realism. A poet of considerable talent, he was at his best during the post-Stalinist thaw when he indulged his rebellious temperament without breaking the Party line.

Selected works: *Moite pesni* (*My Songs*, 1954); *Lirika* (*Lyrics*, 1956); *V minuti na mŭlchanie* (*During Moments of Silence*, 1958); *Prokurorŭt* (*The Prosecutor*, 1965); *Stikhotvoreniya* (*Poems*, 1969); *Izpoved* (*Confession*, 1984); *Ptitsi sreshtu vyatura* (*Birds Against the Wind*, 1985).

[CG/LPG]

E

Eberhart, Richard (United States, b. 1904) Author of over twenty-five books of poetry, Eberhart is known for his unevenness. Only when his editor at New Directions, JAMES LAUGHLIN, made a rigid 112-page selection of poems written between 1930 and 1965 did Eberhart win a Pulitzer Prize (*Selected Poems*, 1965).

Born in Austin, Minnesota, son of a meat-packing executive, he attended the University of Minnesota and graduated from Dartmouth in 1926. He then sailed around the world on a tramp steamer. Arriving in England, he took another B.A. from St John's College, Cambridge, in 1929. The following year he became tutor to the son of the King of Siam. In the 1930s he taught at St Mark's School, outside Boston, where one of his pupils was ROBERT LOWELL. He was a World War II naval aircraft gunnery instructor, which occasioned one of his best-known poems, 'The Fury of Aerial Bombardment'.

For some years he was vice-president of the Butcher Wax Company, before building an academic career at Princeton and then Dartmouth. Other awards include the Bollingen Prize (1962) and the National Book Award (1977). His works have been collected in *The Long Reach. New and Uncollected Poems 1948–1984* (1984) and *Collected Poems 1930–86* (1988).

[RP]

Edmond, Lauris Dorothy (New Zealand, b. 1924) Born in Hawkes Bay, Edmond graduated from the Wellington Teachers' College and Waikato University, Hamilton. Having led a 'traditional' life as wife and mother, Edmond only began publishing in the mid-1970s. In 1985, she won the Commonwealth Poetry Prize for her *Selected Poems* (1984).

Her poetry is often preoccupied with personal experience and asserts a feminine voice in the male-dominated field of New Zealand poetry. She has criticized 'Modernist' poets such as CURNOW, SMITHYMAN, and WEDDE for their intellectualizing verse.

Selected works: *In Middle Air* (1975); *The Pear Tree* (1977); *Wellington Letter: A Sequence of Poems* (1980); *Catching It* (1983); *Summer near the Arctic Circle* (1988); *New and Selected Poems* (1991).

[SH]

Eich, Günter (Germany, 1907–72) In 1929 Eich (co-)wrote his first radio play, a genre which he dominated in the 1950s and 1960s. A German soldier and then an American prisoner of war, Eich was a founding member of the Group 47 back in Germany. Married to fellow writer Ilse Aichinger in 1953, he lived much of his life near Salzburg, Austria.

Eich's post-war poems, beginning with *Remote Farms* (1948), expressed the feeling of loss and guilt but also hope. Their laconic manner was prototypical of a post-war German literature which felt it had to start anew, jettisoning anything remaining from previous German poetry. Eich understood his poems as messages about life, as in *Messages of the Rain* (1955), waiting to be deciphered. His later poems added further reduction, irony, and mistrust of political power, as in *Occasions and Stone Gardens* (1966) and *After Seume's Papers* (1972).

[IRS]

Eielson, Jorge Eduardo (Peru, b. 1924) Although a major part of the Peruvian literary scene, Eielson left Lima for Italy, where his work in plastic arts and his study of Incan art and civilization are well known. His early poetry is characterized by mystic and surrealist tendencies; his later writing becomes increasingly concrete. Like many of the Modernists, Eielson believes in an essential, 'pure', poetic form. In 1945, he won the National Poetry Prize of Peru. Though little of his work has been translated into English, Eielson has inspired new studies of his life and work, increasing both interest in and the reputation of his poetry.

Selected works: *Canción y muerte de Rolando* (*The Song and Death of Roland*, 1943); *Ajax en el infierno* (*Ajax in Hell*, 1945); *Tema y variaciones* (*Theme and Variations*, 1950); *Mutatis mutandis* (1967); *Noche oscura del cuerpo* (*The Dark Night of the Body*, 1989).

[LKA]

Ekelöf, Gunnar (Sweden, 1907–68) Ekelöf's work presents an alternative to his contemporary 'proletarian poets', such as HARRY MARTINSON. The figure of his father, a wealthy stockbroker who suffered from mental illness, arguably influenced young Ekelöf's choice to follow the Freudian circles in Stockholm of the 1930s and show interest in Baudelaire, Rimbaud, and the Surrealists. In 1933 he founded (with Artur Lundkvist) the short-lived surrealistic journal *Karavan*. Meanwhile he published his first poetry collection, *Sent på jorden* (*Sent to Earth*, 1932), followed by *Dedikation* (*Dedication*, 1934) and thirteen more collections, as well as a number published posthumously. His verse is clearly inspired by his extensive travel in Europe as well as his knowledge of Asian literature (he studied Persian in Uppsala and continued his education at the School of Oriental Studies in London). The Asian motifs are often used to criticize what he perceives as the egocentrism of his times. Alluding to Taoist selflessness, Ekelöf describes reality as fragmentary and unfinished and regards the human condition as imperfect, a void that cannot be filled but which must be made sense of. Ekelöf has been widely translated and recognized, as a member of the Swedish Academy since 1958 and a winner of many Swedish prizes, as well as the Grand Prize for Poetry of the Danish Academy (1964) and the Scandinavian Council Prize (1966).

[YB]

Ekelund, Vilhelm (Sweden, 1880–1949) Prolific poet and novelist Ekelund exerted great influence on early Swedish and Swedish-Finnish Modernism. His *Vårbris* (*Spring Breeze*, 1900) won him immediate recognition, and *Antikt ideal* (*Ideals of Antiquity*, 1909) was among the earliest Modernist writings in Swedish. From 1908 to 1921 Ekelund went into self-imposed exile, staying in Berlin, Venice, and Denmark. During this period he came to terms with his bisexual inclinations, eventually marrying the Danish Anne Margrethe Hou. Meanwhile, Ekelund gradually distanced himself from his early lyricism; true to his statement that 'language is philosophy', he started writing fragmented aphorisms, a process completed with the publication of *Lefnadsstämning* (*Mood of Life*, 1925). Ekelund's later style is markedly elitist, self-described as poetry 'for the literate'. The influence of early

Nietzsche shows through his disdain for scholars and total commitment to a philosophy of life based on playfulness and art.

[YB]

Eliot, T. S. (United States, 1888–1965) A leading critic and a playwright, Thomas Stearns Eliot was perhaps the most influential – surely the most famous – poet writing in English during the twentieth century.

Born and raised in St. Louis, Missouri, he attended undergraduate and graduate schools at Harvard, receiving his B.A. and M.A.; he completed doctoral work in philosophy, but refused the degree. Exposed to anti-Romantic ideas at Harvard and to fruitful possibilities of irony and free verse through the French Symbolists, Eliot wrote such early yet accomplished Modernist poems as 'Portrait of a Lady' and 'The Love Song of J. Alfred Prufrock'. In 1914, Eliot emigrated from the U.S., going briefly to Germany and France; in 1915, he settled in England, and married Vivien Haigh-Wood, a disastrous marriage that ended in 1933.

Eliot had 'The Love Song of J. Alfred Prufrock' published through the good offices of EZRA POUND, who took him into his circle and guided his early literary career. To earn a living Eliot taught school and then worked for Lloyds Bank, reaching a position of considerable trust. In 1923, he became the founding editor of the journal *The Criterion* and in 1925 joined the publishing house Faber & Faber.

Eliot's first book, *Prufrock, and Other Observations*, appeared in 1917. In his Sweeney poems and 'Gerontion', written during the next several years, one may find Modernism's double attitude toward Romanticism. There is a contempt for Romanticism's failures: to identify the self more closely with its desires, and to respond effectively to the declining meaningfulness of any desire or sense of self. But there is also a longing for a cleansed Romanticism. From the same years, Eliot's 'Burbank with a Baedeker: Bleistein with a Cigar' raises the issue of anti-Semitism. (See Christopher Rick's *T.S. Eliot and Prejudice* (1988) for a balanced weighing of the accusations.)

The Waste Land (1922) was written in awareness of World War I's damage to a generation and a civilization, and during a time when Eliot suffered overwhelming personal difficulties. Along with images of emotional ruin, *The Waste Land* includes the possibility of renewal – but more as a logical than a necessarily hopeful possibility. One can interpret the relation between death and rebirth in the poem as prophetic, ironic, or futile. The editorial advice Pound offered on the poem emphasized discontinuities of narrative and imagery, and suppressions of the immediate sound – if not the echoing background – of traditional iambic meter.

Beginning with his conversion to Anglo-Catholicism in 1927, as well as his 'Ash Wednesday' and *For Lancelot Andrewes: Essays on Style and Order* (1928), Eliot's religious concerns dominated his poetry. In *The Four Quartets* (1944), the culmination of his religious poetry, Eliot attempts to resolve devotional questions – including whether human life is linked to a transcendent source of value – through a meditation on time, time as history, eternity, and the experience of duration. The four poems seem to suggest that a realized aesthetic vision, a union of measured time with 'timeless' form, is an analogue (some might say heretical) for the Redemption of Christianity. From 1934 to 1959, Eliot wrote six verse plays, also turning on a religious questioning of such concepts as faith, sin, and expiation.

Eliot also achieved wide popularity and authority in the first half of the twentieth century for his criticism. In *The Sacred Wood* (1920) and 'Tradition and the Individual Talent, he presents the encompassing nature of literary tradition as superior to the Romantic interest in writers as individual personalities. In

'Hamlet', with his notion of an 'objective correlative', Eliot claims a causal equivalence between images in poems and emotions in readers. Accordingly, a poet can evoke a particular emotion in a reader by providing the correct imagery. In 'The Metaphysical Poets' and *Homage to John Dryden* (1924), Eliot admires the fused sensibility, the strongly felt thought, of John Donne and his fellow metaphysicals. Eliot contrasts both eighteenth- and nineteenth century poets as suffering from a 'dissociation of sensibility', the lost unity between thought and sensuous or passionate feeling.

In 1948, Eliot was awarded the Nobel Prize for Literature; in 1957, he married Valerie Fletcher.

[CC]

Elliot, Alistair (England, b. 1932) Elliot was born in Liverpool and received a B.A. from Fettes College, University of Edinburgh and an M.A. from Christ Church, Oxford. After starting his career in the theater, he held a number of jobs as a librarian before deciding to write full-time in 1983.

Elliot's verse balances between classical scholarship – Virgil, Horace, Livy – and his own family history, such as a blanket made by his grandmother. His poems are usually in traditional forms (with either full or half-rhymes) and, as a poet, Elliot believes his audience should meet the real whole poem on the page, hence his reputation for writing plainly.

Selected works: *Air in the Wrong Place* (1968); *Contentions* (1977); *Kisses* (1978); *Talking to Bebe* (1982); *Talking Back* (1982); *On the Appian Way* (1984); *My Country: Collected Poems* (1989).

[SS]

Eluard, Paul (France, 1895–1952) Eluard was born in an industrial suburb north of Paris and his poetry was frequently sympathetic towards the working class. From 1926 he was affiliated with the Communist Party, but he is best known as one of the early members of the Surrealist group. His verse from this period, including *Capitale de la douleur* (*Capital of Sadness*, 1926) and *La Vie immédiate* (*The Instant Life*, 1932), is concerned with the possibility of love undergirded by moral concern. Friendly with many leading avant-garde artists, Eluard endowed his poetry with the force of art criticism, composing verses on Picasso, Tanguy, and Dali. A dispute with BRETON over Communism in 1938 led the two to break with one another.

In 1941 Eluard joined the Resistance, and composed war poetry such as 'La Liberté' ('Liberty'), from *Poésie et vérité* (*Poetry and Truth*, 1942), which Allied aircraft dropped to the members of the Underground below. His last years were further occupied with humanitarian works, including his participation in the Mexican Congress of the World Council of Peace (1949).

Selected works: *Poésie ininterrompue* (*Unbroken Poetry*, 1946).

[SJ]

Elytis, Odysseas (Odysseas Alepoudelis; Greece, 1911–96) Elytis was born in Heraklion, Crete, of a well-known family from the island of Lesvos, the homeland of Sappho, whose work he later translated into contemporary Greek. He studied law and political science in Athens and later took literature classes in Paris. The influence of Surrealism is evident in his early collections and through his translations of ARAGON, ELUARD, and APOLLINAIRE. Both *Orientations* (1936) and *The Sun the First* (1943), were rife with a heightened optimism and a joyful glorification of youth and freedom. In these volumes, exhilarating language and a free-flowing stream of images, bathed in blinding sunlight, animate his portrayal of the eroticized landscape of the Aegean world, the locus *par excellence* of his mythopoetic project. With a celebratory mood he fuses the human form with Aegean landscape into an image of youthful and bodily vigor.

More prosaically, between 1940 and 1941 he served as a second lieutenant on the Albanian front. His traumatic experiences were incorporated into his *Heroic and Elegiac Song for the Lost Lieutenant of the Albanian Front* (1945), which constitutes a turning-point in his career. The optimism and joy are tempered in later poetry as the poet becomes aware of the force of destruction and the threat of death. He nevertheless remains faithful to the notion of a spring resurrection which he elaborates in his masterful *The Axion Esti* (1959), which won him the Nobel Prize for Literature in 1979.

The Axion Esti is a relatively long and formally strict and varied poem. Modeled on the Christian Passion and Resurrection, the poem is divided into three parts, 'The Genesis', 'The Passion', and 'The Gloria'. The middle section is further subdivided into three different alternating forms (psalms, song, reading) modeled on Orthodox liturgical elements. In this poem, Elytis confronts the Greek experience of World War II, its defeat and subsequent occupation, with a redemptive and climactic resurrection of the Greek spirit through the ages. This redemptive impulse is conveyed through a multilayered and highly rhetorical language spanning the period from Homeric times to the present, in 'the Greek language that was given to [him], the poor man's house on Homer's shore'. Resonating familiar patterns in the Greek tradition, oral and literary, secular and religious, historical and erotic (Homer, Heracleitus, Sappho, Orthodox hymnography, the Cretan epic *Erotokritos*, folk heroic ballads, the poetry of Dionysios Solomos, the naive idiom of General Markiyiannis), he crowns his magnum opus with an affirmative celebration of all things Greek, 'and Forever this small world the Great'.

No subsequent collection by Elytis managed to exceed the success of *The Axion Esti*. The 1964 musical rendition of excerpts of the poem by Mikis Theodorakis provided unprecedented exposure to the poem and brought Elytis' verses to audiences previously unimagined. Songs such as 'A Solitary Swallow' and 'Intelligible Sun of Justice' achieved such universal recognition in Greece as paeans of freedom that the 1967–74 dictatorship promptly banned them. *The Axion Esti*, poem and folk-oratorio, remain to this day one of Greece's finest contributions to world literature.

English translations of Elytis include *The Axion Esti* and *The Collected Poems of Odysseus Elytis* (1997).

[GSY]

Embirikos, Andreas (Greece, 1901–75) Embirikos was born in Romania to a family of ship owners and shipbuilders from the island of Andros. In 1925 he left his job with his family's business in London and went to Paris where he studied psychoanalysis and became a member of the surrealist group of ANDRÉ breton. In 1935 he published his first collection, *Smelting Furnace*, which established him, along with ENGONOPOULOS, as the founder of Greek surrealism. He introduced psychoanalysis to Greek literature with his second collection, *Inland* (1945), as he combined the surrealist images of the irrational with a psychoanalytic paneroticism. Between 1945 and 1951 he developed the same theme in his long novel *The Great Eastern*, named after the first liner to cross the Atlantic.

[GSY]

Empson, William (England, 1906–84) Born in East Yorkshire, Sir William Empson is probably more famous as a literary critic than he is as a poet. Since his landmark study, *Seven Types of Ambiguity* (1930), Empson regularly contributed important and controversial criticism to the literary world.

Empson was educated at Winchester College and Magdalene College,

Cambridge, where he took his B.A. in mathematics in 1929. He was Professor of English Literature at Sheffield University from 1953 to 1971.

Sometimes considered overly intellectual, Empson's poetry is notably ambiguous and abstruse. More than anything else, the work is passionate, whether desirous for the physical or for justice and kindness. He is an admitted traditionalist, in favor of rhyme and meter, and influenced by AUDEN and SPENDER. Argument is one of his favorite forms. As such, he is essentially a twentieth-century metaphysical poet, his poetic technique always at the service of intellect.

Empson received honorary doctorates from several universities, including his *alma mater*. He was made a fellow of the British Academy and was knighted in 1979 for his services to arts and letters in the U.K. Although his body of poetry is small, Empson's voice is original and memorable, a poetic voice to supplement his large critical achievements.

Selected works: *Cambridge Poetry 1929* (1929); *Poems by William Empson* (1934); *Poems* (1935); *The Gathering Storm* (1940); *Collected Poems* (1949, 1955, 1956).

[EM]

Engonopoulos, Nikos (Greece, 1910–85) Born in Constantinople, Engonopoulos was Greece's foremost surrealist painter as well as the author of eight books of poetry, a professor of architecture at the Athens Polytechnic, and a stage and costume designer. Though tacitly respectful of certain aspects of tradition, he was an experimental revolutionary whose first two volumes, *Do Not Speak to the Conductor* (1938) and *The Pianos of Silence* (1939) – alongside the work of EMBIRIKOS, GATSOS, and ELYTIS – introduced Surrealism to Greece. In 1944, and under Nazi censorship, he published *Bolivar*, inspired by the Argentinian revolutionary Simon Bolivar, in which he parallels South American revolutions with moments of Greek history. In 1958 he was honored with the State Award for Poetry.

[GSY]

Enright, D. J. (England, b. 1920) Born Dennis Joseph Enright, with a Midlands working-class background, Enright created his historical place by rejecting the Modernist tradition during the 1950s. Though sometimes associated with The Movement (see LARKIN, JENNINGS, DAVIE) and sharing some of their dislike for the esoteric, Enright's poetic capacity reaches from the working-class conditions in his native England to countries around the world.

Enright's education positioned this dichotomy between the working class and the international early on. He received many scholarships to attend Downing College, Cambridge, but found that English society expected considerable gratitude on his part for making an exception to the usual rules. Following graduation, he wrote regularly for *Scrutiny* for the next twelve years. After finishing an M.A. in 1946, Enright discovered that many British universities were reluctant to hire 'Scrutineers' because of their reputation for Leavisite zeal, and left England for Egypt, to start a long teaching career overseas.

For the next twenty years, landscapes and the people, especially in the Far East, would provide Enright with the stimulation to create an impressive collection of poems. His travels and teaching assignments emphasized his role as the expatriate in a post-World War II global society. To Enright, the great enemy was not a particular country or ruler, but global indifference to suffering.

Though not overtly political, one of Enright's more controversial poems, 'Confessions of an English Opium Smoker', embarrassed the British Embassy and British Council staff in Bangkok, and contributed to their view that Enright did not fit in. Enright returned to England in 1970. He has maintained a number of honorary lectureships, and edited many books for Oxford University Press.

Selected works: *The Laughing Hyena and Other Poems* (1953); *Some Men are Brothers* (1960); *Addictions* (1962); *Unlawful Assembly* (1968); *The Terrible Shears* (1974); *Collected Poems 1948–98* (1998).

[SS]

Enzensberger, Hans Magnus (Germany, b. 1929) After studying literature and philosophy in Germany and in Paris, Enzensberger has worked in radio, taught as visiting professor, lived abroad, and traveled widely. His lyrical poetry has established him as one of the greatest contemporary German poets. In addition, he has emerged as an important influence on German literary and political culture as an essayist and editor of the magazine *Kursbuch* (*Time-Table*, 1965–75). He is considered an intellectual stimulator of the 1968 student revolt. He currently lives in Munich, working as a writer and editor.

Beginning with his poetic debut, *Defense of the Wolves* (1957), Enzensberger attempted to irritate and to provoke thought about political issues. His early poems were critical of the shallow materialism resulting from the post-war German 'economic miracle'. Satirical tone, critical subjectivity, prose quality, and aggressiveness are reminiscent of both BRECHT and ALLEN GINSBERG. After the particularly aggressive *The Lingo* (1960), the apparently simpler topics in *Braille* (1964) expressed a more melancholy tone.

Enzensberger's distrust of all ideological rigidity, usually displayed in his essays, was expressed poetically by critically assessing historical figures from Machiavelli to Che Guevara in *Mausoleum* (1975), which began Enzensberger's next phase of poetry. The pessimistic tone was even stronger in the *Sinking of the Titanic* (1978). The *Fury of Disappearance* (1980) became more personal, a mood that has continued in the 1990s, in volumes such as *Kiosk* (1995). Enzensberger's current poems still provide a space for skepticism and irritation yet become increasingly self-reflexive.

[IRS]

Erba, Luciano (Italy, b. 1922) Erba was born and raised in Milan, where he eventually became Professor of French Language and Literature at the Università Cattolica. He is the translator of several French poets, such as CENDRARS, REVERDY, and PONGE. A well-disguised expertise in the use of metrical devices, and a casual, yet extremely precise vocabulary characterize Erba's sober and elegant verse. Objects, people, and events are often rendered in his poems with iconic evidence and then wisely juxtaposed in a series of small narratives, observed by the author with detached irony.

Selected works: *Linea K*(*Line K*, 1951); *Il male minore* (*The Lesser Evil*, 1960); *Il prato più verde* (*The Greenest Field*, 1977); *L'ippopotamo* (*The Hippopotamus*, 1989); *L'ipotesi circense* (*The Circesian Hypothesis*, 1995).

[GS]

Erdrich, Louise (United States, b. 1954) Born to a Chippewa-Indian mother and a German-American father, Erdrich is the eldest of seven children. This mixed-blood heritage became the subject matter of much of her writing. In 1971, Erdrich was among the first group of females to be admitted to Dartmouth College, where she met her future husband and co-writer, Michael Dorris, and earned her B.A. Known mainly as a novelist, she began her writing career as a poet, submitting her poems for her thesis at Johns Hopkins University where she obtained her M.A. in 1980. Her first collection, *Jacklight* (1984), appeared the same year as her best-selling novel *Love Medicine*, which earned her a National Book Critics Circle Award, one of the many awards she has won for her writing. Though claiming to be anti-religious, almost half of her poems deal with religious themes in her second collection of poetry *Baptism of Desire* (1989). Other themes she explores include Native American life, parenting, and nature – all in a very realistic voice. Erdrich now lives in Minnesota where she continues to write full-time and raise her three youngest children.

[BRB]

Esenin, Sergei Alexandrovich (Russia, 1895–1925) Esenin was born into and grew up in a peasant family. In 1912 he became a school teacher. Esenin's first published poem, 'A Birch', appeared in the Moscow children's journal, *The Little World*, in 1914. In 1916 he published his first collection of poems, *Radunitsa*, in which he celebrates the peasant Russia. In that year also, his poetry appeared in the most important Russian periodicals: the newspaper, *Birzhevye Viedomosti* (*The Stock Market News*), and the journals, *The Whole World* and *Monthly Journal*. In the second part of 1916, he prepared for publication a new collection of poems, *Goluben'*, and published it in 1918 in Petrograd. His best poetry, however, was written in the 1920s: in 1920, he published the collection of poems, *Treriadnitsa*; in 1923, *Poems of a Brawler*; in 1924, *Moskva kabatskaia* (*Moscow of the Taverns*), reflecting his hard drinking and instability; in 1925, *Soviet Russia, Soviet Country and the Persian Motives*. At the age of 30, partly because of his psychological instability and alcoholism, he ended his life by hanging himself, leaving a poem in his own blood. In spite of the shortness of his poetic career, Esenin left an important poetic heritage. Though his work is not particularly sophisticated, some of his poems are rich in images and emotions and have a deeply captivating effect.

[RN]

Ewart, Gavin (England, 1916–95) Gavin Buchanan Ewart was born in London and educated at Wellington College and Christ's College, Cambridge. His poetry combines an inventive use of form and technique with an irreverent sense of humor. At seventeen, his first poem 'Phallus in Wonderland' was published in GEOFFREY GRIGSON's *New Verse*. Satiric wit and lewd light verse characterize the poet, though his verse is frequently compassionate and genuinely concerned for humanity.

After his first volume, *Poems and Songs* (1939), Ewart served in the Royal Artillery during World War II and then worked for the British Council until 1952. His next book, *Londoners*, did not appear until 1964 and he has been prolific since. He became a Fellow of the Royal Society of Literature in 1981.

Ewart is exceptionally fluent in his command of rhyme, meter, and syntax. Bawdiness permeates his imitations of LARKIN and Hopkins, in which he adopts the persona of an aging though still lusty man. He balances such indulgence with enough sympathy and seriousness to display his versatility.

Selected works: *Pleasures of the Flesh* (1966); *The Deceptive Grin of the Gravel Porters* (1968); *The Gavin Ewart Show* (1971); *No Fool Like an Old Fool* (1976); *Or Where a Young Penguin Lies Screaming* (1978); *The Collected Ewart 1933–80* (1980); *The New Ewart: Poems 1980–2* (1982); *Late Pickings* (1987); *Penultimate Poems* (1989); *85 Poems* (1993); *Selected Poems 1933–93* (1996).

[EM]

Ezekiel, Nissim (India, b. 1924) The foremost English-language poet in India during the mid-century, Ezekiel's work combined European Modernism with Indian scenes and sentiment. Mixing English and Hindi (creating the vernacular 'Hinglish'), his lively poems of Bombay and its people make erudite the everyday.

After graduating from the University of Bombay in 1947, Ezekiel spent a year in London before returning to India to embark upon a career as a journalist, radio broadcaster and, finally, teacher and University of Bombay professor. Throughout each of these jobs his main avocation was writing, beginning with the publication of *A Time to Change and Other Poems* (1952). Rich with Judeo-Christian symbolism (Ezekiel himself is a Jew), explicit love poems, and the language he heard around him, Ezekiel's complex volumes earned him both popularity and critical respect. He was awarded the R.K. Lagu Prize (1947), the Sahitya Akademi Award (1983), and the Padmashri Award (1988). Ezekiel currently lives in a Bombay hospital, a victim of Alzheimer's disease.

Selected works: *Sixty Poems* (1953); *The Third* (1958); *The Unfinished Man* (1960); *The Exact Name: Poems, 1960–64* (1965); *Selected Poems, 1965–75* (1976); *Latter-Day Psalms* (1982); *Collected Poems: 1952–88* (1989).

[MW]

F

Fairburn, A. R. D. (New Zealand, 1904–57) Born in Auckland, Arthur Rex Dugard Fairburn lived in England in 1930–32. He worked as a radio scriptwriter, editor, and university lecturer in art history and was active for community causes.

Both critics and Fairburn himself usually disliked his early poetry, which is marked by Georgian tendencies. After his return to New Zealand in 1932, Fairburn turned to Anglo-American Modernist models to discuss emotional and economic turmoil and issues of identity in New Zealand. He wrote many love poems and his poetry is characterized by epigrammatic turns, lyricism and satire.

Selected works: *He Shall Not Rise* (1930); *Strange Rendezvous* (1952); *Three Poems: Dominion, The Voyage and To a Friend in the Wilderness* (1952); *Collected Poems* (1966).

[SH]

Faiz, Faiz Ahmed (Pakistan, 1911–84) Faiz, the son of a Muslim Punjabi peasant who had become a provincial grandee, had an informal traditional education and a modern one from missionaries and at Punjab University in Lahore, where he earned degrees in English and Arabic.

Naqsh-e-Faryadi (*The Picture of a Dissenter*) was published in 1941, the year in which Faiz married Alys George, an Englishwoman. Its most famous poem says 'love don't ask for the love that was before'. Contrasting romantic emotion with the compulsions of politics, it establishes the lyric and political poles between which Faiz's poetry is spoken. For that poetry and for the figure he cut in India and Pakistan after Partition in 1947, he became the most important Urdu poet of his generation.

Dast-e-Saba (*Hand of the Breeze*) appeared in 1952 just as Faiz was sentenced to four years' imprisonment for his part in an abandoned conspiracy. He published five more books and, while the early work is often singled out, Faiz's best poems are scattered throughout these volumes. Besides the occasional rousing anthem and love poems that conjure a powerful lyric despair, Faiz had a unique ability to evoke the state of mind of a generalized citizen in a predatory political environment.

Faiz was imprisoned a second time, for four months, in 1958. His books were never banned and he was never exiled, but his poems set to music were often kept from being broadcast on state-owned radio and television and Faiz left Pakistan voluntarily in 1962–64 and 1979–82. In 1946, he was made a Member of the British Empire and in 1962 he was awarded the Lenin Peace Prize by Nikita Khrushchev.

[AM]

Fallon, Padraic (Ireland, 1905–74) Born in Athenry, County Galway, Fallon lived much of his life in Wexford working as a farmer and customs officer, as well as a poet. His poems frequently incorporate Irish and world mythologies, as do his verse plays, written for Radio Eireann, including *The Vision of MacConglinne* (1953) and *Diarmuid and Grainne* (1958). In 'Painting of My Father', Fallon blends simple country imagery and diction to create a moving paternal portrait. Although he did not publish many volumes, Fallon's poems frequently appeared in *The Dublin Magazine*.

Selected works: *Poems* (1973); *Poems and Versions* (1983).

[CT]

Fanthorpe, U.A. (England, b. 1929) Ursula Askham Fanthorpe was born in London. She was educated at St Anne's College, Oxford, and later at the University of London Institute of Education. Both a teacher and an administrator in the Department of English at Cheltenham Ladies' College in Gloucestershire, she also did hospital clerical work. The universities of Newcastle and Durham made her an Arts Council Writing Fellow from 1983 to 1985.

Fanthorpe's poetry is known for its commitment to place. These places, along with the solid, common folk that characterize her poems, provide a foundation from which she reaches toward more fantastic myths and prophecy. Obviously influenced by her experiences with illness, death, and dying due to her work in hospitals, her astute poems stress the experiential and the ordinary, but also the profound happenings of life. In these sometimes ironic poems, the reader may be surprised to find poignant emotions which display Fanthorpe's affection for the human race, despite its foibles. Her best poems reveal the connection between desire and existence.

Selected works: *Side Effects* (1978); *A Standing To* (1982); *Voices Off* (1984); *The Crystal Zoo* (1985); *Selected Poems* (1986); *Watching Brief* (1987); *Neck-verse* (1992); *Safe as Houses* (1996).

[MK]

Fargue, Léon-Paul (France, 1876–1947) One of Fargue's best-known titles, *Le Piéton de Paris* (*The Pedestrian of Paris*, 1939), defines the man himself. The French capital occupies a place of choice in the life and works of this dedicated bohemian who, like Baudelaire, APOLLINAIRE, and PRÉVERT, often explored the seamier side of the city. Having frequented Mallarmé's *mardis* (Tuesday gatherings) early in his career, he shared a fascination for Symbolism with an equally young Gide and VALÉRY. In the years immediately preceding World War I, however, Fargue's works took on distinctly Modernist overtones as he moved closer to what Apollinaire called an *esprit nouveau* or new spirit that tended to blur the distinctions between art forms. Fargue's verse remained quintessentially lyrical, but his prose-poems especially contain descriptions that might best be characterized as Cubist in their juxtaposition of images and the fragmented relationship that springs from their descriptions of the magic yet intensely melancholy impressions of the city. Like Verlaine, he often composed in a minor key that conveys to his reader the fundamental unhappiness that underlies his writing.

Selected works: *Poèmes* (1905, 1912); *Pour la Musique* (*For Music*, 1914); *Espaces* (*Spaces*, 1928); *Sous la Lampe* (*Under the Lamp*, 1929); *Haute Solitude* (*High Solitude*, 1941); *Poésies* (preface by SAINT-JOHN PERSE, 1963).

[RSO]

Feher, Ferenc (Yugoslavia, 1928–89) Feher was born into a landless Hungarian peasant family in Žednik, Vojvodina. He studied Hungarian and Russian literature at the University of Novi Sad, then worked as a journalist and editor of many literary magazines. Besides poetry, Feher wrote radio plays and translated Serbian, Croatian, Macedonian,

Slovenian, Russian, and Albanian poetry into Hungarian.

Feher's poetry is strongly influenced by his experiences during early childhood. He repeatedly returns to the themes of hard work and poverty and their effects on people. Memories of his parents and images of himself as a child and a witness to their hard life often permeate Feher's poetry. Much of his poetry is written in a mode of resignation and sadness. Many of his poems are vignettes of his native Vojvodina. In clear and lucid language, Feher succeeds in producing nostalgic and poignant images of his homeland.

Selected works: *Jobbágyok unokái* (*Grandchildren of Serfs*, 1953); *Álom a dülöutak szelen* (*Dreams on the Village Path*, 1956); *Színek és szavak* (*Colors and Words*, 1960); *Delelö* (*On the Pinnacle*, 1966); *Egy kiskirály kunyhójából* (*From a Hut of a Little Prince*, 1972).

[DJ]

Feldman, Irving (United States, b. 1928) Feldman, a MacArthur Fellow, was born in New York, and educated at City College and Columbia. He has lived and taught in many places, and is Distinguished Professor of English at SUNY Buffalo.

Eclectic in its subject matter, structure, and technique, Feldman's poetry is consistently probing. Its allusiveness and mordant wit can be distancing; at their best, his poems provide a perspective for the poet's deep moral concerns. By turns skeptical and optimistic, Feldman explores the outrages of the twentieth century and its culture, and our responsibilities to and for each other.

Selected works: *Works and Days* (1961); *The Pripet Marshes* (1965); *Leaping Clear and Other Poems* (1976); *All of Us Here and Other Poems* (1986); *The Life and Letters* (1994).

[JT]

Fenton, James (England, b. 1949) James Martin Fenton was born in Lincoln and educated at Magdalen College, Oxford, where he won the Newdigate Prize for Poetry in 1968. His poem 'A German Requiem' won the Southern Arts Literature Award for Poetry in 1981 and he also won the 1984 Geoffrey Faber Memorial Prize for *The Memory of War: 1968–82* (1982).

Fenton is an accomplished poet who writes in several styles, including what he calls 'found poetry' consisting of various amounts of quotation. Contained by his powerful vision of recent history, his morally complex poetry is fused with technical cunning and seductive fluency. Fenton's poems are passionate and personal, often funny and violent, and always full of the pleasures of language.

In addition to being a significant poet, Fenton is a well-known critic who has worked for the *Sunday Times* (London), the *Guardian*, and the *New Statesman*. Fenton was made a Fellow of the Royal Society of Literature in 1983 and held the prestigious Oxford Professorship of Poetry (1994–9).

Selected works: *Our Western Furniture* (1968); *Terminal Moraine* (1972); *A Vacant Passion* (1978); *A German Requiem* (1981); *Dead Soldiers* (1981); *Children in Exile* (1983); *Children in Exile: Poems 1968–84* (1984); *Out of Danger* (1993).

[EM]

Ferlinghetti, Lawrence (United States, b. 1919) A native of Yonkers, New York, Ferlinghetti, along with other writers such as ALLEN GINSBERG, KENNETH REXROTH, and Jack Kerouac, founded the Beat movement. Despite his proclaimed aversion to academia, he earned his A.B. from the University of North Carolina, his M.A. from Columbia in 1948, and his doctorate from the Sorbonne in 1951.

Ferlinghetti's poetry delights and assaults with its sarcasm, humor, and irreverent wit. While his early work epitomized the Beat movement, it was Ferlinghetti's vision, his San Francisco bookstore and press, City Lights, that helped shape the Beat movement into a recognizable literary school.

Selected works: *Pictures of the Gone World* (1955); *A Coney Island of the Mind* (1958); *To Fuck is to Love Again* (1965); *Endless Life: Selected Poems* (1981).

[CP]

Finch, Peter (Wales, b. 1947) Finch was born in Cardiff, where he still lives. From 1973 to 1998 he managed Oriel, a grant-supported specialist poetry bookshop. In 1998 he was appointed head of the Academi Agency, an organization devoted to the promotion of Welsh and Anglo-Welsh literature. Finch is prolific, stylistically eclectic, and innovative; his numerous volumes (more than twenty at the last count) include visual texts and 'computer' poems as well as more familiar lyric forms. He has also experimented with audiotapes and established a considerable reputation as a performance poet. Additionally, Finch has written short stories, several guides to publication, and has edited two anthologies, *Typewriter Poems* (1972) and *Green Horse* (1978, with Meic Stephens). A *Selected Poems* appeared in 1987. His most recent collection is *Useful* (1997).

[BS]

Finlay, Ian Hamilton (Scotland, b. 1925) Hamilton Finlay was born in the Bahamas and returned to Scotland as a child. He left school at thirteen and studied briefly at Glasgow School of Art before World War II. His writing career began in the 1950s and he is an avowed concrete poet, best known for his classicism and economy with language, and his outdoor installation pieces: his garden at 'Little Sparta' in the Pentlands is an elaboration on the classical garden. He was shortlisted for the Turner Prize in 1985 and given honorary doctorates by the universities of Aberdeen and Edinburgh.

Selected works: *The Dancers Inherit the Party* (1960); *Poems to See and Hear* (1971); *Ian Hamilton Finlay: A Visual Primer* (1992).

[LKMF]

Fisher, Roy (England, b. 1930) Fisher is a jazz pianist as well as a writer. Born in Handsworth, Birmingham, he remains consciously provincial, though his poetry dwells in the avant-garde. Specifically, he concerns himself with recording the processes of perception in his poems, which he accomplishes with the smooth motions of a jazz musician. Notably, Fisher's poetry comes at the reader with an emphasis on repetition and variation of small structure units giving it a sense of improvisation, much like music.

Visual art as much as music finds a way into this intellectual poet's works. His childhood interest in painting manifests itself in sensual images that complement his preoccupations with the processes of the mind. In fact, the mind's inner space seems complemented by the visual sense of place described in the poems.

Fisher attended Birmingham University, earning a B.A. in 1951 and an M.A. in 1970. Also in 1970, he received the Andrew Kelus Prize for English Poetry, and in 1981, the Cholmondeley Award for Poetry. He retired as Senior Lecturer in American Studies from Keele University in 1982.

Selected works: *City* (1961); *Ten Interiors with Various Figures* (1966); *The Ship's Orchestra* (1966); *Collected Poems* (1968); *Matrix* (1971); *The Thing about Joe Sullivan: Poems 1971–7* (1978); *Poems 1955–80* (1980); *A Furnace* (1986); *Birmingham River* (1994); *The Dow Low Drop* (1996).

[EM]

Flint, F. S. (England, 1885–1960) Growing up in London, Frank Stuart Flint finished his formal education at the age of thirteen because of his family's financial difficulties. He worked at odd jobs until 1904, when he got a civil service job as a typist. During this period he attended the workingman's night school. In 1908, he wrote ten articles and book reviews for the literary journal *New Age*, beginning his career as a critic. Flint had his first book of poetry, *In the Net of Stars*, published in 1909, the year in which he married.

At age twenty-five, Flint had become the best-respected critic of twentieth-century French poetry. His criticism, published in *New Age* as well as in T. S. ELIOT's *Criterion* and many other periodicals, earned him more acclaim than his poetry. *In the Net of Stars* included mostly love poems in conventional rhyming form. In his next two books, *Cadences* (1915) and *Otherworld* (1920), Flint moved more to what he termed 'unrhymed cadence', or free verse, in accordance with the Imagists. In 1919, Flint began working for the Ministry of Labour and continued there until 1951; when he retired, he was awarded the Imperial Service Order. At the age of seventy-four, Flint died in Berkshire.

[BRB]

Follain, Jean (France, 1903–71) Following the publication of *Chants terrestres (Terrestrial Songs*, 1937), Follain received the prestigious Prix Mallarmé in 1939. Follain's origins in Normandy influence his poetic work – he often evokes provincial life at the beginning of the twentieth century. Themes of memory, nature, and the passage of time also reflect the importance of his rural childhood. Moreover, his poetry revolves around concrete, metaphysical imagery and the primacy of objects. His contemporary MAX JACOB claimed that Follain's poetry 'is made with objects', something reflected in the very title (and substance) of his 1955 volume *Objets*. Readers of Follain must grapple with the presence of these objects in order to understand his poems.

In his free verse, Follain interrogates the universal and the eternal, but he also portrays the specific and the instantaneous. Anticipating the 'nouveau roman' in France, he describes his own poetry as 'verbal incantation'. W.S. Erwin, a translator of Follain, views his poems as 'parts of a rite, of an unchanging ceremony heralding some inexorable splendor, over a ground of silence'. Follain received le Grand Prix de Poésie de l'Académie Française in 1970, and died the following year after a road accident.

Selected works: *Ici-bas (Here Below*, 1941); *Usage du temps (The Uses of Time*, 1943); *Exister (To Exist*, 1947); *Territoires (Territories*, 1953); *Des heures (Hours*, 1960); *D'après tout* (1967); *Espaces d'instants (Spaces of Instants*, 1971).

[AD]

Forbes, John (Australia, 1950–98) Forbes had a peripatetic childhood in Queensland, New Guinea, and Malaya (his father was a civilian meteorologist in the RAAF). After a Catholic education in Sydney, Forbes attended the University of Sydney, writing an honors thesis on JOHN ASHBERY and abandoning an M.A. thesis on FRANK O'HARA (both major influences). From the late 1980s he lived in Melbourne, teaching creative writing, holding fellowships and undertaking unskilled work. He edited the irregular *Surfers Paradise*.

A brilliant stylist, Forbes was scornful of romantic models of the poet ('I'd make large claims for the poem but not the poet'). His idiosyncratic mix of high and popular culture, extraordinary gift for simile, and raiding of classical forms (especially the ode) produced a unique style, attending to both Australian and postmodern tropes.

Selected works: *Stalin's Holiday* (1981); *The Stunned Mullet* (1988); *New and Selected Poems* (1992); *Damaged Glamour* (1998).

[DM]

Forché, Carolyn (United States, b. 1950) Forché was born in Detroit, Michigan, graduated from Michigan State, and then received an M.F.A. from Bowling Green. She has worked as a journalist and human rights activist, and has taught at numerous universities.

The poems in Forché's first book, *Gathering the Tribes*(1976), often delve into the poet's past, gender relations and sexuality. Since then, her attention has turned increasingly to exploring where the personal and the political, self and history, intersect, as she does in her chilling second volume, *The Country between Us*(1981). After editing the influential anthology *Against Forgetting: Twentieth Century Poetry of Witness* (1993), Forché has continued to probe the relationship between poetry and politics with her more theoretically informed recent volume, *The Angel of History*(1996). She enjoys more popularity outside academe than within; *The Country Between Us* has sold over 75,000 copies.

[AE]

Fortini, Franco (Franco Lattes; Italy, 1917–95) Fortini, expelled from university because he was Jewish, joined the Resistance Army in 1943. After the war he moved to Milan, where he led an intense intellectual life as political activist and cultural promoter. Fully aware of the deep crisis to which history had condemned post-war literature, Fortini always crafted a verse with strong links to the present, in which landscapes, people, and events are enlightened by a firm and sorrowful meditation on the past and its legacy.

Selected works: *Foglio di via e altri versi* (*Expulsion Order and Other Poems*, 1946); *Poesia ed errore* (*Poetry and Error*, 1965); *Paesaggio con serpente* (*Scenery with Snake*, 1983); *Composita solvantur* (*Orderly Disintegration*, 1994).

[GS]

Fried, Erich (Austria, 1921–88) After losing his family to Nazi atrocities, Fried emigrated to London in 1938, where he worked for the BBC and for magazines. He continued writing prolifically in German and was best known for his poems, which explored human problems and hopes from love to politics in well-executed word plays.

In the mid-1960s, Fried turned to openly political topics with *Poems of Warning* (1965) and especially anti-war poetry in *And Vietnam And* (1966). Increasingly controversial with his criticism of Israeli politics in *Hearken, Israel* (1974) and of German reactions to terrorism in *Thus I Came to Be Among the Germans* (1977), he remained interested in basic human issues. After *Love Poems* (1979), he turned to the political significance of everyday situations, which gained him general recognition. He died of cancer in 1988, during a visit to Germany.

[IRS]

Frost, Robert (United States, 1874–1963) Frost's career presents a number of intriguing tensions: even though Frost is known as the poet of New England, he was actually born in San Francisco and moved to Massachusetts when he was ten years old; even though he is often regarded as America's poet, he was essentially ignored until he went to live in Great Britain for three years; and even though he argued for traditional poetic form – to write poetry without meter, he remarked, was like 'playing tennis without a net' – his career was catalyzed by EZRA POUND and the Imagists, a group of poets who defined themselves in opposition to composing in the 'sequence of the metronome'.

The predominant characteristics of Frost's poetry are his adherence to meter as the necessary form of a poem; his use of dramatic monologues and dialogues to convey a psychological narrative; the dark intensity of his lyrics; and his argument that a poem must strive toward clarity and understanding of the world. Frost's poetry is indebted to Ralph Waldo Emerson and Emily Dickinson, his transcendental forebears, but it also endeavors to capture the diction and cadence of New England, which parallels the imagist adherence to direct language and treatment of the 'thing'.

Frost's professional career as a poet began in 1894 when he received a check for fifteen dollars for a poem published in the *New York Independent*, but it was to take over twenty years for his reputation to become firmly established. In 1912 he moved to England with his family, and his career took a significant turn when he was introduced to Pound, who admired Frost's first book of poetry, *A Boy's Will* (1913). Pound was instrumental in arranging publication of Frost's second book of poetry, *North of Boston* (1914), a book that firmly established Frost as a major American poet.

Frost returned to America in 1915, and the various prizes and academic positions offered to him allowed him to dedicate himself to his poetry. He was awarded the Pulitzer Prize for Poetry four times: in 1924 for *New Hampshire*; 1931 for his *Collected Poems*; 1937 for *A Further Range*; and 1943 for *A Witness Tree*. Moreover, Frost was invited by President John F. Kennedy in 1961 to read a poem at his presidential inauguration. For the occasion, Frost wrote 'The Gift Outright', one of his most popular and widely anthologized poems, and in 1962 the United States Congress bestowed upon Frost the Congressional Gold Medal. Subsequently, he became the unofficial Poet Laureate of the United States.

During his lifetime Frost wrote an immense body of poetry, but the majority of critics seem to agree that the later books of poetry and especially *In the Clearing* (1962) lack the overall intensity of Frost's earlier books, even though the later books include some of Frost's most poignant lyrics such as 'Fire and Ice'.

Frost has been embraced by the American public, and his poetry continues to be a part of an American culture.

[DC]

Fuertes, Gloria (Spain, b. 1918) A member of the Generation of 1956, which infused a zeal for political poetry with a new aesthetic consciousness of poetry as an act of self-discovery. This generation is something of a hybrid, and its poets show a wide range of characteristics, from social activism to hermetic experimentalism.

Fuertes was born into a working-class family in Madrid; her economic circumstances helped shape her literary production. Her poetry embodies the individual's rebellion against oppressive social circumstances. *Anthology and Poems of the Slum* (1954) identifies her major themes and techniques; in straightforward, sometimes prosaic language she asserts the need to rebel against human suffering. *I Advise Drinking Thread* (1954) and *Poet on Call* (1968) are other primary works. A children's author as well as a poet, Fuertes is best known for her use of humor, colloquialisms, and dramatic monologue.

[AB]

Fuller, John (England, b. 1937) John Leopold Fuller was born in Ashford, Kent, in 1937, the son of poet, novelist, and nonfiction writer, ROY BROADBENT FULLER and Kathleen Smith Fuller. He attended New College, Oxford, and became a fellow of Magdalen College in 1966. Fuller followed his father's example and became both a poet and novelist himself.

Fuller's several books of poetry exhibit amazingly varied forms, styles, and content. He moves from lyrical sonnets to monologue to narrative, and from fantasy to post-modernity. In short, Fuller is constantly exploring all of the possibilities for works of poetry and prose.

Selected works: *Fairground Music* (1961); *Cannibals and Missionaries* (1972); *Lies and Secrets* (1979); *The Illusionists* (1980); *Partingtime Hall* (with JAMES FENTON 1987); *The Grey among the Green* (1988); *The Mechanical Body* (1991).

[MK]

Fuller, Roy Broadbent (England, 1912–91) A successful solicitor, by 1969 Roy Fuller had worked his way up to director at the Woolwich Equitable Building Society, where he stayed until 1988. He was also a governor of the BBC from 1972 to 1979, and while fulfilling these heavy obligations he still found time to chair the Literature Panel of the Arts Council of Great Britain and the Poetry Book Society. Fuller also lectured as Professor of Poetry at Oxford from 1969 to 1973; he received both a CBE and a Queen's Gold Medal for poetry in 1970.

Fuller's first books, *Poems* (1939) and *The Middle of a War* (1942), in which AUDEN's influence is apparent, grew out of his experiences in the Royal Navy during the war. He found his own voice in later works, which often explored tensions arising between rational minds and a passionate world through the civilized and savage sides of urban life; these tensions are paralleled in his juxtaposition of formal and gritty language. *Available for Dreams* (1989), published two years prior to his death, showed his verse to be as strong as ever. Besides poetry, Fuller published eight novels, eight children's books, and three volumes of memoirs.

Selected works: *Epitaphs and Occasions* (1949); *Counterparts* (1954); *Brutus' Orchard* (1957); *New and Collected Poems 1934–84* (1985); *Last Poems* (1992).

[JL]

Fulton, Alice (United States, b. 1952) Braiding lyricism with American vernacular, Fulton's poetry complicates relationships between language and ideas. *Palladium* – comprising six sections, each connected to a different definition of the collection's title – demonstrates a reverence for the transgressive; *Sensual Math* experiments further with transmutations of sound and sense, form and content. In poems like 'Some Cool', Fulton challenges the iamb; in other poems, gender and its conventions are subverted.

Born in Troy, New York, Fulton has a graduate degree from Cornell University. Her many honors include a MacArthur Fellowship. She teaches at the University of Michigan in Ann Arbor; she is married to a painter, whose work continues to influence her own.

[RC]

Furnadzhiev, Nikola (Bulgaria, 1903–68) Nikola Yordanov Furnadzhiev was born in Pazardzhik, graduated from the University of Sofia (1930), worked as a high school teacher and, after World War II, as an editor of major literary periodicals.

Although Furnadzhiev began as a Symbolist apprentice, his first book was boldly expressionistic. His stylistically innovative and dynamic verse was inspired by the tragic end of the peasant rebellion of September 1923. The poems brim with metaphoric images of the elemental forces of nature and refractions of folk rituals. After World War II, however, Furnadzhiev was unable to internalize the prescriptions of Social Realism. At its best, his late poetry is bleak, contemplative, and tradition-bound. At its worst, it sounds hollow and rhetorical.

Selected works: *Proleten vyatŭr* (*Spring Windstorm*, 1925); *Dŭga* (*Rainbow*, 1928); *Stikhotvoreniya* (*Poems*, 1938); *Veliki dni* (*Glorious Days*, 1950); *Po pŭtishtata ti vŭrvyakh* (*I Walked along Your Roads*, 1958); *Naytrudnoto* (*The Most Difficult Thing*, 1964); *Sŭchineniya* (*Collected Works*, 1970–73).

[CG/LPG]

G

Ganem, Checri (Lebanon, 1861–1929) Ganem was born in Lebanon and died in Beirut in 1929. He is considered the father of the Lebanese literature of French expression; his masterpiece, the poetic play *Antar* (1910), constitutes the first major example of this type of literature. *Antar* received its pemière at the Odéon in Paris. It put on stage the famous Arabic warrior of the sixth century who was known for his courage, virtuosity, and his poetic talent. Since the play was a mixture of chivalric moments blended into poetic scenes and raised questions of war, love, and death, it was compared with Rostand's *Cyrano de Bergerac*. Representing the Oriental soul, the difficulties of man, of love, and his insatiable quest for truths, *Antar* was considered the most important event of Arabic nationalism organized abroad. The poet worked closely on current events with his brother Khalil Ganem, a journalist and poet, and with the writer Jacques Tabet and the poet Jean Béchara Dagher. Their writing in French conveyed the power to express rebellion against the Ottoman oppression and emphasized the Lebanese identity. Ganem also published *Ronces et fleurs* (*Thorns and Flowers*, 1890) which explored the relationships between men. Echoing the romantic tradition, his poetry and his plays sing lyrics of endurance and hope as well as melancholy.

[MS]

Gardner, Isabella (United States, 1915–81) Isabella Stewart Gardner did not publish a book of poetry until she was forty. She had been an actress in 1939–43, and associate editor of *Poetry* magazine in 1950–56. A painstaking and often blocked lyric writer, she produced just four books in her lifetime, with a fifteen-year gap between the third, *West of Childhood* (1965) and *That Was Then* (1980), the latter a nominee for the American Book Award. She often wrote on the importance and the failure of love (she had four failed marriages and several long affairs).

Shortly before her death of a heart attack in New York City, at age sixty-six, she learned she was to be New York State's first Poet Laureate. A descendant of the wealthy Peabody, Grosvener and Gardner families of New England, and cousin of ROBERT LOWELL, she gave the $10,000 stipend to Yaddo, the writers' colony in Saratoga, New York. A biography of Gardner by Marian Janssen is in preparation. Gardner's *Collected Poems* was published in 1990.

[RP]

Garfitt, Roger (England, b. 1944) Born the son of a magistrate in Wiltshire, Garfitt was educated at Merton College, Oxford. He now lives in Surrey where he both writes and edits poetry.

The year 1973 was a particularly important one for Garfitt's own poetry: he won both the Dorothy Mauger Award at the Portsmouth Festival (for 'Twitchell') and the Guinness International Poetry Award at the Stroud Festival (for 'Spring Grazing'). His volume of poetry *West of Elm* (1974) received the Gregory Award in 1974. His work has appeared in *London Magazine*, *Poetry Nation*, *Poetry Review*, the *Times Literary Supplement*, and in various other anthologies and periodicals. Like that of many post-war poets, Garfitt's work has also been heard on BBC Radio.

Garfitt's writing is known for its breadth and flexibility. His poetic structure varies from free form to classically patterned, which meshes tightly with his exploration of wildlife, basic human nature, and symbols of modern technology. The result is decidedly unexpected.

Selected works: *Caught on Blue* (1970); *Given Ground* (1989).

[MK]

Garioch, Robert (Scotland, 1909–81) Born Robert Garioch Sutherland, the son of an Edinburgh painter and a music teacher, Garioch was educated at the Royal High School and Edinburgh University where he studied English. He spent much of his life as a teacher in Scotland and England, and his writing career began in 1933 with the production of his surrealistic verse play, *The Masque of Edinburgh* (extended and published in 1954). During the war he served in the North Africa campaign until he was captured and spent the rest of the war as a prisoner in Italy and then in Germany. His wartime experience affected him deeply and can be seen in his poetry and his prose description, *Two Men and a Blanket* (1975). He was also a translator, making Scots versions of work by Pindar, Hesiod, the Latin plays of George Buchanan, and the nineteenth-century Italian dialect poet, Giuseppe Giacchino Belli. He was much influenced by the eighteenth-century poet Robert Fergusson, whose work also inspired Burns. During the last decade of his life, when he had retired from teaching, he worked in the School of Scottish Studies at Edinburgh University on Scottish language projects and he was writer-in-residence at Edinburgh University in 1971–73.

Selected works: *17 Poems for 6d* (with SOMHAIRLE MACGILL-EAIN, 1940); *Chuckies on the Cairn* (1949); *Selected Poems* (1966); *The Big Music* (1971); *Doktor Faust in Rose Street* (1973); *Collected Poems* (1977); *Complete Works* (1983).

[LKMF]

Garlick, Raymond (Wales, b. 1926) Garlick was born in London, but raised and educated in North Wales. For most of his professional life he has worked as a teacher and lecturer in English. He has published five volumes of verse: *Poems from the Mountain-House* (1950), *The Welsh-Speaking Sea* (1954), *A Sense of Europe* (1968), *A Sense of Time* (1972), and *Incense* (1976). All five collections focus upon issues of nation, language, and culture; the latter three are also characterized by elaborate stanza forms. Garlick was co-founder (with Roland Mathias) and first editor of *The Anglo-Welsh Review* (then *Dock Leaves*) in 1949; in addition he has written an *Introduction to Anglo-Welsh Poetry* (1970) and edited (again with Roland Mathias) *Anglo-Welsh Poetry 1480–1980* (1984).

[BS]

Garneau, Hector de Saint-Denys (Canada, 1912–43) Garneau is considered to be the founder of modern poetry in Québec. Over the course of his brief life, Garneau's personal life and poetry both drifted from joy to despair. His diary of the years 1935–9, published as *Journal* (1954), show Garneau becoming increasingly, even obsessively, introspective. In 1941, he withdrew from public life, and lived in isolation in his family's manor at Sainte-Catherine-de-Fossambault, where he died two years later.

Garneau was born in Montréal. He published only one book of poetry during his lifetime, *Regards et jeux dans l'espace* (*Gazes and Games in Space*, 1937). Later poems were posthumously published in *Poésies complètes* (*Complete Poetry*, 1949). All of Garneau's poetry is concerned with a search for a radically transformative poetic vision that would break through the limits of the material world. The difficulty of achieving such a vision in a compromised world causes the poet to become increasingly isolated from God, others and himself. Garneau's ultimately destructive, heroically inward search for meaning has been viewed by his poetic heirs as symbolic of the outward cultural limits of a Québécois society stifled by Catholicism and English-Canadian colonialism. Though not explicitly a political poet, he has thus been adopted by the Québécois poets of the 1950s and 1960s as an important spiritual predecessor.

[IS]

Garrigue, Jean (United States, 1912–72) Born Gertrude Louise Garrigus, Jean Garrigue was raised in Indianapolis and educated at the Universities of Chicago and Iowa before settling in New York City.

Garrigue's poetry, particularly in her early collections, presents elaborate surfaces. Rhyme and repetition, circuitous syntax, and, often, a richly arcane vocabulary create sonic and conceptual density. And yet, as with much mid-century poetry, the work is also filled with imagery of water, mirror and dream. Ultimately, Garrigue's poems challenge the stability of both cognition and identity.

Selected works: *A Water Walk by the Villa d'Este* (1959); *Country without Maps* (1964); *New and Selected Poems* (1967); *Studies for an Actress and Other Poems* (1973).

[JT]

Gascoyne, David (England, b. 1916) Born in Harrow, in north-west London, David Emery Gascoyne attended Salisbury Cathedral Choir School and Regent Street Polytechnic. His first volume of poetry, *Roman Balcony and Other Poems* (1932), was published when he was only sixteen. By the time he was twenty, Gascoyne had published a novel, a nonfiction work, and a second book of poetry, *Man's Life is This Meat* (1936). At this point in his career, he had moved from Imagism to Surrealism and translated works by Dali, PERET, and BRETON. Influenced greatly by this movement while living in Paris in the mid-1930s, Gascoyne is credited with introducing the Surrealists into the English-speaking world. Although he broke with the Surrealists in the late 1930s to find his own voice, the sense of rhythm imbued in him from this school left a lasting impression.

Gascoyne wrote a few more volumes in the 1940s and 1950s, but has since produced very little new work. One of his greatest successes was *Night Thoughts* (1956), a verse drama broadcast by the BBC in December 1955. He received the Biella European Poetry Prize in 1982 for *Le Mare de Poeta*.

Selected works: *Holderlin's Madness* (1938); *Poems, 1937–42* (1943); *A Vagrant and Other Poems* (1950); *Collected Poems* (1965, 1988); *The Sun at Midnight: Aphorisms, with Two Poems* (1970); *Three Poems* (1976); *Early Poems* (1980); *Tankers Doft* (1988); *Selected Poems* (1994).

[SS]

Gatsos, Nikos (Greece, 1915–92) Though the author of only one long poem in free verse, *Amorogos* (1941), Gatsos has had a disproportionate influence on Greek literature. Born in a small village in Arcadia, he earned his degree from the Faculty of Letters and Philosophy at the University of Athens. In *Amorogos* he combines the practice of Surrealism with allusions from the Bible and Greek folk ballads in an innovative, lyrical, and elegiac style. Like ODYSSEAS ELYTIS, he was influenced by the pre-Socratic philosopher Heracleitus, whose belief in the dynamic nature of life and art is prominent in Gatsos' poetry. He translated BRETON's *Manifesto* (with ENGONOPOULOS and EMBIRIKOS) and FEDERICO GARCIA LORCA, and contributed to the poetic renaissance of Greek song lyrics, as well.

[GSY]

Gebeyli, Claire (Lebanon, b. 1935) Born in Alexandria, of Greek parents, Gebeyli's ties to Lebanon are personal as well as literary; married to a Lebanese man, she quickly adopted Lebanese culture. She has devoted her time to writing since 1968. News editor at *L'Orient-le Jour*, the French-language Lebanese newspaper, she has introduced poetical comments in current news. She has published *Poésies latentes* (*Latent Poetry*, 1968), *Mémorial d'exil* (*Memorial of Exile*, 1975), and has been awarded several prizes, including the A.C.C.T. in 1980 and the Edgar Allan Poe Prize in 1985. A selection of her texts was published in the yearly magazine *La Corde raide* (*The Tightrope*, 1986) under the title 'Dialogues avec le feu' ('Dialogues with the Fire'). She describes her verse as direct examples of what she has learned in life. Through her echoing, dramatic flashbacks, she explores the disenchantment of war, its constant terror, and its devastation of the simple, happy lives of citizens.

[MS]

Gelman, Juan (Argentina, b. 1930) Though Gelman is one of the major poets in the Spanish language, he has spent almost as much time as a journalist, editing *Panorama* (1969) and *Crisis* (1973), directing the Literary Supplement for *La Opinion* (1971), sitting on the board of the newspaper *Noticias* (1974) and, currently, working as a correspondent for *Pagina 12*. Yet it is his poetry, which draws on medieval sources and uses them as a springboard for reflections on contemporary life, that continues to consolidate his reputation. With passion and tenderness he addresses the issues of modern Latin America. Gelman currently resides in Mexico.

Selected works: *Violins y otras cuestiones* (*Violins and Other Matters*, 1956); *El juego en que andamos* (*The Game in which We Walk*, 1959); *Gotan* (1962); *Los poemas de Sidney West* (*The Poems of Sidney West*, 1969); *Hechos y relaciones* (*Facts and Relations*, 1980); *Citas y comentarios* (*Quotes and Commentaries*, 1982); *La junta luz: Oratorio a las madres de Plaza de Mayo* (*The Light Junta: Speech to the Mothers at the Plaza de Mayo*, 1985); *Interrupciones II* (*Interruptions II*, 1986); *Anunciaciones* (*Annunciations*, 1986); *Unthinkable Tenderness* (1997).

[MN]

George, Stefan (Germany, 1868–1933) Basing his iconoclastic life – self-determined, gay, perhaps egocentric – on poetry and friendship, George was a freelance writer who depended on patronage. His circle of friends developed into a circle of disciples, who addressed George as 'master'. George's role as master and his pose as prophet-poet have caused various controversies, including accusations of proto-Fascism. His poems' vagueness and elitism was easily exploited by National Socialism, although George himself withdrew to Switzerland in 1933.

Exclusively a lyrical poet, George's achievement lies in bringing – after an encounter with the French Symbolist poet Stephane Mallarmé in 1889 – the radically new Aestheticist attitude of art-for-art's-sake to German poetry. After Nietzsche and before Expressionism, it was George who renewed poetic language in Germany; linguistic stylization was paralleled by his books' layout and a special typefont.

A first climax was *Algabal* (1892), which presented beautiful existence within an artificial, self-contained dream world. Beginning in 1900, George emphasized the ethical aspects of beautiful existence which remained highly aestheticized and restricted to a select few. It was also expressed in *The Seventh Ring* (1907) in a highly idiosyncratic myth of a new god, Maximin, the reincarnation of a young poet, dead at sixteen and considered a poetic genius by George. Emphasis on the ethical led George in *The Star of the Union* (1913) and *The New Empire* (1928) to a more prosaic tone in contrast to his perfectly rhythmical and rhymed earlier poems.

[IRS]

Gheorghe, Ion (Romania, b. 1935) Born into a peasant family in the village of Florica in east-central Romania, Gheorge studied Romanian language and literature at the University of Bucharest, then worked as an editor for various farming and literary journals. A poet of great visionary force, Gheorghe represents the orphic direction of neo-expressionism in contemporary Romanian poetry. In the cycle 'Essential Letters' (*Moonlight in the Atlantic*, 1966), he describes his experience working on a fishing boat, attributing mythical qualities to people and events. In *The Grass is Coming* (1968), vegetation apocalyptically erodes the city, while *Megalithical* (1972) and *Political Elegies* (1980) deplore the destruction of traditional peasant civilization. *The Thracian Knight* (1969) announces an attempt unique in Romanian literature to 'explore archaic national spirituality and re-create an original' mythology (M. Popa). Besides minutely investigating vestiges of Dacian (proto-Romanian) culture (*Dacia Feniks*, 1978; *Ashes*, 1980; *The Scriptures*, 1983), Gheorghe 'reconstitutes' Dacian language from the formulaic phrases of magic and children's folklore (*Game of the Game*, 1984).

[GF]

Gibran, Gibran Khalil (Lebanon, 1883–1931) Born in Bsharri to a poor family who emigrated to Boston in 1895, Gibran returned to study the Arabic language and literature in Beirut. In 1912 he moved to New York City. An essayist, novelist, poet, and painter with mystical and philosophical inclination, he became a leading figure in Al-Rabita al-Qalamiyya, the literary society of Arab Mahjar (immigrant) poets, founded in New York in 1920. Together they launched the Romantic movement in Arabic poetry.

Along with MIKHA'IL NU'AIMA's critical pronouncements, Gibran's Arabic poetry brought about a change in sensibility both in immigrant poets and in those living in the Arab world. The famous and influential 'Gibranian style' of his prose poetry and poetic prose fused fluid, sometimes incantatory, rhythms, Biblical and colloquial diction, and symbolically charged imagery. His subjective tone, reverence for nature, and mystical vision offered an alternative to the prevailing attitudes, themes, and moods of the neoclassicists. Ultimately, however, his concern was not escapist retreat into nature, but social reform effected through a new sensibility. Much of his writing assumes the tone of a prophet or sage preaching to an audience.

Selected works: (in Arabic) *A Tear and A Smile* (1914); *Rebellious Spirits* (1920); *The Broken Wings* (1922); *The Processions* (1923). (In English) *The Madman* (1918); *The Forerunner* (1920); *The Prophet* (1923); *Sand and Foam* (1926); *Jesus, Son of Man* (1928).

[WH]

Giguère, Roland (Canada, b. 1929) Born in Montréal, Giguère studied as a printer at the Écoles des Arts Graphiques in Montréal and at the École Éstienne in Paris, and throughout his life he has steadily produced prints that have been exhibited around the world. For a ten-year period beginning in the mid-1950s, Giguère spent time with ANDRÉ BRETON and the Surrealists during frequent trips to France. Giguère has remained one of the most consistent practitioners of Surrealism in Canadian poetry.

Like most of the other Québécois poets writing under the Duplessis regime and during the period of the Quiet Revolution,

Giguère's poetry expresses a desire for a rebellious end to the stifling politics and culture of post-war Québec. For Giguère, however, the situation of Québec is but one specific example of a general and pervasive attack on the imagination waged by modern civilization against the individual. The poetic liberation of the imagination offers the main site of resistance against spiritual deprivation.

Giguère's first collection of poetry appeared in 1949. The books that he produced from 1949 to 1968 have been collected in two volumes, *L'âge de la parole: poèmes 1949–60* (*The Age of the Word: Poems 1949–60*, 1965) and *La main au feu, 1949–68* (*The Hand of Fire, 1949–68*, 1973), for which he won – and refused – the Governor General's Award. *J'imagine* (*I Imagine*, 1975) and *Forêt vierge folle* (*Wild Virgin Forest*, 1978) continue Giguère's experimentation with Surrealist poetry.

[IS]

Gilbert, Jack (United States, b. 1925) Gilbert's first book of poetry, *Views of Jeopardy* (1962), was met with great critical acclaim: it won the Yale Younger Poets Award and was nominated for a Pulitzer Prize. Yet it was over twenty years later that Gilbert published his second collection of poetry, *Monolithos* (1982), which was awarded the Stanley Kunitz Prize, the American Poetry Review Prize, a nomination for the Pulitzer Prize, and the National Book Critics Circle Nomination for best book of poetry.

Directly concerned with perceptions and ideas, Gilbert's poetry explores the boundaries of knowledge, which he renders by using a poetry that insists upon concrete particulars and the force of specific nouns. His poetry, in this regard, is both sparse and evocative.

Born in Pittsburgh, Pennsylvania, Gilbert attended the University of Pittsburgh, the University of California, Berkeley (1958–59), and San Francisco State College (1962). Throughout his career he has worked in numerous universities and has lived in Japan, Europe, and the Greek island of Paros, which supplied the topological backdrop for much of *Monolithos*. He is also known for his relationship to the Beats, and for his mentorship of poet Linda Gregg.

[DC]

Gilbert, Kevin (Australia, 1933–93) Partly of Aboriginal descent, Gilbert started writing in prison. After serving fourteen years for murder he was paroled. In 1971 he was the first Aboriginal to have a play produced in Australia, *The Cherry Pickers*. He became active in Aboriginal causes, particularly land rights and education, and his protest poetry reflects this involvement. Written in free verse, the poetry expresses anger over the hopeless and oppressed condition of the Aboriginal community and attacks white society for its indifference. In spite of its sharp edge and its unabated rage, the poetry is at times witty and always human. It also makes creative use of Aboriginal English.

Selected works: *End of Dreamtime* (1971); *People are Legends* (1978); *Inside Black Australia* (ed., 1988).

[RR]

Gilboa, Amir (Israel, 1917–84) Born in Razywilow, Ukraine, Gilboa wrote Hebrew poetry even before he came to the Land of Israel in 1937. As a young man he found work in various construction and road-building projects initiated by the British, and after moving around the country he joined the British Army in 1942. He served as a driver in Egypt and North Africa, and eventually joined the Jewish Brigade in Italy. He was then involved in its military and humanitarian activities in the Netherlands and Belgium. Back in Israel in 1946, he served in the War of Independence. The experience of his war years is a paramount theme in his poems, which won him both the Bialik Prize (1971) and the Israel Prize for Literature

(1982). Gilboa set the tone for a group of young poets who broke away from the influence of the SHLONSKY-ALTERMAN generation and wove allusions to traditional sources into a deeply personal mode of poetic expression which was characterized by free style and bold colloquialisms. The destruction of European Jewry weighs heavily in his poetry, and his poem 'My Brother Was Silent' is often referred to as a protest against war and its glorification in national contexts. Gilboa's first collection, *For a Sign*, was published in 1942. A collection of his poems, *Blue and Red*, was published in 1963, and a full collection in two volumes was published posthumously in 1987. A collection of translated poems, *The Light of Lost Suns*, was published in New York in 1979.

[ER]

Gilmore, Mary (Australia, 1865–1962) The rural Australia of Gilmore's childhood constituted one staple of her verse, whether as affectionate celebration of pioneering endurance and eccentricities (*The Tilted Cart*, 1925) or as a lament for the destruction wrought by settlement on the environment and its indigenous inhabitants (*The Wild Swan*, 1930, and *Under the Wilgas*, 1932). She was also a poet of social criticism, stimulated in the 1890s by her encounters with the radical nationalist writers associated with the Sydney *Bulletin*, notably Henry Lawson. She participated in William Lane's Paraguayan experiment in communal living (1896–1900), marrying and bearing her only child during this period. Her Socialist sympathies survived the colony's failure, being rooted less in systematic ideology than in sympathy for individual victims of social injustice: the urban poor, the unemployed, the rank-and-file soldier, women suffering under moral double standards or emotional stultification (although she always remained a staunch supporter of the family and of personal stoicism). This strand of her work is most visible in *The Passionate Heart* (1918) and *Battlefields* (1939) and in general in her work as editor and writer for the Women's Page of the *Worker*, a project initiated by her in 1908 and maintained until 1931. Appointment as a Dame of the British Empire (1936) in recognition of her long-term advocacy of Australian literature did not prevent her volunteering as a columnist for the Communist *Tribune* in the Cold War days of the 1950s.

Selected works: *Marri'd and Other Verses* (1910); *Old Days, Old Ways* (1934); *Selected Verse* (2nd edn 1969).

[JST]

Ginsberg, Allen (United States, 1926–97) Ginsberg, perhaps more so than any other American poet in the twentieth century, was a true literary and cultural icon. He embodies the rebellious nature of a poetic temperament, and his influence upon poetry, music, film, television and politics continues to be far-reaching.

Born in Newark, New Jersey, Ginsberg always seemed to be surrounded by the literary life: his father, Louis, was a serious poet whom Ginsberg not only admired but measured himself against. And when Ginsberg became a student at Columbia University, he established long-lasting friendships and correspondences with Jack Kerouac, William S. Burroughs and many of the so-called 'Beat' writers, a small group of poets and novelists who used colloquial language to depict non-traditional topics. Many of the 'Beats' have been immortalized in Kerouac's *On the Road* as well as in Ginsberg's 'Howl'.

His poetry was deeply influenced by Walt Whitman, Herman Melville, Henry David Thoreau, Ralph Waldo Emerson, the mystical-visionary element of William Blake, and WILLIAM CARLOS WILLIAMS. Early in his career Ginsberg began corresponding with Williams, whose style and tone greatly influenced Ginsberg's poetry. Williams acknowledged Ginsberg by including portions of his letters and part of the poem 'Sunflower Sutra' in *Paterson*. Moreover, Williams also wrote the introduction to Ginsberg's first book of poetry, *Howl and Other Poems* (1956), which propelled Ginsberg into the center of the literary and political spotlight.

Adopting Whitman's long poetic lines, 'Howl' is a blatant affront to what Ginsberg perceived as a destructive society, and the poem draws upon homoerotic imagery, excessive metaphoric language, and extensive lists of indictments in order to unveil the corruption of contemporary society. 'Howl' instantly became the 'Beat' manifesto, but more importantly its graphic description of homosexual sex prompted the San Francisco Police Department to deem the work obscene and to arrest LAWRENCE FERLINGHETTI, Ginsberg's publisher. Despite a well-publicized trial, 'Howl' was eventually declared not obscene.

The trial further cemented Ginsberg's interest in the relationship of poetry and politics, and he was often actively involved in various protest movements: in 1968 he was tear-gassed at the Democratic National Convention in Chicago; in 1978 he was arrested for sitting on train tracks in protest at radioactive waste; and he was long associated with the gay rights movement.

Ginsberg emphasized the spiritual element of his poetry; in 1972 he converted to Buddhism. Two years later, he and ANNE WALDMAN co-founded the Jack Kerouac School of Disembodied Poetics as part of the Naropa Institute with the explicit goal of reintegrating spirituality and poetry.

In addition to his prolific writing career, which includes over fifty books, Ginsberg was a recognized political figure, a photographer and an artistic force that has inspired artists such as the composer Philip Glass and others. Ginsberg's place in the American literary and political landscape is firmly established.

[DC]

Giudici, Giovanni (Italy, b. 1924) Born in Le Grazie, in the Liguria region, Giudici moved in the 1930s to Rome, where he took a degree in Classics. He subsequently established himself in Milan, where he currently works as a literary journalist. Since his early collections, Giudici, while clearly continuing the legacy of EUGENIO MONTALE, has shown a sensibility that connected him directly to poetic movements such as 'Crepuscolarismo' (see GOZZANO). His sharp irony about the role of poets within contemporary society is often accompanied by a playful and sophisticated use of metrics within an ostentatiously traditional stanzaic organization.

Selected works: *L'educazione Cattolica* (*The Catholic Education*, 1963); *Autobiologia* (*Autobiology*, 1969); *O Beatrice* (1972); *Prove del teatro* (*Rehearsal*, 1989); *Empie stelle* (*Impious Stars*, 1996).

[GS]

Glatstein, Jacob (Poland/United States, 1887–1971) Glatstein emigrated from Lublin, Poland, in 1914. He soon became a leader in an avant-garde community of Yiddish letters in New York City, where he founded the Yiddish literary magazine, *In Sich*. Eventually, to support his family, Glatstein wrote for Yiddish newspapers under many pseudonyms. Yiddish, with its practical diction and flexible grammatical and verbal constructions, was the perfect language for Glatstein's poetry. His poetic response to World War II is often harsh, but during the war he began to write some of his most amusing poems, *The Poems of the Bratzlaver Rabbi*. These poems draw on village life, Hassidic humor, and mysticism.

Selected works (translated into English): *Poems* (1970); *The Selected Poems of Jacob Glatstein* (1971).

[CV]

Glissant, Edouard (Martinique, b. 1928) An influential author of poetry, novels, and essays, Glissant was born in Sainte-

Marie, Martinique. Before leaving Martinique to study in Paris, he participated in the election campaign of AIMÉ CÉSAIRE in 1945. As a result of his political activities on behalf of Antillean independence, Glissant was banned from leaving France and ended up spending twenty years there before returning to Martinique. While in France, he wrote a number of important volumes of poetry including *Un champ d'îles* (*A Field of Islands*, 1953), *La terre inquiète* (*The Anxious Land*, 1954), and *Le sang rivé* (*Riveted Blood*, 1960), an essay collection, and the novel *The Ripening* (1959). Returning to Martinique in 1965, Glissant participated in many cultural activities, including the establishment in 1974 of the Institut Martiniquais d'Etudes, a private school committed to teaching Antillean culture and history. Since 1988, he has lived in the United States, publishing *Fastes* (*Annals*, 1991) and *Poèmes complets* (*Complete Poems*, 1994).

The focus of all of Glissant's work has been to establish a distinctive Martinician history and culture that is the basis for an equally distinctive Antillean poetics. He is known for his rejection of both Negritude and white, Western culture as models for Martinician identity. Instead, with considerable complexity, Glissant maps out the multiple, infinitely hybrid character of Caribbean identity. He is perhaps best-known for his impressive non-fiction work, *Caribbean Discourse* (1981), which deals with a heterogeneous range of topics in highly theoretical terms.

[IS]

Glück, Louise (United States, b. 1943) Glück's diction is spare, almost unpoetic; her poetry voices the darker emotions, in similar ways to the poems of SYLVIA PLATH. Whether writing about a childhood on Long Island (*Ararat*, 1990), mythology (*The Triumph of Achilles*, 1985), or marriage (*Meadowlands*, 1996), Glück uses plain-spoken description to illustrate how human relationships seem nearly impossible, fraught with sadness and failure. *The Wild Iris*, which won the Pulitzer Prize in 1992, is considered her best book: it intertwines the voices of various flowers, a gardener, and that of a random God. The gardener's will to live comes, ironically, from her despair.

[CV]

Gogarty, Oliver St John (Ireland, 1878–1957) Gogarty is famous as the original for 'stately, plump Buck Mulligan' in James Joyce's *Ulysses*. A major figure of the Irish Literary Renaissance, Gogarty was sometimes considered the embodiment of Dublin: garrulous, passionate, and full of life, laughter, and wit. He studied medicine at Trinity College, Dublin, and became a nose and throat specialist and surgeon. In 1922–36, he served as a senator of the Irish Free State.

At Trinity, Gogarty first became interested in poetry, and much of his early verse is bawdy, improvisational, comic, and often satirical. However, he could also write elegant, well-chiseled lyrics and poignant depictions of slum life in Dublin. In 1923, his volume *An Offering of Swans* was published by W.B. YEATS's Cuala Press. Gogarty's *Collected Poems* came out in 1951.

[CT]

Goldbarth, Albert (United States, b. 1948) Born and raised in Chicago, Goldbarth was educated at the universities of Illinois, Iowa, and Utah. He is now Distinguished Professor of Humanities at Wichita State University.

Words used most often to describe Goldbarth include 'prolific' and 'prolix'. He both writes and publishes copiously, drawing on a stunning store of historical and scientific data. His poems tend to be generous; many run in sequences, and many are long-lined and looping in their syntax and imagery. A number of details repeat from poem to poem: one of the most common is the letter *x*, which often reminds us of all the many things Goldbarth consciously elides.

Selected works: *Jan. 31* (1974); *Comings Back* (1976); *Popular Culture* (1990); *Heaven and Earth* (1991).

[JT]

Goldberg, Leah (Israel, 1911–70) Born in Koenigsburg, Prussia, in 1911, Goldberg began writing at an early age. She received academic training in Kovno, Bonn, and Berlin, and a doctoral degree in Semitic languages from the University of Bonn. Goldberg emigrated to the Land of Israel in 1935 and settled in Tel Aviv, where she became a central figure in a group of poets led by AVRAHAM SHLONSKY. She wrote poetry and children's books, translated works from Russian, Italian, English, and French, and was recognized as a literary editor, essayist, and theater critic. Between 1952 and 1970 she served as the Chair of the Comparative Literature department at the Hebrew University in Jerusalem. Goldberg won the 1970 Israel Prize for Literature for her poetry, which used simple imagery, everyday words, and general themes, and adhered to traditional verse forms and rhyming schemes. She was adamantly opposed to the expression of political and ideological themes in poetry, and focused instead on love, the beauty of nature, and the reprieve which both offer the human spirit. Goldberg's poetry was published in translation in Russian, Polish, and English. Her first collection, *Smoke Rings*, was published in 1935. A nine-volume set of collected works was published in Israel during the 1970s, and collections of translated poems appeared in San Francisco (1972) and London (1976).

[ER]

Goll, Yvan (Isaac Lang; France, 1891–1950) Bilingual and bicultural by virtue of his birth in Alsace, then under German rule, throughout his life Goll felt torn between expressing himself by writing in French or in German. He first undertook university studies in law, art history, literature, and philosophy in Germany where he was greatly attracted to Expressionism. A militant pacifist during World War I, he left for Zurich to avoid German conscription and there befriended early Dadaists such as TZARA and Arp. Moving to Paris in 1919, he actively participated in the activities of Surrealism. As a Jew seeking to escape Nazi persecution, he emigrated with his wife Claire to the United States where they lived from 1939 to 1947 and earned a living through writing and journalism. During this period, he also created a magazine and founded a publishing house, both called *Hémisphères*, and published his most celebrated poem *La Grande Misère de la France* (*The Great Misery of France*, 1940) in *Poet's Message*, a journal which he also founded.

Much of Goll's poetry, especially that written in his later years, features obscure, unusual symbols, and to study it requires specialized knowledge of the esoteric and mystical doctrines of alchemy, cabbalism, theosophism, and other forms of the occult.

[RSO]

Gonzalez, Otto Raul (Guatemala, b. 1921) A member of the 'Generation of 1940', this prolific writer has published over twenty-three books of poetry. He left Guatemala after the fall of the Arbenz government in 1954 and now resides in Mexico. He established himself early as a predominantly lyrical voice faithful to both his Marxist convictions and his Mayan heritage. In this way he occupies a privileged position in the literary imagination of the new generation: that of an exemplary politically committed writer.

Selected works: *Voz y voto del geranio* (*Voice and Vow of the Geranium*, 1943); *Canciones de los bosques de Guatemala* (*Songs of the Guatemalan Forests*, 1955); *Viento claro* (*Clear*

Wind, 1959); *Luna mutilada* (*Mutilated Moon*, 1991); *Diez colores nuevos* (*Ten New Colors*, 1993); *Versos Droláticos* (*Drolatic Verses*, 1993).

[SL]

Goodison, Lorna (Jamaica, b. 1947) Goodison is one of the most gifted poets in the contemporary Caribbean. Born in Kingston, Goodison studied art at the Jamaica School of Art and the School of the Art Students' League in New York; her paintings have graced the covers of all of her books. While Goodison does not see herself as an explicitly political poet, hers is a politics rooted in an attentive, sensuous, and evocative exploration of the Jamaican experience, and in particular, the experiences and struggles of women throughout the West Indies. Her first collection, *Tamarind Season* (1980), displayed what would come to be characteristic strengths of all her writing: an assured, authentic poetic voice; an easy and powerful ability to move between English and Creole; and an honest and loving depiction of the everyday lives of ordinary people in her native land. Her subsequent books do not disappoint. In *I am Becoming My Mother* (1986) and especially *Heartease* (1988), Goodison continues to expand and develop her already remarkable technical skills with form and language.

Goodison's poetry is well-known internationally; some of the poems from *Tamarind Season* are among the most widely anthologized works to have originated from the Caribbean. She has been a visiting professor at Radcliffe College, the University of Michigan, and the University of Toronto, and has traveled throughout the world to give readings of her poems.

Selected works: *Baby Mother and the King of Swords* (1990; stories); *Selected Poems* (1992); *The Book of Amber* (1994); *To Us, All Flowers are Roses* (1995).

[IS]

Gouri, Haim (Israel, b. 1923) Gouri was born in 1923 in Tel Aviv, and currently lives in Jerusalem. He participated in the Israeli War of Independence and was sent to Europe after World War II to work in the displaced persons camps with Holocaust survivors. He studied at the Hebrew University in Jerusalem and the Sorbonne in Paris, and published extensively as an essayist, novelist, and poet. His work won him the Israel Prize for Literature in 1998. His poetry, a staple of the War of Independence generation, was widely recognized and recited during the early years of the state. Its focus gradually moved from the national to the personal and from a heroic, albeit subdued, tone to deep sorrow and an expression of alienation and regret over developments in Israeli society. Gouri's first collection, *Flowers of Fire*, was published in 1949, and subsequently translated into Spanish (1990) and Russian (1992). His novel *The Chocolate Deal* was published in 1965 and translated into English in 1968. A collection of his poems, *Words in My Lovesick Blood*, was published in the United States in 1996.

[ER]

Gozzano, Guido (Italy, 1883–1916) Since the publication of his first poems between 1904 and 1907, Gozzano's poetry evolved around few, recurring themes: a gentle and yet relentless irony toward the role of poets in contemporary society; a peculiar taste for dusty and outdated objects and atmospheres, partly borrowed from French Symbolism; a tragic and yet playful sense of alienation and illness (he died of tuberculosis when he was only thirty-two). To these features, which had become the marks of the poetic movement called 'Crepuscolarismo', he also added a typical prosastic tone, today recognized as a crucial contribution to the evolution of free verse in Italian poetry.

Selected works: *La Via del rifugio* (*The Road to the Shelter*, 1907); *I Colloqui* (*The Colloquies*, 1911).

[GS]

Graham, Jorie (United States, b. 1951) Graham received her B.F.A. from New York University in 1973, and her M.F.A. in poetry from the University of Iowa in 1978. Since that time, her career has remained on a steadily successful trajectory; she received her first teaching job immediately after graduate school and became part of the core of permanent faculty at the University of Iowa in 1983. She has recently accepted a position at Harvard University.

Since 1977, Graham has published six books of poetry – including *Hybrids of Plants and Ghosts* (1980); *Region of Unlikeness* (1985); and *Materialism* (1993). While her poetry engages the world intellectually, she often explores the relation between personal and cultural history; her poems blend analytic intensity, the day-to-day, and the multivalent experience that is consciousness. She may be the most influential American poet under fifty.

Graham's many honors include a John D. and Catherine T. MacArthur Fellowship (1990) and an award from the American Academy and Institute of Arts and Letters.

[DC]

Graham, William Sydney (Scotland, 1918–86) W.S. Graham was born in Greenock, Renfrewshire, the son of a journeyman engineer. He was educated at Greenock High School, then apprenticed to a Glasgow engineering firm at fourteen, and became a journeyman engineer himself at age nineteen. In 1938, a bursary took him to Newbattle Abbey College where he spent a year studying English and Scottish literature and philosophy; there he met Nessie Dunsmuir, whom he married in 1954. During the war Graham worked in Ireland and Glasgow and published his first collection of poems, *Cage without Grievance* (1942), followed by *The Seven Journeys* (1944) and *Second Poems* (1945). He was briefly associated with the Scottish Renaissance, but lost patience with the synthetic Scots of MACDIARMID and his followers; more lastingly, he was associated with the mainly Modernist St Ives artists.

He received an Atlantic Award for poetry in 1947 and in 1947–48 was a lecturer at New York University. In his later years, his writing became more expansively Scottish, incorporating in form and language the influence of the border ballads. His long poem, 'The Nightfishing' (1955), was perhaps overshadowed by the achievements of the Movement poets in England (see LARKIN, JENNINGS) and was followed by fifteen years of relative neglect. His hardship was partly relieved by a Civil List Pension and partly by the gradual purchase of his papers by the University of Victoria in British Columbia. After the publication of his *Collected Poems 1942–77* (1979), his work achieved some late success.

Selected works: *The White Threshold* (1949); *Malcolm Mooney's Land* (1970); *Implements in Their Places* (1977); *Aimed at Nobody* (1993).

[LKMF]

Graves, Robert (England, 1895–1985) A consummate craftsman who produced copious writings, Graves' combination of erudition and emotion marks his verse as some of the most original of the post-Modernist era. The son of a minor Irish lyric poet, Graves was educated at various public schools, which he generally loathed. Graves took a commission in the Royal Welch Fusiliers during World War I, saw action in France and befriended SIEGFRIED SASSOON and, later, WILFRED OWEN. Unlike the work of these two poets, however, Graves' verse of the period, published in *Over the Brazier* (1916) and *Fairies and Fusiliers* (1917), attempted to deny the horrors that he witnessed in the war rather than engage them.

Invalided home in 1918, Graves married Nancy Nicholson, and then wrote his way through an Oxford degree. Publishing some six volumes of poetry between 1920 and 1925 (in addition to fiction and critical pieces), the period is perhaps best represented in the dramatic and controlled poems of *Welchman's Hose* (1925), where the aftermath of war and its psychic tolls were characterized and, hopefully, healed.

Graves' domestic life, however, was as complex as his writings were ample. In 1926, Nancy and Robert invited American poet LAURA RIDING to visit; she was to become Graves' consort, muse, and domina all in one. By 1928, Graves and Riding had taken a flat in London, with Nancy and the four Graves children living on a houseboat on the Thames nearby. Within a year, Nancy had had enough and Riding and Graves moved to Majorca, the island that would be Graves' home for most of his life.

Graves' relationship with Riding is central because some of his most plangent, pointed, and characteristic verse appeared while she was his partner (though not always his lover, since Riding's opinions of sex were frequently negative). His volumes *Poems 1926–30* (1931) and *Poems 1930–3* (1933) were written then, as were both *I, Claudius* and *Claudius, the God* (1934) which established his fame; he won the prestigious Hawthornden and James Tait Black prizes the next year. Even after Riding left him for another man in 1939, her presence can be felt in his work, most notably in his iconoclastic and brilliant *The White Goddess* (1948).

Subtitled *A Historical Grammar of Poetic Myth*, *The White Goddess* was Graves' attempt to reconcile the ambivalent position he saw woman occupying in poetry. She was always the archetypal muse, but that archetype was never simply kind. She was instead tri-partite: 'mother, bride and layer-out'. Inevitably the male poet must fall to the female muse; the White Goddess, though she sustains, also kills. With a wide erudition, Graves makes a case that this is '*the* theme' for all poetry. Although it probably says more about his own writing than any other generalizable trend – the poems of this period embody the very roles and divisions *The White Goddess* describes – it is nonetheless a watershed work of poetic criticism.

Graves' late life was marked by stability and fame. He married his friend Beryl Hodge in 1950, returned to Majorca, and sallied forth only to lecture and to promote writing. During these last years Graves devised the Black Goddess, the more benign and forgiving sister of the White Goddess. This figure could sustain male–female love rather than inevitably kill it (or the male). The result was a more gentle, less fervent and ambivalent poetry. Although his final *Collected Poems* (1977) contained a great deal of the critically ill-received later lyrics, Graves' voluminous learning, precise ear and eye, and seventy-year output mark his as one of the truly remarkable poetic careers of the century.

[MW]

Gray, Robert (Australia, b. 1945) Gray grew up on the north coast of New South Wales near Coffs Harbour, a landscape with which his poems, such as *Creekwater Journal* (1974), are particularly associated. Although he never received a university education, he has worked in a variety of jobs and traveled widely. These experiences have enriched his poetry and made it the opposite of studied, academic verse. With their spare, riddling quality, Gray's poems in *Introspect, Retrospect* (1970) and *Grass Script* (1979) often resemble haiku or Zen parables, reflecting a tactile, concrete, yet philosophical view of nature. *Certain Things* (1993) is more autobiographical and contains prose-poems which look at the world with an observant, flexible eye.

[NB]

Gray, Stephen (South Africa, b. 1941) Born in Cape Town, Gray studied at the University of Cape Town, and then at Queens' College Cambridge, England. He also studied at the Iowa Writers' Workshop and traveled in South America before returning to South Africa where he was senior lecturer in English at Rand Afrikaans

University in Johannesburg. His work as scholar, editor, and historian reflects the changing political, social, and literary climate in his country. A poet in his own right, he has also edited several important works on South African verse and prose: *A World of Their Own: Southern African Poets of the Seventies* (1976), *Modern South African Poetry* (1984), and *Southern African Verse* (1989).

Selected works: *It's about Time* (1974); *Hottentot Venus and Other Poems* (1979); *Love Poems, Hate Poems* (1982); *Apollo Café* (1989).

[KS]

Greacen, Robert (Ireland, b. 1920) Greacen was born in Derry, Northern Ireland, and educated at Trinity College, Dublin. As a young man, he wrote several volumes of poetry, including *The Bird* (1941); *One Recent Evening* (1944); and *The Undying Day* (1948). Later, he published *A Garland for Captain Fox* (1975); *Young Mr Gibbon* (1979); and *A Bright Mask* (1985). He also collaborated with VALENTIN IREMONGER on an anthology, *Contemporary Irish Poetry* (1941). He has lived in London since 1948.

[CT]

Greenberg, Uri Zvi (Israel, 1896–1981) Born in Bialykamien, Galicia, Greenberg received a traditional education and published a collection of Yiddish poetry in 1915. He fought in World War I as a soldier in the Austrian army but later deserted to live in Lvov and Warsaw. He emigrated to the Land of Israel in 1924 and settled in Tel Aviv. Originally associated with the Labor movement, Greenberg, subscribing to nationalist themes and a catastrophic view of the political developments in the region, quickly distanced himself from his comrades, and became one of the ideologists of the Revisionist movement. In his fiery, prophetic style and heavily spiritual poetry, Greenberg called for national revival, heroism, and rebellion against the recurring tragedies of Jewish history. Characterized by an attitude which combined mysticism, messianic fervor, scorn for those who borrow foreign ideologies, and contempt for poetry which does not serve the destiny of the nation, Greenberg established himself as a unique, controversial figure in the Israeli literary pantheon. In 1949 he was elected to the Israeli parliament as a representative of the Herut party. Because of his association with the extreme right, he was shunned for years by the mainstream Israeli public, and only late in his life received national recognition, being awarded the Israel Prize in 1957. Greenberg's first collection, *A Grave Threat and the Moon*, was published in 1925. His complete works were published posthumously in the 1990s.

[ER]

Greenlaw, Lavinia (England, b. 1962) Greenlaw was born in London into a family of scientists and doctors. Although her own muse was poetic, scientific themes and sensibilities are immediately apparent in her verse. Her first published work, *The Cost of Getting Lost* (1991) is a perfect example of her unique temperament and style as a scientific poet.

As a critic, Greenlaw is a contributor of reviews to both the *Independent* and the *Times Literary Supplement*. *The New Yorker* features her work as well. Greenlaw also earned the distinction of being the first British Council Fellow in Writing at Amherst College in Massachusetts. Her first full-length volume of poetry, *Night Photograph*, appeared in 1993, followed by *A World Where News Traveled Slowly* (1997).

[MK]

Grennan, Eamon (Ireland, b. 1941) Born in Dublin, Grennan was educated at University College, Dublin, and Harvard University and is currently the Dexter M. Ferry, Jr. Professor of English at Vassar College.

Invariably combining lyrical and narrative sensibilities, Grennan's poetry always illuminates and preserves what often passes unrecognized in the dailiness of our lives. These luminous acts of preservation stem from the belief, as he has said in a recent interview, that 'every poem is a memory of some kind, a celebratory elegy'.

As well as an accomplished poet, Grennan is also a noted scholar of Renaissance literature and a translator of the Italian poet Giacomo Leopardi.

Selected works: *What Light There Is and Other Poems* (1989); *As if it Matters* (1992); *So it Goes* (1995); *Selected Poems of Leopardi* (trans., 1997); *Relations New and Selected Poems* (1998).

[MO]

Grigson, Geoffrey (England, 1905–85) Born in Pelynt, Cornwall, Geoffrey Edward Harvey Grigson was married three times, the third time to Jane McIntire, a celebrated writer on cooking. Known not only as a poet, but also as an editor, critic, anthologist, journalist, scriptwriter, juvenile fiction writer, nonfiction writer, and autobiographer, Grigson's success in these other genres frequently overshadowed his poetic talent. He founded *New Verse* in 1933 mainly so that he could publish AUDEN, whom he admired greatly. Known widely in literary circles because of the magazine, Grigson found himself in the company of many prominent writers.

He began to publish his own poetry in the magazine under the pseudonym Martin Boldero, but his voice was soon recognized in his verse. Most important to Grigson were the rhythmic and rhyming structure. His poetry was often in the plain style of Auden or compact like that of the Imagists. He received both the Duff Cooper Memorial Prize and the Oscar Blumenthal Prize in 1971. Grigson died not long after the Poetry Society held a celebration for him in honor of his eightieth birthday.

Selected works: *Several Observations* (1939); *The Isles of Scilly, and Other Poems* (1946); *The Collected Poems of Geoffrey Grigson 1924–62* (1963); *Discoveries of Bones and Stones, and Other Poems* (1971); *Sad Grave of an Imperial Mongoose* (1973); *Collected Poems* (1984); *Persephone's Flowers* (1986).

[BRB]

Grochowiak, Stanislaw (Poland, 1934–76) Grochowiak was born in Leszno, lived in Warsaw during the Uprising of 1945, and studied Polish philology at Poznan University after the war, although he never finished his degree. In 1955 he returned to Warsaw, where he was employed briefly at the PAX publishing house, spending the last twenty years of his life working for a number of literary and cultural magazines.

A 'new wave' poet, Grochowiak published his first book of poems, *The Knight's Ballad*, in 1956. This collection attracted immediate attention for its macabre imagery, gallows humor, and use of the grotesque. Some of the harsher critics, such as JULIAN PRZYBOS, accused Grochowiak of 'turpism' (promoting ugliness). However, Janusz Maciejewski has noted that Grochowiak described his own work as 'miserabilism', indicting the mid-twentieth-century powers-that-be for post-war Poland's impoverished emotional and spiritual state. In the mid-1960s Grochowiak's poetics become more moderate, but his political and social consciousness never waned.

Grochowiak was also a notable playwright and prose writer. His *Selected Poems* was published in 1965 and revised in 1978.

[MO]

Grünbein, Durs (Germany, b. 1962) Born in Dresden, East Germany, Grünbein studied theater history and moved to West Berlin in 1985. A master of astute observation and poetic form, he is an important and highly acclaimed poet.

Grünbein's first collections, *Gray Zone in the Morning* (1988) and *Lectures on the*

Lower Skull (1991), presented precise observations that circumscribe the individual subject's unclear position in the gray urban landscapes of postindustrial society. Through reality's shocking and unpleasant quality, Grünbein connects avant-garde tradition with the late twentieth century. Continuing the exploration of the connection between language and physical reality, Grünbein's recent poems emphasize traditional forms, in *Folds and Falls* (1994), and ironic presentation of freak accidents in *Our Dear Dead: 33 Epitaphs* (1994).

[IRS]

Gu Cheng (China, 1956–93) Poet and prose writer, Gu was born in Beijing. At the age of thirteen he was forced to settle in the countryside to raise pigs in Shandong. He returned to Beijing in 1974, working as a carpenter and later as a porter. Gu began to write poems in 1977. His early poems were so controversial that a nationwide debate over them started in the early 1980s, involving dozens of critics and scholars, and almost all the literary journals. As the debate extended to issues not limited to his poetry but discussing every aspect of literature, quite a few new journals emerged as the situation required.

Gu was a major voice in contemporary Chinese verse. His deceptively simple poetry has won wide acclaim for its superb expressiveness of society's real and metaphorical impact on individuals. The frequent images one encounters in his poetry are those that are capable of suggesting the act or state of bending, yielding, and twisting. Actually, one of his dominating themes is the transformation of humans into non-humans.

Gu moved to New Zealand in 1987, and put an end to his life in 1993 after killing his wife. The *Collected Poems of Gu Cheng*, edited by Gu Gong, his father and a poet himself, was published in 1995 in Shanghai. Gu's poems have been translated into all the major languages.

[LG]

Guðmundsson, Tómas (Iceland, 1901–83) Best known for singing the praise of the city of Reykjavík, Guðmundsson's poetry also reflects the changes in twentieth-century Icelandic society. Guðmundsson published his first collection, *Við sundin blár* (*At the Blue Sounds*) in 1924, but the nostalgic lyricism of the poems attracted little attention. After almost a decade of silence came *Fagra veröld* (*Fair World*, 1933), whose introspective insight and irony established the poet's reputation. The focus on urban life also contributed to the collection's success, and Guðmundsson was proclaimed Poet Laureate of Reykjavík. His influence grew as co-editor of the literary journal *Helgafell* in 1942–55, during which period he also published *Fljótið helga* (*The Holy River*, 1950), reflecting the feeling of approaching cataclysm during World War II. Even during the war, however, Guðmundsson continued to reflect on the personal experience of growing older, a theme most pronounced in *Heim til ðín, Ísland* (*Home To You, Iceland*, 1977).

[YB]

Guest, Barbara (United States, b. 1920) Guest was born in Wilmington, North Carolina, and attended the University of California, Los Angeles, and the University of California, Berkeley, but she is known predominantly as a writer of the New York School, a group of poets connected to the New York City art scene of the 1950s and 1960s (see ASHBERY, O'HARA, KOCH).

Art was both an early and an ongoing influence upon her poetry. Throughout the 1950s, Guest worked as a writer for *Art News* magazine, and she has continued to write articles and reviews for numerous art magazines. Guest's poetry often utilizes space as a way to draw attention to the materiality of language. The poem for Guest presents a carefully sculpted site where the visual quality of words are juxtaposed with poignant insights and reflection.

Guest's first book of poetry, *The Location of Things*, appeared in 1960, and since then she has published eleven others. In addition, Guest has gained critical acclaim for a biography of H.D., *Herself Defined* (1984.)

Guest continues to be an important poetic presence, both for her poems and for her integration of the visual arts and poetry.

[DC]

Guillén, Jorge (Spain, 1893–1984) Born in Valladolid, Guillén was a lifelong poet and a professor whose career continued in exile after the Spanish Civil War. He taught at several universities in the United States, including Harvard. In 1977, two years after Franco's death, Guillén returned to Spain, where he remained until his death in 1984.

Guillén is known for finding the poetic in the everyday. His first major work, *Canticle* (1928), follows the aesthetic lines of the Generation of 1927 (see ALEIXANDRE, JIMÉNEZ and LORCA), with carefully crafted poems that use common objects to celebrate life. In *Clamor* (1957) Guillén deals with the injustices of modern life. *Homage* (1967) is his broadest and most philosophical book. *Our Air* (1968) contains Guillén's complete poems.

[AB]

Guillén, Nicolás (Cuba, 1902–89) The greatest Cuban poet of the twentieth century, Guillén's life and work have been synonymous with Cuba's development as a nation. Born in the year Cuba achieved independence, jailed by the British regime in the 1930s, and exiled in the 1950s, Guillén became the nation's poet laureate after the success of the Castro Revolution in 1959.

Guillén was born in Camagüez and first came to prominence with his collection of Afro-Cuban poetry, *Songoro cosongo* (1931), an affirmative depiction of the lives of the impoverished black underclass living in Havana's slums. Through his poetic adaptation of the *son* – an Afro-Cuban popular song form – and his ability to capture black Cuban dialect through the fusion of African rhythms and language with Spanish metrical forms, Guillén's poems helped to establish the centrality of the African contribution to the creation of Cuban culture. In *West Indies Ltd.* (1933), Guillén bitterly depicts the impact of colonialism and slavery on the Caribbean. Influenced by his participation in the First and Second International Congress of Writers for the Defense of Culture, where he met LANGSTON HUGHES, PABLO NERUDA, and other politically committed writers, Guillén became a Communist in 1937.

Guillén's later poetry is characterized by its political and revolutionary tenor, and its demand for social liberation and justice. *Cuba Libre* (*Free Cuba*, 1947), *La paloma de vuelo popular* (*The Dove of Popular Flight*, 1958) and *Elegias* (*Elegies*, 1958) denounce American imperialism and the Cuban dictatorship, and express Guillén's overwhelming sense of loss – of family, of country. *Tengo* (*I Have*, 1959) celebrates the victory of the Revolution but is also cautionary, initiating his diverse post-Revolutionary work concerned with the creation of a new society, a concern particularly expressed in *El Gran Zoo* (*The Great Zoo*, 1967), which marks a formal shift toward free verse and is generally considered to be the finest representation of his work. Guillén, who suffered from Parkinson's disease, died in Cuba at the age of 87.

Selected works: *La rueda dentada* (*The Perforated Wheel*, 1972); *Man-making Words: Selected Poems of Nicolás Guillén* (English, 1972); *Daily Daily* (1972); *Sol de domingo* (*Sunday's Sun*, 1982); *New Love Poetry: In Some Springtime Place: Elegy* (English, 1994).

[IS/LKA]

Guillevic, Eugène (France, 1907–97) Guillevic defied Surrealism, favoring objective realism to metaphor and fantasy. He wrote brief, dense, elliptical poems in an attempt to spark a sense of Being in readers. He began his poetic career at age thirty-five with *Terraque (Landwater*, 1942), followed by *Exécutoire (Writ of Execution*, 1947), *Fractures (Breakages*, 1947), *Élégies (Elegies*, 1948), and *Terre à bonheur (Land of Happiness*, 1952). The 1950s mark a low point in Guillevic's work, when his militant, Marxist leanings lead Guillevic to write didactic, political poetry with traditional meter. Critics often deride Guillevic's *Trente et Un Sonnets (Thirty-one Sonnets*, 1954) for just these failings. Yet Guillevic soon rediscovered his unique voice in later collections such as *Carnac* (1961), *Sphère* (*Sphere*, 1963), *Avec* (*With*, 1966), *Euclidiennes* (*Euclidians*, 1967), *Ville* (*City*, 1969), *Du domaine* (*Of the Domaine*, 1977), *Etier* (*Canal*, 1979), *Autres* (*Others*, 1980), and *Trouées* (*A Patch of Blue*, 1981).

[AD]

Gumiliev, Nikolai Stepanovitch (Russia, 1886–1921) Gumiliev was born into the family of a Moscow doctor, though the family lived in and around St Petersburg after 1895. He studied at the gymnasia of Ia.G. Gurevich and Tsarskoe Selo; at the former he began writing poetry and at the latter he met his future wife Anna Gorenko, who, writing under the name ANNA AKHMATOVA, would become one of the most important Russian poets of the century. His feelings for her are reflected in the feminine images of his first collection of poems, *Put' konkvistadorov* (*The Path of Conquistadors*, 1905). In 1906, Gumiliev studied the arts in Paris. There he published *Romanticheskie tsvety* (*Romantic Flowers*, 1908), dedicating it to Gorenko, whom he would marry in 1910 – and separate from in 1913.

In 1911, Gumiliev, as a reaction to the insistent courtship of Russian Symbolist poet, Viacheslav Ivanov, broke with Symbolism and created the 'Tsekh poetov' ('The Guild of Poets'), the basis of the poetic movement Acmeism. Acmeism believed that poetry should be the precise reflection of an inner experience, balancing image and form, and emphasizing ideas for their emotional effect, rather than their ideological values. Gumiliev's first Acmeist volume was *Chuzhoe nebo* (*Foreign Sky*, 1912), followed by *Kolchan* (*The Quiver*, 1915) and *K sinei zvezde* (*Toward the Blue Start*, 1923). Upon his return to Russia after the revolution, he published *Koster* (*The Bonfire*, 1918) and his best collection, *Ognenny Stolp* (*The Pillar of Fire*, 1920), dedicated to his second wife, A.N. Engel'gardt. In 1921, Gumiliev was arrested by the secret police organization CHEKA and shot.

Though the themes of his poetry vary greatly from one collection to another, taken together Gumiliev's works represent a lyrical diary united through their lyrical constant, the poet's vision of himself.

[RN]

Gunn, Thom (England, b. 1929) Born of successful journalist parents in Kent, Gunn was exposed very early on to social issues. When he was only eight years old his parents divorced and when he was fourteen, his mother died, two events which later greatly affected his poetry. Gunn read widely and began writing at a very early age. After attending the University College School in London, Gunn served two years in the British Army. He then worked at temporary jobs while continuing to write. In 1950, he enrolled in Trinity College, Cambridge where he studied English, earning his B.A. in 1953. He then took an M.A. at Stanford University (1958). Gunn is currently a senior lecturer at the University of California, Berkeley, where he has held various positions off and on since 1958.

Gunn has been identified with the Movement group of poets led by PHILIP LARKIN. He is also associated frequently with TED HUGHES, with whom he collaborated to produce *Selected Poems* (1962). Reading Donne at twenty-one had a great impact on his poetry, most visible in his second work *Fighting Terms* (1954). Other influences include poet and Stanford professor YVOR WINTERS and the philosopher Jean Paul Sartre. Often classified as a controversial poet, Gunn is openly homosexual and has admitted to experimenting with LSD and other drugs since moving to the San Francisco area. His poetry deals with these issues as well as AIDS, American subculture, the Hell's Angels and life in the 1960s and 1970s. Producing a total of over thirty volumes of poetry in Britain and America, Gunn is difficult to categorize with one nationality. He has received awards in both countries, among them, the Levinson Prize (1955), the Maugham Award (1959), Rockefeller Award (1966), a Guggenheim Fellowship (1971), the Sara Teasdale Prize (1988), a MacArthur Fellowship (1993) and the Lenore Marshall Prize (1993).

Selected works: *Poems* (1953); *The Sense of Movement* (1959); *Touch* (1968); *Moly, and My Sad Captains* (1971); *Jack Straw's Castle* (1976); *Selected Poems 1950–75* (1979); *The Passages of Joy* (1983); *The Man with Night Sweats* (1992); *Collected Poems* (1994); *Frontiers of Gossip* (1998).

[BRB]

Guo Moruo (China, 1892–1978) Scholar, poet, translator, and playwright, Guo, a native of Sichuan, was born into the family of a wealthy merchant. After receiving a good traditional education, he went to Japan to study, taking his degree in medicine from Kyushu University in 1921. That year, Guo made his name as one of the leading modern Chinese poets with the publication of his collection *The Goddesses*. These poems, in free form, characterized by an exuberant imagination, bold imagery, and strong rhetoric, express the author's youthful idealism, democratic ideas, and feelings of cosmic union with all that existed. These poems are reminiscent of Whitman in the long, prose-like lines and the catalogues of people, things, places, and natural features, and of Shelley in the intense emotions and ardent revolutionary visions. No sooner had he returned to China in 1925 than he became heavily involved in the activities of the Creation Society. Full of revolutionary ideals, he joined the Chinese Communist Party in the same year, and participated in the failed Nanchang Uprising in 1927. The uprising was crushed and Guo fled to Japan, not returning to China until 1937. During the war years, Guo held several important positions in Chongqing, the wartime capital of the Guomingdang Government. His most famous play, *Qu Yuan*, about the tragic life of an ancient patriotic poet, was written in 1942, when the Chinese people were fighting courageously against the Japanese invaders. After 1949, Guo held more important positions in the People's Republic, including the presidency of the Chinese Academy of Sciences, until his death.

Guo's fame was due not a little to the important role he played in China's cultural life for several decades. As a writer, he was extremely prolific; as a poet, he published eight more collections of poetry after *The Goddesses*; he also translated the works of Kawakami Hajime, the British Romanticists, Goethe, Schiller, Turgenev, Tolstoy, and Upton Sinclair; and as a playwright, he produced several remarkable historical plays. He wrote historical and philosophical treatises as well, the most widely acclaimed of which is his study of the inscriptions on oracle bones and bronze vessels, *Inscriptions on Bronzes from the Two Zhou Dynasties* (1935, 1957), a monumental work in its field. Guo also wrote his autobiography, which is composed of eight volumes.

[LG]

Gurney, Ivor (England, 1890–1937) Ivor Bertie Gurney was born in Gloucester to a tailor and his wife. Young Gurney showed musical talent and in 1911 he received a scholarship to the Royal College of Music in London. In 1915 he volunteered to fight in the war, remaining in service despite injuries that kept him in and out of hospitals until he was discharged after suffering shell shock in 1918. During those three years, and for decades after his discharge, he published both music and poetry. Marion Scott, music historian and editor of the Royal College of Music's magazine and Gurney's longtime friend, worked to keep him writing and publishing and out of asylums and hospitals. As a result, much of Gurney's sustained success is due to his relationship with Scott. Gurney died of tuberculosis the day after Christmas, 1937.

Gurney's poetry is painful and yet somehow satisfying to read, perhaps because of his neat forms. The somber, respectful verses remember lost loves, friends and fellow soldiers, family, Gloucestershire, war, and death. His first works are short and hymn-like, sounding like desperate but strangely lyrical prayers. His later poetry, some of which was to appear in a rejected third volume of verse entitled *Rewards and Wonders*, became longer and more complex, probing his own emotional and psychological experiences. It is Gurney's willingness to bear the soul solemnly which unites both his short- and long-form art, and which distinguishes his work.

Selected works: *Severn and Somme* (1917); *War's Embers* (1919); *Poems by Ivor Gurney* (1954); *Poems of Ivor Gurney* (1973); *Collected Poems* (1982).

[MK]

Gustafsson, Lars (Sweden, b. 1936) Novelist, critic, painter, translator, academic scholar, and poet Lars Erik Einar Gustafsson was born in Västerås. Since the collection *Vägvila* (*Respite*, 1957), Gustafsson has published around sixty literary titles and a dozen scholarly and critical volumes. His literary reviews appeared in *Bonniers Literary Magazine* (which he edited between 1960 and 1972), *Expressen*, and *Svenska Dagbladet*. His literary output has earned him many awards, starting with the *Svenska Dagbladet* Award for 1960 and including the Swedish Novel Prize (1979) and the Bellman Prize of the Royal Swedish Academy (1990). In 1978 he earned his Ph.D. in Philosophy from Uppsala University, writing on the tension between philosophy and language, and has since lectured in many places, dividing his time since 1974 between Uppsala and the University of Texas at Austin.

[YB]

H

H.D. (Hilda Doolittle; United States, 1886–1961) Doolittle was born in Pennsylvania. She attended private school there until she entered Bryn Mawr College in 1904 to study classics. In 1911 she left the home she would later describe to Freud as unhappy and traveled to Europe, eventually joining her friend and mentor EZRA POUND and the other poets living in London who would become the Imagists. She started to lead the movement when work published under 'H.D., Imagiste', began to be recognized as innovative and exceptional. Also at this time H.D. married fellow Imagist RICHARD ALDINGTON. Aldington and H.D. edited *The Egoist* until he joined the army. In 1919 H.D. gave birth to her daughter Perdita; separated from Aldington at the time, the two would finally divorce in 1938. During the 1920s H.D. traveled extensively with her longtime companion, historical novelist Bryher (Winifred Ellerman). This relationship, a move to Switzerland, and her travels, especially those to Greece, fostered H.D.'s creativity, resulting in numerous texts in several different genres published throughout the 1920s, 1930s and 1940s.

Initially working to boil poetry down to its truest image, H.D. flung off the Georgian restraints of long, complicated lines, heavy rhymes and ornamental word choices. In *Sea Garden* (1916) and *Hymen* (1921) the reader sees a clean, concrete image expressed in common language and a free verse produced by careful observation and artistry. She captures moods, emotions, the essence of beauty, and nature so that the reader can study them and see their truths. Later, the trilogy *The Walls Do Not Fall* (1944), *Tribute to the Angels* (1945) and *The Flowering of the Rod*(1946) would chart, in moving triplets, the destruction of World War II and her own reaction – a nervous breakdown – as well as the personal and political recovery of the post-war years. Finally, the long *Helen in Egypt* attempts to craft a feminist heroine via a recuperation of myth.

H.D.'s work was widely celebrated, especially in her earlier years of publication. She broke new ground in the arts as a woman poet. As is often the case, however, H.D. was not formally acknowledged for her genius until later in life. In 1938, she was granted the annual Helen Haire Levinson Prize of *Poetry Magazine*. She also received the Brandeis University Creative Arts Award for Poetry in 1959. In 1960, one year before her death, H.D. was honored by becoming the first woman to be granted the Award of Merit Medal for Poetry of the American Academy of Arts and Letters.

Selected works: *Palimpsest*, (1926); *Hippolytus Temporizes*, (1927); *Red Roses for Bronze* (1931); *Euripides' Ion* (1937); *By Avon River*

(1949); *Tribute to Freud* (1956); *Bid Me to Live* (1960).

[MK]

Haavikko, Paavo Juhani (Finland, b. 1931) Critical consensus views Haavikko as Finland's greatest living poet. Since the publication of his first collection of poetry *Tiet etäisyyksiin* (*The Ways to Far Away*, 1951), he also has published essays, plays for stage and television, libretti for opera, short stories, novels, and aphorisms. Equally worthy of mention is his brilliant and original history of Finland, *The National Line: History of an Unknown Nation 1904–75*. His highly original and radically varied work has led the way into new directions, not only in Finnish lyric and epic poetry, but also in these other fields.

Haavikko was born in Helsinki where he eventually became the literary director of a publishing house and subsequently established his own publishing business. His first book, expressive of vast historical vistas, was suggestive of the individualistic 1950s work to come. His language speaks of great inner tensions; in its drama, irony and wit, warmth and coldness, proximity and distance vie for prominence. His most notable collections of this first creative period are *Synnyinmaa* (*Birthplace*, 1955) and *Talvipalatsi* (*Winterpalace*, 1959) – in JOHN ASHBERY's opinion one of the great poems of the century; both suggest consciousness of poetry as a world of its own, the double of the universe, coexisting with other realities. Stylistically, his mode of writing is noted for quickly shifting wit and seamless change of effects from one level of poetic discourse to another. His subject matter ranges from nature and mythology to history, the latter principally of antiquity and of Tsarist Russia.

Haavikko's language strives to embody rather than merely represent poetic images. We witness emotion and experience synthesized into poetic drama as the border between the internal and the external becomes porous. In his later poetry, notably in *Puut, kaikki heidän vihreytensä* (*Trees in all Their Verdure*, 1966), as well as in the 1976 collection *Viiniä ja kirjoitusta* (*Wine, Writing*), Haavikko fuses his themes of love, human relationships, loneliness, and survival into expressions of great depth and intensity. The longer poems *Fourteen Rulers* (1970), the source of which is Michael Psellus's *Chronographia* of eleventh-century Byzantium, and *Runoja matkalla salmen ylitse* (*Poems from a Voyage across the Sound*, 1973), the 'sound' being the Bosporus, are concerned with power and its use. In his historical series Haavikko is a realist. The historical parallelism in his writing parodies with deft clarity abuses of political power in its ideologically varied forms. The epic *Twenty and One* (1974), bound by a unified plot, is his personal interpretation of the *sampo* myth in *Kalevala*.

Recent comprehensive collections should be mentioned: *Kirjainmerkit Mustat* (Poems 1949–66), *Poems, Poems 1984–92* and *Tyrannin Ylistys, Poems 1970–81*. Haavikko was Decorated Knight First Class of White Rose of Finland 1978; he is the recipient of eight State Prizes for Literature; the Pro Finlandia Medal (1967), a Prix d'Italia (1984), and the Neustadt International Prize for Literature, 1984, to mention the most significant honors. He received an honorary Doctorate in Philosophy from the University of Helsinki in 1969.

[SP]

Hacker, Marilyn (United States, b. 1942) Hacker burst upon the poetry scene in 1974, at the age of thirty-two, when her first collection, *Presentation Piece*, won the National Book Award and the Lamont Poetry Prize. Since then she has produced seven additional books, including *Selected Poems, 1965–90* (1994), which won The Poets' Prize.

Hacker is a formalist who often writes sonnet sequences, and villanelles; lesbian love affairs are a frequent subject for her later poems. Her poems are urbane, nuanced and political, their control and directness indebted to ADRIENNE RICH and MURIEL RUKEYSER.

Hacker attended the Bronx High School of Science and New York University, after which she lived for three years in San Francisco and then in London, with time spent traveling in Mexico, France, and Romania. She was married to the writer Samuel R. Delany, and they have a daughter, Iva. She has co-edited *City*, a poetry magazine, and *Quark*, a science fiction quarterly, as well as *The Kenyon Review*, from which she was controversially dismissed. She divides her time between New York City and Paris.

Selected works: *Winter Numbers* (1994).

[DC]

Hagiwara Sakutaro (Japan, 1886–1942) Hagiwara was born in Maebashi in Gumma Prefecture. When he was a student in Maebashi Middle School, he took an interest in literature. His early poems appeared in the magazine *Bunko*, and became associated with the *Shinshisha* (New Poetry Society). In 1916 he joined with Muro Saisei in founding a magazine entitled *Kanjo*, which rejected abstract and intellectual tones, and introduced to the world of modern poetry a wholly new style. His first collection, *Tsuki ni Hoeru* (*Howling at the Moon*), was published in 1917, and in it Hagiwara created a strange world of morbid sensibility and bizarre fantasy. In 1923 he published *Ao Neko* (*A Blue Cat*), which further consolidated his position as an important poet. In 1933 he founded a magazine called *Seiri*, to which he was one of the major contributors. As a literary theorist, he also published books of criticism such as *Nihon e no Kaiki* (*The Return to Japan*), 1938).

Hagiwara is generally considered the most original of the poets who employed the colloquial language and helped perfect the art of free-style poetry in modern Japan. His works are marked by a masterful handling of colloquial language; in the intrinsic rhythms of his free verse, Hagiwara demonstrates the fullest degree of musicality and beauty of modern colloquial Japanese. Allying piercing imagery with Baudelairian ennui and Buddhist weariness, Hagiwara's works convey the anxiety and anguish of the modern condition. In his later years he showed an increasing interest in traditional Japan.

[LY]

Hall, Donald (United States, b. 1928) Hall was born in New Haven, Connecticut, and educated at Phillips Exeter Academy, New Hampshire, Harvard, and Oxford. After years of teaching, Hall left academia to make his living from his writing. With his wife, the late JANE KENYON, he moved to his ancestral farmhouse in New Hampshire, where he proceeded to write prolifically in a number of genres, perhaps most notably in non-fiction.

Hall is a student of the elegy and a passionate advocate of history in a culture he sees as obsessed with novelty and youth. Preoccupied with cycles – seasonal, familial, and historical -- Hall remains a poet consumed with time and timelessness.

Selected works: *Kicking the Leaves* (1975); *The Happy Man* (1986); *The One Day* (1988); *The Museum of Clear Ideas* (1993); *The Old Life* (1996).

[JT]

Hämäläinen, Helvi Helena (Finland, b. 1907) Hämäläinen is a novelist, dramatist, and poet. Her lyricism draws on seemingly unending folkloric sources as well as keen and detailed observations of nature and the world around her. In her writing, nature and human beings are equal parts of a harmonious world, and her poetic method has been to conjoin images from vastly different spheres of life to form productive associations. Critical consensus views her as an expressionistic poet who strives to objectify inner experiences and to whom internal impressions speak a rich language keenly attuned to the pleasures and pain of form and experience. In her lyricism, basic humanism and extraordinary artistic reverence for beauty join forces. Stylistically, her poetry, embodied in thirteen volumes published during a long and distinguished career, employs free-flowing meter in which rhythm has an important role as the forward carrier of thought.

Among her thirteen collections of poetry, *Voikukkapyhimykset* (*Dandelion Saints*, 1947) stands out for its innovative poetic language. It is her two collections of *Selected Poems* (1973; 1987) which perhaps best reflect the range of her work as a poet. She has won the State Award for Literature three times (1942, 1953, 1958), an Aleksis Kivi Prize (1958) and Finland's most prestigious award, The Finlandic Prize (1988).

[SP]

Hamburger, Michael (England, b. 1924) Born in Berlin to a physician and professor, critic, historian, memoirist and poet Michael Peter Leopold Hamburger emigrated to England in 1933. He obtained an M.A. (1948) in modern languages at Christ Church, Oxford. Shortly afterwards, he married poet Anne Beresford, whom he divorced after nineteen years. He served in the British Army Infantry in 1943–47, becoming a lieutenant, but most of his life has been spent as a freelance writer and lecturer at various universities in England and the United States.

Hamburger is often noted more for his many translations of German poets such as TRAKL, CELAN, and RILKE than for his own poetry. The themes of his poetry rely on his Jewish background, his family life, and war. He is able to merge German and English aspects of literature in his poetry to bring a depth to his experiences and make them accessible to a wider audience. Drawing on his journeys, Hamburger published a seven-volume series of poetry volumes entitled *Travelling* (1952–76). His poetry, viewed sequentially, charts a growing maturity and understanding of himself and his emotions.

Hamburger's work has gained wide acclaim and he has received numerous awards, including the Schlegel-Tieck Prize for Poetry (1967), the Goethe Medal (1986), the Order of the British Empire (1992), and the Petrarca Prize (1993).

Selected works: *Later Hogarth* (1945); *Flowering Cactus: Poems, 1942–49* (1950); *The Dual Site* (1958); *Weather and Season* (1963); *In Massachusetts* (1967); *Ownerless Earth: New and Selected Poems* (1973); *Moralities* (1977); *In Suffolk* (1981); *Collected Poems, 1941–94* (1995).

[BRB]

Hamilton, George Rostrevor (England, 1888–1967) Hamilton was born in London and educated at Exeter College, Oxford. He worked in the Inland Revenue for most of his adult life; indeed, his service was so noteworthy that he was knighted for it in 1951. His prolific writing, including eighteen volumes of poetry, helped him become a Fellow and Member of the Council of the Royal Society of Literature.

In volumes such as *The Making* (1926), Hamilton's poetry is traditional and metaphysical, showing, among other things, the influence of Henri Bergson's philosophy and its emphasis on direct apperception of the world. In particular, the Thames found itself central to Hamilton's stylized nature poetry. His affinity for formality, embraced as early as the well-polished *Epigrams* (1928), developed throughout his career. Hamilton's poems are rhythmically marked and steady as they patrol the realms of the intellect.

Selected works: *Escape and Fantasy* (1918); *Light in Six Moods* (1930); *Unknown Lovers* (1935); The *Sober War* (1940); *Death in April* (1944); *Crazy Gaunt* (1946); *The Carved Stone* (1952); *Landscape of the Mind* (1963).

[EM]

Hardy, Thomas (England, 1840–1928) Hardy was born in Higher Bockhampton, near Dorchester, Dorset. By 1853, Hardy was immersed in the study of Latin and

French while also preparing himself for a career in architecture. In 1856, he was apprenticed to a local architect and six years later moved to London to continue his work under Arthur Bloomfield. It was during his stay in London that Hardy, after first publishing an article titled 'How I Built Myself a House', began to write poetry. However, architecture was the dominant factor in his life and so the young architect eventually returned to Dorset, where he would meet his future wife while working on a local church restoration project. Hardy and Emma Lavinia Gifford, the rector's daughter, married in September 1874.

Shortly before his marriage to Gifford, Hardy gave up his learned profession and became a full-time writer. He published a number of well-received novels during the 1870s and 1880s, including *Far from the Madding Crowd* (1874), *The Return of the Native* (1878), and *The Mayor of Casterbridge* (1886). The early 1890s saw continued success with the publication of *Tess of the d'Urbervilles* (1891). It was, however, only after the publication of *Jude the Obscure* (1895), which was unfavourably received by the critics, that Hardy began to concentrate primarily on writing poetry.

In 1898, *Wessex Poems and Other Verses* was published by Harper and Brothers. Inspired and confident, Hardy would publish poetry broadly during the early 1890s, including his intended masterpiece *The Dynasts*, a verse-play written about Napoleon. The work was released in three parts in 1903, 1906, and 1908.

After receiving the Order of Merit and the Freedom of Dorchester in 1910, Hardy experienced a bittersweet year in 1912. After a thorough revision, Hardy ushered into print a definitive edition of his works, 'The Wessex Edition'. The triumph of this was wholly undercut later that year. On November 27, Hardy's beloved wife Emma died. Although their relationship was often a contentious one, her death was a devastating blow to Hardy. In fact, he spent many days during the next year – despite his remarriage, to his secretary Florence Dugdale – visiting the significant locations of his early life with Emma.

In 1914, Hardy published *Satires of Circumstance: Lyrics and Reveries with Miscellaneous Pieces*, a collection of poetry which included 'Poems of 1912–13', a sequence to his deceased wife. In this elegiac collection, marked by a tone of reverence and regret, Hardy placed great emphasis on recalling the specific places and physical characteristic of his fondest moments with Emma. 'Poems of 1912–13' marked a high point in Hardy's poetry, whose sense of realism and despair would ultimately influence such modern poets as ROBERT FROST, EZRA POUND and DYLAN THOMAS.

After completing only a single book of poetry between 1914 and 1922, Hardy would close his career with a flourish, publishing *Late Lyrics and Earlier* (1922), *The Famous Tragedy of the Queen of Cornwall* (1923), and *Human Shows* (1925). *Winter Words* (1928), Hardy's final collection of poetry, was published after his death on January 11, 1928.

Hardy's heart was buried in Emma's grave in Stinsford Churchyard and his ashes in Poet's Corner, Westminster Abbey.

[BCB]

Harjo, Joy (United States, b. 1951) Known for her unromantic images of urban American Indian life, Harjo focuses on the strength of women and political realities for oppressed peoples of all races. She is among the most widely anthologized contemporary Native American poets.

Born in Tulsa, Oklahoma, to a Cherokee/French–Canadian mother and a Creek (Muscogee) Indian father, Harjo earned her B.A. from the University of New Mexico and her M.F.A. from the University of Iowa. She has taught at the Institute of American Indian Art, Arizona State University, University of Colorado and the University of Arizona. Winner of the Poetry Society of America's William Carlos Williams Award, Harjo has also received an American Book Award, a National Endowment for the Arts Grant, the Delmore Schwartz Memorial Poetry Prize and a Pen Oak Josephine Miles Award.

In addition to her career as a poet, critic, and teacher, Harjo plays the tenor saxophone in the band Poetic Justice. Music, especially jazz and blues, lends form to her poetry. Her most recent collection was sold along with a recording of the poems set to music. Her use of complex stanzas, jazz rhythm and improvisation, and her repetition of sounds and phrases ally her work with that of African-American poets. This alliance extends to her subjects as well: 'Strange Fruit', a tribute to Jacqueline Peters, an African-American activist who was lynched by the Ku Klux Klan in 1986, takes its title from the blues standard made popular early in the twentieth century by blues singer Billie Holiday.

Selected works: *What Moon Drove Me to This?* (1979); *She Had Some Horses* (1983); *Secrets from the Center of the World* (1989); *In Mad Love and War* (1990); *The Woman Who Fell from the Sky* (1994).

[HEE]

Harper, Michael (United States, b. 1938) Harper's poetry is an ongoing negotiation between the personal and African–American history. Born in Brooklyn, New York, Harper attended Los Angeles State College of Applied Arts and Sciences (B.A., 1961; M.A., 1963) and the University of Iowa (M.F.A., 1963). His more than ten books include *Dear John, Dear Coltrane* (1970), his first published book, which draws upon jazz and blues rhythms, and *Healing Song for the Inner Ear* (1985).

Harper has been awarded the Melville-Can Award and was nominated for the National Book Award for Poetry in 1978 for his *Images of Kin: New and Selected Poems* (1977). Kinship is central to his poetry, and he often draws upon his immediate family as well as his ancestors as a way of illuminating issues of race and identity.

Harper has been professor of English at Brown University since 1971.

[CC]

Harris, Wilson (Guyana, b. 1921) Theodore Wilson Harris was born in New Amsterdam, British Guiana (Guyana) and has lived in England since 1959. Before becoming one of the Caribbean's most acclaimed novelists (beginning with the publication of *The Guyana Quartet*, 1960–63), Harris published three books of poetry: *Fetish* (as Kona Waruk, 1951), *The Well and the Land* (1952), and *Eternity to Season* (1954). These poems foreshadow the thematic and formal concerns that define almost all of his novels. Harris writes complex, abstract poems that investigate time, space, memory, belonging, and human creativity, and which blur the lines between dream and reality in a mythological and cosmological investigation of experience. A revised edition of *Eternity to Season*, which contains the best of Harris' poems, was published in 1979.

[IS]

Harrison, Tony (England, b. 1937) Born and educated in Leeds, Harrison's unusual position as a highly educated classicist and linguist from a working-class background permeates his poetry. The resultant works try to speak both to and for the masses, though they acknowledge that the abilities allowing Harrison to do so isolate him from those he would represent.

Unlike many poets who lend their voices to the downtrodden and uneducated, Harrison has tried to reach them directly through television. In 1987 he broadcast his controversial poem *V* (1989), a discussion of death and division set in a vandalized Leeds graveyard that he wrote during the 1984–5 miners' strike. *Loving Memory* (1987) and *The Blasphemer's Banquet* (1989) soon followed it onto the airwaves.

Besides working strong historical and classical ties into his own poetry, Harrison has made translations of Racine, Molière, and Aeschylus, among others; six appear in *Dramatic Verse 1973–85* (1986). He was resident dramatist at the National Theatre from 1977 to 1979.

Harrison has won many fellowships and awards, among them the Cholmondeley Award (1969), the U.S. Bicentennial Fellowship (1979), the European Poetry Translation Prize (1983), and the 1992 Whitbread Award for that year's *The Gaze of the Gorgon*.

Selected works: *The Loiners* (1970); *Dramatic Verse 1973–85* (1986); *Selected Poems* (1984, 1987); *V and Other Poems* (1990); *A Cold Coming: Gulf War Poems* (1992); *The School of Eloquence* (ongoing series).

[JL]

Harsent, David (England, b. 1942) Devon-born Harsent was fiction critic for the *Times Literary Supplement* in 1965–73 and poetry critic for the *Spectator* in 1970–73. He has also worked as a bookseller and has been editor-in-chief and director for publisher Andre Deutsch since 1979.

While Harsent's acclaimed early poems rely on personal experience, he began to deal with more universal themes with the 'Punch' poems in *Dreams of the Dead* (1977), which were later continued in *Mister Punch* (1984). Thematically, at least, aligned with HUGHES, his poems tend to express themes of death, pain, and madness, often through animal imagery. In 1967, Harsent was awarded the Eric Gregory Award for *A Violent Country* (1969). Since that time, he has received numerous honors, including an Arts Council Bursary (1969) and the Faber Memorial Award (1978).

Selected works: *Tonight's Lover* (1968); *Ashridge* (1970); *After Dark* (1973); *Selected Poems* (1989); *Gawain* (a libretto, 1991); *News from the Front* (1993).

[BRB]

Hart, Kevin (Australia, b. 1954) Hart was born in London but came to the Queensland capital of Brisbane at age ten, a transition often evoked in volumes such as *Dark Angel* (1996). For a time a lecturer at Deakin University, Hart accepted a tenured chair at Melbourne's Monash University in the early 1990s. His early poetry is conceptual and intellectual, often using parable to convey difficult cruxes of meaning. From the heavily imagistic *The Departure* (1978), Hart composed poems in *Your Shadow* (1984) that were at once descriptive yet with often staggering philosophical (and religious) implications. After *Peniel* (1990) his style broadened, becoming more emotional and incantatory. As committed to academia as to poetry, Hart has also written well-regarded books on Samuel Johnson and on deconstructive theology.

[NB]

Hart-Smith, William (Australia, 1911–90) English-born, Hart-Smith moved with his family to Auckland, New Zealand, when he was thirteen years old. In 1936, he moved to Australia for the first time; from then on, he moved back and forth between New Zealand and Australia. Although it might be debatable which holds the greater claim to him, he always considered himself to be Australian.

With very little formal schooling, Hart-Smith spent his early career working in various positions at radio stations. He served in the Australian Imperial Forces in 1941–43, but was released after he suffered a cerebral hemorrhage. He was a tutor-organizer in an adult education department at the University of Canterbury (1948–55), an art director for a mail order business (1955–66), and then a writer-in-residence and creative writing instructor at the University of Western Australia for a brief stint.

Hart-Smith's poetry is most often identified with INGAMELL's Jindyworobak movement, which was concerned with putting Australian nature and Aboriginal culture at the center of writing. His first two books of poetry, *Columbus Goes West* (1943) and *Harvest* (1945), were published by the Jindyworobak Club and he was the movement's New South Wales editor shortly after he joined it. In addition to this movement, Hart-Smith was also greatly influenced by D.H. LAWRENCE and the Imagist movement.

Poems of Discovery (1959) received the Crouch Memorial Medal for best book of poems in Australia, while *The Talking Clothes* (1966) took the Grace Leven Prize.

Selected works: *The Unceasing Ground* (1946); *Christopher Columbus, a Sequence* (1948); *On the Level* (1950); *Poems in Doggerel* (1955); *Minipoems* (1970); *Let Me Learn the Steps* (1977); *Selected Poems, 1942–82* (1983).

[BRB]

Hartnett, David William (England, b. 1952) Born in London and educated at Exeter College, Oxford, Hartnett received his B.A. in 1975 and his D.Phil. in 1986. His first book of poems, *A Signalled Love*, appeared in 1985 to critical acclaim, and he has since published two additional collections of poetry, *House of Moon* (1988) and *Dark Ages* (1992). Themes in his poetry include childhood, war, love, and the creative process. He has also written memoriams for artists such as RILKE and GURNEY. In addition to poetry, Hartnett has published one novel and is currently working on another.

[BRB]

Hartnett, Michael (Ireland, b. 1941) Hartnett, an accomplished poet in both the English and Irish languages, was born in County Limerick. He has held many occupations, ranging from civil servant to teacher, from house painter to editor of *Arena* (1963–5). Influenced by the Irish-speaking poets of the eighteenth century, his volume *A Farewell to English* (1975) marks his transition to the Irish language, and until 1985, he did not write any further poetry in English. He has also translated the work of such Irish poets as Daibhi Ó Bruadair and NUALA NÍ DHOMHNAILL. Some critics argue that his Irish poems do not live up to his English-language poems. He often undertakes Irish rural themes, demystifying rustic farm life while celebrating the people who are closest to the earth.

Selected works: *Anatomy of a Cliché* (1968); *Selected Poems* (1971); *Collected Poems* (1985–87); *Selected and New Poems* (1994); *Selected Poems: Rogha Dánta* (1997); *Ó Raithaille* (1988).

[CT]

Harwood, Gwen (also known as Francis Geyer, Walter Lehmann, T.F. Kline, Miriam Stone; Australia, 1920–95) Harwood was born at Taringa, Brisbane, married William Harwood in 1945, and moved to Tasmania. She has written librettos for Larry Sitsky's operas and has also written for other composers. Harwood began writing poetry in her late thirties and her early work reflects a humane breadth of frustration, sadness, and pain.

In some of her well-known poems, Harwood presents a critique of social convention in Australian suburbia, as well as a lament for women whose lives are submerged there. Harwood's poetry has been influenced by the philosopher Wittgenstein and her poetry has been widely acclaimed.

Selected works: *Poems* (1963); *Poems: Volume Two* (1968); *The Lion's Bride* (1981); *Bone Scan* (1988); *Night Thoughts* (1992); *Collected Poems* (1992); *The Present Tense* (1995).

[AP]

Hass, Robert (United States, b. 1941) Hass, a former Poet Laureate of the United States, was born in San Francisco, and received a Ph.D. from Stanford University. A highly regarded critic (*Twentieth Century Pleasures*, 1984) and translator, Hass currently teaches at the University of California, Berkeley.

Hass' clear-eyed poems convey a world of vivid sensations; they are suffused with a palpable sense of the rugged, beautiful landscape of northern California. With a refreshing lucidity and attention to quotidian detail, his best poems explore the pleasures and sorrows of love, work, and family. Hass' most recent work, *Sun Under Wood* (1995), combines lyrical description, narrative, prose, and meditation; the technique is collagist, although hardly Modernist.

Selected works: *Field Guide* (Yale Younger Poets Prize, 1973); *Praise* (1981); *Human Wishes* (1989).

[AE]

Hatem, Jad (Lebanon, b. 1951) Born in Beirut, Hatem currently teaches at the university there. His writing comes from the crossroads of theology, philosophy, and literature. This triple influence and his critical work on Lebanese literature in French have been deeply reflected in his poetry. His first volume, *Enigme et chant* (*Riddle and Song*, 1984) has been widely acclaimed. *Au sortir du visage* (*Beyond the Face*, 1988) and *L'offrande vespérale* (*Vespers Offering*, 1989) share recurrent questions about humankind. Revealing his passionate search for meaning, identity, and the other, this poetry denounces the scandalous ambiguity of man.

[MS]

Hay, George Campbell (Deórsa Caimbeul Hay Deórsa Mac Iain Deórsa Scotland, 1915–84) Hay was born in Argyll, the son of the Scottish novelist J. MacDougall Hay. He studied at Oxford and was fluent in a number of European languages; he settled in Edinburgh, where he was a professional translator. During World War II, service in North Africa and the Middle East left him a semi-invalid. His long poem *Mochtár is Dúghall* (1982) records some of his Middle East experience. His work was included in the influential anthology of Gaelic poetry, *Four Points of a Saltire* (1970) and often revives early Gaelic meters. It describes Scottish landscape and history and, latterly, rawer human experience and injustices.

Selected works: *Fuaran Sleibh, Rainn Ghaidhlig* (1947); *Wind on Loch Fyne* (1948); *O na Ceithir Ardean* (1952).

[LKMF]

Hayden, Robert E. (Asa Bundy Steffy; United States, 1913–80) Robert Earl Hayden has long been recognized as one of the prominent formalist African-American poets. During Hayden's early development, he studied at the University of Michigan with W.H. AUDEN, and Auden's devotion to poetic technique, craft and form influenced Hayden's conception of the poem as a meter-making argument. Hayden was also deeply affected by the Formalist poetry of Stephen Vincent Benet, and in particular Benet's historically based ballad, 'John Brown's Body'.

While Hayden regarded himself first and foremost an American poet – eschewing the label of 'African-American' poet – his most powerful poetry often focuses upon black historical figures such as Nat Turner, Malcolm X, Harriet Tubman and Frederick Douglass, as well as on subjects such as American slavery, the Civil War and the underground railroad.

Hayden's *Selected Poems* (1966) gained him critical recognition and acclaim, and from 1966 onward, his reputation grew with each subsequent book of poetry: *Words in the Mourning Time* (1970), *The Night-Blooming Cereus* (1972), *Angle of Ascent: New and Selected Poems* (1975), *American Journal* (1978), and the posthumous *Robert Hayden: Collected Poems* (1985). In 1976 he was appointed Consultant in Poetry to the Library of Congress, and was nominated as an Academy of American Poets fellow in 1977.

Hayden's reputation as a central poet of the African-American experience is now secure.

[DC]

He Jingzhi (China, b. 1924) He Jingzhi was born in Zaozhuang, Shandong. He went to Sichuan with his classmates in 1939 to join in the National Salvation Movement, and began to write poems thereafter. The next year, he went to Yan'an, the headquarters of the Communist government, and attended Luxun Academy of Humanities there. He made his name as a poet by writing the first new Chinese verse opera in 1945, *The White-Haired Girl*, which is still put on stage occasionally. The majority of his poetry is political lyrics, taking the form of ballads, romantic in sensitivity and optimistic in socialism, yet honest and not heavily affected.

Since the 1950s, depending on the political climate, he has served as Deputy Minister of the Cultural Commission of CPC.

Selected works: *Night in the Countryside*, *Songs of Delight*, and *Selected Poems of He Jingzhi*.

[LG]

Heaney, Seamus (Ireland, b. 1939) Winner of the 1995 Nobel Prize for Literature, Heaney was born in County Derry, Northern Ireland and, at the age of twelve, became a boarder at St Columb's College in Londonderry. This may have initiated Heaney's consciousness of the cultural divisions between the English-influenced Ulster and the rural culture he was born into, a cultural awareness reflected throughout his work. Heaney went on to study English at Queen's University and earned his teaching certificate at St Joseph's College of Education, both in Belfast.

Heaney's education exposed him to the works of both the English literary canon and the rich Irish poetic tradition. His first widely published volume, *Death of a Naturalist* (1966), was a critical as well as a popular success; Heaney received the E.C. Gregory Award, the Cholmondeley Award, the Geoffrey Faber Memorial Prize, and the Somerset Maugham Award for this first book. Its poetry, influenced by ROBERT FROST and TED HUGHES, deals with rural life and nature by using a rich rustic and laboring language with distinctly dialectical tones.

During the 1970–71 academic year, Heaney worked as a guest lecturer at Berkeley and, through the Vietnam War protest movement in the San Francisco Bay area, began to see ways in which poetry can be used to address political issues. Heaney's use of historical and mythical political issues, especially regarding language and land, became a way to address the politically based violence in Northern Ireland without sacrificing his artistic interests to propaganda. *Wintering Out* (1973) and *North* (1975) are his most overtly political works and share the recurrent trope of the peat-bog which, through its unique powers of preservation, can be read as literally and figuratively remembering past lives and history.

Heaney's later works are more mythical and spiritual in tone, calling up ghosts of the past, including James Joyce and the mythical King Sweeney, to address the present.

In addition to his work as a poet, Heaney is a noted essayist and literary critic. He currently teaches at Harvard.

Selected works: *Station Island* (1984); *Field Work* (1979); *New Selected Poems, 1966–87* (1990); *Seeing Things* (1991).

[BB]

Heath-Stubbs, John (England, b. 1918) John Francis Alexander Heath-Stubbs was born in London and raised near Bournemouth on England's south coast. Forced by his poor eyesight to attend a progressive, yet ultimately frustrating, school, Heath-Stubbs finally chose the path of an autodidact before gaining a place at Queen's College, Oxford, in 1939.

A prolific poet, Heath-Stubbs was first published in *Eight Oxford Poets* (1941). Out of the latter would come such brilliant young writers as Sidney Keyes (co-editor of the collection), KEITH DOUGLAS, and Drummond Allison, all of whom would eventually die in service during World War II. Heath-Stubbs' first collection of poetry, *Wounded Thammuz*, was published in 1942 and established the author's sustained use of historical and literary material as subject matter for his poetry. His next collection, *Beauty and the Beast*, was published the following year.

Heath-Stubbs left Oxford after receiving his B.A. with first-class honors in 1943. Initially a teacher, he began writing for *Hutchinson's Twentieth-Century Encyclopedia* in 1945. Heath-Stubbs was primarily a freelance writer until the mid-1950s when he received the Gregory Fellowship in Poetry at Leeds on the recommendation of T.S. ELIOT. After three years, he left to become a visiting professor at the Universities of Alexandria and Michigan. Returning to England in 1961, Heath-Stubbs continued to teach for the next eleven years at the College of St Mark and St John in Chelsea.

Heath-Stubbs continued to write after his departure from Chelsea, publishing *The Watchman's Flute* (1975) and *Naming the Beast* (1982), and a collection of plays titled *Helen in Egypt and Other Plays* (1958).

[BCB]

Hébert, Anne (Canada, 1916–2000) Although known to contemporary readers as a novelist, especially for her four-novel cycle beginning with *Kamouraska* (1970), Hébert also produced several accomplished collections of poetry. She was influenced in her development as a poet by her cousin, HECTOR DE SAINT-DENYS GARNEAU, the great Québécois poet of the inter-war years. His death in 1943 had perhaps just as great an influence on her work, ending her isolation and leading to the theme that has persisted in her work ever since: the struggle against and liberation from the weight of Québécois society. Hébert left Québec in the mid-1950s for Paris.

Les songes en équilibre (*Dreams in Balance*, 1942), Hébert's first collection, comprised poems fairly traditional in form and theme. It is with *Le tombeau des rois* (*The Tomb of the Kings*, 1953), a classic collection of Québécois poetry, that Hébert established a reputation as a poet that would only later be matched by her equally impressive work as a playwright and a novelist. In this collection, Hébert's poems are highly symbolic and explore the difficult liberation of the unconscious from the dead weight of tradition. A new edition of *Le tombeau des rois*, published in 1960 as *Poèmes*, earned Hébert the Governor General's Award.

Three of Hébert's plays were published in the volume *Le temps sauvage* (*Savage Times*) in 1967. In addition to *Kamouraska*, the novel with which she is most readily identified, Hébert has written several other works of fiction, including *Les enfants du sabbat* (*The Children of the Black Sabbath*, 1975), *Héloïse* (1980) and *Les fous de Bassan* (*The Gannets*, 1982). Her last book of poetry was *Day Has No Equal but Night* (1994).

[IS]

Hecht, Anthony (United States, b. 1923) Like many American poets of his generation, Hecht studied at Kenyon College, where he also taught. Other teaching positions include Bard, the University of Iowa, New York University, and the University of Rochester. He has been a Visiting Professor at Harvard, and most recently University Professor in the Graduate School of Georgetown University, where he now has Emeritus status. He is author of seven books of poems. His awards include the Pulitzer Prize, the Bollingen Prize, and the Prix de Rome. He has served as Poetry Consultant to the Library of Congress, the position now called Poet Laureate.

Although he is regarded as a poet of high culture, with his poems shuttling among art treasures, classical myths and neoclassical literature, Hecht's work has also often dwelt upon the horrors of his times. In 'Rites and Ceremonies' he contemplates the Holocaust, as does 'It Out-Herods Herod. . .'. 'The Cost' is about the cost of war; 'Black Boy in the Dark' alludes to Vietnam and President Kennedy's assassination. Not all Hecht's work is so dark: 'The Ghost in the Martini' is a droll self-portrait, and some of the poems in *Flight among the Tombs* are built upon witty puns. He has produced versions of the poems by the Russian-born IOSIF BRODSKY.

Selected works: *Collected Earlier Poems* (1990); *The Transparent Man* (1990); *Flight among the Tombs* (1996); *Obbligati* (essays in criticism, 1986).

[CC]

Hejinian, Lyn (United States, b. 1941) Hejinian was born in San Francisco and educated at Harvard. As one of the central figures associated with Language poetry, Hejinian's writing typically reflects on our inability to separate 'life' from the language we use to conceive it, and is intensely self-conscious about its own processes. She composes her challenging, open-ended texts as collages, weaving together seemingly unconnected, sometimes lyrical, fragments.

Hejinian is best known for her innovative autobiographical prose poem, *My Life* (1980, 1987), in which fractured narrative and repetition offer glimpses of the poet's life, while simultaneously questioning memory, the work's own artifice, and the genre of autobiography itself.

Selected works: *The Cell* (1992).

[AE]

Hénein, Georges (Egypt, 1914–73) Hénein was born in Cairo in 1914 to an important diplomatic family who traveled extensively in Europe. His experimental texts, published after 1934, link him to Surrealism and emphasize his different experience. Soon Hénein became the first representative of Surrealism in Egypt. He published a novel *Déraison d'être* (*Insanity of Being*, 1938). Around the movement 'Art and Liberty', then in the journal *La part du sable* (*The Sand's Share*), Hénein attracted new avant-garde young intellectuals expressing their views in French or Arabic poetry and novels. His second work *Un temps de petite fille* (*Times of a Young Girl*, 1947) was widely praised. In 1948 Hénein separated himself from the Surrealists. His volume, *L'incompatible* (*The Incompatible*, 1949; reissued posthumously in 1981) utilizes puns and dream-images, and reflects his experiences as a native of Cairo. Fleeing Egypt in 1960, he lived in Paris until his death in 1973. He contributed to many French magazines.

[MS]

Herbert, Zbigniew (Poland, 1924–98) CZESLAW MILOSZ has written: 'If the key to contemporary Polish poetry is the collective experience of the last decades, Herbert is perhaps the most skillful in expressing it.' Born in the eastern Polish city of Lvov, Herbert experienced first hand the atrocities of World War II. In 1940 his uncle was executed by the Russians and in 1942–44 Herbert took part in the Home Army's underground activities. It was during this time that Herbert began writing poems, as well as studying Polish language and literature at a clandestine university. After the war, Herbert lived in Cracow, Torun, and Warsaw, obtaining degrees in economics, law, and philosophy. In 1950–56, at the height of Stalinist censorship, Herbert refused to participate in socialist realism and resigned from the official Polish Writers' Union. Instead, he wrote 'for the drawer', supporting himself as a bank clerk, shop attendant, accountant, designer of sanitation equipment for the peat industry, and finally – after the political thaw of the mid-1950s – administrator of the Association of Polish Composers.

In 1956 Herbert published his first book of poems, *Chord of Light*. It immediately established him as one of the most prominent representatives of the Generation of 'Kolumbowie', or Columbuses, those poets 'who first explored the new postwar social and political reality' (John and Bagdana Carpenter). These early poems introduce subjects characteristic of Herbert's oeuvre: classical literature, history, his own past, and quotidian objects. Over the next six years Herbert published two additional books of poems as well as a critically acclaimed volume of essays on European art and architecture, *The Barbarian in the Garden* (1962). His popularity grew in the West, and he received prestigious awards, such as the Lenau Prize (1965) and the Austrian Herder Prize (1973); his *Selected Poems* (1968) was published in the United States.

Throughout the 1970s, Herbert traveled abroad and taught briefly in Berlin and Los Angeles. Meanwhile, the publication of *Mr. Cogito* (1974) brought him even greater international acclaim. Here Herbert found the perfect 'pseudo-persona' – 'a born loser' who is tough minded – to meditate on such topics as dreams, suffering, redemption, and hell. In 1981, after the Solidarity movement lightened the reign of Communism, Herbert returned to Poland. However, later that year, martial law was imposed, and he was forced to remain there. In Herbert's volume *Report from the Besieged City* (1984), Mr. Cogito returns to chronicle life during the turmoil of martial law, promoting the importance of bearing witness to the truth of one's experience, as the best means to combat totalitarianism.

Ill and with little money, Herbert was able to move to Paris in 1986. In 1992, after the toppling of Communism, Herbert returned to Warsaw and resided there until his death in July 1998, after an extended struggle with emphysema. By this time Herbert had been awarded the renowned Jerusalem Prize and the T.S. Eliot Prize. *Elegy for the Departed* was published posthumously in 1999.

[MO]

Hernández, Miguel (Spain, 1910–42) Hernández rose to prominence in the 1930s and became Spain's greatest poet of the Civil War. Ironically, that very war hastened his death and cut short a productive career as poet and dramatist. Hernández was born and raised in Orihuela, in the south-eastern province of Alicante. After an uneventful childhood, he arrived in Madrid and was swept up in the intellectual and aesthetic currents of the Generation of 1927. This group of poets lauded the Baroque poet Luis de Góngora and was also influenced by Ortega y Gasset's *The Dehumanization of Art*. As a result, these poets did not view aesthetic ideals as dependent upon ordinary reality, but instead sought to create artistic worlds that were more profound and real than the world around them. Styles ranged from GUILLÉN's Symbolism to LORCA and ALEIXANDRE's Surrealism. Hernández's own first works were modeled on classical Spanish poets. *Lunar Specialist* (1933) examines the poetic in the everyday but hints at darker, shadow-like imagery which was to dominate later works.

Hernández' friendship with Chilean poet PABLO NERUDA, then a consul in Spain, proved pivotal throughout the remaining years of his life. Neruda's influence was both political (anticlerical) and artistic, as Hernández was drawn to Surrealist techniques. In 1936 Hernández joined the Republican army and experienced firsthand the tragedy of the Civil War. The conflict also inspired his greatest works, from the exuberant *Wind of the People* (1937) to the tragic, dark *The Man is Watching* (1939). Through combinations of epic and lyric modes, of classicism and surrealism, Hernández' Civil War poetry is considered one of the most accomplished artistic expressions of the conflict.

At war's end in 1939 Hernández was arrested and imprisoned for both his support of the Republic and his poetry's political slant. Bitter and dejected, he wrote some correspondence but little poetry from prison. Hernández saw his death sentence commuted to thirty years, but he died in prison in 1942.

[AB]

Hewett, Dorothy (Australia, b. 1923) Born and raised on a remote wheat ranch in Western Australia, Hewett emerged early on as a controversial figure in Australian literature. She once complained that critics focused more on the scandals in her personal life than on her writing. She published her first poetry at age seventeen. In 1942 she joined the Communist Party, but left in 1968, disillusioned by the Soviet persecution of dissidents. She moved to Sydney in 1948 and worked in a factory, then returned to Perth in 1960 to complete university studies. *Bobbin Up*, a proletarian novel based on her Sydney experiences, appeared in 1959. Always a crosser of genres, she is now probably better known as a dramatist than as a poet. Except for a few plays in the realistic tradition, her drama relies heavily on expressionism, allegory, and special effects. She lives in the Blue Mountains west of Sydney, and recently published an autobiography.

In spite of a longstanding commitment to Communism and to feminism, as well as rebellion against traditional mores, her poetry does not espouse causes. Instead, it tends toward the personal and confessional, often focusing on female sexuality. In more recent poems she invokes memory and weighs the contradictions stemming from a fear of and fascination with death. Abundant in imagery, often ribald and witty, at times elusive, always diverse in style, wide in its emotional range, and accomplished in structure, Hewett's poetry may best be described as adventurous.

Selected work: *Dorothy Hewett, Collected Poems 1940–95* (1995).

[RR]

Hewitt, John (Ireland, 1907–87) Hewitt is an Ulster poet known for his finely crafted, balanced lyrics that evoke Ulster in all its troubling complexity. Born a Methodist of planter stock, Hewitt's liberal humanism gave voice to the uneasy, often ambivalent relationship of Northern Irish Protestants to Catholics, to the landscape, and to a history fraught with colonization and bloodshed.

Hewitt was educated at Queen's University, Belfast, and in 1930–57 served as Curator of the Belfast Museum. An early interest in politics led to his participation in civil rights groups in Northern Ireland. Hewitt's poetry is elegant and controlled, as the poet frequently searches for and questions his identity. For example, in 'Once Alien Here', Hewitt describes his Protestant forebears and searches for an 'easy voice to utter each aright'.

He was the Art Director of the Herbert Art Gallery and Museum, Coventry, England, in 1957–72. In 1968, his *Collected Poems* voiced the struggles arising from his Protestant Irish identity. Although writing outside his native land, Hewitt began to look for a shared identity with Irish Catholics. Hewitt also wrote about landscape; his 1969 *The Day of the Corn Crake: Poems of the Nine Glens* focuses on the Glens of Antrim. He returned to Belfast in 1972, one of the worst periods of political violence in contemporary Belfast's history, and became involved with a younger generation of poets such as HEANEY, MONTAGUE, and MAHON. He and John Montague published *The Planter and the Gael* (1971). His *Collected Poems 1932–67* (1988) earned Hewitt widespread respect; his later verse evinces a loosening of style and form.

He married Roberta Black in 1934.

[CT]

Heym, Georg (Germany, 1887–1912) The fame of Heym, a major poet of early Expressionism, rests primarily on more than four hundred poems written during the last two years of his life. Though preparing for a bourgeois career, he felt caged in. In 1910 he joined Kurt Hiller's 'New Club' of poets, which advocated a politically engaged writing. Heym died in an ice skating accident.

Heym's apocalyptic poems, combining ugly reality and demonic visions, express an overpowering sense of threat that clashes with bourgeois society. Lonely, mad, and sick people live in twilight worlds, whose central motif, the modern and industrial city, is ruled by man-eating and fire-spewing demons. Intense metaphors culminate in inescapable destruction.

Selected works: *The Eternal Day* (1911); *Umbra Vitae* (1912).

[IRS]

Hijazi, Ahmad Abdel-mu'ti (Egypt, b. 1935) Born in the village of Tala in the Nile Delta, Hijazi studied in Egypt and France, and taught Arabic literature at the Université de Paris for several years before returning to Cairo in the late 1980s.

Like other Egyptian poets writing free verse after World War II, Hijazi turned to social realism. His early poetry depicts the problems encountered by peasants drawn to Cairo. His later poetry ranges in tone from personal confession to political rhetoric, and reveals his commitment to Arab socialism, Nasserism, and the Palestinian cause. Hijazi's imagery indicates the influence of Surrealism.

Selected works: *Heartless City* (1959); *Only Confession Remains* (1965); *Creatures of Night's Kingdom* (1978).

[WH]

Hikmet, Nazim (Turkey, 1902–63) Politically imprisoned by or exiled from his homeland for most of his life, Hikmet was a poet whose commitment to his Communist beliefs was equaled only by his skill as a free-verse writer. Born the son of an artist and a physician, Hikmet published his first works in his teens; by the time he was twenty, however, his art was already being combined with an interest in politics. This interest took him to Russia in 1922 where he would study for a time at Moscow's University of Workers of the East. He returned to Turkey in 1924 and began writing for the leftist *Resimli Ay* (*Pictorial Monthly*), though his columns there eventually made it necessary to escape again to Russia in 1926, this time meeting MAYAKOVSKY during his stay.

His return to Turkey in 1928 marks the start of his most blatant radical writings – and the start of his political problems as well. After 1928, Hikmet was jailed numerous times on numerous charges. Most were unsubstantiated, but all stemmed from the poet's unrelenting efforts to espouse Marxism and Communism in stridently anti-Communist Turkey. The longest sentence Hikmet served was his last: in 1938 he was convicted of inciting the Turkish army to revolt and began a twelve-year stay.

It is a testament to his art that Hikmet was convicted primarily because those in power feared the effect *Seyh Bedredden destani* (*The Epic of Sheik Bedredden*, 1936), a saga of peasant revolt, might have on their soldiers. Earlier volumes, such as *Jokond ile Si-Ya-U* (*La Gioconda and Si-Ya-U*, 1929), a fanciful tale of a Chinese student talking to the Mona Lisa and convincing her of the probity of Chinese Communism, also received both critical and popular attention, and made the authorities nervous. Yet perhaps Hikmet's greatest work was composed while he was imprisoned; *Memleketimden insan manzaralari* (*Human Landscapes*, 1966–7) charts the interrelatedness of everything: peasants and the wealthy, technologies of stasis and change, the voices of streets, the prisons, the marketplaces, the universities.

Despite his imprisonment, Hikmet's poetry – often circulated in manuscript form – was still read and admired. In 1949 an international campaign was begun for his release, which was effected the next year. That same year he was awarded the World Peace Prize, which he shared with his friend PABLO NERUDA. Despite this high-profile recognition, however, Turkish officials began to persecute Hikmet again almost immediately and so he fled to Moscow in 1951. Eight years later, after extensive traveling and after Turkey finally revoked his national status, he took Polish citizenship. Four years later he died of a heart attack, the third since his release from the Turkish prisons.

Poetically, Hikmet is important for bringing to Turkish verse Modernism's love of vernacular, modification (or defiance) of traditional forms, and consideration of the popular as viable poetic content. From early volumes, such as *1 + 1 =Bir (1 + 1 = One*, 1930), through to his *Secilmis siirler (Selected Poems*, 1967) and the English-language collection *Things I Didn't Know I Loved* (1976), Hikmet wrote a humanistic tale of struggle, endurance, and success. Although often ignored during his lifetime and frequently censored in his native country, Hikmet is a poet whose verse has given him posthumous international fame because of the power of his message and, equally important, the power of his craft.

[MW]

Hill, Geoffrey (England, b. 1932) Hill was born in Bromsgrove, Worcestershire, where he was educated at Fairfield Junior School and County High School. After earning his B.A. (1953) and M.A. (1959) at Keble College, Oxford, Hill taught at the University of Leeds from 1954 to 1980. Since then, the twice-married Hill has held positions at many institutions, including Cambridge, the University of Bristol, and Boston University, where he is presently employed.

Although Hill's poetry has long received wide critical acclaim, his early works, such as *For the Unfallen: Poems 1952–58* (1959), drew mixed responses. Refusing to react with his contemporaries against the inaccessibility of Modernist verse, Hill wrote (and writes) complex, difficult poems packed with scholarly allusions. In *For the Unfallen*, for instance, many of the allusions begin as biblical, then wander through quite contemporary questions of faith and doubt, as well as the paradoxical coupling of suffering and death to life. Such paradoxes, along with puns and wordplays, are favored layering techniques throughout Hill's work.

King Log (1968), Hill's second collection, also revolves around suffering. Its main sequence, 'Funeral Music', draws on the Wars of the Roses to discuss corrupting power and human cruelty, specifically the horrors of battle. Also in this volume are 'Ovid in the Third Reich', an exploration of the role of the poet in society, and 'The Songbook of Sebastian Arrurruz', a set of simply written love poems that manage to combine passion and an impersonal tone.

Mercian Hymns (1971) marked a departure from Hill's earlier style, if not his thematic fixations. These thirty prose poems fuse tales of the historical eighth-century King Offa with Hill's own childhood, invigorating the past with anachronistic infusions of the present. One of the many themes woven into the poetry charts Hill's development as a poet and his inspiration by the Muse of History; as in *King Log*, the relation of past to present and the effect of power on behavior are central. So, too, are suffering and guilt, themes made compelling by the very impersonality of Hill's poetic tone. The suffering that appears throughout Hill's work implies a communal guilt that his impersonal tone compels the reader to share. *Tenebrae* (1978) searches for salvation from this guilt by exploring martyrdoms.

In 1988 Hill moved to Brookline, Massachusetts; he has recently enjoyed an especially prolific period, which he credits to this exterior view of his homeland. The results of this effort are *Canaan* (1997) and *The Triumph of Love* (1998).

Hill has been called the best English poet of the twentieth century. Judging from the stream of honors he has received – which include the Eric Gregory Award (1961), Hawthornden Prize (1969), Faber Memorial Prize (1970), Whitbread Award (1971), Alice Hunt Bartlett Award (1971),

Heinemann Award (1971), Duff Cooper Memorial Prize (1979), and the Ingram Merrill Foundation Award (1985) – it seems likely that his work will endure well into subsequent periods.

Selected works: *Poems* (1952); *Preghiere* (1964); *Somewhere is Such a Kingdom: Poems 1952–71* (1975); *The Mystery of the Charity of Charles Péguy* (1983); *Collected Poems* (1985); *New and Collected Poems 1952–1992* (1994).

[JL]

Hill, Roberta (United States, b. 1947) Hill (formerly Whiteman) is a member of the Oneida Nation of Wisconsin. She grew up in and around Green Bay, Wisconsin, and was educated at the University of Wisconsin and the University of Montana, where she studied with poet Richard Hugo. She earned her Ph.D. from the University of Minnesota and now teaches at the University of Wisconsin, Madison.

Widely anthologized and published in literary journals, Hill has won a number of honors for her work, including a Lila-Wallace Reader's-Digest Award. Her poems are collected in two volumes, *Star Quilt* (1984) and *Philadelphia Flowers* (1996). Themes of her work arise from her careful juxtaposition of domestic and natural subjects. Often referring to her Oneida heritage, her poems consider the continuance of our ancestors as forces in the natural world and our human responsibility as stewards of the earth.

[HEE]

Hill, Selima (England, b. 1945) Hill was born in London, and her parents were artists. She received a special degree in English from New Hall, Cambridge University, in 1967. Hill's poetry reflects her personal interest in travel and in studying world (and particularly ancient) cultures.

Hill published her first book of poetry, *Saying Hello at the Station* (1984), when she was almost forty years old. Since then, her work has quickly become well-represented in anthologies such as the *Chatto Book of Post-Feminist Poetry*. As well as writing poems and reviews for numerous newspapers and magazines, Hill is the author of a script for the television program 'Why Women Write'.

The rhythm of Hill's mostly iambic poetry often appears deceptively relaxed, although the poet is capable of PLATH-like moments of great stress and disturbance. Hill connects apparently unrelated details to reveal states of mind and to study the life of the mind. Her interest in comparative mythology, ancient civilizations, and religions such as Buddhism and Rastafarianism also impacts on her poetry, which often features characters such as various deities from ancient Egypt.

Selected works: *My Darling Camel* (1988); *The Accumulation of Small Acts of Kindness* (1989); *A Little Book of Meat* (1993); *Trembling Hearts in the Bodies of Dogs: New and Selected Poems* (1994).

[LK]

Hillel, Ayin (Hillel Omer; Israel, 1926–90) Born in a kibbutz in the Valley of Jezreel, Hillel served in the Palmach, the elite military unit of the pre-state period; he also became one of the best known poets of that time. He later developed a successful career as a landscape architect and became a leading environmentalist. His literary work which shifted between dramatic poems reflecting the national struggle for identity, light satirical verse which was often set to music, and sophisticated, humorous children's poems, gained him wide recognition and affection. Omer's first collection, *Land of Noon*, appeared in 1950 and his last collection, *Holon Fables*, was published posthumously in 1991.

[ER]

Hippius, Zinaida Nikolaevna (Russia, 1869–1945) Hippius' father was a lawyer of German origin; her mother was the Siberian-born daughter of a local policeman. Hippius was educated mainly at home and spent a very short time in a boarding school for women in Kiev and then in the Fisher Gymnasium in Moscow (1882). From childhood she wrote, maintaining a diary. In 1889, she married the poet Dimitri Merezhkovksi and they moved to St Petersburg; their relationship lasted fifty-two years. In 1894 Hippius met A.L. Volynski, the publisher of the Symbolist journal *The Northern Herald*, in which she published her first important Symbolist poems, 'Dedication' and 'Song'. Her first volume, *Poetry Collection, 1889–1903*, appeared in 1904, and another volume, *Poetry Collection, Book 2, 1903–9*, in 1910. Between 1899 and 1901 Hippius collaborated with many writers and artists at the journal *The World of Art*, where she published her first critical works. Between 1901 and 1904, she organized and ran the Philosophical and Religious Gatherings; in 1903–4, she published the Symbolist journal, *The New Path*, printing poets such as BLOK. Hippius also began to publish prose in the 1890s in journals such as *The Northern Herald*, *The Herald of Europe*, and *Russian Thought*. Very opposed to the October Revolution, which was the subject of her poetry collection *The Last Poems, 1914–18*, Hippius emigrated with her husband to Poland in 1920, moving to Paris one year later. In 1922, *Poems: Diary 1911–21* appeared; *Radiance* came in 1939. One of the important themes in Hippius' poetry is the soul's turmoil, its constant search for harmony, and its inability to achieve this. She died an expatriate in Paris in 1945.

[RN]

Hippolyte, Kendel (St Lucia, b. 1952) Hippolyte was born in Castries. At present, he and his wife, the poet Jane King, direct the Lighthouse Theatre Company in St Lucia, where he also teaches at St Mary's College.

Hippolyte is one of the Caribbean's most original and innovative poetic voices. His poetry is characterized by a high degree of formal experimentation. In collections such as *Island in the Sun, Side Two . . .* (1980), *Bearings* (1986), and *The Labyrinth* (1991), he has produced a thoroughly modern poetry utilizing Caribbean English and exhibiting a deep-felt connection with 'roots-culture'.

[IS]

Hirsch, Edward (United States, b. 1950) MacArthur Fellow and National Book Critics Circle Award winner, Hirsch was born in Chicago, received his B.A. from Grinnell College (1972) and his Ph.D. from the University of Pennsylvania (1979). He teaches at the University of Houston.

Hirsch's work elicits the poignancy of the closely observed, and in so doing meditates upon questions of metaphysics, particularly teleology. Hirsch ably renders otherwise abstract material (such as love and religion) with precise detail, illuminating wisdom, and charismatic wit. In recent work such as *On Love* (1998), Hirsch has begun to explore the dramatic monologue and the dramatic lyric.

Selected works: *For the Sleepwalkers* (1981); *Wild Gratitude* (1986); *The Night Parade* (1989); *Earthly Measures* (1994).

[KM]

Hjartarson, Snorri (Iceland, 1906–86) Winner of the Nordic Council's Literary Prize (1981), and Chief Librarian of the municipal library in Reykjavík, Hjartarson contributed to defining the voice of Icelandic poetry. Born to well-to-do parents in western Iceland, Hjartarson started writing poetry early but abandoned it to study painting in Copenhagen and Oslo, where he also published short stories and a novel. Since his return to Iceland in 1936, however, he has written poetry praising his motherland and expressing joy at coming back to 'dwell by the anvil'. His *Kvædi* (*Poems*, 1944), a hymn to Iceland's independence, won him immediate recognition. While often written in traditional form, the poems surprise the reader with unexpected assonance and jolting rhymes. Hjartarson's second book, *Á Gnitaheiði*

(*On Gnitaheiði*, 1952) mourns Iceland's place in post-war world politics.

[YB]

Hobsbaum, Philip (England, b. 1932) Hobsbaum was born in London, and went on to attend Downing College, Cambridge (B.A. 1955, M.A. 1960), and the University of Sheffield (Ph.D. 1968).

Hobsbaum's poetry is riddled with notions of isolation and alienation, as well as a notable energy. Often melodramatic and admittedly 'incurably romantic', his work is also hauntingly realistic and overtly sarcastic, a paradoxical move no doubt made possible by his own experience of exile. Hobsbaum's confessional, often juvenile, poems have inspired contemptuous reviews, and he has not published a volume of poetry since 1972.

Selected works: *The Place's Fault* (1964); *In Retreat and Other Poems* (1966); *Coming out Fighting* (1969); *Some Lovely Glorious Nothing: A Poem* (1969); *Women and Animals* (1972).

[SG]

Hodgins, Philip (Australia, 1959–95) Hodgins was born in Shepparton, Victoria, where he experienced a country childhood that was to be a major source of his poetic themes. Hodgins resurrected the pastoral poem for his own time, becoming a poet at once thoroughly traditional and utterly contemporary. In *Animal Warmth* (1990) and the verse novel *The Dispossessed* (1994) Hodgins excelled not only in describing landscape but in depicting the psychology and character of the Australian farmer. From his mid-twenties, he knew he had chronic myeloid leukemia, and his own illness became a major theme of his poetry, as in *Blood and Bone* (1986). *Seeing Things* (1995) is filled with images of hospitalization and physical suffering, and is a harrowing if truly rewarding collection. The early loss of Hodgins was widely considered a calamity for Australian poetry.

[NB]

Hoffman, Daniel (United States, b. 1923) Author of nine books of poems, Hoffman writes both formal and free verse, and writes equally well of the natural world and historical subjects, folklore and myth. All these interests coalesce in what may be his signature book, *Brotherly Love* (1980), about William Penn, founder of the city of Philadelphia.

Hoffman is also a considerable critic, having published books on Stephen Crane, Edgar Allan Poe, form and fable in American fiction, and myth in the poetry of W.B. YEATS, ROBERT GRAVES, and EDWIN MUIR.

Currently poet-in-residence at the University of Pennsylvania, he previously taught at Swarthmore College, Columbia University, and University of Cincinnati, and lectured at the International School of Yeats Studies in Sligo, Ireland.

Hoffman was born in Larchmont, New York. He attended Columbia University, with a three-year interruption in 1943–46 to serve in the U.S. Army Air Force. His first book won the Yale Series of Younger Poets Award in 1954. He was the 1973–74 Consultant in Poetry of the Library of Congress.

Selected works: *New and Selected Poems: Hang-Gliding from Helicon* (1988); *Middens of the Tribe* (1995); *Words to Create a World* (prose, 1993).

[RP]

Hofmannsthal, Hugo von (Austria, 1874–1929) Born in Vienna of Austrian, Jewish, and Lombard roots, Hofmannsthal exemplified the multi-ethnic culture of the Austrian monarchy before World War I. Hofmannsthal's first publications at age seventeen brought him early fame. Ending his academic career in 1901, he married and lived as a freelance writer near Vienna until his death.

For poetry, only his first phase is central. Belonging to the 'Young Vienna' group with Arthur Schnitzler and others, Hofmannsthal was influenced by European Aestheticism. However, he found his own Symbolist voice by 1891 with poems whose sounds approach *poésie pure*. In 1892 Hofmannsthal retained his independence from STEFAN GEORGE's circle. The poems written between 1894 and 1896 such as 'Secret of the World' and 'Some of course . . .' are his best because of their added intensity, asserting a magical world beyond the everyday. Initially published in magazines, the poems were later collected in various volumes (first in 1903).

About 1900, Hofmannsthal virtually ceased to write poems. However, the crucial text of this transitional phase, the fictitious Lord Chandos letter (1902), is a core document of Modernism. Articulating doubt in language and hope for a future language to express the totality of existence, it marked Hofmannsthal's shift from the private realm of poetry (and lyrical dramas) in his first phase to his next phase of more publicly oriented, yet still poetic, texts for theater production, including collaborations with Richard Strauss (libretti) and Max Reinhardt (the Salzburg Festival).

[IRS]

Hogan, Linda Hendersen (United States, b. 1947) Born in Denver, Hogan spent part of her childhood in Germany. Much of her writing arises from her ties to the Oklahoma Chickasaw tribe from which she is descended.

Hogan's education includes an M.A. from the University of Colorado and she has taught and lectured at Colorado Women's College and the University of Minnesota. Among her fellowships and awards are an American Book Award, a John Simon Guggenheim Fellowship, and a National Endowment for the Arts grant.

The poetry Hogan has produced between 1978 and 1990 has evolved in its concerns from Hogan's particular Chickasaw perspective to more universal themes that connect humans and the living world. Political in its direct address of environmental, class, and feminist issues, her work also grounds itself in history and landscape. Mother–daughter relationships figure frequently in both Hogan's poetry and prose.

Described as 'intricate' and 'mysterious', Hogan's poems are full of animals, plants, natural places, and art – emblems familiar to Native Americans that she makes available for the healing of all.

Selected works: *Calling Myself Home* (1978); *Daughters, I love You* (1981); *Savings* (1987); *The Book of Medicines* (1993).

[HEE]

Holan, Vladimir (Czech Republic, 1905–80) Coming to prominence with the 1930 publication of *Triumf smrti* (*The Triumph of Death*), Holan established himself as one of the dominant voices of inter-war Czechoslovakia. Though for a time he was a civil servant, it was as editor of the arts journal *Zivot* (1933–38) that he promoted what he called 'poetism', an approach to poetry that eschewed the political in favor of the metaphysical, an approach also favored at the time by JAROSLAV SEIFERT. Censured until 1963 during the Communist regime, Holan published frequently and powerfully until the end of his life.

Selected works: *Cesta mraku* (*Cloudy Way*, 1947); *Four Poems* (1970); *Mirroring: Selected Poems* (1985).

[MW]

Holden, Molly (England, 1927–81) Holden was born in London, and graduated with honors from King's College, where she also earned her M.A. in 1951. Holden is known for her conversational adaptations of conventional poetic forms.

In 1964, Holden published a successful book of poems, *The Bright Cloud*; that same year, she was disabled by multiple sclerosis. Although she continued to publish for many years, the irony of her simultaneous achievement and loss deeply affected her later work.

Holden's poems meticulously describe the natural world and illustrate her faith in the cyclical nature of life's degeneration and regeneration. For inspiration, Holden turned to the English countryside, history, and her family.

Selected works: *A Hill Like a Horse* (1963); *To Make Me Grieve* (1968); *Air and Chill Earth* (1971); *A Speckled Bush* (1974); *The Country Over* (1975); *Selected Poems* (1987).

[LK]

Hollander, John (United States, b. 1929) Hollander was born in New York, attended Columbia University (B.A. and M.A.) and received a Ph.D. from Indiana University. His first volume was selected by W. H. AUDEN for the Yale Younger Poets series in 1958. An important editor, scholar and critic of poetry, Hollander is Professor of English at Yale University.

Hollander is known, like Auden, for his impressive formal skill and urbane wit. The effectiveness of Hollander's work depends on the technical achievement, the subtlety, and the intellectual rigor of his explorations. In his stately, controlled poems, Hollander frequently moves from rather ordinary experiences to broader metaphysical speculations about the human mind and its relationship to the world. His poems have always exuded erudition, well-crafted polish, and a love of wordplay and puns, though in more recent work Hollander has moved toward a more introspective and personal voice.

Selected works: *A Crackling of Thorns* (1958); *Movie-Going* (1962); *Blue Wine* (1979); *In Time and Place* (1986); *Selected Poems* (1993).

[AE]

Holub, Miroslav (Czech Republic, 1923–98) Holub, internationally renowned as an immunologist, travel writer, and poet, was born in Pilsen, Czechoslovakia. He earned an M.D. from Charles University School of Medicine, Prague, in 1953 and a Ph.D. in immunology from the Czechoslovak Academy of Sciences Institute of Microbiology in 1958.

Scientific training gave Holub a spareness and rationality of diction unusual in the lyrical Czech tradition – he pursued, as he has said, 'the energy, tension, and illumination contained in the fact itself'. Additionally, the brutal and often censorial Communist regime led Holub to use surreal imagery and absurdist humor that clash with his objectivity and scientific settings.

Formally, Holub wrote in a free verse modeled on WILLIAM CARLOS WILLIAMS in its compressed, careful diction. Unlike Williams, however, he does not seek simplicity, but rather the clarification of quite complex themes: as Guy Davenport put it, to be 'intelligent rather than wise'.

In 1973 a letter affirming loyalty to the neo-Stalinist authorities appeared in the papers under Holub's name; consequently, he was unable to publish in Czechoslovakia for the next nine years, and his belief in rational progress was shaken. After the 1989 Revolution, Holub advocated a more optimistic tone while continuing his struggle against irrationality and superstition.

Holub received numerous publishers' awards, the Czechoslovak Writers' Union Prize, and the Czechoslovak Academy of Sciences Purkynje Medal in 1988, and a George Theiner Award in 1991. He is the author of more than 120 scientific papers and monographs.

Selected works: *Denní Služba* (*Day Duty*, 1958); *Jdi a Otevři Dveře* (*Go and Open the Door*, 1962); *Zcela Nesoustavná Zoologie* (*A Completely Unsystematic Zoology*, 1963); *Selected Poems* (1967); *Ačkoli* (*Although*, 1969); *Události* (*Events*, 1971); *Notes of a Clay Pigeon* (1977); *Sagittal Section* (1980); *The Fly* (1987); *Poems before and after: Collected English Translations* (1990); *Intensive Care: Selected and New Poems* (1996).

[JL]

Hongo, Garrett (United States, b. 1951) Hongo was born in Hawaii of first generation Japanese immigrants. He writes lush poems that are catalogues of detail – of life in a working-class home within an immigrant community in Hawaii, and of Japanese–Buddhist culture. Hongo's most effective poems are the simpler ones, in which the easy language and precise information combine to illuminate elemental themes of family, fear, and heredity. These poems create an intimate atmosphere without exoticizing Hongo's multicultural identity. He teaches at the University of Oregon, Eugene.

Selected works: *Yellow Light* (1982); *The River of Heaven* (1988); *Volcano: A Memoir of Hawaii* (1995).

[CC]

Hope, A.D. (Australia, 1907–2000) Australia's best-known poet internationally, Hope was nearly fifty when he published his first volume of poetry. He spent his early years in rural Tasmania where his father was a Presbyterian minister. Educated at home until he was fourteen, he went to the mainland to attend preparatory school, then graduated in philosophy with honors from the University of Sydney. After study at Oxford, he returned to Australia in mid-Depression and taught in public schools until he obtained a university position in 1937. In 1951 he became professor of English at the Australian National University where he remained until retirement. In the following years, Hope continued to publish poetry, lecture, and exert his influence and considerable critical ability to promote Australian literature. In one of his later poems, 'Spatlese', he concluded that 'Old men should be adventurous'. He has received numerous awards, both in Australia and abroad.

Although writing in a time when experimentation in Australian poetry prevailed, Hope has always adhered to traditional verse forms. His sophisticated work relies heavily on literary, mythological, and biblical materials. Recognizing the universal application of mythology, he sees it as helping to define humankind's place in the universe. In Hope's view, it is the poet's duty to give modern life meaning through a creative reinterpretation of the timeless stories. This he has done throughout his long career, even though he has been criticized for not writing about Australia and the Australian experience.

Selected works: *A Late Picking: Poems 1965–74* (1975); *Selected Poems* (1986).

[RR]

Hopkins, Kenneth (England, 1914–88) Hopkins was apprenticed to an ironmonger at the age of fourteen, but at John Cowper Powys' urging he chose a life of literature and left his birthplace, Bournemouth, for London in 1938. Hopkins is known primarily for more than two hundred love poems, frequently sonnets, he wrote to his wife, Elizabeth Coward. Besides writing poetry, he founded the Grasshopper Press and served as a visiting professor at the University of Texas.

Selected works: *Love and Elizabeth* (1944); *Collected Poems: 1935–66* (1970); *Collected Poems: 1966–77* (1978); *Introits and Indulgences: Poems* (1982); *The End of a Golden String: Poems* (1984); *She is my Bright and Smiling and Shy Dear: Poems* (1985).

[JL]

Housman, A.E. (England, 1859–1936) Though best remembered as the author of the immensely popular *A Shropshire Lad* (1896), Alfred Edward Housman spent most of his life working as a classical scholar. Early in his life, he was an outstanding scholar, and received a scholarship to St John's College, Oxford. However, Housman failed his final exam in 1881 and in 1882 completed his 'pass' degree. This perceived failure motivated him during the decade that followed to become one of the great classical scholars.

Housman's scholarly work includes a five-volume edition of the *Astronomica* of Manilus, a first-century Latin poet. After his father's death in 1894, Housman turned to poetry and published *A Shropshire Lad*. Although not successful in its first printing, the book later became immensely popular, influencing a generation of English adolescents who frequently memorized the entire book.

Although never well-received by critics, *A Shropshire Lad* enjoyed popular success for many reasons, particularly its appeal to the sensibility of the male adolescent. Housman's favorite theme is time and the inevitability of death, and his poems are filled with stoic bitterness and passionate lyricism. The poetry is always melancholy and frequently pessimistic, with love doomed by infidelity or death. Ballad stanzas with varying rhyme and accent patterns reflect Housman's influences, which include Shakespeare's songs, Scottish border ballads, and the German poet Heinrich Heine.

Selected works: *Last Poems* (1922); *More Poems* (1936); *The Collected Poems of A.E. Housman* (1939); *Complete Poems: Centennial Edition* (1959).

[LK]

Houston, Libby (England, b. 1941) Born in London, Houston was raised in the West Country and obtained her education at Lady Margaret Hall in Oxford. She was married to illustrator Malcolm Dean and currently works as a researcher in Bristol; she also often lends her poetic voice to BBC radio programs.

Houston's poetry displays an affinity with the American Beat poets of the 1960s, particularly in her earlier poems. In later works Houston has created less even rhythms within longer poems of more depth and shadow. Houston's career displays a marked evolution through varied styles and themes as well as broad talent.

Selected works: *A Stained Glass Raree Show* (1967); *Plain Clothes* (1971); *At the Mercy* (1980); *Necessity* (1988).

[MK]

Hove, Chenjerai (Zimbabwe, b. 1954) After graduating from Gweru Teacher's College in 1977, Hove taught English in rural Zimbabwe while pursuing a degree in literature and education through a University of South Africa correspondence course. In 1981 he moved into editing, first at Mambo Press, and then at Zimbabwe Publishing House. In 1984 he helped to found the Zimbabwe Writers Union, and acted as its chairman until 1987. His first poetry collection, *Up in Arms*, was published in 1982. Hove went on to publish *Swimming in Floods of Tears* (1983, with Zambian poet Lyamba wa Kabika), and another book of poetry, *Red Hills of Home* (1985). Hove's Shona poetry appears exclusively in anthologies, such as *Chakarira Chindunduma* (*Rebellion Sounds*, 1985) and *Uyavaya Hwenduri Dzechinyakare* (*A Frenzy of Poems of Long Ago*, 1988); some of his English poetry has been anthologized, as well.

[KT]

Howard, Richard (United States, b. 1929) Richard Joseph Howard is a twentieth-century master of dramatic speech in poetry and perhaps our best living literary translator of French. He is also a noted critic of contemporary poets.

Howard was born in Cleveland, Ohio; throughout his life he has traveled widely. He earned a B.A. and M.A. from Columbia University and also studied at the Sorbonne. After teaching at many universities, Howard has returned, as a teacher, to Columbia. He has long been a prominent poetry editor of *The Paris Review*.

Howard's first collection of poems, *Quantities* (1962), established his strong control over syllabics, partly through highly organized stanza patterns. His third collection, *Untitled Subjects*, a series of dramatic monologues, demonstrates a continuation of Robert Browning's fascination with voice – and won the 1970 Pulitzer.

In 1974, with *Two-Part Inventions*, Howard expanded his domain of voice to include imagined dialogues. Clearly influenced by Oscar Wilde – and including him in one of these poems – Howard made new use of wit as a means of developing an assumed voice to its fullest expression of itself. More recently, Howard has been working with several voices within a single poem – pressing against the border of verse drama.

Akin to W.H. AUDEN and JAMES MERRILL in formal concerns, to WALLACE STEVENS in abstract meditations, Howard is closer to EZRA POUND in efforts to give verbal life to the creative dead. Howard's evocations, however, do not convey faith in the successful resurrection of cultural history. Howard's poetic impulse is tragic insofar as he frames the conflict between history as the essential component of present culture and history as inevitable loss.

[CC]

Howe, Susan (United States, b. 1937) Born to a Harvard law professor and an Irish playwright and actress, Howe is a poet of both historical scholarship and the drama of ideological conflict. Howe attended the Boston Museum of Fine Arts and began her career as a painter. Her first book of poetry, *Hinge Picture* (1974), demonstrated her interest in visual dynamics and the tension between personal and cultural histories. To date, the prolific Howe has published eighteen works of poetry and criticism, and she has been awarded the American Book Award (1980 and 1981) and the Roy Harvey Pearce Award (1996). She is often associated with an avant-garde poetic, and with the Language poets (see BERNSTEIN, PALMER, SILLIMAN).

Howe is married to the sculptor David von Schlegell; she is professor of English at the State University of New York at Buffalo.

[DC]

Hudgins, Andrew (United States, b. 1951) Hudgins was born in Killeen, Texas, and educated at Huntingdon College, Syracuse University, and the universities of Alabama and Iowa. He teaches at the University of Cincinnati.

Hudgins' poetry is drawn from the culture of the South. Focusing on fundamentalist religion, civil war and personal history, and the elaborate rules of family and social interaction, it is consistently disturbing in its analysis of human behavior. Hudgins' use of the bizarre and shocking is often remarked upon, but these devices are not employed for their own sakes; rather, they serve to foreground the moral choices that must be made in the extremity of ordinary life.

Selected works: *The Never-Ending* (1991); *The Glass Hammer: A Southern Childhood* (1994); *Babylon in a Jar* (1998).

[JT]

Hughes, Langston (United States, 1902–67) Often called the Poet Laureate of Harlem, a versatile writer of poetry, fiction, drama, non-fiction, translations and children's books, James Mercer Langston Hughes is the most influential African-American writer of the twentieth century. He was born in Joplin, Missouri, raised in poverty by his mother, and briefly attended Columbia University in 1921. That same year his poem 'The Negro Speaks of Rivers' was published, establishing one of his career's themes: the dignity and unity conferred by African origin.

Although he traveled widely throughout his life, he was always drawn to Harlem, New York, and became a major participant in the Harlem Renaissance, where he was joined by the writers COUNTEE CULLEN and JEAN TOOMER, among others. His first book, *The Weary Blues* (1926), a collection of poems, was helped into print by VACHEL LINDSAY, whom Hughes met as a busboy. This volume marks a strong beginning to his lifelong efforts to bring African-American life and music into poetry.

Fine Clothes to the Jew (1927) shows Hughes' intense use of the blues for its formal qualities and subject matter: the hard lives of African-Americans. The highly effective poems in his first two books refreshed and altered the development of twentieth-century African-American poetry. At the time, however, they were denigrated as unpoetic, that is, insufficiently wrought and improperly obsessed with sexual, racial, and lower-class realism.

Soon after the publication of *Fine Clothes to the Jew*, Hughes attended Lincoln University, in Pennsylvania, graduating in 1929. During the Great Depression, Hughes wrote poetry radically committed to social justice. His *Scottsboro Limited* (1932), for example, takes up the cause of the 'Scottsboro 9', nine African-American men unjustly accused of rape. Hughes continued his use of African-American music, now bebop jazz, in *Montage of a Dream Deferred* (1951). In this collection of poems attacking the persistence of racism, the bebop influence often helps Hughes to a sharp satire, as with the scatting and aggressive discontinuities of narrative in 'Dream Boogie'. The prophetic warnings of further racial violence contained in 'Harlem', an enduringly popular poem, show a more subtle borrowing from bebop, the linked rhetorical questions in the poem suggesting the surprising forward drive generated by the harmonics of bebop.

Although Hughes at times disavowed some of his more radical views, in his last book of poetry, *The Panther and the Lash* (1967), he does not lessen his outrage against racial injustice. His major efforts to change African-American poetry of the twentieth century – to celebrate the miseries and joys of African-American urban life and to incorporate the music as well as the moral protest of his people – have been successful.

Perhaps most important among his other voluminous writings are his short stories, especially those in *The Ways of White Folks* (1934) and his stories of Jesse B. Simple (or Semple). The recurring character, Simple, appears deficient in understanding but proves himself a knowing satirist.

[CC]

Hughes, Ted (England, 1930–98) Edward James Hughes was born in the mill town of Mytholmroyd, Yorkshire, the son of a carpenter. He went to a local school, where he began writing poems. Hughes later attended Cambridge where he met the American poet SYLVIA PLATH, whom he married in 1956. He will be as well remembered for that doomed marriage as for being one of Britain's greatest twentieth-century poets.

His first book, *Hawk in the Rain* (1957), met immediate acclaim for its piercingly direct diction and savagely chaotic language. That volume introduced Hughes' predilection for presenting extreme situations, as represented by his famous animal poems which, in their metaphors and images, are emblematic of human behavior. The negotiation between our animal nature and our denial of it appears as a theme throughout Hughes' prolific career. Many of his works took an unsentimental look at nature, which he saw as beautiful but also as violent and bloody. His early life in the bleak environment of the Yorkshire Pennines in northern England has been pinpointed as a major influence in his poetic vision. His verse is markedly passionate and deeply engaging, and many find this to be at odds with his reticent, ascetic personality.

Hughes won many honors including a Guggenheim Fellowship (1959), the Somerset Maugham Award (1960), the Premio Internazionale Taormina (1973) and the Queen's Medal for Poetry (1974). In 1979, Hughes led a poll as Britain's best poet. In 1984, at age 54, he was appointed Poet Laureate of Britain – the youngest to hold this prestigious post since Alfred, Lord Tennyson. Just thirteen days before his death, Queen Elizabeth honored Hughes with the Order of Merit.

Some months before he died from cancer in 1998, Hughes stunned the literary world with *Birthday Letters*, a series of previously unknown impassioned poems to Plath, who killed herself in 1963 after their separation. A near recluse in later years, Hughes had remained silent about his relationship with the American writer. The work shot to the top of best-seller lists, selling 90,000 copies – almost unheard of for a volume of poetry – and had critics comparing him to Blake, Keats, and AUDEN.

Selected works: *Pike* (1959); *Lupercal* (1960); *Crow: From the Life and Songs of the Crow* (1970); *Selected Poems, 1957–67* (1972); *Gaudete* (1977); *Moortown* (1979); *River* (1983); *New Selected Poems: 1957–94* (1995).

[EM]

Hugo, Richard (United States, 1923–82) Born in Seattle, Hugo spent much of his life in the Pacific Northwest. He served as a bombardier in World War II, before earning his B.A. (1948) and M.A. degrees from the University of Washington; then he took a job with Boeing as a technical writer, until accepting a job as a professor of English at the University of Montana in Missoula.

Hugo's first volume of poetry, *A Run of Jacks*, was published in 1961, but contains his works from the 1940s and 1950s. He published six volumes of poetry in his relatively brief life, including *What Thou Lovest Well* and his highly renowned *31 Letters and 13 Dreams*. In *31 Letters*, Hugo becomes his most personal and psychoanalytic, a move favored by critics. His honors include the Northwest Writers Award (1966) and a Rockefeller Foundation grant (1967).

Hugo was a great teacher of poetry. A collection of lectures from his poetry class entitled *The Triggering Town* instructs young writers how to banish the bad habits that youthful efforts inevitably inspire.

Hugo's subject matter include old Northwestern towns, fishing, and baseball. He creates exquisite landscapes and seascapes with an almost photographic precision. While his works are descriptive of the exterior world, they poignantly present the poet's own psyche and emotions. He has been called a confessional poet – not because he writes strictly about personal experience, but because his works make obvious, sometimes painfully so, how close Hugo's objects are to his circumstances.

[CP]

Huidobro, Vicente (Vicente Garcia Huidobro Fernandez; Chile, 1893–1948) Born into a wealthy Santiago family, the poet, novelist, and playwright Vicente Huidobro published his first book, *Ecos del alma* (*Echoes of the Soul*) in 1911. As with much of his work, these poems are in free verse with no evident rhyme or rhythm. In 1912, with other poets of his generation, he edited the influential magazine *Musa Joven* (*Young Muse*). He is recognized as the father of the poetic movement known as Creacionismo: 'The poem must be a reality in itself, not a copy of external reality'. In 1916 he traveled to Paris and Madrid, where he met and became friends with Picasso, APOLLINAIRE, REVERDY, TZARA, and BRETON. In 1931 he published his most famous poem *Altazor*. He died in Cartagena, Colombia.

Selected works: *Canciones en la noche* (*Songs in the Night*, 1913), *La gruta del silencio* (*The Grotto of Silence*, 1913); *Las Pagodas ocultas* (*Hidden Pagodas*, 1914); *Ver y palpar* (*To See and Touch*, 1941); *El ciudadano de olvido* (*The Citizen of Forgetfulness*, 1941).

[MN]

Hulme, T. E. (England, 1883–1917) Perhaps more important as an essayist and 'philosophic amateur' than as a poet, Thomas Ernest Hulme published only six poems before he died while serving with the Royal Marines Artillery. By influencing such luminaries as EZRA POUND and T. S. ELIOT with his poems and anti-Romantic tracts, Hulme in large part gave impetus to the Imagist school, which rejected Victorian ideals and sought to forge a new aesthetic valuing precise sensory impressions over flowery techniques and Symbolism.

Selected works: *The Complete Poetical Works of T. E. Hulme* (an addendum to Ezra Pound's *Ripostes*, 1912); *Speculations* (1924); *Notes on Language and Style* (1929).

[JL]

I

Ibarbourou, Juana de (Uruguay, 1892–1979) Crowned 'Juana of the Americas' in 1929, Ibarbourou became famous for the spontaneous and sensual Modernist verse of her youth. The poems, mostly sonnets, of *Las lenguas de diamante* (*Tongues of Diamond*, 1919) and *Raiz salvaje* (*Savage Root*, 1922), however, yield to the more restrained, philosophical lyrics of *La rosa de los vientos* (*The Rose of the Winds*, 1930). Later work, deeply religious, uses the vanguardist styles of the prose poem and free verse. Ibarbourou received the prize of the Uruguayan Academy of Letters in 1947 and was nominated for the Nobel Prize in 1959. Her writing is collected in *Obras Completas* (*Complete Works*, 1953).

[LKA]

Ibrahim, Hafiz (Egypt, 1871–1932) Ibrahim achieved greater popularity during his lifetime than his more prominent and better renowned contemporary, AHMAD SHAWQI. Their names are often linked and their work compared. Both wrote within the classical tradition, but Ibrahim was closer than the aristocratic Shawqi to the concerns of ordinary people, treating poverty and other social problems. Ibrahim was also a platform poet in the best sense of the word; his poems on momentous occasions galvanized public opinion. He wrote poetic social commentary using irony and satire.

His poetry is collected in *Diwan Hafiz Ibrahim* (1939).

[WH]

Ieronim, Ioana (Romania, b. 1947) A native of Transylvania, Ieronim was educated at the University of Bucharest and was an editor and translator for the Scientific and Encyclopedic Press for many years. In 1992 she became Romania's cultural attaché to the United States, subsequently working in the Bucharest offices of the Fulbright Soros Foundation.

A 'meticulous observer of everyday scenes' (D. Curticǎ-peanu), Ieronim practices a lyricism in which intellectual distance does not preclude emotional engagement with the material world nor recognition of the sublime amid daily routines. Preoccupied by temporality (*The Curtain*, 1983) and inconsistency (*Monday Mornings*, 1987), Ieronim makes extensive use of geometric, numeric, and alphabetic symbolism (*Poems*, 1986). *The Fool's Triumph* (1992), a delicate series of prose poems reconstituting the poet's childhood, focuses on the dissonance between the individual's inner time and accelerated, oppressive social time. Here, 'Laughter and noise over a well-padlocked silence' ('In the Dining Room') characterize 1950s Stalinist Romania; the child finds refuge in the world of the fairy-tale, but harsh reality is always lurking.

[GF]

Illyés, Gyula (Hungary, 1902–83) If his friend ATTILA JÓZSEF was the poet of Hungary's urban poor, then Nobel Prize nominee Illyés was the poet of its rural peasants. A farm laborer's son, he was nonetheless classically educated, living and studying for a time in Paris; when he returned, he co-edited the progressive magazine *Nyugat* (*West*, 1937–41) and edited its successor *Magyar Csillag* (*Hungarian Star*, 1941–4). 'One Sentence on Tyranny' (1950, published 1956) which criticized the Rákosi dictatorship and despotism in general, was his most famous poem, but it was his prose volume *Puszták népe* (*The People of the Puszta*, 1936) which solidified his reputation as a people's writer. His concerns with domestic and European political developments, particularly with regard to their impact upon oppressed workers, lasted his whole life. His poetic legacy remains one of a 'realist with a lyric disposition' (Joseph Reményi).

Selected works: *Nehéz föld* (*Heavy Earth*, 1928); *Ifjúság* (*Youth*, 1934); *A kacsalaba forgo var* (*The Wonder Castle*, 1936); *Rend a romokban* (*Order in the Ruins*, 1937); *Egy év* (*One Year*, 1945); *Nem volt eleg* (*It Was Not Enough*, 1962).

[MW]

Ingamells, Rex (Reginald Charles; Australia, 1913–55) Born in Orroroo, South Australia, Ingamells first attended Prince Albert College and then studied history at Adelaide University. At the latter, he became strongly interested in Aboriginal culture, which became a focus in all his subsequent poetry. Acting on his interest, in the late 1930s, Ingamells founded the Jindyworobak movement, which sought to establish a uniquely Australian culture and literature by fusing Aboriginal myth and language with European forms and descriptions of the Australian landscape.

The Great South Land (1951) won the Grace Leven Prize; Ingamells died in a car accident four years later.

Selected works: *Gumtops* (1935); *Forgotten People* (1936); *Sun-Freedom* (1938); *Memory of Hills* (1940); *Content Are the Quiet Ranges* (1943); *Year* (1945); *Come Walkabout* (1948).

[JL]

Inkala, Jouni (Finland, b. 1966) Inkala, a poet and a university lecturer in the field of comparative literature, based his licentiate work on E.E. CUMMINGS' poetry. His first collection *Tässä sen reuna* (Herein Its Edge, 1992) received much critical attention and was chosen as a finalist for the prestigious Finlandia Prize. It received the J.H. Erkko Award for the best first collection by a poet. He is generally regarded as a young genius who will lead Finnish poetry in new directions. His second collection *Huonetta ja sukua* (Of Dwelling and Kin, 1994) brilliantly exemplifies the way in which a stultified tradition is overcome by a new living poetic expression. In Inkala's textually conscious writing we encounter the aesthetics of presence, a mind reflecting on its own reflections; in keeping with current theoretical stance, there is in his writing an engagement in the life of the mind without a concomitant mystification of the mind.

[SP]

Iqbal, Shaikh Muhammad (India, 1879–1938) The son of a tailor in the small industrial city of Sialkot in Punjab, Iqbal began his formal education at the local mission school and later studied at Punjab University in Lahore, the provincial capital. He studied philosophy at Cambridge and Heidelberg, where he wrote a dissertation on Persian metaphysics. He returned to Lahore in 1908, having also qualified for the Bar. He taught for several years but resigned to embark on an indifferent career as a lawyer.

Iqbal published three Urdu and three Persian books of poetry and one that combined verse in both languages, as well as a well-known series of English lectures on *The Reconstruction of Religious Thought in Islam*. Although he was identified with the movement for the separate Muslim state of Pakistan, an early poem of his is still sung by Indian schoolchildren as an unofficial national anthem. In another he refers to himself as a rake, yet his poems often gave exegesis of the Quran and he is now usually referred to as Alama Iqbal, the title being a designation for a theologian. In 1922 he was made a British knight.

His journey to the West produced a series of narrative and didactic poems, including 'Shikva', or 'Complaint', which exhorted God to tell his believers why they languished while unbelievers thrived. This poem and others earned a huge following when Iqbal began to recite them on returning to India.

At a time when the Ottoman Empire was in its final decline and Muslim kingdoms were being absorbed by the imperial powers, Iqbal rejected the West, but sought mainly to recall the glory of classical Arabia, lament its decline, and reinvent a Muslim identity, laying great emphasis on the importance of human agency. His work continues to be of great interest, as a bridge between broader humanist impulses and the political Islam of the present day and for its capacity to use classical imagery, diction and meters as a vehicle for ideological innovation.

[AM]

Iremonger, Valentin (Ireland, 1918–91) Trained at the Abbey School of Acting, Iremonger was a member of the Abbey Theatre Company in 1939–40 and the Gate Theatre in 1942–4. He entered the foreign service in 1946 and served as ambassador from Ireland to Norway, Sweden, Finland, and India. *The Bell*, Dublin's literary journal, published his early poems as well as his statement about poetry in 1944: 'Poetry has little to do with truth, sincerity, or what have you'. In 1945 he won the Æ Memorial Award. Iremonger was also an associate editor of *Envoy, A Review of Literature and Art* (1949–51).

Selected works: *Contemporary Irish Poetry* (ed. 1949); *Reservations* (1950); *Horan's Field and Other Reservations* (1972).

[CT]

Ivănescu, Mircea (Romania, b. 1931). Born in Bucharest, Ivănescu studied French language and literature at the University there and for a time was a senior editor at the World Literature Press. He has translated, amongst others, F. Scott Fitzgerald, William Faulkner and *Ulysses*. For Ivănescu, a highly experimental poet, objects and feelings coexist with their representations. Thus the poet becomes a muppet ('mopete') whose gestures and feelings are analyzed in detail with lucid yet subdued irony. In his excursions into his inner life, which turns into memory, the poet decries the relativity of space and time ('the imperial unraveling of time', 'Afternoon Twilight'), skeptical at the 'evocative and institutive power' of words (I. Moldovan). Obsessed by his 'inability to reach the others', Ivănescu brings poetry close to prose and the essay in an attempt to objectivize himself through 'characters' and fictions. As part of his systematic demolition of traditional poetic structures, his volumes are entitled *Verse* (1968), *Other Verse* (1972), *Poems* (1970), *Other Poems* (1973), *Poem* (1973), *New Poems* (1983), *Other New Poems* (1986), *Old, New Verse* (1988).

[GF]

Ivanov, Georgi Vladimirovich (Russia, 1894–1958) Ivanov's father was a colonel in retirement, his mother from the family of a baron. He studied in the Second Military School in St Petersburg and began to publish poetry at the age of sixteen; his first poetry, which he valued most, appeared in the journal *Gaudeamus* in 1911. His first collection, *Departure to the Island of Citera*, also appeared in that year. In January 1912, the poet GUMILIEV invited Ivanov to join his group Tsekh poetov (The Guild of Poets), and the same year Ivanov abandoned the military school. In

1914, he published the collection, *Gornitsa* (*The Chamber*) and, two years later, *Veresk* (*The Heather*), which contains the themes that would become predominant in his later poetry: boredom, cynicism, and the attitudes of an old, wise, life-weary observer of the human drama. In 1918–22, before his emigration from Russia, he published the collections, *Sady* (*The Gardens*, 1921) and *Lampada* (*The Icon-Lamp*, 1922). His first volume published in emigration, *Rozy* (*The Roses*), appeared in Paris in 1931. In his work, Ivanov's lyrical hero is always a divided individual, belonging to both Russia and exile; to the world of a lost past and of an unknown terrifying future; and to passing life and approaching death.

[RN]

J

Jabès, Edmond (France, 1912–91) Jabès was born in Cairo to a French-speaking Jewish family, and his earliest literary efforts include volumes of conventional French verse composed on Romantic and Cubist models. In 1933 he began a correspondence with MAX JACOB who introduced him to the Parisian literary community of avant-garde writers.

Jabès' poetry composed after World War II relied on Surrealist techniques to create startling imagery, but it exhibited greater gravity than the earlier verse. Forced from Egypt with other Jews, French, and English in the midst of the Suez crisis (1956), his multiform writings continually embodied a series of ambiguities that would set him apart from the French literary community in which he found himself. Shortly after settling in Paris, his Cairene poetry was gathered into *Je bâtis ma demeure, poèmes 1943–57* (*I Build My Dwelling*, 1943–57), with a preface by the eminent critic Gabriel Bounoure.

In Paris, Jabès began to consider the meaning of his Jewish identity. He recognized that Surrealism was no longer a valid poetic method, and, as a refugee, began to draft the work for which he is best known today, the seven-volume *Livre des Questions* (*The Book of Questions*, 1963–73). Jabès found in the idea of the 'Book' the possibility of creating a variegated space in which to explore his Jewish identity and the meaning of Jewish history.

Selected works: *Le Livre des Ressemblances* (*The Book of Resemblances*, 1976–80); *Un Étranger avec, sous le bras, un livre de petit format* (*A Foreigner Carrying in the Crook of His Arm a Tiny Book*, 1989); *Le Livre de l'hospitalité* (*The Book of Hospitality*, 1991).

[SJ]

Jaccottet, Philippe (Switzerland, b. 1925) Jaccottet was born in Moudon, but has lived in Grignan, a village in the Drôme, France, since his marriage in 1954. He has translated writers from several languages (including Homer, Holderlin, UNGARETTI, and MANDELSHTAM), and has produced critical studies of RILKE and Gustave Roud.

Jaccottet's poetry is distinguished by its lack of artifice; some critics attribute the strength of his lyrical voice to his inattention to Symbolism. His preferred subject is the study of man within his natural environment. His journal notes, published as *La Semaison, carnets 1954–79* (*Scatterings 1954–79*) and *La Seconde Semaison, carnets 1980–94* (*Further Scatterings*, 1980–94), show his continuous engagement with an unusual combination of the natural world, translation, and literary criticism.

He has received several prizes, including the Prix Rambert (1956), the Grand Prix Ramuz (1970), the prize of the city of Lausanne (1970), the Grand Prix de Poésie of Paris (1986), the Grand Prix National de Traduction (1987), and the Prix Prétarque (1988).

Selected works: *L'Effraie* (*The Screech Owl*, 1953); *Airs* (1967); *Paysages avec figures absentes* (*Landscapes with Absent Figures*, 1970); *La Promenade sous les arbres* (*The Walk through the Trees*, 1988).

[SJ]

Jacob, Max (France, 1876–1944) Born in the Breton town of Quimper to a middle-class Jewish family, Jacob wrote many books, including poetry, prose, art criticism, and moving spiritual meditations on the vicissitudes of the soul in the material world.

In 1894 he moved to Paris to study law and thought of becoming a civil servant. However, the arts attracted him and, although his family disapproved, he pursued a painting career; simultaneously he began composing poetry. In 1905 he met Picasso, who introduced him to GUILLAUME APOLLINAIRE. The trio became a regular feature in the Montmartre and Montparnasse circles of the Cubist avant-garde.

Many of Jacob's contemporaries saw him only as a clown, not as a serious artist. They were unprepared, then, to accept his quite sincere turn to Christianity following a vision of Christ in October 1909. He recounted his experiences of the divine, including his conversion to Catholicism, in *La Défense de Tartuffe* (*The Defense of Tartuffe*, 1919). After 1920, Jacob regularly retreated to the abbey of Saint-Benoît-sur-Loire in order to escape the debilitating influences of urban life; however, his homosexuality continued to challenge his effort to remain a good Christian, as he understood the term.

With the onset of World War II, Jacob retreated definitively to Saint-Benoît. Though a Christian, he nevertheless wore the yellow star identifying him as a Jew. In February 1944 he was arrested while leaving a church and was interned at the transit camp of Drancy north of Paris. He died there the following month as a result of bronchial pneumonia.

In the years following the war, many writers to whom he generously gave of himself, including Jean Cocteau, André Billy, Marcel Béalu, as well as younger ones such as EDMOND JABÈS and Jean Grenier published letters they had received from him.

Selected works: *Cornet à dés* (*The Dice Cup*, 1917); *Le Cabinet noir* (*The Black Cabinet*, 1922); *Morceaux choisis* (*Selected Pieces*, 1937); *Méditations religieuses* (*Religious Meditations*, 1947).

[SJ]

Jamie, Kathleen (Scotland, b. 1962) Born in Renfrewshire, Jamie grew up in Midlothian and read Philosophy at Edinburgh University. She won a Gregory Award at the age of eighteen which she used for travel in Israel. Her love of traveling has since informed her poetry and resulted in a travel book about Pakistan, *The Golden Peak* (1992). *The Autonomous Region* (1993) was a collaboration with the photographer Sean Mayne Smith and her interest in different media continues in her installation work with artists. She held the post of writer-in-residence at Dundee University in 1990–93. *The Queen of Sheba* (1994) won the Geoffrey Faber Memorial Prize in 1996.

Selected works: *Black Spiders* (1982); *A Flame in Your Heart* (with Andrew Greig, 1986); *The Way We Live* (1987).

[LKMF]

Jammes, Francis (France, 1868–1938) Jammes spent most of his life in the Basque country. His poetry celebrates the beauty of the nature of that region, and the daily life of the men and animals that inhabit it. *An Early Manifesto* (1897), written with some irony and in the cause of poetic truth, resulted in the neologism *jammisme*. His first volume of poetry, *De l'Angélus de l'aube à l'Angélus du soir* (*From the Dawn Angelus to the Evening*

Angelus, 1888), reflects his belief that poetry should not solely symbolize the human condition, but that it should paint the state of the soul simply as it is. A meeting in 1900 with CLAUDEL was to prove influential; under his guidance Jammes returned to Catholicism. In 1917 the Académie Française awarded him the Grand Prix de Littérature. He repeatedly attempted to gain entrance to the prestigious academic body, but failed each time.

Selected works: *Géorgiques chrétiennes* (*Christian Georgics*, 1912); *Feuilles dans le vent* (*Leaves in the Wind*, 1913); *Le Rosaire au soleil* (*Rosary in the Sun*, 1916); *Le Pèlerin de Lourdes* (*The Pilgrim of Lourdes*, 1936).

[SJ]

Jandl, Ernst (Austria, 1925–2000) Jandl taught German and English at high school. During the 1950s he was affiliated with the 'Viennese Group' of writers and began a close friendship (and collaboration) with fellow writer Friederike Mayröcker.

A major experimental writer, Jandl became famous for his avant-garde sound poems, which he began crafting in the 1950s. He read his poems at London's Royal Albert Hall in 1966. Using reductions and repetitions, they imitate actual sounds. For example, Jandl eliminated all vowels from the German word for 'trench' in 'trench warfare', then combined and recombined the remaining fragmented consonants to evoke successfully the sounds of machine gun fire. Despite a poem's sound character, it is tied to meaning, often expressing self-irony or even bitterness, themes that Jandl also explored in less experimental poems.

Selected works: *Laut und Luise* (1966); *speech bubbles* (1968); *the yellow dog* (1980); *peter and the cow* (1996).

[IRS]

Janés, Clara (Spain, b. 1940) Janés was born in Barcelona and raised in the intellectually stimulating environment of Catalonia. Her father's death in 1959 was to have an impact on her poetry, as was her career as a student activist during the 1960s. Her poetry is characterized by brevity and intensity. *Conquered Stones* (1964) initiates the Existentialist reflections that dominate her work. *Book of Alienations* (1980) and *To Live* (1983) ponder the absence of a true, knowable reality and poetry's role in filling that void. Janés has also explored the erotic in *Eros* (1981) and Muslim culture in *Fertile Crescent* (1989). She remains a leading poet and novelist today as well as an active translator of Czech poetry.

[AB]

Jarrell, Randall (United States, 1914–65) Jarrell was born in Nashville, Tennessee. His family moved to California soon after he was born; when his parents divorced, he and his brother returned with his mother to Tennessee, but he went back to live with his paternal relatives for a short time–a period that would be vividly evoked in his final collection of poems. He was educated at Vanderbilt, where he studied with ROBERT PENN WARREN and JOHN CROWE RANSOM.

Jarrell's early poetry was heavily influenced by that of W.H. AUDEN, but lacked Auden's technical and humorous virtuosity. Few of these early poems appeared in his *Selected Poems* of 1955, but much of what was collected is notable for the traits that would characterize Jarrell's most brilliant work – among them his fascination with fairy tales and the world of childhood, his persistent use of cross-gendering, and his preoccupation with the loneliness and anxiety of mid-century, middle-class American life. This volume also includes many of the unaffectedly moving war poems for which he may be best known.

Jarrell was one of his period's most famous and influential critics; his reputation as a poet remains in danger of eclipse, although the publication of *The Woman at the Washington Zoo* (1960) and *The Lost World* (1965) began to redress that imbalance. The poems of these collections fulfill the promise of the best of Jarrell's early work.

[JT]

Jeffers, Robinson (United States, 1887–1962) Jeffers was born in Pittsburgh to highly educated Presbyterian parents who began tutoring him when he was three years old, then sent him to private schools in Pittsburgh, Switzerland, and Germany. He continued his education in the classics and sciences at the University of Western Pennsylvania and Occidental College in Los Angeles, took graduate courses in literature and studied medicine for three years at the University of Southern California, and studied forestry at the University of Washington.

Jeffers' studies in science and Greek tragedy and admiration for W.B. YEATS had strong effects. Jeffers' conception of the insignificance of humanity in a beautiful universe, set forth in his doctrine of Inhumanism, led him to eschew both the Modernist tendencies of his contemporaries and their predilection for living in Europe; with his wife, Una, Jeffers went to live on the Pacific coast in the then-isolated Carmel, a place that seemed to him akin to Homeric Greece. Here he built a stone house and tower and settled for life. In his poetry, he uses continuously the structures, measures, and themes of Greek tragedy. Other influences include the Bible, an important text in his upbringing, and Old English literature, from which he adopted the device of alliteration.

His work continues to have its admirers, most notably poet ROBERT HASS.

Selected works: *The Roan Stallion, Tamar, and Other Poems* (1928); *The Women at Point Sur* (1927); *Dear Judas and Other Poems* (1929); *The Double Axe and Other Poems* (1948).

[JT]

Jennings, Elizabeth (England, 1926–2001) Jennings grew up in Oxford, and graduated from the university there in 1949. She established her literary reputation during the 1950s as part of the Movement, a group of writers including KINGSLEY AMIS and PHILIP LARKIN, who used their writing as social protest. Although Jennings was a part of the group, she and her poetry stand apart for many reasons, including her lifelong Christianity and love of Italy.

Jennings' poems are short lyrics that meditate on subjects such as the experience of artists, aging, relationships, and religion. The poems are marked by lucid diction contained in regular, often rhymed meters. In 1953, Jennings received the Arts Council award for her first book, *Poems*. She followed that achievement with the Somerset Maugham Award for her second book, *A Way of Looking* (1955). Jennings used the prize money to travel to Italy and study culture for three months, and her 1958 book, *A Sense of the World: Poems*, includes poems written during her stay in Rome.

In her later work, which includes poems for children, Jennings' technical control and variety has increased, and religious themes appear more frequently. In *Moments of Grace for Listener* (1980), Jennings searches for moments of grace by examining life details. Her poetry, as always, balances its lyric force with moments of philosophical rumination.

Selected works: *Recoveries: Poems* (1964); *Collected Poems* (1967, revised 1987); *Lucidities* (1970); *Relationships* (1972); *Selected Poems* (1980); *Celebrations and Elegies* (1982); *Times and Seasons* (1993); *Familiar Spirits* (1995).

[LK]

Jensen, Johannes Vilhelm (Denmark, 1873–1950) Laureate of the Nobel Prize for Literature in 1944, Jensen is equally known for his verse and prose. Born to an old peasant family and the son of a veterinarian, Jensen started by writing short stories, travel tales and what he called 'myths'. With the publication of his *Digte*

(*Poems*) in 1906 he introduced new forms and original images that changed the course of Scandinavian poetry. Consciously diverging from the lyrical and decadent poetry of the turn of the century, Jensen's language is rough, resembling Old Norse sagas, which he also translated into Danish. The poems' coarseness also expressed Jensen's admiration for primitive nature and physical force, which the poet associated with a 'Northern culture'. His racial mysticism came short, however, of identifying with German National Socialism. His poetry remained personal by finding the poetic in modern life and technology.

[YB]

Jiménez, Juan Ramón (Spain, 1881–1958) Jiménez is one of the most influential and internationally known Spanish poets of the twentieth century. Born in Moguer, a small town in rural Andalusia, Jiménez was a vintner's son who retained a lifelong love of nature. It was in Madrid, however, that Jiménez met the Nicaraguan poet RUBÉN DARÍO and was inspired to write his first works, *Violet Souls* and *Water Lilies* (1900). He remained in Moguer until 1912, when he returned to Madrid and lived there until the outbreak of the Civil War in 1936. Jiménez was highly regarded by the poets of the Generation of 1927 in Spain (see ALEIXANDRE, GUILLÉN and LORCA) as well as by younger poets in Latin America. His literary reputation, in fact, led him to be elected to the Royal Spanish Academy, an offer he declined. In Madrid he published anthologies of earlier works–in his zeal for perfection he constantly edited and re-edited his poetry–as well as the key work of his middle period, *Diary of a Newly Married Poet* (1916), upon his marriage to Zenobia Camprubí Aymar. In 1936 Jiménez left Spain for good. He would live for brief periods in the United States and Cuba but resided principally in Puerto Rico. Jiménez taught and lectured at universities and continued to write until his death, two years after that of his wife, in 1958. In 1956 he received the Nobel Prize for Literature.

Jiménez's poetic output falls into three broad periods. Works written before 1916 reflect the poet's Moguer years, and his love of nature and of the commonplace. His style evolved from Symbolist imitation to a personal quest for beauty. Though melancholy pervades his first books – Jiménez battled against depression during this period, particularly after his father's death in 1901 – in *Sad Airs* (1903) the poet displays an intimate style reminiscent of Bécquer. Other works of this period, notably *Spring Ballads* (1910), owe much to Verlaine and the Symbolists for their use of auditory and impressionistic imagery. As in all of Jiménez' work, one finds in this period a mixture of the alexandrine, made popular by the Modernists, and the traditional (eight-syllable line) forms.

Jiménez' marriage begins his second period, which lasts from 1912 to his exile from Spain in 1936. The *Diary of a Newly Married Poet* shows the poet's newfound metaphysical leanings as well as his use of the sea to embody both timelessness and change. With increasing frequency, poetry itself becomes a theme during this period, as Jiménez awakens to the transcendence of his creative powers. *Eternities* (1918) seeks a poetry that is 'naked' or 'pure', stripped of unnecessary elements to develop a single, central image. Unlike the sterile, intellectual quality of much verse from the period, however, Jiménez' work depends on the power of emotion.

The poetry of exile makes up Jiménez' third phase. *Total Season* (1948) displays a confident awareness of beauty in the world around. Other works continue this theme of fulfillment but couple it with a growing preoccupation with finality and death. The *Third Anthology* (1957), Jiménez' last book, is the most comprehensive collection of his poetry.

[AB]

Johnson, Linton Kwesi (England, b. 1952) Johnson came to England from Jamaica in

1963. After studying sociology at the University of London, he joined the Black Panther South League, where he was inspired to write poetry by W. E. B. DuBois' *Souls of Black Folk*. Drawing on his Caribbean background for his anti-colonial, anti-racist lyrics, he read percussive, alliterative poems over a reggae bass line and called it 'dub poetry'.

By choosing to write in Jamaican creole, Johnson continued the efforts of EDWARD KAMAU BRATHWAITE to use Caribbean, jazz, and blues rhythms as an alternative to standard English poetry's iambic pentameter. His experiment was both a popular and a critical success, and Johnson toured the world with the Dennis Bovell Dub Band, recording twelve albums, as well as publishing volumes of verse.

He was made an Associate Fellow of Warwick University in 1985, an Honorary Fellow of Wolverhampton Polytechnic in 1987, and received an award from the city of Pisa for his contribution to poetry and popular music in 1990.

In recent work, such as 'Mi Revolutionary Fren', Johnson moves his focus away from the black experience in Britain to explore a more global view; he still sees himself as an activist first and a poet second.

Selected works: *Voices of the Living and the Dead* (1974); *Dread Beat an' Blood* (1975); *Inglan is a Bitch* (1980); *Tings and Times: Selected Poems* (1991).

[JL/IS]

Johnson, Louis (New Zealand, 1924–88) Johnson was educated at the Teachers' Training College in Wellington, where he was born. From the late 1940s onwards, Johnson was a teacher and editor in the Department of Education. In 1968, he spent a year in New Guinea, then taught creative writing in Australia during the 1970s.

Together with JAMES K. BAXTER, Alistair Campbell, W.H. Oliver, and Hubert Witheford, Johnson formed the 'Wellington school'. He founded and edited the *New Zealand Poetry Yearbook* (1951–64) and established *Numbers* (1954–60), two journals which provoked lively literary debates. As a member of the 'Wellington school', he was suspicious of ALLEN CURNOW's Modernist-nationalist poetics and proposed a poetry that would reflect New Zealand in its international post-war context.

Johnson's poetry before 1968 deals with suburban life – a New Zealand experience that was often ignored – in a sardonic, yet sympathetic way. *Fires and Patterns* (1975) won the first New Zealand Poetry Book of the Year Award. When he returned to New Zealand in the 1980s after lecturing abroad, Johnson found the literary scene changed, and his sense of alienation finds expression in his late volumes, which are also characterized by a greater formal tightness than his earlier writings.

Selected works: *Stanza and Scene* (1945); *The Sun among the Ruins* (1951); *New Worlds for Old* (1957); *Bread and a Pension* (1964); *Coming and Going* (1982); *True Confessions of the Last Cannibal* (1986); *Last Poems* (1990).

[SH]

Jones, Bobi (Robert Maynard Jones; Wales, b. 1929) Jones was born in Cardiff, and lectures at the University of Wales, Aberystwyth, where he was appointed Professor of Welsh in 1980. Repudiating what he saw as the moribund conventions of Eisteddfod culture and 'popular' Welsh verse, Jones established himself at the forefront of the Welsh avant-garde with his first book, *Y Gan Gyntaf* (*The First Song*, 1957). This was followed by five more volumes before 1976. Jones's imagery can seem deliberately difficult, but is often brilliantly startling. He is also perhaps the most prolific Welsh language author of the post-war period; besides poetry, Jones has published two novels, five collections of short stories, a linguistics textbook, numerous works of literary criticism, stories for children, and several guides for students of Welsh.

[BS]

Jones, David (Wales, 1895–1974) Although Jones's centrality within the Anglo-Welsh canon is well established, the importance of his work within the tradition of Anglo-American Modernism remains under-appreciated. T.S. ELIOT, however, ranked Jones alongside Joyce and POUND, describing his first book, *In Parenthesis* (1937), as 'a work of genius'. A richly allusive and prismatic response to the experience of World War I, *In Parenthesis* is also Jones's most accessible text. His second volume, *The Anathemata* (1952) – or 'the blessed things that have taken on what is cursed and the profane things that somehow are redeemed' – is a still more abstract reflection upon the author's lifelong interest in the historical materiality of cultural artifacts, including the artifacts of language.

Jones was born in Brockley, Kent, of a Welsh father and an English mother. He strongly identified with Wales, and his poetry frequently alludes to Welsh literature and folklore. Formally educated as a visual artist, Jones served in the Royal Welch Fusiliers during World War I before converting to Catholicism in 1921, after which he spent some years among the religio-artistic communities of Eric Gill at Ditchling, Sussex, and Capel-y-ffin, Wales. In 1933 Jones suffered the first in a series of nervous breakdowns, and from 1946 he led an increasingly solitary life in a succession of small Harrow boarding houses, surrounded by his books and pictures. His posthumous publications include *The Sleeping Lord and Other Fragments* (1974); and in 1981 a retrospective exhibition of his paintings was held at the Tate Gallery.

[BS]

Jones, Glyn (Wales, 1905–95) Merthyr-born Jones worked as a Cardiff schoolteacher for most of his life. He established his reputation as a writer of short stories; his early collections, *The Blue Bed* (1937) and *The Water Music* (1944), are characterized by poetic prose replete with unusual descriptive similes. His verse shows a similar propensity for verbal play (a 'gift for logopoeic dance' as he would write in the much anthologized 'Merthyr'), but Jones' gift also came with a compassionate sensibility. His longest poem, *The Dream of Jake Hopkins* (1944), a verse drama written for radio, was inspired by his teaching career. Jones also wrote novels, Welsh verse translations, and a volume of autobiographical criticism, *The Dragon Has Two Tongues* (1968). His *Collected Poems* appeared in 1996.

[BS]

Joseph, Jenny (England, b. 1932) Joseph was born in Birmingham and was educated at St Hilda's College, Oxford, where she developed a keen and observant eye as a newspaper reporter. Although at one time Joseph lived in South Africa, she currently makes her home in Gloucestershire.

JOHN LEHMANN published Joseph's poetry for the first time in the 1950s. Since then Joseph has won numerous prizes for her creative work, including the Eric Gregory Award for *The Unlooked-for Season* (1960). In 1986 her novel-length prose poem exploring ancient Greek myths, *Persephone*, was the winner of the James Tait Black Memorial Prize. Joseph also publishes children's books.

Joseph's poetry is known for its way of ardently mixing everyday, honest moments with mystery and myth. Her neatly crafted stanzas strive to uncover all of the intricacies hidden within the human heart. Joseph's poetry sometimes reveals an intense searching, sometimes an acquired numbness, and sometimes rare and startling beauty. Often in the longer format, Joseph writes of the domestic, the seasons, landscapes, mythology, mirrors, ghosts and history/History (lived experience versus the record as people come to know and accept it). All of these diverse subjects are woven together in her volumes to create a unified and earnest whole.

Selected works: *The Thinking Heart* (1978); *Beyond Descartes* (1983); *The Inland Sea* (1989); *Beached Boats* (with photographer Robert Mitchell, 1991); *Selected Poems* (1992); *Ghosts and Other Company* (1995); *Extended Similes* (1996).

[MK]

Jouve, Pierre Jean (France, 1887–1976) Jouve began his career as a Symbolist, but a personal crisis, the result of the horror of World War I, led to a repudiation of his early work. *Noces* (*Wedding*, 1931) bridges his twin interests in Christianity and psychoanalysis. His mystical love lyric, *Matière céleste* (*Heavenly Matter*, 1937), introduces Hélène, a figure of nothingness. Through her, Jouve probes the unconscious depths of eros, death, and spirituality. Without dismissing the influence of Baudelaire and Rimbaud, this poem exhibits an affinity with the verse of St John of the Cross. A mystical wisdom, emanating from the orient, lightens the poetry composed after World War II.

His writings on music include studies of Mozart and Alban Berg; in addition to his criticism and verse, he wrote prose narratives, including *Paulina 1880* (1925) and *Vagadu* (1931).

Selected works: *Sueur de sang* (*Blood-red*, 1935); *La Vierge de Paris* (*The Virgin of Paris*, 1946).

[SJ]

József, Attila (Hungary, 1905–37) Though his life was brief, József's influence in Hungarian poetry has been immense. Detailing the poverty he witnessed and lived through, József's work is some of the finest proletarian poetry ever written; when it was combined with his late, introspective verse, it became the work of one of the twentieth century's greatest poets.

József was born into abject poverty in Budapest. His washerwoman mother had to provide for her family and, when she could not, József and his sisters were moved into an orphanage. He still managed to get an education, though he worked at various odd jobs while he was in high school and during a period at the University of Szeged (1924).

Poetry intervened in his academic career, however, and not simply by providing a more interesting diversion than scholarship. After placing poems in Hungary's leading progressive literary magazine, *Nyugat* (*West*), he published 'Tiszta szívvel' ('Song of Innocence') in 1924 and it caused a national stir because of its revolutionary ideas; he was forced to leave the university, though he would continue studying in Vienna and at the Sorbonne. While there, he wrote and also read widely in continental philosophy, economics, psychoanalysis, and the contemporary literary avant-garde.

Returning to Hungary in the late 1920s, József joined the Communist Party, though he was dismissed from it in 1932 because he found party-line Socialist Realism constricting. This dismissal coincided with a pair of ill-fated love affairs, all of which combined to take their toll on József's already fragile mental state. He developed schizophrenia in 1932 and was plagued with bouts of it for the rest of his life. Little of this madness is reflected in his verse, however. Remarkably consistent in the face of the poet's breakdowns, the work continues József's concern with the plight of the poor and oppressed, deepening his sentiments with a simultaneous dose of Marx and Freud, whom he had encountered both in his readings and in his own experiences of psychoanalysis in the early 1930s. In a post-institutional depression, he killed himself by thrusting his arm under a passing train.

What differentiates József's work from that of other 'proletarian' poets is, first of all, the sophistication with which he depicts the poor. Frequently embodied in the figure of his mother, the working classes are shown in their full complexity, and

József's anger at their treatment, her treatment, is palpable. Yet in the poems after 1932, critics have noted that the underlying intellectual strains found in the early verse are heightened, so that his combination of Magyar folk songs and Freud, for instance, made for mesmerizing verse. József's wide reading came into full play in volumes such as *Medvetánc* (*The Bear's Dance*, 1934), *Nincs bocsánat* (*There is no Pardon*, 1936–7) and *Utolsó versek* (*Last Poems*, 1937). As a poet of touching sensibility, great erudition, and metaphoric power, József influenced all generations of Hungarian poets who followed him.

Selected works: *A szépség koldusa* (*Beggar of Beauty*, 1922); *Nem én kiáltok* (*No Shriek of Mine*, 1925); *Nagyon fáj* (*It Hurts So Much*, 1936).

[MW]

Justice, Donald (United States, b. 1925) Born and raised in Miami, Florida, Justice pursued seriously his interests in both poetry and music. He received his undergraduate degree from the University of Miami, his M.A. from North Carolina, studied at Stanford for a year under YVOR WINTERS, and proceeded to earn his Ph.D. from Iowa in 1954. Justice has received many awards including the Pulitzer Prize for his *Selected Poems* (1979). For many years, he was a mainstay on the faculty of the renowned University of Iowa Writers' Workshop.

Justice is noted for his masterful use of forms such as the sestina and sonnet, especially in *The Summer Anniversaries* (1960). Later collections such as *Departures* (1973) adopt freer verse. Even when formally loose, Justice's works cultivate harmonies of musical order and cadence.

[CP]

K

Kaneko Mitsuharu (Oga Yasukazu; Japan, 1895–1975) Kaneko was the son of a sake dealer near Nagoya, but was adopted by the prosperous Kaneko family and brought up in Kyoto and Tokyo. He attended two universities and an art academy without completing any of his studies. By 1919 he had published a book of poems at his own expense; after a year's sojourn in Europe he published *Koganemushi* (*A Gold Beetle*, 1923), a collection of glittering romantic poetry intended as his farewell to youth.

Later travel in China, southeast Asia, and Europe added to his growing sense of alienation and his opposition to imperialism. Upon his return, he became a major poet whose rich symbolist technique veiled a bitterly critical view of colonialism, militarism, and ultranationalism. He was the only major Japanese poet to write and publish anti-war poems during the war. A fourteen-volume *Complete Works* appeared a few months after his death in June 1975.

[LY]

Kantaris, Sylvia (England, b. 1936) Kantaris uses a keen eye for detail to twist everyday scenes in unsettling ways while maintaining a conversational, sometimes even prosaic, tone and gentle humor. Her unusual take on life may stem from her study of French Surrealists, on whom she did her master's and doctoral theses at the University of Queensland, Australia.

She received a Poetry Magazine Award (Australia) in 1969 and a Poetry Society Competition Award in 1982.

Selected works: *Time and Motion* (1975); *Stocking Up* (1981); *The Tenth Muse* (1983); *News from the Front* (with D. M. THOMAS, 1983); *Dirty Washing: New and Selected Poems* (1989); *Lad's Love* (1993); *Lost Property* (1998).

[JL]

Karelli, Zoe (Chrysoulla Argyriadhi; Greece, 1901–98) Karelli was born in Thessaloniki where she studied foreign languages and music. Her first poems were published in the journal *The Third Eye* and later collected in a volume entitled *The March* (1940), which established her as the most prominent woman poet of the post-World War II period. She received the second State Award for Poetry for *Cassandra and Other Poems* (1955) as well as France's 'Palmes Academiques'. Her poetry, though lyrical, tends toward abstraction and idealism and is especially preoccupied with the spiritual disintegration of human experience, particularly in relation to love and God.

Selected works: *Seasons of Death* (1948); *Fantasy of Time* (1949); *Of Solitude and Arrogance* (1951); *The Mirror of Midnight* (1958).

[GSY]

Kariotakis, Kostas (Greece, 1896–1928) Though born in Tripoli, Kariotakis grew up in different locations throughout Greece but spent most of his troubled adolescence in Hania, Crete. He took his law degree in 1917 from the University of Athens but became a government clerk. Though he tried to remain in Athens by entering the Ministry of Public Welfare he was transferred to Patras and eventually 'exiled' to Preveza where he shot himself after trying unsuccessfully to drown. His suicide consequently influenced the interpretation of his poetry by the 1930s Generation that followed him. Influenced by French Symbolism, his poetry speaks of a pervasive melancholy, pessimism, hopelessness, and loneliness. Considered a precursor of Greek modernism, he remains an important figure.

Selected works: *The Pain of Man and of Things* (1919); *Nepenthe* (1921); *Elegies and Satires* (1927).

[GSY]

Karpowicz, Tymoteusz (Poland, b. 1921) Born near Wilno, Karpowicz moved to Silesia after the war. Although he published three books of poetry in 1941–48, Karpowicz first gained critical attention with his volumes *Bitter Sources* (1957) and *Stone Music* (1958). In 1957–61 he was president of the Wroclaw division of the Union of Polish Writers, and from 1958 to 1974 he worked as a journalist and helped edit a number of literary magazines. In 1973 Karpowicz left Poland and since then has held various teaching positions in Austria, Germany, and the United States.

Often referred to as a 'linguistic poet', Karpowicz was influenced by the Cracow Vanguard movement, in particular the work of JULIAN PRZYBOS. His poems are compressed and concise. CZESLAW MILOSZ has compared them 'to miniature ink drawings'. Karpowicz likes to juxtapose nature imagery with human action, highlighting the atrocities mankind has committed through the twentieth century.

Selected works: *Three Slavic Poets* (1975); *Tymoteusz Karpowicz: The Poetry of Survival* (1991).

[MO]

Kaštelan, Jure (Yugoslavia, 1919–90) A Croatian writer, Kaštelan graduated from the University of Zagreb, where he later taught at the Department of Yugoslav Literatures. He lived in Zagreb for most of his life. In addition to his work as a poet, essayist, and translator, he was a journalist, editor, and political and cultural activist.

Kaštelan's poetry is full of youthful enthusiasm and spontaneity. His verse is clear and sharp and often full of melodious resonances. His themes include love and death, as well as patriotic feelings for his country, especially in his early poems.

Selected works: *Crveni konj* (*A Red Horse*, 1940); *Pijetao na krovu* (*A Cock on the Roof*, 1950); *Malo kamena i puno snova* (*A Few Rocks and a Lot of Dreams*, 1957); *Zvezdana noć* (*A Starry Night*, 1966); *Krilati konjanik* (*A Winged Horseman*, 1991).

[DJ]

Kavadias, Nikos (Greece, 1910–75) Born in Manchuria of a merchant family from the island of Cephalonia, Kavadias spent his life working as a radio operator on merchant ships. Though he published only three short collections of poems, *Marabou* (1933), *Fog* (1947), and *Traverso* (1975), he remains one of Greece's most popular poets with many of his poems set to music. Unlike other poets for whom the sea journey had a symbolic function, Kavadias' exoticism, cynicism, and occasional melodrama were inspired by his real life experiences. With a predilection for narrative and description, he writes in rhymed verse about the loneliness, bitterness, disillusionment, and erotic longing of the sailor. His language is an exotic blend of Greek, Italian marine terms, and foreign words.

[GSY]

Kavanagh, Patrick (Ireland, 1904–67) Kavanagh is one of the most influential Irish poets of the twentieth century, despite the unevenness of his work. He provided future generations of Irish poets with a vision of rural Ireland that was liberated from YEATS's romanticized idealism. In contrast to the mythologized landscape of early revivalist writers, the Ireland he portrays is claustrophobic, repressed, frustrated, impoverished, and insular. But Kavanagh also celebrates – as no other Irish poet does – the quiet simplicities and earthy pieties of country life.

Born and raised in County Monaghan, Kavanagh left school at age twelve. His first volume of poetry, *Ploughman and Other Poems* (1936), gave voice to Kavanagh's early experiences in Monaghan. In 1939 he went to Dublin, hoping to become part of its vital literary world, but he quickly became disillusioned. His poetry, reflecting his disenchantment with the city, became bitter, ironic, and satirical. *The Great Hunger* (1942), perhaps Kavanagh's finest work, tells the story of Patrick Maguire, an impoverished Catholic farmer and poet crippled by the overwhelming provincialism of mother, church, and society.

His volume of poems *A Soul For Sale* (1947) is also a work of disenchantment and satire. In 1952, Kavanagh was admitted to hospital to be treated for lung cancer. Upon his release, his poetry grew less caustic, more gentle – glorying in simplicities – an innocence reborn. *Come Dance with Kitty Stobling and Other Poems* was published in 1960.

[CT]

Kavanagh, Patrick Joseph (England, b. 1931) Before writing for the *Spectator* and the *Times Literary Supplement*, P.J. Kavanagh did National Service in Korea, acted, and worked in publishing and television. The death of his first wife, Sally Philips, just two and a half years after their marriage, shaped his early work; a melancholy tone that remains warm and eschews self-pity underlies later pieces. Though occasionally careless technically, Kavanagh struggles powerfully with religious belief in such poems as 'Real Sky'.

Selected works: *One and One* (1960); *On the Way to the Depot* (1967); *About Time* (1970); *Edward Thomas in Heaven* (1974); *Life before Death* (1979); *Real Sky* (1980); *Selected Poems* (1982); *Presence: New and Selected Poems* (1987); *Collected Poems* (1992).

[JL]

Kees, Weldon (United States, 1914–55) Kees was born in Beatrice, Nebraska. In addition to being a poet, he was a painter, jazz pianist and composer, and filmmaker. This varied and adventurous life is presumed to have ended in 1955, when his abandoned car was found near the Golden Gate Bridge.

Kees' output of poems was small, totaling perhaps 150 (gathered, in 1975, into *Collected Poems*). His work was informed by the Depression and World War II and by film noir; his voice is detached, sometimes eerily passive, and within it a satiric note waxes and wanes. Kees' best-known poem, the chilling sonnet 'For My Daughter', shows the poet at his enigmatic peak.

Selected works: *The Last Man* (1943); *The Fall of the Magicians* (1947); *Poems 1947–54* (1955).

[JT]

Keesing, Nancy (Australia, 1923–93) Keesing was born in Sydney, and married A.M. Hertzberg in 1955. She received her Diploma of Social Studies from the University of Sydney.

Keesing was an extremely prolific writer of poetry, literary criticism, biographies, novels, and memoirs. While she considered herself to be a poet first, claiming that she wrote criticism and history only secondarily, she is better known for her critical work which deals with such varied topics as Australian Jewish stories, Australian motherhood, women's use of slang, and

Australian gold-miners. Keesing was awarded the Order of Australia in 1979.

Selected works: *Imminent Summer* (1951); *Three Men and Sydney* (1955); *Australian Bush Ballads* (ed., 1955); *Showground Sketchbook and Other Poems* (1968); *Hails and Farewells* (1977).

[SG]

Kell, Richard Alexander (Ireland, b. 1927) Born in Youghal, County Cork, Kell graduated from Trinity College, Dublin, in 1952. Kell has worked as a lecturer in universities for most of his life: Brunel College of Technology in Middlesex, England (1956–59); Isleworth Polytechnic (1960–70); and Newcastle-upon-Tyne Polytechnic (1970–83). A fine technician and prosodist, Kell writes poems that often show the struggle between intellect and passion, moral control and emotional intensity. One of his poems, the tender and stirring 'Spring Night', is dedicated to his wife, and set on Killiney Hill, just outside Dublin.

Selected works: *The Control Tower* (1962); *Differences* (1969); *Humours* (1980); *The Broken Circle* (1985); *Rock and Water* (1993).

[CT]

Kennedy, X.J. (United States, b. 1929) Upon reading with DONALD JUSTICE at the 92nd Street Y.M.H.A. in Manhattan, Kennedy joked that it was 'Old Formalists' Night Out'. Like much of Justice, Kennedy's work is highly polished and in meter and rhyme. From his first volume, *Nude Descending a Staircase* (1961), he has proven to be a technical virtuoso, writing in every form. It is unfortunate that his enormously popular textbooks, *Literature* and *An Introduction to Poetry*, have overshadowed his poetic reputation. The fact that his work is often satirical or humorous has also caused him to be considered, by some, less than serious.

Born Joseph Charles Kennedy in Dover, New Jersey, he attended Seton Hall, Columbia, and University of Michigan. At the latter he dropped his studies before writing his doctoral dissertation. For years he was a professor at Tufts University, a position he relinquished in 1977 in order to write and edit full-time.

Selected works: *Cross-Ties: Selected Poems* (1985); *Dark Horses: New Poems* (1992).

[RP]

Kennelly, Brendan (Ireland, b. 1936) Kennelly is considered the quintessential Irish poet; he has published all his poetry in Ireland and, apart from a few short stays abroad, the bulk of his career has been spent lecturing at Trinity College, Dublin. Kennelly was born in Ballylongford, County Kerry, and educated at Trinity College, receiving his B.A. in 1961, his M.A. in 1963, and Ph.D. in 1967.

Kennelly is known throughout Ireland as a poet, a literary critic, as well as a brilliant reader of his poems. Until recently, however, Kennelly had been regarded as a 'popular' poet and ignored by much of the literary establishment. Influenced by the oral tradition in Irish, as well as such Anglo-Irish poets as YEATS and KAVANAGH, much of Kennelly's writing deals with Irish themes and local people. His *Islandman* (1977), for example, describes the Island of Carrig, conveying images in accessible, emotional, and personal poetry. *Cromwell* focuses on the life and motivations of Oliver Cromwell, the early colonizer of Ireland, in such poems as 'Reading Aloud', 'Therefore, I Smile', and 'Mud'. Kennelly received the Æ Memorial Prize for Poetry in 1967.

Selected works: *Selected Poems* (1969); *A Time for Voices: Selected Poems* (1990); *Breathing Spaces* (1992); *Love of Ireland: Poems from the Irish* (1997).

[CT]

Kenny, Maurice (United States, b. 1929) Probably the most prominent poet of the Native American Renaissance, Kenny was born to a mother of Senecan Indian ancestry and a father of Mohawk Indian descent. He received his B.A. from Butler University before moving to New York City where he had contact with the best-known poets of the 1950s, including LOUISE BOGAN with whom he had a particularly significant association. A long-time editor and publisher, Kenny founded *Contact II* magazine and Strawberry Press. During the 1970s and 1980s, Kenny traveled extensively in promotion of Native American writing. It is generally acknowledged that Kenny's work created a mainstream interest that allowed many contemporary Native American poets to begin publishing in the late 1970s.

Nominated for the Pulitzer Prize in 1983, Kenny has won a national Public Radio Award, an American Book Award and other honors.

In the more than fifteen volumes of poetry and prose Kenny has written, he has always chosen Native American subjects, be they social, musical or historical. Many of his poems reflect traditional tribal literature and song from his Iroquois heritage. Often his highly spiritual poems contrast the Native American sense of the past with that of the Euro-American. In his most recent work, Kenny has created portraits of historical figures such as Jesuit missionaries and Molly Brant, a Mohawk leader. Kenny's portrayal of the past is always informed by contemporary Native American experience and is infused with a strong sense of human beings' place in the natural world.

Selected works: *Dead Letters Sent* (1958); *I Am the Sun* (1976); *North: Poems of Home* (1977); *Dancing Back Strong the Nations* (1979); *Only as Far as Brooklyn* (1979); *The Smell of Slaughter* (1982); *Blackroabe* (1983); *The Mama Poems* (1984); *Humans and/or Not So Humans* (1988); *Last Mourning in Brooklyn* (1991); *Tekonwatonti: Molly Brant* (1992).

[HEE]

Kenyon, Jane (United States, 1947–95) Kenyon was born in Ann Arbor, Michigan, and educated at the University of Michigan. Married to the poet DONALD HALL, she lived with him in his ancestral farmhouse in New Hampshire.

Kenyon's poetry meditates on life in the country, focusing on the details of daily domesticity and the cycle of seasons. She is known as an exquisite crafter of poems. Her luminous details and the quiet, prayer-like music of her lines are heightened by an ability to shift seamlessly between a present scene and a deeply felt recollection.

Selected works: *The Boat of Quiet Hours* (1986); *Let Evening Come* (1990); *Constance* (1993); *Otherwise: New and Selected Poems* (1996).

[JT]

Khlebnikov, Velimir (Russia, 1885–1922) Son of an ornithologist, Viktor Vladimirovich Khiebnikov was born in Astrakhan province on the Volga. He began studying math and natural sciences at university in Kazan in 1903 and five years later went to study at St Petersburg University, though he never graduated. Khlebnikov attended meetings of Vyacheslav Ivanov's literary group 'The Tower' but became disillusioned and fell into avant-garde artistic circles. In 1910 Khlebnikov was the nominal leader of the Russian Cubo-futurists, and by 1912 he and VLADIMIR MAYAKOVSKY were at the center of the Futurist movement. Khlebnikov was drafted into the army in 1916 and lived an itinerant existence until his death from malaria and typhus-related exhaustion six years later.

Khebnikov was a very productive writer but he edited rarely and published even less. Much of his work is still quite unpolished, yet is Dostoyevskian in its brilliance and rawness. A devout Slavophile, Khlebnikov abandoned his Latin name Viktor in favor of the Slavic Velimir. Mysticism and a belief in the unity of the universe abound in Khebnikov. In his poetics, he experimented with 'zaum' or trans-sense language – a belief that there are essential units of sound which transcend all languages. Outside of his art, Khlebnikov endlessly sought the mathematical formula which he believed would predict history and control the functioning of the universe.

[TW]

Khodasevich, Vladislav Felitsianovich (Russia, 1886–1939) Khodasevich was born into a family of Polish lineage and grew up during cataclysmic political change, attending university in Moscow. In 1907 he divorced his first wife, Marina Ryndina, and later married Anna Chulkova, sister of the Symbolist poet Georgy Chulkov. In 1920 he moved to Petrograd where he was an important part of 'Petersburg Poetics', which would later have a strong influence on BRODSKY. In 1922 Khodasevich moved abroad, living in Czechoslovakia, Italy, and Berlin, where he edited the journal *Table Talk*. Finally, living in Paris (where he died) Khodasevich was editor and critic for *Vozrozhdenie* (*Renaissance*). Among the most productive of the Symbolist poets, Khodasevich was also a Pushkin scholar, literary critic, and biographer of Derzhavin. His style is aligned with GUMILIEV's Acmeism and Clarism and strongly at odds with the Futurists. Khodasevich's classical education and grounding in Pushkin are evident in his work, but his subject matter and sensibility are quite contemporary. The theme of a unifying order in the universe is combined with a fascination with the moment of change or destruction in Khodasevich's poetics.

[TW]

Khoury-Ghata, Vénus (Lebanon, b. 1937) A native of Beirut where she was raised, Khoury-Ghata has lived in France since 1973. She has written in different genres and her poetry is widely acclaimed. She published in 1968 *Terres stagnantes* (*Stagnant Land*), a collection roughly based on her everyday experiences. *Au sud du silence* (*From the South of Silence*), published seven years later, explores the years of war; *Les Ombres et leurs cris* (*Shadows and Their Cries*, 1980) further investigates the cruelty of war and was awarded the Prix Apollinaire in 1980. *Un faux pas au soleil* (*A Mistake of the Sun*, 1982) and *Fables pour un peuple d'argile* (*Fables for People of Clay*, 1992), narrate the destruction of Lebanon during the war, the problems of negotiating between French and Arabic, the 'Franbanais', and the problems of everyday life. Reflecting the lyric tradition and renewing academic forms, her varied verse addresses current issues of the twentieth century, and intellectualizes poetry.

[MS]

Khristov, Boris (Bulgaria, b. 1945) Arguably the best Bulgarian poet of the last three decades, Boris Kirilov Khristov was born in the village of Krapets, Pernik area, graduated from the University of Tŭrnovo, and has worked as teacher, journalist, and editor. Before the collapse of the totalitarian government in 1989, however, his works were frequently banned from publication or withdrawn from circulation.

Khristov's poetry thrives on irony and paradox. He combines realistic detail, mythological archetypes, and biblical symbolism to convey his visions of troubled childhood, resentful solitude, death as an end and a new beginning, and poetry as prophecy and liberation.

Selected works: *Vecheren trompet* (*Evening Trumpet*, 1977); *Chesten krŭst* (*Cross My Heart*, 1982); *Dumi i grafiti* (*Words and Graffiti*, 1991); *Dumi vŭrkhu drugi dumi* (*Words on Words*, 1991); *Cherni bukvi vŭrkhu cheren list* (*Black Letters on a Black Page*, 1997).

[CG/LPG]

Kinnell, Galway (United States, b. 1927) Born on February 1, 1927, in Providence, Rhode Island, Kinnell began studying poetry while in high school in Massachusetts. He continued his studies at Princeton University, where his roommate was W.S. MERWIN, and at the University of Rochester.

Kinnell published his first book of poetry, *What a Kingdom it Was*, in 1960, but it was not until his third collection, *Body Rags* (1968) that he received recognition as a major American poet. Ever since, Kinnell has been a strong and consistent presence in the American literary world – publishing over fourteen books of poetry, five translations, and one novel. Kinnell's poetry explores mortality, as well as the primal violence and wildness that surge beneath the veneer of 'civilization'.

Visceral and intelligent, Kinnell's free verse has earned him justifiable distinction. His numerous awards include a Fulbright Scholarship, Guggenheim Fellowships, the London Translation Prize, and the Cecil Hemley Poetry Prize for his translation of YVES BONNEFOY's *On the Motion and Immobility of Douve*, an American Book Award, the Pulitzer Prize, and a National Book Award for his *Selected Poems* (1982). Kinnell teaches poetry at New York University.

[BRB/DC]

Kinsella, John (Australia, b. 1963) Kinsella grew up in the countryside of Western Australia and studied at the University of Western Australia. His poetry has two distinct modes: the pastoral of *The Silo*(1995) and *The Hunt* (1998), reflecting the landscape and customs of Western Australia; and the experimental of *Eschatologies* (1991) and *SYZYGY* (1993), reflecting Kinsella's wide learning and travel, and his affinities with language, poetry and with deconstruction. With his wife, Tracy Ryan, he has edited the poetry magazine *Salt* as well as contributing to and editing a number of anthologies. Widely considered a poetic *wunderkind*, he became a fellow of Churchill College, Cambridge, and has attracted the attention of world-famous critics such as Harold Bloom and George Steiner.

[NB]

Kinsella, Thomas (Ireland, b. 1928) Kinsella is considered a challenging, even difficult poet – but also one of the important post-World War II Irish poets. Born in Dublin, Kinsella attended University College, Dublin, on grants and scholarships, and in 1946 joined the Irish Civil Service.

Influenced by AUDEN and YEATS, Kinsella's early poetry shows technical skill, fluidity, and innovation. *Another September* (1958) won the Guinness Poetry Prize and the Poetry Book Society Selection of the Year. Kinsella continued to work in the Finance Department of the Irish Civil Service while publishing three volumes of poems: *Moralities* (1960); *Poems and Translations* (1961); and *Downstream* (1962). In 1965, Kinsella accepted a post as poet-in-residence at Southern Illinois University at Carbondale in the United States. His subsequent volumes were highly regarded: *Wormwood* (1966) won the Denis Devlin Memorial Award and *Nightwalker and Other Poems* (1968) adopts looser, more radical forms – under the influence of WILLIAM CARLOS WILLIAMS, ROBERT LOWELL, and THEODORE ROETHKE.

Kinsella received a Guggenheim Fellowship to translate the *Táin Bó Cuailnge*, a saga of Cuchulain, as *The Tain* (1969). In 1970, he accepted a position at Temple University, Philadelphia, where he published *The Butcher's Dozen* (1972), a moving volume about Bloody Sunday. Kinsella set up his own publishing press in Dublin, Peppercanister Press, and published *Notes from the Land of the Dead* (1972).

In 1976 Kinsella taught at Temple University's School of Irish Tradition in Dublin, and was able to divide his academic year between Philadelphia and Dublin. His *Peppercanister Poems 1972–78* (1979) brings together all his work, including *The Tain*. Recent publications include *From Centre City* (1989) and *Collected Poems 1956–94* (1997).

[CT]

Kirsch, Sarah (Germany, b. 1935) Kirsch attended the Institute of Literature in Leipzig, East Germany, from 1963 to 1965. Her protests against WOLF BIERMANN's exile led to her leaving East Germany in 1977. A prolific writer, she is perhaps the most important female poet of her generation in Germany.

Despite affinities with other poets, Kirsch's poems on love and nature are innovative, starting with the collections *Magic Spells* (1973) and *Tailwind* (1976). In an original intensity and with an emphasis on female subjectivity, her poems center on the precarious balance between humankind and nature, between trust and melancholy. Resisting the threat to humane existence caused by emotional isolation, as in *Catlives* (1984), her poetry is laconic but also humorous, as best shown in *Erlking's Daughter* (1992).

[IRS]

Kizer, Carolyn (United States, b. 1925) An important member of her generation of American poets, Kizer for several years was without a publisher until the small press BOA Editions Limited issued *Yin* in 1984; it was awarded the Pulitzer Prize.

Kizer's work is marked by good humor, humanity and a strong sense of identity. Her second book, *Knock Upon Silence* (1965) contained the sequence 'Pro Femina', which remains an important feminist work. To date she has published seven volumes of her poetry, a book of translations (*Carrying Over*, 1988), and two books of prose (*Proses*, 1993; *Picking and Choosing*, 1995).

Born in Spokane, Washington, she was educated at Sarah Lawrence College, after which she was a Fellow of the Chinese Government in Comparative Literature at Columbia University. Subsequently she lived in Nationalist China for a year. In 1959 she founded *Poetry Northwest* magazine. In 1964–65 she was a Specialist in Literature for the U.S. Department of State, dealing with Pakistan. In 1960–70 she served as the first Director of the Literature Program for the National Endowment for the Arts. She divides her time between Sonoma, California, and Paris.

Selected works: *Mermaids in the Basement* (1984); *The Nearness of You* (1986); *Harping On: Poems 1985–95* (1996).

[RP]

Knight, Etheridge (United States, 1931–91) Identified with the Black Arts Movement, Knight's work exceeds his oft-noted autobiographical subjects of prison life and drug use, and affirmatively treats love, nature, and human frailty. Although he received little formal education, Knight attends to poetic tradition, and writes in various dictions and styles, in metrical stanzas, and in haikus and even as toasts.

Born in Corinth, Mississippi, as an Army-trained medical technician he was wounded in the Korean War; later convicted of armed robbery, Knight began writing poetry in Indiana State Prison. His awards include grants from the National Endowment for the Arts and the Guggenheim Foundation, as well as the National Book Award for *Born of a Woman* (1980) and the American Book Award for *The Essential Etheridge Knight* (1981).

[HE]

Kocbek, Edvard (Yugoslavia, 1904–81) Kocbek was born in Sv. Jurij ob Scavnici-Ljutomer in Slovenia. After his studies of Romance languages and literature in Ljubljana and Berlin, he worked as a professor of French. Despite his strong Christian inclination, he was active in the partisan movement during World War II, and he continued to be politically active in the Yugoslav government after the war. He also worked as an editor of literary journals. After the appearance of his first collection of short stories, *Strah in pogum* (*Fear and Courage*, 1951), and its hostile reception, he withdrew from political life and focused on writing and translating. His works include poetry, memoirs, translations, and novels.

Kocbek's poetry depicts the down-to-earth yet lyrical reality of the everyday world. His images are simple and beautiful, with numerous visual emphases. Kocbek's language is precise and clear; he conveys different moods and sentiments with ease and tender immediacy.

Selected works: *Zemlja* (*The Earth*, 1934); *Groza* (*Horror*, 1963).

[DJ]

Koch, Kenneth (United States, b. 1925) Born in Cincinnati, Koch served in World War II, graduated from Harvard, and became a founding poet of the 'New York School', along with JOHN ASHBERY and FRANK O'HARA. After earning a Ph.D. at Columbia, Koch became a professor there, and has remained at Columbia for almost forty years.

Koch's bright, inventive poems – written in an astonishing variety of forms – are filled with an infectious excitement and joy in words. Although widely regarded as one of the most amusing contemporary poets, Koch always strives to be serious while never being overly somber. His often wistful later work is increasingly reflective about time and memory, without sacrificing any of his earlier imaginative vigor. Koch has also written several influential books about teaching poetry to children.

Selected works: *Thank You and Other Poems* (1962); *One Train* (1994); *On the Great Atlantic Rainway: Selected Poems 1950–88* (1994).

[AE]

Kolbe, Uwe (Germany, b. 1957) Growing up in close proximity to the Berlin Wall (built in 1961), Kolbe belongs to the first generation literally born into the new Communist state. His poetic formulation of life in East Germany established him very early as a major new poetic voice. The title of his collection *Born Into* (1980) even supplied the phrase for the way his generation felt about the state.

The skepticism and irony of his poems caused difficulties with the authorities. Consequently, Kolbe left East Germany during the mid-1980s on a long-term visa. The fall of the Berlin Wall, which Kolbe experienced from afar while visiting the United States, changed the political basis of his poetic creativity. Still, he has remained a prolific writer exploring all topics of human existence with poetic mastery in volumes such as *Not Really Platonic* (1994) and *Vineta* (1998).

[IRS]

Kolmar, Gertrud (Germany, 1894–1943?) Born into a wealthy Jewish family, Kolmar worked as an interpreter and taught deaf-mute children. After the Nazis assumed power in 1933, she became increasingly isolated but stayed in Germany because of her father. She was sent to forced labor; after her deportation in 1943, she was never seen again.

In *Poems* (1917), Kolmar reflected her conflicts with gender roles, while they became more historical and mythological in *Prussian Coats of Arms* (1934). A central theme of her verse was survival of animals and women, especially Jewish women, by way of transformation. Centering on nature and her isolation after 1933, Kolmar's third book, *The Woman and the Animals* (1938), was pulped by the Nazis.

[IRS]

Komunyakaa, Yusef (United States, b. 1947) Winner of the 1994 Pulitzer Prize for Poetry, Komunyakaa was born in Louisiana and served in Vietnam as a war correspondent. He is currently Professor of English at Princeton University.

Komunyakaa writes in a compressed, terse style, and moves fluidly through a range of idioms, from more formal lyricism to blues-inflected colloquial language. His poems often explore memory, the past, and history, as well as questions of family, identity, and race. He also frequently ponders the difficulties of love, and celebrates jazz music and culture. In his highly praised volume

Dien Cai Dau (1988), Komunyakaa writes movingly about his Vietnam War experiences.

Selected works: *Copacetic* (1984); *I Apologize for the Eyes in My Head* (1986); *Neon Vernacular: New and Selected Poems* (1993).

[AE]

Kornhauser, Julian (Poland, b. 1946) Born in Gliwice, Kornhauser studied Slavistics at Jagiellonian University and published his first collection of poems in 1972. A representative of the 'Generation of '68', Kornhauser is perhaps best known as the co-author, along with ADAM ZAGAJEWSKI, of the contentious collection of essays titled *The Non-Represented World* (1974), which, as STANISLAW BARANCZAK has said, 'advocated a return to reality and straightforward speaking in Polish literature'.

Kornhauser's poetry is never divorced from politics. His work is historical but contemporary. He speaks directly about Lenin, Kruczonych, and MAYAKOVSKY, as well as the weaver, the machinist, and the farm worker.

Kornhauser is the author of over a dozen books of poetry, fiction, and criticism. His work has also been anthologized in Polish and East European poetry collections translated into English.

[MO]

Kovner, Abba (Israel, 1918–87) Kovner was born in Sebastopol, Crimea, in 1918, and as a young man lived through the Nazi occupation of the Vilna ghetto. After hiding in a convent, he returned to the ghetto and led its armed revolt. After the fall of the ghetto he became involved with illegal immigration to the Land of Israel. He was arrested by the British in Egypt, and later served in the Israeli military during the War of Independence. A member of kibbutz Ein Hachoresh, he became an active novelist, poet, and essayist, who dedicated his life to the commemoration of Holocaust victims and their heroism. From his poetry through his documented testimonies to the monumental Diaspora Museum in Tel Aviv which bears his signature, Kovner became a voice of the victims and a living question mark on the ability to sustain humanity in a world full of hatred and evil. His poetry, which combines drama, irony, and colorful imagery of wandering through forests and dark seas, earned him the Israel Prize for Literature (1970). Kovner's first collection, *While There is Still Night*, was published in 1947. His widely read novel about the life of Israeli pioneers, *Face to Face*, appeared in 1953. Two children's books and a volume of testimonies which he wrote were published posthumously. Some of his well-known collections appeared in English translation, among them *A Canopy in the Desert* (1973) and *My Little Sister* (1986).

[ER]

Koziol, Urszula (Poland, b. 1931) Koziol was born in Rakowka, south-east Poland. Educated at the University of Wroclaw, she taught Polish literature at a number of secondary schools and colleges throughout provincial Poland, and in 1971 she was appointed editor of the literary magazine *Odra*. Her first book of poems, *Blocks of Rubber*, appeared in 1957. Since then she has published several selections of poetry, fiction, and literary essays.

Koziol says in her poem 'A Polish Lesson': 'Between "I know" and "I don't know"/there's a zone of possibilities . . .'. Her poetry occupies this 'zone', often meditating on the possibility of understanding such subjects as death, truth, and our relationship with the natural world, especially in the aftermath of the atrocities that took place in Poland during the first half of the twentieth century.

[MO]

Kristensen, Tom (Aage Tom Kristensen; Denmark, 1893–1974) Poet, novelist, literary critic, and translator, Kristensen was born in London but received his education in Denmark. After graduating from Copenhagen University, he failed the practical teaching examination and started working for various newspapers, including *Politiken*, a major daily. His most productive period was the decade beginning with the publication of his first poetry book, *Fribytterdrømme* (*Freebooter Dreams*) in 1920. The following year witnessed the publication of his first novel, after which Kristensen continued writing in both genres and became best known for his introspective autobiographical novel, *Hærværk* (*Havoc*, 1930). Like his friend Emil Bønnelycke, Kristensen was influenced by the Italian futurist MARINETTI, yet Kristensen's poetry is more reserved and skeptical. He describes the world of thugs and pimps with which he was familiar in his childhood and draws from them a positive revolutionary model, contrasted with a Christian morality which he rejects. Travel to China in 1922, however, drove Kristensen away from Communism, and his poetry afterwards became more introspective.

[YB]

Krmpotić, Vesna (Yugoslavia, b. 1932) Krmpotić, born in Dubrovnik, has spent most of her life in Zagreb, where she graduated in psychology and English language from the Faculty of Philosophy of the University of Zagreb. She has lived in India (where she studied Bengali), Ghana, Egypt, and the United States.

Strongly influenced by Indian philosophy, Krmpotić writes poetry and lyrical prose of extraordinary style and beauty. Human existence and its angst are the focus of her poetry. Besides love as a sensuous experience, Krmpotić examines love as a means of understanding the world and ordering the universe. In her poetry, Krmpotić incorporates her knowledge of old Indian and Egyptian texts, as well as old Slav and Greek myths and legends.

Selected works: *Poezija* (*Poetry*, 1956); *Plamen i svijeća* (*A Flame and a Candle*, 1962); *Čas je, Ozirise* (*It's Time, Osiris*, 1976); *Jednina i dvojina* (*Singular and Plural*, 1981); *Stotinu i osam* (*One Hundred and Eight*, 1991).

[DJ]

Kroetsch, Robert (Canada, b. 1927) Born in Heisler, Alberta, and educated at the University of Alberta, Middlebury College, McGill University, and the University of Iowa, from 1961 to 1978, Kroetsch was a professor at the State University of New York in Binghamton, where he helped found *Boundary 2: A Journal of Postmodern Literature*. He is presently a professor at the University of Manitoba.

Kroetsch began writing poetry only after successfully establishing himself as an innovative novelist and critic, receiving the Governor General's Award for Fiction for *The Studhorse Man* (1969). Kroetsch's first collection, *The Stone Hammer Poems: 1960–75* (1975), offers an autobiographical exploration of his rural prairie roots in language that is formal and philosophical. He persists in his examination of the essential ambiguity of definitions of self, nation, place, and landscape in *Field Notes: 1–8, A Continuing Poem* (1981). With *Completed Field Notes* (1989), Kroetsch shows himself to be one of the contemporary innovators of the long poem.

Selected works: *Badlands* (1975); *Seed Catalogue* (1977); *The Lovely Treachery of Words: Essays Selected and New* (1989).

[IS]

Krolow, Karl (Germany, 1915–99) Krolow lived in Darmstadt, Germany. He began writing traditional nature poetry in *Affliction* (1948). Then, influenced by Modernist French and Spanish poetry (which Krolow translated himself), his poems became more playful and surrealistic in *Days and Nights* (1956) and *Foreign Bodies* (1959).

In the mid-1960s, Krolow turned to the

basics of human existence – such as love and love gone wrong – in *Landscapes for Me* (1966) and *Everyday Poems* (1968). His poems became more matter-of-fact in tone and addressed the limitations of language. In the process, he found his way to stricter poetic forms. During the 1980s, Krolow added open social criticism to his repertoire and increasingly pondered death, something continued in his most recent publication, *The Second Time* (1995).

[IRS]

Krynicki, Ryszard (Poland, b. 1943) Born in Sankt Valentin, Austria, Krynicki was educated at Poznan University and played a significant role in the 'Generation of '68' movement, publishing his first two books of poems in 1969 and 1975. From the mid-1970s until the late 1980s, though, Krynicki was prohibited from publishing in Poland, turning instead to underground and emigré presses which published his work. Mr Cognito Press has put out a collection of his poems translated into English, *Citizen R. K. Does Not Live*.

Linguistically experimental and politically minded, Krynicki's early poems are often expansive, while his more recent work, influenced by BERTOLT BRECHT's aphorisms, tends to be terse and morally concerned. Krynicki is also an adept translator of German and Austrian poetry.

[MO]

Kumin, Maxine (United States, b. 1925) Pulitzer Prize-winner Kumin was born Maxine Winokur in Philadelphia and educated at Radcliffe College. She has taught at a number of universities and been a poetry consultant to the Library of Congress.

The physical world has always been important to Kumin's poetry; she observes it closely and reports what she sees in exquisite detail. Family and ancestry, in a sense that she has spoken of as 'tribal', are also important. Kumin prefers the power of traditional forms, especially when working with material that is close to her.

Selected works: *The Nightmare Factory* (1970); *Up Country* (1972); *The Retrieval System* (1979); *Our Ground Time Here Will Be Brief* (1982).

[JT]

Kunitz, Stanley (United States, b. 1905) The career of Stanley Jasspon Kunitz is a lesson in endurance. His first book, *Intellectual Things* (1930), received little attention. His second, *Passport to the War*, was not published until 1944. His third, *Selected Poems 1928–58*, followed his second by another fourteen years and took years to find a publisher. When it did appear, it won the 1959 Pulitzer Prize.

Kunitz began by writing tight metaphysical poems on love and art, life and death. But in the early 1960s his style and subjects changed. A fourth book, *The Testing-Tree* (1971), contained many free-verse poems on highly personal matters, including his father's suicide, a volume that demonstrates the influence of his friend, ROBERT LOWELL, and Lowell's book *Life Studies* (1959). Kunitz's *Passing Through: The Later Poems New and Selected*, won the National Book Award in 1995. He has also translated several major Russian poets, including ANNA AKHMATOVA and OSIP MANDELSHTAM. Kunitz was appointed Poet Laureate of the United States in 2000.

[RP]

L

Labiş, Nicolae (Romania, 1935–56) Labiş' youth in north-eastern Romania was marked by war, famine and the onset of Communism. After formally studying literature in Bucharest, he edited the *Gazeta literara*; unfortunately, in the year of his literary debut, Labiş was struck by a street car and killed. Labiş wrote under conditions of maximum political pressure, having to subordinate art to communist ideology (proletcultism). Nevertheless, he had the force to break away from politically induced clichés and stereotypes and create a genuine poetry vibrating with candor, emotion, and freshness. An enthusiastic romantic, he believed in the myth of new beginnings, and saw revolution as a 'tumultuous, instinctive unfettering' (I. Milea). Simultaneously he introduced love and confession in his repertoire, reorienting poetical investigation toward the lyrical self (*First Loves*, 1956). In *Fight with Inertia* (1958), he revealed a surprising melancholy, an existential anxiety, signs of his search of self. Labiş's return to the foundations of poetry made possible the rediscovery of lyricism in the 1960s and the emergence of NICHITA STĂNESCU, the founder of a new tradition.

[GF]

Lalić, Ivan V. (Yugoslavia, 1931–96) Born into a well-known and educated family in Belgrade, Lalić finished Law School at the University of Zagreb. In addition to his work as a poet, Lalić was also a translator and literary critic.

Lalić's poetry focuses on culture, history (Yugoslav and classical, especially Greek and Byzantine), and the metaphysical search for man's place in the universe. His central themes include the experiences of childhood, love and loss, despair, suicide, and death, all often situated within a Mediterranean context. His poetry is often highly formal, written in sonnets, rhymed verse, or hexameters. His later poems are free verse.

Selected works: *Vetrovito proleće* (*A Windy Spring*, 1956); *Vreme, vatre, vrtovi* (*Time, Fires, Gardens*, 1961); *Smetnje na vezama* (*Miscommunications*, 1975); *Vizantija* (*Byzantium*, 1987); *Četiri zakona* (*Four Laws*, 1996).

[DJ]

Larbaud, Valery (France, 1881–1957) Born at Vichy into a wealthy family, Larbaud traveled extensively throughout Europe beginning in 1898. His travel-inspired writings, such as those contained in the collections *Jaune, bleu, blanc* (*Yellow, Blue, White*, 1927) and *Allen: Aux Couleurs de Rome* (*Allen: The Colors of Rome*, 1938), are of considerable literary interest. A gifted linguist, Larbaud immersed himself in the literature of the countries he visited and probably exerted greater influence on French literary life as a critic and translator (of Coleridge,

Whitman, Butler, Joyce, Faulkner, Gómez de la Serna, Svevo) than as a poet. Attributed to a fictitious South American millionaire, Archibaldo Olson Barnabooth, Larbaud's verse exhibits a typically modern cosmopolitanism, tinged with nostalgia for places once visited and charged with the restless energy of a life spent in luxury hotels and the sleeping cars of express trains criss-crossing Europe at night. Larbaud was left paralyzed by a stroke in 1935.

Selected works: *Poèmes d'un riche amateur* (*Poems of a Multimillionaire*, 1908); *A.O. Barnabooth: Ses œuvres complètes* (*A.O. Barnabooth, His Diary*, 1913).

[ML]

Larkin, Philip (England, 1922–85) The son of the city treasurer, Larkin grew up in Coventry, spending much of his youth in solitude suffering from poor eyesight and stammering. He became a student at St John's College, Oxford in 1940 where he studied literature and became lifelong friends with KINGSLEY AMIS. In 1943 Larkin earned his B.A. and in 1947, his M.A. He began his career as a librarian in 1943 at the Wellington Public Library and continued to work in various libraries over a forty-year span.

Larkin was considered the foremost member of 'The Movement', a group of British poets (see DAVIE, GUNN, JENNINGS, WAINWRIGHT) who favored traditional forms and concerned themselves first and foremost with clarity, and who were often criticized for being narrow-minded. Referred to as England's unofficial poet laureate, Larkin was a very private person who avoided the fame his poems brought him, declining to succeed Sir JOHN BETJEMAN as Poet Laureate because of the attention it would bring him. Living alone all of his life, many of his poems deal with society and its intrusion on solitude, while some of his later poems contain a more desolate look at his solitude in their contemplation of loneliness and approaching death. His poetry contains humanistic themes of love and a concern with time and its role in society. He developed in his later works a mature voice that allowed him to experiment with humor and irony while maintaining continuity, which he felt was of utmost importance (as did other members of The Movement).

Larkin's first two collections of poetry, *The North Ship* (1946) and *In the Grip of Light* (1948) were not received favorably by critics and the small third collection, *XX Poems* (1951), which he had privately printed received hardly any attention. However, he gained notoriety with his next two collections, *The Less Deceived* (1955) and *The Whitsun Weddings* (1964), which placed him among the best of the modern British poets. He published his last collection of poetry *High Windows* in 1974, and this was also largely successful.

Larkin received numerous awards including the Queen's Gold Medal for Poetry (1965), the Cholmondeley Award (1973), the Benson Medal and the CBE (1975); he was made Companion of Literature by the Royal Society of Literature in 1978. He received the Order of the Companion of Honour in June 1985, his final and highest honor.

Unable personally to receive this last honor because he was suffering from cancer of the esophagus, Larkin died following surgery in 1985 at the age of sixty-three. Published posthumously, his *Collected Poems* (1988) contained many of his unpublished pieces and was an instant success and best-seller.

[BRB]

Lasker-Schüler, Else (Germany, 1869–1945) Else Schüler's first marriage generated her more famous hyphenated surname, but it was her second marriage, to Herwarth Walden (editor of the important Expressionist magazine *The Storm*), which strengthened her extant ties to the German artistic community, including her friendships with BENN, TRAKL, and Franz Marc. Sensing things to come, she fled Nazi Germany in 1933, finally emigrating to Palestine in 1937.

Lasker-Schüler's literary work combined Judaic, Christian, and Middle Eastern elements into a personal mythology. Her poems displayed both her Jewish faith and formal experimentation, fitting in well with Expressionism. After 1917 she emphasized religion and love; her late phase added the themes of poverty and lonely exile.

Selected works: *Styx* (1902); *The Seventh Day* (1905); *Hebrew Ballads* (1913); *Collected Poems* (1917); *My Blue Piano* (1943).

[IRS]

Laughlin, James (United States, 1914–97) Laughlin was born on 30 October 1914, into a wealthy family in Pittsburgh, Pennsylvania. During a leave from Harvard University, Laughlin met EZRA POUND in Rapallo, Italy, and Pound offered to tutor Laughlin. Soon after, Pound discouraged Laughlin from writing, but encouraged him to establish a publishing firm.

Upon graduating from Harvard in 1939, Laughlin used the $100,000 his father had given him as a present to start New Directions, which he dedicated to publishing experimental writing as well as foreign authors in translation. Though once supported by family money, Laughlin's New Directions has become one of the most profitable independent presses.

While Laughlin is known primarily as a publisher, he has written over thirty-two books of poems, short stories, and essays. Despite his status as a minor poet, Laughlin's free verse is often fresh, and his lyrics can possess a resonant concision that blends Imagist and Objectivist poetics with personal experience.

[DC]

Lawrence, D. H. (England, 1885–1930) Long recognized as a major twentieth-century English novelist, David Herbert Lawrence's substantial work as a poet was largely underrated and ignored while he was alive. Lawrence's ten books of verse were finally recognized in the early 1960s, when A. Alvarez stated, 'The only native English poet to survive the First World War was D. H. Lawrence'. Since then, his poetry has been increasingly influential, with major contemporary writers acknowledging its authority.

Born in 1885 outside Nottingham, Lawrence journeyed from the industrial Midlands to the artistic and intellectual circles of Europe and North America. He attended Nottingham University College on a two-year teacher-training course. After completing his training in 1908, Lawrence taught at the Davidson Road School in the London suburb of Croydon and published his first poems in the *English Review* (1909).

His early poetry, *Love Poems and Others* (1913) and *Amores* (1916), clearly demonstrates the struggle between a young man and his 'demon', a romantic figure associated with mystery and darkness, and in concert with another side, the novelist. Together with *New Poems* (1918) and *Bay* (1919), this quartet makes up the future *Collected Poems of D. H. Lawrence* (1928). These books reflect an early phase of Lawrence's development, influenced by his childhood and youth in the colliery town of Eastwood. As in most of his writing, Lawrence does not attempt to disguise that his personal life and poetry were related. The *Collected Poems* were purposely ordered chronologically to reflect a biography of an emotional, inner life.

Lawrence's poetic style changed abruptly in 1912, when he abandoned a rhyming method for a more 'organic' or 'unrhyming' manner. Many critics suggest this stylistic shift was caused by Lawrence's meeting with Frieda von Richthofen Weekley, his future wife. Lawrence's book, *Look! We Have Come Through!* (1917) chronicles his first years with Frieda.

Despite a happy beginning with Frieda, World War I kept Lawrence from traveling and he was regularly harassed by the British authorities who tried to draft him, despite his ill health and pacifism. He and Frieda left England permanently in 1919 to settle in Italy; they would eventually travel to Mexico and the United States.

Although Lawrence was embittered after the war, his next book of verse, *Birds, Beasts and Flowers* (1923) expressed a positive affirmation, a 'pure life-rapidity'. Based on his post-war experiences, these poems are notable for visionary accuracy of metaphor and simile, as well as profound detail.

Lawrence's health continued to decline, and his poetry sharpens to its 'wittiest, slangiest and most acerbic' in his final two volumes, *Pansies* (1929) and *Nettles* (1930). Stricken with tuberculosis, Lawrence wrote one last volume, *Last Poems*, published posthumously in 1932. His acknowledgment of his pending death is clear, as the verse comprises a set of prayerful meditations. D. H. Lawrence died in Bandol, Provence, in March 1930.

[SS]

Layton, Irving (Canada, b.1912) One of Canada's most revered and reviled poets, Layton is the author of over fifty volumes of poetry, essays, and letters including *Red Carpet for the Sun* (1959), winner of the Governor General's Award for Poetry in English. Layton is as well known for the considerable body of work he has produced over six decades of writing as for the outspoken, controversial, public persona that has made him a recognizable cultural figure since the 1960s.

Born Israel Lazarovitch in Tirgu Neamt, Romania, at the age of one Layton moved with his parents to Montréal. Early in his career, Layton co-founded the important modernist journal *First Statement* (1942–5; later *Northern Review*, 1945–56), with which LOUIS DUDEK was also later associated; in 1952 Layton co-founded Contact Press with Dudek and RAYMOND SOUSTER. Layton's first collection of poetry, *Here and Now* (1945), introduces what will become characteristic themes: frank sexuality and aggressive masculine energy; direct, angry attacks on the philistinism of Canada's colonial society, and dramatization of the belief that the poet should confront and disturb society.

Layton's willingness to play the role of public gadfly has unfortunately tended to deflect attention from what is a remarkably strong and consistent body of work. The numerous prizes and awards he has received, including two Nobel Prize nominations (1981 and 1983), and the translation of his poetry into numerous languages attest to the continuing significance of his work.

Selected works: *The Collected Poems of Irving Layton* (1971); *The Darkening Fire: Selected Poems, 1945–68* (1975); *The Unwavering Eye: Selected Poems, 1969–75* (1975); *A Wild Peculiar Joy 1945–82* (1982); *Final Reckoning: Poems 1982–6* (1987).

[IS]

Lee, Dennis (Canada, b. 1939) Lee is as well-known for his inventive and witty verse for children as for an influential, if relatively small, body of criticism and poetry. Lee was born in Toronto, attended the University of Toronto, and has been an important figure in the poetry scene of that city since he co-founded the House of Anasi Press.

Lee's first book of poems, *Kingdom of Absence* (1967), was an attempt in the manner of JOHN BERRYMAN or ROBERT LOWELL to rework the sonnet form. *Civil Elegies* (1968; republished with additions in 1972), Lee's most acclaimed work, is a serious and insightful examination of dilemmas of Canadian nationalism in response to the pessimistic pronouncements of the philosopher George Grant. *Alligator Pie* (1974) and *Nicholas Knock and Other People* (1974) are the first of Lee's many books for children; the title poem of the former collection is known by nearly all Canadian children. In addition to a number of important uncollected essays, *Savage Fields* (1979) is a landmark study of MICHAEL ONDAATJE and LEONARD COHEN.

[IS]

Lee, Li-Young (United States, b. 1957) Born of Chinese parents in Indonesia, Lee was only two years old when his father became a political prisoner in President Sukarno's jails. The family fled, and for the next five years traveled in Hong Kong, Macao, and Japan, finally settling in America. Lee's romantic, almost baroque poetry deals with themes of country and identity through descriptions of his family's journey. He has won a Whiting Award, a Guggenheim Fellowship, and a writer's grant from the NEA; his second book, *The City in Which I Love You*, was the 1990 Lamont Poetry Selection of the Academy of American Poets.

[CV]

Lehmann, John (England, 1907–87) John Frederick Lehmann was born at Bourne End in the Thames Valley and educated at Eton and Trinity College, Cambridge. As important an editor as he was a poet, especially because of his receptivity to new talent, he began his association with the Hogarth Press in 1931, becoming a partner in 1938. He is perhaps best known, however, as the editor of *New Writing* and of *London Magazine*. His early poetry is remarkably detached in both tone and subject matter. From an early stage, his poetry was technically adroit, presenting carefully constructed cadences, subtle assonance, and well-timed internal rhyme. Lehmann's poetry was often eclipsed by his other activities and is now somewhat neglected, despite its unostentatious rhythms and direct treatment of experience.

Selected works: *A Garden Revisited and Other Poems* (1931); *Forty Poems* (1942); *Collected Poems 1930–63* (1963); *Christ the Hunter* (1965); *Photograph* (1971); *New and Selected Poems* (1985).

[EM]

Leino, Eino (Finland, 1878–1926) Armas Eino Leopold Leino was a poet, novelist, dramatist, essayist, journalist, and translator. His first published collection *Maaliskuun Lauluja* (*March Songs*, 1896) raised the language of poetry to new heights. The subsequent *Helkavirret* (*Whitsuntide Hymns*, 1903) belongs to the early years of his mature period; in this volume he employs material from folk poetry's legends and ballads, but Leino's 'modernized' *Kalevala* meter makes the work uniquely his own. Symbolism of death, desolation, and loneliness often dominates his later collections. His later work culminates in *Helkavirret II* (1916) with elements of theosophic mysticism. A unique work of this period is the skillfully wrought, stanzaic collection of love lyrics *Juhana herttuan ja Catharina Jagellonican lauluja* (*The Songs of Duke Juhana and Catharina Jagellonica*, 1919). Lyric poetry forms a relatively small part of Leino's poetic oeuvre; of the sixteen parts of his *Collected Works*, only five are of lyric poetry. Among Leino's many translations of classics from Runeberg to Corneille's *Le Cid*, Dante's *Divina Commedia* is the most significant. Leino was awarded the State Literature Prize eleven times.

[SP]

Leonard, Tom (Scotland, b. 1944) Leonard was born in Glasgow, educated at Lourdes Secondary School and as a mature student studied English and Scottish literature at Glasgow University. He has since held a number of writer-in-residence posts in Glasgow. In the language of urban Glasgow, his poetry grapples head-on with social hypocrisy with equal amounts of fury and humor; his influences are wide-ranging, from government reports to WILLIAM CARLOS WILLIAMS. He has also written a radio play, revues with LIZ LOCHHEAD and Alasdair Gray, and organized two sound-poetry festivals.

Selected works: *Six Glasgow Poems* (1969); *Intimate Voices: Selected Work 1965–83* (1984);

Situations Theoretical and Contemporary (1986); *Nora's Place* (1990); *Reports from the Present: Selected Work 1982–94* (1995).

[LKMF]

Levertov, Denise (United States, 1923–97) Even though Levertov was born in Ilford, Essex, England, she is usually considered an American poet. After serving as a nurse during World War II, Levertov married Mitchell Goodman in 1947 and emigrated to the United States in 1948, becoming a citizen in 1955.

Throughout her career, Levertov remained politically active in her poetry; during the Vietnam War, along with MURIEL RUKEYSER and others, she formed the Writers and Artists Protest Against the War in Vietnam. Her poetry never wavered in its focus on community, and she often integrated environmental concerns and women's issues into her meditations upon daily life.

Levertov published her first book of poetry, *The Double Image*, in 1946, and thereafter more than thirty books of poetry, translations, and essays. In 1976, she received the Lenore Marshall Poetry Prize for *The Freeing of the Dust*.

Levertov continued to write, publish, and protest until her death in 1997 from complications from lymphoma.

[DC]

Levi, Peter (England, b. 1931) Peter Chad Tigar Levi, a former Jesuit priest, was Professor of Poetry at Oxford from 1984 to 1989. Levi taught Greek and Latin for twenty-five years and is the author and editor of more than forty books. His writing includes biographies of Shakespeare, Milton, Pasternak, and, most recently, *Horace: A Life* (1989).

Like his major influences, WALLACE STEVENS and GEORGE SEFERIS, Levi writes poetry characterized by graceful rhythms, casual rhyme schemes, and a subdued tone. Using language that is simple and natural, Levi reflects in his poetry his concerns for nature, death, and relationships.

Selected works: *Collected Poems 1955–75* (1976); *Five Ages* (1978); *Private Ground* (1981); *The Echoing Green* (1983); *Shadow and Bone* (1989); *The Rags of Time* (1994); *Reed Music* (1997).

[EM]

Levine, Philip (United States, b. 1928) Levine is the best-known stylist of a prominent school of late-century American poetry. Autobiographical, often narrative, his poems describe everyday events in a lyric vernacular that is deceptively simple in its progression. Levine's poetry focuses mostly on his immigrant family, the difficulties of their working-class life in Detroit, and World War II. His *What Work Is* won the 1991 National Book Award; he teaches at New York University.

Selected works: *They Feed The Lion* (1972); *Selected Poems* (1984); *A Walk with Thomas Jefferson* (1988); *New Selected* (1991); *The Simple Truth* (1994).

[CV]

Lew, Emma (Australia, b. 1962) Lew's poetry has been widely published in journals throughout the world. Her first collection, *The Wild Reply* (1997), was co-winner of The Age of Poetry Book Award (with PETER PORTER), was awarded the Mary Gilmore Award, and was shortlisted for the New South Wales Premier Prize. In the absence of linear, or even fragmented, narrative, Lew's poetry is like a postmodern drama: intense, urgent, and wild. Lew brings a startling unfamiliar voice to Australian poetry.

[DCO]

Lewis, Alun (Wales, 1915–44) Lewis was born in the mining village of Cwmaman and studied History at the University of Aberystwyth. In 1937 he decided to train as a teacher. In the same year his first poems were published in newspapers and magazines. In 1938 he joined the faculty at Lewis' Boys School in Pengam, and in 1939 he became engaged to Gweno Ellis, whom he had met as an undergraduate.

When World War II broke out, Lewis was divided over the appropriate course of action. Like many Welsh men of letters, he favored pacifism but, eventually, in the spring of 1940, he left his school for the Royal Engineers.

Separated from his beloved Gweno and unhappy with military life, Lewis continued to write. His circumstances inspired him to new heights; within a few months he had written several significant poems, including the grimly prophetic 'All Day it Has Rained'. After marrying Gweno in 1941, Lewis applied for a commission, which he attained by the time of his first book, *Raider's Dawn* (1942). A short story collection, *The Last Inspection*, appeared in the same year. In the winter of 1942 his unit (the 6th Battalion South Wales Borderers) was transferred to India, where Lewis entered another creatively productive phase. He had already prepared his second volume of poems for publication when he was killed in a firearms accident in Burma; *Ha! Ha! among the Trumpets* (1945) appeared posthumously, along with *Letters from India* (1946), and his second collection of short stories, *In The Green Tree* (1948).

[BS]

Li Guangtian (Xi Cen; China, 1906–68) Poet and critic Li was born into the family of a poor peasant in Zouping, Shandong. Adopted by his maternal uncle, who was able to give him a decent education, Li went to the First Normal School of Shandong and then, in 1929, to Beijing University, where he was classmate to BIAN ZHILIN. Li began to publish during his college years, but became famous only after the appearance of *The Han Garden*, a collection of poems by him, Bian, and He Qifang in 1936. Li's poems are characterized by a highly refined sensibility: he was one of the first Chinese poets at the time to sense the futility and fragmentation of life in the small towns and villages. His major books of poetry include *The Han Garden* (1936), *The Spring City* (1958), *Ashima* (1960), and *Xianxiu* (1962). The last two are long narratives based on the folk tales of the Dai minority.

[LG]

Li Jinfa (Li Shuliang; China, 1900–76) Li went to France to study fine arts in 1919. Highly influenced by the French Symbolists, Baudelaire in particular, Li began to write Symbolist poems. His first collection of poetry, *The Drizzle* (1925), published with the encouragement of the Cultural Minister Zhou Zuoren, blew an exotic wind into Chinese verse, a wind so exotic for the unprepared audience that Li has ever since been called a 'genius of absurd poetry'. This nickname bears much truth: he deliberately destroys all syntax, writes quite a number of poems with only emotionally charged nouns and adjectives, and is able to suggest multiple layers of meaning. Although the unique strength of this type of poetry derives partially from the intrinsic property of the Chinese language which is typically pictographic, Li was the first to take successful advantage and to revolt against conventional poetic form. Li is the first Chinese Symbolist poet and the most innovative of modern Chinese poets. His other books of poetry include *Songs of Happiness* (1926), *Parasites and Murderers* (1929), and *Collected Poems of Li Jinfa* (1986). Li died in New York on December 25, 1976.

[LG]

Li Ying (China, b. 1926) A native of Fengrun, Hebei, Li was born into the family of a poor railroad worker. She went to Beijing University in 1945, majoring in Chinese. After graduation, she joined the Liberation Army in 1949, and since then has worked in the military cultural institutions as journalist, editor, and freelance writer. Li is a prolific poet, writing mainly about life in the military. She has published over two dozen books of poetry, such as *Festivals in the Battle Field* (1953), *The Quiet Sentry Post* (1963), and *The*

Burning Battle Field (1984). *The Smiling Face of Spring* (1951) won her belated recognition with National Poetry Awards in 1982 and 1984. Her talent in expressing the bold and unconventional nature of army life in graceful language and from a clearly feminine perspective is rarely surpassed.

[LG]

Liehu, Rakel Maria (Finland, b. 1939) Rakel Liehu is first and foremost a poet, although she has also written plays and novels, and been a newspaper columnist and a lecturer of Finnish language and history. Her early poetry employs decidedly religious themes and representative imagery. Critics see the influence of French feminist Poststructuralism in her more recent work; hence, her writing has undergone a significant change, setting her apart among contemporary Finnish poets. Liehu is seen as a Postsymbolist mythographer whose language affects shifts in reader consciousness. In abandoning the idea of a stable text, her language is continuously transforming itself. While it reflects the disunity in human existence, it gives the reader the chance to discover an abundance of associative images.

Among Liehu's ten collections of poetry, the following three are particularly noteworthy: *Kubisseja* (*Cubisms*, 1992), *Murehtimatta! Smaragdinen* (1993), and *Skorpionin sydän* (*Scorpion's Heart*, 1997). Among her awards, Finland's Association of Authors' Prize in 1992 is the most significant.

[SP]

Lindegren, Erik (Sweden, 1910–68) Poet and art critic Lindegren grew up in northern Sweden and settled in Stockholm in the 1930s. His first collection, *Posthum ungdom* (*Posthumous Youth*, 1935) shows the influence of Symbolism and fin-de-siècle fascination with ennui and death. Yet it was not until *Mannen utan våg* (*The Man without a Way*, 1942), which Lindegren had to have printed privately, that the author gained wide reputation. The volume introduced an innovative form of poems comprising seven non-rhyming couplets. These 'exploded sonnets' heralded a new trend in Swedish poetry. The fragmented, unharmonic form was combined with themes of disorientation and may well have reflected the poet's reaction to the horrors of World War II. Lindegren's absurd and abstract tone mellowed somewhat in later collections, such as *Sviter* (*Suites*, 1947) and *Vinteroffer* (*Winter Sacrifice*, 1954). In 1962 Lindegren was elected a member of the Swedish Academy.

[YB]

Lindsay, Vachel (United States, 1879–1931) Nicholas Vachel Lindsay has been an out of favor yet persistently influential poet for much of the twentieth century. Ignored because of his sincere enthusiasms – a lack of irony – and unenlightened racial views, he nonetheless contributed to the language of conversation and folk song in American poetry.

Born in Springfield, Illinois, Lindsay was raised as a fundamentalist Christian. He attended Hiram College, Ohio, the Chicago Art Institute, and in 1905 finished his formal education at the Chase School, New York.

Lindsay's first book of poems, *The Tramp's Excuse and Other Poems* (1909), followed the first of several voluntary tramps through the country. *The Congo and Other Poems* (1914) was his most popular book. For years, he was in demand as a reader and lecturer. In his early fifties, he killed himself.

[CC]

Lipska, Ewa (Poland, b. 1945) Lipska was born in Krakow, and studied painting and art history at the Krakow Academy of Fine Arts. Like ADAM ZAGAJEWSKI, she is one of the New Wave poets whose writing reflects the democratic movement in Poland during the 1960s and whose art has been influenced by the Polish poets born in the 1920s, including Lipska's friend and mentor, WISLAWA SZYMBORSKA. Lipska published five volumes of poetry between 1967 and 1978, and had an English-language edition of selected poems, *Poet? Criminal? Madman?* appear in 1991. Like her surrealistic novel *The Storeroom of Darkness* (1985), her poems frequently use dream logic to address the madness of daily life and express her skepticism that language can effect social justice.

Selected works: *Living Death* (1978); *Home of Peaceful Youth* (1979); *Not a Matter Here of Death, but of a White Purl* (1982).

[RD]

Livesay, Dorothy (Canada, 1909–96) Livesay is best known for her socially committed verse written in the 1930s and 1940s, which earned her two Governor General Awards for Poetry. Born in Winnipeg, her family moved to Toronto when she was twelve. She attended the University of Toronto, where she began to write and publish poetry while still an undergraduate. While her early work was influenced by Imagism, her horror at the Depression led her to become a Marxist and a social worker, and to produce poetry that forcefully articulated radical political and social themes.

Livesay's poetry has retained this political side ever since, even while it has undergone other changes over the decades, becoming more personal in the 1950s and then in the 1960s being influenced by both the Black Mountain poets and those associated with the Vancouver magazine *Tish*. Livesay is important for being one of the first Canadian poets to write directly and frankly about the experiences of women.

Selected works: *Collected Poems: The Two Seasons* (1972); *The Phases of Love* (1983); *The Self-Completing Tree: Selected Poems* (1986).

[IS]

Livingston, Douglas James (South Africa, 1932–96) Douglas Livingston is widely recognized as one of the leading Modernist poets from South Africa. The son of a colonial officer and born in Kuala Lumpur, Malaya, he moved with his family to South Africa in 1942. Trained in Harare as a bacteriologist, he worked in Zambia before returning to South Africa in 1964. There he continued to balance his scientific and literary careers, publishing poems and medical articles in numerous British, American, Rhodesian, and South African journals until his untimely death in 1996. He was awarded the Guinness Poetry Award in 1965, the Cholmondeley Award in 1970, the Olive Schreiner Prize in 1974, and the South African English Association Prize in 1977.

Writing largely within a non-political framework, his poetry is nonetheless grounded in the contemporary South African experience and he is often compared with the earlier South African poet, ROY CAMPBELL. Using strict syllabic counts and complicated rhyme schemes, language itself plays a significant factor in Livingston's early work. Although he utilizes a wide variety of styles and personae, his early childhood memories of war seem to have influenced him as a great deal of his poetry reflects struggle, destruction, and violence; death in the animal world and the destruction of the physical world figure prominently. Similarly, isolation and the reality of isolation is another recurring motif, resulting in a verse that reflects fragmented social, ethical, and humanistic values.

Selected works: *The Skull in the Mud* (1960); *Sjambok and Other Poems from Africa* (1964); *Poems* (with THOMAS KINSELLA and ANNE SEXTON, 1968); *Eyes Closed against the Sun* (1970); *The Sea my Winding Sheet and Other Poems* (1971); *A Rosary of Bone* (1975); *The Anvil's Undertone* (1978); *A Littoral Zone* (1991).

[KS]

Lochhead, Liz (Scotland, b. 1947) Lochhead was born in Motherwell, grew up in a largely Protestant mining village close by, and was educated at Dalziel High

School. She studied painting and drawing at Glasgow School of Art in 1965–70 and it was during those years that she began to write poetry. After art school she worked as an art teacher at Bishopriggs High School; and in 1972 she published her first collection, *Memo for Spring*. She won a Writers Exchange Fellowhip to Canada in 1979 after which she became a full-time writer, holding several writer-in-residence posts. As well as six collections of poetry, she has written plays and performance pieces, collaborated on two revues with TOM LEONARD, and made a successful translation into Scots of Molière's *Tartuffe* (1985). She is firm in the belief that poetry for readings should be selected with the audience in mind, with accessible pieces which can be put across to her listeners. This has stood her in good stead for radio and television work, and often results in rhythmical, sensuous, and direct poetry. Her pieces written specially for performance are collected in *True Confessions and New Clichés* (1985). Her writing relishes bravura movement and evinces particular strength in her evocations of women's lives.

Selected works: *Memo for Spring* (1972); *Islands* (1978) and *The Grimm Sisters* (1981) collected in *Dreaming Frankenstein and Collected Poems* (1984); *Bagpipe Muzak* (1991).

[LKMF]

Lodeizen, Hans (The Netherlands, 1924-50) One of the most widely read poets of The Netherlands, Lodeizen's nostalgic poetry of longing is still popular, especially among younger readers. He wrote melancholic poems in which the contrast between dream and reality is the predominant theme.

Lodeizen went to law school in Leiden, but he moved to the United States (Amherst, Massachusetts) to pursue his real interest: biology. However, existential restlessness and a premonition of his disease – he died of leukemia – led him to quit his studies in 1948.

During his short life, Lodeizen published only one collection, *Het innerlijk behang* (*The Inner Wallpaper*, 1949). In some of his posthumously published works, including *Verzamelde gedichten* (*Complete Poems*, 1997) he bears witness to his homosexuality.

[TV]

Logue, Christopher (England, b. 1926) Logue is lauded for his free adaptations of Homer's *Iliad* in four separate books: *Patrocleia* (1962), *Pax* (1967), *War Music* (1981), and *Kings* (1991), praised for their originality. Logue, who served in the British Army and has acted in plays, films, and television productions retells the epic tale with a modern, cinematic flair, while exposing the violence of war. Despite acting, translating, and writing plays, children's literature, and prose, Logue makes his living primarily from his poetry, which he has both recorded and adapted into illustrated posters. He is also a contributor to *Private Eye* and *The Times* (London).

Logue's early poetry was influenced by EZRA POUND and he is known as a writer of populist lyric and satiric verse, a 'comic poet', who is wry and self-deprecating. Other major works include: *Wand and Quadrant* (1953); *The Man Who Told His Love* (1958); and *Ode to the Dodo* (1981).

[JS]

Lokhvitskaia, Mirra (Maria) Alexandrovna (Russia 1869–1905) Lokhvitskaia's father was the law professor, A.V. Lokhvitski, and sister was a well-known writer, N.A. Teffi. Lokhvitskaia was educated at home, then studied in 1888 at the Aleksandrovski Institute in Moscow. In 1892–5 she lived in the provincial towns of Iaroslav' and Tikhvin, then returned to Moscow, finally settling in St Petersburg in 1898. She had five children. Her first poems 'Sila vera' ('The Power of Faith') and 'Den' i noch' ('Day and Night'), were published in Moscow in 1888. After *The Russian Survey* published the poem 'By the Sea', her name became known in literary circles; espousing passionate, sensual love, she was labeled immoral and decadent – and her poetry's notoriety was established. The year 1896 saw the publication of a collection of early work, *Poems*, a volume that received critical praise. Four additional volumes of *Poems* followed in 1898, 1900, 1903, and 1904. In her poetry, she rejects the civic way of thinking and proclaims the worship of beauty and sensuality; like other Modernist poets, she also manifests an interest in the past and in folklore. Her work expresses the subtlety of feelings and an interest in exotic sensations.

[RN]

Longley, Michael (Ireland, b. 1939) A suburban Belfast poet, Longley is frequently associated with the group of Northern Irish poets such as DEREK MAHON, SEAMUS HEANEY, and James Simmons, who earned their reputations in the late 1960s and early 1970s. Longley received his B.A. from Trinity College, Dublin, in 1963, and for six years taught school in Dublin, London, and Belfast. He took a position at the Arts Council of Northern Ireland in 1970, where he worked until 1991.

Much of Longley's early work examines the political upheaval of Northern Ireland. *No Continuing City* (1969) and *An Exploded View* (1973) address the ambiguous and difficult position of a Northern Irish Protestant, who, while sympathizing with the Catholic's desire for civil rights, cannot abandon his own Protestant past. However, unlike Protestant poet TOM PAULIN, Longley shows no ambivalence in identifying himself as part of the British tradition. *The Echo Gate* (1979) struggles with the necessary healing and reconciliation between these two communities.

Longley's poems are carefully crafted and formal, technically precise, often using world mythologies and themes to illustrate local situations. In 1994, his poem 'Cease Fire' was published in the *Irish Times* on the day of the historic IRA cease fire; the poem utilizes the final scenes of *The Iliad* to suggest the heroic necessity of forgiveness and reconciliation. In 1991 he won the Whitbread Prize for Poetry

Selected works: *Selected Poems 1963–80* (1981); *Poems 1963–83* (1985); *Gorse Fires* (1991); *The Ghost Orchid* (1995).

[CT]

Lopez Vallecillos, Italo (El Salvador, 1932–86) Journalist, essayist, and historian Lopez Vallecillos was a founder of the 'Committed Generation', a significant group of poets that organized themselves in the mid-1950s to redefine the political responsibilities of the modern writer. He also founded two very important presses: EDUCA and UCA Editores, through which he exercised an enormous influence in shaping the literary culture of Central America.

Although known for his historical and political writings during El Salvador's civil war years, his poetry remains the marker of his international literary profile.

Selected works: *Biografía del hombre triste* (*Biography of a Sad Man*, 1954); *Imágenes sobre el otoño* (*Songs about the Autumn*, 1962); *Puro asombro* (*Pure Astonishment*, 1970); *Inventario de soledad* (*Inventory of Loneliness*, 1975).

[SL]

Lorca, Federico García (Spain, 1898–1936) One of Spain's most accomplished poets and dramatists of the twentieth century, Lorca was born near Granada in Andalusia. The south of Spain would become a central theme of his work. A lover of art, Lorca studied drawing and painting and was a close friend of Salvador Dalí. He was also a fine musician, and the influence of Spanish popular songs can be seen in his poetry. In the 1920s Lorca lived at the students' residence in Madrid and became a central figure of the Generation of 1927. This group of poets lauded the Baroque poet Luis de Góngora and was also influenced by Ortega y Gasset's *The Dehumanization of Art*. As a result, these poets did not view aesthetic ideals as dependent upon ordinary reality, but instead sought to create artistic worlds that were more profound and real than the world around them. Styles ranged from GUILLÉN's Symbolism to Lorca and ALEIXANDRE's Surrealism.

Lorca began to write plays and was active in the workers' theater groups during the Second Republic (1931–36). Lorca went to New York in 1929 and there wrote the surrealist *Poet in New York* (1931). In 1936, Lorca, a Republican supporter, was executed near Granada.

Lorca's fame as a poet rests on *Gypsy Ballads* (1927), *Poem of the Deep Song* (1931), and *Poet in New York*. *Deep Song* combines flamenco-type rhythms with everyday images to create simple yet transcendent poems. The stunning *Gypsy Ballads* uses popular Andalusian culture and the figure of the gypsy to represent the primordial themes of love and lust, life and death. *Poet in New York* remains one of the finest examples of Surrealist poetry in Spain. Depression-era New York City embodies the poet's despair and loneliness upon his separation from the motherland. The book's disturbing imagery symbolizes humankind's fall from grace into the *danse macabre* of a world in upheaval.

[AB]

Lorde, Audre (United States, 1934–92) Lorde grew up in Harlem, New York, and earned degrees from Hunter College and Columbia University. She published nine books of poetry that are wild, poignantly insightful, and sometimes rhetorically grand. She writes ardently on personal and political subjects, and also creates mythologies; however, her self-declared identities as African-American, feminist, and lesbian have attracted the most scholarly interest.

A co-founder of Kitchen Table/Women of Color Press, Lorde won three National Endowment of the Arts grants, and was the New York State poet laureate in 1991–92.

Lorde's first collection, *The First Cities*, was published in 1968; her last, *Undersong: Chosen Poems Old and New*, was published just before her death, in St Croix, of cancer; *The Marvelous Arithmetic of Difference* (1993) is a collection of posthumously published poems.

[HE]

Louis, Adrian C. (United States, b. 1947) Louis was born and raised in northern Nevada and is an enrolled member of the Lovelock Paiute Tribe. Since 1984 he has taught at Oglala Lakota College on the Pine Ridge Reservation in South Dakota.

A long-time editor of Native American newspapers including *Indian Country Today*, the Indian newspaper with widest circulation in the United States, Louis has written two works of prose that have been translated into French. He is primarily known, however, as a poet, publishing nine volumes and winning a Pushcart Prize, as well as fellowships from the Bush Foundation, the National Endowment for the Arts and the Lila Wallace-Reader's Digest Foundation for his writing. In 1989 he was awarded the Poetry Center Book Award from San Francisco State University.

His poetry is often characterized as angry, tough, honest and hard-bitten. Louis takes the realist view of reservation life as he sees it and lives it. His poems reflect the violence, alcoholism and despair as well as the tenacity, humor and love that make up life for many Native Americans today.

Selected works: *The Indian Cheap Wine Seance* (1974); *Muted Ward Drums* (1977); *Sweets for the Dancing Bears* (1979); *Fire Water World* (1989); *Among the Do Eaters* (1992); *Blood Thirsty Savages* (1994); *Vortext of Indian Fevers* (1995); *Ceremonies of the Damned* (1997).

[HEE]

Lowell, Amy (United States, 1874–1925) Lowell is best remembered for her experiments in technique and form. A foster-parent of the Imagist movement, she traveled to England in 1914, where she met EZRA POUND and H.D. (Upon Pound's defection from Imagism, he began to call such poetry 'Amy-ism'.) Lowell's first collection, a forgettable volume, appeared in 1912, when she was thirty-eight. Subsequent volumes showed originality, vitality, and motion.

Born into a distinguished family – one brother was president of Harvard University and another charted the canals on Mars, while ROBERT LOWELL was a distant cousin–her education was acquired privately, and through travel. Among her admirers was THOMAS HARDY; her death was occasion for nation-wide tributes.

Selected works: *The Complete Poetical Works* (1955).

[RP]

Lowell, Robert (United States, 1917–77) If Robert Lowell had not appeared on the American poetry scene when he did, critics would have invented him. He began to publish at exactly the time when a new 'Major American Poet' was needed. ROBERT FROST's poetry after World War II was mainly occasional and relaxed. EZRA POUND was held on treason charges. T.S. ELIOT had become more British than the British. And WALLACE STEVENS' last major work had not yet appeared. So when Lowell's difficult-to-read and even more difficult-to-come-by (it was a small press publication) *Land of Unlikeness* appeared in 1944, poets and critics applauded. When *Lord's Weary Castle* was published in 1946, reprinting some of the same poems but from a trade publisher, Lowell was given the Pulitzer Prize. Before he was thirty he held a Guggenheim Fellowship and was appointed Poetry Consultant to the Library of Congress. He also won a grant from the National Institute of Arts and Letters.

This is rare recognition for a poet whose early work was at best difficult. The first two books contained clotted and baroque imagery, esoteric allusions, a fierce rhetoric, and promoted the necessity of finding faith in a secular country. Like that of Robert Frost, Lowell's work had deep roots in New England; the difference was that Frost was a failed poultry farmer and Lowell the descendant of urban patricians.

Lowell's third book, *The Mills of the Kavanaughs* (1951), containing a 'symbolic monologue by an insane woman' (according to Lowell's account), was met with puzzlement. It has since tended to be neglected by Lowell critics even today. Its reception was perhaps one reason why Lowell turned his back on his early manner and themes and wrote the poems and prose in *Life Studies* (1959) – although he also was taken by the openly confessional poems W.D. SNODGRASS was writing for his own first book, *Heart's Needle* (1960). In either event, the *Life Studies* poems are the freest verse Lowell was to write. There are poems on his relatives, his marriage, his poet friends, politics, and his own mental instability. The book contains what arguably is his most famous poem, 'Skunk Hour', and a prose autobiographical fragment, '91 Revere Street'. It is the book of Lowell's which has worn the best.

It was followed by *Imitations* (1961), a collection of seventy poems derived from poems by eighteen other writers, some in languages Lowell did not read. Some felt he coarsened the originals. But then came *For the Union Dead* (1964), which continued in the *Life Studies* mode and contains another of his best poems, the title piece. Numerous other books followed but none occupied Lowell as much as his 'sonnet sequences', *Notebook 1967–68* (1969), a series of fifty-eight sequences, which he later revised and extended as three separate books, *History* (1973), *For Lizzie and Harriet* (1973), and *The Dolphin* (1973) – revised, in part, with the advice of his friend ELIZABETH BISHOP.

Robert (Traill Spence) Lowell was born in Boston of a family whose members included James Russel Lowell and AMY LOWELL. He attended St Mark's School,

Harvard University, Kenyon College, and Louisiana State University. As a conscientious objector to World War II, he served five months in a Federal prison. His first two marriages, to fiction writer Jean Stafford and critic Elizabeth Hardwick, ended in divorce. In 1972 he left New York and Hardwick to live in England. He married novelist Lady Caroline Blackwood in the same year. A final book, *Day by Day* (1977), published just before he died of a heart attack in Manhattan, marked a return to his powers of the 1950s and 1960s. He left one daughter, Harriet, by Hardwick, and a son, Sheridan, by Blackwood.

Selected works: *Selected Poems* (1987); *Collected Prose* (1987); *Collected Poems* (2000).

[RP]

Loy, Mina (England, 1882–1966) Born Mina Gertrude Lowry, the avant-garde poet Mina Loy lived and traveled extensively in Europe and the Americas before becoming a naturalized U.S. citizen in 1946.

Although she published relatively little in her lifetime, she has recently been 'rediscovered' and recognized for having made an important contribution to her art. She has been read by recent scholars as a lost literary gem of American Modernist poets. Her often satirical poetry reflects her interest in the nature of artistic creation, a sharp sense of feminine oppression, and 'savage truth-telling'. An actress and visual artist as well as a writer, Loy also received recognition for her painting, but it is as a poet that she survives.

Selected works: *Lunar Baedeker* (1923); *Lunar Baedeker and Time Tables* (1958); *The Last Lunar Baedeker* (1982); *Insel* (1991); *The Lost Lunar Baedeker* (1996).

[JS]

Lucebert (Lubertus Swaanswijk, The Netherlands, 1924–94) Although he is world famous as a painter from the Cobra group, in his own country Lucebert's double talent is mainly recognized as a poet and principal character of the Movement of the 1950s (also known as the 'Experimentalists'), the group of poets who changed the face of Dutch poetry after World War II. In exuberant, rich and often humorously absurdist poems he searches for a primal form of language. The romantic Lucebert expects to find a deeper wisdom here than in the narrow-minded spiritual climate of the post-war Netherlands. His poetry is characterized by an irregular composite of images. His metaphors are heavily physical: he emphasizes the sensuality of the body, not the intellect.

In 1953, BERTOLT BRECHT invited Lucebert to spend some time in East Berlin. After his return to The Netherlands Lucebert did not move back to Amsterdam, but instead chose Bergen, a small town near the North Sea. There he concentrated more and more on painting, mainly because his faith in poetry as a positive force in the world had waned. In the period after 1965 he wrote very little, though during the 1980s his poetic production regained its strength. Lucebert's later poems are more accessible and calmer: the vital elan of his first period is overshadowed by an essentially pessimistic worldview.

His unconventional and rebellious debut, *Apocrief/ De analphabetische naam* (*Apocryphal/ The Analaphabetical Name*, 1952) was received with amazement and generate controversy. Subsequent volumes, such as *Van de afgronden de luchtmens* (*About the Abyss and the Air Man*, 1953) and *Troost de hysterische robot* (*Comfort the Hysterical Robot*, 1989), showed the excellence of his verse and garnered him all major poetry prizes of The Netherlands and Flanders.

[TV]

Luo Fu (Mo Luofu; Taiwan, b. 1927) Luo, a native of Hunan, China, went to Hunan State University to study English in 1948, but left for Taiwan a year later. He served in the Taiwan Marine Corps for quite a few years, and was sent to Vietnam in 1965 as English Secretary of the Taiwan Military Consultative Group.

Luo is famous both as editor of the leading poetry magazine *Epoch*, and as an original poet. *Epoch* is to modern Chinese verse in Taiwan what *Poetry* is to modern American verse: it is engaged in introducing the local modernist poets, and modern Western literary trends to the general public. Its contribution to the process of modernizing Chinese poetry in Taiwan cannot be overestimated.

In Luo's own poetry, veins of French Surrealism and Existentialism can be easily traced. *Death of the Stone Room* (1965), his best-known long poem in dozens of stanzas, is generally regarded as monumental and inspirational in the development of modern Chinese poetry.

Selected works: *Soul, Beyond Outside* (1967); *Songs of the Devils* (1982); *The River Without Banks* (1986).

[LG]

Luzi, Mario (Italy, b. 1914) Luzi was born and raised in Florence, where he eventually became Professor of French Literature. His early collections, deeply influenced by Ermetismo (see UNGARETTI, QUASIMODO), showed all the typical themes and idiosyncrasies of this movement: an intense spirituality, a contemptuous attitude toward reality, an 'orphism' leading directly to Mallarmé and ELUARD. His late collections, while displaying praiseworthy metrical innovations, developed Luzi's metaphysical interest toward a dark and passionate Christian sensibility.

Selected works: *La barca* (*The Boat*, 1942); *Nel magma* (*In the Magma*, 1963); *Al fuoco della controversia* (*At the Fire of Controversy*, 1978); *Il silenzio la voce* (*The Silence, the Voice*, 1984); *Viaggio terrestre e celeste di Simone Martini* (*The Earthly and Celestial Voyage of Simone Martini*, 1994); *Ceneri e ardori* (*Ashes and Burnings*, 1997).

[GS]

M

MacBeth, George (England, 1932–92) A prolific poet and novelist, MacBeth was born in Shotts, and educated at New College, Oxford. He was a member of a loose-knit group of British poets known as The Group. From 1957 to 1976 he worked as a producer for the BBC.

MacBeth has been described as a 'public poet' whose poems are consistently open to audience, appealing directly to the common reader. Although he is not viewed as avant-garde, he liked much of the work of such writers. His finest volume was the early *The Broken Places* (1963), for which he was co-recipient of the Faber Award in 1964. His later poetry sought new ways to combine modern approachability with the technical skills of the Victorians.

A poet of diverse interests and changing styles, MacBeth wrote with a consciously chosen and pursued form. His works reveal a common aspect: the ordering of feeling by means of rules and regulations, principles of construction which go beyond the traditional meter, rhyme, and stanza pattern.

When motor neurone disease debilitated him before his death in 1992, MacBeth wrote a collection of poems which described with painful candor the stages of his illness and the heartbreak of his wife, exploring their shared and separate torments. Posthumously published, *The Patient* (1992) has been seen by some as MacBeth's own apotheosis.

Selected works: *A Form of Words* (1954); *The Colour of Blood* (1967); *The Night of Stones* (1968); *A War Quartet* (1969).

[JS]

MacCaig, Norman (Scotland, 1910–96) MacCaig was born in Edinburgh. His father was from Dumfriesshire and his mother from Scalpay; the mixture of the two cultures and connection through his mother with the Gaelic-speaking community influenced much of his work. He went to the Royal High School in Edinburgh and read Classics at Edinburgh University. During the war he was a conscientious objector. On retiring as a primary schoolteacher after nearly forty years, he first became Fellow in Creative Writing at Edinburgh University in 1967–69, then at Stirling was Lecturer in English Studies in 1970–72 and Reader in Poetry in 1972–77. He was awarded the OBE in 1979 and Queen's Gold Medal for Poetry in 1986.

His first two collections, *Far Cry* (1943) and *The Inward Eye*(1946), were aligned with the New Apocalypse school but he later disowned them, excluding these works from his *Collected Poems* (1990). His prolific and successful later poetry was, contrastingly, wittily descriptive and compact. His poems are often passionately precise–dealing with human and animal peculiarities, the landscape of Assynt, and the cityscape of Edinburgh. The contained oppositions of the poetry reflect his love of debate, a love fed in the Edinburgh writers' circles of the 1950s and 1960s, especially in conversations with his friends HUGH MACDIARMID and SORLEY MACLEAN (SOMHAIRLE MACGILL-EAIN).

Selected works: *Riding Lights* (1955); *The Sinai Sort* (1957); *Surroundings* (1966); *Rings on a Tree* (1968); *A Man in My Position* (1969); *The World's Room* (1974); *The Equal Skies* (1980); *Voice-Over* (1988).

[LKMF]

MacDiarmid, Hugh (Christopher Murray Grieve; Scotland, 1892–1978) A lowland postman's son, MacDiarmid became the greatest poet and cultural nationalist of modern Scotland. Returning from Salonika during World War I, Grieve took up a career as a journalist and freelance writer. In 1921, he launched a series of letters denouncing Scots as a language incapable of intellectual achievement; only a year later, Grieve began his powerful poetic career – in Scots – publishing 'The Watergaw' under the name Hugh MacDiarmid (which combined the lowland 'Hugh' with the Clan Campbell surname). MacDiarmid's subtlety and craft erased the sentimental and maudlin qualities of a great deal of nineteenth-century Scots verse. His two volumes of shorter Scots lyrics, *Sangschaw* (1925) and *Penny Wheep* (1926), achieved a combination of Romantic imagery with Modernist technique and content. The book-length *A Drunk Man Looks at the Thistle* (1926) was his greatest poetic achievement in Scots; its ditch-bound drunkard intellectualizes poetry, the shifting metaphors of the moon and the thistle, and the political and artistic state of Scotland itself.

Although enjoying considerable artistic success with his poetry and his proselytizing for the 'Scottish Renaissance' in the arts, this period of MacDiarmid's life was fraught with personal trauma. Professionally, he failed during a brief stint as editor of the London radio journal *Vox*. Personally, he failed as a husband; after an acrimonious divorce in 1931, his wife denied him access to their two children. Soon after, however, he married Valda Trevlyn, whom he had met during his sojourn in London. Valda was MacDiarmid's life-mate, financially supporting the family when necessary and shielding MacDiarmid from visitors and critics as his physical health weakened toward the end of his life. They had a son, Michael (b. 1932), who would edit his father's *Complete Poems* (1978).

Poetically, with *Stony Limits and Other Poems* (1934), MacDiarmid eased away from Scots to what he called 'synthetic English' which drew on other languages and disciplines, such as science. This multi-lingual assemblage comprised much of his later work, including the great, long *In Memoriam James Joyce* (1955). Its sweeping passages on philosophy and language mark a high-point in MacDiarmid's late English-language poetry.

Like his famous drunken narrator, MacDiarmid was always interested in a Scottish resurgence. He helped found the National Party of Scotland in 1928, yet his commitment to international social causes also led him to membership of the Communist Party of Great Britain. During the next twenty years he was in and out of favor with each party because of his activity in the other. His political dedication was firm, however, and despite official vacillations regarding his membership, he remained committed to both causes. Despite personal hardship, including poverty, a breakdown in 1935, a stint on the Shetland island of Whalsay to dry out (1933–42), and being conscripted to work in the Clydeside shipyards during World War II, MacDiarmid managed to keep writing and remain actively involved in the political causes of his day.

In 1950, MacDiarmid was granted a Civil List pension. His life-long poverty abated, he devoted himself to being the official and unofficial spokesman for

Scottish arts at home and abroad. He died of cancer in September 1978.

Selected works: *To Circumjack Cencrastus* (1930); *First and Second Hymns to Lenin* (1931–2); *Lucky Poet* (1943); *Collected Poems* (1962).

[MW]

MacDonagh, Thomas (Ireland, 1878–1916) A native of County Tipperary, MacDonagh became a Lecturer in English Literature at University College, Dublin, and helped poet Padraic Pearse found St Enda's College in 1908. MacDonagh, with Edward Martyn and Joseph Plunkett, was a co-founder of the Irish Theatre in Dublin. His nationalistic play *When Dawn is Come* was produced by the Abbey Theatre in 1908. Poetically, MacDonagh was influenced by early Irish verse and translated 'The Yellow Bittern' by Cathal Buidhe Mac Giolla Ghunna. *Literature in Ireland* (1916), posthumously published, describes how Anglo-Irish literature has been affected by the Irish language.

A participant in the Irish Volunteer movement, MacDonagh was a signatory to the 1916 Proclamation of the Irish Republic. He was executed by the British after the Easter Rising, events memorialized in YEATS's well-known poem 'Easter 1916'.

Selected works: *Through the Ivory Gates* (1903); *Lyrical Poems* (1913); *Poetical Works* (1916).

[CT]

MacEwan, Gwendolyn (Canada, 1941–87) In her brief life, MacEwan wrote short stories, children's books, radio plays, documentaries, and two novels, but she is best remembered as a poet possessing a unique voice and considerable literary gifts. If MacEwan's poetry has not attracted the critical attention that it deserves, it is perhaps because her attention to magic, ceremony, imagination, and especially myth has been seen as naive or unsophisticated, even while essentially the same characteristics have been celebrated in contemporaries such as LEONARD COHEN and MICHAEL ONDAATJE.

MacEwan was born in Toronto, and published her first poem in *The Canadian Forum* while still in her teens. Leaving school at the age of eighteen to embark upon a career as a writer, MacEwan spent a short time in Montréal, where in 1960–62 she edited *Moment* with AL PURDY and Milton Acorn, to whom she was later married for a short time. In 1963 she published her first book of poetry, *The Rising Fire*, and the novel *Julian the Magician*. *A Breakfast for Barbarians* (1966) established her as a promising young poet. This promise was fulfilled with *Shadow-Maker* (1969), which was awarded a Governor General's award; MacEwan posthumously received a second for the collection *Afterwords* in 1988. A second novel, *King of Egypt, King of Dreams*, based on the life of Akhenaton, appeared in 1971. MacEwan's interest in mythic, larger-than-life characters was further exhibited in three works that she completed before her death: the short stories about the eponymous magician in *Noman* (1972), her treatment of the Franklin Expedition in the verse-play *Terror and Erebus* (1974), and finally, her portrayal of T.E. Lawrence in her most complex and complete work, *The T.E. Lawrence Poems* (1982).

[IS]

MacGreevy, Thomas (Ireland, 1893–1967) A Modernist poet who spent many years in Paris, MacGreevy was influenced by French avant-garde writers as well as by T.S. ELIOT. MacGreevy was born in County Kerry and served in World War I as an artillery officer. After the war, he lived in Paris in 1927–33, where he became part of an expatriate literary community that included James Joyce, James Stephens, Brian Coffey, and the young SAMUEL BECKETT. MacGreevy wrote fractured and innovative free verse, with sophisticated, cosmopolitan themes. Upon his return to Dublin in 1941, MacGreevy became Director of the National Gallery (1950–64). Some critics suggest he ceased writing poetry in Ireland because Irish provincialism and insularity at the time was not conducive to his Modernist style. His *Collected Poems* appeared in 1971, and he also published several books on art, including *Jack B. Yeats* in 1945. *Collected Poems of Thomas MacGreevy: An Annotated Edition* was published in 1991.

[CT]

Machado, Antonio (Spain, 1875–1939), Machado combines the love of traditional Spain with intimate personal portraits in his work. He was the leader of the generation of 1898, which attempted an intellectual regeneration of Spain through frank examination of its political and social reality. The poetry of this period incorporated the Symbolists' musicality with profound philosophical themes.

Machado was born in Seville but spent most of his life in Castile: Soria, Segovia, Madrid. He visited Paris frequently and knew well the work of French poets and philosophers, Bergson in particular. Machado was educated at the liberal Free Institute and taught French. The death of his beloved wife Leonor in 1912 inspired some of his most poignant verse. In the 1920s he would meet another woman, the subject of the *Songs for Guiomar* (1928). During the Civil War Machado fought for the Republican cause, and at war's end he fled to France, where he died in 1939.

Machado was initially influenced by Symbolism but soon embraced a more direct and natural expression of emotion. He defined poetry as 'the essential word in time' ('Poetics'), and the effect of the latter on human existence would remain his central theme. Two major periods in Machado's poetry are marked by *Solitudes, Galleries and Other Poems* (1907) and *Castilian Fields* (1912). The former contains childhood memories and generally shows the poet looking inward for his inspiration, often contrasting his present, time-ravaged existence with images of youthfulness. The latter renders the poet his place in the Generation of 1898, as he looks outward at present-day Castile and describes it in stark contrast to its past greatness, much as essayists Ganivet, Barjoa, and Unamuno had done. Machado re-edited and published collections of his work throughout his life. His later years were dedicated to the *Guiomar* poems and to the philosophical *Juan de Mairena* (1937).

[AB]

Mackey, Nathaniel (United States, b. 1947) The poetry of Mackey blends jazz, philosophy, folklore, and experimental aesthetics. Born on 25 October 1947, in Miami, Florida, Mackey attended Princeton University, where he received his A.B. in 1969, and Stanford University, where he received his Ph.D. in 1975.

Mackey has published six volumes of poetry including the intensely musical *Song of the Andoumboulou* (1994). He has also published two volumes of his ongoing prose composition, *From a Broken Bottle Traces of Perfume Still Emanate, Bedouin Handbook* (1986) and *Djbot Baghostus's Run* (1993). The strength of Mackey's poetry stems from his blending of personal and historical narratives into a deeper interrogation of cultural subjectivity. In this sense, he contributes to the image of the poet as a cultural historian and ethnographer, which has its roots in the epic poem.

Mackey has also completed two works of criticism on experimental poetry and edits *Hambone*, an influential journal that blends experimental poetry and jazz. Since 1977, Mackey has taught at University of California, Santa Cruz.

[DC]

MacLean, Sorley (Somhairle MacGill-Eain; Scotland, 1911–96) MacLean, the best-known Scottish Gaelic poet, was born on Raasay. He went to Portree High

School on the Isle of Skye and studied English at Edinburgh University in 1929–33. After earning a teaching diploma at Moray House College of Education in Edinburgh, he spent his earlier professional life as a teacher in Portree, Edinburgh, and Wester Ross. He served in the Signal Corps (1940–43) until he was wounded in action. He was writer-in-residence at the University of Edinburgh (1973–4) and at Sabhal Mór Ostaig Gaelic College, Skye (1975–6). MacLean, MACCAIG, and MACDIARMID often dominated the Edinburgh literary scene and 'passion and intensity' was often used to describe both MacLean's life and his poetry; he was unable for family reasons to fight in the Spanish Civil War, although he altered this in his poetry, saying he stayed for the sake of a lover. His work combined political conflict and social criticism with a skillful reworking of the complex formal Gaelic style. He made his own translations into English, most of which were published in *O Choille gu Bearradh / From Wood to Ridge: Collected Poems in Gaelic and English* (1989).

Selected works: *17 Poems for 6d* (with ROBERT GARIOCH) (1940); *Dàin do Eimhir agus Dàin Eile* (1943), translated by IAN CRICHTON SMITH as *Poems to Eimhir and Other Poems* (1971); *Reothairt is Contraigh: Taghadh de Dháin 1932–72 / Spring Tide and Neap Tide: Selected Poems 1932–72* (1977).

[LKMF]

Macleish, Archibald (United States, 1892–1982) Three time Pulitzer Prize winner MacLeish was born in Glencoe, Illinois, graduated from Yale (1915), voluntarily served in World War I, and received a law degree from Harvard (1919). After three years of practicing law in Boston, he moved his family to Paris and devoted himself to writing poetry. Upon his return home in 1928, he worked as a journalist for *Fortune* magazine. Then in 1939 he was appointed Librarian of Congress, a position he held until 1944 when he was named Assistant Secretary of State under Roosevelt. He eventually left politics, and in 1949–62 he was Boylston Professor of Poetry at Harvard.

MacLeish's early work was indebted to French Symbolists such as Laforgue and Mallarmé and to the modernist poetics of T.S. ELIOT and EZRA POUND. Preoccupied with the hopelessness of the postwar world, these poems, as James E. Miller has said, reflected 'the sense of loss and futility of the lost generation'. MacLeish's poetry evolved throughout the 1930s and 1940s. The Great Depression and the atrocities of World War II prompted him to turn his attention toward social and political concerns. His poems and verse plays of this period promoted New Deal sensibilities and exposed the hypocrisy and false prophecy of totalitarian regimes. From the late 1940s on, his work remains politically aware, but it also becomes 'more personal'(Nicholas Everett). His later meditations on old age are often referred to as his finest work. Along with numerous literary awards and prizes, MacLeish won an Oscar for his screenplay *The Eleanor Roosevelt Story* (1965).

Selected works: *Tower of Ivory* (1917); *Conquistador* (1932); *Poems 1924–33* (1933); *America Was Promises* (1939); *Collected Poems 1917–52* (1952); *The Wild Old Wicked Man and Other Poems* (1968); *New and Collected Poems* (1976).

[MO]

MacNeice, Louis (Ireland, 1907–63) A self-named 'radio practitioner', Frederick Louis MacNeice worked as both a script writer and producer for the BBC, where he published some of the one hundred and fifty stage, radio, and television plays that he wrote. Most noted is his 1946 dramatic masterpiece, *The Dark Tower*.

Also a highly esteemed poet, MacNeice has been classified as a '1930s poet' and is thus associated with the left-wing Oxford Group, AUDEN, SPENDER, and DAY LEWIS. Yet MacNeice's writing differs in that it is less political. He uses a more colloquial tone than his colleagues, which he mingles with both sensory and temporal qualities, particularly in his earlier works. He received criticism for being a detached observer, a journalistic 'reporter of experience' who, though descriptively vivid, lacked emotional depth.

The ideas and images of MacNeice's poetry span a wide range of subjects, but his later, post-war pieces embody less energy, turning toward more somber material imbued with a sense of destruction and loss. Several of his works were published posthumously, including *The Burning Perch* (1963), his unfinished autobiography *The Strings are False* (1965), *Collected Poems* (1966), *Selected Literary Criticism* (1987), *Selected Poems* (1989), and *Selected Prose* (1993).

Widely renowned as both a teacher and a writer, MacNeice taught at Birmingham and at Bedford College of the University of London; wrote *Letters from Iceland* with Auden; was a visiting lecturer in English, poetry, and drama; was granted an OBE in 1958; received the Italia Prize for radio plays; and gave the Clark Lectures at Cambridge in 1963.

Selected works: *The Agamemnon* (1936); *Autumn Journal* (1939); *The Poetry of W.B. Yeats* (1941); *Holes in the Sky* (1948); *Autumn Sequel*(1954); *Solstices* (1961).

[JS]

Mahapatra, Jayanta (India, b. 1928) Though he did not publish his first volume of poetry until he was forty-three, Mahapatra has been an unusually prolific poet, with over thirty volumes to his credit. A physics teacher for many years, his poetry evinces a keen intellectual quality, the voice of a scientist exploring the exterior spaces of his home and the interior ones of the self. Unlike many of his peers, Mahapatra remained in the rural area, Orissa, in which he was born and it figures centrally in his poetry. Setting the poetry's moods – deep or light, ingrained or flighty – Orissa's landscape is a constant in his work. Moreover, the contradictions between modernity and the traditionalism of the rural people infuse Mahapatra's verse.

Mahapatra was born in the city of Cuttack, was educated at English-language schools there, attended university there, taught there, and, except for periods lecturing or teaching abroad, still resides there. His traditional education allowed him to read English poetry, though, more than the literature itself, it was the language which fascinated him. Despite the ambivalences of being an Indian poet writing in English, Mahapatra's work has been uniformly well-received; he was the first English-language Indian writer to win the prestigious Sahitya Akademi Award (1981).

Mahapatra's first two volumes emphasized his love of language, sometimes at the expense of clarity. However, with *A Rain of Rites* (1976), he came into his own. This volume, rich in imagery and sentiment and centered on the landscape of his native Orissa, caught the attention of domestic and foreign readers alike. Publication and reviews in journals such as *The Hudson Review* led to Mahapatra's sojourn at the Iowa Writers' Workshop (1976); he won *Poetry*'s Jacob Glatstein Memorial Award in 1975.

Some critics, however, found in *A Rain of Rites* and *Waiting* (1979) a poetry edging toward, but not yet achieving, a larger vision. As he has continued to write, this 'larger vision' has, conversely, proven to be introspective. Not confessional in a traditional sense, Mahapatra's examinations of Orissa and India, of his father, family and friends, and of his own life – what Madhusudan Prasad calls his 'hermit-like meditativeness' – have enabled him to unify his poetic vision in precise, if necessarily effusive, expression of the vast contradiction that is India: modern and antiquated, Hindu and Christian, private and public, poetic and prosaic.

Selected works: *Close the Sky, Ten by Ten* (1971); *Svayamvara and Other Poems*(1971); *A Father's Hours* (1976); *Relationship* (1980); *Life Signs* (1983); *Selected Poems* (1987); *A Whiteness of Bone* (1992); *Shadow Space* (1998).

[MW]

Mahon, Derek (Ireland, b. 1941) Born in Belfast, Mahon received his B.A. from Trinity College, Dublin, in 1965. He taught English in Belfast in 1967–68, co-founded *Atlantis* magazine with SEAMUS DEANE in 1967, and worked at the Language Centre of Ireland in Dublin in 1968–70. He has been an editor, a journalist, and a lecturer at many universities, including University of East Anglia, Norwich; Emerson College, Boston; and the New University of Ulster, Coleraine.

Mahon's poetry has been described as cosmopolitan, alienated, and detached, less rooted than the work of such contemporaries as HEANEY and MONTAGUE. However, he shares with them a fraught relationship with his native Northern Ireland. Mahon's early poems reflect his voluntary exile, an estrangement from a city to which he felt he never truly belonged. Many poems relate to international exiles, ranging from Irishmen LOUIS MACNEICE and SAMUEL BECKETT to the classical Ovid and the French existentialist Albert Camus. Mahon's poetic vision, however, is grounded in the space between artistic freedom and quotidian stagnation, between beauty and violence, between the purity of the imagination and the nightmare of history. The structure of Mahon's poetry also adopts this dialectic; his use of traditional forms is invaded by a vernacular ease and informality. In his widely anthologized 'A Disused Shed in Co. Wexford', the thousands of mushrooms that crowd to one keyhole and plead for emancipation are compared with the dispossessed of the world.

Selected works: *Night-Crossing* (1969); *Lives* (1972); *The Snow Party* (1975); *Courtyards in Delft* (1981); *The Hunt by Night* (1982); *Antarctica* (1985); *Selected Poems* (1991); *The Hudson Letter* (1995); *The Yellow Book*(1998).

[CT]

Maiden, Jennifer (Australia, b. 1949) Born in Penrith, New South Wales, Maiden left school at thirteen, working at casual jobs in offices and factories before returning to study. In 1974 she graduated from Macquarie University, Sydney (B.A.); her first volume of poetry, *Tactics*, was published in the same year. Her volume *The Winter Baby* (1990) won the New South Wales Premier's Award (the Kenneth Slessor Award) and the Victoria Premier's Award (the C.J. Dennis Award). A full-time writer, she conducts numerous writing workshops and seminars in and around Sydney.

Maiden's early volumes use a densely laden, non-referential language generative of a world interior to the text, what Martin Duwell calls 'Maidenland'. Later volumes incorporate local landmarks and public events and figures, thus engaging social commentary. The publication of her *Selected Poems* (1990) with a laudatory endorsment from A.D. HOPE, and *The Acoustic Shadow*'s (1993) inclusion in the Penguin Poetry Series establish her as a poet of note on the Australian scene.

[FD]

Maj, Bronislaw (Poland, b. 1953) Born in Lodz, Maj studied Polish at the University of Krakow and has worked in teaching and publishing. Most notably, Maj helped organize and edit *Na Glos* (*Out Loud*), a vital independent forum for literature in mid-1980s Poland.

Though in 1984 Maj received an honorary prize from Solidarity, his poems' political elements are often muted, transformed into an attentive, ethical examination of human conscience and the surrounding world. Attempting to uncover human motives and discover the world's subtle structures, Maj's poems meditate on specificities of time and place. Using minimal description, they enact a longing to preserve the vanishing moment and determine the possibility of human happiness.

Selected works: *Wiersze* (*Poems*, 1980); *Taka wolnosc* (*That Sort of Freedom*, 1981); *Wspolne powietrze* (*The Air we Breathe*, 1981); *Zmeczenie* (*Fatigue*, 1986); *Zaglada swietego miasta* (*The Annihilation of the Holy City*, 1986).

[MT]

Maksimović, Desanka (Yugoslavia, 1898–1993) Maksimović is perhaps the most popular Yugoslav poet of the twentieth century. Her poems, non-fiction, children's stories, and translations from Russian, Slovenian, Bulgarian, and French are well known among Yugoslav readers of all ages. She was the beloved doyenne of Yugoslav belles lettres, admired and honored throughout her long and prolific career.

Maksimović graduated from the University of Belgrade and studied at the Sorbonne. She returned to Belgrade, where she began working as a teacher, and stayed there for the rest of her long career. In 1924, Maksimović published her first collection of poems, *Poezija*, characterized by extraordinary lyricism and freshness. This collection immediately established her as one of the major young poets of Yugoslavia. During the 1920s and 1930s, her poetry was predominantly confessional, imbued with the imagery of her native land and its beauties. Maksimović continued her prolific poetic career for over seventy years, and every new collection was an important literary event in Yugoslavia.

In her poetry, Maksimović drew strongly upon the cultural heritage of the Serbian people. At the same time, she established a new poetic discourse, thoroughly fresh and recognizable as her own. Her style is deceptively simple and clear, yet her rich poetic language is full of metaphors and other stylistic figures based upon traditional Serbian language, archaisms, and folklore. Her exceptional linguistic sensuality employs a rich register of intonations, emotions, and tones.

World War II and its horrors made an indelible impact on Maksimović. She began writing patriotic poems which expressed her support for the struggle for the liberation of Yugoslavia from German occupation. Her powerful poem 'Krvava bajka' ('A Bloody Fairy Tale'), written after the massacre of high school students and their teachers in Kragujevac in 1941, expressed her outrage and is among the best known poems in the Serbian language.

Even in her most patriotic mode, Maksimović's poetry is gentle and lyrical, stressing compassion and anguish for the suffering and pain of her people. Poems from the collection *Tražim pomilovanje* (*I Seek Mercy*, 1964) express a strong sense of social justice, often emphasizing the miseries and inequality that people suffer. Her poems written during the 1950s and 1960s explore issues of human history and the struggle it entails.

Her later works, written during the 1970s, were inspired by deaths in her family and by her own old age; the poems of the 1980s are her coming to terms with the end of her life. These poems are infused with an awareness that death is an inevitable part of life and nature; they establish her sense of belonging to a universe larger than any individual life and suggest a necessary return to it. These poems are a farewell to life and a calm preparation for her impending death.

Selected works: *Zeleni vitez* (*A Green Knight*, 1930); *Otadžbino, tu sam* (*Motherland, here I am*, 1951); *Miris zemlje* (*The Scent of Earth*, 1955); *Ne zaboraviti* (*Not to be Forgotten*, 1969); *Nemam više vremena* (*I Have No More Time*, 1973); *Ničija zemlja* (*No One's Land*, 1979); *Pamtiću sve* (*I Will Remember Everything*, 1990).

[DJ]

Mălăncioiu, Ileana (Romania, b. 1940) Born in the village of Godeni, Mălăncioiu received her doctorate in philosophy from the University of Bucharest, then worked as an editor in Romanian television and at the leading literary magazine, *Viața românească* (*Romanian Life*).

There is nothing of the traditional feminine sensitivity in Mălăncioiu's verse. She expresses fear, anxiety, sadness, void, humiliation, the fantastic, and the grotesque in harsh, unpolished, almost physically painful verse. Her dense expressionism thrives in somber hues, rotting landscapes, nightmarish situations, and universal carnage (*Total Burning*, 1976). In *The Slaughtered Fowl* (1967), modern civilization intrudes in the rural universe. In later volumes, extinction becomes the dominant theme (*Across the Forbidden Zone*, 1979; *My Sister Beyond*, 1980); even in love the poet suffers (*To Ieronim*, 1970; *The Queen's Heart*, 1971; *Lilies for the Bride*, 1973). In *Climbing the Mountain* (1985), Mălăncioiu indicts the Communist dictatorship in powerful language, without rhetorical subterfuge. Throughout, the form is neoclassicist, the tone elegiac, and the condition of the lyrical subject 'accepted solitude' (D. Micu).

[GF]

Mandel, Eli (Canada, 1922–92) The rough prairie landscape of Mandel's childhood in Estavan, Saskatchewan, has figured prominently in his poetry. Mandel earned a Ph.D. from the University of Toronto, and has taught literature at both the University of Alberta and York University, Toronto. He has been important as a literary critic, theorist and anthologist in addition to writing a number of fine volumes of verse.

Mandel's poetry is influenced by the mythopoetic criticism of Northrop Frye. While Mandel's second collection, *Idiot Joy* (1967), won a Governor General's Award for Poetry, it is perhaps only with *Stony Plain* (1973) and *Out of Place* (1977) that Mandel found his true subject–poems about his prairie roots. As an editor of *Five Modern Canadian Poets* (1969) and *Eight More Canadian Poets* (1972), Mandel was influential in establishing canonical figures in Canadian poetry as well as bringing attention to deserving but lesser known writers. *Dreaming Backwards: Selected Poetry 1954–81* is the definitive collection of Mandel's work.

[IS]

Mandelshtam, Osip Emil'evich (Russia, 1891–1938) Considered one of the premier Russian poets of the century (alongside AKHMATOVA, TSVETAEVA, PASTERNAK), Mandelshtam was raised in Pavlovsk and St Petersburg. After attending schools there, he studied literature at the Sorbonne (1907–8), attended the University of Heidelberg (1909–10), and finally studied for six years in the Department of History and Philology at the University of St Petersburg, though he did not take a degree. In 1911, he was baptized in the Vyborg Methodist Church.

While in Paris, in 1907–08, he read BRIUSOV and the French Symbolists and began to write as well; *Apollon* published his first poems in 1910. One year later, Mandelshtam became a member of the Guild of Poets, the future Acmeist circle founded by GUMILIEV, where he befriended Akhmatova. His early publishing history is a series of issues and reissues. He published *Kamen'* (*Stone*, 1913), enlarged it in 1916, and published a third edition as *Pervaia Kniga Stikhov* (*The First Poetry Book*). This book was very much criticized. The poems of 1916–20 are collected in *Tristia*, but it was published under the title *Kniga Vtoraia* (*Second Book*) in 1922, and then again in 1923 with Mandelshtam's chronological disposition of poems. In 1928, Mandelshtam published *Stikhotvoreniia* (*Poems*). It included a cycle of twenty new poems composed between 1921 and 1925 along with *Kamen'* and *Tristia*.

Mandelshtam welcomed the February Revolution of 1917 but was reticent about the October Revolution. He perceived

Kerensky, the head of the provisional government, as a follower of the Decembrist ideas. Moreover, he was critical of Stalinism; in 1934, after writing an epigram about Stalin himself, Mandelshtam was arrested and exiled for three years to Voronezh. Upon his return from exile he was again arrested and sentenced to five years in a labor camp for 'counter-revolutionary activity'. Mandelshtam died in that camp.

Mandelshtam's powerful 1930s poems, drawing primarily on his complicated, constrained life, were saved by his widow, Nadezhda. Although these poems began to appear in samizdat form in Russia during the 1950s, with American volumes in the 1950s and 1960s, it was not until 1973 that a large selection appeared in the Soviet Union.

Mandelshtam's poetry is unusually musical, and quite philosophical. His inner search and world view change from one collection of poetry to another, though the dynamic power of the word is constant. He links the attitude of the poet toward the word to that of the architect toward stone. The stones of Rome, in particular, were objects and images that reflected his interest in Catholicism and the embodiment of Rome's historical and religious tradition. Personal and historical time were also important themes. Taken as a whole, Mandelstham's poetry is unusual, complicated, profound, sharp, precise, elegant, and stylistically rich.

Selected works: *The First Moscow Notebook* (1930–1); *The Second Moscow Notebook* (1932–4); *The First Voronezh Notebook* (1935); *The Second Voronezh Notebook* (1936–7); *The Third Voronezh Notebook* (1937).

[RN]

Manhire, Bill (New Zealand, b. 1946) Born in Invercargill, Manhire was educated at the University of Otago and University College, London. Since 1973 he has been a lecturer and professor at Victoria University, Wellington.

His poetry, together with that of IAN WEDDE and Murray Edmond, appeared in the Auckland journal *Freed* in the late 1960s. In his verse, Manhire deliberately broke free from British models and turned to post-war American poetry, especially ROBERT CREELEY's. With its often tantalizing and enigmatic word play, and its manipulation of clichés and minimalist style, Manhire's output has been influential for a new generation of poets.

Selected works: *Malady* (1970); *The Elaboration* (1972); *How to Take off Your Clothes at the Picnic* (1977); *Good Looks* (1982); *Zoetropes, Poems 1972–82* (1984); *Milky Way Bar* (1991).

[SH]

Mann, Chris (South Africa, b. 1948) Born in Port Elizabeth, Christopher Michael Zithulele Mann was educated at the University of Witwatersrand. While a Rhodes Scholar at Oxford he won the Newdigate Prize for Poetry and then took a degree in African Studies at the School of Oriental and African Studies in London. He lived and taught in a Swaziland village before moving to Grahamstown where he lectured in English at Rhodes University. He has also worked on a medical and agricultural project at Both's Hill outside Durban. His first book of verse, *First Poems* was published in 1977 and he co-edited (with GUY BUTLER) *A New Book of South African Verse in English* in 1979.

His second volume of poetry, *New Shades* (1982), draws on both European and African traditions, touching on themes of politics, sports, ancestral spirits, religion, and violence. While living in Grahamstown, Mann was a member of Izinkonjane ZaseRhini, a local band which performed different types of township and traditional music. This musical influence is felt in his later poems, which also reflect his interest in oral literature and tradition.

[KS]

Manner, Eeva-Liisa (Finland, 1921–94) Manner was a distinguished poet of Finnish Modernism, prose writer, dramatist, critic, essayist, and highly acclaimed translator of Shakespeare, Joyce, and Kafka. It is not an exaggeration to say that her accomplishments amount to a life's work in each of those areas. Manner was also a poet in exile; while living in Helsinki, Spain, and principally in Tampere, she longed for Viipuri, the cosmopolitan Karelian city of her birth, which was lost in World War II to the then Soviet Union.

Manner's notable erudition influenced her writing and earned her the critical assessment of being Finland's most openly intellectual wordsmith. Manner's writing is characterized by intelligent passion, intensive and transparently expressive diction, and the aspect of musicality. She has said that Bach's polyphony is the key to her lyricism.

Her early years were marked by dire financial difficulties resulting in life under what now is unimaginable stress; hence, she found her poetic voice at the relatively late age of 35. Manner's collection *Tämä matka* (*This Journey*, 1956) was a breakthrough, one which inspired and gave a direction to change in Finnish lyricism. The volume's rich subject matter gave birth also to *Eros and Psykhe* (1959), a sensitive love story in free verse, one more notable for its rhythm and metaphors than its action. Subsequent so-called 'Spanish collections' tell of renewed modes of expression and shifts in subject matter and focus. Among the 1960s collections are *Kirjoitettu Kivi* (*The Written Stone*, 1966) and *Fahrenheit 121* (1968), as well as the principally contemplative poetry of *Niin vaihtuivat vuoden ajat* (*So Changed the Seasons*, 1964) and *Jos suru savuaisi* (*If Sorrow Were to Turn to Smoke*, 1968). Her many awards and grants include the Aleksis Kivi Prize in 1961, the State Literature Prize in 1967, and the Institute of Culture Award in 1967.

[SP]

Manninen, Otto (Finland, 1872–1950) Manninen is considered one of the greatest Finnish lyric poets of all time. He was also a Professor of Finnish language, a recipient of honorary doctorates of Philosophy and Theology, and the most significant Finnish-language translator; his exceptional translations of *The Iliad* and *The Odyssey* are viewed as two of the greatest Homeric translations anywhere.

Manninen's critically acclaimed poetic oeuvre remained relatively limited, principally because of vigorous self-criticism and the exceptional demands his translation work made on his time. Manninen's collections *Säkeitä* (*Verses*, 1905), *Säkeitä II* (1910), *Virrantyven* (*Stream's Calm*, 1925), and *Matkamies* (*Traveling Man*, 1938) are characterized by virtuosity and polish. The posthumously published *Muistojen tie* (*Path of Memories*, 1951) speaks of depth of emotion and wisdom of a lived life; Manninen's poems belong to Finnish lyricism's most enduring expressions.

He was an honorary member of the Finnish Association of Writers and received The State Award for Literature three times (1905, 1910, 1938) and the Aleksis Kivi Prize in 1936.

[SP]

Mansour, Joyce (Egypt, 1928–86) Born in England of Egyptian parents, Mansour was nicknamed 'l'enfant du conte oriental' by ANDRÉ BRETON, leader of the French Surrealists. The only recognized woman in this movement, she started to publish in *Acte sud* (1950). She wrote with great liberty about subjects that were 'taboo' at the time, such as sex, death, disease, and marital relationships. Her poems *Cris* (*Cries*, 1953) express her own interior confusion and are often framed as interior dialogs. Subversive, caustic, and full of surrealistic humor, her article-poems were published in *Déchirures* (*Tears*, 1955) and then in *Les Gisants satisfaits* (*The Satisfied Dead*, 1958). They mock the traditional standards of the women's press (health, fashion, and love). Her complete works were collected after her death in 1986 in *Prose et poésie* (1991). Today her influence remains strong among Lebanese poets and Francophone readers, as well as feminists worldwide.

[MS]

Mapanje, Jack (Malawi, b. 1944) Mapanje was born of Yao and Nyanja parents and went to Catholic schools before attending the University of Malawi, where he earned a B.A. and a Diploma in Education. Mapanje also has an M.Phil. from the University of London. He is a founder and editor of *ODI*, a journal of Malawi literature started in 1971, and contributed to *MAU: 39 Poems from Malawi* (1971). In 1975, he began lecturing in the English department at Chancellor College, University of Malawi. In 1983, two books of poetry that Mapanje co-edited were released, *Oral Poetry from Africa: an Anthology* and *Summer Fires: an Anthology of Modern African Poetry*.

His first book of poems, *Of Chameleons and Gods* (1981), was published while he was a student in linguistics at University College, London. Its introduction states that the volume spans some ten turbulent years in which 'I have been attempting to find a voice or voices as a way of preserving some sanity'. The chameleonic regime of Hastings Banda eventually banned the book and incarcerated Mapanje in 1987, without charge or trial, for over three and a half years. A concerted international campaign worked for his release. His second book of poetry, *The Chattering Wagtails of Mikuyu Prison* (1993), focuses on this prison experience, and includes poems written before and after his incarceration. Mapanje currently resides in England, and has spent the 1990s working against censorship. A new book of poetry, *Skipping without Ropes*, was released in 1998.

[KAC]

Marechera, Dambudzo (Zimbabwe, 1952–87) Born near Rusape in 1952, Charles Dambudzo Marechera grew up in the ghetto. He attended various mission schools until 1972, when he began his undergraduate work in English literature at the (then) University of Rhodesia. Expelled in 1973, he went to New College, Oxford, but was again expelled in 1976. For several months in 1979, he was a writer-in-residence at the University of Sheffield, during which time he published a few poems in *West Africa* magazine. He returned to Zimbabwe in 1982, and died of an AIDS-related lung collapse in 1987. Most of his poetry was published posthumously in *Cemetery of Mind*, but other poems are scattered among his prose, which is better known.

Selected works: *Mindblast, or The Definitive Buddy* (1984); *An Articulate Anger* (1988); *Dambudzo Marechera 4 June 1952–18 August 1987: Pictures, Poems, Prose, Tributes* (1988); *The Black Insider* (1990).

[KT]

Marinetti, Filippo Tommaso (Italy, 1876–1944) The founder of Futurism, Marinetti was highly influential upon writers (see APOLLINAIRE, POUND) and cultural movements, such as Surrealism and Russian Cubism. Beginning with the first Manifesto's publication in Paris in 1909, and his 'Parole in Libertà', mixtures of poetry, visual art and political slogans, conducted a relentless struggle against literary rhetoric and metrical traditionalism. His linguistic experimentation and his celebration of modernity (even in the controversial shape of war and Fascism), still stand as crucial and springboard contributions to the evolution of twentieth-century poetry.

Selected works: *Il monoplano del Papa* (*The Pope's Monoplane*, 1912); *Zang-tumb-tumb* (1914); *Spagna Veloce e Toro Futurista* (*Fast Spain and Futurist Bull*, 1931); *Il poema non umano dei meccanismi* (*The Non-human Poem of Mechanisms*, 1941).

[GS]

Marlatt, Daphne (Canada, b. 1942) Born Daphne Buckle in Melbourne, Australia, Marlatt moved with her family first to Malaysia and then at the age of nine to Vancouver. Marlatt became involved with the Tish group of poets (which included GEORGE BOWERING) in Vancouver in the early 1960s while still a student at the University of British Columbia. *Leaf Leaf/s* (1969), her second book of poetry, shows the beginnings of Marlatt's particular poetics: the transformation of image into sound and a meticulous attention to the world of raw sense experience.

As well as being one of the leading figures in a new generation of Canadian poets, Marlatt is an important figure in Canadian feminism. In 1982–83, she co-founded the Anglo-Quebec feminist journal *Tessera*, and in 1983 she published the collection *How to Hug a Stone*, a work whose examination of the female body and language has drawn deserved critical attention.

Selected works: *Vancouver Poems* (1972); *Stevenson* (1974); *In the Month of Hungry Ghosts* (1979); *Ana Historic* (1988).

[IS]

Marson, Una (Jamaica, 1905–65) Marson is the first prominent female writer in the Caribbean. She was born in St Elizabeth, Jamaica. In 1928, after working at the leading Jamaican newspaper, *The Daily Gleaner*, Marson founded and edited *The Cosmopolitan*, the first women's publication in Jamaica. Her first book of poetry, *Heights and Depths* (1931), was awarded the Institute of Jamaica's Musgrave Medal. In 1932–6, Marson lived in England, where she served for three years as secretary for the League of Coloured People, before becoming Haile Selassie's personal secretary during his exile from Ethiopia.

Returning from England in 1936, she became a social worker and founded the newspaper *Public Opinion*, and the journal *Jam Standard*, both of which hold articulated progressive political positions. Marson was interested throughout her life in issues of social justice and in the treatment and social status of women. These themes, as well as her resistance to colonial representations of Caribbean identity, characterize the poems in *The Moth and the Star* (1937) and *Towards the Stars: Poems* (1945). Marson is also important for the use of creole in her poetry, which had an impact on subsequent generations of Caribbean writers.

[IS]

Marti, Kurt (Switzerland, b. 1921) Marti was born in Bern, where he now lives. A minister at the Nydegg Church in Bern from 1961 to 1983, he began writing poetry to find a freer language than the church allowed. While some poems are in the local dialect, most are in standard German, and all have been popular, controversial, and influential.

Marti's books combine religious, political, and literary themes. *Poems in the Margins* (1963) and *Necrologies* (1969) stressed the religious. *Republican Poems* (1959) and especially *Hail-Vetia* (1971) showed a political thinker who, in New Testament tradition, emphasized the power of the word over violence. Marti focused on linguistic experimentation in *Paraburi* (1972) and *Occident* (1980). Marti's latest works, such as *There Goes Existence* (1993), are more aggressively humorous and generally human.

[IRS]

Martinson, Harry (Sweden, 1904–78) Laureate of the Nobel Prize for Literature (1974, shared with Eyvind Johnson), Martinson is best known for his leading role among the so-called 'proletarian poets', a group that dominated Swedish poetry in the 1930s. After the death of his father and the emigration of his mother to the US, the young Martinson was left in the care of various relatives and orphanages. He often ran away from these places, and at sixteen became a sailor, a work which he continued intermittently for the next seven years. In his early twenties he started publishing his poetry, which often made autobiographical references to his experience at sea. In 1929 he began a ten-year marriage to writer Helga Johansson (Moa Martinson), a relation crucial to Martinson's development. After volunteering in 1940 for the Finnish war, Martinson came back and remarried in 1942.

After the collection *Nomad* (1931), Martinson commanded a large readership; in 1949 he was elected to the Swedish Academy. Martinson's work is noted for its experimentalism in form and ideas as well as sensuous imagery balanced by stark realism. Unlike many of his contemporaries, he refers relatively little to concrete circumstances. Many of his works are set in far-away places such as the Congo and China. His epic poem *Aniara* (1956), which has also been rewritten into an opera (1959, libretto by ERIK LINDEGREN), takes place in a spaceship whose travellers are informed of the step-by-step destruction of humanity by a nuclear war. In the introduction, Martinson explains that *Aniara* is about pain and disappointment, as well as about using imagination to fill in for what we cannot achieve. Martinson is also known for his travel sketches, novels, and drama.

[YB]

Masaoka Shiki (Japan, 1867–1902) Masaoka was born in Matsuyama. He started writing prose and verse at a very early age. In 1890 he entered Tokyo Imperial University to major in literature. Around the same time, he traveled around the country and wrote a considerable amount of travel literature. He also published *Dassai Shooku Haiwa* (*Talks on Haiku from the Otter's Den*) serially in the newspaper *Nippon*, in which he criticized the intellectualized, stereotyped approach to *haiku*. He advocated a new fashion of naturalism, insisting that the subject of the poem should be described honestly and realistically. He left the university in 1893 and soon afterwards published *Basho Zatsudan* (*Remarks of Basho*), in which he criticized the idolized concept of the poet *Basho*. In 1897 he founded the *haiku* magazine *Hototogisu*. As a literary theorist, he also published a critical work on *haiku* entitled *Haijin Buson* (*The Haiku Poet Buson*). In 1901 and 1902 he published such pieces as *Bokuju Itteki* (*A Drop of Ink*), *Byosho Rokushaku* (*A Six-foot Sickbed*), and *Gyoga Manroku* (*Stray Notes While Lying on My Back*), continuing vigorous activity until his death in September 1902.

Masaoka was mainly known for the movement for modernizing the *haiku*, although he was also a prolific writer of *tanka*, poetic diaries, and critical essays. He maintained the important place of the *haiku* in Japanese literature and advocated a new, more realistic style as a way of rescuing it. He also joined in the movement to reform the *tanka* and helped its rebirth as a modern form by advocating a realism similar to that he stressed in the *haiku*. He also created a new prose style based on realism, his championing of realism in various fields of literature having a great effect on the literary world of his day.

[LY]

Masefield, John (England, 1878–1967) Born in Herefordshire, Masefield's childhood was difficult: after his parents died when he was young, his guardians forced him to train for the merchant navy. At seventeen, Masefield deserted ship in New York; financially cut off, he lived on the streets, writing poetry. Two years later, suffering from both tuberculosis and malaria, he was reconciled with his family and returned to England.

Soon after his return, Masefield met YEATS, who became a close friend and mentor. Although many thought Yeats or Kipling more qualified to be England's Poet Laureate, the prolific Masefield was appointed to this position in 1930 and continued in it until his death in 1967, a tenure unmatched by anyone except Tennyson. His other honors include the

William Foyle Poetry Prize and the Presidency of the Society of Authors.

Masefield's early difficulties caused him to write a great deal on the tragedy in human life, expressing empathy toward the misfortunate. His most successful poems, however, are those based on his experiences at sea. He wrote many humorous poems which, though tainted with pathos, made his reputation; his more philosophic poems, intermingling beauty and tragedy, were not widely read. Although his poetry was a great success during his lifetime, most of his works are out of print now.

Selected works: *Ballads* (1903); *Philip the King and Other Poems* (1914); *Reynard the Fox: Or, the Ghost Health Run* (1919); *The Dream* (1922); *Madsummer Night and Other Tales in Verse* (1928); *A Tale of Troy* (1932); *Some Verses to Some Germans* (1939); *I Want! I Want!* (1944); *Poems* (1953); *Old Raiger and Other Verse* (1961).

[BRB]

Mason, R. A. K. (New Zealand, 1905–71) Born in Auckland, Ronald Allison Kells Mason studied Classics. In the 1930s he became a member of the Communist Party and was politically active during the Depression. He devoted much of his energy to trade union activities and left-wing political journalism.

Mason's poetry is influenced by his classical education and his struggles with the (im)possibility of faith. His position as a Pakeha New Zealander and his introduction to the first volume of TUWHARE's poetry make him a central figure in indigenous New Zealand poetry.

Selected works: *The Beggar* (1924); *No New Thing* (1934); *End of Day* (1936); *This Dark Will Lighten* (1941); *Collected Poems* (1962).

[SH]

Masters, Edgar Lee (United States, 1868–1950) Masters wrote *Spoon River Anthology*, his masterpiece, first under the pseudonym Webster Ford in *Reedy's Mirror* (1915). It was then enlarged in 1916, and revised in 1944. Although he wrote prolifically in several genres in 1920–50, only *Spoon River Anthology* attained lasting importance, becoming a national bestseller and drawing praise from CARL SANDBURG and EZRA POUND.

The collection of over 200 epitaphs, delivered as monologues in the voices of deceased citizens of a small Midwestern town, was controversial in its time for its forthrightness. The poems crack the façade of smug, small-town America, and reveal immorality, hypocrisy, class injustice, and petty cruelties, while also affirming individualism and sexuality.

Born in Garnett, Kansas, Masters spent his formative years in Lewistown, Illinois, and practiced law in Chicago, 1892–1920.

[HE]

Mastoraki, Jenny (Greece, b. 1949) Poet and translator Mastoraki was born in Athens and studied Byzantine history and literature at the university there. She has written essays on literature and translation and has translated widely from American, Italian, German, and South American literature and criticism. Her first collection, *The Legend of Saint Youth* (1971), was about growing up in Greece in the 1950s and 1960s. Her next collection, *Tolls* (1972), was published under the Colonels' dictatorship of 1967–74 and explored writing under censorship. *Kin* (1979) expanded her grappling with censorship by focusing on family control. Her two most recent books, *Tales of the Deep* (1983) and *With a Crown of Light* (1989) assume a more erotic tone. An English translation of *Tales of the Deep* can be found in *The Rehearsal of Misunderstanding* (1998).

[GSY]

Matić, Dušan (Yugoslavia, 1898–1980) Matić is one of the best known and most influential Yugoslav poets and essayists. Born in Cuprija and educated in Belgrade, Matić began his literary career as a founder of the Yugoslav Surrealist group after several years spent in France (1916–23), where he came under the influence of Henri Bergson. Between the wars, Matić edited and published various Yugoslav Surrealist magazines.

During the 1930s, Matić's radical political and aesthetic activism became even more pronounced. In his writing, he frequently dealt with important contemporary events such as the Spanish Civil War. After World War II, Matić continued his prolific literary production and became an important literary and cultural figure. His works, including *Bagdala* (1954), *Budenje materije* (*The Awakening of the Matter*, 1959), and *Laža i paralaža* (*A Lie and a Metalie*, 1962), are an impressive testimony to Matić's erudition, skill, and poetic imagination; his essay 'Anina balska haljina' ('Ana's Ball Gown') is considered one of the classic Yugoslav texts on poetry.

Always suspicious of the conventional and banal, Matić writes poetry characterized by inventiveness, paradox, and creativity. His work is intellectual and sophisticated, yet his writing often successfully incorporates ordinary, everyday language, transforming it into an effective poetic idiom.

Selected works: *Prošlost dugo traje* (*The Past Lasts a Long Time*, 1977); *Najmladi Jagodić neće u roman* (*The Youngest Jagodic won't Go into a Novel, 1988*).

[DJ]

Matthews, William (United States, 1942–97) Matthews was born in Cincinnati, Ohio, and educated at Yale and the University of North Carolina. In addition to writing prolifically and teaching, he served as president of both the Poetry Society of America and the Associated Writing Programs.

Matthews' poetry is known for its striking imagery and startling aphorisms. Romantic love and the psychology of human interactions are major concerns, and Matthews' treatment of them is insightful and sensitive. His lyric line, maintained through free and formal verse, maintains an Augustan grace – with a playful quality borrowed from American blues and jazz. He was much admired personally for his astonishing wit.

Selected works: *Ruining the New Road* (1970); *Rising and Falling* (1979); *A Happy Childhood* (1984); *Foreseeable Futures* (1987).

[JT]

Maxwell, Glyn (England, b. 1962) Born in Welwyn Garden City, Maxwell studied English at Oxford University and then took an M.A. in poetry at Boston University. With his wife and their daughter, he currently lives in Massachusetts, where he teaches at Amherst College.

Garnering comparisons with AUDEN, LARKIN, and even ROBERT FROST, Maxwell is one of the most promising young poets of his generation, and is consistently well-reviewed. His work is filtered through a deep-seated concern for England past and present, and his themes are often specifically masculine. His frequently colloquial language adds a freshness to his poetry yet never undermines the seriousness of his themes. Maxwell is also a playwright and a novelist.

Selected works: *Tale of the Mayor's Son* (1990); *Out of the Rain* (1992); *Rest for the Wicked* (1995); *The Breakage* (1999).

[SG]

Mayakovsky, Vladimir Vladimirovich (Russia, 1893–1930) Although his initial education was obtained in the usual series of gymnasia, by 1909 Mayakovsky was a member of Moscow's Bolshevik committee and had been arrested three times. That year, at age fifteen, he spent eleven months in Buterskaia prison. Upon his release, he eschewed politics in favor of the Moscow Institute for the Study of Painting, Sculpture, and Architecture. There he encountered the futurist group 'Gileia', whose eponymous journal would eventually publish his poetry. His first fully fledged volume, *Ya* (*I*), appeared in 1913, the year he participated in the first Futurist poets' meeting.

Before the revolution, Mayakovsky produced four reputation-making narrative poems, amazing for their poetic quality and originality, their provocation, their revolt against the imperfect world, their despair and idealism: *Oblako v shtanakh* (*A Cloud in Pants*, 1915), *Fleita pozvonochnik* (*The Backbone Flute*, 1915), *Voina i mir* (*War and the World*, 1917), and *Chelovek* (*Man*, 1918). The two first poems address love, but *A Cloud in Pants* also touches on the questions of art and religion via the perceptions of the rejected lover. *War and the World* is filled with fantastic images, but its theme is the reality of World War I. *Man*, as its title hints, is a philosophical poem.

Mayakovsky accepted the October Revolution of 1917 with enthusiasm, thereafter alternating political verse with lyric poetry. He also wrote plays and produced graphic art as a propagandist for the revolution. His inner conflict over the path of Soviet life, his own religious revolt against God, and his love pains led him to commit suicide at Easter 1930, an unfair end for one of the greatest Russian poets.

[RN]

M'Baye d'Erneville, Annette (Senegal, b. 1926) M'Baye d'Erneville became one of the first African women published in French, when her *Poèmes africains* (*African Poems*) appeared in 1965. These poems revive the oral Wolof songs of Kassacks (circumcision), motherhood, arranged marriage, Khaware (musical gathering), and traditional dances. She received the 1964 prize from the Senegalese Poets Society. Her volume *Kaddu* was published in 1966.

Founder of the magazine *Awa* (in 1963), she encourages female writers to go beyond sporadic publications by bringing some manuscripts to the attention of publishers. This was the case of Mariama Bâ and Mariétou M'Baye (Ken Bugul). Magazine editor, teacher, administrator, journalist for *Soleil* (*Sun*) and *Jeune Afrique* (*Young Africa*), poet, and author M'Baye d'Erneville was educated in Senegal and France.

[LF]

McAuley, James (Australia, 1917–76) Poet, founding editor of the Australian cultural journal *Quadrant* (1956), and one half of the notorious 'Ern Malley' literary hoaxers, McAuley worked in the Australian Army Directorate of Research during World War II, and experienced post-war administrative duty in New Guinea, a place which deeply influenced his personal and religious beliefs.

McAuley published six volumes of highly crafted lyrical poetry: *Under Aldebaran* (1946), *A Vision of Ceremony* (1956), *Captain Quiros* (1964), *Surprises of the Sun* (1969), *Music Late at Night* (1976), and *Time Given* (1976), as well as a *Selected* (1963) and a *Collected* (1971). McAuley was a professor of literature at the University of Tasmania (1961–76), publishing four volumes of critical prose on modern and Australian literature.

In the infamous 1944 Ern Malley hoax, McAuley and fellow poet Harold Stewart concocted a series of sixteen poems, *The Darkening Ecliptic*, a pastiche of fragments from various sources, in an attempt to parody the excesses of Modernist verse. They attributed the work to one Ern Malley, a mechanic who had died tragically young, and whose sister Ethel had submitted his poetry to literary editor Max Harris' avant-garde journal *Angry Penguins*. *The Darkening Ecliptic* has come to be celebrated in itself, though the hoax is seen by some as indicative of McAuley's growing cultural, religious, and political conservatism.

[LM]

McClatchy, J. D. (United States, b. 1945) Born in Bryn Mawr, Pennsylvania, Joseph Donald McClatchy, Jr. graduated from Georgetown *summa cum laude* and received his Ph.D. from Yale in 1974. He has taught at many schools, including LaSalle, Yale, and Princeton, and has received numerous grants and fellowships, from the Ingram Merrill and Guggenheim Foundations and the National Endowment for the Arts, among others. He has been awarded prizes from the American Academy and Institute of Arts and Letters, *Poetry* magazine, the Poetry Society of America, and the Academy of American Poets. He is editor of *The Yale Review*, an influential journal.

McClatchy is a remarkably adept technician, melding aesthetic and moral considerations into an intricate whole. Although the dazzling polish of his craftsmanship can be distracting, his poems are elegantly intelligent, sensitively exploring themes of religion, language, and self-representation.

Selected works: *Stars Principal* (1986); *The Rest of the Way* (1990); *The Vintage Book of Contemporary American Poetry* (ed., 1990); *The Ten Commandments* (1998).

[JDS]

McFadden, Roy (Ireland, 1921–99) A lawyer by profession, McFadden has never received the critical acclaim he deserves. He was born in Belfast and graduated from Queen's University, Belfast, in 1944. After co-editing *Ulster Voices* (1941–42), McFadden published his first volume of poems, *Swords and Ploughshares* (1943), a powerful work that takes war as its theme. Other early volumes include *Flowers for a Lady* (1945) and *The Heart's Townland* (1947). McFadden also co-edited *Rann: An Ulster Quarterly of Poetry* (1948–53). A frequent contributor to *The Bell*, McFadden often complained that the Dublin-based journal was too concerned with stereotypical 'Irish' themes. Indeed, McFadden's own poetry was initially influenced by YEATS, whose sweeping rhetorical style was in many ways antithetical to McFadden's slightly ironic and more distanced voice. *A Watching Brief* (1979), an important volume, makes use of McFadden's knowledge of the legal profession.

Selected works: *The Garryowen* (1971); *Verifications* (1977); *The Selected Roy McFadden* (1983); *Letters to the Hinterland* (1986); *After Seymour's Funeral* (1990); *Collected Poems 1943–95* (1996).

[CT]

McGinley, Phyllis (United States, 1908–78) When McGinley won the Pulitzer Prize for Poetry in 1960, many were surprised, considering her merely a practitioner of light verse writing exclusively in conventional meters and forms. If a comparison were to be made, it would be with the droll verses of Dorothy Parker. McGinley's subjects included such quotidian affairs as the Blue Plate Special, the elevators at Altman's Department Store, and her six toothbrushes. Yet her work was admired by W.H. AUDEN, who wrote a foreword to the winning volume, *Time Three* (1960). Auden placed her within the genre written by Hood, Praed, Calverley, BELLOC, and Chesterton, and admired her sense of play.

McGinley was born in Oregon and received her education at the University of Utah and University of California. She lived in suburban Westchester County, north of New York City.

Selected works: *The Love Letters of Phyllis McGinley* (1954); *The Province of the Heart* (prose, 1959).

[RP]

McGuckian, Medbh (Ireland, b. 1950) A native of Belfast, McGuckian was educated at Queen's University, Belfast, and received her B.A. in 1972, and M.A. in 1974. Since the publication of her first volume, *The Flower Master* (1982), McGuckian's poems have received wide critical attention; she was the first female poet in Northern Ireland to be recognized during the 1970s and 1980s alongside her male contemporaries. Although her poems often tackle domestic subjects, they are never easily categorized; indeed, their dense imagery, complicated syntax, and often startling, difficult metaphors have been criticized for their obscurity. Because McGuckian rarely writes about conditions in Northern Ireland, some critics argue that obliquity itself is her 'mode of resistance' to politics. Sometimes compared with Emily Dickinson, McGuckian portrays female sexuality, eroticism, and domestic interiors with insight and originality–always 'at a slant'.

Selected works: *Venus and the Rain* (1984); *On Ballycastle Beach* (1988); *Marconi's Cottage* (1991); *Captain Lavender* (1994).

[CT]

McHugh, Heather (United States, b. 1948) McHugh is the American poet who best represents the convergence of American Realism and French Surrealism. Her poems often begin with her manipulation of language and revel in the striking images, puns, and ideas this word play reveals. McHugh's consideration of the human condition is a springboard into the fantastic in order to better reveal the impossibility of a singular notion of truth, and the ultimate importance of play. One of the more remarkable poets/essay writers, her latest collection of essays, *Broken English: Poetry and Partiality* (1999), presents the multiplicity of her passions – from modern art to medieval physics and French post-structuralist theory. Her selected works, *Hinge and Sign: Poems, 1968–93* embodies her strongest work of the past thirty years.

[CV]

McKay, Claude (United States, 1889–1948) Born in Jamaica, McKay published his first books in his early twenties. These books were primarily political in nature, and in them he used dialect to portray the social problems of his people. Eventually emigrating to New York, McKay was one of the instigators of the black culture movement called the Harlem Renaissance. Maintaining his interest in the plight of blacks, his verse of this period became more and more formal, as if the free verse of other Harlem Renaissance writers could not maintain the tension he desired for his politically charged poems. These are the poems that hold up today; they are still fresh, witty, and solemn. He died a Roman Catholic schoolteacher in Chicago in 1948.

While a good selected works begs to be published, a strong collection is *The Passion of Claude McKay: Selected Poetry and Prose, 1912–1948* (1973).

[CV]

Mehren, Stein (Norway, b. 1935) One of Norway's true renaissance men, poet, essayist, illustrator, novelist, and playwright Mehren studied philosophy in Norway and biology in Norway and Germany. In his debut volume, *Gjennom stillheten en natt* (*Through the Silence One Night*, 1960), Mehren emerged as a Modernist. Free verse, enjambment, half-sentences, and double entendres characterize his poems. Mehren's work thematizes man's relationship with reality. According to Mehren, language, because it is a construct of culture, is a barrier to our understanding of reality. He has won numerous awards for his writing, most recently the Anders Jahres Pris in 1993.

Selected works: *Gobelin Europa* (*Goblin Europe*, 1965); *Den store søndagsfrokosten* (*The Great Sunday Breakfast*, 1976); *Nattmaskin* (*Nightmachine*, 1998).

[AC]

Mekuli, Esad (Yugoslavia, 1916–93) Mekuli is the founder of modern Yugoslav poetry in the Albanian language. Born in Montenegro, he studied veterinary science in Belgrade, where he received a Ph.D. in parasitology. He was an active participant in the Partisan movement during World War II. Mekuli had two careers: he was a professor at the Veterinary Institute in Kosovo, and he was an established poet.

In the latter role he was an editor of an Albanian journal and actively encouraged other Albanian poets. He translated many canonical works of Yugoslav writers into Albanian. He was also a major translator of Albanian poetry into Serbo-Croat.

Mekuli's works reflect exceptional lyrical sensibility, while his style is refined and sophisticated. His pre-war poems are intimate reflections of the world around him. The poems after World War II are focused on social issues, with an emphasis on patriotism.

Selected works: *Për ty* (*For You*, 1955); *Dita e re* (*New Day*, 1966); *Vjersha* (*Poems*, 1973); *Midis dashurise dhe urrejtjes* (*Between Love and Hate*, 1981); *Brigjet* (*The Hills*, 1981).

[DJ]

Melissanthi (Hebe Skandalaki; Greece, 1910–91) Author of nine books of poetry and a children's play, Melissanthi was born in Athens where she received diplomas for the study of German, French, and English. She is also known as a translator, particularly of ROBERT FROST and Emily Dickinson. In 1936 she received the Athens Academy of Arts and Science Award for *Return of the Prodigal* and in 1946 the Palamas Award for *Lyric Confession*. A lyrical and often pessimistic poet, her work has been described as an affirmation of death, rife with metaphysical agony and empathic humanism.

Selected works: *Insect Voices* (1930); *Prophecies* (1931 and 1932); *Human Shape* (1961); *The Barrier of Silence* (1961).

[GSY]

Meredith, William (United States, b. 1919) A native of New York City, Meredith graduated from Princeton in 1940 and was a naval aviator in World War II. His war poems are characterized by decorous language and good humor. His first collection, *Love Letter from an Impossible Land* (1944) was a Yale Younger Poets Series winner while he was still a Lieutenant (JG) in the Navy. The volume was selected by ARCHIBALD MACLEISH.

Meredith has published nine books, most in metrics, but *Hazard, the Painter* (1975) is a book-length poem in free verse. His *Partial Accounts: New and Selected Poems* (1987) won the Pulitzer Prize, and *Efforts at Speech: New and Selected Poems* (1997) won the National Book Award.

For many years he taught at Connecticut College. His later years have been plagued with ill health, including a stroke suffered in 1983, which left him with expressive aphasia. He lives in Uncasville, Connecticut.

Selected works: *Poems are Hard to Read* (prose, 1991).

[RP]

Merrill, James (United States, 1926–97) Born to the founder of the prestigious brokerage firm, Merrill Lynch, Merrill always had the liberty to write and travel as he pleased. This wealthy upbringing also influenced his poetic aesthetics: he wrote a poetry that was highly mannered and decadent in style. His books of the late 1940s and throughout the 1950s exhibit Merrill's genius for metrics and form. While the verse was occasionally dismissed as too ornate and about nothing important, one can see his facility with language, his unfailing ear for rhythm, his extensive knowledge of poetry, and finally, the wit and playfulness that his financial freedom might have allowed him. Some of these poems, especially those dealing with his struggles with his parents' divorce, and with his feelings of loneliness, verge on the 'poor little rich boy' in tone, perhaps due to the combination of their subject matter and his high-blown style.

Written in the 1970s, Merrill's masterwork is *The Changing Light at Sandover*. It comprises three book-length poems, 'The Book of Ephraim', 'Mirabell: Books of Number', and 'Scripts for the Pageant'. In these poems, Merrill and his longtime lover, David Jackson (DJ) use the ouija board to contact friends, famous writers and thinkers in the spirit world. This premise allows Merrill to develop a variety of voices, to discuss a range of topics from the personal to the historical, and adds to his writing a depth and seriousness of purpose. He and DJ use the ouija to make connections beyond their world of privilege – and these connections transcend time, creating for the artistic, homosexual couple a family of sorts. The scientific content of much of *The Changing Light at Sandover* is rooted in genetics, and suggests to the reader that these two men, with their ouija board, are expanding the notion of procreation. The spirit world enters their small home, and they report physical signs from, for example, their friend Maya Deren, the filmmaker who mysteriously died after making a documentary about voodoun. Likewise, they affect the spirit world in their discussions with its emissaries.

This book is practically a primer of poetic styles; whole sections are written in uppercase, run-on lines, some borrow from his earlier, formal work, and others use psalm structures and alphabetical methods of organization. The cast of characters in *The Changing Light at Sandover* attempts reconciliation between the physical and the spiritual.

His later work never quite matched these three poems (one of his last poems was an ode to the laptop computer), but *The Changing Light at Sandover* is the great epic of the twentieth century, a form that had been previously thought dead. The journey of this epic could only move inward, since the discoveries of the external world had already been made. His predecessors in this form are perhaps Tennyson and W.H. AUDEN.

Merrill also wrote two novels and much non-fiction, collected in *Recitative* in 1986. When Merrill died in 1997 poetry in English lost one of its most agile and, finally, original practitioners.

[CV]

Merwin, W.S. (United States, b. 1927) William Stanley Merwin has had a long, consistently strong and celebrated career as a poet, his late books showing continued mastery. He has also translated with distinction from French and Spanish.

Born in New York City, Merwin graduated in 1948 from Princeton, where he was taught by JOHN BERRYMAN, and studied Romance languages in graduate school. Merwin worked several years as a tutor overseas, including a turn with the son of Robert Graves.

Merwin's first book, *A Mask for Janus* (1952), was chosen for the Yale Series of Younger Poets Award by W.H. AUDEN, who praised Merwin's formal craft. He followed with several more volumes, loosening his formality along the way, and in 1970 won a Pulitzer for *The Carrier of Ladders*. That same year, he published *The Miner's Pale Children*, a remarkable series of autobiographical prose poems.

After many years in France, Merwin moved to Hawaii. Since 1970, he has published an average of almost a book of poems a year – books that seem to be getting stronger. These include most notably *The Rain in the Trees* (1988). He received the Bollingen Prize in 1979.

It is unfair to call Merwin an environmentalist poet, given that his passion for the natural world has not usurped his writing gifts. In *The Vixen* (1995), his concern for the environment extends his awed exploration of the radical context of human consciousness, the mysterious fullness and emptiness at the edge of our ken. With his spare syntax and puzzling yet compelling line breaks he creates his own vehicle for this exploration.

[CC]

Mew, Charlotte (England, 1869–1928) Mew was born in Bloomsbury to a typical middle-class couple. Her first published work, a short story, appeared in 1894 but Mew is now known primarily for her poetry. Mew published her first, and warmly received, volume of poetry, *The*

Farmer's Bride in 1915. Successive deaths of her mother and sister – to whom she was extremely close – poverty and depression combined to lead Mew to commit suicide in 1928, a decade after she received a Civil List pension through the endeavors of THOMAS HARDY. *The Rambling Sailor*, her second book-length work of poetry, was published posthumously in 1929.

Mew's poetry displays flexibility of style and quiet, intense emotion. Recent publications featuring Mew and her poetry include a *Collected Poems and Prose* (1981).

[MK]

Michaux, Henri (France, 1899–1984) Belgian by birth, Michaux is best known for his explorations of interior and exterior space. He traveled widely, and recounted his voyages in *Ecuador* (1929) and *Un Barbare en Asie* (*A Barbarian in Asia*, 1931). But for Michaux travel was an occasion to probe his inner life, and to produce writings on imaginary countries and peoples.

After World War II Michaux turned to painting and calligraphy, which further developed his original style of magical perception. To deepen his self-analysis, he took hallucinogenic drugs which served, he believed, not as an escape from reality but as a means to heighten it. Among the works in which his visions are recounted are *Connaissance par les Gouffres* (*Knowledge from the Abyss*, 1967) and *Les Grandes Epreuves de l'esprit* (*Great Trials of the Spirit*, 1966).

Selected works: *Qui je fus* (*Who I Was*, 1927); *Plume* (1938); *L'Espace du dedans* (*The Space Inside*, 1966).

[SJ]

Middleton, Christopher (England, b. 1926) Middleton was born in Truro, Cornwall, and attended Merton College, Oxford, and came to the United States in 1966.

Middleton's poetry closely follows the innovations of Modernism. Rooted in Surrealism and German Expressionism, his works are consistently original, and he sees the poet as one who tries to shape language into new ways of seeing and understanding. Critical of the 'suave poetry' which he sees as dominating British literature, he is sometimes at odds with the British poetry mainstream.

Although he has lived in Texas for over thirty years, Middleton is still a vital part of the contemporary English poetry scene, and is viewed by some as an increasingly important influence on English writing since the 1950s.

Middleton's awards and honors include: Sir Geoffrey Faber Memorial Prize in 1964 for *Torse 3: Poems, 1949–61*; Guggenheim Fellowship, 1974–75; National Endowment for the Humanities Fellowship, 1980; Schlegel-Tieck Translation Prize, 1986; Max-Geilinger-Stiftung Prize, 1987–88, for translations; Neustadt Prize nomination, 1992.

Selected works: *The Lonely Suppers of W. V. Balloon* (1975); *111 Poems* (1983); *Selected Writings* (1989); *The Balcony Tree* (1993); *Intimate Chronicles* (1996).

[JS]

Miles, Josephine (United States, 1911–85) Miles was born in Chicago and raised in California. She studied at UCLA and Berkeley, where she remained to teach. She was a well-known scholar of the conventions of grammar and vocabulary through different periods of English literature.

Miles' scholarly studies echo in the precision of her observations and idiomatic language, as does the debilitating arthritis which began in her childhood. Treated explicitly in a number of poems, the influence of her physical condition can be sensed in other works as well, in the current of pain which underlies many of her calm portrayals of individuals and situations.

Selected works: *Lines at Intersection* (1939); *Local Measures* (1946); *Prefabrications* (1955);

Kinds of Affection (1967); *Coming to Terms* (1979).

[JT]

Miljković, Branko (Yugoslavia, 1934–61) Miljković, the Yugoslav 'prince of poets', rose to prominence in his youth in the 1950s. His premature death by suicide at the age of twenty-seven further nurtured a legend already in the making and reinforced his powerful influence and popularity among Yugoslav poets and readers. His fame has continued unabated to this day, and his name still resonates powerfully in Serbian culture.

A prolific essayist and translator from many languages, Miljković, who studied philosophy at the University of Belgrade, wrote poetry that was highly intellectual and erudite. His poems reflect an intense preoccupation with death, loss, and the futility of life; his poetic world is the world of individual alienation, loneliness, and torments. Some critics have tried to explain these interests by citing Miljković's traumas during World War II, when he witnessed two massacres.

Miljković drew upon both traditional forms (often the sonnet, his favorite form) and Modernist elements, Symbolist and Surrealist. He experimented with the expressive possibilities of the Serbian language, introducing experimental techniques into a traditional milieu. Some of his formally and stylistically innovative poems are about elements from Serbian mythology, history, and culture. His often successful experiments in form included free verse and prose poems. Leaving a legacy belied by his youth, some of his poems are considered among the best in the Serbian language.

Selected works: *Uzalud je budim* (*I Wake Her up in Vain*, 1957); *Smrću protiv smrti* (*With Death against Death*, 1959); *Poreklo nade* (*A Source of Hope*, 1960); *Krv koja svetli* (*Blood that Shines*, 1961).

[DJ]

Miller, Ruth (South Africa, 1919–69) Born Ruth Friedjohn in Uitenhage, in the Cape Province, Miller grew up in Petersburg but spent most of her life in Johannesburg. She worked as a secretary and later taught English at St Mary's Convent in Johannesburg until 1965. Although she is perhaps South Africa's best-known female poet, only two volumes of her verse were published in her lifetime. Her first book, *Floating Island* (1965), won the Ingrid Jonker Prize for Poetry in 1966. The second, *Selected Poems*, was published in 1968. Her friend and executor, Lionel Abrahams, published fifty of her previously uncollected poems in a 1991 volume: *Ruth Miller: Poems, Prose, Plays*. This volume includes her earlier two volumes, two radio plays, a short story, and an essay. Her work considers issues of alienation not only as poet and artist, but also as a woman and a liberal South African living under apartheid rule. Images of death, tragedy, and mortality perhaps suggest she knew something of her own impending death from cancer.

[KS]

Milosz, Czeslaw (Poland, b. 1911) Lithuanian-born Milosz has been defined as catastrophist, pantheist, dissident, and ecstatic, but above everything, Milosz will stand as a poet of struggle: through two World Wars, through Communism and defection, through politics and beauty.

The son of an engineering officer in the Tsarist army, Milosz was born to Polish-speaking gentry in Szetejnie, Lithuania. He explored Socialism as a student at the University of Vilna in 1929–34, where he studied law and began to write poetry. A leftist sympathizer, Milosz was fired from a position as programmer for Polish radio in 1937. He moved to Warsaw, joined a Catastrophist poetry circle, and published underground texts of poetry. After the war, Milosz remained in Soviet-occupied Poland as a consular officer until his defection from the Communist government in 1951 to France.

Chagrined by the support of Marxism in Paris, Milosz moved to California in 1960 to accept a position at Berkeley in Slavic Languages. He did not return to Poland until 1980, when he was awarded the Nobel Prize for Literature; his works, banned since 1945, began to appear in print in Poland again, a fitting balance to Milosz' many struggles.

Milosz' early works depict the ambivalence of Poland itself at the beginning of the century. He explored the artist's distance from the world in *Three Winters* (1936); illustrated his moral reactions to Socialism in *Rescue* (1948) with the famous 'Voices of Poor People'; spoke against absolutism and explored the dangers of Communism in *Captive Mind* (1953); and yearned for an independent Poland in *Seizure of Power* (1955). His first collection after his defection, *Light of Day* (1954), exposed his concern with the connection between history and identity. In his later life, Milosz would reveal himself as a reserved Modernist, a foreigner in isolation amid the peace and freedom movements of 1960s America. Poems written in California would enhance America's understanding of Milosz' ecstatic visions, his search for self-definition, and his faith in God, with *Bobo's Metamorphosis* (1965), *City without a Name* (1969), and *From the Rising of the Sun* (1974), where he wrote about everything from angels to astronomy, art to irony, and flowerbeds to table tops. Milosz' *Collected Poems: 1931–87* was published in 1988.

Milosz' poetry is often confessional, but the social and political history of Europe dominates his own history in the early autobiography *Native Realm* (1959), which revealed the story of his defection. The later *Year of the Hunter* (1990) shows a more abstract emphasis on beauty. His newest works, including the poignant observations of *Road-Side Dog* (1998), offer testimony to a poet in a constant state of renewal; Milosz' prose and poetry seem compelled by history and beauty alike. With over thirty books in multiple translations, the essence of Milosz' current struggle is the Polish people's desire for freedom, a world where catastrophism, totalitarianism, and death are merely ravages of time. Milosz' new search is one of simplicity, of experience in the everyday, of what comprises the commonplace beautiful.

[MF]

Miron, Gaston (Canada, 1928–96) Miron is an influential figure in the development of Québécois poetry in the second half of the twentieth century, in part because of his involvement with the Les Éditions de l'Hexagone, a press committed to the publication and distribution of Québécois poetry. Although Miron's position as an editor at the press and his commitment to political activities in support of an independent Québec have limited his poetic output, the work that he has produced has earned him numerous literary awards and accolades, and comparisons to poets such as AIMÉ CÉSAIRE and PABLO NERUDA.

Miron was born in Sainte-Agathe-des-Monts, Québec. He moved to Montréal in 1946, where in 1953 he co-founded L'Hexagone. It was in this year that his first collection of poems appeared in *Deux Sangs*, a volume that also contained the poems of Olivier Marchand. *L'homme rapaillé* (*The Agonized Life*, 1970), which collected numerous pieces that had appeared in magazines, literary reviews, and journals, established Miron's reputation as a poet and political essayist. The works collected in this volume describe the traumas of Québec's vexed history and politics, and argue for an independent Québec limited neither by a stifling regionalism nor by an abstract universalism. As a result of his political views, Miron was briefly jailed during the 1970 October Crisis. *Contrepointes* (*Counter-Points*, 1975) is a volume of previously uncollected poetry that appeared between the publication of *Deux Sangs* (*Two Bloods*) and the late 1960s.

[IS]

Mistral, Gabriela (Chile, 1889–1957) Trained as a teacher, Mistral first became known for her pedagogical work in rural Chile. In 1914, however, three of her poems entitled 'Sonnets of Death' won a prestigious literary competition in Santiago. These were included in her first collection of poetry, *Desolación* (*Desolation*, 1922). That same year, Mistral became an educational consultant for the Mexican government and thereafter spent much of her life in Europe and the United States promoting human rights and Latin American literature and culture.

Though Mistral experienced the loss of many loved ones in her life, and though she addresses death and suffering in her poetry, she also expresses belief in the creative forces of motherhood and poetry. Initially influenced by Modernism, Mistral eventually created a more direct, personal poetic voice. Much of her imagery involves landscape, nature, and a religious, metaphysical view of death. Her second work, *Ternura* (*Tenderness*, 1924), is a book of children's poems; she dedicated her third work, *Tala* (*Feeling*, 1938), to orphaned children of the Spanish Civil War. The poems of *Lagar* (*The Wine-Press*, 1954) express her agony over the Holocaust and the death of her nephew. Mistral's diverse and innovative versification as well as her distinctive tone influenced much of Latin America's subsequent poetry. She was awarded the Nobel Prize for Literature (1945) and Chile's National Prize for Poetry (1951). The most recent English translation of her work is entitled *A Gabriela Mistral Reader* (1993). Mistral died of cancer while acting as a diplomat in the United States. Her literary reputation remains solid and she will long be considered one of Latin America's canonical poets.

[LKA]

Miyazawa Kenji (Japan, 1896–1933) Miyazawa was born in Iwate, the son of a pawnbroker. He grew up in a family of the Buddhist True Pure Land faith, and later he became a fervent Nichiren devotee. He studied at Morioka Higher School of Agriculture and Forestry and after graduation in 1918 stayed on for further research on the subject of soil and fertilizers. In 1924 he published a collection of poems, *Haru to Shura* (*Spring and the Asura*), and a collection of juvenile stories, *Chumon no Ooi Ryoriten* (*The Popular Restaurant*).

His poems are characterized by a rich vocabulary which absorbs and enhances dialect and scientific terminology to create a unique poetic effect. His works, imbued with the mystical spirit of his faith, also demonstrate a vast extension of the imagination.

[LY]

Monro, Harold (England, 1879–1932) Harold Edward Monro was both a publisher and a poet. Born in Brussels, he moved to England at age seven and was educated at Radley, and at Gonville and Caius College, Cambridge. Monro is most remembered for the Poetry Bookshop, which he established in 1913, to publish, sell, and organize readings of work by contemporary poets. He founded *The Poetry Review*. T.S. ELIOT, who described Monro's work as isolated between the Georgians and the Moderns, introduced his *Collected Poems* of 1933.

Selected works: *Poems* (1906); *Evolution of the Soul* (1907); *Judas* (1907); *Chronicle of a Pilgrimage: Paris to Milan on Foot* (1909); *Before Dawn* (1911); *Children of Love* (1914); *The Earth for Sale* (1928).

[EM]

Montague, John (Ireland, b. 1929) Although he was born in Brooklyn, New York, Montague is very much an Irish poet – one of the most widely read today. Montague lived with his parents and uncle in New York City until he was four years old, when he was sent back to live with his aunts in Garvaghey, Northern Ireland. Montague studied at University College, Dublin, and then attended Yale University as a Fulbright Scholar in 1953–54. In 1955, he received an M.F.A. from the University of Iowa, where he met his first wife, Madeleine de Brauer. They were married in 1956, and Montague worked as a journalist in Dublin and in Paris. After their divorce in 1972, Montague accepted a position at University College, Cork, where he remained until 1988. He married Evelyn Robinson in 1973.

Perhaps because of Montague's 'complex fate'–straddling two cultures–he has been able to address Ulster's history more directly than many of his Northern Irish compatriots. *The Rough Field* (1972) is a sequence of poems about Ulster, past and present. But in Montague's poetry, the historical is often personalized. He also writes poignant and lyrical love poems, such as 'Do Not Disturb', 'Talisman', 'Gone', and 'Legendary Obstacles', where acts of intimacy become inseparable from the anticipation of loss. Indeed, Montague's most stirring poems are about loss – losing a family, a language, a lover, or a nation – and how poetry itself allows 'absences to flower'.

Selected works: *Death of a Chieftain and Other Stories* (1964); *A Chosen Light* (1967); *Tides* (1970); *A Slow Dance* (1975); *Selected Poems* (1982); *The Dead Kingdom* (1984); *Time in Armagh* (1993); *Collected Poems* (1996).

[CT]

Montale, Eugenio (Italy, 1896–1981) Born in Genoa, where he studied accounting and music, Montale published his first poems in the early 1920s. His first collection of poetry, *Ossi di seppia* (*Cuttlefish Bones*, 1925), was destined, along with QUASIMODO and UNGARETTI's first volumes, to set the standards for contemporary Italian verse.

After moving to Florence in 1927, Montale became director of the rare book library Gabinetto Viesseux (a position he had to resign in 1938 because of his anti-Fascist beliefs). In 1939 his second collection, *Le Occasioni* (*The Occasions*) was released, followed by *Finisterre* (1943), published in Switzerland. These two collections further outlined the personality of Montale as one of the great metaphysical poets of the twentieth century, whose radically negative attitude toward reality was simultaneously an expressive urge and a political statement. In search of clues that might disclose the riddle of human existence, Montale thoroughly explored the world, like the Mediterranean landscape of his early poetry, only to find enigmatic signs of an incumbent catastrophe, both historical and existential. Only Clizia, his interlocutor in several of the poems of this collection, seemed to represent a chance to see through an otherwise opaque reality.

In 1948 Montale moved to Milan, where he worked as a publicist and music critic for the newspaper *Corriere della Sera*. A new collection entitled *La Bufera e altro* (*The Storm and Other Poems*, 1956), besides deepening Montale's merciless investigation of a universe marked by pain and failure, further embodied the contrast between a godlike female presence and the meaningless sterility of the world. In the same year a collection of essays, *La farfalla di Dinard* (*The Butterfly of Dinard*), was released.

After receiving honorary degrees from the Universities of Rome, Milan, Cambridge, and Basel, and following the release of another collection of critical prose, *Auto da Fé* (1966), Montale was appointed senator in 1967. His later collections *Satura* (1971), *Diario del '71 e del '72* (*Diary of '71 and '72*, 1973) are charged with a sharp irony which is only partially attenuated by the tender lyrical tone of 'Xenia', a series of short compositions dedicated to his deceased wife. After a life of literary exploration and success, he was awarded the Nobel Prize in 1975.

With *Quaderno di quattro anni* (*It Depends: A Poet's Notebook*, 1978) and *Altri versi* (*Other Poems*, 1980) Montale inclined to a prose-like verse, in which irony takes the shape of a bitter, often epigrammatic sarcasm toward any existential categories – time, life, death, as well as the triviality of daily routine. The last edition of *Diario Postumo: 66 poesie e altre* (*Posthumous Diary: 66 poems and other things*, 1996), a collection of the poems Montale gave to his friend Annalisa Cima, raised a vigorous debate on their philological authenticity.

Fully in line with the most accomplished achievements of twentieth-century Western poetry, Montale's work stands today as a lucid witness of the deep transformation of post-war European culture, as well as a firm reflection on the metaphysical origin of evil.

[GS]

Moore, Marianne (United States, 1887–1982) Moore's early passion was biology; she majored in it at Bryn Mawr, graduating in 1909. Contemporaries to Moore describe her famous Brooklyn apartment as a sort of museum of natural history; in fact, ELIZABETH BISHOP, during her years in Brazil, was always on the lookout for interesting specimens and amusing facts for Moore. This passion for the animal world is reflected in her work. Moore wrote whole series of poems about fish, birds, and lizards–and this focus allowed her to write about an internal life of passion, without resorting to autobiography or to modernist self-aggrandizement. In some ways, her work captures, too, the Darwinian urges to catalogue existence, to present the world within clearly defined parameters; her use of syllabics is one way in which she captures language and the line. There is an almost Victorian sensibility to Moore's work, in its precise diction and formal presentation.

Moore, however, was the darling of American Modernism, with her early poems appearing in influential journals such as *The Egoist* and *The Dial* in the 1920s, and she was celebrated by the avant-garde even before her first collection was published in 1921. Over a period of twelve years in the 1940s and 1950s, she won a Guggenheim Fellowship, an American Academy of Arts and Letters grant, the Bollingen Award, a National Book Award, and the Pulitzer Prize.

Moore remained a New Yorker her whole life, seldom leaving Brooklyn, and though she never taught, she encouraged the younger writers of her day. Moore's most famous protégé was Elizabeth Bishop who wrote about their friendship in the essay, 'Efforts of Affection: A Memoir of Marianne Moore'. The essay reveals the tendency of many poets of the time to adopt a somewhat patronizing attitude toward Moore, perhaps due to her rather eccentric ways. She was just as popular for her boisterous manner, flowing capes, and tricorne hat as she was for her poetry. Perhaps Moore herself participated in this image of herself, remaining as she did largely unsexual, living with her mother until her mother's death. Moreover, 'Miss Moore' refused to take on the mantle of feminism, insisting on a secular humanism (for a fine example of this stance, see the long poem, 'Marriage', or the poem, 'The Steeplejack'). Still, the best of Moore's poems fracture language to achieve an effect that has not to this day been matched. The splintering of diction and the density of her language do not dilute the power of meanings. Meticulous, and a perfectionist, Moore published on her own schedule: her *Selected Works*, which she edited in 1961, is a slim volume. One of the problems for her readers is Moore's perfectionism, which engendered the wholesale rewriting and often even frank rejection of early works considered significant.

[CV]

Moraes, Dom (India, b. 1938) Moraes was born in Bombay and educated at the University of Bombay and at Oxford. The youngest poet to win the Hawthornden Prize, for *The Beginning* (1957), he published early romanticist lyrics, in volumes such as *Poems* (1960). After the publication of *John Nobody* (1965) and *Poems: 1955–65* (1966), Moraes entered into a period of poetic silence, though he kept writing as an international journalist. Finally settling in Bombay, where he still lives, Moraes gained new poetic recognition with the publication of his *Collected Poems: 1957–87* (1987) and *Serendip* (1990).

[MW]

Morgan, Edwin (Scotland, b. 1920) Morgan was born in Glasgow and educated at Rutherglen Academy and Glasgow High School. His M.A. in English at Glasgow University was interrupted in 1940–46 by Royal Army Medical Corps service in the Middle East. After the war, he was appointed lecturer at Glasgow, eventually becoming Professor in English in 1975–80. His first book, *The Vision of Cathkin Braes and Other Poems*, was published to critical acclaim in 1952, as was his translation of *Beowulf*. Honors include awards for translation, honorary degrees from Glasgow, Edinburgh, Loughborough, Stirling, and Waikato, New Zealand and an OBE (1982). His output is prolific, including criticism, plays, libretti, and poetry translation ranging from Anglo-Saxon to Russian, as well as formidable collections of his own poetry. His widely-varied work is mostly characterized by an enjoyment of media and fascination with the strangeness of familiar subjects. While earlier poems were more strictly separated into formal experimentation, like the concrete poems of *The Second Life* (1968), or more traditional forms, like the 'Glasgow Sonnets' of *From Glasgow to Saturn* (1973), later collections thrive on a fusion of approaches, taking both audible and visible enjoyment in serious game-playing.

Selected works: *The Cape of Good Hope* (1955); *Instamatic Poems* (1972); *Wi' the Haill Voice: 25 poems by Vladimir Mayakovsky* (1972); *Poems of Thirty Years* (1982); *Sonnets from Scotland* (1984); *From the Video Box* (1986); *Collected Poems* (1990); *Hold Hands among the Atoms* (1991); *Collected Translations* (1996).

[LKMF]

Morgenstern, Christian (Germany, 1871–1914) Morgenstern worked for magazines and book publishers. Philosophically, he turned in 1909 to the anthroposophy of Rudolf Steiner, who is best known today as the founder of the Waldorf school. Due to poor health, Morgenstern spent much time in spas during the last years of his life.

Although he also wrote poetry about serious topics, especially influenced by Nietzsche and Steiner, Morgenstern is best known for his grotesque and humorous poems, especially in *Gallows Songs* (1905), *Palmström* (1910), and *Palma Kunkel* (1916). Not mere nonsense, these poems use language to create its own meaning in opposition to a meaningless world. They are reminiscent of Lewis Carroll's 'Jabberwocky' and predate avant-garde (Dada) attempts at playing with language.

[IRS]

Morris, Mervyn (Jamaica, b. 1937) Morris was born in Kingston, Jamaica. He attended Oxford University as a Rhodes Scholar, and since 1966 has been a faculty member at the University of the West Indies, Mona, Jamaica. He is an important figure in contemporary Caribbean letters not only as a poet, but as a leading literary critic and an editor of numerous volumes and anthologies of Caribbean poetry, including LOUISE BENNETT's *Selected Poems* (1982).

Morris' poems cover a wide range of themes, including race, politics, the problems of colonialism, and the challenges posed by cultural hybridity. He is perhaps best known, however, in the words of EDWARD KAMAU BRATHWAITE, as the Caribbean's 'leading poet of domesticity'. This is especially true of the poems in his first collection, *The Pond* (1973). Morris' second collection, *On Holy Week* (1976), takes the Christian Gospel as a framing device for its exploration of sin and redemption. In *Shadowboxing* (1979), poems are reduced to their essence in the hope of revealing the truth at the center of things. In 1976, Morris received the Institute of Jamaica's Musgrave Medal, an acknowledgment of the consummate craftsmanship exhibited by his poems.

[IS]

Morrison, Blake (England, b. 1950) Philip Blake Morrison was born in Burnley, Lancashire, in 1950 and educated in Nottingham and at University College London where he received his Ph.D. in 1978. His first of only two poetry collections, *Dark Glasses*, was published in 1989.

A literary journalist and critic, he worked for the *Times Literary Supplement* and *Observer* before becoming literary editor of the *Independent on Sunday* (1990–95). He is now a freelance writer. While his writing packs the disquieting punch of a social critic – the long title-poem of his second collection, *The Ballad of the Yorkshire Ripper* (1987), is about the serial killer Peter Sutcliffe – he is also a literary critic of the Movement poets and of SEAMUS HEANEY. With ANDREW MOTION he coedited *The Penguin Book of Contemporary Poetry* (1982).

[LKMF]

Motion, Andrew (England, b. 1952) Named TED HUGHES's successor as Poet Laureate in 1999, Motion was born in London and educated at Radley College and University College, Oxford, where he received his B.A. in 1975, the year he won the Newdigate Prize. His first volume, *Goodnestone: A Sequence*, appeared in 1972. He was a lecturer in English in 1977–81 at the University of Hull, where he met PHILIP LARKIN; his exhaustive biography of Larkin won the Whitbread Award in 1994. After lecturing at Hull, Motion became poetry editor and then editorial director for Chatto and Windus Publishers. He also served as the editor of *Poetry Review* (1990–92) and then, like ELIOT before him, as editor for Faber and Faber. In 1995, he became Professor of Creative Writing at the University of East Anglia.

First inspired to write after reading THOMAS HARDY, Motion has been prolific ever since, producing two novels in addition to his seven volumes of poetry. He writes of personal experience, such as his mother's death following a riding accident, and of contemporary England, as in his poetry about Princess Diana's death, but only as vehicles to universal ideas.

Selected works: *The Pleasure Steamers* (1978); *Independence* (1981); *Dangerous Play: Poems 1974–84* (1984); *The Price of Everything* (1994); *Salt Water* (1997); *Selected Poems 1976–97* (1999).

[BRB]

Mouré, Erin (Canada, b. 1955) Mouré was born in Calgary, Alberta, attended the Universities of Calgary and British Columbia, and lived for ten years in Vancouver before moving to Montréal. She writes sophisticated, political verse that attacks hegemonic structures at the level of linguistic practice. Mouré's poetry is self-reflexive and emphasizes the necessity of a plurality of interpretations, and she is known for powerful articulations of feminist positions.

Both her first and most recent books – *Empire, York Street* (1979) and *Search Procedures* (1996) – were nominated for Governor General's awards. With *Furious* (1988), her strongest collection of poems to date, Mouré won the first of what will no doubt be several Governor General's awards for poetry.

[IS]

Mtshali, Oswald (Joseph) Mbuyiseni (South Africa, b. 1940) Mtshali was born at KwaBhanya, near Vryheid in northern Natal. One of the early Soweto, or township, poets, he has worked as journalist, teacher, and theater critic. In the late 1960s his work began appearing in various journals, local newspapers, and anthologies: *The Classic*, *New Coin*, *The Purple Renoster*, *Ophir*. In 1971 the poems were collected as *Sounds of a Cowhide Drum* and became an instant bestseller. He won the Olive Schreiner Prize for Literature in 1975. In 1980 his second volume of verse, *Fireflames*, which included several translations of original work from the Zulu, was banned in South Africa. Like the work of SEPAMLA, Mtshali's poetry becomes a social and political commentary recording the violent, precarious conditions in township life.

[KS]

Muir, Edwin (Scotland, 1887–1959) A farmer's son, Muir was born in Deerness, Orkney, the youngest in a family of six, and grew up in a close-knit community on the island of Wyre. When he was fourteen, the farm failed and the family moved to Glasgow where Muir worked as an office boy and clerk. His mother, father, and two of his brothers died within a short space of time and Muir was deeply affected by the misery of this period, later writing about it in *The Story and the Fable* (1940) and *An Autobiography* (1954). He was fervently religious as a boy and later wrote that he spent his Glasgow youth in an atmosphere of evangelicalism but eventually 'escaped into Socialism'. During this period he read Shaw, Ibsen, Heine, Blatchford, and particularly Nietzsche; his early poetry was an unsuccessful combination of Socialist propaganda and Nietzschian aphorism, published as *We Moderns* (1918). In 1919 he married Willhelmina (Willa) Johnstone, a gifted linguist, and moved to London to work on Orage's *New Age*. However, the effects of the Glasgow years brought him close to breakdown and finally necessitated a course of psychoanalysis. Partly to aid his recovery, he and Willa traveled to Prague, Germany, Italy, and Austria during 1921–24, working jointly on translations of Kafka and Feuchtwanger and contributing to *Freeman*. After living in the south of France for several years, the couple returned to Britain in 1927; Muir produced substantial quantities of criticism and reviews, as well as writing three novels and a study of John Knox. Living in Surrey, Sussex, and Hampstead, and later moving to St Andrews, he also continued to work with Willa, mainly on German translations (nearly forty volumes of them).

Muir published *First Poems* in 1925, returning to poetry relatively late and maturing as a poet towards the end of his life. He published the bulk of his poetry in the 1930s and 1940s. Unlike MACDIARMID, who both admired and attacked his work, Muir did not adopt synthetic Scots and instead wrote poetry of a quieter yet nonetheless visionary nature, returning to some of the religious impulse of his youth.

During the war, he worked for the British Council and then became director of the British Institute in Prague (1945–48), and in Rome (1948–50). As Warden of Newbattle Abbey Adult Education College in 1950–55, he encouraged the poetry of GEORGE MACKAY BROWN, who remembered him in *Edwin Muir: A Brief Memoir* (1975) as a softly spoken, slightly reserved man. He was Eliot Norton Professor of Poetry at Harvard in 1955–56, and retired to Cambridgeshire.

Selected works: *The Labyrinth* (1949); *Selected Poems*, ed. T.S. Eliot (1965).

[LKMF]

Muldoon, Paul (Ireland, b. 1951) Muldoon is considered the most innovative, imaginative, and skillful Irish poet of his generation. He was born and raised in County Armagh, Northern Ireland, and educated at Queen's University, Belfast. A precocious young poet and an avid reader, Muldoon was encouraged early in his career by SEAMUS HEANEY. His first volume, *New Weather* (1973), heralded by critics, sets up many of Muldoon's poetic subjects and themes: he transforms and modernizes mythologies, particularly Gaelic; he draws comparisons between the Celt and the Native American; he demonstrates the influence of such poets as ROBERT FROST and Byron; and he delights in the playful and postmodern interplay of language – both its limits and its possibilities.

From 1973 to 1986 Muldoon worked as a radio and television producer for BBC Northern Ireland. During that time he published several well-received volumes: *Mules* (1977); *Why Brownlee Left* (1980); and *Quoof* (1983). In 1987 he began a series of one-year lectureships at U.S. universities. Since 1990 he has lectured in and directed the creative writing department at Princeton University. In 1999 he was elected Oxford Professor of Poetry, a position previously held by AUDEN, GRAVES, and FENTON.

Like so many Irish poets, Muldoon writes about Northern Ireland obliquely; he often uses American history, myth, landscape, and dialect as a way of looking at his native Ulster. In *Meeting the British* (1987), '7, Middagh Street' is concerned with W.H. AUDEN's emigration to New York City and questions the artist's responsibility to his or her homeland. *Madoc–A Mystery* (1990), an epic poem that compresses U.S. history, science fiction, and philosophy, takes as its starting point the plan of Southey and Coleridge to move to America and start a utopian community. His latest volumes include *The Annals of Chile* (1994) and *Hay* (1998).

[CT]

Murphy, Richard (Ireland, b. 1927) A highly regarded poet, Murphy was born in County Galway, and educated at Oxford University. Murphy's career is characterized by one-year academic positions, particularly in the United States. He won the Æ Memorial Award in 1951, the Guinness Award in 1962, and the American-Irish Foundation Award in 1983.

Sailing to an Island (1963), Murphy's early and perhaps most celebrated volume, takes the West of Ireland with its rugged, heroic, sea-faring inhabitants as its theme. In the historical sequence *The Battle of Aughrim* (1968), Murphy's various speakers narrate the Roman Catholic versus Orange conflict in which the Catholics were defeated. 'Casement's Funeral' from this work is a stirring elegy to Roger Casement (1864–1916), an Irish nationalist who died for his cause. *The Price of Stone* (1985), a 50-poem sequence, compares the process of building structures, particularly houses, to building poems.

Selected works: *The Last Galway Hooker* (1961); *New Selected Poems* (1989); *The Mirror Wall* (1989).

[CT]

Murray, Les (Australia, b. 1938) Murray was born and raised in the Bunyah region of northern New South Wales, to which he returned in middle age. In the interim, he studied at the University of Sydney, which he left in 1961 without receiving a degree. After working as a freelance translator and in administration, he took to writing full-time in 1970.

His first volume, *The Ilex Tree* (1965), was co-written with GEOFFREY LEHMANN and won the Grace Leven award for poetry. By *The Vernacular Republic* (1976) Murray had established his characteristic mix of empathy for the landscape, freewheeling erudition, and a casual yet determined solidarity with the rural working class. This last side of him was reflected in the verse novel *The Boys Who Stole the Funeral* (1980) while his growing interest in Christianity emerges in *The Daylight Moon* (1987), perhaps his single most important collection, as well as *Dog Fox Field* (1991). *Ethnic Radio* (1977) includes 'The Buladelah-Taree Holiday Song Cycle' in which Murray explores his spiritual kinship with Aboriginal Australians.

Murray has become known as one of the leading poets writing in English, and is frequently mentioned alongside his friends JOSIP BRODSKY, SEAMUS HEANEY, and DEREK WALCOTT, all Nobel Prize winners. In 1996, Murray had a serious illness which required extensive hospitalization. *Subhuman Redneck Poems* (1996) provoked both admiration and ire in its sharp, satiric attacks against what Murray saw as the secular leftist hegemony in Australian culture. The volume also included 'It Allows a Portrait in Line-scan at Age Fifteen', a moving portrait of Murray's autistic son. *Fredy Neptune* (1998) is a verse-novel featuring a German-born Australian who accidentally finds himself serving on the opposing side during World War I, and develops unique defenses against the social maladies of the twentieth century. Murray traveled widely in Europe and North America to promote the book, which has established him as a truly popular poet not only in Australia but worldwide.

Selected works: *Poems against Economics* (1972); *Translations from the Natural World* (1990).

[NB]

Mutran, Mutran Khalil (Syria, 1872–1944) A Syro-Lebanese Catholic from Baalbek, Mutran received missionary education which introduced him to Western, particularly French, literature. In 1892, having written a nationalistic poem, he fled to Egypt from Ottoman persecution and lived there for the rest of his life. He was officially honored there in 1913 and 1947.

Mutran is considered a link between neoclassical and Romantic Arabic poetry. He retained the classical form but introduced many innovations, such as narrative, the concept of organic unity in the poem, and the stress on spontaneity, though not subjective experience like the Western Romantics and younger Arab poets whom he influenced.

Selected works: *Diwan al-Khalil* (1948, 1949).

[WH]

N

Naffah, Fouad Gabriel (Lebanon, 1925–83) Born in Beirut, Naffah lived all his life in Lebanon where he loved writing every day in small cafés in the city. Considered the first Lebanese poet of French expression who not only imitated his predecessors but tried to reach what he called 'pure creation', he produced poetry where formal research intermingled with a mystical quest, haunted by death and the absolute. Committed several times to an asylum, he pursued his writing nonetheless. He has translated his personal experience to cosmic dimensions. His writing is often associated with Gérard de Nerval and Stephane Mallarmé. *La description de l'homme, du cadre et de la lyre* (*Portrait of a Man, Surroundings, and Lyre*, 1950) offers a sense of hope – the possibility of reaching understanding through the knowledge that poems reveal. This René Laporte Prize winner (1964) is written in Alexandrine lines, with no rhymes and no punctuation. Since his death, Naffah's reputation as a 'strong Lebanese poet' has been widely endorsed.

[MS]

Nash, Ogden (United States, 1902–71) Frederic Ogden Nash wrote widely popular light verse, much of which remains entertaining, some of the lines of which rise to distinguished wit and epigram. A famous example: 'Candy/ Is dandy,/ But liquor/ Is quicker'. His slapstick metrics clash agreeably with his double, triple, even quadruple rhymes – often amusingly forced.

Born in Rye, New York, of a wealthy Southern family, Nash studied briefly at Harvard (1920–21) and joined *The New Yorker* staff in 1929.

Nash's first two books of poems, *Hard Lines* and *Free Wheeling*, appeared in 1931, the year he married. He lived to write twenty-one more volumes of poetry, many delightful children's books, and lyrics for stage musicals (including *One Touch of Venus*, 1943, with Kurt Weill and S.J. Perelman).

[CC]

Nastasijević, Momčilo (Yugoslavia, 1894–1938) Not very well known in his lifetime, the Serbian poet Nastasijević came to prominence in the 1950s. He studied French and Comparative Literature at the University of Belgrade and spent most of his life in Belgrade working as a French teacher. Besides poetry, Nastasijević also wrote essays, fiction, and drama.

Nastasijević's poetry has often been described as hermetic, full of extremely private symbols inaccessible to ordinary readers. He focused on sound (trying to approximate the effect of music) more than meaning. His poems are terse and compressed, but feature a stretched and attenuated syntax reminiscent of the work of Gerard Manley Hopkins; what

Hopkins did with English, Nastasijević did with Serbian.

Selected works: *Pet lirskih krugova: Jutarnje, Večernje, Bdenja, Gluhote, Reču kamenu* (*Five Lyrical Circles*, 1932); *Magnovenja* (*Moments*, 1938); *Odjeci* (*Echoes*, 1938).

[DJ]

Ndebele, Njabulo Simakahle (South Africa, b. 1948) Ndebele was born in Western Native Township in Johannesburg and grew up in Niger. He was educated at the National University of Lesotho, Cambridge University, and the University of Denver. His poetry first appeared in various journals and anthologies which helped to launch the South African black poetry revival and the Black Consciousness Movement: *Izwi*, *Classic*, *Stuffrider*, *Black Poets in South Africa*. A collection of short stories, *Fools*, was published in 1983. He received the Noma Award for Publishing in Africa in 1984. In 1991 he returned to Lesotho, where he lectured and served as Pro-Vice Chancellor. After the end of apartheid, he served as President of the Congress of South African Writers and head of the department of African literatures at the University of Witwatersrand. Perhaps better known as a cultural critic and reviewer, Ndebele is particularly concerned with the role of language, discourse, and the changing literary terrain in his native South Africa.

[KS]

Nemerov, Howard (United States, 1920–91) Nemerov was a highly skilled poet who could easily move from seamless form poetry to epigrammatic free verse. Born in New York City, Nemerov attended Harvard University, served as a fighter bomber pilot during World War II, and taught at numerous colleges before joining Washington University, where his colleagues included MONA VAN DUYN.

The body of Nemerov's writings includes fifteen novels and collections of essays, and eighteen books of poetry. His mature verse can be seen after 1966 – especially in *The Blue Swallows* (1967) and *Gnomes and Occasions* (1973), two volumes that seek the glimmers of transcendence in the quotidian. In this regard, Nemerov's poetry offers a sustained meditation upon the spiritual residing within the material.

Nemerov's poetry has been widely acclaimed, and he won numerous awards including the National Book Award, the Pulitzer Prize, the Bollingen Prize, and the National Medal of Honor – all for *The Collected Poems of Howard Nemerov*. Nemerov was appointed Poet Laureate of the United States in 1988. Although his reputation has diminished with his death, Nemerov continues to be regarded as a fine example of American academic poets.

[DC]

Neruda, Pablo (Ricardo Eliezer Neftali Reyes y Basoalto; Chile, 1904–73) Neruda is widely recognized as the greatest Latin American poet of the twentieth century. Born in Parral, Chile, and raised in Tamuco, Neruda was a career diplomat whose life might be charted as points on a map: Burma and India from 1927 to 1933; Buenos Aires in 1934, where he met FEDERICO GARCÍA LORCA and other poets of the Generation of 1927; Barcelona in 1934–37; Mexico until 1943; Chile in 1943–49, including a term as a Communist Senator which ended when the Videla administration accused him of sedition and he escaped across the Andes; exile, until his 1953 return to Chile; twenty years of public service and recognition at home and abroad, including a 1970 Communist Party nomination for Chile's presidency and a two-year ambassadorship to France – and the 1971 Nobel Prize for Literature.

No matter how diverse, points on a map reflect neither the worldwide influence nor the scope of Neruda's writing. The private, 'impure', and passionately erotic poetry of early volumes such as *Twenty Poems of Love and a Song of Despair* (1924; trans. 1969) established Neruda's reputation and prompted his 1930 appearance in T.S. ELIOT's *The Criterion*. By that time, however, Neruda's sensualism was becoming Surrealism. Turning his *Residence on Earth* (1933) into wildly imaginative poetry, he indulged both image and metaphor.

By the third volume of *Residence on Earth* in 1947 (1973), however, Neruda's poetry had assumed a plainer diction and more pointed political direction. Affected by the atrocities of the Spanish Civil War, Neruda became a public poet, writing candidly about oppression. Whether praising the foreign – Stalin and Stalingrad in *Nuevo canto de amor a Stalingrado* (1943) – or mourning the domestic-decimated Incan civilization in *The Heights of Macchu Picchu* (1948; 1954) – Neruda's poetry of the 1940s was an overtly political forum. This phase culminated in 1950's *Canto General de Chile*, one of the greatest historical-political poems ever written.

Elementary Odes (1954; 1961) showed the surfacing of Neruda's sense of humor and joy in the mundane, as he wrote 'odes' to such things as socks, tomatoes, and artichokes. *Extravagaria* (1958) followed this trajectory as he took his simple diction and discriminating eye and turned them upon himself, treating with irony his previous personae, subjects, and interests; the verse autobiography *Isla Negra: A Notebook* (1964) extended this trope.

Eight volumes of poetry were in progress when Neruda died in 1973; like the posthumous *Jardin de invierna* (1974), many of these added consideration of death's approach to characteristic themes of joy in language and love of life.

[MW]

Neto, Agostinho (Angola, 1922–79) Neto is perhaps the most famous of all the Lusophone poets. Like LÉOPOLD SENGHOR, Neto became the first president of his native country. His writing exemplifies the perfect fusion of poetic eloquence and the struggle for independence. Angola's independence came in 1975, fifteen years later than many African nations (including Senghor's Senegal), and only after a brutal struggle with the Portuguese colonialists.

Neto's life began in Kaxikane, approximately forty miles from Luanda, the capital. He was raised in a Christian household, and in 1947 earned a grant to study medicine in Portugal. By the time he received his medical degree in 1958, he had already been imprisoned twice by the Portuguese authorities. International writers repeatedly spoke out against his unjust incarcerations. The poems that make up *Sagrada Esperana* (*Sacred Hope*, 1963), his only book of poetry, were written between 1945 and 1960.

Sagrada Esperana was first published in an Italian translation, entitled *Con Occhi Asciutti* (*With Dry Eyes*). The first Portuguese edition came out in 1974, and included more poems. By then, Neto had been working extensively with the MPLA (Peoples' Movement for the Liberation of Angola) for many years. In 1962, he became the Movement's president. He was also imprisoned during the 1960s. Poems such as 'O choro do Africa' remind the world that the crying of Africa is a symptom invented by servitude, and that Africans have in their hands other lives and joys. According to Neto's vision, the future must be built with love and dry eyes.

[KAC]

Nguyen Chi Thien (Vietnam, b. 1939) Born in Hanoi, Nguyen Chi Thien received a good education in French and Vietnamese before the Communists came to power in 1954. He developed a love of poetry early, and this caused him trouble with the authorities as he, innocently enough at first, turned his considerable talent to making fun of the system. Satiric verses of his were passed from mouth to mouth, and soon he was arrested on a drummed up charge and put in jail for more than three years (1961–64). It was in jail – where he was to spend two more long terms, for a total of 27 years – that he found his own distinct voice: a social conscience that embraces humanity tinged with deep love for family and a keen awareness of the passing of time.

Unable to secure pen, ink, and paper to put down his thoughts and poetry, he had to ponder and compose poems in his head. As a consequence he developed a phenomenal memory which to this day allows him to recite by heart some 800 poems that he composed in prison.

In 1979, during a brief respite when the Communist authorities allowed him out of jail for health reasons, Nguyen Chi Thien wrote down some four hundred poems in a manuscript which he managed to hand over to some British diplomats who subsequently smuggled it out of Vietnam. This collection, first published under the title *Echoes from the Abyss* (1980), caused a sensation around the world. When it was learned who the author was, several national P.E.N. Clubs and human rights organizations championed his cause and demanded his release. He was not freed until twelve years later, in 1991. In November 1995 Nguyen Chi Thien was finally allowed out of the country to be resettled in the U.S.

In prison, Nguyen Chi Thien almost singlehandedly revolutionized a moribund tradition of modern Vietnamese poetry which was suffocating under slogans and war-calls demanded by the Communist authorities intent on taking over the southern part of the country. 'Having nothing to lose', as he later confessed, he could confront the regime, the Communist Party, and its leader directly. His poetry shines by its wit, its irreverence, its brilliant conceits – calling the regime 'The Swamps' full of croaking frogs (in the poem of that name), or stating with conviction that 'baby diapers', the metaphor for innocence, would one day be victorious over 'the Red Flag' ('There will Come a Day') – and its tenderness for all victims of man's inhumanity to man.

Nguyen Chi Thien's poetry is contained in two major collections, *Hoa Dia Nguc* (*The Flowers of Hell*, the correct title of *Echoes from the Abyss*) and *Hat Mau Tho* (*Blood Seeds Become Poetry*, 1997). Major selections from the first book, translated into English, have been brought out by Yale University Press (Huynh Sanh Thong, translator, 1984) and VICANA (Nguyen Ngoc Bich, translator, 1995). VICANA has also published a short selection from the second collection. Nguyen Chi Thien's poetry has been translated into several other languages including German, French, Japanese, Chinese, and Czech.

In 2000 Nguyen Chi Thien is on a sabbatical as a writer-in-residence in France and guest of the Parlement des écrivains. He is working on a memoir of his six years as an unwilling guest at the 'Hanoi Hilton'.

[BN]

Niatum, Duane (United States, b. 1938) Born Duane McGinniss in Seattle, Washington, and later changing his name to reflect his ancestry, Niatum is a member of the Klallam tribe of the American Northwest.

After serving in the Navy, Niatum earned his B.A. at the University of Washington and his M.A. at Johns Hopkins University. He also holds a Ph.D. in Northwest Coast Indian Art.

Niatum has published seven books of poetry and edited two works that are considered major anthologies in American Indian studies: *Carriers of the Dream Wheel* (1975) and *Harper's Twentieth Century Native American Poetry* (1988).

Niatum fills his own poetry with a sense of place. The forest of the Northwest figures prominently in his work, as do the names and spiritual roles of animals that inhabit that landscape. Niatum's poetry is one of connectedness and relatedness in all things, be they Native or Euro-American, human or animal. He sometimes employs traditional English forms to lend a musical or chanted quality that evokes his Klallam heritage and simultaneously reveals his sophisticated poetic ability.

Selected works: *After the Death of an Elder Klallam* (1970); *Toas Pueblo* (1973); *Ascending Red Cedar Moon* (1973); *Digging our Roots* (1977); *Pieces* (1981); *Songs for the Harvester of Dreams* (1981); *Stories of the Moons* (1987).

[HEE]

Nichol, bp (Canada, 1944–88) An enormously influential and productive writer during his short life, Nichol was perhaps Canada's most avant-garde and radical literary voice in the twentieth century, experimenting widely with poetic and other forms of writing. Born Barrie Phillip Nichol in Vancouver, it is in Toronto, where he moved in 1963, that he became known for his original and inventive verse.

Nichol's first 'collection', *bp* (1967), was distributed in a box containing a book, a record of sound poetry, a flip book of poems, and an envelope of concrete poems, a form with which he is especially associated. In 1970 he won the Governor General's Award for Poetry for four books that he published that year: *The True Eventual Story of Billy the Kid*, *still water*, *Beach Head*, and *The Cosmic Chef*, an edited anthology of concrete poetry. Nichol's greatest work, *The Martyrology* (1972–88, in 10 volumes; volumes 7–10 appearing posthumously), offers both an intimate biographical portrait of the poet and a postmodern investigation into the dissolution of self and meaning in the modern world.

[IS]

Nichols, Grace (Guyana, b. 1950) Nichols is best-known for *i is a long memorized woman* (1983), her remarkable volume of poetry, which won her the Commonwealth Poetry Prize and spawned award-winning film and radio adaptations. The poems in this collection trace out the experience of a single African woman taken as a slave to the Caribbean. Nichols explores the condition of slavery with an incredible degree of complexity and detail, showing both its multiple horrors and degradations and the seemingly limitless capacity of the human spirit to endure against all odds.

Born in Georgetown, British Guiana (Guyana), Nichols emigrated to England in 1977. Her more recent volumes of poetry, *The Fat Black Woman's Poem* (1984) and *Lazy Thoughts of a Lazy Woman* (1989) are more humorous in tone, and are generally thought to be less successful than her debut. She has also produced numerous volumes of children's stories that draw on non-Western myths and legends for their inspiration.

[IS]

Niedecker, Lorine (United States, 1903–70) Although she was not widely read until after her death, Niedecker's reputation has continued to grow. Born in rural Wisconsin, she spent most of her life on Black Hawk Island there, far from literary circles, working at a variety of often arduous jobs. Through her extensive correspondence with poets like LOUIS ZUKOFSKY and WILLIAM CARLOS WILLIAMS, Niedecker became associated with the Objectivists, among whom her work most resembled GEORGE OPPEN's.

For Niedecker, to write was 'to sit at desk and condense'. Carefully compressed, Niedecker's fragmentary poems often focus with great clarity on the perception of local places and moods. Her finely constructed writing exhibits unusual syntax, sound patterns, and visual arrangements of words.

Selected works: *The Granite Pail: The Selected Poems* (1985); *From This Condensery: The Complete Writings* (1985).

[AE]

Nijhoff, Martinus (The Netherlands, 1894-1953) The son of a religious mother and a father who ran a major (eponymous) publishing house, Nijhoff is generally considered one of the greatest Dutch poets. He studied law in Amsterdam and married the novelist A.H. Nijhoff-Wind in 1916. Although they had a son, their marriage did not last long. In 1952 he married the actress G. Hagedoorn. Afier studying Dutch language and literature in Utrecht later in his life, Nijhoff worked for his father's publishing house for a short time and he was frequently asked to advise the government in linguistic matters.

Nijhoff's poetry and poetics are strongly linked with representatives of international Modernism, such as T.S. ELIOT and PAUL VALÉRY. His work is characterized by a very simple wording of extremely complex themes. He chooses common words and employs almost classic verse forms for his intricate poems. In his best work Nijhoff achieves a degree of inscrutability that, even with repeated readings, yields its meaning only slowly and in small portions. His poetry is 'open' in the best modern tradition, always making it possible to interpret his work in different, but equally valid ways.

Nijhoff's first collection *De Wandelaar* (*The Walker*) was published in 1916 and contains sometimes black-romantic, sometimes melancholic verse. His later work, collected under the seemingly bland, but in fact very telling titles *Vormen* (*Forms*, 1924) and *Nieuwe gedichten* (*New Poems*, 1934), showed his mastery of his craft.

Some of his most famous poems, such as the epic 'Awater' (which has been compared with Eliot's 'The Waste Land') and 'Het Veer' ('The Ferry') deal with Nijhoff's struggle to reconcile himself to the Protestant heritage of his mother. His earlier work deals with the theme of estrangement for the modern individual; later he stresses the value of the down-to-earth view, the tangible. Vague metaphysics are shunned in favor of concrete, modern life. Poems are no longer situated in an imaginary space or in the bucolic countryside, but often are set in the city.

After 1924, Nijhoff's poetry grows more and more anti-idealistic and anti-symbolist. Whereas other poets from his generation, such as A. Roland Holst and H. Marsman, try to surpass modernity's existential doubt and uncertainty through a (religious) philosophy of life, Nijhoff truly tried to be modern, by making doubt an all-important part of his poetics and poetry. The idealist escape from reality practiced by some of his colleagues was, for Nijhoff, not an honest response to that reality.

Nijhoff was also an important translator and his translations of Shakespeare, Eliot, Gide and others, are unanimously praised – the major Dutch prize for translations is named after him. He was also editor of the authoritative literary journal *De gids* (*The Guide*), and a literature reviewer for several newspapers. He was a major figure in Dutch literature and is still considered one of the greatest, whose work is an inspiration for every poet, even among the youngest generations.

[TV]

Nims, John Frederick (United States, b. 1913) Educated at DePaul and Notre Dame universities, Nims earned a Ph.D. in 1945 from the University of Chicago. He taught at various American and European institutions from 1939 through the mid-1980s.

Nims' technically proficient poems risk, but do not always succeed in, marrying colloquial language with elevated themes, often resulting in an uneasy mix of erudition and obtrusive wit.

Nims' most significant influences on American poetry are as Editor of *Poetry* (1978–84) and as a translator. He is author of the praiseworthy textbook, *Western Wind: An Introduction to Poetry* (4th edition, 1999); his translations include *Sappho to Valery: Poems in Translation* (1990), and *The Complete Poems of Michelangelo* (1998).

[HE]

Nishiwaki Junzaburo (Japan, 1894–1982) Nishiwaki was born in Ojiya, Niigata Prefecture. He had a talent for drawing and wanted to be an artist, but his father's death led him to study economics at Keio University. Around the time, he read a great deal, notably the work of EZRA POUND, T.S. ELIOT, and the French Symbolists. When he studied abroad in England in 1922, he encountered Modernism, Surrealism, and Cubism. In 1925 he published *Spectrum*, a collection of poems in English. After returning to Japan he continued to publish poems in Japanese as well as criticism. An anthology, *Fukuikutara Kafu yo!* (*You, Fragrant Fireman!*, 1927), which he compiled with six other poets, was the first book of surreal poetry published in Japan. Besides composing in Japanese, he wrote a considerable amount of poetry in English and French.

[LY]

Nortje, Arthur (South Africa, 1942–70) Nortje was born in Oudtshoorn and educated at the University College of the Western Cape. After studying at Jesus College, Oxford, he taught in Hope, British Columbia and in Toronto. He returned to Oxford to work on a doctorate and died in 1970 of an overdose of barbiturates. His work reflects the personal erosion of self-identity, confidence, and the alienation of the exile. His early poems critique the social and political structure of apartheid on an intensely personal level while the later poems, written primarily in England, explore the themes of loneliness, solitude, and isolation. Two collections of his verse have been published posthumously: *Lonely against the Light* and *Dead Roots* (both 1973).

[KS]

Nu'aima, Mikha'il (also known as Na'imah, Nouayme, Naimy; Lebanon, 1889–1988) Nu'aima studied at a Russian school in Nazareth, Palestine, before going on a scholarship to the University of Poltava in Russia. In 1911 he emigrated to Washington, where he studied law. In 1920 he went to New York and became the critical voice of Al-Rabita al-Qalamiyya, the society of immigrant poets who launched the Romantic movement in Arabic poetry. He returned to settle in Lebanon in 1932.

Nu'aima's education gave him scant knowledge of classical Arabic literature, despite his wide reading in European, particularly Russian, literatures. More influential as a critic than as a poet (he also wrote plays and short stories), Nu'aima began to contribute articles to the North American Arab magazine *Al-Funun* (*The Arts*) in 1913. He rejected classical poetry wholesale in favor of Romanticism and attacked neoclassical poetry as 'mummified literature'. Those articles, later collected in *The Sieve* and published in Cairo, played an important role in changing many attitudes toward language, technique, and form in Arabic poetry. Nu'aima's own poetry, written mainly between 1917 and 1926, was innovative in theme and technique, and mystical and meditative in tone.

Selected works (in Arabic): Critical essays: *The Sieve* (1923); *The Idols* (1958); *Roads* (1963). Poetry: *Whispers of Eyelids* (1943). Biography: *Gibran Khalil Gibran* (1934).

[WH]

O

O'Brien, Sean (England, b. 1952) O'Brien was born in London and attended Selwyn College, Cambridge, Birmingham University, Hull University, and Leeds University. He won the Eric Gregory Award in 1979, the Somerset Maugham Award in 1984, the Cholmondeley Award in 1988; he co-founded *The Printer's Devil* literary magazine in 1990.

O'Brien's poetry is urban, with emphasis often on social and political subjects. *The Frighteners*, for instance, speaks about dire economic circumstances in England. O'Brien's work is often satirical, with wry twists, and full of comment and *bon mots* alike.

Selected works: *The Indoor Park* (1983); *Boundary Beach* (1989); *HMD Glasshouse* (1991); *A Rarity* (1993); *Ghost Train* (1995).

[JS]

O'Hara, Frank (United States, 1926–66) O'Hara was born in Baltimore, Maryland, and raised in Grafton, Massachusetts. After serving in the Navy during World War II, he received his B.A. from Harvard, and his M.A. from the University of Michigan. Once settled in New York, starting at the Museum of Modern Art's front desk, O'Hara quickly rose to be an influential Assistant Curator at the museum, a keen art critic and close friend to many famous painters. O'Hara also found himself at the center of a dynamic world of painters, dancers, composers, and writers – and along with JOHN ASHBERY and KENNETH KOCH formed the nucleus of the 'New York School' of poets. He was killed at age forty in a strange accident when struck by a beach taxi on Fire Island, New York State. Always somewhat unconcerned with publishing his work, it was not until the posthumous *Collected Poems* was published that the extent of his ambitious and influential oeuvre became clear.

O'Hara's poetry typically fuses surrealistic, rapidly shifting imagery with an informal, conversational voice. In both kaleidoscopic long poems and briefer renderings of quotidian action and emotion, O'Hara chronicles with breathtaking immediacy the dizzying experience of daily life, often conveying the swirl of his beloved Manhattan. Beneath the deceptively charming, bright surfaces of his work, however, run strong undercurrents of irony, sadness, anxiety, and awareness of time's passing; this recognition of transience lends O'Hara's poems a gravity and density that is even more effective because of their apparent spontaneity, exuberance and humor.

Selected works: *Meditations in an Emergency* (1957); *Lunch Poems* (1964); *Collected Poems* (1972).

[AE]

O'Sullivan, Vincent (New Zealand, b. 1937) Born in Auckland, O'Sullivan was educated at Oxford and the University of

Auckland. He traveled widely, living in Greece and Central America. He has taught at the University of Waikato and the University of Wellington.

O'Sullivan's early poetry reworks classical and mythical subjects. In his later poetry, his taste for the dramatic and the satiric and his ear for the New Zealand vernacular find expression. 'Butcher', O'Sullivan's best-known character, who incorporates insensitivity and a preoccupation with material possessions, portrays a somewhat cynical yet complex vision of twentieth-century man.

Selected works: *Our Burning Time* (1965); *Revenants* (1969); *From the Indian Funeral* (1976); *Butcher and Co* (1977); *Brother Jonathan, Brother Kafka* (1980); *The Butcher Papers* (1982); *The Pilate Tapes* (1986).

[SH]

Okara, Gabriel (Nigeria, b. 1921) The poetry of Okara incorporates imagery from both Western and African sources, as well as from Moslem, Christian, and indigenous African religious traditions. His poem 'The Mystic Drum' connects the speaker with natural and supernatural forces. 'The Snowflakes Sail Gently Down' links snowfall and wind-like/white-robed Moslems salaaming at evening prayer with a dream of black birds nesting on oil palms with suns for fruit.

Okara worked as a printer and bookbinder in Nigeria, and also studied journalism at Northwestern University in the United States. He was first published in the initial issue of *Black Orpheus*, a Nigerian literary magazine begun in 1957. His first collection of poetry, *The Fisherman's Invocation* (1978), won the Commonwealth Poetry Prize. He has also written a novel entitled *The Voice* (1964).

[KAC]

Okigbo, Christopher (Nigeria, 1932–67) Okigbo is perhaps the most written-about and yet most enigmatic figure in modern African poetry.

Born in the town of Ojoto in eastern Nigeria, Okigbo was a member of the Igbo ethnic group. Raised as a Roman Catholic, but also being told that he was the reincarnation of his grandfather, a priest of the river goddess Idoto, Okigbo wrote poetry which draws heavily from both traditions.

Okigbo was educated at some of the best schools in colonial Nigeria, and at University College, Ibadan, where he graduated with a degree in Classics in 1956. Although his academic career was not exceptional, he was recognized by students and teachers alike as a bright, engaging young man, showing much promise if somewhat bohemian in his tastes. His time at Ibadan overlapped with that of many future literary luminaries, including renowned novelist Chinua Achebe, JOHN PEPPER CLARK, and WOLE SOYINKA.

Following graduation he worked as a civil servant, secondary school teacher, librarian, and publisher's agent. He also served as West Africa Editor of the literary journal *Transition*. Active in various student groups and publications at Ibadan, only after he left University College did he begin to give serious attention to his poetry. In interviews he cites 1957 as the year he received the literary equivalent of the call to the priesthood: from then on he thought of himself as a poet and worked accordingly.

He was, however, a sporadic poet, working on impulse and inspiration rather than by any set schedule. He could go months without writing and, though he took the art quite seriously, felt no remorse at such long, fallow intervals: 'Poetry is not an alternative to living; it is only one way of supplementing life', he told one interviewer. He was, however, an almost compulsive editor of his own work, constantly revising previously written, and sometimes already published, poems. Prior to his death he had planned to pull together four of his already published poetic cycles: *Heavensgate* (1962), *Limits* (1964), 'Silences' and 'Distances' – the latter two having appeared in *Transition* in 1962 and 1964 respectively. He substantially reworked each and prepared an introduction which provides a basic framework for understanding these dense, allusive, and many-layered poems.

Okigbo draws on numerous traditions for both imagery and poetic structure, citing as influences his own Igbo heritage, French Symbolist poetry, French Impressionist composers, Near Eastern history and mythology, and English and American poets such as T.S. ELIOT, EZRA POUND, and Gerard Manley Hopkins. Okigbo, Soyinka, and others have been accused of suffering from 'the Hopkins disease', characteristic of those who are perceived to write poetry that is willfully obscure and rooted in a personal ethos closed to the average reader. But Okigbo was unapologetic, famously retorting that he wrote for other poets, not the average man in the street who had no interest in poetry.

Okigbo returned to eastern Nigeria from Lagos in 1966 after a series of coups and massacres and volunteered for the rebel army soon after civil war broke out in July 1967. He was killed in battle a month later. The planned collection of his poetry, *Labyrinths*, was published posthumously in 1971 and was made up of his introduction, four poetic cycles, and his final set of poems titled 'Path of Thunder', subtitled 'Poems Prophesying War' and completed in 1966. This slender, 72-page collection continues to exercise considerable influence over poets and critics alike and stands as a monument to a poetic talent cut short.

[MLL]

Olds, Sharon (United States, b. 1942) Olds was born in San Francisco, graduated from Stanford University, and earned a Ph.D. at Columbia University. The author of seven books of poetry and the recipient of numerous awards, she teaches at New York University.

Olds' gripping, confessional poems gaze unflinchingly at the private horrors and pleasures of family life and sexuality. With visceral, explicit language and a flair for metaphor, she writes about bodily experience, sexual abuse, dysfunctional family relationships, oppressive political situations, and the redemptive power of love. Olds' controversial work has been praised for its narrative force and wrenching candor.

Selected works: *The Gold Cell* (1987); *The Dead and the Living* (1984); *The Father* (1992).

[AE]

Olson, Charles (United States, 1910–70) After receiving his B.A. and M.A. from Wesleyan University, Olson was among the first three candidates in Harvard's then new doctoral American Studies program, an interest that can be seen in much of his later work. He also uncovered many previously unknown books of Melville's own library, leading eventually to Olson's influential if not unconventional critical study of *Moby Dick*, entitled *Call Me Ishmael* (1947).

As a leading member of the 'Black Mountain Poets', a group whose name derived from their association with the Black Mountain College located near Asheville, North Carolina, Olson advocated a shift in poetry away from formalism and the then prevalent New Criticism. In his 1950 essay 'Projective Verse', Olson proclaimed that a poem's line lengths should correspond to a poet's breath, that 'FORM IS NEVER MORE THAN AN EXTENSION OF CONTENT', and 'ONE PERCEPTION MUST IMMEDIATELY AND DIRECTLY LEAD TO A FURTHER PERCEPTION'.

His lasting achievement, the epic *The Maximus Poems* (1983), uses Gloucester, Massachusetts, as a model of the ideal 'polis', what Olson calls 'a form of mind' which rejects the sweeping trends of commercialism and industrialism he believed were undermining the small town's self-sufficiency and individual character. Despite the Black Mountain Poets' anti-academic approach to poetics, *Maximus*, with its mixture of history, mythology, and spirituality, is the result of a lifetime of reading and study, informed by Olson's scholarly training.

Selected works: *Collected Poems* (1987); *Collected Prose* (1997).

[JM]

Ondaatje, Michael (Canada, b. 1943) Born in Colombo, Ceylon (now Sri Lanka), Ondaatje emigrated to Canada in 1962. At Bishop's University, where he began his B.A., Ondaatje started to write poetry under the guidance of poet D.G. Jones, a former Governor General's award winner. Ondaatje's first collection, *Dainty Monsters* (1967), consists of short poems that show both modernist and lyrical influences. *The Man with Seven Toes* (1969) and *The Collected Works of Billy the Kid: Left Handed Poems* (1970), are long prose poems that mark the beginning of Ondaatje's interest in finding hidden histories, or in inventing and creating histories in the midst of 'official' stories about the past. The latter book won a Governor General's Award for Poetry (1970); Ondaatje won a second Governor General's award for *There's a Trick With a Knife I'm Learning to Do* (1979).

Internationally, Ondaatje is best known as the writer of a number of critically acclaimed novels, beginning with *Coming Through Slaughter* (1976), the magical-realist story of Buddy Bolden, a forgotten New Orleans jazz figure. His novel, *The English Patient* (1992), won both the Governor General's Award for Fiction (1992) and the Booker Prize in that same year, and was made into an Academy Award-winning film. Ondaatje's novels may be seen as extensions of his prose poems; they are lyrical, poetic, and continue his interest in the reinvention and rediscovery of lost or forgotten histories. Ondaatje is one of Canada's most celebrated contemporary writers. The next step in his much-acclaimed career is eagerly awaited.

Selected works: *Running in the Family* (1982); *Secular Love* (1984).

[IS]

Oodgeroo of The Noonuccal Tribe (Kath Walker; Australia, 1920–93) Oodgeroo of the Noonuccal Tribe spent her childhood on Stradbroke Island, off the coast of Queensland, and has little formal education. Born Kath Walker, she later changed her name in order to disregard the remnants of a European colonial past.

Oodgeroo's work is overtly political (with poems such as 'Assimilation – No!' and 'Integration – Yes!') and deals almost exclusively with the plight of Aboriginal peoples. Her first book of poems, *We Are Going* (1964), was the first to be published by an Aboriginal poet, and her work has consistently brought (inter)national attention to Aboriginal oppression and human rights.

Selected works: *The Dawn is at Hand* (1966); *My People: Oodgeroo* (1970); *Father Sky and Mother Earth* (1981); *Stradbroke Dreamtime* (1993).

[SG]

Ooka Makoto (Japan, b. 1931) Ooka was born in Shizuoka Prefecture. His father, Ooka Hiroshi, was an educator and a noted *tanka* poet. Ooka Makoto graduated from Tokyo University with a major in Japanese literature and had an interest in the work of PAUL ELUARD and Surrealism. With TANIKAWA SHUNTARO, he was an early member of the *Kai* (Oar) group; he was also one of the first poets to practice Surrealism in Japan. His first book of criticism, *Essay on Modern Poetry*, appeared in 1955, and his first book of poems, *Memory and Presence*, in 1956.

Ooka is one of the most important and prolific contemporary poets with fifteen volumes of his *Complete Works* currently in print, including plays, movie scripts, poetry, and criticism. Ooka has recently led a revival of traditional Japanese *renga* and *renku* linked verse.

[LY]

Oppen, George (United States, 1908–84) Associated with the Objectivist poets (WILLIAM CARLOS WILLIAMS, LOUIS ZUKOFSKY, LORINE NIEDECKER), Oppen had quite an unusual career. Profoundly troubled by the poverty caused by the Depression, he ceased writing after publishing his first book, and joined the Communist Party. Under pressure during the McCarthy era, Oppen moved to Mexico, where he remained for almost a decade. After twenty-five years of silence, Oppen resumed writing in the early 1960s, and began creating his most important, powerful work.

Seriousness, honesty, and the struggle for clarity are the hallmarks of Oppen's spare, terse poems. His work often confronts moral issues: war, the nuclear threat, the possibility of community, the relations of art and politics, and the attempt to locate meaning in our words and lives.

Selected works: *Discrete Series* (1934); *The Materials* (1962); *Of Being Numerous* (1968, Pulitzer Prize).

[AE]

Ormond, John (Wales, 1923–90) Born at Dunvent, and educated at Swansea University, Ormond began to publish poetry in his late teens. Harshly critical of his own work, he subsequently gave up literature for an extended period, instead pursuing a journalistic career. In 1957 Ormond joined BBC Wales, where he produced several distinguished television documentaries about Welsh artists and writers. He returned to poetry in the 1960s; *Requiem and Celebration* (1969) was well received, and with its sequel, *Definition of a Waterfall* (1973), he was heralded as a major force in Anglo-Welsh verse. Ormond's style and themes are eclectic; however, he often focuses upon material forms (man-made and natural) as an inspiration for profound meditative speculation. A *Selected Poems*, containing earlier and previously unpublished later works appeared in 1987.

[BS]

Ormsby, Frank (Ireland, b. 1947) Born in Enniskillen, County Fermanagh, Northern Ireland, Ormsby received his B.A. (1970) and M.A. (1971) from Queen's University, Belfast. He was editor of *The Honest Ulsterman* in 1969–89, and since 1971 has taught at the English Royal Belfast Academical Institution. Ormsby's poetry often reflects and revels in the ordinary – highlighting and reporting tenderly on everyday relationships, details, and events with a skilled, exacting eye and ear. Often his poems reveal how larger political events influence personal lives in minute but significant ways. His *A Store for Candles* (1977) was a Poetry Book Society Choice. Ormsby won the Eric Gregory Award in 1974 and the Cultural Traditions Award in 1992. As well as publishing several volumes of poems, including *Ripe for Company* (1971), *Being Walked by a Bog* (1978), and *A Northern Spring* (1986), Ormsby has edited many anthologies of Northern Irish poetry, including *A Rage for Order: Poetry of the Northern Irish Troubles* (1992).

[CT]

Orozco, Olga (Argentina, b. 1920) One of the most important poets of the 'Generación del '40', together with Enrique Molina, Alberto Girri and others, Orozco has published continuously since the appearance of her first book *Desde lejos* (*From afar*) in 1946. Her most important collections of poems are *Las muertes* (*Deaths*, 1952), *Los juegos peligrosos* (*Dangerous Games*, 1962), *Museo salvaje* (*Wild Museum*, 1974), *Cantos a Berenice* (*Songs for Berenice*, 1977), *Mutaciones de la realidad* (*Mutations of Reality*, 1979) and *En el reves del cielo* (*On the Back of Heaven*, 1987). Her poetry is characterized by its elegiac tone, and prevalent recurrent themes: death, childhood, a sense of loss, love, and a certain yearning for the absolute. In 1961 she received a fellowship from the Fundación Nacional de las Artes to travel to Europe where she wrote an essay on the occult and the sacred in modern poetry. She currently lives in Buenos Aires.

[MN]

Ortiz, Simon J. (United States, b. 1941) Born in Albuquerque, New Mexico, Ortiz was raised in an Acoma (Pueblo) village. He attended Fort Lewis College, the University of New Mexico, and the University of Iowa. He has taught at San Diego State, Navajo Community College, and the University of New Mexico. A poet and editor who greatly influenced emerging Native American writers in the 1980s, Ortiz has turned increasingly to writing prose in the past decade.

A storyteller and poet of the oral tradition, Ortiz was raised speaking his Native language and hearing the Acoma storytelling tradition. Formally, songs, chants, and ceremonial stories are reflected in Ortiz's published poems. Thematically, his work is also overtly political in that it defies historically accepted versions of events and calls for unity between peoples of color.

Selected works: *Going for Rain* (1976); *A Good Journey* (1977); *A Poem is a Journey* (1981); *From Sand Creek* (1981).

[HEE]

Osherow, Jacqueline (United States, b. 1956) Born in Philadelphia and educated at Harvard, Oxford and Princeton universities, Osherow writes from and of her urban, Jewish background. Often grouped with the New Formalists – although her use of rhyme and meter stems from personal, rather than ideological reasons – Osherow infuses her discussions of movies, Italian art, and domestic life with her exploration of Jewish identity. Her poems are often quite long by contemporary standards (up to twenty pages) as she navigates terza rima with a chatty aplomb, an ease similar to that of EDWARD HIRSCH or AMY CLAMPITT. Osherow has received a Guggenheim Fellowship, the Witter-Bynner Award, and a National Endowment for the Arts Fellowship. She directs the creative writing program at the University of Utah.

[CV]

Ostriker, Alicia (United States, b. 1937) Ostriker is an important feminist literary critic as well as a poet, who integrates her politics into her poetry and scholarly prose. Born in New York, Ostriker attended Brandeis University (B.A., 1959) and the University of Wisconsin (Ph.D., 1964.) She became a professor of English in 1965 at Rutgers University, where she continues to teach.

Deeply influenced by ALLEN GINSBERG'S blending of the personal, spiritual, and political, Ostriker has published six books of literary criticism, which include the highly influential *Stealing the Language* (1986) as well as much-acclaimed recent work on feminism and the Bible, and eight books of poetry, most of which address broad-based political themes as well as her experiences as a woman and mother. Among Ostriker's poetry awards are the William Carlos Williams Prize for *The Imaginary Lover* (1986), and the Anna David Rosenberg Poetry Award (1994).

[DC]

Osundare, Niyi (Nigeria, b. 1947) Osundare took a degree in English from the University of Ibadan in 1972, and eventually earned a Ph.D. from the University of Toronto in 1979. In 1986, he started writing two poems weekly for the *Nigerian Tribune* – 'verse journalism', according to the poet. His work has a consistently strong political urgency, distancing his approach from the more obscure stylings of WOLE SOYINKA or CHRISTOPHER OKIGBO.

Osundare has won many literary awards, and has the distinction of being the first Anglophone poet to win Africa's most prestigious book award, the Noma Prize (in 1991). A very prolific writer, Osundare's nine collections are: *Songs of the Marketplace* (1983), *Village Voices* (1984), *A Nib in the Pond* (1986),*The Eye of the Earth* (1986), *Moonsongs* (1988), *Songs of the Season* (1990), *Waiting Laughters* (1990), *Selected Poems* (1992), and *Midlife* (1993).

[KAC]

Otero, Blas de (Spain, 1916–79) De Otero, born in Bilbao in the Basque region, belongs to the Generation of 1936 which returned poetry to its social and historical roots. Turning away from the avant-garde, depersonalized aesthetic of the Generation of 1927 (see HERNÁNDEZ, JIMENEZ and LORCA), these new poets wrote in colloquial, realistic language about social and historical conditions, and denounced the status quo. Otero, a Marxist, openly opposed the right-wing government; from 1958 to 1970 his works were not published in Spain. Otero first wrote about the reality of postwar Spain in *Spiritual Song* (1942). His anguished view eventually led him to religious disillusionment. *Fiercely Human Angel* (1950) reinterprets the fall of humankind in a positive light, as the result of questioning society's limits. Otero remained unrepentant for his political and religious views in *I Ask for Peace and the Right to Speak* (1955). Otero, like GLORIA FUERTES, saw the poet as an agent in the service of humanity.

[AB]

Øverland, Arnulf (Norway, 1889–1968) Together with Sigurd Hoel, Helge Krog and others, poet, essayist, and playwright Øverland marked the awakening of a socially committed literature in Norway between the two world wars. Although he started by studying philology, Øverland soon took to writing poetry. His first collection, *Den ensomme fest* (*The Lonely Feast*, 1911) won immediate success for its clear, terse style. Already his early poems sided with the oppressed, but it was only after World War I, in his *Brød og vin* (*Bread and Wine*, 1919), that his socialist message came to maturity, confronting bourgeois values and criticizing the Christian establishment. In the 1930s Øverland turned his pen against Fascism, and during World War II he became a major inspiration for the Norwegian resistance. For this reason he was imprisoned in a Nazi concentration camp for four years, returning at the end of the war to publish collections titled, significantly, *Vi overlever alt!* (*We Survive Everything!*, 1945) and *Tilbake til livet* (*Back to Life*, 1946).

[YB]

Owen, Wilfred (England, 1893–1918) Owen was born in Oswestry, England. His father, a railway worker, claimed to have Welsh roots leading back to the time of Henry VIII. His mother, a devout Christian who was devoted to her son, encouraged his literary ambitions from an early age. Owen entered university, but lack of funds forced him to withdraw before he could complete his degree. He considered the priesthood for a time, but decided he did not share his mother's faith, and in 1913 he took up a position at the Berlitz School, Bordeaux. At the outbreak of World War I he returned to England, and in 1915 he enlisted in the Manchester Regiment. After being exposed to extreme weather conditions on the Western Front, Owen met SIEGFRIED SASSOON in military hospital. Sassoon recognized Owen's talent, and urged him to write more. Owen eventually returned to the Front, and was awarded the Military Cross for bravery in October 1918. A month later – just one week before the Armistice was declared – he was killed.

In his earlier poems Owen had affected Keatsian mannerisms. However, the experiences of the Front transformed his idiom. Although he retained an interest in traditional forms, his diction became less self-consciously poetic; in particular, he began to favor the device of half-rhyme (snow/renew, toil/all, war/year, etc.). Half-rhymes dominate 'Strange Meeting', his most famous poem, and perhaps the greatest single English lyric of the war. The standard modern edition of his work is JON STALLWORTHY'S *The Poems of Wilfred Owen* (1986).

[BS]

P

Page, P.K. (Canada, b. 1916) Patricia Kathleen Page was born in Swanage, Dorset, England, and moved to Calgary, Alberta, at the age of three. Born into a military family, Page lived in numerous places in Canada while still a child, and spent time as well in England, where her first poem appeared in print in *The Observer* (London) in 1934. Back in Canada, her poems began to appear in a number of journals and magazines in the late 1930s and early 1940s. In 1941, Page moved to Montreal where she met the poets A.M. Klein, F.R. SCOTT, and A.J.M. SMITH, and helped to edit the influential journal *Preview*. In contrast to the modernism of the Montreal Group, Page's early work consisted primarily of poems of social protest which expressed sympathy for the disadvantaged and disenfranchised.

Under the pseudonym Judith Cape, Page published the novel *The Sun and the Moon* (1944), later reissued as *The Sun and the Moon and Other Fictions*, a collection edited by MARGARET ATWOOD. *The Metal and the Flower* (1954), Page's first individual book of poetry, won a Governor General's award. While living in Brazil, Mexico, and Guatemala from 1956 to 1964 as the wife of Canadian ambassador William Arthur Irwin, Page did not publish or even write much poetry, but turned her creative energies exclusively to drawing and painting. A journal that she kept during this period was published in 1987 as *Brazilian Journal*. Since 1967, with the publication of *Cry Ararat*, Page has pursued her work as both a poet and painter. Under the name of P.K. Irwin, her paintings have been collected by a number of major Canadian museums and galleries, while her achievements as a poet have earned her admission to the Order of Canada (1977) and widespread acclaim as one of Canada's major poets.

[IS]

Pagis, Dan (Israel, 1930–86) Born in Bukovina, Romania, young Pagis lived through the horrors of World War II in Europe. He was interned in a Ukrainian concentration camp and, after escaping and wandering, came to Israel in 1946. He received a doctoral degree from the Hebrew University in Jerusalem, where he taught medieval Hebrew literature. His scholarly publications on medieval secular poetry have gained him international recognition. So has his poetry, which deals with the dreadful realities of war and genocide as well as the endless, persevering struggle of the human spirit for freedom, forgiveness, acceptance of fate, and submission to the inevitable chagrin of human experience. Pagis' words are ironic, strong, controlled and concise, often dwelling on a small number of images which interact with intensity in his poems. His verse makes frequent allusions to Biblical, rabbinical, and medieval elements of Hebrew literature, thus pointing to the richness of his inner world and the tight interplay between his academic, spiritual, and poetic assets. Pagis' first collection, *The Shadow Dial*, was published in 1959. Collections of his poems were published posthumously in 1987 and 1991. His poetry was translated into English (*Selected Poems*, 1976; *Points of Departure*, 1981; *Variable Directions*, 1989; *Poems*, 1996) and German.

[ER]

Palamas, Kostis (Greece, 1859–1943) A prolific and erudite writer, Palamas had a profound effect on the Greek literature of his time. Though a contemporary of CONSTANTINE P. CAVAFY, he was considered the most important figure of his generation and the founder of the New Athenian School of literature. His impact on Greek cultural life was felt for decades. He wrote a total of eighteen volumes of poetry, fiction, drama, translation, criticism, and articles.

Heavily influenced by Dionysios Solomos (1798–1857), he defended the literary use of vernacular Greek which he elaborated upon and embellished. Palamas' style was eloquent, grandiose, and highly rhetorical, writing in most verse forms and on themes from the ancient, Byzantine, and modern era, especially of the 1821 Greek revolution. His influences were many and varied, ancient and contemporary, including Nietzsche, the French Parnassians, and Symbolists. His collections *The Songs of My Country* (1886) and the lyrical lament for his dead son, *The Grave* (1898), bear the marks of the folkloric and romantic tradition. In *Life Immovable* (1904) and *The Ascrean* (1904) he turned toward mysticism and this move culminated in his great visionary epics, *The Twelve Words of the Gypsy* (1907) and *The King's Flute* (1910). During his lifetime he was honored as Greece's national poet and often nominated for a Nobel Prize though he gained the international recognition he deserved only posthumously. His funeral in Nazi-occupied Athens was an event of national significance and turned into a defiant and spirited demonstration against oppression and tyranny.

[GSY]

Palmer, Michael (United States, b. 1943) Palmer is the author of numerous collections of poetry, essays on poetry, poetics, and the visual arts, as well as translations of South American and French writers. Born in New York in 1943, Palmer received his B.A. and M.A. in Comparative Literature from Harvard University. After traveling in Europe for a year after graduation, Palmer moved to San Francisco in 1969, and has lived there since.

Palmer, a self-acknowledged Modernist whose work has also been associated with the Language poets, published his first book, *Plan of the City O*, in 1971, and continued to write poetry steadily throughout the 1970s and 1980s – including *Notes for Echo Lake* (1981), *First Figure* (1984), and his pivotal *Sun* (1988) – and then nothing more until *At Passages* (1995). His poems are fragmented, lyrical and meditative; they contain more accessible semantic units than the work of other Language poets, perhaps because of Palmer's affection for the work of Charles Baudelaire.

[DC]

Parra, Nicanor (Chile, b. 1914) The son of a schoolteacher – and one himself for a number of years – Parra received graduate degrees in mathematics and physics from Brown University (1945), and Oxford (1951), eventually taking a position as a Professor of Theoretical Physics at the University of Chile in Santiago. His first book of poetry, *Cancionero sin nombre* (*Songbook without a Name*, 1937), received praise, but Parra did not publish any more poetry until *Poesías y antipoesías* (*Poems and Antipoems*, 1954) appeared seventeen years later. With its concept of 'antipoetry', this work revolutionized Latin America's avant-garde. Antipoetry rejected an elite, metaphysical poetics, and used colloquial speech, elements of popular Chilean folklore, and almost no metaphor. It was also an attempt to revitalize language. Parra's antipoetry is characterized by parodic intertextuality, irony, and humor which lends itself to social commentary and criticism. Many works combine visual elements with words, such as his book *Artefactos* (*Artifacts*, 1972), which is a published collection of 242 postcards. His exhibited 'public works' or 'object poems' of the 1990s combine three-dimensional figures taken from everyday life with sayings or titles. *Obra gruesa* (*The Thick Book*, 1969) collects work to 1969 and *Hojas de Parra* (*Leaves of Parra*, 1985) that of 1969–85. In 1969, Parra received the Chilean National Poetry Prize.

Selected works: *Emergency Poems* (1972); *Sermons and Homilies of the Christ of Elqui* (1984); *Antipoems: New and Selected* (1985).

[LKA]

Parry, Robert Williams (Wales, 1884–1956) Parry was born at Tal-y-sarn, Caernarvonshire, and spent most of his professional life as a teacher and lecturer. In 1910, his poem 'Yr Haf' ('The Summer') won the Chair at the National Eisteddfod, and Parry was regarded as a central figure of the Welsh poetic revival, alongside T. Gwynn Jones and W. J. Gruffydd. 'Yr Haf' self-consciously echoed the fourteenth-century love poet, Dafydd ap Gwilym; however, even before the publication of *Yr Haf a Cherddi Eraill* (*The Summer and Other Poems*, 1924), Parry had developed a more bleakly elegiac rhetoric, in response to the losses of World War I, losses he had witnessed firsthand during his military service in 1916–18. He would continue to develop away from his early optimism, repudiating mankind altogether in his last volume, *Cerddi'r Gaeaf* (*Winter Poems*, 1952).

[BS]

Parun, Vesna (Yugoslavia, b. 1922) Parun, a prominent Croatian poet, spent her childhood and adolescence in the Dalmatian towns of Zlarin and Split. She studied philosophy and Romance languages and literature in Zagreb, where she lives now as a freelance writer. A prolific poet, she also writes children's verse, plays, screenplays, and essays.

Her early poems are interesting social and patriotic comments, engaged with the present and full of belief in the future. Later, she focused on the personal, and her poetry became more intimate. Themes addressed in her later poetry have included love, intimate and sensual emotions, woman's erotic desires and longing. Parun's poetry, often confessional, also displays her Mediterranean origin, an intense sense of nature and its beauty, and distinct ties with her country and its people.

Parun's style marked a departure in Croatian poetry from a traditional poetic form. Her poems are striking for their formal perfection, immediacy, and unorthodox linguistic expression. While Parun's early poetry is written in free verse, her later work is an attempt (often very successful according to numerous critics) to combine the immediacy of free verse with the more formal demands of traditional forms, especially the sonnet.

Selected works: *Zora i vihori* (*A Dawn and Storms*, 1947); *Crna maslina* (*A Black Olive Tree*, 1955); *Vjetar Trakije* (*A Thracian Wind*, 1964); *Sto soneta* (*A Hundred Sonnets*, 1972); *Salto mortale* (1981); *Kasfalpirova zemlja* (*The Land of Kasfalpir*, 1989).

[DJ]

Pascoli, Giovanni (Italy, 1855–1912) Born and raised in poverty, especially after the mysterious murder of his father in 1867, Pascoli struggled to complete his studies, though he eventually became a Professor of Italian Literature in Messina and later in Bologna. In his first collection, *Myricae* (1891), his use of onomatopoeia, synesthesia, dialectics, linguistic 'pastiche', and his intuitive discovery of the role played by the subconscious in the creative process, made him one of the most original voices of his time. His essay 'Il Fanciullino' ('The Young Boy', 1897), in which Pascoli describes the poet as an astonished child in front of an inexplicable universe, still represents the best exposition of his poetics.

Selected works: *Canti di Castelvecchio* (*Castelvecchio Songs*, 1903); *Primi Poemetti* (*First Poems*, 1904); *Nuovi Poemetti* (*New Poems*, 1909).

[GS]

Pasolini, Pier Paolo (Italy, 1922–76) Poetry represents merely a stage of Pasolini's intense and eclectic exploration of reality. While formally in debt to earlier authors such as PASCOLI or D'ANNUNZIO, Pasolini's poetry soon focused on the broader subject of the evolution (or rather involution) of Italian civilization in the tormented post-war era. To that end, Pasolini used poetry either as a powerful research tool on language (as in his poems in Friuli dialect) or as a painful investigation of the fate of Italian culture, to him doomed by the conformist attitude of the growing Italian petit bourgeoisie.

Selected works: *La meglio Gioventù* (*The Best Youth*, 1954); *Le ceneri di Gramsci* (*Gramsci's Ashes*, 1957); *L'usignolo della Chiesa Cattolica* (*The Catholic Church Nightingale*, 1958); *La religione del mio tempo* (*The Religion of My Age*, 1961); *Poesia in forma di rosa* (*Poetry in the Shape of a Rose*, 1964); *La nuova Gioventù* (*The New Youth*, 1975).

[GS]

Pasos, Joaquin (Nicaragua, 1914–47) One of the most important poets of the Nicaraguan avant-garde, Pasos started to write at an early age. He was the youngest founding member, at age sixteen, of the literary magazine *Vanguardia* (*Vanguard*) which published notable poets such as Pablo Antonio Cuadro and JOSÉ CORONEL URTECHO. Known for his sense of humor and rebellious nature, he was instrumental in the founding of the Nicaraguan Anti-Academy, an entity that served to criticize the Modernist and foreign influences in Nicaraguan poetry. His literary page entitled 'Mondays' was a place from which the opposition mocked the Somoza dictatorship. His poetry was collected and published posthumously for the first time fifteen years after his premature death due to illness.

Selected works: *Poemas de un joven* (*Poems of a Young Man*, 1962).

[SL]

Pasternak, Boris (Russia, 1890–1960) Though best-known for his prose – *Doctor Zhivago* (1957) brought him the Nobel Prize for Literature in 1958 – Boris Leonidovich Pasternak is more impressive as a poet. He began his writing career as a poet and continued to publish stylistically diverse poetry throughout his life.

The son of a painter and a concert pianist, Pasternak studied both music and philosophy, but eventually turned to poetry, publishing *Bliznets v tuchakh (Twin in the Storm-clouds)* in 1914. That same year, Pasternak met MAYAKOVSKY, whose Futurism influenced the young writer's style for a time. The critically well-received *Sestra moia zhizn' (My Sister Life*, 1922) drew on both public politics and the private turmoil of love. After exhausting the lyricism of these early volumes, Pasternak changed his poetic style to longer narrative verse, eventually publishing a novel in verse, *Spectorsky*(1931).

Pasternak had married Eugenia Lourie in 1922; by the time *Spectorsky* was published he had divorced her and married Zinaida Neuhaus, publishing *Vtoroe Rozhdenie* (*Second Birth*, 1932). Yet the imposition of social realism cut short this 'birth'; Pasternak moved to translation, particularly the work of (Stalin-pleasing) Georgian writers. He also published the meditative and somewhat patriotic volumes *Na rannikh poezdakh* (*On Early*

Trains, 1943) and *Zemnoi prostor* (*Breadth of Earth*, 1945), which primarily describe the daily life of the Soviet people.

However, political disfavor followed *Doctor Zhivago*: Pasternak was forced to decline the Nobel Prize and was expelled from the Union of Soviet Writers. It was only after *glasnost* that Pasternak was officially recognized and *Doctor Zhivago* published in Russia. With this official recognition has come a reconsideration of his poetry and acknowledgment that it stands as some of the most significant of this century.

[RN]

Patchen, Kenneth (United States, 1911–72) Patchen was born in Niles, Ohio, into a steelworker's family. Attending the University of Wisconsin briefly, Patchen's experience covers the map: his occupations range from steelworker to writer for the *New Republic*; his creative output ranges from drama to graphic art; he himself ranged from Boston to San Francisco.

His work, originally published in fine volumes such as *The Journal of Albion Moonlight* (1941) and now collected in *Awash with Roses: The Collected Love Poems* (1991) and *The Memoirs of a Shy Pornographer* (1999), is seldom anthologized. However, it won several awards during Patchen's lifetime, including the Shelley Memorial Award (1954) and a lifetime contribution award from the National Foundation on the Arts and Humanities (1967). In the 1950s Patchen was one of the first to set his poetry to jazz, touring the country and making recordings for Cadence and Folkways. Patchen's poetic ranges from the sentimental and romantic (seen in simple, lyrical love poems employing antiquated forms and diction) to the cynical and overtly political, which manifests his indignation toward humanity's inhumanities during World War II.

[VB]

Paterson, A. B. (Australia, 1864–1941) Andrew Barton Paterson was born in Narambla, New South Wales, moving at age five to Illalowg, both in Australia's bush country. His early education was provided at home and at a small bush school. In 1874, Paterson was sent to Sydney to live with his grandmother in order to attend Sydney Grammar School.

While working as a lawyer, and later a journalist, 'The Banjo' (a nom de plume taken from a horse owned by the family) wrote verse in the form of the Bush Ballad, a style of folk song developed by rural Australian settlers. Despite other claims of authorship, it is generally held that in 1895 Paterson wrote the lyrics to quite possibly the most famous bush ballad, 'Waltzing Matilda'. This piece was followed by the extremely popular collection *Man from Snowy River and Other Verses* (1895) and numerous other volumes and novels published well into the twentieth century. Barton went on to serve during World War I, continuing his writing career after returning to Australia.

[MP]

Paterson, Don (Scotland, b. 1963) Paterson was born in Dundee in 1963. He left school at the age of sixteen and worked in Scotland and England as a jazz musician, now leading the jazz-folk band Lammas. He received a Gregory Award in 1990 and in 1993 won the Forward Prize for *Nil Nil* (1993). He held the post of writer-in-residence at the University of Dundee (1993–95) and is poetry editor for Picador. His second collection, *God's Gift to Women*, was published in 1997, winning a Scotish Arts Council Book award. Both collections show a love of philosophical games, exploring how far he can plunge his readers into artifice before retrieving them with sometimes brutal directness. Paterson firmly maintains a Scottish voice, writing for and about the Scottish working class.

[LKMF]

Patten, Brian (England, b. 1946) Patten was born in Liverpool, and attended secondary school at Sefton Park in Liverpool.

Many of Patten's works, especially those for children, demonstrate his interest in fantasy, which, he says, he always sets against realistic backgrounds putting the everyday world into different perspective. Patten believes that reality is not constant and that people create their own version of it, according to their needs.

In addition to poetry, Patten has written several children's books and plays. He won the Mystery Writers of America special award for his novel, *Mr Moon's Last Case* (1975).

Selected works: *Penguin Modern Poets* (1967); *Little Johnny's Confession* (1967); *The Irrelevant Song and Other Poems* (1980); *The Unreliable Nightingale* (1973); *Vanishing Trick* (1976); *Love Poems* (1981); *Grinning Jack: Selected Poems* (1990); *Armada* (1996).

[JS]

Paulin, Tom (Ireland, b. 1949) Although Paulin was born in Leeds, England, he grew up in Belfast and belonged to the group of poets and intellectuals who emerged from Northern Ireland in the 1960s and 1970s, which included MONTAGUE, HEANEY, DEANE, and MAHON. Paulin was educated at the University of Hull and Oxford University. In 1972, he became a lecturer in English at the University of Nottingham, England. A Protestant with liberal-minded parents, Paulin rejected Unionist politics in favor of a republican and nonsectarian vision of a unified Ireland.

From the beginning, Paulin's work was characterized by his commitment to the humanistic, rationalist ideals of the Enlightenment as well as a sensitivity toward linguistic differences and cultural diversity. Influenced by W. H. AUDEN, his early volumes, such as *Theoretical Locations* (1975), *A State of Justice* (1977), and *Personal Column* (1978), frequently use metaphor to allude to political conflicts in Northern Ireland. However, as his poems evolved, he responded more directly and critically to Ulster politics. His poems, too, made use of Ulster dialects resulting in a freer and, for non-Ulster readers, perhaps a more difficult style. *A State of Justice* (1977) was the choice of the Poetry Book Society. *Fivemiletown* (1987) expresses the diverse voices of the Ulster conflict, as in 'An Ulster Unionist Walks the Streets of London'.

As well as producing such powerful volumes of poetry, Paulin was a director of the Field Day Company and published *Ireland and the English Crisis* in prose in 1984. Paulin's work juxtaposes politics and aesthetics powerfully and provocatively.

[CT]

Pavese, Cesare (Italy, 1908–50) One of the leading figures of Italian Neorealism, Pavese's early poetry – prose-like and mimetic, owing much to the subject of his dissertation, Walt Whitman – sharply contrasted the fragmented, concentrated verse made fashionable by Ermetismo (see UNGARETTI, QUASIMODO). His paratactic verse, quite close to a recitative, evolved around the same themes found in his narrative: urbanization versus the rural world, loneliness, and the impossibility of political commitment in the face of failed social relationships. His late work, published soon after his suicide, displayed a more traditional language and imagery and has enjoyed continued success.

Selected works: *Lavorare stanca* (*Hard Labor*, 1936); *Verrà la morte e avrà i tuoi occhi* (*Death Will Come and Will Have Your Eyes*, 1951); *Poesie edite e inedite* (*Poetry, Edited and Unedited*, 1962).

[GS]

Pavlov, Konstantin (Bulgaria, b. 1933) Recipient of the poetry prize of the International Academy of Arts (Paris, 1992), Konstantin Mirchev Pavlov was born in the village of Vitoshko, Sofia area, and graduated from the University of Sofia.

Before the fall of the totalitarian regime (1989), he worked for *Bulgarian Radio, Television, and Cinematography*, a leading literary magazine and for a publishing house. His intellectual and artistic independence, however, pitted him against the government. He was frequently fired and his poems were banned from publication.

Pavlov's works synthesize contemplation and satire, parable and grotesque, obsession with the absurdity of the human condition and an implicit optimism that fuels his indignation at any assault on personal freedom.

Selected works: *Satiri* (*Satires*, 1960); *Stikhove* (*Verses*, 1965); *Poyavyavane* (*Appearance*, 1989); *Ubiystvo na spyasht chovek* (*Murder of a Sleeping Man*, 1992); *Repetitsiya za gala tants* (*A Gala Dance Rehearsal*, 1995); *Spasenie* (*Deliverance*, 1995).

[CG/LPG]

Pavlović, Miodrag (Yugoslavia, b. 1928) A well-known Serbian poet, essayist, and playwright, Pavlović was born in Novi Sad, Vojvodina. He has spent most of his life in Belgrade, where he finished Medical School. However, he devoted himself to a literary career and worked as an editor, theater director, journalist, and writer. An avid traveler, Pavlović incorporates many of his experiences and impressions into his writings.

Pavlović's poetry is characterized by an acute, at times ironic, awareness of world mythology, culture, and history. His poems are replete with allusions to ancient Greece, Rome, Persia, and Scythia in addition to references to medieval Serbian culture and Orthodox Christianity, to which he feels a strong affinity. In his later poems, Pavlović presents a critical picture of urban life. Pavlović creates surreal, bizarre, and often absurd metaphors and similes which at times come close to magic realism. His use of unconventional language and fantastic symbols conveys the loss of meaning and sense in the modern world.

Selected works: *87 Pesama* (*87 Poems*, 1952); *Velika Skitija* (*The Great Scythia*, 1969); *Svetli i tamni praznici* (*Bright and Dark Holidays*, 1971); *Divno čudo* (*A Beautiful Wonder*, 1982); *Knjiga staroslovna*; *Knjiga horizonta* (*An Ancient Book; A Book of Horizons*, 1993).

[DJ]

Paz, Octavio (Mexico, 1914–98) One of the most prolific and prominent intellectual figures in Latin America, Paz is well known both for his poetry and for his essays. He has received many literary awards including Belgium's International Poetry Prize (1963); Mexico's National Prize in Letters (1977) and its Ollin Yoliztli Prize (1980); Spain's Miguel de Cervantes Prize (1981); and the Nobel Prize for Literature (1990).

Although born in Mexico City, Paz grew up in nearby Mixcoac, where he read deeply in his grandfather's library and eventually attended one of the most prestigious preparatory schools in Mexico. Among his teachers were poets from the great vanguardist literary group centered around the literary magazine *Contemporáneos*. At seventeen, Paz published his first poem and founded his first literary magazine, *Barandal*. Influenced by, but rejecting, the idea of 'pure' art held by the Contemporáneos, Paz envisioned a less esoteric and more socially engaged poetics.

Much of Paz' thinking and writing reflects the time he spent outside Mexico – as a participant in the Second Congress of Antifascist Writers in Civil War Spain (1937); as a Guggenheim Fellow in the United States (1944–45); and as a diplomat in France (1946–51; 1959–62), Japan (1952), and India (1962–68). Highly sensual but also philosophical, Paz' poems are influenced by Surrealism, Existentialism, the haiku, and Buddhist and Hindu thought. His first path-breaking volume of poetry – *Libertad bajo palabra* (*Freedom under Parole*, 1949) – bears the stylistic fragmentation of North American Modernist poetry while the prose poems of

Eagle or Sun? (1951) reflect the influence of Surrealism. His study of the haiku resulted in *Seeds for a Hymn* (1954). *Sun Stone* (1957), a circular poem whose structure is based on the Aztec calendar, reflects his interest in Mexican history and culture. While in India, Paz wrote in even more experimental structure and language: *White* (1967), for instance, is considered one of his most ambitious undertakings because of its innovative use of the blank page and its incorporation of multiple textual sequences. Later works, such as *A Draft of Shadows* (1975), *Vuelta* (1981), and *A Tree Within* (1987), return to a more lyrical style. For Paz, poetry was an act of transcendence, something which could momentarily overcome the limits and essential solitude of human existence.

Attentive to culture and to the universal qualities of human existence, Paz' writing achieves a penetrating, comparative synthesis of diverse cultural and aesthetic movements. In 1950, Paz published his now-classic essay on Mexican cultural identity, *The Labyrinth of Solitude*. Other important prose works include two essays on aesthetics, *The Bow and the Lyre* (1956) and *Children of the Mire* (1974). The former discusses the nature of poetry itself and the second the romantic roots of Modernist art and its attitude toward history and tradition. In 1983, Paz published a significant historical study and interpretation of the work and life of the great seventeenth-century Mexican poet, Sor Juana Inés de la Cruz. He also founded and edited three very important literary magazines, *Taller, Plural*, and *Vuelta*. Paz died in Mexico City of an undisclosed illness; his funeral was attended by thousands.

[LKA]

p'Bitek, Okot (Uganda, 1931–82) p'Bitek is best known for his four prose poems, *Song of Lawino: A Lament* (1966), *Song of Ocol* (1970), *Song of (a) Prisoner* (1971), and, that same year, *Song of Malaya* ('malaya' means prostitute). Very early in his career, he published a novel in Acholi, *Lak tar miyo kinyero wi lobo?* (*Are your teeth white? Then laugh!*, 1953). His most famous work, *Song of Lawino*, was also originally written in Acholi and translated by the author. Though many African writers write solely in European languages, p'Bitek actively promoted the use of his native language for literary purposes. He precedes the Kenyan writer Ngũgĩ wa Thiong'o, who started writing fiction in his native Gikuyu in 1977. Both writers have ardently espoused the creation of literature in indigenous African languages.

p'Bitek's poetry is inspired by traditional Acholi songs that he heard throughout his childhood. His father was a schoolteacher and storyteller, and his mother was a gifted traditional singer and composer. He studied at Kings College, Budo, and played soccer for Uganda's national team. When Uganda's soccer team attended the 1956 Olympics in London, p'Bitek stayed to earn degrees in education (at Bristol), law (at Aberystwyth), and social anthropology (at Oxford). He wrote a thesis on traditional Acholi and Lango songs.

Returning to Uganda, p'Bitek lectured in sociology at University College in Makerere. In 1966, he became the director of the Uganda National Theatre and Cultural Center, and founded the Gulu Arts Festival. He endeavored to shift the predominant emphasis on British art forms to that of African styles. He stated that Ugandans should 'look to the village . . . and see if we cannot find some root there, and build on this'. In *Song of Lawino*, the protagonist Lawino represents this unschooled knowledge of Acholi culture, a knowledge that Africans obsessed with modernization (such as her husband Ocol) want to destroy. The English translation concludes 'Let no one uproot the/ Pumpkin', a plea to maintain Acholi cultural identity. The shorter response poem, 'Song of Ocol', illustrates the intolerance of educated 'city' Africans to their own cultural heritage as Ocol asserts that the pumpkins of custom and tradition are meaningless in the face of (European) modernity.

p'Bitek's criticism offended the Ugandan government, and he was forced to emigrate. While at the Nairobi University College, he initiated the Kisumu Arts Festival. He then accepted a one-year fellowship from the University of Iowa's International Writing Program for 1969–70. He taught at the University of Nairobi for most of the 1970s, during which time he held visiting appointments at the University of Texas, Austin and the University of Ife, Nigeria. After Idi Amin's regime was overthrown, p'Bitek returned to Uganda. He accepted a position as professor of creative writing at Makerere University, but died five months after taking up the appointment.

In addition to two works of nonfiction dealing with African religion, p'Bitek translated Acholi folk songs and folk tales, collected as *The Horn of My Love* (1974) and *Hare and Hornbill* (1978), respectively.

[KAC]

Péguy, Charles (France, 1873–1914) Born to humble parents in Orléans, and raised by his mother and grandmother after the early death of his father, Péguy was educated in Paris at the École Normale Supérieure. Like SPIRE, during the Dreyfus Affair (1894–1906) he sided with Alfred Dreyfus, the Jewish army captain falsely accused of passing military secrets to Germany. *Notre jeunesse* (*Our Youth*, 1910) records his subsequent disillusionment with Dreyfus' supporters. From 1897 he was a Socialist, but in 1908 he returned to the Catholic church. He came to prominence as a publisher and a polemicist with the founding of the *Cahiers de la Quinzaine* (*Fortnightly Review*, 1900–1914). Among the best expressions of his willingness to understand Christ's Passion is the *Mystère de la charité de Jeanne d'Arc* (*Mystery of the Charity of Jeanne d'Arc*, 1910).

He was killed in the first weeks of World War I in the Battle of the Marne.

Selected works: *Jeanne d'Arc* (1897), a dramatic trilogy; *Le Porche du mystère de la deuxième vertu* (*The Portico of the Mystery of the Second Virtue*, 1911); *Le Mystère des Saints-Innocents* (*The Mystery of the Holy Innocents*, 1912); *Eve* (1913).

[SJ]

Penna, Sandro (Italy, 1906–77) Like UMBERTO SABA, who was among the first Italian poets to appreciate his work, Sandro Penna holds a rather anomalous position within twentieth-century Italian verse. Openly devoted to celebrating gay love and a physical, almost pagan closeness to the world, his verse seems to have no predecessors in Italian literature, to the point that several critics have mentioned classical Greek poetry as his only verifiable source of inspiration. In his collections, a traditional frame of rhyme and precise stanzaic organization counters the unconventionality of his themes, and is combined with a circumscribed and yet extremely refined use of the language.

Selected works: *Una strana gioia di vivere* (1956); *Croce e delizia* (1958); *Stranezze* (1976); *Il viaggiatore insonne* (1977).

[GS]

Peralta, Bertalicia (Panama, b. 1939) A Panama City-born essayist, poet, journalist, and music teacher, Peralta founded and coedited the literary magazine *El Pez Original* (1961–68), dedicated to the new literature of Panama. She is well known in Central America for her outspoken feminist position and for her dedication to children's literature. Her poetry embraces women's struggles for freedom and is often characterized by a subtle irony that aligns her with the poetry of the Mexican poet ROSARIO CASTELLANOS.

Selected works: *Sendas Fugitivas* (*Fugitive Paths*, 1962); *Los Retornos: poesía* (*Returns: Poems*, 1966); *Himno a la Alegría* (*Hymn to*

Happiness, 1973); *Ragul* (*Ragul*, 1976); *Casa Flotante: poesía* (*Floating House: Poems*, 1979); *Piel de Gallina* (*Goosebumps*, 1982).

[SL]

Péret, Benjamin (France, 1889–1959) Given the choice of jail time or joining the army when he was caught defacing a public statue in his home town near Nantes, Péret reluctantly chose the army and was sent to the Balkans during World War I. After the war, Péret went to Paris, where he came into contact with ANDRÉ BRETON, to whom he was to remain loyal throughout his life. He participated in hypnosis experiments (see DESNOS) and worked on the journal *La Révolution surréaliste*, briefly as editor (though his most famous contribution was a photograph of himself insulting a priest). A representative of the political side of Surrealism and a confirmed Trotskyite, Péret nonetheless believed that poetry should never be used for the purpose of mere propaganda. Following World War II, he published *Le Déshonneur des poètes* (*The Disgrace of Poets*, 1945), a harsh attack on the Communist poets of the Resistance. In *La parole est à Péret* (*Péret Speaks*, 1943), Péret proclaimed that magic was the 'flesh and blood' of poetry and argued that poetry's revolutionary effect depended on its ability to express the marvelous, which, hidden from the eyes of the vulgar, explodes like a 'time bomb', shattering the established bourgeois world view. His own verse was remarkable for its satirical wit and poetic treatment of everyday objects placed in striking juxtapositions. Péret lived for a time in Brazil and Mexico and compiled an *Anthologie des mythes, légendes et contes populaires d'Amérique* (*Anthology of Myths, Legends, and Folktales from America*, 1960), published posthumously.

Selected works: *Le Passager du transatlantique* (*The Transatlantic Passenger*, 1921); *Le Grand Jeu* (*The Great Game*, 1928); *Je ne mange pas de ce pain là* (*I Don't Eat that Bread*, 1936); *Je sublime* (*I Sublime*, 1936); *Feu central* (*Central Fire*, 1947).

[ML]

Perse, Saint-John (Alexis Saint-Léger Léger; France, 1887–1975) Léger was born on his family's estate on a small island off the coast of Guadeloupe. His collection of poems *Étoges* (1911) is a nostalgic evocation of memories of his lush boyhood home. Léger studied law at Bordeaux and chose a diplomatic career on the advice of PAUL CLAUDEL. His long poem *Anabase* (*Anabasis*, 1924), which chronicles a fictitious expedition to an exotic oriental land, was the last major work he published before devoting himself to his diplomatic career. Léger served in China and was Aristide Briand's chief-of-staff from 1925 to 1932. He then served as Secretary General of the French Ministry of Foreign Affairs until forced into exile in 1940 by the pro-Nazi Vichy regime. Léger went to the United States and settled in Washington, where he found work as a consultant on French literature at the Library of Congress. *Exil* (*Exile*, 1942) is a powerful meditation on the plight of exile. Known for its epic scope, difficult language, brilliant imagery, and elegant epiphanic touches, the poetry of Saint-John Perse is a celebration of the eternal yearnings of the spirit and human communion with the forces of nature. Natural themes became prevalent in the poet's later works: *Pluies* (*Rains*, 1944), *Neiges* (*Snows*, 1945), *Vents* (*Winds*, 1946), and *Amers* (*Seamarks*, 1957). Léger returned to France for the first time in 1957 and received the Nobel Prize for Literature in 1960.

[ML]

Pessoa, Fernando (Portugal, 1888–1935) The foremost Portuguese poet of the century, and one of the most acclaimed Modernists anywhere, Pessoa remained relatively obscure until recently. Though he published regularly in journals and magazines, he put out only three volumes during his lifetime and one of these, *35*

Sonnets (1918), was a collection of Shakespearean-styled school poems. It has only been since his death that his fame has grown and the complexity of his poetry begun to be understood.

Pessoa was born into a well-to-do Lisbon family. His father, a music reviewer, died when Pessoa was five, however, and the family moved to South Africa in 1895 when Pessoa's mother married a consulate official there. Pessoa's childhood was thus polylingual; when he started writing poems, he composed in Portuguese, Spanish, English, and German. Returning to Lisbon in 1905, Pessoa entered the university but never completed his degree. Instead, he took a lifelong position as a commercial translator, even as he wrote poetry (and prose) continuously. His work first appeared in journals in 1912; within three years he had helped to found the influential literary magazine *Orpheu*. In 1934 he published the masterpiece *Mensagem* (*Message*), though it was not until well after his death that its influence in Portugal and elsewhere was felt. Pessoa translated professionally, wrote passionately, and lived quietly until his death from liver dysfunction at age forty-seven.

It is a critical commonplace, however, that these biographical details are not the real life of Fernando Pessoa. Unlike other Modernists, such as MACDIARMID, who took pseudonyms to craft a single masked self to write from and through, Pessoa took forty-four such personalities over the course of his career. Complete with biographies, philosophical viewpoints, and stylistic consistencies, these 'heteronyms' account for more than two-thirds of Pessoa's output. Although he also published marvelous symbolic poetry under his own name (which critics have called an 'orthonym', since hetronymy suggests that 'Fernando Pessoa' is a constructed identity as well), he shared his poetic life with numerous other 'poets'.

There are three primary heteronyms which dominate Pessoa's work. All date to 1918 – indeed, if his letters are to be believed, to a single day in 1918 – and all bear a relationship to the others. There was the modernist Alvaro de Campos, a free verse poet whose copiousness echoes Whitman. There was Ricardo Reis, a cosmopolitan formalist influenced by contemporary continental philosophy. Primary among the heteronyms, including Pessoa himself, was Alberto Caeiro, 'the master'. A pastoralist and free verse writer, Caeiro was the ur-spring of Pessoa's work. As OCTAVIO PAZ put it: 'Reis believes in form, Campos in sensation, Pessoa in symbols. Caeiro doesn't believe in anything: he exists.'

The combination of these four writers – and the other forty Pessoa invented – crafted a distinct and memorable art, canvasing the world from different poetic, personal, and philosophical viewpoints. When he died, Pessoa left over 20,000 pieces of writing for posterity. Time will only tell how much more complex and fascinating his oeuvre will be as these materials continue to come to light.

[MW]

Peters, Lenrie (The Gambia, b. 1932) After receiving his basic education in the Gambia, Peters moved to Sierra Leone in 1949. Three years later, he began medical school in England, and obtained his degree from Trinity College, Cambridge in 1959. He spent several years practicing medicine in England before returning to Africa. He has worked as a surgeon in the Gambia, both for the government and privately. He has also practiced in Sierra Leone, where his novel *The Second Round* (1965) is set. Peters is also an accomplished singer.

Many of Peters' poems are concerned with the isolation of spirit in the postcolonial African world. His collections are: *Poems* (1964), *Satellites* (1967), *Katchikali* (1971), and *Selected Poetry* (1981), which includes 58 new poems. Like SYL CHENEY-COKER, he represents West Africa's important contribution to Anglophone literature.

[KAC]

Petrov, Valeri (Valeri Nisim Mevorakh; Bulgaria, b. 1920) Author of numerous short lyrics and long narrative poems, two travelogues, five plays, fifteen movie scripts, and an accomplished translator from English (all of Shakespeare's plays and sonnets), Italian, and Russian, Petrov was born in Sofia. He earned a medical degree in 1944, but soon became a professional writer. Raised in a family of intellectuals with leftist political views (his father was a professor of law and former Bulgarian ambassador to the United States), Petrov has been a life-long supporter of Communist ideas and an equally ardent opponent of any form of dictatorship. Consequently his works were severely criticized, banned from publication, and he was expelled from the Communist Party. After the fall of the totalitarian regime in 1989, he was a member of parliament representing the Socialist Party.

Petrov's poetry is a highly original blend of delicate lyricism and superb wit (ranging from playful humor to piercing satire). It is widely acclaimed for its formal virtuosity, especially of his fresh and expressive rhymes, and for its emotional and intellectual sophistication and honesty.

Selected works: *Stikhotvoreniya* (*Poems*, 1949); *V mekata esen* (*In the Mild Autumn*, 1961); *Dŭzhd vali, sluntse gree* (*Rain is Falling, the Sun is Shining*, 1967); *Satirichni poemi* (*Satirical Poems*, 1988); *Izbrani proizvedeniya* (*Selected Works*, 1990).

[CG/LPG]

Phillips, Carl (United States, b. 1959) Phillips studied classical philology while an undergraduate at Harvard and then spent eight years teaching high school Latin. After his first book, *In the Blood* (1992), won the Morse Poetry Prize, Phillips earned an M.A. in creative writing from Boston University. Currently, he is an associate professor of English and African and Afro-American Studies at Washington University, St Louis.

Well-known for his poetry's eroticism, Phillips writes verse often imbued with a 'wild and rigorous prosody', as Alan Michael Parker notes, which creates a kind of 'breathlessness'. Eroticism does not degrade into sentimentality, however; rather, Phillips writes with an elegant reserve, a 'reticence', according to MARILYN HACKER, reminiscent 'of the young JAMES MERRILL, even AUDEN'.

Selected works: *Cortege* (1995); *From the Devotions* (1998).

[MO]

Pilinszky, Janos (Hungary, 1921–81) Born to a middle-class family in Budapest, Pilinszky studied law and literature at the university there before being drafted into the army in 1944. Called to help in the liberation of the concentration camps in Germany, Pilinszky's wartime duty forever changed his world view; his religious faith was shaken by the realities of what man might do to man. When he returned to Budapest, he edited *Újhold* (*New Moon*), published the Baumgartner Prize-winning *Trapéz és korlát* (*Trapeze and Parallel Bars*, 1946), and, in 1957, began a long tenure as editor of the Catholic weekly *Új Ember* (*New Man*). Publishing regularly until his death, Pilinszky established himself as one of the primary post-war Hungarian poets, winning the Attila József Prize in 1971.

The confessional works of *Trapéz és korlát* chart a world of post-concentration camp alienation. This nihilism was a fundamental aspect of Pilinszky's work; over time it would modulate and moderate, as the power of Hungary's Communist regime lessened and Pilinszky's own distance from his war experiences grew. By the time of *Harmadnapon* (*On The Third Day*, 1959), images of the Holocaust are mixed with Christian symbols, coloring each for a hard, but at least partially redemptive, vision. At the height of his powers in his collected works, *Nagyvárosi ikonok* (*Big City Icons*, 1970), Pilinszky reconciles history to his religious beliefs, finding harmony again, even if it is still tinged with his experiences thirty years before.

Selected works: *Szálkák* (*Splinters*, 1972); *Végigfejlet* (*Denouement*, 1974).

[MW]

Pilon, Jean-Guy (Canada, b. 1930) Pilon was born in St Polycarpe, Québec. One of the poets published by GASTON MIRON's press, Les Éditions de l'Hexagone, Pilon is known for his support for Québec nationalism. Unlike the strident, explicitly political tone that characterizes the poetry of some of his contemporaries, Pilon's nationalism is articulated through a romantic appeal to nature and to the land. The communal project of building a French country on the North American continent is for Pilon part of a more general quest for spiritual wholeness and transcendence.

Pilon's first two books of poetry, *La fiancée du matin* (*Engaged to the Morning*, 1953) and *Les cloîtres de l'été* (*Cloisters of the Summer*, 1953) consist of lyrical celebrations of nature and the body. His calls for the creation of a new country can be found in *La mouette et le large* (*The Gull and the Open Sea*, 1960), *Recours au pays* (*Resort to the Country*, 1961) and *Pour saluer une ville* (*To Greet a City*, 1963). With *Saisons pour la continuelle* (*Seasons for the Faithful*, 1964), Pilon has turned to a search for simple satisfactions. In 1959, Pilon founded the important journal *Liberté*. In 1968, he was awarded the Governor General's Award for *Comme eau retenue: poèmes 1954–63* (*Retained like Water: Poems 1954–63*, 1968). In the same year, he was elected a member of the Royal Society of Canada.

[IS]

Pinsky, Robert (United States, b. 1940) Pinsky, Poet Laureate of the United States, was born in New Jersey, and received a B.A. from Rutgers. At Stanford, where he earned a Ph.D., Pinsky was influenced by his teacher YVOR WINTERS. A noted critic and translator as well as a highly regarded poet, Pinsky is currently a professor at Boston University.

Pinsky is a ruminative poet of incisive clarity and reason. A champion of the discursive, he waxes abstractly and thoughtfully about his subjects in gently flowing stanzas. With a voice that is conversational and calm, wry and serious, Pinsky often ponders the relationships that both bind and separate us.

Selected works: *The Want Bone* (1990); *The Figured Wheel: New and Collected Poems* (1996).

[AE]

Pitt-Kethley, Fiona (England, b. 1954) Pitt-Kethley is a prolific author, publishing travel books, novels, anthologies, and journalism, in addition to books of poetry. She currently works as a critic for the *New York Times*. Her first book of poetry, *London* (1984), was published privately and contains the explicit, everyday poetry that marks most of her work.

Pitt-Kethley's poetry uses satire to confront and exploit contemporary social problems. The author is an activist for social change, working to improve the rights of writers and to end discrimination in poetry publishing and literary awards.

Her recent work includes *Private Parts* (1987), *Abacus* (1989), *The Perfect Man* (1989), and *Dogs* (1993). She also publishes work in periodicals such as *New Statesman*, often using her father's name, Rupert Singleton, as her pseudonym.

[LK]

Pitter, Ruth (England, 1897–1992) Pitter was born in Ilford, Essex, and worked as a furniture painter. Her first poems were published in *New Age* magazine when she was still a pupil at the Coborn School for Girls, and her *First Poems* (1920) was financed by HILAIRE BELLOC. A poet of an often deceptively simple vision of nature, and religious to boot, she rarely indulges in sentiment but instead uses the natural world to explore what she has described as 'the mysteries of things'. Honors included being the first woman recipient of the Queen's Gold Medal for Poetry in 1955 and a CBE in 1979.

Selected works: *A Mad Lady's Garland* (1934); *A Trophy of Arms* (1936); *The Spirit Watches* (1939); *The Bridge* (1945); *The Ermine* (1953); *Still by Choice* (1966); *The End of Drought* (1975); *Collected Poems* (1990).

[LKMF]

Pizarnik, Alejandra (Argentina, 1936–72) Born in 1936 of a Russian Jewish family, Pizarnik committed suicide at the age of 36. Despite the tragic brevity of her life, she is considered one of the most important female voices in Latin American poetry of the twentieth century. Her early poetry, in such volumes as *La tierra mas ajena* (*The Most Foreign Land*, 1955) and *Las aventuras perdidas* (*The Lost Adventures*, 1958), is characterized by its intense brevity and luminosity. In addition to these powerful works, she published a piece of poetic prose, *La condesa sangrienta* (*The Bloody Countess*, 1971), which is a re-writing of Valentine Penrose's gothic novel of the same title (1971). After her death, OLGA OROZCO and Ana Becciu edited her unpublished work in *Textos de sombra y ultimos poemas* (*Texts of Shadow and Final Poems*, 1982), which included *Los poseidos entre lilas* (*The Possessed among Lilacs*, 1969) and *Hilda la poligrafa o la bucanera de Pernambuco* (*Hilda, the Polygraph or the Buccaneer of Pernambuco*, 1971). Radically different from her previous poetry, these texts are an explosion of obscenity and excess. Recently her correspondence has been published in Buenos Aires and her diaries and notebooks are soon to be published in Spain.

Selected works: *La ultima inocencia* (*The Last Innocence*, 1956); *Arbol de Diana* (*Diana's Tree*, 1962); *Los trabajos y las noches* (*The Work and the Night*, 1965); *El infierno musical* (*The Musical Inferno*, 1971).

[MN]

Plath, Sylvia (United States, 1932–63) Although she took her own life at thirty-one and published only one book of poems during her lifetime, Plath has been one of the most influential and widely read postwar American poets. While enhanced by the shocking details of her brief life and tragic death, her tremendous posthumous fame rests most firmly upon the tense, masterful poems in the volume *Ariel*, published after her death.

Born in Boston, Plath was a precocious and talented young girl whose father, an entomologist and professor at Boston University, died of diabetes when she was eight – by most accounts a crucial blow with lasting implications on her emotional life. As a young woman, she demonstrated remarkable success, attending Smith College on a scholarship, winning writing awards from women's magazines and publishing many poems and short stories, being elected to Phi Beta Kappa, graduating *summa cum laude*; however, these external signs of achievement masked profound anxieties and strains which began to emerge toward the end of college. As her junior year ended, Plath suffered a breakdown and attempted suicide, an experience she later rendered in her harrowing novel, *The Bell Jar* (1963). Upon her apparent recovery and successful graduation, Plath left on a Fulbright Fellowship to Cambridge, where she earned an M.A.; at Cambridge, she met the British poet TED HUGHES, whom she married in 1956. The couple returned to the U.S., where Plath taught at Smith for a year (1957–8), and took a poetry writing seminar with ROBERT LOWELL at Boston University that would prove to be influential on the development of her writing.

Her early work, while containing the seeds of her originality, reveals the strong and lasting influence of poets such as Lowell, THEODORE ROETHKE, DYLAN THOMAS, and W. H. AUDEN. In 1959, the couple returned to England, where Plath had her first book of poems published (*The Colossus*, 1960) and had two children, in 1960 (Frieda) and 1962 (Nicholas). By the summer of 1962, she had learned of Hughes's infidelity and their marriage had ended in ruins. During the next several months, Plath lived alone through an unusually arctic English winter with their two small children, writing at a frantic pace, composing the visceral, gripping poems that would eventually be collected in *Ariel*, and descending deeper into depression. On February 11, 1963, Plath committed suicide in a London flat.

Though Plath has often been associated with 'Confessional' poetry, known for its candor about occasionally lurid personal suffering, her best poems, such as 'Metaphors', 'Morning Song', 'Daddy', 'Lady Lazarus', 'Tulips', 'Cut', and 'Poppies in October', transcend vulgar self-expression through their combination of genuine pain, jarring honesty, and verbal control, as well as through Plath's witty self-dramatization and self-mockery. Her poems often express a sensitive young woman's struggle with domesticity and the rigid stereotypical roles and expectations placed upon women in the 1950s; they are driven by furious rage and sardonic irony against various forms of confinement. Plath's genius lies in her ability to transform specific, personal experience into myth and larger-than-life drama in convincing, profoundly moving ways. Much of her work hovers around death, suicide, and suffering, but the poems are always animated by her tendency to make the familiar chillingly strange. The crisp diction and blunt colloquial phrasing, rapid tonal shifts and compression, the sharply etched images, playful rhythm and aural repetition – in general, what Hughes called her 'crackling verbal energy' – bring these anguished poems unforgettably to life.

Selected works: *The Colossus* (1960); *Ariel* (1965); *Crossing the Water* (1972); *Collected Poems* (1981).

[AE]

Plutzik, Hyrum (United States, 1911–62) Born in Brooklyn of Russian/Yiddish-speaking parents, Plutzik combines a love of nature and science with a Shul-like devotion to the history of his chosen form. He began writing during World War II: enlisted for two years, Plutzik explores his wartime experiences indirectly, through the figure of Hamlet or characters from Greek mythology. His lyricism, while reminiscent of ROBERT FROST, stems from Plutzik's interest in Jewish mysticism. He taught for many years at Trinity College in Hartford, Connecticut.

Selected works: *Collected Poems* (1992).

[CV]

Ponge, Francis (France, 1899–1988) Born in Montpellier to a bank director, Ponge was a member of no movement or school of poetry, though he was briefly affiliated with the Surrealists in the early 1930s. In the 1940s, he became a member of the Communist Party for a short stint, even serving as the editor of their newspaper. During World War II, Ponge was a member of the French Resistance. Yet his work does not reflect these associations and activities, standing apart from other poetry. Mostly idiosyncratic prose poems, Ponge's writing displays his love of language in his use of wordplay and antiquated diction. His subjects are often common objects, to which the reader is introduced through humor and the poet's creative process, with Ponge's inclusion of mistakes and revisions. This innovative poetry won Ponge many awards, including the International Poetry Prize (1959), Grand Prize for Poetry from the French Academy (1972), French National Poetry Prize (1981), and Grand Prize from Société de Glées de Lettres (1985).

Selected works: *Le Parti pris des choses* (*The Voice of Things*, 1942); *Proèmes* (*ProsePoems*, 1948); *La Rage de l'expression* (*The Fury of Expression*, 1952); *Le Grand Recueil* (*The Great Anthology*, 1961); *La Fabrique du 'pré'*

(*The Making of 'pre'*, 1971); *Dix poèmes* (*Ten Poems*, 1983).

[BRB]

Popa, Vasko (Yugoslavia, 1922–91) Popa has often been described (especially in the West) as one of the most prominent Serbian poets of the twentieth century. He was certainly one of the most visible Serbian poets in the West. Born in a small village in Vojvodina, he was educated in Vienna, Bucharest, and Belgrade, where he graduated from the Faculty of Philosophy in 1949. He participated actively in Yugoslav literary life as editor of a number of literary journals and magazines and as a translator from French.

Popa's painful experiences of concentration camps where he was interned during World War II found ways into his poetry. His first collection, *Kora* (*Crust*, 1953), explores the tragic fate of man faced with the destruction and annihilation of war. Themes of violence and destruction, of human helplessness in an absurd (and threatening) universe continued to engage Popa's imagination throughout his career.

Strongly influenced by the themes, rhythms, and cadences of Serbian folk art, Popa's poetry often focused on the fantastic, absurd, and grotesque. He delves into the mythology and folklore of the Serbian people in his next anthology, *Nepočin-polje* (*The Nepočin-field*, 1956), and from then on, elements of the Serbian mythic past find ways into most of his poems. His themes also include a passionate interest in the cosmic order of things, its existential significance, and its relation to people. In *Sporedno polje*, Popa examines the origin of the world and conditions of human existence and attempts to find solutions to and ways to escape from those conditions. His collections *Uspravna zemlja* (1972) and *Vucja so* (1975) explore Serbian (pre-Christian) national mythology, as well as Serbian history, traditions, and culture (especially those related to Serbian struggles against the Ottoman empire). Popa's late collection, *Kuča nasred druma* (1975), arises from his interest in the national and mythological histories of the Serbian people. It addresses events from the distant Serbian past and relates them to events from the more recent past (World War II) in an attempt to establish a continuation in Serbian national identity.

Popa's language is light and concise, stripped down to its bare essentials. In his terse, occasionally even ascetic poems, this 'magician of language' succeeds in invoking a world rich in images and emotions, and occasionally even playful. Most of his poems are written in a free verse which abounds in innovative use of language. While exploring the poetic possibilities of Serbian traditional language and establishing a style based on Serbian folklore (fables, myth, and riddles), Popa maintained firm ties with the Modernist (including Surrealist and experimental) sensibilities of Serbian poetry of the nineteenth and twentieth centuries. His fame and popularity, both in Yugoslavia and abroad, indicate Popa's success in conveying to his readers the mystery of the world and its infinite charm, play, and intrigue, as well as its dark underbelly of occasional threats and violence.

Selected works: *Urnebesnik* (1960); *Ponoćno sunce* (*Midnight Sun*, 1962); *Sporedno nebo* (1968); *Mala kutija* (*A Small Box*, 1984).

[DJ]

Porta, Antonio (Antonio Paolazzi; Italy, 1935–89) One of the leaders of the neo-avant garde movement called 'Gruppo '63', Porta soon moved from its programmatic manifesto of a permanent linguistic revolution toward a more articulated and ultimately more communicative form of poetry. From that early experience Porta retained a carefree attitude toward syntactical combination, as well as the systematic erasure of the grammatical subject, combined with a certain dose of surrealistic violence. Porta was an active journalist and literary critic, and taught at various universities.

Selected works: *I rapporti* (*The Relationships*, 1966); *Quanto ho da dirvi* (*All I Have to Tell You*, 1977); *Passi passaggi* (*Paces Passages*, 1980); *Invasioni* (*Invasions*, 1984); *Il giardinere contro il becchino* (*The Gardener against the Grave-Digger*, 1988).

[GS]

Porter, Dorothy Featherstone (Australia, b. 1954) Porter completed her B.A. at the University of Sydney and has taught creative writing and poetry for many years, most recently at Sydney's University of Technology. She enjoys the Australian bush, being interested in Australia's native birds and history, all things which figure in her verse.

Though Porter has published five collections of poetry, it is her innovative verse novels that have won her international success and popularity, particularly the crime thriller *The Monkey's Mask* (1994), winner of the 1994 *Age* Book of the Year Award, which is being made into a film. She has also written two novels for young adults, *Rookwood* (1991) and *The Witch Number* (1993). Porter regularly contributes as a critic and reviewer to various Australian literary journals, and is highly regarded as a performer of her poetry.

Selected works: *Little Hoodlum* (1975); *Bison* (1979); *The Night Parrot* (1984); *Driving Too Fast* (1989); *Crete* (1996).

[DCO]

Porter, Peter (Australia, b. 1929) Porter was born in Brisbane. After his mother died in 1938, Porter, an only child, was sent to boarding school. He was a cadet journalist (1947–48) before moving to England in 1951 where he became associated with 'The Group' (see ADCOCK, BROWNJOHN, REDGROVE), and published his first collection, *Once Bitten, Twice Bitten* (1961).

Before 1968, when he became a full-time freelance writer, Porter worked as a bookseller and advertising copywriter. He has edited anthologies, written libretti, collaborated with the artist Arthur Boyd (1920–99), and translated Martial. Porter has a major international reputation and has won considerable literary awards, such as the Duff Cooper Memorial Prize for his 1983 *Collected Poems*, which was recently supplemented with a two-volume *Collected Poems* (1999). Yet, since 1974 he has regularly returned to Australia for short stays, where his acceptance as an 'Australian poet' has grown steadily.

While concerned with wit, many of Porter's poems are statements on culture and self-contained ethical imperatives. The emotions associated with the suicide of his wife (also in 1974) led to the elegiac poems of *The Cost of Seriousness* (1978), generally considered Porter's best single volume. 'An Exequy' and 'The Delegate' are important additions to modern elegy and are widely anthologized. Both an urbane and an urban poet (he still lives in London), Porter habitually invokes a plethora of references to European high culture, often music, and has become increasingly concerned with stanzaic forms and the linguistic construction of reality. His interest in poets such as STEVENS and ASHBERY has not meant a reduction in his ethical concerns. Porter, like WALLACE-CRABBE, writes poetry that mediates between the nationalist and postmodernist wings of Australian contemporary poetry.

[DM]

Pound, Ezra (United States, 1885–1972) Undisputedly one of the most influential twentieth-century poets and cultural icons, Ezra Weston Loomis Pound remains a much-discussed figure. Born in Hailey, Idaho, moving to Pennsylvania at four, he later attended the University of Pennsylvania – where he met WILLIAM CARLOS WILLIAMS – and Hamilton College. He had hardly begun teaching at Wabash College in Indiana before he was fired over clashing standards of sexual behavior.

Pound moved to Venice in 1908, publishing his first book, *A Lume Spento* (*Spent Light*), and a few months later moved on to London, where he lived for a dozen years. Pound quickly made himself well-known to such writers and visual artists as W.B. YEATS, Ford Madox Ford, T.E. HULME, Wyndham Lewis, RICHARD ALDINGTON, and H.D. But he worked at least as hard to make many others well-known, including T.S. ELIOT, ROBERT FROST, and James Joyce.

In 1912, in co-founding the Imagist movement, he turned from Provençal poetry toward an Oriental model. From the vigorous 'Sestina: Altaforte' of his earliest work, he transformed his poetry into the modernity of 'In a Station of the Metro', free of meter yet restrained in imagery, if not in juxtaposition.

In 1914, as a co-founder of the Vorticist movement, he worked toward aggressive irony and a use of conceptually disparate images or poetic elements. That same year he married Dorothy Shakespear. In 1915, his attractive volume *Cathay* strengthened his lifelong interest in translation. At times, Pound approached literary translation as a resurrecting or invoking – in a mystically literal sense – of historical writers from such disparate cultures as Chinese, Greek, and American.

His ambitions were immense; he wanted to create a twentieth-century renaissance. But he also sought a fusion of civic life and high culture in which the great creators of past or distant civilizations would be living presences. By 1920, partly in reaction to World War I, Pound's 'Homage to Sextus Propertius' and 'Hugh Selwyn Mauberley', show a revulsion from the values of civic life and Western civilization – a revulsion he seems to have overcome when he later met Mussolini. In 1920, Pound moved to Paris for four years, where he gave Eliot shrewd editorial advice on 'The Waste Land'.

In Italy from 1924 to the end of World War II, Pound worked on his central poetic effort, *The Cantos*, started in 1915 and appearing in a final unfinished version in 1970. The range of the 117 cantos covers the full spectrum, from incomprehensibly dim stretches to lyrical clusters, e.g., *The Pisan Cantos* (1948), that have given some light to the century.

Pound defended the Fascist Axis and advocated the 'social credit' economics of C.H. Douglas. Pound's version of 'social credit', weakened by his lack of training in economics and befouled by his anti-semitism, is widely regarded as crack-pot. Allied victors jailed and indicted him for treason, but before trial, he was declared insane and committed to an asylum until 1958. Released, Pound returned to Italy and lived in relative seclusion, speaking infrequently in public and entertaining doubts about his effectiveness as a poet and raconteur. He died in Venice in 1972. Though these last years were generally spent in quietude and reflection, it is as a maverick that Pound will be remembered, restless in his poetics and passionate in his politics.

[CC]

Prado, Adélia (Brazil, b. 1935) Born to a family of laborers, Prado stayed in her native town, Divinópolis, to receive her degree in Philosophy and Religious Education and become a teacher. Though she had published poems in various literary supplements, her first collection, *Bagagem*, was not published until 1976. Since then she has published other books of poetry, including *O coraçao disparado* (*O Desperate Heart*, 1978) and *Terra de Santa Cruz* (*The Land of Santa Cruz*, 1982), as well as prose and has had her work adapted for the stage.

Prado's poems express a longing to communicate with the world she experiences as a woman and the God she understands as a poet. These attempts at communication lead her to address the nature of language and poetry, as well as religion, throughout her work.

[VW]

Pratt, E.J. (Canada, 1882–1964) Edwin John Pratt is recognized as a seminal figure in Canadian poetry. A poet with a Victorian sensibility who wrote epic, rhyming verse even as Modernism was making its influence felt, Pratt's verse was important in providing the founding literary myths for Canadian nationalism. His epic poems depicting the stoic struggles of groups of men against an overpowering nature mirrored the struggles of the nation itself to locate its identity in the twentieth century.

Pratt was born in Western Bay, Newfoundland, and spent his early years traveling to the small coastal parishes served by his father, Reverend John Pratt. Educated in St John's, Pratt was first a teacher before becoming a preacher-probationer in a Methodist ministry, a position which allowed him to gain an intimate knowledge of the difficult lives of the Maritime fishermen and the awesome power of the sea. Both insights would later find their way into his poetry. In 1907, Pratt attended the University of Toronto, where he received a B.A. and M.A. in philosophy, a Bachelor's degree in Divinity, and, in 1917, a Ph.D. for a dissertation on Pauline eschatology.

That year also marked the publication of Pratt's first book, *Rachel: A Sea Story of Newfoundland in Verse*. Pratt published a collection of poetry, *Newfoundland Verse* (1923), before finding the epic form in which he would establish his reputation. *The Witches' Brew* (1925) is a mock epic that parodies the brief period of prohibition in Canada. *Titans* (1926) depicts earth-shattering struggles between enormous creatures, such as the fight between the whale and the kraken in the well-known poem 'The Cachalot'. The direct confrontation between opposing forces would become a subject characteristic of Pratt's poetry, as in the human struggles with the sea in *The Roosevelt and the Antinoe* (1930) and *The Titanic* (1935), and those depicting military antagonists in Pratt's epics concerning World War II – *Dunkirk* (1941) and *Behind the Log* (1947).

Brébuf and His Brethren (1940) and *Towards the Last Spike* (1952) are Pratt's classic contributions to Canadian literature. *Brébuf* traces the harrowing experiences of Jesuit missionaries in New France in the seventeenth century, and their eventual martyrdom at the hands of hostile Iroquois. If this poem acts as an account of the prehistory of the Canadian nation, Pratt's story of the building of the Canadian Pacific Railway over the vast, alien landscape of the country, metaphorically shows the emergence of Canada into nationhood.

Though he was never a particularly experimental or formally innovative poet, Pratt nevertheless encouraged and assisted younger Canadian poets whose aesthetic concerns were often directly opposed to his own more traditional style. The recipient of three Governor General's Awards for poetry and nine honorary degrees, Pratt has left an indelible mark on Canadian poetry.

[IS]

Prévert, Jacques (France, 1900–77) Born in Neuilly-sur-Seine and educated in Paris, Prévert began his career as a writer of screenplays, for which he became widely known. It was not until 1945 that his first volume of poetry, *Paroles* (*Language*), was published and it was an instant best-seller. A collection of poetry that he had been writing for twenty years, its wordplay and intense imagery showed the early influence of the Surrealists. Prévert's work focuses on universal experiences and ordinary, everyday life. Quite lyrical, several of his poems have been set to music. Prévert remained a prolific poet and screenwriter until his death in 1977, a loss to both the literary and theatrical world.

Selected works: *La Pluie et le beau temps* (*Rain and Fine Weather*, 1955); *Histoires* (*Stories*, 1960); *Choses et autres* (*Things and Others*, 1972); *Grand Bal du printemps* (*The Great Dance of Spring*, 1976).

[BRB]

Prynne, J.H. (England, b. 1936) Jeremy Halvard Prynne has been highly influential in bringing American post-modern poetry to England, both as a teacher and mentor to younger poets and through his own poetry. Prynne studied at Jesus College, Cambridge, spent one year at Harvard as a Frank Knox Fellow, and, in 1962, received a fellowship at Gonville and Caius College, Cambridge, where he remains.

Prynne's examination of questions of language, subject position, and power relations closely ally his poetry with postmodern theory. Prynne's second collection, *Kitchen Poems* (1968), is concerned with the gaps and relationships between language and meaning and attempts to create a poetry of the real. Perhaps inspired by this exploration of signification, Prynne explores subjectivity and its role in the construction of meaning in *Day Light Songs* (1969). His work also confronts the impact of materialistic concerns, power relationships, and the physical body on the subject. His later work seems to examine the space between language and the real and attempts to place the reader in this space.

Selected works: *Brass* (1971); *High on Pink Chrome* (1975); *News of Warring Clans* (1977); *Poems* (1983).

[BB]

Przybos, Julian (Poland, 1901–70) Born into a poor peasant family in Gwoznica, Przybos was a foot soldier, a student of Polish philology, a teacher, a farmer, an editor, and an ambassador to Switzerland. Constantly engaged in material and ideological struggles, Przybos supported and practiced political and aesthetic innovation and revolution. A central theoretician of the 'avant-garde', he derived from modern technology and thought a modern poetry of economy and function.

Though Przybos' poetry is roughly divided into two phases – a convulsive, hysteric, explosive, enthusiastic pre-war phase influenced by Italian and Russian futurism and constructivism, and a more didactic, communicative post-war phase – it constantly celebrates energy and potential through texts expanded by sound experiments, multiple meanings, and precise, proliferating metaphors.

Selected works: *Sruby* (*Screws*, 1925); *W glab las* (*In the Depth of the Wood*, 1932); *Poki my zyjemy* (*So Long as We Live*, 1944); *Miejsce na ziemi* (*A Place on Earth*, 1945); *Najmniej slow* (*The Fewest Words*, 1955); *Wiecej o manifest* (*More about the Manifesto*, 1963); *Kwiat nieznany* (*Unknown Flower*, 1968).

[MT]

Pugh, Sheenagh (Wales, b. 1950) Pugh was born in Birmingham and studied modern languages at Bristol. She moved to Wales in 1971 and published her first collection, *Crowded by Shadows*, in 1977. Six more books have followed, including *Earth Studies and Other Voyages* (1983), a *Collected Poems* (1990), and, most recently, *Id's Hospit* (1997). She has utilized a wide range of traditional forms in her work, which is descriptive in character and wide ranging in content (but perhaps most predominantly concerned with issues of travel, particularly her own travels to Iceland). Pugh has also published a book of verse translations, from the French and German, entitled *Prisoners of Transience* (1985).

[BS]

Purdy, Al (Canada, 1918–2000) Considered Canada's most Canadian poet, Purdy was at one and the same time a national poet who traveled widely and repeatedly across the country, and a regional one whose poetry reflects the concerns and landscape of Loyalist Eastern Ontario where he was born and continued to live. The vocation of poetry was one into which Purdy gradually grew. Unlike most Canadian poets of the twentieth century, Purdy had no academic background; he was a part of no school or group, which permitted him a degree of freedom in pursuing the form and themes his poetry would take.

Born in Wooller, Ontario, Purdy's early

life was characterized by intermittent jobs as a laborer, including a stint in the RCAF, in which he served six years. His first book of poetry, *The Enchanted Echo*, appeared in 1944. *Poems for All the Annettes* (1962) was Purdy's breakthrough collection, a highly original body of work that announced the appearance of a major poet. *The Cariboo Horses* (1966) won a Governor General's award, as did his *Collected Poems* (1986). During the 1960s and 1970s, Purdy's international travels served as inspiration for a number of works.

Purdy's reputation as a writer has grown steadily over the decades. He achieved fame only in middle age, and so perhaps it is not surprising that the volume and quality of his poetry has only increased with time. In the 1980s and 1990s, his publications included volumes of letters to CHARLES BUKOWSKI and George Woodcock, a book of collected plays, and his first novel, *Splinter in the Heart* (1990). He remained a vibrant and important voice in Canadian letters until his death in 2000.

[IS]

Q

Quasimodo, Salvatore (Italy, 1901–68) After spending his childhood in Sicily and living in several cities throughout Italy, Quasimodo finally established himself in Milan where, along with intense activity as journalist, editor, and translator, he taught Italian literature at the local Conservatory. From his first collection, *Acque e terre* (*Waters and Lands*, 1930), and followed by *Oboe sommerso* (*Sunken Oboe*, 1932) and *Ed è subito sera* (*And Suddenly it's Evening*, 1942), Quasimodo earned the reputation of being the leading poet of 'Ermetismo', originally a derogatory label used by some critics to describe the apparent obscurity of the generation of poets born after World War I (see UNGARETTI). After the war his poetry encountered strong opposition from younger authors, who interpreted Quasimodo's precious and often convoluted verse as a fossilization of the 'new poetry' into a mannerist repertoire of images. Those doubts seem confirmed today since, despite his success – he was awarded the Nobel Prize in 1959 – there is only a small legacy passed by Quasimodo onto the next generations of poets, especially when compared with authors such as EUGENIO MONTALE or even the younger VITTORIO SERENI. His later collections including *Il falso e il vero verde* (*The False and True Green*, 1954), *La terra impareggiabile* (*The Incomparable Earth*, 1958), or *Dare e avere* (*To Give and To Have*, 1966), although easily falling into rhetoric, witness a sincere desire to find new inspiration in political commitment. Undoubtedly among his best and still unsurpassed achievements are his poetic translations from classical Greek poetry.

[GS]

Queneau, Raymond (France, 1903-76) Although he is more famous for his prose than for his poems, Queneau resists boundaries between genre and desires to 'make of the novel a sort of poem' by incorporating neologisms, deviations in spelling, and onomatopoeia. Taking an experimental, often comical approach to writing, Queneau allied himself with BRETON and the Surrealists from 1924 to 1929. His first poetic work was an autobiography in verse, *Chêne et chien* (*Oak Tree and Dog*, 1937), that derided 'good literature' and 'good sentiments'. Indeed, much of Queneau's poetry is also parody: *Bucoliques* (*Bucolic Poems*, 1947), *L'Instant fatal* (*The Fatal Moment*, 1948), *Petite Cosmogonie portative* (*A Portable Little Cosmology*, 1950), *Sonnets* (*Sonnets*, 1958), *Le Chien à la mandoline* (*The Dog with the Mandoline*, 1965), and *Fendre les flots* (*Cleave through the Seas*, 1969). His *Cent Mille Milliards de poèmes* (*One Hundred Trillion Poems*, 1961) draws on mathematical principles, as does his first novel, *Chiendent* (*Quack Grass*, 1933). Queneau resists the pull of lyricism and beautiful language in his poetry.

In 1960, Queneau co-founded l'Oulipo (Ouvroir de Littérature Potentielle), a group that defined precise rules of composition. He also worked as editor for Gallimard and *Encyclopédie de la Pléiade* (*Encyclopedia of the Pleiade*). Sardonic word play pervades Queneau's writings, which often reflect the influence of James Joyce and Lewis Carroll. Queneau's black humor and derision, however, reveal serious philosophical concern with themes of death and language.

[AD]

R

Raboni, Giovanni (Italy, b. 1932) Born and raised in Milan, Raboni has been relentlessly exploring the expressive potential of poetry within contemporary urban landscape since his early collections. The result is a composite language that draws its inspiration from literary tradition as well as technical and bureaucratic jargons. His recurring themes of social isolation and self-annihilation caused by the alienating dynamics imposed by mass culture are often accompanied by a deep and painful awareness of incumbent death. In addition to editing and translating, he works as a literary critic for various newspapers.

Selected works: *L' insalubrità dell'aria* (*The Insalubrity of the Air*, 1963); *Il più freddo anno di grazia* (*The Coldest Year of Grace*, 1977); *Nel grave sogno* (*In the Heavy Dream*, 1982); *Nel libro della mente* (*In the Book of the Mind*, 1997).

[GS]

Racin, Kočo (Kosta Apostolov Solev; Yugoslavia, 1908–43) Racin was a Macedonian poet, whose poetry, as well as his other literary endeavors, was dedicated to the liberation of the working class and the Macedonian nation. With little formal education, Racin learned his craft through independent study of various writers. As an active member of the Communist Party, he wrote poetry that reflected his revolutionary thoughts and activism. He worked as an editor and copy-editor on Marxist and Communist newspapers and journals in Serbia and Macedonia. He was killed in combat during World War II.

Racin's early poetry is primarily lyrical, intimate, and sensual. These poems are modernist, often Expressionist in form. After 1928, his poetry became socially and politically engaged, advocating total revolution and addressing contemporary issues (for example, the Spanish Civil War). He eventually completely departed from expressionism, and espoused ideas influenced by Maxim Gorky's views of socialist literature.

Selected works: *Beli mugri* (*White Dawns*, 1939); *Pesme* (*Poems*, 1952); *Stihovi i proza* (*Verse and Prose*, 1954).

[DJ]

Radnóti, Miklós (Hungary, 1909–44) One of the most frequently translated of the Hungarian poets, and certainly one whose life elicits sympathy from any reader, Radnóti was a rising star in the Budapest literary scene until the advent of World War II. Born of Jewish parents, Radnóti was originally educated at a trade school but eventually matriculated into the University of Szeged, graduating in 1934. By that time he had already published two volumes of verse and separated himself from the dominant, traditionalist literary scene centered on *Nyugat* (*West*), the journal which had published ADY, JÓZSEF, and ILLYÉS, among others. Working as a translator during the 1930s, Radnóti published six volumes of poetry, ranging from the love poems he wrote to his wife Margit in *Újhold* (*New Moon*, 1935) to the stark meditations on pre-World War II Hungary and Europe in *Járkálj csak, halálraítélt!* (*Walk On, Condemned!*, 1936). Of course, the nascent political catastrophes that Radnóti foresaw came to pass with the advent of Fascism, Nazism, and the war. From 1940 to his death in 1944, Radnóti worked in Axis labor camps, shifted about from Hungary to Yugoslavia and back. At the end of one such forced march the workers were summarily executed; Radnóti's body was found in a mass grave two years later by his widow, a parcel of poems still in his pocket.

Selected works: *Pogány köszöntö* (*Pagan Salute*, 1930); *Újmódi pásztorok éneke* (*Song of the Modern Shepherds*, 1931); *Lábadozó szél* (*Convalescent Wind*, 1933); *Meredek út* (*Steep Road*, 1938); *Naptár* (*Calendar*, 1942); *Tajtékos ég* (*Clouded Sky*, 1946).

[MW]

Raičković, Stevan (Yugoslavia, b. 1928) One of the major contemporary Serbian poets, Belgrade resident Raičković studied literature at the university there. He came to prominence soon after publishing his early work in 1945, and has since received numerous literary awards. He also writes children's poetry, fiction, and nonfiction; he is a prominent translator from Russian.

Raičković employs both traditional and modernist forms, though in his own idiosyncratic style. Most of his poetry is lyrical, confessional, occasionally written in the form of comments to a beloved or a friend. His themes include urban landscapes (the suburbs, city streets, pubs, and parks) and nature with its powerful, but indifferent, elements (rivers, wind, fire, the sun). Some of his poems are reflexive examinations of the relationship between the poet and poetry.

Selected works: *Detinjstvo* (*Childhood*, 1950); *Kasno leto* (*Late Summer*, 1958); *Prolazi rekom lada* (*A Boat Passing on the River*, 1967); *Zapisi o crnom Vladimiru* (*Notes About Dark Vladimir*, 1971); *Slučajni memoari* (*Accidental Memoirs*, 1978); *Svet oko mene* (*The World around Me*, 1988); *Stihovi iz dnevnika* (*Verses from the Diary*, 1990).

[DJ]

Raine, Craig (England, b. 1944) Raine is known particularly for his unique perspective, which he uses to present the ordinary in an unusual way through his writing. He first demonstrated this technique, looking through alien eyes in *A Martian Sends a Postcard Home* (1979), which is a description of Earth from an alien viewpoint. This approach earned Raine, as well as his followers, particularly CHRISTOPHER REID, membership of the 'Martian school' of poets, as it was termed by JAMES FENTON. This 'defamiliarization' figured prominently in English poetry of the late 1970s and early 1980s and distinctly characterizes Raine's work.

Especially early on, as in *The Onion, Memory* (1978), Raine's writing was criticized for a detached inhumanity. However, *Rich* (1984), a prose memoir with luxury as its subject and containing autobiographical family material, shows Raine's developing maturity as a writer. It is a quieter piece, yet one that remains committed to Raine's familiar uses of metaphor and simile. In *History: the Home Movie* (1994), a novel in verse that took ten years to create, Raine uses a hand-held movie camera, as he did his earlier Martian, to reveal information and let the story unfold.

Raine was poetry editor at Faber and Faber in 1981–91, and won the Cholmondeley Poetry Award in 1983. He lectures at Oxford.

[JS]

Raine, Kathleen (England, b. 1908) Raine was born in London and first educated at Miss Hutchinson's School in Bavington.

She attended Girton College, Cambridge, where she received an M.A. in natural sciences in 1929 and later became a research fellow (1955–61). She married twice, first Hugh Sykes Davies and later Charles Madge, with whom she had two children.

Raine is a prolific and influential writer, both as poet and critic. She has been deemed a romantic lyricist whose writing is permeated with a sense of the ethereal. Her poetry was influenced by the literary tradition of Plato, YEATS, and especially Blake, for whom she felt a close affinity and on whom she wrote extensively. Her monumental recontextualization of his thought was a labor of love, taking her twenty years to complete. Additionally, Raine wrote her autobiography, originally published in three volumes but later united into one complete text.

Raine is also founder of the Temenos Academy of Integral Studies (1990), a program committed to studying traditional thought, art, and literature through lectures and seminars, and served as editor of the Temenos bi-annual review. Raine's numerous other distinctions include: Harriet Monroe Memorial Prize (1952); Arts Council Award (1953); Oscar Blumenthal Prize (1961); Andrew Mellon lecturer (1962); Cholmondeley Award (1970); W. H. Smith Literary Award (1972); D. Litt. Leicester (1974), Durham (1979), Caen (1987); Foreign Book Prize for non-fiction (France, 1979); Queen's Gold Medal for Poetry (1992); Officier, Ordre des Arts et des Lettres (France, 1995); Royal Society of Literature Fellow.

Selected works: *Stone and Flower* (1943); *Selected Poems* (1952); *Defending Ancient Springs* (1967); *The Lost Country* (1971); *The Oval Portrait* (1977); *The Oracle in the Heart* (1980); *Autobiographies* (1992).

[JS]

Rakosi, Carl (United States, b. 1903) Rakosi, who legally changed his name to Callman Rawley but publishes under his given name, was born in Berlin, Germany in November 1903. In 1910 his family emigrated to the United States.

Known primarily for his connections with the Objectivists GEORGE OPPEN, LOUIS ZUKOFSKY, and others, Rakosi attended the University of Wisconsin where he received his B.A. (1924) and M.A. (1926). In 1940 he received a Master of Social Work from the University of Pennsylvania. After publishing *Two Poems* (1933) and *Selected Poems* (1941) Rakosi, like Oppen, ceased writing poetry because he felt that it was incongruent with the desperation of daily life in the aftermath of the Depression and World War II. For decades he focused instead on his career as a psychiatric social worker.

In 1965 Rakosi was prompted to write again, and since then he has published eleven books of poetry and prose. His chiseled and spare poems, which are by turns plain spoken, wittily ironic, meditative, and lyrical, address themselves with an attentive eye and ear to the empirical particulars of our experience. Like the other Objectivists, Rakosi prizes clarity, precision, and honesty in verse, opposes all pretense and showy ornamentation, and grapples with how the mind perceives and understands the physical world.

[AE/DC]

Ralin, Radoy (Dimitur Stefanov Stoyanov; Bulgaria, b. 1923) Born in Sliven and educated at the University of Sofia, Ralin is a national legend, a symbol of resistance against any form of oppression. A Communist, member of the anti-Fascist underground (1942), and a volunteer during World War II (1944–45), Ralin became increasingly disillusioned as he witnessed the Communist Party consolidate its grip on power. He worked as a journalist and editor for various newspapers and literary publishing houses and as a screen writer for the Bulgarian Cinematography, but was frequently fired because of his witty criticism of life in socialist Bulgaria. In 1968, his support for the Prague Spring and his book of epigrams *Lyuti chushki*

(*Hot Peppers*), the entire printing of which was destroyed, led to Ralin's house arrest and exile to the city of Silistra. An immensely popular dissident, he participated in the demise of the totalitarian regime in 1989.

Ralin is an interesting lyrical poet whose deliberately low-key works refract tensions and passions concealed within the experience of ordinary urban life. His national and international reputation, however, rests on his sparkling, witty, and formally innovative satirical verse and prose.

Selected works: *Voynishka tetradka* (*Soldier's Notebook*, 1955); *Strogo poveritelno* (*Top Secret*, 1956); *Nepredvideni chuvstva* (*Unforeseen Feelings*, 1959); *Khalosni patroni* (*Blanks*, 1962); *Molya, zapovyadayte!* (*Please Help Yourselves!*, 1966); *Epigrami v ramki* (*Epigrams in Frames*, 1983); *Koilo-galena treva* (*Feather Grass – Caressed Grass*, 1989).

[CG/LPG]

Ramanujan, A.K. (India, 1929–93) One of India's most influential poets, Attipat Krishnaswami Ramanujan wrote his verse in Kannada and in English, translated classic Tamil and Kannada works into English, and translated from English into Kannada. Working as a trilingual artist, Ramanujan's presence is wide and deep in a diverse Indian society. Being rooted in such a heritage has an obvious effect; the author must simultaneously address a breadth of personal and national concerns.

Born into a Srivaishnava Brahmin family in Mysore, Ramanujan attended the local Maharaja's College and received his B.A. and M.A. in English literature. It was during this period that he started writing poetry in both Kannada and English. In 1958–59 he was in Poona after obtaining a fellowship in linguistics at Deccan College. A Fulbright Fellowship followed, sending him to Indiana University; he received his doctorate in 1963. For the rest of his academic career, Ramanujan was a professor at the University of Chicago.

Proverbs, Ramanujan's first collection, was written in Kannada and published in 1955. It was not until *The Striders* (1966), which became a Poetry Book Society Recommendation, that he released a volume of his work in English. He returned to English poetry with *Relations* (1972) and *Second Sight* (1986).

Along with his work as a poet, Ramanujan was renowned for the translations he made, often of classic text in the Tamil and Kannada traditions. One of his Kannada translations, a book of devotions entitled *Speaking of Siva*, was nominated for the 1974 National Book Award in the United States. Ramanujan's final work, published posthumously under the title *Flowering Tree and Other Oral Tales from India* (1997), is another collection of Kannada translations, this time of folktales. For Ramanujan, the translation process was not just changing languages. He would interpret the work to meld with the modern world, finding ways to give ancient techniques in writing a similar result for today's reader.

Key to Ramanujan's writing is his connection with India. Though most of his academic career was spent in the United States, he never detached himself from his native land, as can be seen throughout his writing. However, Ramanujan did break from his religious upbringing. He rejected his family's religion and the traditions associated with it, favoring instead many points of Buddhism, especially meditation. Another break from Hinduism occurred when he married a Christian woman. This distancing allowed Ramanujan not only to be devoted to the customs of India, but also to be critical of what he felt needed to change.

[MP]

Ranasinghe, Anne (Sri Lanka, b. 1926) Born Anneliese Katz in Essen, Germany, Jewish poet Anne Ranasinghe was sent to England at the age of 13 without her parents, who were subsequently murdered. There, she lived with relatives and was training to be a nurse when she met her Sri Lankan husband. She became a Sri Lankan citizen in 1956 and today is esteemed as one of the foremost poets from that country writing in English. Her work has been translated into eight languages. She was an Executive Secretary for Amnesty International South Asia Publication Service for fifteen years.

Ranasinghe's first book of poetry, *And the Sun that Sucks the Earth to Dry*, was published in 1971 and since then she has written *Against Eternity and Darkness* (1985); *Not Even Shadows* (1991); *At What Dark Point* (1991); *Desire and Other Short Stories* (1994); and *Mascot and Symbol* (1997). The violent persecution of the Holocaust is a common theme in Ranasinghe's work and she believes that patriotism is dangerous. Her poetry expresses a bleak realism.

[JS]

Ransom, John Crowe (United States, 1888–1974) Ransom was born in Pulaski, Tennessee and was educated at Vanderbilt University and Christ Church College, Oxford, where he was a Rhodes Scholar. He won the Bollingen Prize for Poetry (1951), and the National Book Award for *Selected Poems* (1964).

While on the faculty of Vanderbilt, in 1914–37, Ransom was a founding member of the Fugitives, a leader in the Agrarian movement, and a progenitor of the New Criticism.

His significance in American poetry stems more from his status as an influential critic (*The New Criticism*, 1941) than from his three volumes of determinedly archaic formal verse. In 1939 he founded the *Kenyon Review*, which he edited until 1959 and with which he was associated until his death.

[HE]

Ravikovitch, Dahlia (Israel, b. 1936) Ravikovitch was born in Ramat Gan, Israel. After graduating from the Hebrew University in Jerusalem, she worked as a journalist and a high-school teacher, and published poetry, children's books, translations of poetry and prose, and short stories. Ravikovitch is considered one of Israel's leading poets. A recipient of the Bialik Prize for Literature, she writes personal poetry which gives expression to the great despair inherent in human existence; to the pain experienced by human beings whose creativity and eroticism are suppressed; to madness, hallucination, and disorientation. She frequently writes in a meticulously formal style which creates great tension between content and form. Her poem 'Clockwork Doll' is often presented as a powerful voice decrying the precarious existence of dehumanized women. Ravikovitch's first volume, *The Love of an Orange*, appeared in 1959, and her most recent book, *Half an Hour before the Monsoon*, in 1998. Her collection of stories, *Death in the Family*, appeared in 1977. Two translated volumes of poetry appeared in English, *Dress of Fire* (1978) and *The Window* (1989).

[ER]

Raworth, Tom (England, b. 1938) Thomas Moore Raworth is a prolific writer both of novels and of poetry, the first collection of which was *Weapon Man* (1965). Since 1969, Raworth has been writer-in-residence at numerous United Kingdom and American universities.

Raworth is known for his independent form, which involves an acute attention to detail, a lack of narration, and a continuing exploration of discontinuous language. His poetry has been compared both to the French Surrealists and to the work of JOHN ASHBERY, and is among the most difficult of any published by contemporary English poets.

In *The Relation Ship* (1966), which earned him the Alice Hunt Bartlett Award, Raworth's poems condense incidents of daily life to rapid accumulations of imagery. Raworth published *Writing* (1982), which is composed of approximately 2,500 short lines that can be read forward or backward.

[LK]

Redgrove, Peter (England, b. 1932) A poet, novelist, essayist, and short story writer, Redgrove was born in Kingston, Surrey, and educated at Queens' College, Cambridge, where he studied natural science and where he also met TED HUGHES, who became a lifelong friend. From 1954 to 1961, Redgrove was a scientific journalist and editor. He then became a visiting poet at the State University of New York (1961–62), after which he was the Gregory Fellow in Poetry at Leeds University. He finally settled as poet-in-residence at Falmouth School of Art in Cornwall (1966–83). Since that time, he has mostly supported himself by his writing alone. During the time he was at Falmouth, he divorced his first wife and met poet Penelope Shuttle, with whom he collaborated on several works and whom he later married.

In the first four years of publishing his works, Redgrove produced three volumes of poetry. Since that time, he has not slowed in his output. His early work is often criticized for over-use of images and verbal wordplay. Throughout his poetic career, Redgrove has dealt mainly with reconciling the human conscience with the natural world, clearly influenced by his studies in natural sciences. Though he began writing in accordance with Imagism, he has since moved to more personal exploration and then to Surrealism. Redgrove's work at times has been met with mixed, and sometimes quite negative, criticism, as is to be expected from such a prolific writer. He has earned many awards for his work, however, including a Fulbright Fellowship (1961), several Arts Council grants, the Cholmondeley Award (1985), and election as a Fellow of the Royal Society of Literature (1982).

Selected works: *The Collector and Other Poems* (1960); *The Force and Other Poems* (1966); *Dr Faust's Sea-Spiral Spirit and Other Poems* (1972); *The Weddings at Nether Powers and Other Poems* (1979); *The Moon Disposes: Poems 1954–87* (1987).

[BRB]

Reed, Henry (England, 1914–86) Born in Birmingham, Reed earned a B.A. from the university there (1934) and later took an M.A. (1937). While there he met LOUIS MACNEICE, who was an assistant lecturer in Classics and who had a great impact on Reed. After university, he spent most of his time writing, working on a biography of THOMAS HARDY and contributing poems to literary journals. In 1941 he served in the Royal Army Ordnance Corps for a year, and then transferred to the Foreign Office until 1945.

Much of Reed's poetry was concerned with the events leading up to and during World War II. His collection, *A Map of Verona* (1946), revealed a mastery of blank verse that was instantly popular. He published his second and final collection, *Lessons of War*, in 1970, containing five poems, three of which were in his previous work. Aside from his poetry, Reed was immensely successful in writing radio scripts and translating from Italian.

[BRB]

Reeves, Gareth (England, b. 1947) Reeves earned his B.A. at Trinity College, Oxford, in 1968. The following year, he published his first book of poems, *Pilgrims*. Reeves' life and poetry then changed when he moved to California for studies at Stanford University in 1970–75.

Reeves was a Wallace Stegner fellow while at Stanford, and he earned his Ph.D. there in 1981. While in America, Reeves' poetry continued to focus on his native country, but when he returned to England, his focus frequently became the experiences he had in California.

In 1984, Reeves published his second book of poetry, *Real Stories*, which explores physical landscapes, as well as the landscape of memory. Reeves, who published *Listening In* in 1993, is the founder and co-editor of *Poetry Durham*, and he is a frequent contributor of articles and poems to a wide variety of magazines and journals.

[LK]

Reeves, James (John Morris Reeves; England, 1909–78) Now better remembered for his children's verse and his many years spent as an editor and anthologist, Reeves was nonetheless a vital voice in pre- and post-war British poetry. Influenced by ROBERT GRAVES, whose press published his first volume, *The Natural Need* (1936), Reeves offered an alternative private voice to the public, portentous verse of AUDEN and the Oxford Poets. A self-described 'quiet' poet, Reeves wrote often ironic lyrics which reflected upon his own perceptions rather than the social fabric as a whole.

Selected works: *The Imprisoned Sea* (1949); *The Password* (1952); *The Talking Skull* (1958); *Collected Poems: 1929–59* (1960); *Selected Poems* (1967); *Subsong* (1969).

[MW]

Reid, Christopher (England, b. 1949) Reid was born in Hong Kong and attended Exeter College, Oxford. He has held various types of employment – from librarian to actor – none of which appears in his poetry. This indicates his resistance to the autobiographical in his work, an aversion which spills over into his criticism of poets who do use their own lives in their writing.

Reid's work is closely associated with the poetry of CRAIG RAINE, with whom he shared the Prudence Farmer Award for poetry in 1978 and 1980. Reid is part of the so-called 'Martian' movement, 'originated' by Raine, which is characterized by its rich use of simile and metaphor to open up to the reader new avenues for perception. Reid's work uses metaphor to make commonplace objects alien and is notable for the playful way in which he approaches his subjects.

Selected works: *Arcadia* (1979); *Katarina Brac* (1985); *Expanded Universes* (1996).

[BB]

Rekola, Mirkka Elina (Finland, b. 1931) Rekola, a poet and critic, studied literature at the University of Helsinki at the time when Anglo-Saxon New Criticism was the prevailing theoretical school of thought. Her career as a poet began at the age of twenty-three. In her lyricism she has progressed from expressing dualism's limits and the poetic persona's sense of alienation toward open experience of the actual and the genuine, as well as toward broad, intelligent mysticism. Eastern classicism has had a fertile effect on her poetic viewpoint and imagination, particularly in her aphoristic poetry.

Among more than twenty published collections the following should receive special mention as representative of Finnish Modernism, specifically representative of poetic language that strives to join concrete images and abstract ideas: *Vedessä palaa* (*Water on Fire*, 1954), *Anna päivää olla kaikki* (*Let Day be All*, 1968), *Kuutamourakka* (*Mooncontract*, 1981), and *Runot 1954–1978* (*Poems, 1954–1978*) as well as a collection of aphorisms, *Tuoreessa muistissa kevät* (*In Fresh Memory, Spring*, 1987). Rekola is the recipient of three City of Tampere Prizes for Literature (1958, 1962, 1965) and four State Awards for Literature (1966, 1969, 1973, 1982).

[SP]

Revard, Carter (United States, b. 1931) Born in Pawhuska, Oklahoma, Revard is part Osage Indian on his father's side. He grew up among Osage and Ponca relatives and was given an Osage name, Nompehwathe, or Fear Inspiring. He often refers to Osage traditions, including naming ceremonies, in his poetry.

Revard's poems have been published in a dozen anthologies and collected in three volumes. His work is as likely to reflect his Native heritage as not. A specialist in medieval literature, Revard earned degrees from the University of Tulsa, Oxford University where he was a Rhodes Scholar, and Yale University. He is a professor at Washington University in St Louis, Missouri.

Selected works: *My Right Hand Don't Leave Me no More* (1970); *Nonymosity* (1980); *Ponca War Dancers* (1980).

[HEE]

Reverdy, Pierre (France, 1889–1960) Born at Narbonne into a family of sculptors and carvers noted for their work on religious subjects, Reverdy went to Paris in 1910 to pursue his dream of becoming a writer. He lived at the Bateau Lavoir and counted GUILLAUME APOLLINAIRE, Pablo Picasso, Georges Braque, and Juan Gris among his friends. Like the Apollinaire of 'Zone' (1913), BLAISE CENDRARS, and MAX JACOB, he is often considered a 'Cubist' poet. Reverdy edited the journal *Nord–Sud* and had a profound influence on the Surrealists. In *Le Gant de crin* (*The Horsehair Glove*, 1927), Reverdy proclaimed that poetic images were pure creations of the spirit. He also compared the poet with an oven: the senses merely provided combustible materials to be changed into the flames of poetry. In such collections as *La Lucarne ovale* (*The Attic Window*, 1916), *La Guitare endormie* (*The Sleeping Guitar*, 1919), *Epaves du ciel* (*Wreckage of Heaven*, 1924), and *Flaques de verre* (*Pools of Glass*, 1929), the austerity and intense solitude of Reverdy's verse is coupled with a yearning for an absolute reality beyond the realm of the senses. The result is often an eerie sense of metaphysical suspense. Beginning in 1926, Reverdy led a life of solitary contemplation (while continuing to write) near the abbey of Solesmes.

Selected works: *La Plupart du temps: Poèmes 1915–1922* (*Most of the Time: Poems 1915–1922*, 1945); *Main-d'oeuvre* (*Handiwork*, 1949).

[ML]

Rexroth, Kenneth (United States, 1905–82) Eclectic and broad in his scope, Rexroth's range and interests are far reaching and include Christian mysticism and Eastern philosophy. Rexroth's poetry seeks out the hints of the spiritual and the metaphysical within the human world; he is one of the most prominent religious American poets of the twentieth century.

Born on December 22, 1905, Rexroth was largely self educated, although he briefly attended the Chicago Art Institute and the Art Students League in New York City. Even in his teens, Rexroth was a prolific painter and writer who blended elements of Modernism with labor politics, but his poetry came to maturity in the 1940s and 1950s in San Francisco when he published *The Phoenix and the Tortoise* (1944) and *The Signature of All Things* (1950). Rexroth also played a key role in the Beat movement, which was centered in San Francisco.

In addition to his twenty-four works of poetry, Rexroth published numerous translations of Japanese and Chinese texts, which deeply influenced his own sensibilities.

[DC]

Reznikoff, Charles (United States, 1894–1976) Reznikoff was born in Brooklyn, New York. He studied journalism for a year, but ended up earning a degree in law at New York University. A first generation American, Reznikoff found inspiration in the urban immigrant experience. Much of his work emerged from his observations of everyday life in urban ethnic neighborhoods.

His preference for objective statement over introspective rumination situates Reznikoff in the Objectivist movement. Fellow Objectivist poets include LOUIS ZUKOFSKY, GEORGE OPPEN, and CARL RAKOSI.

Reznikoff's most celebrated works are his two longest ones, *Testimony* (1965) and *Holocaust* (1975). He employed similar technique in writing both, editing and ordering verbatim quotes from legal testimonies as a means of creating an objective narrative. The most complete collection of his works is *1918–1975: The Complete Poems of Charles Reznikoff* (1989).

[CP]

Rich, Adrienne (United States, b. 1929) In one of the most famous examples of misapprehension in twentieth-century U.S. literature, W.H. AUDEN lauded Adrienne Rich's first book of poetry, *A Change of World*, selected by him for the Yale Younger Poets Prize, in the following terms: 'The poems . . . are neatly and modestly dressed, speak quietly but do not mumble, respect their elders but are not cowed by them, and do not tell fibs . . . '. Rich has herself spoken of the esteem in which she held her poetic elders of the largely white, male canon at the time, and if she could not see what was ahead it is unfair to suggest that Auden should have; still, his words provide an unwitting window into the sources of a career that has formed and continues to form a remarkable trajectory of possibility and transformation.

Rich's first two collections, *A Change of World* (1951) and *The Diamond Cutters and Other Poems* (1955), contained tightly controlled formal poems notable for their technical virtuosity and intimations of what was to come. A period of emotional desperation in the late 1950s and early 1960s culminated in the breakthrough volume *Snapshots of a Daughter-in-Law* (1963), in which a critical deployment of canonical texts and probing focus on female experience depart strikingly from her earlier work.

Necessities of Life (1966) commenced an exploration of the uses and limits of dialogue that would ultimately carry Rich's work into a rhetorical dimension. *Leaflets* (1969) continued the formal experimentation begun with *Snapshots of a Daughter-in-Law* and probed the boundary between female and male forces of love and egoism, respectively – a dichotomy that Rich later rejected.

With *The Will to Change* (1971), Rich finally closed the gap between 'the woman in the poem and the woman writing the poem'. The rhetorical element deepens in this and subsequent volumes: *Diving into the Wreck* (1973) winner of the National Book Award, which Rich shared with AUDRE LORD 'in the name of all women', *The Dream of a Common Language* (1978), and *A Wild Patience Has Taken Me This Far* (1981). These collections chart Rich's attempts to redefine women's relationship with language and the canon, and to ground poetry in a broader cultural matrix. In *Your Native Land, Your Life* (1986) and *Time's Power* (1989), she began an examination of aspects of her relationship with her Jewish heritage and of the course of her own work that would be continued in *An Atlas of the Difficult World* (1991). The title poem of this collection also continues Rich's engagement of the canon, specifically with a tradition represented by Whitman and CRANE. *The Dark Fields of the Republic* (1995) broods on personal and communal experience and responsibility. The sense of foreboding in its poems was further expressed in Rich's refusal of a 1997 National Medal for the Arts on the grounds that 'the very meaning of art . . . is incompatible with the cynical politics of this [Clinton] administration'.

Rich is also an important essayist, having published several collections of critical essays on poetry and cultural institutions, including the widely read and taught 'When We Dead Awaken: Writing as Re-Vision'.

[JT]

Rickword, Edgell (England, 1898–1982) Rickword, whose poetic career spanned only about a decade, is perhaps best known as a critic and the editor of *Left Review* and *Our Time*. Rickword's poetry was inspired and influenced by the work of fellow World War I poet SIEGFRIED SASSOON. Both use direct language and visual harshness in their war poetry, though

Rickword's work is characterized by the rejection of the sentimental in favor of French Symbolisme. In the 1930s Rickword joined the Communist Party, founded the *Left Review* and *Our Time*, and virtually stopped writing poetry, though 'To the Wife of any Non-interventionist Statesman' (1938) was an especially important political poem of the time and was translated into many languages.

Selected works: *Behind the Eyes* (1921); *Invocations to Angels* (1928); *Twittinopan, and Some Others* (1931).

[BB]

Riding, Laura (United States, 1901–91) During her lifetime, Laura Jackson Riding published poetry, novels, essays, short stories, and studies of linguistics under a number of names: Laura Riding Gottschalk, Madeleine Vera, Laura Riding, and Laura Riding Jackson.

Born on January 16, 1901 in New York City, Riding gained acclaim during the 1920s through her affiliation with the 'Fugitives', a group whose members included JOHN CROWE RANSOM and ROBERT PENN WARREN. Late in the 1920s Riding lived with ROBERT GRAVES, with whom she started a literary press.

Riding published thirteen works of poetry, including *Collected Poems* (1938). The principle that the poem must not be a shadow of truth informed all of Riding's poetry and eventually prompted her abandonment of the art, although she continued to write novels, short stories, and essays as well as to translate the works of others. Upon her death from cardiac arrest on September 2, 1991 Riding had published over forty books.

Many consider Riding to be one of the most important American woman poets of the twentieth century, although her status as a 'major' poet remains debatable.

[DC]

Ridler, Anne (England, b. 1912) Barbara Anne Ridler was born in London and educated at Downe House School, in Italy, and at King's College London, where she took a diploma in journalism in 1932. She worked in the editorial department at Faber & Faber, as assistant to T. S. ELIOT and also as a freelance reader.

A poet concerned with the metaphysical, and often writing about family love, she shows the influence of Eliot and AUDEN. She is a translator of Italian opera libretti, a playwright, and her work as an editor includes *The Faber Book of Modern Verse* (1951) and the poetry of James Thomson (1963) and Thomas Traherne (1966).

Selected works: *Poems* (1939); *The Nine Bright Shiners* (1943); *A Matter of Life and Death* (1959); *Some Time After* (1972).

[LKMF]

Rifbjerg, Klaus (Denmark, b. 1931) A versatile writer of poetry, short stories, novels, and drama, Rifbjerg shaped the Modernist, international bent of post-World War II Danish poetry. *Under vejr med mig selv* (*Getting Wind of Myself*, 1956) demonstrated his willingness to challenge literary traditions. As suggested by the book's subtitle, 'a premature autobiography', Rifbjerg wrote with self-assured wit and playfulness. The sarcastic social criticism became more pronounced in his next collection, *Efterkrig* (*Postwar*, 1957), an insight into the bourgeoisie of mid-century Copenhagen. After this volume Rifbjerg started experimenting with dissonance and syntactic fragmentation, a stream of consciousness in verse. In 1959 he took over editorship of BJØRNVIG's *Heretica*, together with Villy Sörensen (b. 1929), and used it to promote the work of BECKETT, Robbe-Grillet, and other contemporary avant-garde writers. Rifbjerg's aggressive style came to a climax with *Fådrelandssange* (*Patriotic Songs*, 1967), as the poet continued to address the ruptures and unreality of modern life.

[YB]

Riis, Annie (Norway, b. 1927) After working as a homemaker and a French teacher for twenty years, Riis decided to attend Oslo University. There she studied French, literature, and history. Encouraged by an enthusiastic teacher, she published her first collection of poetry, *Satura*, in 1975 at the age of forty-eight. Since then Riis has been a prolific author not only of poetry but also of novels and children's literature including *Alice i eventyrland* (1990), a Norwegian translation of *Alice in Wonderland*. She often writes short, satiric verse with a feminist viewpoint.

Selected works: *Vet du Hva?* (*Do You Know What?*, 1976); *Fridafrank* (1991); *Satirens tid* (*Age of the Satire*, 1994); *Ravlys* (*Amber Light*, 1998).

[AC]

Rilke, Rainer Maria (Austria, 1875–1926) Born René Karl Wilhelm Johann Josef Rilke, Rainer Maria Rilke is the equal of ELIOT and YEATS as a major Modernist poet. He cultivated a lifestyle in the aestheticist tradition of the dandy, travelling much, never having a real home, and always – successfully – depending on 'often female' patrons. The outsider's lifestyle enabled him to relate to the alienation typical of his times, though not to its social source. Rilke's themes and tones were determined by his answers to the Modernist quest toward a new meaningful totality of life, which he saw in a fragile harmony between the world of tangible objects and the world of the unspeakable.

In 1899 and 1900 Rilke traveled to Russia, experiences that informed, after an insignificant early phase, his second phase of poetry. The three parts of the *Hour Book* (1899, 1901, 1903), express subjective mysticism beyond traditional religiousness voiced through the persona of a fictitious Russian monk.

Rilke married the painter Clara Westhoff in 1901, but they separated in 1902. Rilke moved to Paris, traveled, and for several months in 1905 and 1906 worked as a secretary for French sculptor Auguste Rodin. The attempt to apply Rodin's artistic method to poetry effected a triumphant first climax of Rilke's career in *New Poems* (1907 and 1908) with the innovative object poem that transforms a simple thing into the manifestation of an abstract idea.

Seeking eternal truths, Rilke seemed to feel that the triumph of the object poems did not present an answer to alienation because both presuppose objectification. His next creative phase was defined by doubts, expressed in *The Notebooks of Malte Laurids Brigge* (1910). With this seminal work about alienated life in the big city, Rilke created the genre of the lyrical novel and the first truly modern German, if not European, novel. The same year, a guest at Duino Palace, he began working on his *Duino Elegies*, but he suffered writer's block.

It was not until about 1921 that Rilke's creative energy erupted again. At Muzot Palace in 1922, he finished the *Duino Elegies* (1923) and its companion volume, *Sonnets to Orpheus* (1923). These high Modernist poems represent Rilke's ultimate achievement both in theme and tone. In the *Elegies*, Rilke transcended the human condition by using lyrical poetry itself as a means to ensure meaning by way of a new mythology: 'Nowhere can world exist but within'. The necessary transformation was to be achieved by acknowledging suffering (and joy) in song. The poet-singer was established as a prophet, which in turn became the main theme of the *Sonnets*.

Rilke probably believed that he had found the answers to his quest for eternal truths; however, he continued to write probing yet relaxed poems until his death from complications caused by leukemia.

[IRS]

Ríos, Alberto (United States, b. 1952) Ríos was born in Nogales, Arizona, and educated at the University of Arizona. He teaches at Arizona State University, in Tempe.

The son of a Mexican-American father and an English mother, Ríos grew up in a border town, living in two cultures. Drawing on Hispanic oral traditions, Ríos' poetry does much of the same, and in it magical realism figures prominently. Simultaneously, it draws on the reading in English of Ríos' schooldays – comic books, science fiction, the *World Book Encyclopedia*. Ríos' view is both communal and intimate, presenting the quiddities of individuals within complex social relations.

Selected works: *Whispering to Fool the Wind* (1982); *Five Indiscretions* (1985); *The Lime Orchard Woman* (1988); *Teodoro Luna's Two Kisses* (1990).

[JT]

Risset, Jacqueline (France, b. 1936) Risset was born in Besançon and currently lives in Rome, where she teaches French literature at the University of Rome. One of the most widely known poets in a renaissance of French women poets who emerged between 1970 and the early 1990s, Risset is known as part of the 'écriture feminine' movement.

Risset writes frequently on love, concentrating on the individual moments that create life's various 'beginnings'. Her work employs minimal narrative, focusing instead on rhythm; she often cites music as the earliest influence in her poetry. As a critic, she has also written extensively on Dante.

Selected works: *Jeu* (*Game*, 1971); *La Traduction Commence* (*The Translation Begins*, 1978); *Sept Passages de la Vie d'une Femme* (*Seven Passages from the Life of a Woman*, 1985); *L'Amour de Loin* (*Distant Love*,1988); *Petits Elements de Physique Amoureuse* (*Small Elements of a Passionate Physique*, 1991).

[SG]

Ritsos, Yannis (Greece, 1909–90) Born in Monemvasia on May 1, a symbolic day for the poet, Ritsos spent his troubled life in sanitariums, suffering from tuberculosis, or in prison or political exile, persecuted for his Communist beliefs. Undoubtedly the most prolific of Greek poets, he published twenty-three books of poetry, three volumes of *Collected Poems* (1961–64), two plays, a poem for dance, and a number of translations of primarily East European poetry. He won the Lenin Prize for poetry in 1977, the Greek State Award in 1956, and was nominated for a Nobel Prize. His first two collections *Trakter* (1934) and *Epitaphios* (1936), reveal a fiery and militant temperament which was later subdued into a more personal, humanitarian mode devoid of anger and partisanship. Though his later poetry sought recourse in mythological images and allusion, his works remained sensitive and relevant to contemporary realities. In *Romiosini* (1966), he welds the peasant figures of World War II resistance fighters with austere images of the landscape in which they live, fight, and die, evoking in the process the continuous resurrection of past heroic figures who function as bastions of Greek freedom and integrity throughout the ages. His eloquent and inspiring readings of his poetry, along with the musical renditions by Mikis Theodorakis, brought his work to the masses and it remains a symbol of Greek resistance to internal oppression and foreign domination.

Selected works: *Spring Symphony* (1938); *Moonlight Sonata* (1956); *Testimonies* (1963); *12 Poems for Cavafy* (1963); *Eighteen Little Songs of the Bitter Motherland* (1974).

[GSY]

Roberts, Lynette (Wales, 1909–95) Roberts was born in Argentina, of Welsh-Australian parents. After finishing her education at an English boarding school she lived on the fringes of literary London before marrying the writer/editor, Keidrych Rhys, and moving with him to Llanybri, Carmarthenshire. There she wrote most of her published poetry. Her work –

syntactically compressed, allusive, visual – was admired by T.S. ELIOT, who published her *Poems* (1944) and *Gods with Stainless Ears* (1951). In 1956 Roberts gave up poetry and became a Jehovah's Witness. Apart from the much anthologized 'Poem from Llanybri', Roberts has been overshadowed by her male Anglo-Welsh contemporaries – including DYLAN THOMAS, DAVID JONES, and GLYN JONES – but recently she has received greater attention. A 1983 special issue of *Poetry Wales* on Roberts contains previously unpublished works, as well as a critical reappraisal.

[BS]

Robinson, E. A. (United States, 1869–1935) Few careers illustrate the fickleness of fame as does that of Edwin Arlington Robinson. Early in his career he was given a sinecure by President Theodore Roosevelt. During his lifetime he won three Pulitzer Prizes, the last for a single poem of over forty thousand words, which became a Book-of-the-Month selection and out-sold most best-selling novels. His work was included in all the major anthologies. It is unfortunate that today Robinson seems largely forgotten, as is his contemporary ROBINSON JEFFERS. Robinson created an entire gallery of psychological portraits: Richard Corey, Miniver Cheevy, Aaron Stark, Luke Havergal, Reuben Bright, and many more. He produced admirable sonnets as well as highly polished blank verse.

Robinson was born on December 22, 1869 in Head Tide, Maine. His family moved to Gardiner, Maine, when he was a child, and that is the town which became 'Tilbury Town' in many of his poems. He entered Harvard College in 1891 but departed without a degree in 1903. He self-published his first book, *The Torrent and the Night Before* (1896), and three other books followed before he found his stride in *The Man Against the Sky* (1916). He produced twenty-four collections during his lifetime. A second *Collected Poems* appeared posthumously in 1937. He died of pancreatic cancer in New York City in 1935.

[RP]

Rodgers, William Robert (Ireland, 1909–69) An Ulster Presbyterian, Rodgers was born in Belfast and educated at Queen's University, Belfast. Ordained in 1935, Rodgers was a practicing Presbyterian minister in Armagh until 1946. He then worked as a BBC producer and scriptwriter in 1946–52. Rodgers associated with such poets as LOUIS MACNEICE and DYLAN THOMAS. With MacNeice he collaborated on an unpublished work, 'The Character of Ireland'. In 1966, Rodgers became writer-in-residence at Pitzer College, Claremont, California.

His early works include *Awake! and Other Poems* (1941) and *Europa and the Bull* (1952), the latter of which appeared to great critical acclaim. However, many later volumes, including *Ireland in Colour* (1956) and *Collected Poems* (1971), were considered uneven and less accomplished. Initially, Rodgers' poems were popular not only in Ireland, but in England and the United States as well, but in recent years his reputation has declined.

[CT]

Roethke, Theodore (United States, 1908–63) Roethke was born in Saginaw, Michigan, the son of a florist who owned a greenhouse. He was educated at the University of Michigan and took graduate courses at Harvard. Despite struggles with mental illness, periodic breakdowns, and alcoholism, Roethke became an influential teacher at several schools, including Lafayette College, Bennington College, and then permanently at the University of Washington. Widely regarded during his lifetime as one of the central poets of his generation, he received the Pulitzer Prize, two National Book Awards, and a Bollingen Prize.

Roethke's highly musical poetry is intimately connected with the rhythms of the natural world. He masterfully conveys a vital, pulsing, almost terrifying world of continual growth and decay. A famous early sequence returns to explore the frightening yet Edenic world of his father's greenhouse; other important autobiographical sequences such as 'The Lost Son' experiment with fragmented syntax and childlike rhyming in order to inhabit the depths of the poet's psyche and past as a step on the way toward regeneration. Roethke's profound connection with the physical world is fused with a deeply romantic symbolism; his poems frequently use nature to chart spiritual and psychological journeys, in which the despairing self progresses and regresses through darkness and suffering, as it strives towards mystical vision – a transcendent, momentary union with being itself.

Selected works: *The Lost Son* (1948); *The Waking* (1953); *The Far Field* (1964); *The Collected Poems* (1966).

[AE]

Romer, Stephen (England, b. 1957) Romer was born in Bishops Stortford and graduated with honors from Trinity Hall, Cambridge, in 1978. After a year of graduate study at Harvard, Romer returned to England, where he earned his Ph.D. from Cambridge in 1985.

In 1986, while teaching English literature at the British Institute in Paris, Romer received the Eric Gregory Trust Award for young poets from the Society of Authors. The award came in recognition of his first book, *Idols*, which is filled with Romer's customary irony in a variety of forms, including couplets, blank verse, and off-rhyming tercets.

Romer's poetry reflects an awareness of death and the value one must place on time. He continues to publish poems, translations, and reviews, and has served as editor of *Smale Fowls* since 1987.

[LK]

Rose, Wendy (United States, b. 1948) A painter as well as a poet, Rose was born in Oakland, California; she is Hopi and Miwok Indian. Rose holds a Ph.D. in anthropology and she has taught at the University of California Berkeley and at California State College Fresno.

In Rose's six collections of poetry and three chapbooks, her assertion of her Hopi identity and her focus on women on the margins of society have held as main themes. Poems of social protest and outrage are presented in poignant language, often through a persona. Rose writes out of place as well as history, giving voice to forgotten figures, such as Julia the 'Ugliest Woman in the World', a Mexican Indian woman who toured with a freak show, or Truganniny, the last Tasmanian who was stuffed and mounted after her death.

Selected works: *Hopi Roadrunner Dancing* (1973); *Academic Squaw* (1977); *Builder Kachina: a Home-Going Cycle* (1979); *Lost Copper* (1980); *What Happened When the Hopi Hit New York City* (1982); *The Halfbreed Chronicles* (1985).

[HEE]

Rosenberg, Isaac (England, 1890–1918) Rosenberg was born in Bristol and moved to the Jewish quarter in Whitechapel, London, at the age of seven. His family was poor, but he was fortunate to be sponsored at the Slade School of Art and began his studies in 1911.

Though his painting was influenced by the Pre-Raphaelites and William Blake, his first volume of poetry, *Youth* (1918), revealed a more immediate influence: Imagism. Rosenberg vacillated about whether he should concentrate his energy on painting or poetry until he joined the army when his creativity became focused on poetry by default – he could not paint in the trenches of France.

Rosenberg's war poetry differs from that of other World War I poets, such as WILFRED OWEN and SIEGFRIED SASSOON; while their work reflects a conflict between patriotic idealism and the stark realities of war, this irony is absent from Rosenberg's work. Perhaps because of his lower-class background, Rosenberg never seems to have felt betrayed by elite politicians and military strategies as, for instance, Sassoon had. Instead, Rosenberg appears to have gone to the front with a more realistic idea of what war entails and that is reflected in his verse. So, too, is his Jewish background; his poetry is informed by Old Testament themes and a sense of spirituality. Rosenberg was killed in a battle in France; his body was never recovered.

Selected works: *Night and Day* (1912); *Youth* (1915); *Poems* (1922).

[BB]

Rosselli, Amelia (Italy, 1930–96) Rosselli holds a unique place within Italian twentieth-century verse. Isolated from the Italian literary arena (she was born in Paris and spent long periods of time abroad), she accumulated an irregular and eclectic intellectual background ranging from music to literature, and many of her poems were written in languages other than Italian (they include several in English). Praised by PASOLINI and ZANZOTTO, among others, Rosselli's powerful, non-academic verse seems to spring from a deliberate and yet spontaneous operation on the language, conceived as an unrestrained reflection of the human psyche. She committed suicide in 1996.

Selected works: *Variazioni Belliche* (*Wartime Variations*, 1964); *Serie ospedaliera* (*Hospital Series*, 1969); *Documento* (*Document*, 1976); *Appunti sparsi e persi* (*Loose and Lost Notes*, 1983); *Sleep. Poesie in inglese* (*Sleep: Poems in English*, 1992).

[GS]

Rothenberg, Jerome (United States, b. 1931) Rothenberg's writing investigates the possibilities of verbal and non-verbal poetic form in search of an art that more closely approximates the root of human existence. Consequently, his poetic interests are eclectic and range from Native American poetry to FEDERICO GARCÍA LORCA, and from Jewish poetry to Dadaism.

Born on December 11, 1931, in New York City, Rothenberg's first published book was a translation of *New Young German Poets* (1959); he published his first work of poetry, *White Sun Black Sun*, in 1960. Since then he has published over sixteen books of poetry, eight works of translation, two books of prose, and has edited nine anthologies. His writings include such works as *Poland/1931* (1974), *Vienna Blood* (1980), *The Lorca Variations* (1993), and the widely used poetry anthologies *Technicians of the Sacred* (1968) and the two-volume *Poems for the Millennium* (1996, 1998).

Associated with performance and concrete poetry, Rothenberg's writing has been consistently praised for its precision, musicality, and power. He teaches at the University of California at San Diego.

[DC]

Rozewicz, Tadeusz (Poland, b. 1921) Rozewicz was born in Radomsko. His childhood was spent during an optimistic era, in a Poland which had regained its independence for the first time in 150 years, but as a young man Rozewicz bore witness to the horrors of World War II. In 1943–44 he served in the underground Home Army, and in 1944 his brother was killed by the Gestapo. After the war, Rozewicz studied art history at the Jagiellonian University in Cracow, but eventually he moved to Wroclaw and devoted himself to writing.

Often considered the most influential Polish poet of the immediate post-war period, Rozewicz gave voice to a generation who had lost 'faith in man and all man's works' (M.J. Krynski and R.A. Maguire). He developed a somber poetry of spartan imagery, bereft of metaphor, stripped of rhetorical flourishes, and skeptical of all aesthetic values. He set out to chronicle what was left of the world for those who were 'led to the slaughter' and survived.

In the mid-1950s and 1960s, Rozewicz's

emaciated style did not change, but his subject matter evolved. He turned his attention away from the ruinous wake of the war and focused on the disparity of the individual, the immense suffering and subtle joys.

Since the 1970s Rozewicz has continued to live and write in Wroclaw, away from the literary scenes of Warsaw and Cracow. However, his poetry has never again reached the heights it attained in the middle decades of this century. Several selections of Rozewicz's work have been translated into English, most notably *'The Survivor' and Other Poems* (1975) and *Reading the Apocalypse in Bed: Selected Plays and Prose* (1998).

[MO]

Rumens, Carol (Carol-Ann Lumley; England, b. 1944) Winner of the 1984 Cholmondeley Award for Poetry, Rumens was born in south London. She enrolled in Bedford College to study philosophy in 1964, but left in 1965 to get married. Aside from writing, she has worked in publishing and advertising. Elected Fellow of the Royal Society of Literature in 1984, Rumens serves as the writer-in-residence at the University of Kent.

Her first publication, *A Strange Girl in Bright Colours* (1974), introduced the themes of women's and children's liberation that she continues throughout her subsequent volumes. These early poems were not much of a success and it was not until her 1981 volume *Unplayed Music* that she began to develop her own style and mature poetic voice. This volume earned her the Alice Hunt Bartlett Prize for the most promising volume by a new writer. *Scenes from the Gingerbread House* (1982) tells of Rumens' childhood, describing her life at age eleven. Her following two works, *Star Whisper* (1983), which was a Poetry Book Society Choice, and *Direct Dialling* (1985), move to themes of human suffering by concentrating on events of the Holocaust. Rumens continues to write poetry focusing on historical events of Eastern Europe and on her travels, as seen in her descriptive, metaphysical 1989 collection *From Berlin to Heaven* and in *Thinking of Skins: New and Selected Poems* (1993).

[BRB]

Ryan, Gig (Australia, b. 1956) English-born Elizabeth Ryan has lived most of her life in Australia, presently in Melbourne where she is poetry editor for *The Age* and singer with the band Disband. Ryan's poetry is composed of dramatic monologues, satire, parody, knife-edged wit and feelings. Political and personal, her verse is sharply aware of the hostile world with which it engages. The influences of the Australian poets known as the 'Generation of '68', such as JOHN TRANTER, JOHN FORBES, and JENNIFER MAIDEN, are evident in Ryan's poetry. However, it is Ryan's distinct voice that has shifted the boundaries of Australian poetry, especially for women poets, and her influence is now emerging in new poets such as EMMA LEW and Cassie Lewis.

Selected works: *The Division of Anger* (1981); *Manners of an Astronaut* (1985); *The Last Interior* (1986); *Excavation* (1990); *Pure and Applied* (1998).

[DCO]

S

Saarikoski, Pentti Ilmari (Finland, 1937–83) Saarikoski studied classical languages and began his writing career at the age of twenty. As a notable representative of Finnish Modernism, both mainstream lyricism and political radicalism, he advanced modern poetic expression toward high/postmodernism. His knowledge of antiquity expresses itself as reverence for tradition, the presence of which is found in the smallest of details. His rebellious voice – a German critical sentiment sees him as 'The Finnish Rimbaud' – is not directed at literary authorities, many of whom were misfits themselves; rather, Saarikoski's opponent is eternal mediocrity.

Saarikoski's first collection already included an impressive component of translations of work by Sappho, Euripides, and Aristotle, among others. His true breakthrough came with the 1962 publication, *Mitä tapahtuu todella* (*What's Really Going on*), which includes three collections of poems and a study of his poetic methodology and theory. In it he denies the cohesiveness of texts. A poem is not a unified work of art, a matter of symmetry and closure; such cohesion would not reflect the modern, fragmented world, a noteworthy development in Finnish lyricism at the time.

He breaks down conventional hierarchies of the elevated and the mundane, and strives to interweave what the previous view saw as separate in the world of subject matter and stylistics. His later 1960s collections contain intimate minimalistic poems as well as ones he believed were the result of spontaneous, automatic writing, the latter an appropriate expression of his bohemian period. His unrestrained mode of living, particularly his alcoholism, resulted in degenerating health and long periods of depression.

Saarikoski is the author of over sixteen collections of poetry and the highly esteemed translator of, besides Greek Classics, modern prose by Joyce, Henry Miller, and J.D. Salinger. Among his many awards should be mentioned three State Awards for Literature (1963, 1966, 1981) and Pro Finlandia medal (1972).

[SP]

Saba, Umberto (Italy, 1883–1957) Born Umberto Poli, this poet later chose the pseudonym Saba ('bread' in Hebrew) in honor of his Jewish heritage. Always reluctant to leave Trieste, where he was born, Saba consciously lived at the margins of the cultural debate of his time, and such an eccentric position became the typical feature of his unique poetry. His verse clearly shows the legacy of the metrical and linguistic tradition of eighteenth-century Italian literature (poetry, as well as prose and opera librettos). In such a traditional frame Saba encased his passions and his tormented autobiography, both rendered with extremely modern accents (like the numerous symbolic references borrowed from psychoanalysis, sharing with Italian novelist Italo Svevo, also from Trieste, this city's exposure to the culture of Mitteleuropa). When language became the crucial issue for younger poets, especially after the two wars, Saba's 'poesia onesta' ('honest poetry', as he used to define his work) stood as one of the last examples of Italian verse fruitfully connected to a traditional language and still capable of achieving an aesthetically accomplished result. His major works are *Coi miei occhi* (*With My Eyes*, 1912), *Cose leggere e vaganti* (*Light and Wandering Things*, 1920), *Preludio e Canzonette* (*Prelude and Songs*, 1923), *Parole* (*Words*, 1934), *Ultime Cose* (*Last Things*, 1945), *Uccelli* (*Birds*, 1951) and *Quasi un racconto* (*Almost a Tale*, 1957). In 1961 all of his collections were published together in a definitive edition bearing the title *Canzoniere* (*Songbook*).

[GS]

Sachs, Nelly (Germany, 1891–1970) Leonie Sachs grew up in an upper middle-class Jewish family in Berlin. An intercession by Swedish author Selma Lagerlöf enabled Sachs to leave Nazi Germany and emigrate to Sweden. Filled with a sense of the Holocaust's horrors and her responsibility as a survivor to remember these horrors, Sachs wrote poems that questioned the meaning of Jewish suffering and suggested transformation to an existence without hatred. These poems earned her the 1966 Nobel Prize (shared with Josef Agnon).

Although arriving at a more universal mysticism, Sachs' poetry developed from the specific traditions of Judaic and Christian mysticism in *In the Dwellings of Death* (1947) and *Star Eclipse* (1949), which directly addressed the Holocaust in free-rhythmical diction. While her poems in *And No One Knows Where to Go* (1957) and *Journey into Dustlessness* (1961) still clearly showed the influence of Judaic tradition, Sachs' late poetry emphasized her personal mystic vision over tradition, in *Still Death Celebrates Life* (1961) and *Glowing Enigma* (four parts: 1963–67).

[IRS]

Saint-Aude, Magloire (Clement Magloire, Jr.; Haiti, 1912–72) In 1941 Saint-Aude legally adopted his mother's maiden name as a way of establishing an identity separate from his father who, as director of the newspaper *Le Matin (The Morning)*, was a well-known public figure in Haiti. His first two collections of poetry, *Dialogue de mes lampes* (*Dialogue of My Lamps*) and *Tabou* (*Taboo*), appeared in that same year. Known for writing dark, difficult poetry, Saint-Aude was one of the major writers of Surrealist verse in the Caribbean. He was influenced by the French Surrealist poet ANDRÉ BRETON, who wrote about Saint-Aude in *Le Clef des champs* (*The Key to the Fields*, 1956). Other works include the novel *Veillée* (*Vigil*, 1956) and the collection of poems entitled *Déchue* (*The Deposed*, 1956).

[IS]

Šalamun, Tomaž (Yugoslavia, b. 1941) The Slovenian Šalamun is among the most influential poets of his generation in both Slovenia and Yugoslavia. He was born in Zagreb and educated at the University of Ljubljana, where he studied history and art history.

During the 1960s, he focused his interest on language, experimentation, and conceptual and pop art. After he visited the United States during the 1970s, Šalamun's writing became strongly influenced by American society which, for him, becomes a source of creative energies and freedom. His visit to Mexico in the 1980s further contributed to his interest in the Americas. His later work is permeated by images of Mexico, its mythology, and its native cultures.

An heir to Futurism, Surrealism, and Expressionism, Šalamun is close to contemporary Language poetry. His poetry contests conventional meanings and symbols. He experiments with language, free linguistic associations, and displaced metaphors in an attempt to challenge literary tradition.

Selected works: *Poker* (1966); *Namen pelerine* (*The Purpose of a Cape*, 1968); *Druidi* (*Druids*, 1975); *Balada za Metko Krasovec* (*A Ballad for Metko Krasovec*, 1981); *Sonet o mleku* (*A Sonnet on Milk*, 1984); *Otrok in jelen* (*A Child and a Deer*, 1990); *Mera časa* (*Measure of Time*, 1990).

[DJ]

Salinas, Pedro (Spain, 1891–1951) Like many of his contemporaries from the Generation of 1927 (see LORCA, JIMENEZ, ALEIXANDRE), Pedro Salinas was a poet, critic, and professor who lived abroad after the Civil War. Salinas sought to transform reality by looking at it in unusual and unfamiliar ways. His early poetry frequently uses objects from the mechanized world, as in *Steadfast Chance* (1929) and *Fable and Sign* (1931). Salinas is known above all for his love poetry, in which the beloved becomes an extended metaphor. *My Voice Owed to You* (1934) and *Love's Reason* (1936) belong to this cycle. Later, in *A Contemplation* (1946), he would turn to the sea as a central image. Salinas was teaching in the United States at the time of his death.

[AB]

Sanchez, Sonia (United States, b. 1934) While Sanchez' roots in the 'Black Arts' movement are readily apparent to readers, her grounding in Formalism is not always clear. Much of her early education as a writer in New York City was with Formalists, and to this day she credits them with developing her understanding of sound. This lyricism, manifest in rhythmic speech patterns and colloquial word combinations, also borrows heavily from urban English.

Born in Birmingham, Alabama, Sanchez has spent most of her adult life in and around American inner cities. She has written many plays, edited many collections, and records her poems periodically. Often the placement of her poems reminds one of a musical score, an orchestral arrangement that is to be read vertically as well as horizontally.

Selected works: *Shake Loose My Skin: New and Selected Poems* (1999).

[CV]

Sandburg, Carl (United States, 1878–1967) Sandburg is considered a distinctively American poet. Born in Galesburg, Illinois, into a family where the father worked as a railroad blacksmith and the mother could not read English, Sandburg developed a poetic style, tone, and idiom that sought to embody American ideals.

Sandburg's connections with the Zeitgeist may be related to two facets of his life: first, he was an adamant social democrat concerned with the larger fabric of American society, who helped organize the Wisconsin Socialist Democratic party; and second, his primary income from 1910 onwards came from working as a reporter.

Despite the fact that he worked full time as a reporter, Sandburg still published in excess of sixty texts during his lifetime, including poetry, history, biography, fiction, and music. Sandburg was awarded the Pulitzer Prize twice – first in 1939 for his biography *Abraham Lincoln: The War Years*, and again in 1951 for his *Complete Poems*. He was also an accomplished guitar player, and he has the distinction of being a pupil of the legendary Andres Segovia.

Sandburg died in Flat Rock, North Carolina in 1967, but he was buried at his birthplace in Illinois. In September of that year, a National Memorial Service for Sandburg was held at the Lincoln Memorial in Washington, D.C., testifying to his place in the American literary landscape. Although his literary reputation has faded, Sandburg remains an important cultural and popular figure.

[DC]

Santa Maria, Angel Cruchaga (Chile, 1893–1964) Santa Maria began writing poetry during the literary climate represented by VICENTE HUIDOBRO and the journal *Azul*. Cruchaga worked in the Banco Español, the Biblioteca Nacional, and was president of the Alianza de Intelectuales.

The poet's concern with Symbolism, the mystical, and suffering – seen in the early volumes *Las Manos Juntas* (*Joined Hands*, 1915), *La Ciudad Invisible* (*Invisible Cities*, 1928), *Afán del corazón* (*Eagerness of the Heart*, 1933) – did not limit the subject matter of his poems. These elements are present in his religious *Job* (1922) as well as his patriotic *Rostro de Chile* (*The Face of Chile*, 1955). The imbuing of elements from the real world, and in particular from Chile, with divine meaning, earned the interest of NERUDA, who selected and introduced the poems for Cruchaga's *Antologia* published in 1946. Cruchaga received the Premio Nacional de Literatura in 1948.

[VW]

Sarajlić, Izet (Yugoslavia, b. 1930) Sarajlić is a Bosnian poet firmly tied to his land and especially to the city of Sarajevo, where he resides. Like many other Yugoslav poets, Sarajlić was scarred by World War II, and his poetry is a reminder of the horrors of war and a lament of the destruction that the war wrought on his generation. Regarding the twentieth century as the age of cynicism and alienation, Sarajlić maintains a nostalgia for the nineteenth century. Sarajlić's poetry is gentle and romantic, partly in response to a modern epoch he sees as skeptical and inimical to poetry (especially love poetry).

His poetry is strongly influenced by literature, especially Russian; it is allusive and full of references to other poets, including BRECHT, LORCA, PASTERNAK, and Yesenin. Acutely aware of the world around him, Sarajlić writes poetry about small things, everyday life in the contemporary world, and intimate moments of love.

Selected works: *U susretu* (*A Meeting*, 1949); *Sivi vikend* (*A Gray Weekend*, 1955); *Minutu ćutanja* (*A Minute of Silence*, 1960); *Posveta* (*Dedication*, 1961); *Tranzit* (*To Search*, 1963); *Intermeco* (*Intermezzo*, 1965); *Godine, godine* (*Years, Years*, 1965); *Portreti drugova* (*Portraits of Comrades*, 1966); *Vilsonovo šetaliste* (*Wilson's Promenade*, 1968); *Stihovi za laku noć* (*Good Night Poems*, 1971); *Pisma* (*Letters*, 1974); *Sarajevska ratna zbirka* (*A War Collection from Sarajevo*, 1995).

[DJ]

Sarton, May (United States, 1912–95) Sarton's parents came to the United States following the German invasion of Belgium in 1914, and she grew up speaking English at home. After high school, she joined Eva de Galienne's Civic Repertory Theater in New York City as an apprentice in 1929, staying with the company until its dissolution in 1937. She held many jobs, including a position at the Office of War Information, but always said writing was her true priority. For many years she was the Briggs-Copeland Instructor in Composition at Harvard.

Feminist critics have been Sarton's greatest enthusiasts, applauding her explorations of female artistry and a lesbian's experience in American society. Her work has gained a wider audience in the past twenty years, with readers appreciating her deft and sensitive studies of memory, dreams, and ideas of self-knowledge.

Selected works: *Mrs Stevens Hears the Mermaids Calling* (novel, 1965); *Collected Poems: 1930–1973* (1974); *Circles on the Water* (1982); *Available Light* (1988).

[JDS]

Sassoon, Siegfried (England, 1886–1967) Sassoon is best known as a World War I trench poet. Born in Kent and educated at Clare College, Cambridge, Sassoon's published pre-war poetry was influenced by the Pre-Raphaelites. This early poetry is characterized by a pastoral atmosphere and reflective of a love of nature.

In 1915 Sassoon went to France where the mechanistic killing and horrors of trench warfare influenced the growing sense of realism in his work. The love of nature found in his early poetry is not absent from his war poems; rather, Sassoon uses the beauty and life represented by nature to contrast the death and destruction in the trenches. He frequently employs satire to criticize the powerful elite, such as politicians and military officials, whom he held responsible for prolonging the war (as in *Counter Attack and Other Poems*, 1918). Sassoon's war poetry was highly criticized for its flagrant anti-patriotism.

In the twenty-five years after the war, Sassoon wrote relatively few poems. Perhaps inspired by his conversion to Catholicism, in the 1950s and 1960s he turned his poetic attention to religious themes. These later poems tend to be meditative and short and, stylistically, Sassoon returns to his pre-war affinity with the Pre-Raphaelites.

Selected works: *The Daffodil Murderer* (1913); *The Old Huntsman and Other Poems* (1918); *Satirical Poems* (1923); *The Path to Peace: Selected Poems* (1960); *Collected Poems, 1908–56* (1961).

[BB]

Scammell, William (England, b. 1939) Scammell was born in Hythe, Kent, educated at the University of Bristol, and has lectured at the University of Newcastle since 1975. He has received many awards, including the Cholmondeley Award (1982), British Arts Council Award (1985), and the Poetry Society National Poetry Competition Prize (1989).

Scammell's poetry has been noted for its Audenesque qualities, the mixing of registers as well as a developed sense of wordplay. Also influenced by Whitman, many of Scammell's poems revolve around lists of European cultural elements – taking in philosophy, twentieth-century history, music, Victorian writers, and modern poetry – as well as the indexing of names.

Selected works: *Yes and No* (1979); *A Second Life* (1982); *Time Past* (1982); *Jouissance* (1985); *Eldorado* (1987); *The New Lake Poets* (ed. 1990); *Bleeding Heart Yard* (1992).

[SS]

Scannell, Vernon (England, b. 1922) Although his poetry frequently discusses private themes, such as his family and creative life, Scannell's work also reflects the diverse public life he has lived. The time he spent in the 51st Division Gordon Highlanders of the British Army in 1941–45 reveals itself in the images of violence and war that run throughout his poetry. Likewise, the idea of danger and risk-taking as a part of daily life reflects upon his experience as a professional boxer from 1945 to 1946. Scannell attended the University of Leeds in 1946–47 and taught English at a preparatory school from 1955 to 1962. Since that time he has been both a freelance writer and a broadcaster.

Scannell has received numerous awards for his work, including the Heinemann Award for Literature, a Royal Society of Literature Award in 1961 for *The Masks of Love* (1960), and the Cholmondeley Award in 1974 for *The Winter Man* (1973). He received a Civil List pension in 1981 for his contribution to literature.

[BRB]

Schnackenberg, Gjertrud (United States, b. 1953) Perhaps one of the finest Christian poets working today, Schnackenberg turns her portraits of historical characters into a conversation about permanence and faith. Her first two books established her as one of the foremost modern practitioners of the New Formalism; her third book, *A Gilded Lapse of Time* (1992), presents Italian Renaissance art as vehicle for modern religious meditation. There, refraining from commentary on content, Schnackenberg chooses to abstract the highly representational art through descriptions of color, and of the experience of viewing. Once a student of IOSIP BRODSKY, Schnackenberg is married to the philosopher Robert Nozick.

[CV]

Schuyler, James (United States, 1923–91) Pulitzer Prize-winning poet James Schuyler was born in Chicago, attended college in West Virginia, and served in World War II. He settled in New York and became a central figure in the 'New York School' of poets through his close friendships with JOHN ASHBERY, KENNETH KOCH, and FRANK O'HARA.

Schuyler's work features a bracing clarity, incisive wit, and painterly dedication to concrete detail. As they chart the on-going movements of the poet's feelings and thoughts, Schuyler's casual, conversational poems combine precise observations of the natural world with an openness to the flux and randomness of the quotidian.

Selected works: *Freely Espousing* (1969); *The Crystal Lithium* (1972); *The Morning of the Poem* (1980, Pulitzer Prize); *Collected Poems* (1993).

[AE]

Schwartz, Delmore (United States, 1913–66) A Brooklynite, Schwartz graduated from New York University in 1935 and (like T.S. ELIOT) attended Harvard as a graduate student in philosophy. His first book, *In Dreams Begin Responsibilities* (1938), marked him as a leading writer of his generation. He translated Artur Rimbaud's *A Season in Hell* (1939) and wrote a verse play, *Shenandoah* (1941).

'The Heavy Bear Who Goes with Me', one of Schwartz's most remembered poems, shows his fascination with individual identity and its paradoxical relation to physical existence and desire. The language Schwartz uses, fusing allegorical directness with ironic distance, reflects the vexed nature of the poem's philosophical issues.

Among his many academic positions, Schwartz taught briefly at Princeton University with JOHN BERRYMAN and RANDALL JARRELL. In 1943, he became the editor of *Partisan Review* and remained a strong voice there for more than a decade. His short stories (see *The World is a Wedding*, 1948) often depict and satirize Jewish intellectuals and their middle-class immigrant backgrounds. *Selected Essays* (1970) contains much of his criticism and cultural observations.

Although mental illness and alcoholism isolated him during the later years of his life, in 1959 Schwartz received the Bollingen Prize for *Summer Knowledge: New and Selected Poems, 1938–1958*. He is widely considered a prime example of the supposed type of American writer: someone with brilliant promise, early success, and a tortured decline into failure. Saul Bellow used him as the model for the poet Fleisher in *Humboldt's Gift*.

Schwartz was married twice but died alone.

[CC]

Schwitters, Kurt (Germany, 1887–1948) Schwitters traveled much, especially in Norway where he emigrated in 1937. Fleeing the German occupation of Norway, he finally went to England.

A multi-talented artist, Schwitters used various media and techniques. Belonging to the international avant-garde movement, in the context of Expressionism and Dadaism, he developed his own MERZ-Art, a name reportedly created in Schwitters' typical collage style by truncating the name 'Commerz Bank'.

'Anna Flower' from *Anna Blume* (1919) is the best-known work of Schwitters' early phase. Originally published in his own *Merz*-journal, the idiosyncratic word usage points to Schwitters' further development toward concrete poetry; see *Anna Blume and I* (posthumous collection, 1965). After the mid-1920s, Schwitters primarily wrote prose.

[IRS]

Scott, Dennis (Jamaica, 1939–91) Poet and dramatist Scott was born in Kingston, Jamaica. He was educated at Jamaica College and the University of the West Indies, Mona, Jamaica. As a member of the Jamaican National Dance Theatre and as principal of the Jamaican School of Drama, Scott has been an important figure in the development of theater in the Caribbean. He has also served as the chair of the Yale School of Drama.

Scott's poetry is known for its visceral depiction of the urban poor and its examination of the consequences of a society deeply divided by class. His work produces its deepest effects by its tension between form and theme, and between standard English and Jamaican dialect. Scott's bursts of simple, expressive, seemingly effortless verse are used to celebrate the world lyrically, but also to evoke the horror of a world that hides a nightmarish reality below its surface. In his later poetry, his tone softens somewhat, and life no longer appears for Scott inevitably to involve an encounter with pain, whether physical, psychic or metaphorical.

His collections include *Journeys and Ceremonies: Poems 1960–1969* (1969), *Uncle Time* (1973), *Dreadwalk: Poems 1970–1978* (1982) and *Strategies* (1989). In 1974, he was the recipient of the Commonwealth Poetry Prize.

[IS]

Scott, F. R. (Canada, 1899–1985) Francis Reginald Scott is an important figure not only in the development of Canadian poetry but also in the evolution of Canadian political life in the twentieth century. Scott was born in Québec City. After studying in England as a Rhodes Scholar, he returned to McGill where he received his law degree in 1926. Scott was Dean of the School of Law at McGill from 1961 to 1964, a representative at the United Nations in the early 1950s, a member of the Bilingualism and Biculturalism Committee from 1963 to 1971, a founding member of the CCF – the precursor of today's New Democratic Party – and the author of numerous books on Canadian politics. He is the one of the few individuals to have won a Governor General's Award in different categories: for *Collected Poems* (1980) and for the non-fiction volume *Essays on the Constitution* (1977).

Scott has been an influence on Canadian poetry both through his own work and as a catalyst for a number of poetic projects. With A.J.M. SMITH, Scott founded the *McGill Fortnightly Review* in 1925, one of the first outlets for Modernist poetry in Canada. In 1942, Scott, A.M. Klein, and P.K. PAGE founded the journal *Preview*, which later merged with IRVING LAYTON's *First Statement*. The quality of Scott's own poetic output has been the subject of some debate. While he has produced several fine poems, including the nationalist poems 'Trans Canada' and 'Laurentian Shield', Scott struggled throughout his life to find a poetic voice that fused his interests in Modernism, social protest, and satire. That he failed as much as he succeeded does not diminish his overall contribution to Canadian letters.

Selected works: *Overture* (1945); *Events and Signals* (1955); *Eye of the Needle* (1957); *Signature* (1964); *Collected Poems* (1980).

[IS]

Seferis, George (George Seferiadis; Greece, 1900–71) Seferis was born in Smyrna and moved to Athens in 1914. He studied law in Paris and in 1924 joined the Greek foreign service where he worked until his retirement in 1962. He served as ambassador to Lebanon, Syria, Jordan, Iraq, and finally to Great Britain (1957–62), a country with which he always had a very close relationship. During World War II he accompanied the Greek government in exile, first to Crete and then to Egypt, South Africa, and finally Italy. He served as a member of the Greek delegation to the United Nations and was involved in the discussions of the Cyprus question; British imperialist policy and Cyprus feature prominently in his collection *Logbook III* (1955). He wrote twelve books of poetry, essays, translations, diaries, and fiction, most of which were composed abroad. He was awarded the William Foyle Poetry Prize in England (1961) and in 1962 became Greece's first Nobel Prize laureate for literature.

A leading figure of 'the Generation of the Thirties', Seferis is credited with the revival of Greek poetry after the political impasse of the tumultuous 1920s and the suicide of poet KOSTAS KARIOTAKIS in 1928. His first collection, *Strophe* (*Turning Point*, 1931), revolutionized Greek poetry and inaugurated modernism in Greece. Though both *Strophe* and its follow-up, *The Cistern* (1932), adhered to traditional forms, Seferis is better known in Greek literature as a master of free verse. Influenced by the French Symbolists, T.S. ELIOT, and EZRA POUND, his verse is often sparse, hermetically obscure, and elliptical. This semantic density, unprecedented in Greek literature, may be partly attributed to Seferis' erudition and to his frequent allusions to Greek history, literature, and mythology through the ages. On the question of Greek diglossia – the conflict between *katharevousa*, an archaizing Greek 'cleansed' of foreign vocabulary and dialectical variation, and *demotic*, more colloquial idiom with access not only to dialectical diversity but also to the Greek language throughout history – Seferis declared the issue closed as early as 1937 and proceeded to write in refined demotic.

The main preoccupations of Seferis' poetry are the relationship of memory, tradition, and the present in modern Greece (a primary theme in Greek literature in its modern phase) and the vicissitudes and alienation of love. His post-World War II poem 'Thrush' (1946) introduces a mystical dimension to his poetry and locates mythological figures such as Odysseus and Aphrodite on a contemporary stage of an arid, deserted landscape and a hostile sea. Other major collections include *Mythistorima* (1935), *Book of Exercises* (1940), *Logbook I, II* and *III* (1940, 1944, 1955), and *Three Secret Poems* (1966). During his lifetime he was translated by Henry Miller, LAWRENCE DURRELL, Rex Warner, and later by Edmund Keeley and Philip Sherrard (*Collected Poems*, 1967).

In the spring of 1969 he issued a public condemnation of the Papadopoulos dictatorship (1967–74). His funeral in September 1971 drew a vast crowd and was linked to the protest movement against the regime. Despite the inaccessibility of Seferis' verse, several selections from *Mythistorima* and *Epiphania* were set to music by Mikis Theodorakis with phenomenal critical and popular success, and became emblematic of Greek poetry's intimate relationship with popular song culture.

[GSY]

Seifert, Jaroslav (Czech Republic, 1901–86) Seifert, winner of the 1984 Nobel Prize for Literature, was born in Prague, the son of a blacksmith. Until 1950 he was a journalist and the editor of a number of Czech periodicals, including the literary monthly *Kytice* (*The Bouquet*). A writer whose verse reverberated through Czechoslovakia's German occupation and Communist rule, Seifert combined lyricism with social criticism into an art of surpassing beauty.

After publishing his first volume, *Mesto v slzach* (*City in Tears*, 1921), Seifert continued to publish poetry regularly, in addition to his journalistic pieces. He began his professional and poetic careers as a member of the Communist Party, but the increasing Sovietization during the 1920s caused him to break with the party in 1929. For a period eschewing the political altogether in his verse, he participated with VLADIMIR HOLAN in the 'poetist' movement, which sought a 'pure' poetry of aesthetic beauty removed from earthly ties. He won the State Prize for Literature in 1936 for *Ruce Venusiny* (*The Hands of*

Venus), a volume engaging and embracing love.

After World War II, during Seifert's editorial tenure of *Kytice* (1946–48), he became more and more vocal about the ills of Socialist realism; the Communists eventually declared him a 'traitor to his class' and banned his poetry. Instead, then, he turned to writing children's literature, emphasizing the themes that had become increasingly prevalent in his poetry: the village, the rural workers, domesticity. Seifert's prominence in Czech letters was firmly established in 1956, when he spoke out against Communist censorship; he was once again prevented from publishing but had also managed to convey the sense of outrage and disgust which his fellow writers felt toward the government.

One can chart the dominant themes of modern Czech history in Seifert's poetry, from the annexation of Czechoslovakia to Germany (*Zhasnete svetla*, *Switch off the Lights*, 1938) through the Prague Uprising in 1945 (*Prilba hliny*, *The Helmet of Clay*, 1945) to the renewed Communist crackdown of the 1960s and 1970s (*Morovy sloup*, *The Plague Monument*, 1977). This last volume is regarded by many critics as Seifert's finest. Coming some fifty-six years after his first, it combines a sense of Czech history – modern and ancient alike – with the images of post-war celebration, and hope.

In addition to being awarded the Nobel Prize, Seifert was named the Poet of the Nation in 1966. A lyricist, a Surrealist, a patriot in the face of Nazism, and a man who possessed an uncommon understanding of his homeland, Seifert stands as the major figure in twentieth-century Czechoslovakian poetry.

Selected works: *Na vlnach T.S.F.* (*On Radio Waves*, 1925); *Osm dni* (*Eight Days*, 1937); *Kamenny most* (*The Stone Bridge*, 1944); *Mozart v Praze* (*Mozart in Prague*, 1951); *The Selected Poetry of Jaroslav Seifert* (1986).

[MW]

Senghor, Leopold Sédar (Senegal, b. 1906) Born in Joal to a Serer father and Peul mother, Senghor was sent at age seven to a Catholic missionary school in (then) French West Africa. He excelled in his studies in Africa, and continued at Lycée Louis-le-Grand in Paris. He was the first black African to earn French aggregation at the Sorbonne in 1935, the first president of independent Senegal in 1960 and, in 1983, was elected as the first black Immortal to the French Academy.

The foremost Francophone African poet of his time, Senghor founded the Negritude movement and the journal *The Black Student* with AIMÉ CÉSAIRE of Martinique, BIRAGO DIOP of Senegal, and Léon Damas from French Guyana, all of whom were students in Paris in the 1930s. Senghor's vision of this literary and social movement was to affirm the values and traditions of people of black color.

In 1947, he published *Anthologie de la nouvelle poésie nègre et malgache de langue française* (*Anthology of New Black and Malgache Poetry in French*) with an introduction entitled 'Black Orpheus' by Jean-Paul Sartre. This important collection helped establish a canon of francophone black writers who reflected the principles of Senghor's vision of Negritude. Senghor's poetry and academic work in language reflect his sincere appreciation of the French literary tradition. From Charles Baudelaire to PAUL CLAUDEL, Senghor's poetic influences go beyond the French school to the then contemporary black writers and musicians of the Harlem Renaissance such as LANGSTON HUGHES and CLAUDE MCKAY. His poems are often dedicated to places and people influencing him at the time.

His first collection *Chants d'ombre* (*Shadow Songs*, 1945) consists of poems written mostly while imprisoned by the Nazis. This collection was dedicated to the many fallen black men in World War II. Senghor remembers his early childhood experiences in Joal, the village that for him symbolizes an ideal place, and develops a romantic vision of his and so many other black people's motherland. These experiences and this ideal vision of Africa provide an important foundation for Senghor's idealization of black people and of Africa, present in much of his work.

Despite being harshly criticized for essentializing black character as emotional, Senghor continued to demonstrate his ideas for a universal civilization in his works *Liberté* (*Freedom*), Volumes I–V. His poetry continued to develop along the same lines with 'Ethiopiques' which prophesizes a brighter tomorrow for Africa. *Chansons pour Naëtt* (*Songs for Naëtt*, 1949), love poems written for Senghor's first wife, Ginette, helped establish Senghor as one of the foremost French-language poets.

Senghor's political life began after he served with the French and was taken prisoner by the Nazis during World War II. He was elected Senegalese deputy to the French Constituent Assembly in 1945 and in 1960 became the first president of Senegal. He remained president until stepping down in 1980. Since then, he has resided in France with his second wife.

Selected works: *Hosties noires* (*Black Hosts*, 1948); *Nocturnes* (*Nocturnes*, 1961); *Elégie des Alizés* (*Elegy of the Trade Winds*, 1969); *Lettres d'hivernage* (*Winter Letters*, 1973); *Elégies majeures* (*Major Elegies*, 1979); *Poèmes* (*Poems*, 1982).

[LF]

Sepamla, Sipho (South Africa, b. 1932) Born in Krugersdorp on the Rand and trained as a teacher, Sydney Sipho Sepamla has also worked as a personnel officer. In the 1970s he became active in the Black Consciousness Movement, organizing various workshops, poetry readings, and conferences, and serving as editor of the journals *New Classic* and *S'ketch*. He was often subjected to various forms of censorship. As director of the Federated Union of Black Arts (FUBA) Center in Johannesburg, he founded the program to provide an alternative education for blacks and colored in South Africa after the Soweto uprising in 1976. He won the Pringle Award for poetry in 1977 for *The Soweto I Love*. His work reflects his complex love–hate relationship with South Africa, and particularly with urbanized society; he also expounds the absurdities of white power and, in his earlier poems, the inevitability that apartheid and white rule would eventually come to an end.

Selected works: *The Blues is You in Me* (1970); *Children of the Earth* (1983); *Selected Poems* (1984).

[KS]

Sereni, Vittorio (Italy, 1913–83) Born in Luino, a small town on Lake Maggiore, Sereni moved to Milan in 1932 to complete his education at the local university which was, despite the severe restrictions imposed by Fascism, one of the main centers of cultural debate in Italy at the time. Soon after publishing his first collection, *Frontiera* (*Frontier*, 1941), deeply influenced by MONTALE and 'Ermetismo' poetry (see UNGARETTI, QUASIMODO), Sereni was drafted to join the Italian troops fighting in the war fronts of the Mediterranean. First sent to Greece, he was later captured in Sicily by an Anglo-American division, and subsequently confined for two years in a military prison in Africa (an experience which served as a main source of inspiration for his second collection, *Diario di Algeria* (*Diary of Algeria*), published in 1947). After his return to Italy, in spite of his brilliant career in a pre-eminent Italian publishing house and his intense editorial activity as a translator and editor for several literary journals, Sereni, unlike PASOLINI and FORTINI, shied away from the vigorous debate surrounding Italian post-war poetry. After a long and painful silence, his third collection, *Gli Strumenti Umani* (*The Human Instruments*), finally appeared in 1965, followed by *Stella Variabile* (*Variable Star*) in 1982. These two works gained him immense status among younger poets, who saw in Sereni one of the few pre-war poets still capable of evolving from the mannerisms which were Ermetismo's legacy to contemporary Italian verse.

[GS]

Serote, Mongane (South Africa, b. 1944) Wally Mongane Serote was born in Sophiatown and was educated at both Alexandra Township and Leribe, Lesotho, completing his education at the Morris Isaacson High School in Soweto. He became actively involved in the Black Consciousness Movement and was imprisoned for nine months in 1969, only to be released without having been officially charged. Serote was a Fulbright Scholar and completed a fine arts degree at Columbia University in 1979 before moving in exile to London and Botswana, becoming involved in the Nedu Art Ensemble. His poetry has been published in various journals and in 1972 he published his first anthology *Yakhal'Inkomo*. In 1973 he was awarded the Ingrid Jonker Poetry Prize; the next year *Tsetlo* was published and subsequently banned in South Africa. As a member of the 'township' or 'Soweto' poets, Serote's poetry typically contains elements of consciousness-raising, political commitment and images of violence, revolt, and resistance.

Selected works: *No Baby Must Weep* (1975); *Behold Mama, Flowers* (1978); *Selected Poems* (1982); *A Tough Tale* (1987).

[KS]

Sexton, Anne (United States, 1928–74) Sexton received a minimal education. After boarding school she attended a Boston 'finishing school' in 1947, and later worked as a fashion model. Following a series of depressions and mental breakdowns, a doctor advised her to attempt writing as therapy. She enrolled in a class taught by ROBERT LOWELL in Boston, and thus began in 1957 a spectacular literary career.

Just three years later her first book, *To Bedlam and Part Way Back*, was published. *All My Pretty Ones* followed two years after that. Her third book, *Live or Die*, received the Pulitzer Prize. Her *Selected Poems* (1964) was published in the U.K. and was a Poetry Book Society Recommendation, after which she was elected a Fellow of the Royal Society of Literature in London. She was also awarded the first traveling fellowship of the American Academy of the Arts and Letters, and was Phi Beta Kappa poet at Harvard. She had a play, *Mercy Street*, produced at the American Place Theater in New York. She often gave dramatic poetry readings accompanied by a rock group, 'Anne Sexton and Her Kind'. The group's name came from the poem with which Sexton usually began her readings, 'Her Kind', in which the poet confessed to being a possessed witch.

The range of Sexton's work is narrow. Her subjects were usually herself, her family, her lovers, her illnesses. For this reason she was labeled one of the 'Confessional Poets', together with her friends Robert Lowell and SYLVIA PLATH. Yet unlike some confessional writers, the emotions conveyed in her first three books were highly controlled, often through strict form. The result was a powerful poetry, as in the first poem from her first book, 'You, Doctor Martin', in which she speaks of a psychiatrist at a mental hospital who walks 'from breakfast to madness', and sees his patients as 'large children'. Her imagery was often breath-taking, as when she describes life as 'a kitten in a sack'. Her use of rhyme was skillful, as in the poem 'Elizabeth Gone'. Further, she had a fine sense of humor, which often made her dark subjects bearable. This is in sharp contrast to Sylvia Plath, with whom Sexton is often compared.

After her first three books, however, Sexton's poems increasingly became loose, and for many readers, less interesting. She had less to 'confess', and her voice rarely varied. An exception is the volume *Transformations* (1971), a droll retelling of fairy tales by the Brothers Grimm. It was made into an opera by Conrad Susa.

Anne Sexton was born in Newton, Massachusetts. In 1948 she married Alfred Muller (Kayo) Sexton II, from whom she separated in 1972. She had two daughters, Joyce Ladd and Linda Gray. In 1972 she held the Crashaw Chair in Literature at Colgate University. She received three honorary doctoral degrees. At the time of her suicide, she was Professor of Creative Writing at Boston University. A play based on her writings, *Anne Sexton: My Own Stranger*, was adapted by Linda Laundra and Marilyn Esper in 1980. Her *Complete Poems* was published in 1981.

[RP]

Seymour, A. J. (Guyana, 1914–90) Arthur James Seymour was born in Georgetown, British Guiana (Guyana). A career civil servant, he was nevertheless a prolific poet, producing forty-two collections of poetry over his lifetime, including *The Guiana Book* (1948), *Selected Poems* (1965), and *Images of Majority* (1978). His importance to Caribbean letters does not derive from the originality of his verse, but rather from his lifelong commitment to the cultivation and development of a unique and independent Caribbean culture and literature. He was the founder and editor of the important literary journal *Kyk-over-al* (1945–61), which published the work of MARTIN CARTER, WILSON HARRIS, and Ian McDonald. In 1973, he was named deputy chair of the Department of Culture in Guyana. In this role, and as a critic, reviewer, and anthologist, he helped the careers of numerous writers and established the beginnings of a confident, self-assured literary culture in the Caribbean.

[IS]

Shapcott, Thomas (Australia, b. 1935) Born in Ipswich, Queensland, Shapcott worked as an accountant until 1978. Immensely active, Shapcott was a foundation member (1973–76) and then director (1983–90) of the Literature Board. In addition to thirteen poetry collections, he has published anthologies, two volumes of short stories, children's books, libretti, a memoir, a history of the Literature Board, two studies of the artist Charles Blackman, and six novels. He was executive director of the National Book Council, has won numerous major awards, and in 1989 was awarded the Order of Australia. He is married to the poet Judith Rodriguez and is currently Professor of Creative Writing at the University of Adelaide.

Shapcott's own importance is sometimes obscured by his encouragement of the younger 'revolutionary' poets of the 1960s and 1970s known as the 'Generation of '68' (see TRANTER, DUGGAN, FORBES, MAIDEN). His anthology *Australian Poetry Now* (1970) is a key document in that group's evolution. Shapcott's own poetry, however, has ranged widely, from the relatively conventional early work, to the experimentation of the 1970s. His best collections, *Shabbytown Calendar* (1975) and *The City of Home* (1995), show the importance of place and autobiography. His *Selected Poems: 1956–1988* was published in 1989.

[DM]

Shapiro, Karl (United States, 1913–2000) Today Karl (Jay) Shapiro's reputation is in disrepair. In the 1940s and 1950s he was one of the golden boys of American poetry, and his work featured in all the leading anthologies with that of JOHN BERRYMAN, ROBERT LOWELL, and THEODORE ROETHKE. It is likely his outspoken criticism caused his eclipse. He called T. S. ELIOT a failed poet and D. H. LAWRENCE 'Gandhi with a penis'. One hopes that his reputation will be revived; poems such as 'Auto Wreck', 'Barber Shop', 'University', and 'Buick' should long be admired.

Shapiro was born in Baltimore, Maryland, and educated at the University of

Virginia and Johns Hopkins. He never took a degree. He won both the Pulitzer Prize and the Bollingen Prize, edited both *Poetry* magazine and *Prairie Schooner*, and served as Poetry Consultant to the Library of Congress – a position now called Poet Laureate. He died in New York City where he lived with his third wife, the translator Sophie Wilkins.

Selected works: *The Poetry Wreck: Selected Essays 1950–70* (1975); *Collected Poems, 1940–78* (1978); *The Wild Card: New and Selected Poems* (1998).

[RP]

Shawqi, Ahmad (Egypt, 1868–1932) Shawqi is widely recognized as the greatest modern Arab poet. In grand pan-Arab celebrations held in his honor in Cairo in 1927, his contemporaries named him 'The Prince of Poets', a title by which he is still known.

Shawqi was born to an aristocratic family of mixed Arab, Circassian, Turkish, and Greek ancestry. He attended the Law School in Cairo before Khedive (King) Taufiq sent him to the University of Montpellier in France in 1887 to study law. Shawqi returned to Egypt in 1891 to be appointed to an important position in Khedive Abbas' court, quickly gaining the Khedive's favor because of his poetry. Shawqi occupied that position until World War I broke out and Khedive Abbas was deposed by the British, who appointed another king and declared Egypt a British Protectorate. Shawqi was exiled to Spain in 1915. He took no public office upon his return in 1919, but instead devoted himself to poetry, which he employed in the service of social and political issues and the nationalist, anti-colonial struggle.

Shawqi's poetry was the culmination of the neoclassical revival begun in the mid-nineteenth century, after the age of decadence in Arabic literature suffered under Ottoman rule. He restored to poetry the vigor, polish, and intensity of the best examples of pre-Islamic and Abbasid poetry. He demonstrated that the traditional qasida (ode) form – with its two-hemistich lines, monorhyme, grandeur of tone, and tidal flow of emotion – was perfectly capable of expressing the spirit of the age. In fact, his confirmation of the classical style, idiom, and method was so powerful (and so popular among Arab readers), and he adapted it so well to modern times, that the task of Romantic and Modernist innovators who came after him became very difficult.

Most of Shawqi's poems appeared first in daily newspapers, and this accounts for the immediacy of his impact on public life. A public poet in the classical sense, his poems were inspired by momentous national events and often galvanized public sentiments. His exile by the British had more to do with his poetry than with his loyalty to the deposed Khedive Abbas or to direct political involvement. Shawqi also wrote traditional panegyrics, elegies, lyrics, love poems, as well as bucolic, descriptive, didactic, and devotional verse. A great craftsman, many of his poems were set to music because of their sonorous, rhythmical quality. Toward the end of his life, he wrote several verse plays on historical themes. Those plays exhibit a certain romantic nostalgia and lyricism unmatched in his poetry. Overall, Shawqi's work is considered a cornerstone of modern Arabic poetry.

Selected works: *Al-Shawqiyyat* (1898); *Al-Shawqiyyat* 4 vols. (1926, 1930, 1936, 1943 collected poems); *The Unknown Shawqiyyat* (1961).

[WH]

Shéhadé, Georges (Lebanon, 1910–89) The most translated poet and playwright, and the most acclaimed Lebanese writer in France and Francophone countries, Shéhadé was born in Alexandria in 1910. From his early childhood, he was interested in words and fascinated by writing. He published his first poems when he was twelve years old, in *La Revue du Com-*

merce (1922). Immediately noted by the Surrealists, he was encouraged by them to develop his poetry, writing in French. Soon he published a play influenced by the Surrealists, *Rodogune Sinne* (1936), and poems, *Poésie zéro ou l'Écolier sultan* (*Poetry Zero, or the Schoolboy Sultan*, 1936), which Saleh Stétié called 'the book of an ingenious and scholarly childhood'. Shéhadé received his B.A. in Law at the University of Alexandria and moved to Lebanon where he became a professor of French Literature at the École Supérieure des Lettres de Beirut. Although attached to Lebanon, he moved to France in 1978, fleeing the terrible conflicts. He received *Le Grand Prix de la Francophonie* in 1987 and died two years later in Paris.

Poésie I (1938) was an immediate success, reflecting different French literary movements, in particular Symbolism and Surrealism. The volume reflects current events, the Lebanese nature, and the passage of time. *Poésie II*(1948) confirmed his approach to writing using interior rhythms, alliteration, metaphors, and vivid images. Though the words are simple, they convey a great originality and audacity through their musical effects and arrangements. By the third volume, *Poésie III* (1949), the traditional epic and romantic themes of love, faith, and war are conveyed in more universal tones. *Si tu racontes un ramier* (*While You Tell a Turtledove*, 1951) translates the new problems of Lebanon and the Lebanese theme of the Oriental soul to a deeper level, where poetry reflects the ambiguity of man, and his irresolvable quest for truth and understanding of the world. Some of Shéhadé's poems show the tragic destiny of emigrants, the torment over paradise lost, and nostalgia, as well as contemplation of new questions in life. These four volumes of poetry were gathered together in *Poésies* (1952).

In the early 1950s Shéhadé stopped writing poetry in order to concentrate on the theater. Yet when his last volume of poetry, *Le Nageur d'un seul amour* (*The Swimmer of a Single Love*, 1985), was published, it was very well received. His work has had an unparalleled legacy since he was able to free himself from traditional themes and literary currents in order to reveal new trends and universal themes in his poetry.

[MS]

Shlonsky, Avraham (Israel, 1900–73) Shlonsky was born in Karyokov, Ukraine, came to study in Jaffa in 1913, spent the war years in Russia, and returned to the Land of Israel in 1922 to work as a road builder and agricultural laborer. He was a poet, essayist, editor, and translator, and quickly became the voice of pioneers' aspirations, the leader of the literary Left in Tel Aviv of the 1930s and 1940s, and a mentor to the younger generation of poets. In his rebellion against classicists such as BIALIK, he produced poetry which was rich in symbols and imagery and relied heavily on the spoken language and neologisms. His poetry, representing the dichotomy between the certainty of the developing Zionist endeavor and strong doubts of both the individual and the collective, was characterized by a sense of alienation and isolation, and, after the Holocaust, by themes of fear and terror. Shlonsky translated works from Russian and English, and was also known as a children's poet. His first collection, *Distress*, was published in 1924, and his collected works in the 1970s.

[ER]

Shu Ting (China, b. 1952) One of the best-known poets in contemporary China, whose name is frequently mentioned alongside BEI DAO, Shu was born in Shimazhen, a small town in Fujian, but grew up in Xiamen, the largest city in the province. Like most people of her generation, and before graduating from junior high school, Shu was sent to live in the countryside, 'to be re-educated by the farmer', as it was known at the time. After returning to Xiamen, Shu did all kinds of odd jobs and, at intervals, began to write poems. The publication of her 'To the Oak Tree', a literary sensation in the early 1980s, has brought her great fame, which she has continued to enjoy. That single poem established her position as a major contemporary poet, who is now a member of the Fujian Association of Writers. In 1985, Shu was invited to the Horizontal Art Festival in Germany. A year later, she was invited by the Saint Joseph Poetry Research Center (U.S.) to read her poems.

Her tender and genuine romantic sensitivity, which had been denied in Chinese verse for a few decades, gives her poetry a distinctive voice at the age of valuing personal concerns over commitment to public duties. Her books of poetry include *A Double-Mast Boat* (1982), and *Selected Lyrics of Shu Ting and Gu Cheng* (1982). Her poems have been translated into many languages.

[LG]

Sigurjónsson, Jóhann (Iceland, 1880–1919) Born at Laxamýri in northern Iceland to an established family, Sigurjónsson studied in Reykjavik. Soon, though, he left Iceland to mix with the bohemia in Copenhagen that formed around Georg Brandes. While winning recognition for his play in Danish, *Fialla-Eyvindur* (*Eyvind of the Hills*, 1911), Sigurjónsson also started composing in Icelandic, among the first writers to use the modern idiom. Although he is mostly known in his capacity as a playwright of folk-based drama, Sigurjónsson started composing poetry as early as 1905 and should be counted among the pioneers of twentieth-century Icelandic poetry. Using simple meters or free verse, he expressed a Nietzschean appetite for life. His collected works, *Rit*, were published in two volumes in 1940–42.

[YB]

Sikelianos, Angelos (Greece, 1884–1951) The author of nine books of poetry and seven poetic dramas, Sikelianos was a visionary and inspiring personality with prophetic and utopian ambitions. He was born in Lefkas of a distinguished family and studied law in Athens. He married Eva Palmer, who financed his ambitious Delphic festivals (1927 and 1930), in which he tried to revive the ancient spirit by staging plays, poetry recitations, and lectures at the site of the Delphic oracle. A revolutionary democrat and mystic, his sometimes inaccessible poetry, characterized by a philosophical lyricism, was pantheistic and panhellenic, with a broad rhetorical sweep and an impressive command of Greek. Among his most important collections are *The Visionary* (1909) and *Greek Easter* (1922); his collected work was published in 1947 under the title of *Lyrical Life*.

[GSY]

Silkin, Jon (England, 1930–97) Founder and co-editor of the acclaimed literary magazine, *Stand*, Silkin was born in London, and was educated at Leeds University while simultaneously teaching as the Gregory Fellow in Poetry.

Silkin's Jewish heritage, army experience, personal challenges with his children and relationships, and living in the US and Israel inform his poetry. He believed that literature has moral dimensions as well as aesthetic qualities, and our language places and defines us as human beings by affecting the thoughts and feelings of others. This belief echoes through his verse, as well as anchoring *Stand* with a distinctive social commitment.

Selected works: *The Peaceable Kingdom* (1954); *Nature with Man* (1965); *Amana Grass* (1971); *The Psalms with their Spoils* (1980); *Autobiographical Stanzas* (1984); *The Penguin Book of First World War Poetry* (ed., 1979).

[SS]

Silliman, Ron (United States, b. 1946) Silliman has lived primarily in and around the San Francisco area. He has degrees from the University of California and San Francisco State, and has worked as an educator and lobbyist. His political involvement in prison reform and such periodicals as *The Socialist Review* is part and parcel of his poetic, which insists upon the politics inherent in language.

Silliman is in part responsible for Language poetry (alongside CHARLES BERNSTEIN among others), through his creation of unusual formal structures and reassessment of prose narrative. Poems such as *Tjanting* (1981) and his on-going, unfinished poem *Alphabet* – including the volumes *ABC* (1983), *What* (1989), and *Toner* (1992) – reflect his work's resistance to traditional hermeneutic readings by rejecting closure and linearity.

[VB]

Simic, Charles (United States, b. 1938) An immigrant to the U.S. from Yugoslavia when he was eleven, Simic remains an East European poet in his sensibility. His deceptively simple language, the brilliant, magical realism of his imagery, and the abruptness of his transitions are his main connections with the poetry of ZBIGNIEW HERBERT and WISLAWA SYMBORSKA. In Simic's poems, the ordinary becomes not so much divine, but a talisman against the forces of confusion, atrophy, and despair. His poems tend to be short and spare, and their narrator often plays the buffoon, increasing the pathos of the performance. His awards include the 1989 Pulitzer Prize. Simic teaches at the University of New Hampshire.

Selected works: *Selected Poems 1963–1983* (1985); *The World Doesn't End* (1989); *Book of Gods and Devils* (1990); *Walking the Black Cat* (1996).

[AE]

Simpson, Louis (United States, b. 1923) Pulitzer Prize-winning poet Simpson, like JAMES WRIGHT and ROBERT LOWELL, radically altered his style in mid-career. His early poems are tightly constructed lyrics. But during the 1960s he became dissatisfied with expressing himself in form and meter, and his lines became loose. After writing about American society in *At the End of the Open Road* (1963), he turned to his Russian ancestry in *Adventures of the Letter I* (1971). His work is full of compassion for the lonely and unfortunate, as in his poem 'The Boarder'.

Simpson's mother was Russian, his father Scottish. He was born in the West Indies. The family emigrated to America when Simpson was 17. He worked as an editor with a publishing house, then studied at Columbia University, where he took a Ph.D. For years he taught at Columbia, then became Professor of English at the State University of New York at Stony Brook.

Selected works: *People Live Here: Selected Poems 1949–1983* (1983); *Collected Poems* (1988); *Selected Prose* (1989).

[RP]

Sissman, E. L. (United States, 1928–76) Edward Louis Sissman grew up in Detroit but made Boston his lifelong home. As a student poet, he won Harvard's Garrison Prize in 1948; he had a career in advertising, was a columnist for *Atlantic Monthly*, and wrote reviews for *The New Yorker.*

Sissman responded to a 1965 diagnosis of cancer with a flurry of creative activity, publishing *Death: An Introduction* (1968), *Scattered Returns* (1969), and *Pursuit of Honor* (1971). A posthumous collection, *Hello, Darkness*, was published in 1978. His awards included a grant from the National Institute of Arts and Letters.

Sissman's work has elicited faint praise from critics, some of whom suggest that his adman background adversely overwhelms the poems. Eclectic and full of irrepressible wordplay, his urbane formal poetry is laced with specifics, including brand names.

[HE]

Sisson, C.H. (England, b. 1914) Charles Hubert Sisson was born in Bristol and earned his B.A. from the University of

Bristol. He did graduate work at the Universities of Berlin and Freiburg, and the Sorbonne. In government service for much of his life, Sisson was made Fellow of the Royal Society of London in 1975, and was named a Companion of Honour in 1993. He currently resides in Somerset.

God Bless Karl Marx! (1987) is perhaps his best known book of poetry. Although some critics have seen Sisson's poetry as a desperate grasp at 'the good old days', the poems represent a culmination of Sisson's lifelong, careful study in literature. In addition to his role as poet, Sisson has been editor, novelist, translator, and a writer of non-fiction.

Selected works: *Poems* (1959); *The London Zoo* (1961); *the Trojan Ditch: Collected Poems and Selected Translations* (1974); *Exactions* (1980); *Selected Poems* (1981); *Night Thoughts and Other Poems* (1983); *Collected Poems* (1984); *Nine Sonnets* (1991); *What and Who* (1994).

[MK]

Sitwell, Edith (England, 1887–1964) Dame Edith Louisa Sitwell was born the daughter of Sir George and Lady Ida Sitwell, and the granddaughter of the Earl of Landesborough. She was born in Scarborough, Yorkshire, and raised in her ancestral home at Renishaw Hall with brothers and fellow poets Sacheverell and Osbert, but spent most of her life in London. Sitwell and her two brothers were perhaps the most famous literary family of their time. Remembered as an eccentric woman of medieval tastes, Sitwell converted to Roman Catholicism as an adult. In addition to poetry, she wrote fiction, biographies, critical anthologies, and social histories. Her first published poem appeared in 1913, and she spurred on the English Modernist movement in the anti-Georgian magazine, *Wheels*.

Her poetry received most acclaim in the 1940s with volumes such as *Street Songs* (1942), *Green Song* (1944), *The Song of the Cold* (1945), and *The Shadow of Cain* (1947). When her outlandish poetic effects became less than fashionable, Sitwell's poetry faded, but it survives today as a testament to her power as poet of the moment. She died in 1964.

Sitwell's poetry inhabits a fabricated world of bright colors and harsh effect. Although varied in form and rhyme, her subject matter lies in legend and ideals overshadowed by a technological strain. She seems to prophesy a dark new world that she does not necessarily find unpleasant.

Selected works: *The Mother and Other Poems* (1915); *Clown's Houses* (1918); *The Wooden Pegasus* (1920); *Façade* (1922); *Bucolic Comedies* (1923); *Troy Park* (1925); *Rustic Elegies* (1927); *Collected Poems* (1930).

[MK]

Sjöberg, Birger (Sweden, 1885–1929) Although only two of his collections appeared during his lifetime, Sjöberg has been recognized as one of the pioneers of modern Swedish poetry. After very little formal education, Sjöberg tried his hand at journalism in Stockholm, then settled in Helsingborg. He was known only as a minor figure until the publication of *Fridas bok* (*Frida's Book*, 1922). Establishing Sjöberg's debt to the Swedish lyric tradition of Bellman, Wennerberg, and Taube, the collection combined lyrics and music and earned the author the title 'modern troubadour'. With witty parody as well as tenderness, it describes the naive, self-complacent provincial community of Sjöberg's native Vönersborg. Its follow-up, *Kriser och kransar* (*Crises and Laurel Wreaths*, 1926), shocked Swedish circles with its innovative modern poetic forms and rhythms. The poems in this collection presented Sjöberg's reaction to World War I by bringing language to its breaking point in jarring phrases, strident tones, and nervously pounding rhythms. Sjöberg left behind more than 3,000 poetic fragments, which were published posthumously in multiple volumes including *Minnen fren jorden* (*Memories from the*

Earth, 1940) and two sequels to *Frida's Book*.

[YB]

Slessor, Kenneth (Australia, 1901–71) Slessor was born to a middle-class family in New South Wales. His family name was originally 'Schlosser', and this German origin caused Slessor anxiety in his youth, especially since his adolescence coincided with World War I. As a boy poet, he wrote verse strongly supporting the Australian participation in the struggle against German aggression, an early sign of his becoming the quintessential poet of the Australian military.

Although Slessor did well in school, he never went to university. Slessor spent the 1920s and 1930s working in Sydney as a journalist for several newspapers and magazines. This exposed him to a mixture of literary and demotic influences similar to that experienced in the U.S. by HART CRANE (whom Slessor read avidly). He also became involved with the circle around Norman Lindsay's journal *Visions* and its ideology of romanticism, populism, and sexual vitalism. His first volume, *Thief of the Moon* (1924) was influenced by Lindsay to the point of repressing Slessor's own voice. *Earth-Visitors* (1926) contains much more of Slessor's native strangeness.

Cuckooz Country (1932) represents Slessor's greatest engagement with experimental Modernism. *Five Bells* (1939) is much more romantic in tone but with a despairing eloquence all Slessor's own. The title poem, a lament for the death of a friend in Sydney Harbor, is one of the great elegies of the English language, expressing, as critic Paul Kane has shown, both negation and transcendence. The poem concerns not only mourning but the inability to mourn, and not just the pathos of death but the isolation of the poetic voice from the currents of life and death around it.

Slessor married Noela Senior in 1922; she predeceased him by many years. He later remarried, but then divorced in 1961. Although according to his biographers Slessor seems to have had, even more than most heterosexual men, a tremendous need for female company, his relations with women were never satisfactory, a condition that frequently found its way into his poetry, especially his light verse.

Slessor spent World War II as a war correspondent, spending time at both the Pacific and Mediterranean fronts. The latter setting provided the scene for his last major lyric, *Beach Burial*. This meditation on the graves of sailors, at once somber and soft-spoken, is seen by many as Slessor's signature poem, and is one of the best-known works of Australian literature.

Slessor wrote no more significant poetry after the war's end. He did, though, continue his career as a journalist, eventually becoming editorial writer for the *Sydney Daily Telegraph*. In the 1960s, he wrote several pieces supporting the Vietnam War which made him a target for attack by a younger generation of Australian writers, though he was also a source of encouragement for younger poets such as LES MURRAY. Slessor remained active on the literary scene as reviewer and anthologist until his death of a heart attack in 1971.

Selected works: *Trio* (1931); *Darlinghurst Nights* and *Morning Glories* (1933).

[NB]

Smith, A.J.M. (Canada, 1902–80) Although Arthur James Marshall Smith produced only a modest number of poems by the standards of his contemporaries, he is certainly one of the most important and influential Canadian poets of the century. Known along with A.M. Klein and F. R. SCOTT as part of the 'Montréal Group' of poets that struggled against Canadian provincialism and conservatism, Smith's role as a poet, critic, and anthologist was crucial to the mid-century establishment of Canadian poetry as a distinct and vital literary concern.

Born in Westmount, Québec, Smith

attended McGill University, where he and Scott founded *The McGill Fortnightly Review* (1925–27), which published some of the first poems by members of the Montréal Group. After earning an M.A. in 1926 from McGill for a thesis on W. B. YEATS, Smith traveled to the University of Edinburgh, where he would eventually earn his Ph.D. in 1931. His stay in Edinburgh secured his commitment to the modernisms of Yeats and T.S. ELIOT. Returning to Canada in 1929 at the height of the Depression, Smith eventually secured an academic position in 1936 at Michigan State University, where he remained for thirty-six years. In the same year, Smith published his first anthology of poetry, *New Provinces* (1936), which included the work of Scott, Klein, and E. J. PRATT. Subsequent anthologies, especially *The Book of Canadian Poetry* (1943) and the bilingual *Oxford Book of Canadian Verse* (1960) were landmark works that helped to established the canon of Canadian poetry. Of Smith's own work, which appeared piecemeal in poetry journals and magazines, the most important is *News of the Phoenix and Other Poems* (1943), recipient of the Governor General's Award for Poetry.

Selected works: *Collected Poems* (1962); *Towards a View of Canadian Letters: Selected Critical Essays 1928–1971* (1973).

[IS]

Smith, Iain Crichton (Iain Mac a'Ghobhainn; Scotland, 1928–98) Smith was brought up on the island of Lewis in the Outer Hebrides. He read English at the University of Aberdeen, graduating with an M.A. in 1949, followed by a year at teacher training college. After National Service in the Education Corps in 1950–52, he was a teacher in Clydebank and Oban from 1952 to 1977, when he became a full-time writer. His first collection, *The Long River*, was published in 1955.

Smith was bilingual in English and Gaelic, often torn between the two languages when he felt that Gaelic could no longer provide the 'linguistic athleticism' he needed. His work includes criticism, plays, short stories, and novels as well as Gaelic and English translations of his own work and that of SORLEY MACLEAN (SOMHAIRLE MACGILLEAIN) and the eighteenth-century Gaelic poet Duncan Bán MacIntyre. A passionate critic of Scottish antipathy and also of what he saw as the suffocating restrictions of Calvinism, he was an unsentimental poet of place and identity. He was the recipient of many literary awards and of honorary doctorates from the universities of Dundee (1983), Glasgow (1984), and Aberdeen (1988). In 1985–91 he was on the Literature Committee of the Scottish Arts Council. He was made an OBE in 1980.

Selected works: *Deer on the High Hills* (1962); *From Bourgeois Land* (1969); *Love Poems and Elegies* (1972); *The Notebooks of Robinson Crusoe* (1975); *In the Middle* (1977); *The Exiles* (1984); *A Life* (1986); *The Village, and Other Poems* (1989); *Collected Poems* (1992).

[LKMF]

Smith, Ken (England, b. 1938) Kenneth John Smith, born in Rudston, East Yorkshire, earned his B.A. in English Literature from the University of Leeds, in 1963. Smith served in the Royal Air Force from 1958 to 1960, the year he married. His marriage was dissolved in 1978 and this troubled relationship contributed to his discussions of human relations and attitudes in his later poetry.

Smith's first collection, *The Pity* (1967), received the Gregory Award and was noted for its nature imagery. Although he claims not to be a nature poet, much of his verse contains environmental themes. In his 1987 collection, *Terra*, Smith draws upon his experience as a writer-in-residence at Wormwood Scrubs Prison in west London. These poems discuss the isolation of the convicts generalized to a larger audience of isolated people imprisoned in daily life.

[BRB]

Smith, Stevie (England, 1902–71) Florence Margaret Smith ('Stevie' was the nickname she adopted later) was born in Hull, Yorkshire, and lived a life both unremarkable and extraordinary. She lived in her aunt's home for more than sixty-five years, worked for the same company for thirty years, and freely admitted that her poetry never changed significantly from the time she started writing as a young woman. While Smith once considered marriage fleetingly, she came to view matrimony and independence as mutually exclusive, and opted to remain single and care for her aunt instead of marrying and raising a family. Despite the sedentary and relatively uneventful life she lived, Smith has earned a reputation as one of the most intangible and elusive – as well as gifted and unique – poets of her generation.

Smith began writing poetry in her early twenties, and much of her early work (including her three novels) was particularly autobiographical; she wrote repeatedly about abandoned or lost children, making direct and indirect references to her father's abandonment of her own family in poems such as 'Papa Love Baby' and her first novel *Novel on Yellow Paper* (1936). Using poetry as a kind of sounding board, she went on to explore her paradoxical religious beliefs and to indulge her fascination with death, the combination of which provides the reader with an almost uneasy insight into Smith's life. Her work is often dialogic, and she frequently wrote from opposing viewpoints on the same subject – as she did brilliantly in 'The House of Usher', the opening poem of *A Good Time Was Had by All* (1937) – creating an unusual richness and an envelopment to the body of her work.

Smith is perhaps best remembered as an aural poet who placed considerable emphasis on the sound of each word and poem. She was prone to experimenting with her work in public readings, often singing her poems to her own melodies or setting them to popular music of the times. Like the Pre-Raphaelites and Blake, she was also wont to accompany her work with illustrations designed to complicate the poems themselves, pushing readers to formulate their own interpretations of her work.

Critics often remarked upon Smith's propensity to tackle serious – even morbid – themes with sing-song devices and humor. While Smith did not read her peers' work, she was heavily influenced by the folk stories of the Brothers Grimm and she blended her delight in fairy tales with her interest in history and theology to a charming and sometimes disarming effect. That effect may have been what critics found unattractive in her work in the 1940s, but it is also what pushed her back into critical favor in the 1950s – and has caused a critical reappraisal since her untimely death from a brain tumor in 1971.

Selected works: *Tender Only to One* (1938); *Not Waving but Drowning* (1957); *The Frog Prince and Other Poems* (1966); *Scorpion and Other Poems* (1972).

[SG]

Smith, Sydney Goodsir (Scotland, 1915–75) Born in Wellington, New Zealand, Goodsir Smith and his parents settled in Edinburgh in 1928 when his father, Sir Sydney Alfred Smith, was appointed to the Chair of Forensic Medicine at the University of Edinburgh. Goodsir Smith was sent to school in England, and while at Malvern College he wanted to be a painter. His parents did not consider painting a suitable career, and he began to study medicine in Edinburgh. After barely a year he left Edinburgh for Oriel College, Oxford, to study English and history. In 1938 he married Marion Walsh. During World War II, he taught English to the Polish Forces stationed in Scotland, then worked for a year for the British Council. After the publication of *Skail Wind* (1941), *The Wanderer and Other Poems* (1943), and *The Deevil's Waltz* (1946) he was given the 1947 Rockefeller Atlantic Award for poetry; from then on he worked freelance as a radio, television, and newspaper journalist and critic. He was also an artist and cartoonist, and cut a distinctive figure in the Edinburgh literary scene with NORMAN MACCAIG and HUGH MACDIARMID, establishing a reputation as one of the best Lallans poets after MacDiarmid. His twin aims of 'intellectualizing' Scots and Gaelic and inspiring the left wing of Scottish Nationalism came together most successfully in his controversial play in Scots verse, *The Wallace*, produced at the 1960 Edinburgh International Festival.

Selected works: *Under the Eildon Tree* (1948); *Figs and Thistles* (1959); *Kynd Kittock's Land* (1965); *Collected Poems* (1975).

[LKMF]

Smithyman, Kendrick (New Zealand, 1922–95) Born near Northland, William Kendrick Smithyman worked as a primary school teacher before becoming a tutor in the English Department at the University of Auckland. He started publishing verse in the 1940s and proved himself a prolific poet. Smithyman's *Stories about Wooden Keyboards* (1985) won the 1986 New Zealand Book Award for Poetry.

Smithyman was the most revolutionary poet of his day, sometimes alienating his readers with his stylistic obscurity. Even though ALLEN CURNOW admired his poetry, Smithyman did not share Curnow's preoccupation with nationalistic themes and considered himself to be a regionalist poet, while simultaneously retaining an international perspective. He also did not follow the dominant neo-romanticism of post-war New Zealand, but found the poetry of British and American Modernists more appealing.

His poetry of the late 1960s is less obscure. These poems are marked by a strong sense of both old and new places. His famous 'Reading the Maps an Academic Exercise' (in *Stories about Wooden Keyboards*) is a poem that draws on the metaphor of maps to express the unstable nature of truth and Smithyman's perceived limitation of language.

Selected works: *The Blind Mountain and Other Poems* (1950); *Inheritance* (1962); *Flying to Palmerston* (1968); *Earthquake Weather* (1972); *The Seal in the Dolphin Pool* (1974); *Dwarf with a Billiard Cue* (1978); *Are You Going to the Pictures?* (1987).

[SH]

Snodgrass, W. D. (United States, b. 1926) William DeWitt Snodgrass made one of the most brilliant debuts in post-modern American poetry with the publication of *Heart's Needle* (1959), which won high praise and the Pulitzer Prize. The 'heart' of the book was a formal poetic sequence on his separation from his daughter. He followed this collection with an equally strong second, *After Experience* (1967), containing more confessional poems and a group of ekphrastic poems. The book also displayed his translation skills.

Many critics have never forgiven him his collection of monologues, *The Führer Bunker Poems* (1977), about Nazi leaders and the Holocaust. A reviewer in *The New York Times Review of Books* lamented, 'Why Snodgrass should be wasting his gift on attempts to outdo "the banality of evil" I can't begin to guess . . .'. In recent years Snodgrass has returned to the lyric, writing on love, the seasons, animals, and humans in *Each in His Season* (1993).

Selected works: *Selected Poems, 1957–1997* (1987); *The Führer Bunker Poems: The Complete Cycle* (1995); *Selected Translations* (1998).

[RP]

Snyder, Gary (United States, b. 1930) Snyder was born in San Francisco, grew up in Washington State, and was educated at Reed College and Berkeley. He became associated with Beat writers such as ALLEN GINSBERG and Jack Kerouac, and from 1956 to 1968 lived mainly in Japan, where he studied Zen Buddhism. Since then, he has lived and taught in northern California and has also become an influential environmental activist.

Snyder's crisp, clear poems typically offer precise images juxtaposed with little authorial comment. They meditate on the dangers of modern civilization and return often to his major concerns, which he says are the 'most archaic values on the earth': the wildness of nature; the magic inherent in primitive cultures; and the pleasures and mysteries of physical work, sex, love, and language.

Selected works: *Riprap* (1959); *Turtle Island* (1975, Pulitzer Prize); *Axe Handles* (1983); *No Nature: New and Selected Poems* (1992); *Mountains and Rivers Without End* (1996).

[AE]

So Chong-ju (also known as Midang; Korea, b. 1915) The foremost poet in Korea for much of the twentieth century, Nobel nominee So Chong-ju embraces the historic and mythic past to create a modern poetry. Expelled from high school when he was fifteen, So eventually became a professor at Dongguk University in Seoul. Although he was a committed poet – living in exile during World War II – his poetry is more lyrical than combative. His initial volumes, such as *Flower Snake* (1938) and *Cuckoo* (1946), show a realism frequently based on western models. However, the late volumes tend more toward metaphysics and autobiography. Throughout his long career, So Chong-ju has consistently written popular and moving verse.

Selected works: *Winter Sky* (1968); *Collected Poems* (1972); *Poems of a Wanderer* (1976); *With the Westering Moon* (1980); *Poems after the Crane Left* (1982); *Selected Poems* (1989).

[MW]

Södergran, Edith (Finland, 1892–1923) Daughter of a Swedish-speaking Finnish family, Edith Irene Södergran was born in St Petersburg, Russia, where her father was conducting business. Three months after her birth the family moved to the neighboring resort of Raivola, in Finnish territory. Södergran was sent to the German school in St Petersburg, where she received a cosmopolitan education and started writing poetry in Swedish, French, Russian, and (mostly) German; after the age of sixteen, however, she wrote in Swedish exclusively. When Södergran was fifteen, her father died of tuberculosis, and soon afterwards she contracted the same disease, spending much of 1913 in Davos, Switzerland. She returned to Raivola to live with her mother a year later, but continued to struggle with recurrent bouts of tuberculosis.

In 1916, Södergran published her first book, *Dikter* (*Poems*), which demonstrates her knowledge of a wide range of European poets, including German Expressionists and Russian Futurists, anticipating the Finnish-Swedish modernist movement. This collection was followed by *Septemberlyran* (*The September Lyre*, 1918), which signaled a new, Nietzschean period in her writing, while reflecting upon the upheavals of the Russian Revolution. Later volumes include *Rosenalteret* (*The Rose Altar*, 1919), *Framtidens skugga* (*The Shadow of the Future*, 1920), and *Landet som icke är* (*The Land That Is Not*, 1925). As the precursor and portal figure for all Nordic modernism – allowing it to be aligned with the works of T.S. ELIOT, EZRA POUND, and VLADIMIR MAYAKOVSKY – Södergran has won posthumous recognition as one of Northern Europe's leading poets.

[YB/SP]

Šopov, Aco (Yugoslavia, 1923–82) Born in Macedonia, Šopov attended the University of Skopje; he lived in Skopje for most of his life and was politically active throughout his adult life. During World War II, he fought against the Nazis. After the war, he continued to be active in Yugoslav political life as a government minister and diplomat, serving for a time as the Yugoslav ambassador to Senegal. He was also a cultural and literary activist, translating into Macedonian works such as *Hamlet* and *Cyrano de Bergerac*, as well as numerous Yugoslav works.

Šopov's early poetry, published during the 1940s, is full of revolutionary enthusiasm. He emphasizes Macedonian culture and supports the class struggle and the building of Socialism in Macedonia. His later poetry turns more toward intimate experiences such as personal loss, grief, and resignation of a life-weary poet. Melancholy and sadness are the prevailing feelings. In this later poetry, Šopov addresses the questions of love and beauty, the meaning of art, and the necessity of self-examination and self-expression.

Selected works: *Pesni* (*Poems*, 1944); *Veterot nosi ubavo vreme* (*The Wind Brings Nice Weather*, 1957); *Gledac na pepelta* (*The Ember Gazer*, 1970).

[DJ]

Sorescu, Marin (Romania, 1936–96) Born into a peasant family in Bulzeşti, southwestern Romania, Sorescu studied at the University of Jassy before taking up various editorial duties and working as a script-writer for the Romanian film industry. In the early 1990s he served as the Minister of Culture within the first post-Communist government of the country.

The most widely recognized contemporary Romanian poet, with numerous translations and international prizes, Sorescu rejected the prevalent hyperlyricism of the 1960s by resorting to parody, irony, and the burlesque. *Alone among the Poets* (1964) and *Poems* (1964) shocked yet delighted the public through the desacralization of serious themes and parables elevating the commonplace, through the innovative use of colloquial phraseology. The poet of an 'upside-down world' (M. Mincu), Sorescu perfected his post-avant-gardist anti-lyrical approach in *By the Lilac Fence, Books I–VI* (1972–98). By returning to nature and his own origins, he opposed standardization, alienation, and dehumanization. The events, characters, and scenes from his native village belong to an elementary, archaic world whose vitality rests to a great extent on its power to retell itself.

[GF]

Sosa, Roberto (Honduras, b. 1930) Sosa became the most important poet of his country after winning Spain's Adonais Prize for Poetry for his book *Los Pobres* (*The Have-nots*, 1969), and the Casa de las Américas Prize for *Un mundo para todos dividido* (*A World Divided*, 1971). Never mincing his words when it came to political denunciation, Sosa's books were banned in Honduras during the wars in Central America in the 1980s. His poetry is close in tone to that of VALLEJO and NERUDA, revealing a clear commitment to social justice and a very tight, economical use of language. He has ventured more recently, with great acclaim, into erotic poetry.

Selected works: *Caligramas* (*Caligrams*, 1959); *Muros* (*Walls*, 1966); *Mar Interior* (*Interior Sea*, 1967); *Secreto Militar* (*Military Secret*, 1985); *El Llanto de las Cosas* (*The Cry of Things*, 1994); *Máscara Suelta* (*Loose Mask*, 1994); *Sociedad y poesía: los enmantados* (*Poetry and Society: The Blanketed Ones*, 1997).

[SL]

Soto, Gary (United States, b. 1952) Born in Fresno, California, to second-generation Mexican-Americans, Soto was educated at California State and the University of California. A writer of poetry, memoirs, children's books, and librettos and a producer of films, Soto's concern is an authentic portrayal of Hispanic experience. His work encompasses the life of itinerant field laborers, the violence of urban existence, and the importance of community.

His poetry in volumes such as *The Tale of Sunlight* (1973) tends toward the narrative, anecdotal, and earthy. Moreover, his use of pronouns confronts the reader in the reading, suggesting a participation in the events related in the poem. Knowledge in his poems, such as 'Making Money:

Drought Year in Minkler, California' and 'How Things Work', becomes the currency by which community is created; readers leave the poem implicated in that community and commodification.

Soto is currently a professor at the University of California; his *New and Selected Poems* appeared in 1995.

[VB]

Soupault, Philippe (France, 1897–1990) Born near Paris into a conservative middle-class family, Soupault came to despise the values of the French bourgeoisie. During World War I, Soupault became acquainted with GUILLAUME APOLLINAIRE and ANDRÉ BRETON and was involved with the Paris Dadaists. He was co-founder of the Surrealist journal *Littérature* and co-author, with Breton, of the first important piece of automatic writing, *Les Champs magnétiques* (*Magnetic Fields*, 1920). After breaking with Breton, Soupault traveled widely and turned increasingly to writing novels, including *Le Bon Apôtre* (*The Good Disciple*, 1923), *Les Frères Durandeau* (*The Brothers Durandeau*, 1924), *Les Dernières Nuits de Paris* (*Last Nights of Paris*, 1928), and *Le Grand Homme* (*The Great Man*, 1929) – a biting satire of his uncle by marriage, the automobile magnate Louis Renault. Soupault also published critical works on literature, painting, and the cinema, and worked in radio. In such collections as *Westwego* (1922), *Georgia* (1929), and *Chansons du jour et de la nuir* (*Songs of Day and Night*, 1949), Soupault's verse exhibited greater simplicity and gracefulness – and less verbal audacity – than that of his better-known Surrealist counterparts. After World War II, Soupault worked for UNESCO.

Selected works: *Poèmes et Poésies, 1917–1973* (1973); *Odes, 1930–1980* (1980).

[ML]

Soutar, William (Scotland, 1898–1943) Soutar was born in Perth, the son of a joiner. He went to Perth Academy, but under the 1916 Military Service Act he was conscripted into the Royal Navy from 1916 to 1919. During his service, he contracted the ossification of the vertebrae (spondylitis) which later confined him to bed for the last thirteen years of his life. He began studying medicine at Edinburgh University, but changed to English, graduating in 1923 with the anonymously published *Gleanings by an Undergraduate* newly to his credit. In 1924 his illness was diagnosed, and in 1930 he was operated on unsuccessfully. After a ten-year interlude, he published a collection of 'bairnrhymes', poems in Scots for children, called *Seeds in the Wind* (1933, with a revised edition in 1949). He believed that if Scots were to be rejuvenated it would be through writing for children, and the bairnrhymes are what he is justly best remembered for. They and his 'whigmaleeries' – short poems often with a grotesque edge or bleak humor – are the simplest of his work and the richest in their use of Scots language. He also wrote 'variations' on poems, which were reinterpretations of poems in other languages into Scots.

Selected works: *Poems in Scots* (1935); *In the Time of Tyrants* (1939); *But the Earth Abideth* (1943); *The Expectant Silence* (1944); *Poems of William Soutar: A New Selection* (1988).

[LKMF]

Soyinka, Wole (Nigeria, b. 1934) Born in Abeokuta, Nigeria, to Yoruba parents, Soyinka was educated in Nigeria and England. Best known for his plays and his outspokenness on the social and political state of Nigeria, Soyinka received the Nobel Prize for Literature in 1986, the first African to win the award. His first collection of verse, *Idanre and Other Poems* (1967), draws heavily on Yoruba imagery and modern poetic forms. Criticized by many as willfully obscure, Soyinka's poetry has become increasingly cosmopolitan in its thematic focus, drawing its imagery from numerous cultures and contemporary political events while adhering to the often complicated formal structures of his earliest work. Imprisoned and harassed by successive military regimes, Soyinka has lived and taught in his native Nigeria, Ghana, Britain, France, Germany, and the United States.

Selected works: *A Shuttle in the Crypt* (1971); *Ogun Abibiman* (1976); *Mandela's Earth and Other Poems* (1988); *Outsiders* (1999).

[MLL]

Spaziani, Maria Luisa (Italy, b. 1924) Born in Turin, Spaziani lived in Milan and Paris before moving to Rome, where she currently directs the Eugenio Montale International Center of Poetry. Since her literary debut in the 1950s, the short, almost epigrammatic poems of the early collections have been replaced by a more articulated expression, without giving up a typical irony which involves personal life as well as social perspective.

Selected works: *Le acque del sabato* (*Saturday Waters*, 1954); *Utilità della memoria* (*The Usefulness of Memory*, 1966); *L'occhio del ciclone* (*The Eye of the Hurricane*, 1970); *Geometria del disordine* (*Geometry of Disorder*, 1981); *La stella del libero arbitrio* (*The Star of Free Will*, 1986); *I fasti dell'ortica* (*The Splendor of the Nettle*, 1995).

[GS]

Spencer, Bernard (England, 1909–63) Born in Madras, British India, Spencer spent much of his life traveling from country to country and job to job: teaching, advertising, working in the theater, journalism, and radio. After joining the British Council in 1940, he was sent to Greece, but was forced to leave during World War II. From Greece he went to Egypt, helped LAWRENCE DURRELL publish *Personal Landscape*, a magazine of expatriate writers, and then moved on to Madrid at the end of the war. He lectured in England, Turkey, Spain, and Austria, traveling often. He published several collections of poetry as well as various contributions to literary magazines. Spencer was found dead by railroad tracks in Vienna, apparently the result of an accident.

Selected works: *Aegean Islands and Other Poems* (1946); *With Luck Lasting* (1965); *Collected Poems* (1965).

[BRB]

Spender, Stephen (England, 1909–95) The son of a prominent journalist, Sir Stephen Spender attended private schools, then went up to Oxford in 1928. It was there that he met Christopher Isherwood, CECIL DAY LEWIS, and W.H. AUDEN. Together, the four men would become known variously as the Auden Generation, the Oxford Poets, the Thirties Poets or, drawing on the title of one of Spender's poems, the Pylon Poets. Straddling the years between Modernism and World War II, and locked into the political upheavals of the 1930s, they each contributed to an artistic yield marked by social engagement and leftist politics.

Unlike some of his peers, however, Spender's commitment to the left was ambivalent, at best. Though the lyrical works in *Poems* (1933) and *Vienna* (1934), influenced by RILKE and LORCA, depict the downtrodden and oppressed, they also reveal a personal, rather than social, focal point. That is, the individual remained the locus of interest for Spender, a legacy of Romanticism which characterizes his work as a whole. Spender joined the Communist Party to show his sympathy for struggling peoples across the globe, but left it relatively quickly fearing the strident pragmatism of the Communist Party's use of art. By the time *The Still Center* (1939) was published, Spender had moved away from the left, embracing instead a tradition of English liberalism: as much as possible, art was to be autonomous and the individual self-determined.

During the 1940s, Spender's poetic output lessened as he began two important editorial tenures, first at *Horizon* (1939–41), then at *Encounter* (1953–67), an anti-Communist political and literary magazine (originally funded by the CIA). Having already published two volumes of incisive criticism, *The Destructive Element* (1935) and *The New Realism* (1939), Spender's connection with these two magazines allowed him to continue his literary commentaries. *Poems of Dedication*(1946) and *The Edge of Being* (1949) comprised Spender's primary poetic output for the decade, volumes full of his usual clear-eyed imagery and emphasis upon the body and self as existential and poetic subjects.

Spender lectured, taught, and traveled for the rest of his life; he was named a Commander of the British Empire in 1962 and knighted in 1983. Although Auden has rightfully received the most critical attention of this group and Day Lewis was named Poet Laureate, Spender's legacy is to remain the romantic balance to the popular vision of the exacting Thirties Poet. Committed via belief in the individual, not the collective, Spender crafted a poetic and critical defense of the grand liberal tradition.

[MW]

Spicer, Jack (United States, 1925–65) Spicer was born in Los Angeles to relatively affluent parents. He earned degrees from the University of California where, with ROBERT DUNCAN and Robin Blaser, he formed a group known as the 'Berkeley Renaissance'. Spicer continued at Berkeley, all but completing a Ph.D. in linguistics. Spicer supported himself as an academic, and published little in his own lifetime; his *Collected Books* (1975) and *One Night Stand . .* (1980) were both published posthumously. He died in 1965 from severe liver damage.

With Duncan and Blaser, he asserted that a poem existed a priori to language, and that language attempted to embody that poem. In an attempt to turn American poetry away from the Whitmanesque, and toward a more impersonal Modernist poetics, Spicer claimed his poetry originated outside himself, something especially true of his later work. Although he also insisted that the political did not impinge upon the poetic, his work was unapologetic in its open homoeroticism in a time when such lifestyles were unpopular.

[VB]

Spire, André (France, 1868–1966) Born in Nancy to a family of the Jewish bourgeoisie with ancestry dating to the seventeenth century, Spire was a child of republican values in progress and reason.

Like PÉGUY, Spire experienced an awakening in the aftermath of the Dreyfus Affair (1894–1906), which brought to the fore the problematic Jewish presence in France. In 1902, during his stay in the Jewish quarter of London's East End, he discovered for himself what he believed was an authentic, proletarian Jewish population. After 1908 he became a vocal proponent of Zionism, and he remained skeptical about the possibility of Jewish assimilation into the French Republic. He spent World War II teaching in New York City. Speaking neither Yiddish nor Hebrew, it was in French that he wrote poignantly about Jewish identity.

Selected works: *Poèmes juifs* (*Jewish Poems*, first edition, 1907; definitive edition, 1959); *Quelques juifs* (*Some Jews*, 1913); *Quelques juifs et demi-juifs* (*Some Jews and Half Jews*, 1923); *Plaisir poétique et plaisir musculaire* (*Poetic Pleasure and Muscular Pleasure*, 1949); *Souvenirs à bâtons rompus* (*Rambling Memories*, 1961).

[SJ]

St John, David (United States, b. 1949) St John was born in Fresno, California, and educated at California State University and the University of Iowa. He teaches at the University of Southern California. His awards include a Prix de Rome fellowship.

St John's elegant poems explore the tensions between the contradictory desires for individual autonomy and intimate communion with another. Epistolary, narrative, confessional, and elegiac elements are not so much interwoven as layered, through a use of lush imagery, lyrical process, and subtly modulated tones.

Selected works: *Hush* (1976); *The Shore* (1980); *No Heaven* (1985); *Study for the World's Body: New and Selected Poems* (1994); *The Red Leaves of Night* (1999).

[JT]

St Vincent Millay, Edna (United States, 1892–1950) No American poet was more popular between the two World Wars than Edna St Vincent Millay. Her oft-quoted quatrain, 'My candle burns at both ends; / It will not last the night. / But ah, my foes, and oh, my friends – / It gives a lovely light', was a rallying cry for the new Bohemians living in Greenwich Village, as well as for the new 'free women', for whom she became unofficial feminine laureate.

Millay was born on February 22, 1892 in Rockland, Maine. She attended Vassar College, graduating in 1917, the year of her first volume, *Renascence*. The long title poem was written when the author was just nineteen, and it remains one of her best works. Her second collection, *A Few Figs from Thistles* (1920) was very popular, but not as fine as her third, *Second April*, which followed a year later. That collection dealt with more serious matters, and in a more serious tone.

During her lifetime she was to publish eight more collections and four plays. Of these, *Fatal Interview* (1931), a group of over fifty sonnets, was best received by critics. She was compared with Dante Gabriel Rossetti, Elizabeth Barrett Browning, Petrarch, and even Shakespeare. The least appreciated were *Conversations at Midnight* (1937), in which she assumed various male personae; and *Make Bright the Arrows* (1940), anti-war diatribes disguised as poems. When it came to political poetry, the Muse deserted her.

In her younger years, Millay lived in New York City and supported herself by writing short fiction, translating, and working with the Provincetown Players as both playwright and performer. She had numerous love affairs, among them one with critic Edmund Wilson. In 1923 *The Harp Weaver* won the Pulitzer Prize, and at the end of that year she married Eugene Boissevain, a businessman. For a time they remained in Manhattan, but her precarious mental state caused a retreat to a hilltop farmhouse in Austerlitz, upstate New York. Boissevain predeceased her, and she lived her remaining years alone, writing productively but in poor health. She died one evening in 1950, attempting to ascend the stairs to her room. She was found seated on the stairs, a glass of wine beside her – projecting a romantic image to the end. Sixty-six uncollected poems were published posthumously as *Mine the Harvest* (1954).

Her finest work were her sonnets, which at their best were moving and technically brilliant. These include 'What Lips My Lips Have Kissed', 'Pity Me Not', 'I Shall Go Back', 'Euclid Alone Has Looked on Beauty Bare', 'On Hearing a Symphony of Beethoven', 'Love Is Not All; It Is Not Meat or Drink', and 'Well, I Have Lost You, and Lost You Fairly'.

Selected works: *Collected Sonnets* (1941); *Collected Lyrics* (1943); *Collected Poems* (1956).

[RP]

Staff, Leopold (Poland, 1878–1957) Staff was born in Lvov. He studied law, philosophy, and Romance languages at the university there, and after World War I he moved to Warsaw where he resided for the rest of his life. From 1901 to 1954 Staff published sixteen books, and a posthumous volume appeared in 1958. In 1983 a selection of post-war poems was translated into English under the title *An Empty Room*. Staff was the recipient of numerous awards and honors, including a P.E.N. Club prize for his work as a translator.

A prominent presence in the 'Young Poland' movement which revolutionized Polish poetry prior to World War I, Staff, however, did not align himself with any group or school. Instead, as Adam Czerniawski noted, 'Staff was the benign spirit who presided over Polish poetry during the first half of this century'. TADEUSZ ROZEWICZ has gone so far as to call Staff 'the god of poetry'.

Always a philosophical poet with a Renaissance sensibility, Staff exhibited a formal yet provocative elegance in his early poems, but most critics and poets, including CZESLAW MILOSZ, find the 'sophisticated simplicity' of his later work, where he 'rejected meter and rhyme', to be 'his highest accomplishment'.

Selected works: *Still Weather* (1946); *Osier* (1954); *The Nine Muses* (1958).

[MO]

Stafford, William (United States, 1914–93) Stafford has been called the ROBERT FROST of the West since his poetry is honest, plain, and concerned with the relationship between the human and nature. Moreover, his poetry also addresses the separation between the individual and nature as well as the loneliness that pervades human relationships. But unlike Frost, Stafford's poems often strive to find an equilibrium between people and nature in order to uncover a sense of peace in an otherwise turbulent and chaotic world.

Born in Hutchinson, Kansas, Stafford attended the University of Kansas (B.A., 1937; M.A., 1945) and the University of Iowa (Ph.D., 1955). Except for a brief period during the 1950s, Stafford was a professor at Lewis and Clark College in Portland, Oregon, until his death in 1993.

During World War II, Stafford served as a conscientious objector and worked in various civilian public service camps, which reinforced his belief that poetry must strive toward peace.

A prolific author who published over thirty-three books of poetry, five works of non-fiction, and one of translations, Stafford was the Poet Laureate of Oregon from 1975 to 1990. His collection, *Traveling through the Dark* (1962), was awarded the National Book Award.

[DC]

Stainer, Pauline (England, b. 1941) Born in Burslem, Pauline Stainer was educated at St Anne's College, Oxford (B.A., 1963) and Southampton University (M.Phil., 1967).

While Stainer has yet to receive much international attention, she is well-known and well-regarded in England for the elusive nature of her poetry's emotional overtones and her resuscitation and enhancement of poetic clichés. Her work examines the relationship between the profound and the mundane, often elevating the status of the latter to that of the former. She was awarded a Hawthornden Fellowship in 1987, and the National Poetry Competition Prize in 1992.

Selected works: *The Honeycomb* (1989); *Little Egypt* (1991); *Sighting the Slave Ship* (1992); *The Ice-Pilot Speaks* (1994); *The Wound-Dresser's Dream* (1996).

[SG]

Stallworthy, Jon (England, b. 1935) Born in London to a prominent surgeon, Stallworthy later detailed the history of his family life in *A Familiar Tree* (1978). Stallworthy is noted for his biographical and critical studies of poet WILFRED OWEN, as well as his translations of BLOK and PASTERNAK. After serving in the Oxfordshire and Buckinghamshire Light Infantry in 1953–55, he attended Magdalen College, Oxford, where he earned his B.A. (1958) and B.Litt. (1961). His role as a husband and father influenced his poetry, which largely draws on personal themes. Stallworthy was editor for Oxford University Press, London, from 1959 to 1971, and went on to teach at Cornell University for almost a decade. He has since taught at Wolfson College, Oxford. Among his many awards are the Newdigate Prize for English Verse (1958), the Duff Cooper Memorial Prize (1974), and the National Institute and American

Academy of Arts and Sciences E.M. Forster Award (1976).

Selected works: *The Earthly Paradise* (1958); *The Astronomy of Love* (1961); *The Almond Tree* (1967); *Hand in Hand* (1974); *The Apple Barrel: Selected Poems, 1955–1963* (1974); *The Anzac Sonata: New and Selected Poems* (1986); *Guest from the Future* (1997).

[BRB]

Stănescu, Nichita (Romania, 1933–83) Born in the oil city of Ploeşti, north of Bucharest, Stănescu studied at the University of Bucharest and worked as an editor after graduation. A poet who opened new paths in Romanian verse, Stănescu was equally praised and denigrated initially. Eventually, however, his status was recognized. He received several Poetry Prizes from the Romanian Writers' Union, the Herder Prize for poetry (1978), and a nomination for the Nobel Prize (1979). When he died, the poet was buried next to Mihai Eminescu, Romania's greatest poet, and Stănescu's idol. Recognized as a distinct voice in world poetry, as capable of song (*The Sense of Love*, 1960) as elegy (*Eleven Elegies*, 1966), Stănescu has been translated widely.

The most important post-war poet, on a par with the pre-war greats—BACOVIA, BARBU, BLAGA, and ARGHEZI—Stănescu was initially an exalted adolescent singing love in pre-war metaphors (*A Vision of Feelings*, 1964). However, he soon became disappointed with the inadequacy of the word, laden as it is with tradition. Therefore existing poetic forms had to be crushed and recharged with significance for a new discourse to be created. Stănescu's agony over the rupture between reality and its linguistic expression, between meaning and its form, led to *Unwords* (1969). 'Unwords' speak themselves defying all rules of grammar; they change meaning as they engage the self in speech and become 'knotted' to lived meaning (*Knots and Signs*, 1982). As Ş. Mincu puts it, throughout his work, 'Stănescu makes a dramatic attempt, not at metapoetry, a discourse in which the Self becomes impersonal, but at transcending the poetic perceived as a convention, not outside of itself, in a production of ars poeticas, but toward life'.

Selected works: *The Right to Time* (1965); *The Egg and the Sphere* (1967); *Laus Ptolemaei* (1968); *In the Sweet Classic Style* (1970); *Epica Magna* (1978); *Unfinished Work* (1979).

[GF]

Stead, C. K. (New Zealand, b. 1932) Born in Auckland, Christian Karlson Stead earned his M.A. from the University of Auckland and his Ph.D. from the University of Bristol. He has traveled widely and was Professor of English at the University of Auckland until 1986. He is now a full-time writer. Stead is also a prominent critic, novelist, and short story writer, but considers himself to be primarily a poet.

Stead's early poems have strong romantic characteristics and are marked by his stylistic skill and musical sense. His *Crossing the Bar* (1972) constitutes a transition to his later, Modernist style, influenced especially by the poetry of EZRA POUND. Stead's interest in New Zealand society is reflected in a frequent exploration of its political themes even as his poetry is infused by a strong consciousness of poetic tradition. His frequent travels often surface as a continuing contrast of place, of 'here' and 'there'. His Modernist poetry attempts to relate life 'as it occurs', in a loose fragmentary structure in the form of what he has called a long 'process poem'. Stead adapted the Baxterian sonnet and translations of other poems, for example those of Catullus.

Selected works: *Whether the Will is Free* (1962); *Quesada* (1975); *Walking Westward* (1979); *Geographies* (1982); *Poems of a Decade* (1983); *Between* (1988); *Voices* (1990).

[SH]

Ştefan, Florika (Yugoslavia, b. 1930) Ştefan was born into a Romanian family in

Lokve, Vojvodina. After attending the University of Belgrade, she moved to Novi Sad, Vojvodina, where she lives now. She writes poetry and essays in both Romanian and Serbo-Croat. In addition to editing several literary journals, she has worked as a journalist for various radio-stations, newspapers, and publishing companies.

Štefan's earlier poetry was focused on social issues and themes. Her later poems are more confessional, focused on intimate themes (such as love and death), and written in a penetrating, stylized idiom which is at times passionate and melancholy. She creates her own vision of the world in which life occurs as a drama that necessarily creates questions, dilemmas, and tragedies.

Selected works: *Cîntecul tineretii* (*Poems of Youth*, 1949); *Dozvolite suncu* (*Let the Sun*, 1962); *Jutarnji hleb* (*Morning Bread*, 1979); *Prelomne godine* (*Crucial Years*, 1980); *Zebnja* (*Dread*, 1990); *Beleg* (1998).

[DJ]

Stefánsson, Davíð (Iceland, 1895–1964) The leading Icelandic romantic poet of the 1920s and 1930s and the most prolific poet of his time, Stefánsson is also known for his plays and the novel *Sólon Islandus* (1940). Born to a cultured farmers' family (his father was a Member of Parliament), Stefánsson traveled extensively in Europe, then spent half of his life (from 1925) as a librarian in the small town of Akureyri. His hobby as book collector also shows in his poetry. His verse, ranging from the lyrical to the epic, combines social criticism with a stylistic homage to Icelandic folklore. The debt to folk themes and love lyrics is especially clear in Stefánsson's early poetry, beginning with *Svartar Fjaðrir* (*Black Feathers*, 1919), which brought him wide recognition. His work since *Í byggðum* (*Among Human Habitations*, 1933) shows a growing social involvement and stresses social themes, including a critique of capitalism and religious institutions and a darker vision in the aftermath of World War II. The last collection published during his lifetime, *Ný kvædabók* (*A New Book of Poems*, 1947), contains some of his finest poems.

[YB]

Stern, Gerald (United States, b. 1925) Stern was born in Pittsburgh and educated at the University of Pittsburgh and at Columbia. He has taught at a number of universities, including the University of Iowa.

Nostalgic and celebratory, Stern's poetry follows in the tradition of Whitman; many have observed the technical similarities between the two poets, but Stern attributes them to a mutual reading of the Old Testament. To the Whitman tradition Stern brings Jewish humor and a playful sensibility. The result is a distinctive voice, proceeding from a central speaker who is at once ironically self-absorbed and generously empathic. Stern's *This Time: New and Selected Poems* received the National Book Award in 1998.

Selected works: *Rejoicings* (1973); *Lucky Life* (1977); *The Red Coal* (1981); *Leaving Another Kingdom: Selected Poems* (1990).

[JT]

Stevens, Wallace (United States, 1879–1955) Unlike most poets who decide to dedicate their lives to their poetry, Stevens decided while he was a sophomore at Harvard University to enroll in the New York School of Law in order to secure a financial stability that could support his literary endeavors. Stevens graduated in 1903, was admitted to the New York Bar in 1904, and slowly began a career that would culminate as vice-president of the Hartford Accident and Indemnity Co. Once he achieved a sense of financial security, he not only focused his attention upon his poetry, but he also began to consider the possibility of marriage. With a stable job, in September of 1909 he married Elsie Viola Kachel.

Since Stevens placed such importance upon establishing himself financially, it is perhaps hardly surprising that his first book of poetry, *Harmonium* (1923) was not published until he was forty-four years old. Largely ignored, *Harmonium* included a number of significant poems, such as the imagistic 'Thirteen Ways of Looking at a Blackbird', 'Peter Quince at the Clavier', and 'Sunday Morning', a pivotal poem that outlines the central argument that would drive the whole of Stevens' poetic career. Stevens perceives Christianity as spiritually, emotionally, and intellectually bankrupt, and he argues that poetry as a mode of aesthetic existence is and must be the force that provides a sense of fulfillment for society.

From 1923 until 1933 Stevens wrote little poetry. His daughter Holly was born in 1924, and her birth may have contributed to this prolonged lull in his writing. None the less, *Ideas of Order*, Stevens' second book of poetry (1935), continues his earlier argument for the primacy of an aesthetic mode of existence, and in the poem 'The Idea of Order at Key West', one of his most important works, Stevens praises the artist as the maker of order and as the vehicle that brings the vitality of existence into sharp relief.

Ideas of Order earned Stevens recognition as a poet, and critical attention slowly shifted in his favor. From 1935 onward he was considered one of America's greatest living poets. Five notable collections of poetry followed: *The Man with the Blue Guitar* (1937), a long poem meditating upon Pablo Picasso's painting of the same name; *Parts of a World* (1942); *Notes Towards a Supreme Fiction* (1942); *Transport to Summer* (1947); and *The Auroras of Autumn* (1950).

Throughout his career, Stevens often returned to the role of the artist as the person most capable of delineating the inextricable relationship of reality and imagination; his collection of essays, *The Necessary Angel: Essays on Reality and the Imagination* (1960) emphasizes that poetry is the ultimate fusion of imagination and objective reality – an idea shared with MARIANNE MOORE, with whom Stevens corresponded for years.

At his death in 1955, Stevens was one of the leading voices of American poetry, and he is often regarded as the American poet par excellence.

[DC]

Stewart, Douglas (Australia, 1913–85) A New Zealander by birth, Stewart moved to Sydney in 1938 to work for the *Bulletin*. He was editor of that publication's literary page from 1940 until 1961, then became a literary editor for publishers Angus & Robertson until his 1971 retirement, during which he continued his literary career as an editor, dramatist, anthologist, and poet.

Stewart's early books of verse dealt with the New Zealand landscape; after moving to Australia he was forced to come to terms with a new physical and cultural landscape. In this struggle he was greatly influenced by the Australian nature poetry of the 1940s. In *Sun Orchids* (1952) and *The Birdsville Track* (1955), Stewart attained the spare, witty observational voice for which he was to become known.

Some of Stewart's finest poems, such as 'B Flat' and 'Silkworms', examine wise passivity as an antidote to violent fanaticism. The meaning of heroism was another common theme: first examined in his verse plays, such as *The Fire on the Snow* (1944), this topic resurfaced in *Rutherford* (1946). In these poems, however, the plays' historical explorer-heroes have been replaced by scientists.

Stewart received an OBE in 1960, and won the Britannica Australia Award in 1968.

Selected works: *Green Lions* (1936); *The White Cry* (1939); *Elegy for an Airman* (1940); *Sonnets to the Unknown Soldier* (1941); *The Dosser in Springtime* (1946); *Glencoe* (1947); *Selected Poems* (1963, 1973); *Collected Poems, 1936–67* (1967); *Selected Poems* (1992).

[JL]

Storni, Alfonsina (Argentina, 1892–1938) Storni was born in Sala Capriasca, Switzerland, shortly before her family emigrated to Argentina. In 1907 she joined a theatrical company for one year. After having an illegitimate son, she moved to Buenos Aires and was the first woman accepted into intellectual circles where she befriended Horacio Quiroga whose suicide in 1937 greatly affected her. Storni drowned herself in Mar del Plata in 1938.

Storni's presentation of the female as well as her direct condemnation of gender biases, as found in *El dulce daño* (*The Sweet Harm*, 1918), *Irremediablemente* (*Irremediably*, 1919), and *Languidez* (*Languor*, 1920), earned her the title of first Latin American feminist. She was awarded the Primer Premio Municipal and the Segundo Premio Nacional de Literatura in 1920.

[VW]

Strand, Mark (United States, b. 1934) Born in Canada in Summerside, Prince Edward Island, Strand took a B.A. at Antioch College and a B.F.A. at Yale University, where he studied painting. He completed his M.A. in 1962 at the University of Iowa, where he taught for three years. He has been a Fulbright scholar in Italy and a Fulbright lecturer in Brazil. He has translated poems by Carlos Drummond de Andrade and RAFAEL ALBERTI, in addition to writing several children's books and a volume of short fiction.

His awards include the Pulitzer Prize (1999), and fellowships from the Ingram Merrill, Rockefeller, and Guggenheim Foundations and from the National Endowment for the Arts. In 1987 he received a MacArthur Fellowship, and in 1990 he was named Poet Laureate of the United States. While noted for his surrealistic poems, such as 'Eating Poetry', his best work is autobiographical, including 'Elegy for My Father' and 'Shooting Whales'. Currently he teaches at the University of Chicago.

Selected works: *Selected Poems* (1989); *The Continuous Life* (1990); *Dark Harbor* (1993); *Blizzard of One* (1998).

[RP]

Suárez, Clementina (Honduras, 1902–91) Suárez worked to encourage interest in the arts in Central America. She owned art galleries, read her poetry in public, and traveled extensively to experience the intellectual climate of other countries. Suárez founded the magazine *Mujer* (*Woman*) that published articles on literature and art; she also contributed to many other journals.

Despite her many cultural interests, she is best known for the poetry found in *Corazón Sangrante* (*Bleeding Heart*, 1930), *Engranajes* (*Meshings*, 1935), *Creciendo con la hierba* (*Growing in the Grass*, 1957), *and El poeta y sus señales: Antologia* (*The Poet and Her Signs: Anthology*, 1969). Her poetry treats the subjects of motherhood, revolution, and of course the role of the arts in society. Suárez held a seat in the Academia de la Lengua and received the Premio Nacional de Literatura in 1970.

[VW]

Swenson, May (United States, 1913–89) Anna Thilda May Swenson was born in Logan, Utah, and educated at Utah State University. The eldest of ten children in a close-knit Mormon family, she did not inform her parents that she was moving permanently when she left for New York in 1936. She lived there for the rest of her life, working at various office jobs to support herself while writing until she began to receive the numerous awards – among them an Amy Lowell Scholarship, and a Bollingen Prize – which allowed her to devote herself full-time to her craft.

In its meticulous examination of physical phenomena, Swenson's work is reminiscent of MARIANNE MOORE and ELIZABETH BISHOP (she carried on a long-term correspondence with the latter), but departs from them in the individuation and identification of its speaker. While Swenson's eye is pressed so closely against the world as almost to merge with it – she spoke of 'a craving to get through the curtains of things as they *appear*, to things as they *are*, and then into . . . things as they are *becoming*' – she remains distinct, bounded, and overtly present.

Swenson's poetry is predominantly free-verse, and often experimental. Her book *Iconographs* is a collection of shape poems constructed to represent the objects or dynamics on which they focus. Her collections of 'poems to solve' are riddles.

Selected works: *A Cage of Spines* (1958); *To Mix with Time: New and Selected Poems* (1963); *Half Sun Half Asleep* (1967); *New and Selected Things Taking Place* (1978); *In Other Words* (1987).

[JT]

Swir, Anna (Poland, 1909–84) Anna Swirszczynska was born in Warsaw, to a family whose poverty forced her to work early in her life. The images of her first poems, published in the 1930s, reflect her university study of medieval art and baroque Polish literature.

Swir's experience as a military nurse and underground worker in Warsaw during World War II radically changed her poetry. *Building the Barricade* (1974) renders the Warsaw Uprising of 1944 in a cycle of one hundred poem-pictures. Her contemporary CZESLAW MILOSZ sees flesh as the central theme of her mature, feminist poems: 'flesh in love-ecstasy, flesh in pain, flesh in terror, flesh afraid of loneliness'.

Selected works: *Wind* (1970); *I Am a Woman* (1972); *Happy as a Dog's Tail* (1978); *Talking to My Body* (1996).

[RD]

Szirtes, George (England, b. 1948) Szirtes was born in Budapest in 1948 and moved to England in 1966. Although visits to his native Hungary in the mid-1980s have influenced his later writing, it is his training as a painter and graphic artist which informs his work as a whole. Throughout his career as a poet, much of his work has been visually surrealistic, which is often combined with traditional English poetic form characterized by his attention to meter and stanza. This seeming paradox between traditional form and surrealistic content seems to complement Szirtes' tendency to couple feelings of optimism with an atmosphere of impending doom. In addition to his work as a poet, Szirtes edits and translates Hungarian poetry.

Selected works: *The Slant Door* (1979); *Short Wave* (1984); *The Photographer in Winter* (1986); *Metro* (1988); *Bridge Passages* (1911).

[BB]

Szymborska, Wislawa (Poland, b. 1923) 'The premier Polish woman poet' (STANISLAW BARANCZAK) and recipient of the 1996 Nobel Prize for Literature, Szymborska was born in Kornik, near Poznan in western Poland. She has lived most of her life in Krakow, where she attended school illegally during the German occupation, afterward studying philology and sociology at the Jagiellonian University. From 1952 to 1981 she worked on the editorial staff of the weekly publication *Zycie Literackie* (*Literary Life*). Early in this tenure she published *That Is Why We Live* (1952) and *Questions Asked of Oneself* (1954), though Szymborska now rejects these first two volumes as participating in the falsehood of the official language imposed by Communist ideology. *Calling Out to Yeti* (1957) is the first book she recognizes as her own. She has published nine collections of poems in Polish and three English translations. Her most recent English volume, *Poems New and Collected, 1957–1997*, includes her Nobel Lecture, delivered in Stockholm in December 1996.

Like other poets of her generation, Szymborska is essentially a metaphysical poet forced by the events of World War II toward a historical poetry. Like TADEUSZ ROZEWICZ and ZBIGNIEW HERBERT, she is an involuntary witness of the Holocaust, the Stalinist occupation of Poland, and the eventual imposition of martial law in 1981. She simultaneously seeks the nature of philosophical truth and bears a devastating historical knowledge. Her poems are primarily lyrical meditations motivated by the human existential situation and the individual's relationship to history. The work is ironic, skeptical, and combines a sardonic voice with delicacy of imagery. Often a poem begins by positing an intellectual concern, a simple paradoxical assertion which it then sets out to explore. These meditations reveal the interior life of a woman who examines our external existence with the compassion of one who holds this earthly world dear, and with the skepticism of one who has witnessed just how foolish, cruel, and vulnerable, we who dwell among its raptures can be.

Poems such as 'The Sky' and 'Writing a Resumé' illustrate Szymborska's characteristic rejection of, and reconciliation to, the divisions manufactured by human consciousness. In the latter poem, the pragmatic title delineates a task, but the poem itself explores and illuminates the gap between the public personae social institutions demand of us and the actual experience of our individuality: 'Of all your loves, mention only the marriage; /of all your children, only those who were born.' Szymborska recognizes first-hand that language co-opted by a totalitarian force can become the vehicle for cultural aberration, an instrument used to mask truth. She distrusts a poetry of witnessing, recognizing the danger of speaking on behalf of a people – and she distrusts a poetry devoid of irony, its humor. Like much of Szymborska's verse, these poems meet human folly with both lamentation and laughter.

Selected works: *Salt* (1962); *No End of Fun* (1967); *Could Have* (1972); *A Large Number* (1976); *Sounds, Feelings, Thoughts: Seventy Poems* (1981); *The People on the Bridge* (1986); *The End and the Beginning* (1993); *View with a Grain of Sand* (1993).

[RD]

T

Tada Chimako (Japan, b. 1931) Tada was born in Fukuoka and lives in Kobe. She graduated from Keio University with a major in English literature. Her first book of poems, *Hanabi* (*Fireworks*, 1956), drew favorable attention, and she has published extensively since.

Tada is considered one of Japan's foremost intellectual poets. With refined and intellectual style, her works show an attempt at combining intellect and the senses, bringing some freshness of language into a Japanese poetry that has tended toward excessive sentimentality. As a student of the Classics, she has shown special interest in Homer's *Odyssey*. Tada is also recognized as a highly cultivated and intelligent translator; she has translated works by SAINT-JOHN PERSE, Georges Charbonnier, ANTONIN ARTAUD, Marguerite Yourcenar, and Claude Lévi-Strauss.

[LY]

Tagore, Rabindranath (India, 1861–1941) Tagore was born in Calcutta into a family of prominent aristocrats. Among his uncles were important painters and his father, a Sanskrit scholar, was a leader of a Hindu reform movement. He left school at fourteen and later attended Calcutta's Presidency College for just one day. An attempt at further studies in England during 1878–80 was similarly abortive.

Tagore published at least 21 collections of poetry and songs in Bengali, as well as novels, short stories, and plays. He also painted, in a naive style that is wholly his own. Paradoxically, his international reputation rests mainly on a single English volume of poetry, *Gitanjali*, or 'Song-Offering', for which he was given the Nobel Prize for Literature in 1913. Tagore's own translation of this work, which does not exactly correspond to the Bengali original, was taken up, amended, and championed by WILLIAM BUTLER YEATS. For a brief while Tagore was in vogue in literary London, counting EZRA POUND among his admirers, until an inevitable reaction set in. Tagore's poetry for a long while survived abroad mainly in spiritualist circles, though PABLO NERUDA and Herman Hesse were also moved to translate him.

In India, Tagore was a much more dynamic poet. Styling himself a *baul*, one of a band of itinerant singers whose songs mingled Muslim and Hindu and mystical and devotional vocabularies, he engendered a genuine discovery of rich troves of folk poetry in Bengali and other Indian languages. His songs, set to his own innovative melodies, became a fondly enacted domestic genre of their own. His more ambitious verse adopts a varied line and draws on both Bengali's Sanskrit inheritance and its colloquial vocabulary. This combination was initially regarded as unmetrical and jarring but eventually became the dominant style of Bengali poetry.

In addition to his literary pre-eminence, Tagore was a figure in the reimagining of India's cultural heritage that accompanied the rise of political nationalism. In 1901 he founded a school at Shanti Niketan, which in 1924 became Vishwa Bharati University. He engaged in a long, but friendly, polemic with Mahatma Gandhi, whose economics, based on cottage industries like cotton spinning, disturbed him. He wrote songs that became the official national anthems of both India and Bangladesh. (The Indian anthem was composed to replace a nationalist hymn in which Muslims, and Jawaharlal Nehru, found an objectionable Hindu chauvinism.) Tagore was knighted in 1915, renouncing the award in 1919 immediately after British troops fired on Indian nationalists at Jalianwala Bagh in Amritsar, Punjab.

[AM]

Taha, Ali Mahmoud (Egypt, 1901–49) Born in al-Mansura, Taha graduated from a technical institute in 1924. He achieved great fame throughout the Arab world as the leading Romantic poet of the 1930s and 1940s. His poetry balances a fine sense of music with powerful emotion. His themes revolve around love, women, wine, and poetry, and Europe figures in his work as the locus of the exotic. His influence and corpus exhausted many of the possibilities of Romanticism, so that later in his life, Taha himself moved toward national and political themes, like so many mid-century Arabic poets.

Selected works: *The Lost Mariner* (1934); *Nights of the Lost Mariner* (1940); *Flowers and Wine* (1943); *East and West* (1947).

[WH]

Takamura Kotaro (Japan, 1883–1956) Takamura was born in Tokyo, the son of a noted sculptor. At first he wrote only in the *tanka* form; after leaving Japan in 1906 to study sculpture in the United States, he started writing free verse. He lived for a time in France, where he read such poets as Verlaine, Baudelaire, and Rimbaud and was influenced by Rodin. Known as a strong humanist, his interest in socialism is often expressed in his works, such as *Dotei* (*A Journey*, 1914). After his wife Chieko died, *Chieko Shyo* (*Poems for Chieko*), a book of poems about her, was published and became his most popular work. Takamura is also highly respected for some half-dozen other volumes of poetry as well as his lifelong activity as a sculptor.

[LY]

Tamura Ryuichi (Japan, b. 1923) The son of a restaurateur, Tamura was born in Tokyo in the year of the Great Kanto Earthquake. He began writing self-consciously avant-garde poetry at the age of fourteen, mainly affected by the European literature of the 1920s. After graduating from Meiji University in 1943, he served in the Imperial Navy; unlike most of his friends, he managed to survive World War II on shore duty. Returning to the devastated Tokyo, he helped to found the influential poetry magazine *Arechi* (*The Wasted Land*, 1947–8, revived as an annual in 1951–8), which dominated the poetic scene of this period.

Tamura's first collection, *Yosen no hi to your* (*Four Thousand Days and Nights*, 1956), was characterized by bleak images of autumn, rain, and death. His second book, *Kotoba no nai Sekai* (*World without Language*, 1962), showed a colder concern with language than the first. Like other Wasteland poets, by employing the abstract and esthetic aspects of data and surrealism, Tamura managed to criticize modern culture. A *Collected Poems* appeared in 1966, and this has been followed by *Midori no Shiso* (*A Green Thought*, 1967) and *Shinnen no Tegami* (*New Year's Letter*, 1973). In some half-dozen later volumes, Tamura has gone beyond the unrelieved despair toward a new lyricism opening out, although tentatively, on a landscape suffused with music. He remains one of the most distinguished Japanese post-war poets.

[LY]

Tanikawa Shuntaro (Japan, b. 1931) Tanikawa was born in Tokyo, the only son of the distinguished philosopher Tanikawa Tetsuzo. He disliked school from the start, constantly rebelled against his high school teachers, and never even considered going to college. By the age of eighteen he was writing poetry and had several poems published in the prestigious literary magazine *Bungakkai* (*Literary World*), as a result of the influence of Miyoshi Tatsuji, who was one of the leading poets of the day and had a high opinion of Tanikawa's talent. Tanikawa's first book, *Niju Oku Konen no Kodoku* (*Twenty Billion Light Years of Loneliness*), appeared in 1952 and it marked a clear new direction in post-war Japanese poetry. As indicated by the title, Tanikawa's early poems were marked by a unique cosmic sensibility, by which he merged his personal feelings of youth with the infinite expanses of the universe.

In 1953 his second book, *Rokujuni no Sonetto* (*Six-Two Sonnets*), came out; and at the time he joined the *Kai* (Oar) group. This group, which was soon joined by OOKA MAKOTO, Yoshino Hiroshi, Tomotake Shin, Iijima Koichi, and others, made a lasting contribution to post-war Japanese poetry. Instead of depicting the intensity of war as the Wasteland poets (see TAMURA RYUICHI) did, Tanikawa's works present an innocent world without the shadow of war and defeat, providing an alternative version of post-war poetry. Yet his poems importantly involve philosophical elements, which is surely due to the influence of his father.

Tanikawa is one of the most prolific and the most celebrated poets in Japan. Almost every year a new book of poetry has appeared but he does not limit himself to verse as he is also well-known as a playwright, script-writer for film, television, radio, and a video producer. He has also written many collections of verse specially for children, experimenting with a variety of technical devices to create a huge range of new metrical forms. His titles are numerous, with several of his collections also being translated into English and many other languages.

Selected works: *Ai ni Tsuite* (*Concerning Love*, 1955); *Rakushu Kujuku* (*Ninety-nine Lampoons*, 1964); *Tabi* (*Travel*, 1968); *Utsumuku Seinen* (*The Downcast Boy*, 1971); *Kotoba Asobiuta* (*Word Play-Songs*, 1973); *Teigi* (*Definition*, 1975); *Sonohoka ni* (*Something Else*, 1979); *Kokakora Ressun* (*Coca-Cola Lesson*, 1981).

[LY]

Tate, Allen (United States, 1899–1979) A well-respected formal and learned poet, John Orley Allen Tate was most influential as a critic who helped establish New Criticism as a major interpretative approach to literature and 'close reading' as the dominant form of critical activity during the twentieth century.

Born in Winchester, Kentucky, and educated at Vanderbilt University, where he was taught by JOHN CROWE RANSOM, Tate admired the history, stability, and culture of the ante-bellum agrarian South. His first book of poems, *Mr Pope and Other Poems*, appeared in 1928, followed by such volumes as *Three Poems* (1930), *Poems, 1928–31* (1932), *The Mediterranean and Other Poems* (1936), *Poems: 1928–1947* (1948).

As a conservative he was concerned with the individual's attachment to received culture and traditional values. With the source and sanction of these values no longer whole, Tate saw that regarding persistent faith as individual heroism was contradictory. With a dignified rhetoric, Tate's best-known poem, 'Ode to the Confederate Dead', meditates on this tension, and attempts to affirm a heroism of belief within an aesthetic structure of ritual. In 1950, he converted to Catholicism, using its systematic values to inform his later poetry, as in *The Swimmers* (1970).

Tate wrote biographies of Stonewall Jackson and Jefferson Davis, an antebellum novel, *The Fathers* (1938), and edited *The Sewanee Review* in 1944–46. His books of criticism include *Reactionary Essays on Poetry and Ideas* (1936), *Reason in Madness* (1941), *On the Limits of Poetry* (1949), and *The Forlorn Demon* (1953). Tate was married four times, twice to the same woman, the novelist Caroline Gordon.

[DC]

Tate, James (United States, b. 1943) Tate was born in Kansas City, Missouri, and received an M.F.A. from the University of Iowa. He teaches at the University of Massachussets; he was awarded the 1992 Pulitzer Prize for *Selected Poems*.

Tate creates strange worlds wherein the unexpected and absurd jostle with the commonplace. Carried along by his deadpan, colloquial voice and his surrealistic juxtaposition of odd images, Tate's poems are often funny, enigmatic narratives full of verbal energy and adventure. Tate's buoyant humor is in constant tension with an undercurrent of loneliness, loss, and disillusionment, which makes his best work playful and moving.

Selected works: *The Lost Pilot* (Yale Younger Poets Prize, 1967); *Absences* (1972); *Distance from Loved Ones* (1990); *Selected Poems* (1991)

[AE]

Tati-Loutard, Jean-Baptiste (Congo, b. 1938) Tati-Loutard spent his childhood in the countryside with his mother and his sisters, and the sea greatly influenced his early poetry. He finished his undergraduate work at the University of Bordeaux in 1963, and later earned degrees in Italian and comparative literature. Since 1966, Tati-Loutard has led an academic life in the Congo, as professor, dean, director, minister, and critic.

He has described a poem as a vague element of the instinct for survival. He cites many international influences, and has soundly rejected the poetic theory of the Negritude movement. In his opinion, its essentialist preoccupations do not correspond with contemporary African experiences.

Selected works: *Les Poèmes de la mer* (*Poems of the Sea*, 1968); *Les Racines Congolaises* (*The Roots of the Congo*, 1968); *L'Envers du soleil* (*The Far Side of the Sun*, 1970); *Les Normes du temps* (*Standards of the Times*, 1974).

[KAC]

Tchernichovsky, Shaul (Israel, 1875–1943) Born in the village of Mikhalovka on the border between Crimea and Ukraine in 1875, Shaul (Saul) Tchernichovsky received a broad education which included both traditional Jewish and general topics, among them Russian, Modern Hebrew, and a number of European languages. In Odessa, where he lived for short periods, he became associated with literary and political Hebrew and Zionist circles, and established himself as poet and translator. Tchernichovsky studied medicine in Germany, returned to Russia in 1905, served as a military physician during World War I, and left in 1922 to settle in Berlin. In 1931 he emigrated to the Land of Israel and settled in Tel Aviv, where he served as a doctor.

Tchernichovsky's wide array of translations was unprecedented and unmatched by any of his Jewish contemporaries, and his poetry was unique in its breadth. It presented an unusual affinity with nature and pagan cultures combined with deep empathy for the human condition and understanding of both strength and tragedy embedded in the Jewish experience past and present. While in the Land of Israel he began writing poetry cast in the Sephardic rather than the Ashkenazic accent, thus establishing himself as one of the greatest poets of the Land of Israel as well as a great European poet. Tchernichovsky's first book, *Melodies and Liturgy*, was published in Warsaw in 1898. Collections of his poems were published in the early 1930s, 1966, and 1990.

[ER]

Thomas, Dylan (Wales, 1914–53) Thomas' talent was prodigious and precocious. Born on October 27, 1914, in Swansea, he left school at seventeen, forgoing further education to pursue his ambitions as a writer; even before the appearance of his first volume (*Eighteen Poems*, 1934) he had written over two hundred poems in notebook form. These notebooks provided the basis for many of the poems in his next two collections, *Twenty-five Poems* (1936), and *The Map of Love* (1939). Thomas' prolonged quarrying of material composed in late adolescence probably contributed to his image as a youthful visionary of high Romantic aspiration, an image re-confirmed for many by the nostalgic tone of his fourth volume, *Deaths and Entrances* (1946), which included 'The Hunchback in the Park' and 'Fern Hill' among its contents. However, others argue that Thomas' Romanticism is only superficial, and should not be allowed to overshadow his commitment to Modernist aesthetic principles. Certainly his work resists literal paraphrase, and owes as much to French Symbolism as to Keats or Shelley.

In 1949 Thomas settled in the Welsh coastal town of Laugharne with his wife Caitlin (whom he had married in 1937) and their three children. Although increasingly preoccupied with genres other than the poetic, his lyrical gift is fully evident in his late great 'play for voices', *Under Milk Wood* (1954); his best-known single poem, 'Do Not Go Gentle into That Good Night', also dates from this period.

By the 1950s Thomas had achieved international recognition, supplementing his income from reading tours of the United States. His skill as a reader was legendary, but so too was his capacity for drink, and one New York night in November 1953, after a particularly heavy binge, Thomas slipped into an alcoholic coma and never regained consciousness. In the resonant language of the official coroner's report, his death resulted from 'a massive insult to the brain'. His recently published *Collected Poems* (1952) would go on to win the Foyle's Prize.

Since then, Thomas' linguistic exuberance and rhetorical flights of sensual fancy have been criticized as well as praised: his positive influence is clear in the early PLATH or later BERRYMAN. The Movement poets, however, reacted against his 'excesses' by embracing irony and understatement and the attitude of many Anglo-Welsh authors toward their most famous literary countryman is also ambivalent (Dylan is often negatively contrasted with R.S. THOMAS, for example). It is true that when Thomas did employ devices derived from Welsh verse forms such as *cynghanedd* (literally, 'harmony': a technique of balancing consonantal sounds and meter across a single line) he had learned them from Hopkins rather than from any Welsh-language author. However, essentialist arguments about the authenticity of Thomas' 'Welshness' seem wrongheaded when considered from the other side: his work is no more readily assimilable to the English tradition, after all, and his best poems are unlike anything else in the language. As such, he remains one of the most distinctive and original voices of twentieth-century poetry.

[BS]

Thomas, Edward (Wales, 1878–1917) Thomas was born in London, of Welsh parents. He identified himself as Welsh, and as a boy made frequent holiday trips to his father's relatives in Carmarthenshire. It is perhaps ironic, therefore, that he found lasting fame as the quintessential celebrant of the English 'South country'.

Thomas read history at Lincoln College, Oxford, and married his childhood sweetheart while still a student. His marriage was not always happy (he felt that he could not equal his wife's love for him), but he worked hard as a writer and reviewer to support his rapidly growing family (in his short life he published some thirty prose volumes; they are predominantly works of rural observation with titles like *The Heart of England* (1906) and *Beautiful Wales* (1905). Thomas came to poetry late in his career, after being profoundly affected by ROBERT FROST's *North of Boston* (1914); he struck up an important friendship with Frost, who once said that 'The Road Not Taken' was inspired by Thomas' dreamy indecisiveness. Once he had chosen the path of poet, however, Thomas did not look back: between December 1914 and April 1917, he wrote more than 140 lyrics. His best work combines Frost's low-key diction with the nostalgic sensibility of THOMAS HARDY. A well-known reviewer of other people's poems, Thomas was slow to publish his own, and he would live to see only a handful in print; he had enlisted in the Army in 1915, and in 1917 he was killed on the battlefields of Arras.

[BS]

Thomas, R.S. (Wales, 1913–2000) Ronald Stuart Thomas was born in Cardiff, raised in Anglesey, read Classics at University College of North Wales, Bangor, and studied theology at St Michael's College, Llandaff. Ordained in 1936, he married the painter Mildred E. Eldrige soon afterward, and in 1942 became rector at Manafon, Montgomeryshire. There he wrote his first three volumes of verse (collected in *Song at the Year's Turning*), and also learned Welsh. He was the vicar at Eglwys-fach, Cardiganshire, from 1954, and at Aberdaron, Caernarvonshire (a primarily Welsh-speaking community) from 1967. After retiring from the church in 1978, Thomas moved again, to Y Rhiw, just outside Aberdaron.

The phases of Thomas' poetic career roughly conform to his geographical movements. His earliest poems, inspired by the tough hill-farming life of Manafon, are frequently as grim and dour in tone as the subjects they portray. Thomas was not above describing his parishioners as ignorant 'peasants,' and when he asks his reader not to be 'taken in / By stinking garments or an aimless grin' ('Affinity') he also seems to be admonishing himself. During this period Thomas invented the character of Iago Prytherch, a peasant *persona* to whom he would frequently return, and through whom he would continue to explore his feelings of ambivalence toward his countrymen.

Poetry for Supper (1958) saw Thomas extending and developing his earlier themes, while also exploring the politics of Welsh nationalism; and political concerns dominate middle period collections such as *The Bread of Truth* (1965). However, after moving to Aberdaron, religion gradually came to replace nation as Thomas' primary inspiration. Beginning with *H'm* (1972) and continuing through to *Frequencies* (1978) and beyond, Thomas produced some of the finest religious lyrics in twentieth-century English. They are also somewhat unorthodox – Thomas' God can seem as harsh and silent as the bleak countryside of his earliest work.

Upon retiring from the church, Thomas continued to write, examining the relation between poetry and painting in *Between Here and Now* (1981), and *Ingrowing Thoughts* (1985), and further developing his religious thematic in the extraordinary *Experimenting with an Amen* (1986). By now in his seventies, it seemed that he was just reaching the height of his powers. Thomas has won several awards, including the Heinemann Award of the Royal Society of Literature (1955), the Queen's Gold Medal for Poetry (1964), and the Cholmondeley Award (1978). In Wales his current reputation is at least equal to that of Dylan Thomas in the 1950s; indeed, some consider him to be the more authentically Welsh of the two poets. His work is certainly darker than Dylan's, and at times more obviously politicized, but it also has clear antecedents in the English literary tradition. (Thomas has edited selections of the two English-language poets he most resembles, George Herbert and William Wordsworth, and his introductions to those volumes provide valuable insights into his own aesthetic.) A *Collected Poems: 1945–90* was published in 1993.

[BS]

Thomson, Derick (Ruaridh Mac Thómas, b. 1921) Thomson was born on Lewis and studied at Aberdeen and Cambridge. He taught at the universities of Edinburgh, Glasgow, and Aberdeen, and was Professor of Celtic at Glasgow from 1963 to 1991. He founded the Gaelic magazine *Gairm* in 1952 and the Gaelic Books Council in 1968, of which he was Chairman from then until 1991. He was awarded the Ossian Prize in 1974 and *Creachadh na Clársaich / Plundering the Harp* was joint winner of the Saltire Society Book of the Year in 1982. In addition to his poetry, his critical work includes the important *Introduction to Gaelic Poetry* (1974).

Selected works: *An Dealbh Briste* (1951); *Eadar Samhradh is Foghar* (1967); *An Rathead Cian* (1970); *Saorsa agus an Iolaire* (1978); *Smeur an Dóchas / Bramble of Hope* (1993); *Meall Garbh* (1995).

[LKMF]

Thorpe, Adam (England, b. 1956) Poet, novelist, and dramatic artist Thorpe was born in Paris and raised in Beirut, Calcutta, Cameroon, and the south of England. He attended Magdalen College, Oxford.

Thorpe published his first book of poetry, *Mornings in the Baltic*, in 1988. The works in the collection are primarily poems which address diverse experiences and issues narrated through personae speaking about themselves. His second collection, *Meeting Montaigne* (1990), is shorter and models London upon images from Dante's *Inferno*.

In addition to his poetry, Thorpe has published novels and founded the Equinox Travelling Theatre and, in 1984, won the *Time Out* Mime Street Entertainer of the Year Award. Thorpe has taught mime at secondary schools in London, and English at the Polytechnic of Central London.

[BB]

Tomlinson, Charles (England, b. 1927) A noted translator as well as poet, Alfred Charles Tomlinson was born in the working-class midlands to middle-class parents, and went up to Cambridge in 1945. After jobs as a personal secretary and elementary school teacher, he became a lecturer, later professor, at the University of Bristol.

Tomlinson claimed that his poetry was always interested in depicting things as they were, being 'more interested in blackbirds than in ways of looking at them'. This reference to WALLACE STEVENS was fitting, since Tomlinson's work shows the influence of modern American poetics, particularly the work of Stevens. Just as influential, however, were the poets that Tomlinson would translate, including UNGARETTI, MACHADO, and PAZ.

Selected works: *Relations and Contraries* (1951); *Seeing is Believing* (1958); *A Peopled Landscape* (1963); *American Scenes and Other Poems* (1966); *Collected Poems* (1985); *Annunciations (1989)*; *The Door in the Wall* (1992).

[MW]

Toomer, Jean (United States, 1894–1967) Born Nathan Pinchback Toomer in Washington, D.C., Toomer was the maternal grandson of the first black governor in the U.S. and was raised in his grandfather's affluent household.

Toomer's family was of mixed racial ancestry and moved fluidly between white and black worlds. This fact was of defining importance for Toomer, who throughout his life resisted being categorized by race (unless it served his immediate interests). He saw himself as an American, one of the first conscious members of a new amalgamate race being produced by the melting pot of U.S. society.

After attending a number of universities briefly and working at various jobs, Toomer resolved to be a writer. In 1923, he published *Cane*, the impressionistic collection of poems, prose sketches, and stories on which his reputation rests. This volume had grown out of two months spent in Sparta, Georgia, where Toomer had experienced rural black culture for the first – and only – time. The book and its author were hailed as brilliant new additions to the Harlem Renaissance, but Toomer was uninterested; shortly after *Cane*'s publication, he left the world of literature to become a disciple of the mystic George Gurdjieff. Though Toomer continued to write prolifically for decades, he was unable to publish most of his work. The one poem outside *Cane* to receive attention was 'Blue Meridian', a Whitmanesque long poem laying out his transracial vision.

[JT]

Trakl, Georg (Austria, 1887–1914) Born into a wealthy family in Salzburg, Trakl was long tormented by alcohol and drug problems. He left school and became a pharmacist, which gave him easy access to drugs, and in 1912 he started working as an army pharmacist. When he experienced the horrors of World War I, as depicted in his poem 'Grodek', he attempted suicide. He later died of a cocaine overdose.

His early poetry was influenced by the French Symbolists; however, after 1912, Trakl wrote unique poems that belong to the ultimate achievement of early Expressionism, although he was less an Expressionist revolutionary than an eccentric individualist. The poems prefer ellipsis to traditional syntax and utilize illogical word combinations as though words had lost their communicative function; Trakl often replaced words with completely different ones during revisions of the same poem, exploiting sound over meaning.

While his poetry is hermetic, it is thematically focused on universal suffering and personal and general guilt. These themes are objectified in a dualism encompassing good and evil, i.e., the yearning for harmony that gives way to a sense of decay and loss of meaning, or god in an 'infernal chaos of rhythms and images'. Here metaphors with color adjectives 'black dew' are particularly challenging. Although formal changes (free verse and nominal style) mark his last poems, the themes and images provide such a cohesiveness that Trakl's poems can be seen as *one* long poem.

[IRS]

Tranströmer, Tomas (Sweden, b. 1931) Often mentioned as a candidate for the Nobel Prize and translated into more than thirty languages, Tranströmer has been the most influential Swedish poet since the 1950s.

While still a student of History of Religion at Stockholm University, he published his first collection, *17 dikter* (*17 Poems*, 1954). This volume describing childhood impressions from Runmarö in the Stockholm archipelago, was immediately recognized as the work of a gifted poet. In 1960 Tranströmer began working at the Roxtuna correctional institution for adolescents, where he stayed for six years. This period saw the publication of *Hemligheter pä vägen* (*Secrets on the Road*, 1962) and *Den halvfärduga himlen* (*The Half-made Heaven*, 1962), which reflect on the poet's travel abroad and reveal his interest in music, which would become a major theme in his writings. (Tranströmer would later claim to hold music as more important than poetry.) While moving to Västerås, the poet was guaranteed a writer's salary from the State, yet he continued to work as an occupational psychologist. In his fourth collection, *Klanger och spår* (*Echoes and Traces*, 1966), Tranströmer moves further toward abstract concerns, and in the following volume, *Mörkerseende* (*Seeing in the Dark*, 1970), he comes to grips with the death of his mother, a teacher who had raised him since divorcing the poet's father. A steady, though relatively small output followed: *Östersjöar* (*Baltics*, 1974), *Sanningsbarriären* (*The Truth Barrier*, 1978), *PS* (1980), *Det vilda torget* (*The Wild Marketplace*, 1983), and *För levande och döda* (*For the Living and the Dead*, 1989). In 1990 Tranströmer had a stroke which left him partly paralyzed and unable to speak. The appearance of the autobiographical novel *Minneva ser mig* (*The Memories See Me*) in 1993 was seen by some as sealing the poet's career, a fear that was dispelled with the publication of *Sorgegondolen* (*The Gondola of Sorrow*, 1996). The collection won the August Prize, awarded by the Swedish Writers' Association.

[YB]

Tranter, John (Australia, b. 1943) Born in Cooma, New South Wales, Tranter interrupted his university studies to travel. He graduated in 1970, the year he published his first collection, *Parallax*. In 1971–73 he was Asian editor for Angus & Robertson publishers. He worked for ABC Radio in the 1970s and 1980s, and has taught creative writing, undertaken editorial work (being poetry editor of *The Bulletin*, 1990–93) and been involved in publishing. He has won numerous prizes and fellowships and has toured widely. Since 1978 he has lived in Sydney, which features in his poetry. In 1997 he established *Jacket*, a free Internet quarterly.

Tranter's early poetry is difficult, autotelic, and concerned with the generative powers of form. Although critics emphasize his internationalism, postmodern style, and knowledge of French and American poets, Tranter is recognizably Australian in his idiom. In *Under Berlin* (1988) he evokes and satirizes Australian tropes and myths. Tranter's interest in style, popular culture, and literary theory has produced some of the most interesting and uncompromising modern Australian verse. Especially notable is *The Floor of Heaven* (1992), four verse tales concerned with ekphrasis, violence, childhood, memory, and nostalgia.

Tranter has edited poetry anthologies, with *The New Australian Poetry* (1979) being a definitive document for the 'Generation of '68' (see DUGGAN, FORBES, MAIDEN). Interested in computer-generated writing, he produced a collection of 'computer-assisted short stories', *Different Hands*, in 1998. While literary history has presented Tranter in ideological terms (with LES MURRAY as Pope and Tranter as anti-pope) it is clear that Tranter's energies and interests are more wide ranging and less programmatic than was initially apparent. His poetry is both highly original and deeply aware of antecedents.

Selected works: *Selected Poems* (1982); *At the Florida* (1993).

[DM]

Trayanov, Teodor (Bulgaria, 1882–1945) The father of Bulgarian Symbolism, Teodor Vasilev Trayanov, born in Pazardzhik and educated in Sofia and Vienna (1901–08), fought in the Balkan Wars (1912–13), held diplomatic posts in Vienna (1914–20) and Warsaw (1922), edited *Khiperion* (1922–31), the most influential Symbolist literary magazine, and taught literature in high school (1926–33).

Trayanov's poem 'Nov den' ('A New Day', 1905) marks the beginning of the Symbolist movement in Bulgaria. His finely crafted poetry, more philosophical than lyrical in terms of mood, imagery, and themes, negotiates between individual self-awareness and supra-individual phenomena such as history, myth, cosmic forces, national destiny, artistic creativity, and freedom. Denounced during the heyday of Social Realism, Trayanov was gradually reintroduced into the canon.

Selected works: *Regina mortua* (1909); *Khimni i baladi* (*Hymns and Ballads*, 1902–09); *Bŭlgarski baladi* (*Bulgarian Ballads*, 1921); *Pesen na pesnite* (*Song of Songs*, 1923); *Romantichni pesni* (*Romantic Songs*, 1926); *Osvobodeniyat chovek* (*Liberated Man*, 1929); *Panteon* (*Pantheon*, 1934).

[CG/LPG]

Treinin, Avner (Israel, b. 1928) Treinin was born in Tel Aviv in 1928. He earned a doctoral degree from the Hebrew University in Jerusalem, where he later served as Dean of the Faculty of Natural Sciences. A professor of physical chemistry, Treinin the poet speaks of the world in scientific terms, and draws attention to its flaws and to the limitations of humans in their futile attempts to grasp it in its perfection. His poems, which are often a reflection of the harsh Israeli desert landscape, won him the Bialik Prize for Literature. Treinin's first collection, *Moss on the Wall*, was published in 1957, and his most recent book, *The Ascents of Ehaz*, in 1996.

[ER]

Tripp, John (Wales, 1927–86) Tripp, a farrier's son, was born at Bargoed and raised in Cardiff. He was a journalist in London for several years before returning to Wales in 1969 to work as a freelance writer and poet. From his first short booklet, *Diesel to Yesterday* (1966), to his final collection, *Passing Through* (1984), Tripp was concerned with the condition of modern Wales, and the historical roots of that condition; although critical of what he saw as empty materialism, his observations are more compassionate than judgmental. His style is colloquial, his idiom resolutely contemporary, his tone sometimes angry, but mitigated by an introspective and self-mocking wit. A selection of his poems appeared in the *Penguin Modern Poets* series; a *Selected Poems* was published in 1989.

[BS]

Tsvetaeva, Marina Ivanovna (Russia, 1892–1941) Tsvetaeva lived a life of poetic triumph and personal tragedy. Her parents belonged to the cultured elite – her father founded Russia's first fine arts museum, the Alexander III Museum (the Pushkin Museum) – and Tsvetaeva's early life was privileged and promising: she wrote her first poem at age six.

Her first poetry collection, *Vecherni Albom* (*Evening Album*, 1910), attracted the attention of such poets as BRIUSOV, GUMILIEV, and VOLOSHIN. Voloshin in particular became Tsvetaeva's mentor and invited her into his literary circle in Koktebel. While there, Tsvetaeva married military cadet Sergei Yakovlevich Efron, who helped her publish *Volshebny Fonar'* (*The Magic Lantern*, 1912) and *Iz dvukh knig* (*From Two Books*, 1913). The couple had three children: Arianda (b. 1912), Irina (b. 1917), and a son, Georgy (b. 1925).

After the 1917 Revolution, Efron entered the White Army, and Tsvetaeva returned to Moscow, writing a number of poems, the most important of which is her tribute to the tzar and the Whites (and her rejection of the Soviets), *Levedinyi stan, Stikhi 1917–21* (*The Swans' Demesne*, published only in 1957). She suffered greatly during the Moscow famine, not being able to provide enough for her family, and placing her daughters in an orphanage, hoping that they would have food during the winter of 1919–20. Nevertheless, she continued to write poetry and published some of her poems in the Paris emigré journal *Sovremennye Zapiski* (*Contemporary Notes*). Her younger daughter, Irina, died of malnutrition in the orphanage in 1920.

Two years later, Tsvetaeva and Arianda left Soviet Russia to be reunited with Efron, who was then in Berlin. There she published *Razluka* (*Separation*, 1922), *Stikhi k Bloku* (*Poems to Blok*, 1922) and *Tsar-devitsa: Poema-skazka* (*The Tsar-Maiden*, 1922). Late in the year, the family moved to Prague where she published a collection of lyric poetry, *Remeslo* (*Craft*, 1923). In 1925, the family finally settled in Paris, which became Tsvetaeva's home for the next fourteen years, although she kept in touch with Russian poetry through her correspondence with PASTERNAK and her open support for the non-émigré MAYAKOVSKY. Still, though she published *Posle Rossii* (*After Russia*, 1928) in Paris, the rest of her time there was spent writing prose, which earned more.

Meanwhile Efron had developed Soviet sympathies; he began to spy for the NKVD, the precursor of the KGB. In 1937, Efron decided to return to Russia and Arianda went with him. Both were arrested upon their return, Efron to be shot in 1941 and Arianda to serve eight years in a labor camp.

Unaware of the situation, Tsvetaeva returned in 1939. She found herself without any emotional and financial support: in terrible poverty, politically fearful, rejected by all her literary colleagues and even her friends, and badly treated by her beloved son, Georgy. On August 31, 1941 in Yelabuga, where she was evacuated to escape the German invasion, she hanged herself. She was buried unmourned, in an anonymous grave.

Different people in Tsvetaeva's life, with whom she had very intense relationships, or whose work was spiritually or artistically close to her, played an important role in inspiring her poetry. An example is her lyrical diary *Versty* (*Mileposts*, 1922), the result of her passionate affair with OSIP MANDELSHTAM.

Thematically and stylistically varied, Tsvetaeva's poetry experimented with rhythm, syntax, and archaisms, trying to find those which best expressed the melody of her soul in each moment of her life. She will be remembered as one of the greatest Russian poets with one of the most tragic lives.

[RN]

Tuéni, Nadia (Lebanon, 1935–83) Tuéni was born in Beirut and died in a car accident in 1983. She devoted her time and soul to poetry. Her quest for harmony and balance, the marriage of sensual elements and spiritual elements, was constantly reflected in her poetry, which often recalls the logic of Surrealism. She published *Le Rêveur de terre* (*Dreamer of Earth*, 1975) and four years later *Liban, vingt poèmes pour un amour* (*Lebanon: Twenty Poems for a Love*). Surprising images, inspired by the subconscious and raising metaphysical questions, constitute both frame and content for her poetry.

[MS]

Tuqan, Ibrahim (Palestine, 1905–41) Born in Nablus to a literary family, Tuqan received an excellent education before he went to the American University in Beirut in 1923. He became the greatest Palestinian poet of the first half of the twentieth century.

Tuqan wrote neoclassical poetry which gave powerful expression to the Palestinian national struggle against the British Mandate and Zionism, often voicing a sense of impending doom and exile. His tone in those poems is as personal as that of his love poems and his meditations on his approaching death of an incurable disease. In this he modernized poetry without abandoning the classical tradition.

His poetry is collected in *Diwan Ibrahim Tuqan* (*Collected Works*, 1966).

[WH]

Turkka, Sirkka Annikki (Finland, b. 1939) Turkka is considered a major poet of her generation whose work has been published in anthologies and literary magazines throughout the world, and translated into twelve languages. In her writing, the fragmentation of structures, self, and language search for their limits, pushing at the point where meaning breaks down and incoherence results. By her dramatized language and poetic forms, she has advanced and enriched Finnish lyric modernism. Her poetry is characterized by sharp humor, the richness of folkloric sources, and an unusual sensitivity to nature.

Turkka's first collection was *Huone Avaruudessa* (*A Room in Space*, 1973). One of the subsequent nine collections, *Tule Takaisin Pikku Sheba* (*Come Back, Little Sheba*, 1986) received the Finlandia Prize.

At that time she was the only woman and the only poet to have received her country's most prestigious literary award. She is also the recipient of two State Awards for Literature (1980, 1984).

[SP]

Tuwhare, Hone (New Zealand, b. 1922) Maori poet Tuwhare was born in Kaikohe into the Nga Puhi tribe. He was initially apprenticed as a boiler maker and later worked on hydro-electric power projects. He was a member of the Communist Party, where he met the New Zealand poet R. A. K. MASON, who encouraged and influenced his poetry. Tuwhare was involved in Maori cultural and political causes.

Tuwhare's *No Ordinary Sun* (1964) gained international acclaim. The poems are influenced by his Maori and working-class background and present a mixture of vernacular rhythms, English and Maori, and biblical language.

Selected works: *Sap-Wood and Milk* (1972); *Something Nothing* (1974); *Making a Fist of it: Poems and Short Stories* (1978); *Mihi: Collected Poems* (1987); *Deep River Talk: Collected Poems* (1994); *Shape-Shifter* (1997).

[SH]

Tuwim, Julian (Poland, 1894–1953) Tuwim was the cofounder and chief representative of the Skamander group. Though he studied law and philosophy briefly at the University of Warsaw, he quickly turned to writing and editing.

From his first publication, *Czyhanie na Boga* (*Lying in Wait for God*, 1918), Tuwim showed himself a poet capable of combining emotional tension with explosive, lyric power. While his typically short poems are rhythmic and strong, Tuwim employed unexpected associations and clusters of symbols, images, and poetic techniques to evoke a fantastic – sometimes phantasmagoric – power. Writing from positions of vitalism and biologism, Tuwim employed what Ryszard Matuszewski called a 'poeticalchemy' to reveal proletariat misery and to unmask the monstrosity of the bourgeoisie.

Selected works: *Sokrates tanczacy* (*Dancing Socrates*, 1920); *Slowa we krwi* (*Words in Blood*, 1926); *Rzecz czarnoleska* (*The Czarnoles' Case*, 1929); *Biblia cyganska* (*The Gypsy Bible*, 1933); *Tresc gorejaca* (*Burning Matter*, 1936); *Kwiaty polskie* (*Polish Flowers*, 1949).

[MT]

Tzara, Tristan (Samuel Rosenstock; France, 1896–1963) The Cabaret Voltaire in Zürich was the site of the 1916 founding of the multilingual Dada movement by Hugo Ball, Richard Huelsenbeck, and Romanian-born Tzara. The movement's initial impetus was World War I; its anti-rationalism, its violence and nihilism, found expression in the performance art and 'noise poetry' of Tzara and his friends. By 1918, with the *Manifeste Dada* (*Dada Manifesto*), Tzara was writing solely in French, which he continued to do for the remainder of his life.

He moved to Paris in 1920. However, by then, BRETON's Surrealism, which had drawn some of its initial energy from Dada, had established itself as the foremost movement of the French and European avant-garde. Tzara joined the Communist Party in 1936, and entered the French Resistance during World War II.

Selected works: *L'Homme approximatif* (*Approximate Man*, 1931); *Grains et issues* (*Seeds and Bran*, 1935).

[SJ]

U

U Tam'si, Tchicaya (Congo, 1931–88) Born Gerald Flix Tchicayu, U Tam'si remains one of the Congo's foremost writers (U Tam'si, according to Lilyan Kesteloot, means 'who speaks for one's country'). Starting in 1946, he spent most of his life in Paris. He returned to Kinshasa during the brief leadership of Patrice Lumumba. His work with UNESCO allowed him the opportunity to return to Africa frequently.

He is known for six books of poetry published over a fifteen-year period: *Le Mauvais sang* (*Bad Blood*, 1955), *Feu de brousse* (*Brush Fire*, 1957), *A triche-coeur* (*A Cheating Heart*, 1960), *Epitome* (1962), *Le Ventre* (*The Belly*, 1964), and *L'Arc musical* (*The Musical Bow*, 1969). He has also written plays and prose. He was influenced by Surrealism, including that of AIMÉ CÉSAIRE. For English-speakers, Gerald Moore's translations and criticism are considered the early and authoritative work on U Tam'si.

[KAC]

Ujević, Tin (Yugoslavia, 1888–1955) Many Yugoslav critics acknowledge the extraordinary power of Augustin Ujević's poetry. He was acclaimed as one of the great Yugoslav poets throughout most of his career. A famous bohemian, he was well-known for his aversion to authority and rigid social norms. As a young man, Ujević was politically active. However, due to his high moral and ethical standards, he often faced disappointments, which eventually led to his withdrawal from both social and political life. His famous poem 'Svakidašnja jadikovka' is a brilliant testament of this disillusionment. His collection *Lelek sebra* (*A Serf's Lament*, 1920), which focused on the horrors of war and on personal disillusionment, is powerful evidence of his rejection of conventional life.

Ujević drew upon the Croatian literary tradition, but he instilled this tradition with the spirit of European Modernism and with his own individual style and vision. His enchantingly beautiful poetry set a standard for the generations of Yugoslav poets who followed him.

Selected works: *Kolajna* (*A Necklace*, 1926); *Auto na korzu* (*A Car on a Corso*, 1932); *Rukovet* (*A Handful*, 1950).

[DJ]

Ungaretti, Giuseppe (Italy, 1888–1970) Born and raised in Alexandria, Egypt, Ungaretti moved to Paris in 1912, where he had his first contacts with the European literary scene, particularly with the French avant-garde (APOLLINAIRE, above all). Before moving to Brazil in 1936, where he taught Italian literature at the University of São Paulo, he had already published some of his most influential collections, such as *Il porto sepolto* (*Buried Harbor*, 1916), *Allegria di naufragi*

(*Gaiety of Shipwrecks*, 1919), *L'allegria (Gaiety*, 1931), *Sentimento del tempo* (*Feeling of Time*,1933). Being considered one of the fathers of 'Ermetismo', originally a derogatory label used by some critics to describe the apparent obscurity of the generation of poets born after World War I, Ungaretti soon earned an official status within the Italian literary arena, and he was responsible for the most radical metrical renovation in the history of Italian poetry. The extreme brevity of his compositions (particularly evident in his early collections), resulting from a clever fragmentation of traditional meters, carried a lyrical power never experienced before in Italian verse. Dissolving authorial trust in the rationality of discourse, Ungaretti explored words almost as magical utterances in which pauses and silences were as important as the sound of language. Even though his later collections, such as *Il dolore* (*Pain*, 1947), *La terra promessa* (*The Promised Land*, 1950), and *Il Taccuino del Vecchio* (*The Old Man's Notebook*, 1960), did not bring any substantial innovations, his work has always been regarded as highly influential by many later poets, including FRANCO FORTINI and VITTORIO SERENI.

[GS]

V

Valente, José Angel (Spain, b. 1929) Valente, from Galicia (Orense), is a leader of the Generation of 1956. This group of poets, which also includes GLORIA FUERTES, infused a zeal for political poetry with a new aesthetic consciousness, that of poetry as an act of self-discovery. This generation is something of a hybrid, and its poets show a wide range of characteristics, from social activism to hermetic experimentalism.

Besides writing poetry, Valente has worked as a professor, critic, and translator and serves as a United Nations official. Though his work is diverse, Valente's constant themes are the poem as process of creation (and of self-awareness) and the role of intertextuality in establishing links with other times, places, and peoples. Valente combines a concern for social and temporal circumstance with a complex, allusive style. His principal works are *Poems to Lazarus* (1960), *Memory and Signs* (1966), and *To the God of Place* (1989).

[AB]

Valéry, Paul (France, 1871–1945) Unlike most poets who dominate their time, Valéry was not prolific (as a poet at least) nor markedly public for much of his life. Yet his position as the pre-eminent French poet of the early decades of the twentieth century is indisputable. Combining wide erudition, philosophic contemplation, and the technical inheritances of the Symbolists and Surrealists into his own complex and innovative verse, Valéry was unique among twentieth-century writers.

Born in Sète, on the Mediterranean coast, Valéry studied law in Montpellier before taking a civil service job; eventually he secured a position as the personal secretary to the director of the French Press Association, a job he held for twenty-two years (1900–22).

By 1892, Valéry had written a great deal of verse influenced primarily by the Symbolists and the writings of Mallarmé. That year, however, after the dissolution of an ill-fated love affair, Valéry had an epiphanic moment that would affect the next twenty years: he decided that verse was not the proper way to express his intellect – his central concern, always – and so gave up writing poetry. Instead he concentrated on what would become his multi-volume *Cahiers* (*Notebooks*), records of his morning ritual quietly contemplating everything from mathematics and science to domestic relationships and art. In 1912, however, his friend André Gide encouraged him to gather the earlier poetry. Valéry got no further than his new valedictory poem; after five years of writing and revision he published his masterpiece *Le Jeune Parque* (*The Young Fate*, 1917).

Like much of Valéry's work, this poem centers on the balance between contemplation and action, embodied here in the seaside gazing of the youngest of the three Fates. Curious about mortality, with its vaster possibilities of sensation and the pleasures of limited time, she looks both inward and outward. A metaphysical poem, complex in its construction and sometimes abstruse in its symbolism and thought, *La Jeune Parque* is nonetheless a landmark in the century's poetry. It marked a move beyond the dominant Surrealism and also introduced a towering intellect to wide readership.

Valéry's only subsequent volumes, *Album de vers anciens, 1890–1900* (*Album of Old Verse*, 1920) and *Charmes* (*Songs*, 1922), showed how remarkably consistent he was in the quality of his verse. The former gathered his earlier work, ably crafted in those modes current at the fin-de-siècle. The latter volume contains poems equal to *La Jeune Parque* in technical grace and intellectual force; of these, 'Le Cimetière marin', translated in a famous version by C. DAY LEWIS as 'The Cemetery by the Sea,' is one of his most anthologized poems, reiterating his heady poetics yet again.

In 1922, upon the death of his employer, Valéry assumed a public presence that lasted for the final twenty years of his life. Succeeding Anatole France as a member of the French Academy in 1925, Valéry was appointed to the first Chair of Poetry at the Collège de France in 1937. His importance to French literature and culture was signified to the world when he was given a state funeral upon his death in 1945.

[MW]

Vallejo, César (Peru, 1892–1938) Born of Spanish and Indian descent in Santiago de Chuco, in the mountains of Peru, Vallejo is one of Latin America's most startling poets. Influenced by Modernist poets such as DARÍO and Herrera y Reissig, Vallejo nevertheless transcended these roots to become associated with the literary avant-garde. His style remains unique, however, as he never adopted any of the codified schools, such as Surrealism or Creationism, but strove to expose the universal and intimate quality of human feeling, especially suffering, in his own fashion. Deeply in touch with the agonies of human existence, Vallejo's language is filled with biblical vocabulary (the influence of his childhood devotion to Catholicism) and, in his later writings, with the Marxist philosophy to which he was partial.

Finishing his university education in literature with a thesis entitled *Romanticismo en la poesía castellana* (*Romanticism in Castilian Poetry*, 1915), Vallejo moved to Lima, where he began law school and worked as a teacher. *Los Heraldos negros* (*The Black Heralds*, 1918), his first volume of poetry, was published during this time. The book marks Vallejo's break with Modernism through an incorporation of mundane language into its aesthetic. Returning to his hometown from Lima in 1920, Vallejo spent four months in jail after being accused of arson during a popular revolt. In prison, he wrote *Escalas melografiadas* (*Musical Scales*, 1923) and published his second, extremely hermetic, volume of poetry entitled *Trilce* (1922). Like its title, the book makes use of neologisms and other strategies to push language to its limits, creating an abundance of interpretive possibilities without losing its intimate rapport with the reader.

In 1921, at the instigation of his friends and colleagues, Vallejo was released from prison. Two years later, he published a short novel entitled *Fábula salvaje* (*Savage Fable*, 1923), and departed for France where he eked out a meager living as a translator and a journalist (contributing to his compatriot Mariátegui's magazine *Amauta* (1926–28)). He was then exiled from France for his political involvement, including two trips to the Soviet Union and his official enrolment with the Communist Party. Vallejo lived in Madrid from 1930 to 1932 and was greatly moved by the events of the Spanish Civil War. While supporting the Spanish Republic, Vallejo published two volumes on his experiences in the Soviet Union, along with drama, short stories, and a novel (*Tungsteno*, 1931) about the exploitation of miners in Peru.

Although nostalgic for his home country, Vallejo never managed to return. He died in extreme poverty in Paris, where he had returned to live upon the defeat of the Spanish Republic. *España, aparta de mi ésta cáliz* (*Spain, Take this Cup from Me*, 1938), the last book-length collection of poems put together by Vallejo, was originally published by the soldiers of the Republican Army in Spain and later included in the posthumously collected *Poemas humanos* (*Human Poems*, 1939). The poems of this volume are more hopeful than the obscure and dark work of *Trilce*. *España, aparta de mi ésta cáliz* offers readers a sense of redemption in the potential of human solidarity. Translations of Vallejo's work include *Four Poems of César Vallejo* (1960), *Trilce* (1973), *César Vallejo: The Complete Posthumous Poetry* (1978), and *Selected Poems* (1981).

[LKA]

Van Duyn, Mona (United States, b. 1921) Van Duyn was born in Waterloo, Iowa, and educated at the University of Northern Iowa and the University of Iowa. Her many awards include the Bollingen and Pulitzer Prizes, and an appointment as Poet Laureate.

Van Duyn's poetry is striking for its ability to encompass habitual, even chatty, speech within a formal structure. The dailiness of its concerns – love between aging spouses is a particularly notable theme, as are the challenges of mental and physical illness – reflects the ongoing and provisional nature of sense-making. She is married to the critic Jarvis Thurston; they live in St Louis, where they both taught at Washington University for many years.

Selected works: *To See, to Take* (1970); *Bedtime Stories* (1972); *Letters from a Father and Other Poems* (1982); *If It Be Not I: Collected Poems, 1959–1982* (1993).

[JT]

Van Ostaijen, Paul (Flanders, 1896–1928) Van Ostaijen is the most important avant-garde poet to write in Dutch and his work is linked to movements such as Dadaism, Expressionism, and Cubism. His first collection was *Music Hall* (1916), which betrays a fascination for modern city life. His experiences in Antwerp during World War I were used for the collage collection *Bezette stad* (*Occupied City*, 1921). After the war he moved to Berlin, where he met several key figures of the international avant-garde. Back in Antwerp he wrote his most important poetry, which was published posthumously in the volume *De feesten van angst en pijn* (*The Feasts of Fear and Agony*).

In addition to being a poet, Van Ostaijen also wrote short, Kafkaesque stories and incisive essays, in which he proves to be an erudite observer of artistic developments of his day (poetry, painting). He died of tuberculosis, after a stay in a sanatorium.

[TV]

Varela, Blanca (Peru, b. 1926) Born in Lima to an artistic family, Varela is one of few Peruvian women poets to receive international attention. She attended the Facultad de Letras at the Universidad de San Marcos before moving into the international arena by contributing to journals in Mexico and the United States.

At her friends' suggestion, she consented to publish her first collection of poems, *Ese puerto existe* (*And that Port Exists*), for which OCTAVIO PAZ wrote the prologue. Like EIELSON and Sologuren, Varela tests the limits of the world's order and meaning, thus building on the Surrealist concerns of Cesar Moro. She attempts to find and discuss the realities of life without allowing the nature of language to affect their form.

Selected works: *Luz de día* (*Light of Day*, 1963); *Valses y otras falsas confesiones* (*Waltzes and Other False Confessions*, 1972); *Canto villano* (*Peasant Song*, 1978); *Ejercicios materiales* (*Material Exercises*, 1991).

[VW]

Varnalis, Katsos (Greece, 1884–1974) Varnalis was born and raised in Bulgaria where he later worked as an elementary school teacher. He studied literature in Athens and subsequently philosophy, literature, and sociology in Paris. Heavily influenced by the Russian Revolution, his literary work is profoundly Marxist in ideology and revolutionary and humanistic in spirit. These features characterize his most important collections, *The Light that Burns* (1922) and *Slaves Besieged* (1927), an allusion to Solomos' (1798–1857) *The Free Besieged*. He remained faithful to traditional forms and, influenced by PALAMAS, proclaimed a vision of the poet as prophet and messenger of the people.

[GSY]

Velarde, Ramón López (Mexico, 1888–1921) López Velarde was born in Jerez, Zacatecas, and was educated at the Seminario Conciliar in the same state. He later continued his studies at the Instituto Científico Literario in San Luis Potosí from which he received his law degree in 1911.

López Velarde's work displays elements of mysticism, erotic love, and the pastoral life of the provinces. His work stands at the doorway between Modernism and the avant-garde movement which flourished shortly after his untimely death. López Velarde's place in the genesis of contemporary Mexican poetry as well as his patriotic 'La suave Patria' (1921) make him one of the most important poets of Mexico.

Selected works: *La sangre devota* (*Devout Blood*, 1916); *Zozobra* (*Anxiety*, 1919); *El minutero* (*The Minutehand*, 1924); *El son del corazón* (*Sound of the Heart*, 1932); *Poemas* (*Poems*, 1935).

[VW]

Vesaas, Tarjei (Norway, 1897–1970) Better known for his many novels, short stories, and plays, Vesaas has become increasingly recognized for his poetry. Vesaas was born to an old farming family and was expected to inherit the farm, a burden which is felt in his early work. His first novels, published in 1923 and 1924, described life on a country farm and brought the author immediate success. The novel *Kimen* (*The Seed*, 1940), exploring the darker side of mass psychology, marked Vesaas' growing social involvement. It was not until Vesaas was forty-nine that he published his first poetry collection, *Kjeldene* (*The Springs*, 1946). Influence by the folk ballad form, the poems in this volume are written in conventional rhyme and meter, which disappear in the next collections, *Leiken og lynet* (*The Game and the Lightning*, 1947), *Lykka for ferdesmenn* (*Wanderers' Happiness*, 1949), *Lýyende eldars land* (*Land of Hidden Fires*, 1953), *Ver ny vår draum* (*May Our Dream Be New*, 1956) and *Livet ved straumen* (*Life by the River*, 1971). The lyrical quality of Vesaas' prose is amplified in his poems, which present unorthodox nature imagery and uncanny symbols, and are generally considered less accessible to readers than his novels. Vesaas received the Nordic Literary Prize in 1963.

[YB]

Voiculescu, Vasile (Romania, 1884–1963) Born in the village of Pârscov in east-central Romania, Voiculescu studied philology, then medicine, in Bucharest. A military doctor during World War I, he wrote patriotic war poems in a traditionalist vein (*From the Country of the Bison*, 1918). The volumes which Voiculescu published in the 1920s and 1930s – *Poems with*

Angels (1927), *Destiny* (1933), *Ascent* (1937), *Poems* (1939) – define him as a religious and mystical poet. Using symbol, allegory, and parable, he finds answers to tensions between the human and the divine in traditional peasant ethics, ancient magic practices, and Christian spirituality. In 1941 Voiculescu won the National Prize for Poetry. After World War II he stopped publishing but continued to write, his short stories and poems (*The Last Sonnets of Shakespeare in Imaginary Translation by Vasile Voiculescu*, 1964) appearing posthumously. At the age of 74, Voiculescu was imprisoned by the Communists for four years, the 'victim of a legal error'.

[GF]

Voigt, Ellen Bryant (United States, b. 1943) Voigt was born in Danville, Virginia, and educated at Converse College, in South Carolina, and the University of Iowa. She is a member of the faculty for the graduate creative writing program of Warren Wilson College.

Rural life and family relations play an important role in Voigt's elegant and forceful poetry. While much of her work draws on her own life, an increasingly communal emphasis comes to the fore in her most recent book, a sequence of poems dealing with the Spanish Influenza epidemic of 1918. Throughout, the poems precariously balance loss and abundance.

Selected works: *The Forces of Plenty* (1983); *The Lotus Flowers* (1987); *Two Trees* (1992); *Kyrie* (1995).

[JT]

Vold, Jan Erik (Norway, b. 1939) A poet, novelist, critic and translator, Vold studied language and literature in Oslo, Uppsala, and at University of California, Santa Barbara. His first two poetry collections, *Mellom speil og speil* (*Between Mirror and Mirror*, 1965) and *Blikket* (*The Glance*, 1966), were well received. Vold's poetry took, however, a distinctive turn with *Spor, snỳ* (*Tracks, Snow*, 1970), which presents *haiku*-like three-line poems. Each poem is printed on a separate page, so that the words leave their track on the expanse of snow-white paper. This 'new simplicism' (*nyenkelhet*) is clearly inspired by WILLIAM CARLOS WILLIAMS, ROBERT CREELEY, and FRANK O'HARA. Also known for his essays on politics, society, religion, and women's issues, Vold has received many awards and has been nominated for the 1999 Scandinavian Council's Literary Prize. He lives in Stockholm, Sweden.

[YB]

Voloshin, Maximilian Aleksandrovich (Russia, 1877–1932) Voloshin's mother was a translator; after the death of his father, who had been a lawyer, the family moved to Moscow where Voloshin began both attending school and writing poetry. In spring 1901, he traveled abroad, encountering Parisian literary society, but soon returned to Russia. Upon his return, he was accepted into the milieu of Russian Symbolists, befriending BRIUSOV and BELY, and visiting the Wednesday salons held by Diaghileff's journal *The World of Art*. In 1906, Voloshin married the painter Sabashnikova, describing the complexity of their relationship in his poems such as 'Ia zhdal stradaniia stol'ko let' ('I Waited for Suffering for Such a Long Time') and 'Otryvki iz poslanii' ('Extracts from Letters'); in 1907, he separated from his wife. Three years later, his first collection, *Poems, 1900–1910*, was published in Moscow, followed by another collection, *Anno mundi ardentis* (1915), which condemned World War I. He accepted the Russian February Revolution of 1917 'without any special enthusiasm', and the October Revolution as an inevitable evil. After the revolutions he published various volumes, including *Neopalimaia Kupina* (*Unburned Kupina*, 1921), *Putiamni Kaina* (*By the Ways of Cain, 1921–23*), and *Vladimirskaia Bogomater'* (*The Vladimir's Madonna*, 1929). His poetry is beautiful but cold; its form seems often to be more important than its emotional connotation. Like the poetry of the Parnassians, it carries a philosophical meaning, but is entirely devoid of mysticism.

In 1931, a year before his death, Voloshin bequeathed his house in Koktebel – a long-time meeting place for Russian artists and writers – to the Union of Soviet Writers. Today, Voloshin is considered by many to be one of the most refined, and finest, Russian poets.

[RN]

Voznesensky, Andrei Andreevich (Russia, b. 1933) Though he graduated from the Institute of Architecture in 1957, Voznesensky was encouraged by BORIS PASTERNAK to continue to write poetry. Like the narrative poems which preceded them, *Parabola* (1960) and *Mosaic* (1960) garnered critical praise and, despite accusations of being a 'bourgeois formalist' poet, Voznesensky became a member of the Presidium of the USSR Writers' Union in 1967. He was awarded the State Prize for poetry in 1979.

Rhythmically and stylistically experimental, Voznesensky has long been thematically concerned with the balance between the positive potential of technology and its physical and social risks, including totalitarianism. Although artistically more limited and thematically poorer than AKHMATOVA, TSVETAEVA, or MANDELSHTAM, Voznesensky remains important for his role in bringing to public attention, and questioning, critical moments of modern Soviet life.

Selected works: *Antimiry* (*Antiworlds*, 1964); *Akhillesovo serdtse* (*Heart of Achilles*, 1966); *Ten' zvuka* (*Shadow of Sound*, 1969); *Vzgliad* (*A Look*, 1972); *Soblazn* (*Temptation*, 1979); *Gadanie po knige* (*Telling by the Book*, 1994).

[RN]

Vrettakos, Nikiforos (Greece, 1911–91) Vrettakos was born of a poor family in a village near Sparta and worked as a laborer, public servant, and editor. Self-taught, he wrote twenty-one poetry collections in free verse and with unelevated thematic simplicity. His sincerity has put him at risk of being termed 'sentimentalist', as a profound humanism and empathy for humanity's toils permeates his poetic oeuvre; for Vrettakos love and goodness constitute the highest ordering principles of human relations. Between 1967 and 1975 he worked as a special advisor at the Institute of Byzantine and Modern Greek Studies in Palermo (Sicily). He was twice awarded the State Award for Poetry, for *Grimaces of Man* (1940) and *Poems, 1929–1951* (1956).

[GSY]

Vysotsky, Vladimir Semenovich (Russia, 1938–80) Though a collection of Vysotsky's poem-songs never appeared during his life, he was one of the most important Russian singer-songwriter/poets of the 1960s. When the Soviet authorities stopped his public performances, his audiences dubbed tapes of his private performances and circulated the recordings. His poignant and pointed works address universal problems of human existence, as well as the hidden problems of Soviet society: prostitution, alcoholism, theft, and the falsity of banal 'bourgeois' existence. With a poet's crafted language and style, he found a way to express a large variety of themes and concerns, and to touch universally his audiences' humanity.

Selected works: *Pesni russkikh bardov* (*Songs of the Russian Bards*, 1977–78); *Nerv* (*Nerve*, 1981); *Pesni i stikhi* (*Songs and Poems*, 1981, 1983); *Sobranie stikhov i pesen* (*A Collection of Poems and Songs*, 1988).

[RN]

W

Wain, John (England, 1925–94) John Barrington Wain was born in Stoke-on-Trent, Staffordshire, and was educated at Newcastle and St John's College, Oxford. He lectured at the universities of Reading, Bristol, Paris, Cincinnati, and Oxford.

Wain's poetry is an expression of his decidedly anti-Modernist stance, and some of his poems exhibit his alliance with the Movement poets (see LARKIN, AMIS, GUNN, JENNINGS) in the early 1950s. He is perhaps best known for his long poems. However, all of his poetry tends to circle around his chosen topics of alienation, compassion, integrity, and love within images that provide fresh insights into the everyday.

Honored any number of times throughout his life, he won the Somerset Maugham Award in 1958 and was appointed to the prestigious Oxford Professorship of Poetry in 1973, a position he held for five years. Wain died of a stroke at age sixty-nine after suffering from debilitating diabetes for several of the last years of his life.

Selected works: *Mixed Feelings* (1951); *A Word Carved on a Sill* (1956); *Weep before God* (1961); *A Song about Major Eatherly* (1961); *Letters to Five Artists* (1969); *The Shape of Feng* (1972); *Feng* (1975); *Poems, 1949–1979* (1981); *Mid-week Period Return: Home Thoughts of a Native* (1982).

[MK]

Wainwright, Jeffrey (England, b. 1944) Wainwright was born in Staffordshire in 1944. He received both his B.A. and his M.A. from the University of Leeds where he wrote his Master's thesis on WILLIAM CARLOS WILLIAMS. He currently teaches at Manchester Polytechnic.

Wainwright's poetry merges diverse aspects of life into compact coherency. A recurring theme is history as transcendent over time rather than as a moment frozen in the past. For Wainwright, the impact of the past and the political, particularly as they relate to class, are omnipresent in the personal life of the individual.

Selected works: *The Important Man* (1970); *Heart's Desire* (1978); *Selected Poems* (1985); *The Red-Headed Pupil and Other Poems* (1994).

[BB]

Walcott, Derek (St Lucia, b. 1930) Walcott was born in Castris, St Lucia. He comes from an artistic family: his father, Warwick, who died when he was one, was a writer and a painter; his mother staged amateur theatricals; and his twin brother, Roderick, has become a well-known playwright. Walcott is of mixed racial origins, a fact that many critics have probably too reductively identified as the source of the dichotomies that characterize his work. The sense of being neither black nor white, but 'brown', 'red', or colored – and so out of step with the mainstream of

Caribbean society – is only the most obvious of these dichotomies. Walcott's poetry enacts the continual drama that comes from the uncertainty of being between fixed categories – between North and South, colonial and indigenous cultures, the tradition of Western poetry and the poetry of folk culture, history and 'historylessness', the language of 'standard' English and Caribbean dialect, the space of the local and that of the global. It is through his continual willingness to explore this difficult in-between space, the void that exists between the opposites that have both left their mark on him, that Walcott fashions both an identity and a poetry uniquely suitable to the conditions of the New World.

By his twentieth birthday, Walcott had written two volumes of poetry, *25 Poems* (1948) and *Epitaph for the Young* (1949), as well as the play, *Henri Christophe* (1950). From 1950 to 1954, he studied at University College of the West Indies in Jamaica, earning a degree in English, French, and Latin. After spending a year studying theater in New York City in 1958, he moved to Trinidad where in 1959 he founded the Trinidad Theatre Workshop. His themes of the 'historylessness' of the Caribbean peoples and the colonial subject's struggle for self-definition emerge in three impressive volumes written in the 1960s: *In a Green Night: Poems 1948–1960* (1962), *The Castaway and Other Poems* (1965), and *The Gulf and Other Poems* (1969). *Another Life* (1973) makes explicit the autobiographical character of Walcott's poetry, in its examination of the growth and development of the Caribbean artist to adulthood. In *Sea Grapes* (1976) and *The Star-Apple Kingdom* (1979), Walcott's verse becomes angrier and more plain-spoken, while thematically it turns to a direct examination of post-independence politics. The volumes that Walcott has written while living in the United States, *The Fortunate Traveller* (1982), *Midsummer* (1984), *The Arkansas Testament* (1987), and *Omeros* (1989) repeat and recapitulate many of the themes that have concerned him throughout his life: the desperate life of the world's poor, the loss of home, and the power of poetic imagination to overcome all oppositions.

Although Walcott has been the recipient of major awards, including a MacArthur Award (1981) and the Nobel Prize for Literature (1992), and is widely considered to be one of the great poets of the twentieth century, there are aspects of his work that can be seen as at least potentially troubling. Walcott's liberal humanism, his appeals to a common humanity, his rejection of Negritude, and his commitment to the Western poetic forms, have made it all too easy for Western critics and audiences to appropriate and assimilate his poetry, which has caused questions to be raised about the degree to which it speaks of and to genuine Caribbean experience. Nevertheless, his formidable output, impressive range, and commanding grasp of the English language have ensured him of a place among the very best poets of the century.

[IS]

Waldman, Anne (United States, b. 1945) Waldman was born in Millville, New Jersey, into a family devoted to poetry. Her father was a professor of English and her mother translated the works of others.

Waldman received her B.A. from Bennington College in 1966, where she studied with HOWARD NEMEROV. Immediately upon graduation, she returned to New York City to become assistant director of the Poetry Project at St Mark's Church-in-the-Bowery, which placed her in daily contact with poets such as ALLEN GINSBERG. In 1974, Waldman co-founded with Ginsberg the Jack Kerouac School of Disembodied Poetics at the Naropa Institute, of which she became Director of Writing and Poetics in 1984.

Throughout the 1960s and 1970s, Waldman published nine books of poetry and edited three collections. In the 1980s, Waldman's work became more performance oriented, and she frequently gave mesmerizing readings for radio, television, and film. To date, Waldman has published and edited over twenty books, but her acclaim stems mostly from energetic televised performances and readings.

[DC]

Wallace-Crabbe, Chris (Australia, b. 1934) Wallace-Crabbe is deeply associated with Melbourne, the city of his birth. Educated at Melbourne University, he became lecturer, reader and, in 1988, professor there. One of the 'Melbourne University poets', Wallace-Crabbe was one of the first poets in the late 1950s to represent Australian suburbia, but he also has a notably cosmopolitan aspect. He has held international academic fellowships (for instance, at Yale and Harvard), and has traveled widely. Cosmopolitan poetic interests are visible in his engagements with American poetry and prose poetry, both notably early in the Australian context. Published from the mid-1980s by Oxford University Press, Wallace-Crabbe is one of the few living Australian poets with an international reputation.

Wallace-Crabbe has long been a central figure in Australian culture. He was inaugural director of the Melbourne University Australian Centre (1990–94); general editor of the Oxford University Press Australian Writers series (1992–96); editorial board member of *Australian Book Review* and *Meanjin*. He is an important critic and anthologist and has won numerous prizes.

Wallace-Crabbe's poetry has developed from ethical-formalist beginnings, to a widening interest in politics and the self. His work in the Oxford Poets series, especially, is important and accomplished. Strongly attracted to the Australian vernacular and the quotidian, Wallace-Crabbe's lyrics often contain more sombre, metaphysical concerns. This is seen in *For Crying out Loud* (1990), with its moving elegies for the poet's adult son. Ultimately, however, the poet looks to the multiplicity of daily life, the world of ideas and nature as sources of replenishment and joy.

Selected works: *The Emotions Are Not Skilled* Workers (1980); *I'm Deadly Serious* (1988); *Selected Poems: 1956–1994* (1995); *Whirling* (1998).

[DM]

Walwicz, Ania (Australia, b. 1951) Walwicz was born in Swidnica Slaska, Poland, arrived in Australia in 1963, and lives in Melbourne. A visual artist, Walwicz is a graduate of the Victorian College of the Arts, Melbourne. Her poetry and prose has been widely published in periodicals and anthologies in Australia and Europe. She has also written plays.

Walwicz is probably best known for her performance poetry, which she has performed in Australia, Britain, France, and Switzerland. Her poetry is repetitious and incantatory. Frequently it attempts to give the reader or listener the experience of being outside the spoken language, thereby enacting the experiences of migrants who are cut off from English. Focusing on the theme of migrant alienation and racism in the new country, Walwicz's work also embraces feminism and its interconnection with immigration.

Selected works: *Writing* (1982); *Boat* (1989).

[AP]

Warren, Robert Penn (United States, 1905–88) Warren's literary career parallels that of THOMAS HARDY. Both wrote fiction and poetry, and both wrote their best poetry in their later years. Indeed, Warren began to produce his most significant work in the mid-1950s, with *Promises: Poems 1954–1956* (1957), a book published when he was fifty-two. It was his first book of lyric poetry to appear since publication of his *Selected Poems* in 1944. It was quickly followed by *You, Emperors and Other Poems 1957–60*. Other important collections were *Incarnations. Poems 1966* and *Now and Then* (1979). Also like

Hardy, Warren's work revealed a pessimism and violent world-view.

Warren was the only American writer to receive the Pulitzer Prize for both fiction and poetry. His other awards include the National Book Award in poetry, the Bollingen Prize for poetry, the Presidential Medal of Freedom, and a MacArthur Fellowship.

Warren was born in Guthrie, Kentucky, and graduated *summa cum laude* from Vanderbilt University in 1925. He took a Master's degree from the University of California (1927) and did graduate work at Yale University (1927–28) and at Oxford as a Rhodes Scholar (B. Litt., 1930). For many years he taught at Yale and lived in Connecticut with his wife, the writer Eleanor Clark. They had two children.

Selected works: *New and Selected Poems 1923–1985* (1985); *Brother to Dragons: A Tale in Verse and Voices* (1979); *New and Selected Essays* (1989).

[CV]

Wat, Aleksandr (Poland, 1900–67) Wat was born in Warsaw to a cultured Polish-Jewish family and studied philosophy at the University of Warsaw. His interest in Dadaism and his revolutionary use of Polish syntax initiated the Polish Futurist movement. He published his first poems, the Futurist collection *Me from One Side and Me from the Other Side of My Pug Iron Stove*, in 1920. After that, he worked for the avant-garde magazines *New Art* and *Almanac of the New Art* and, in 1929–31, was co-editor of *The Literary Monthly*, the most important Communist journal between the world wars.

After the outbreak of World War II, Wat was arrested by the Soviet secret police, sent first to the Moscow prison Lubianka, and then to Kazakhstan, where he remained in various prisons and camps until the amnesty of 1941. He returned to Poland in 1946 where he was active in literary life for three years – then withdrew in protest against the political constraints placed on writers. He became increasingly ill, traveled in France and Italy in the hope of improved health, and was invited in 1963 to teach in the Center for Slavic and Eastern European Studies at the University of California at Berkeley. Wat's disappointment in America led CZESLAW MILOSZ to tape a series of conversations in which Wat recounts his experience of and insights into twentieth-century Soviet Communism, *My Century* (1978).

Wat's two volumes of lyric poems, *Poems* (1957) and *Mediterranean Poems* (1962), as well as the posthumous collections *Dark Trinket* (1968) and *With the Skin: Poems* (1989), interweave his long-time illness and suffering, reflections on art and history, and references to the Old Testament, with his poetic vision.

[RD]

Watkins, Vernon (Wales, 1906–1967) Born in Maesteg, the son of a bank manager, Watkins was educated at Repton, and Magdalen College, Cambridge. Dreaming of a poet's life in Italy, he abandoned the academy, only to find himself working for Lloyds Bank in Cardiff. Depressed, Watkins suffered a nervous collapse, but he eventually returned to the bank, remaining in that employment (with the exception of military service) until his retirement.

Watkins described the purpose of poetry as 'the conquest of time', by which he meant both the recovery of childhood bliss and the immortalization of the fleeting moment. His two most successful collections in this regard were *The Lady with the Unicorn* (1948) and *The Death Bell* (1954). A mass of material was published posthumously, including a *Collected Poems* in 1986.

[BS]

Wazyk, Adam (Poland, 1905–82) After studying mathematics at the University of Warsaw and publishing work with new artistic sensibilities, Wazyk became a functionary of the Communist regime and a central theoretician of Socialist realism. However, in 1956, after publishing *Poemat dla doroslych* (*Poem for Adults*) which expressed his disappointments with Communism, Wazyk dropped his political affiliations and pursued literary endeavors, including the writing of an important collection of essays, *Dziwna historia awangardy* (*The Strange History of the Avant-Garde*, 1976).

Influenced early by APOLLINAIRE and Surrealism, Wazyk's best-known poems – published in *Semafory* (*Semaphores*, 1924) and *Oczy i usta* (*Eyes and Lips*, 1926) – reject single-point perspective and chronological order and emphasize instead juxtapositions, employing subconscious leaps and film-like montages. Though anti-traditional, Wazyk's poems attempt faithful presentations of realistic, urban existence and of anti-transcendental experience which dissolves fixed hierarchies of subject and object.

[MT]

Webb, Francis (Australia, 1925–73) Born in Adelaide, Webb grew up with grandparents in Sydney. After a Catholic schooling, he joined the wartime Royal Australian Air Force, completing his training in Canada. After 1942 he published regularly in the *Sydney Bulletin*. Quitting university in 1946, Webb again worked in Canada and visited England, then traveled in Australia from 1950 to 1953. Much of his remaining life was spent in mental hospitals, first in England then, from 1960, mainly in New South Wales.

Webb's style was influenced by Hopkins, ELIOT, HART CRANE, and early LOWELL, and is remarkable for its musicality, rhythmic mastery, and intense power of image-making. The poems are basically religious, but with a broad intellectual and cultural range. Early work often centers on Australian explorer myths; later St Francis, Hitler, Socrates, the painter Anthony Sandys, Bruckner, and numerous others also figure. Many items in *Collected Poems* (1969) are visionary meditations on isolation, pain, and death. 'Around Costessey' shows Webb's painterly love of landscape; 'Ward Two' is a stark, characteristically compassionate observation of life in a Sydney psychiatric hospital. Webb has achieved limited general popularity, but remains an influential and much admired figure among other Australian poets.

[AL]

Webb, Harri (Wales, 1920–95) Born in Swansea and educated at Magdalen College, Oxford, Webb worked as a librarian after World War II. A lifelong Welsh Nationalist and an active member of Plaid Cymru (the Welsh Nationalist Party) from 1959, Webb's verse reflected his politics; many of the poems in *The Green Desert* (1969) and *A Crown for Branwen* (1974) deal with Welsh social history. Webb himself claimed to have 'only one theme', but this self-deprecating description belies his tonal range – he can be extremely funny as well as moving. A prolific journalist and pamphleteer, Webb was associated with Meic Stephens in the 1965 launching of *Poetry Wales*, as well as writing several scripts for television, two collections of ballads, and an adaptation for children of stories from the medieval prose tales known as *The Mabinogion*. His *Collected Poems* appeared in 1995.

[BS]

Wedde, Ian (New Zealand, b. 1946) Born in Blenheim, and educated at the University of Auckland, Wedde spent a great part of his early life traveling in Asia, the Middle East, North Africa, Europe, and North America before he returned home to study and publish. Wedde is active as a novelist, poet, critic, translator, and editor of two anthologies of New Zealand poetry, which include poems in Maori and writings by previously neglected women poets. Wedde won the National Book Award for Poetry (with BILL MANHIRE in 1977) and for fiction (in 1976). He now works as a Concept Curator, Humanities, at the Te Papa Tongarewa, the new National Museum of New Zealand.

Together with Manhire, Alan Brunton, Murray Edmond and Russell Haley, David Mitchell and Bob Orr, Wedde contributed to the Auckland student magazine *Freed*, which encouraged a new kind of New Zealand poetry, 'free' from British models embraced by the previous generation of writers such as ALLEN CURNOW and JAMES K. BAXTER. The influence of experimental, post-war American poetry and the media on this diverse group of poets is strong. Wedde's poetry is influenced especially by WILLIAM CARLOS WILLIAMS and revolves around important events in his life, such as the birth of his first son. His poems investigate the relation between the personal and the political and the possibility of poetry having an impact on broader social issues. His poetry is characterized by a controlled style and an energetic, informal voice.

Selected works: *Homage to Matisse* (1971); *Earthly: Sonnets for Carlos* (1975); *Spells for Coming out* (1977); *Castaly* (1980); *Tales of Gotham City* (1984); *Tendering* (1988); *The Drummer* (1993).

[SH]

Wen Yiduo (Wen Jiahua; China, 1899–1946) Wen, a native of Xishui County, Hubei, was born into the family of a late Qin Dynasty scholar, on November 24, 1899. His father began to teach him classic Chinese poetry when he was five years old. Wen's interest in the Chinese classics never faded. He attended Qinghua University, where he was the student editor of the *Qinghua Weekly*, and *The Journal of Qinghua*. From 1922 to 1925, he studied painting, first in Chicago and then in Colorado. During his stay in the U.S., he met several outstanding poets of the time, including AMY LOWELL. Wen's taste in poetry leaned more toward Shelley, Keats, and Tennyson than the modern, however. Still, he won fame as an eminent modern poet with two collections, *The Red Candle* (1923), and *The Dead Water* (1928). He used the red candle as a symbol to express his cultural nationalism, to lighten up the then economically and politically backward China by burning itself out. In both collections, he superbly gave shape in melodious vernacular Chinese to his unyielding patriotism and sympathy for the Chinese people struggling for independence. The poems in *The Dead Water* are more mature, well-balanced between his strong Confucian sense of public duty and his unconstrained romantic sensitivity. His belief in cultural nationalism – a combination of Confucian doctrines and Western democratic ideas – often brought him into conflict with the authorities over political issues. He was assassinated in Kuming by the Guomindang (The Nationalist Party) on July 15, 1946, after delivering a speech at the Memorial Ceremony for one of his colleagues who had been murdered four days before.

Wen Yiduo taught at a number of universities, and has been held in high esteem not only for his poetic achievement, but for his research on classic Chinese literature as well. He is a recognized authority on many Chinese classics.

[LG]

Weöres, Sándor (Hungary, 1913–88) Born to an estate-holder in Szombathely, Weöres studied law at the University of Pécs, but eschewed that subject in favor of poetry. The time that elapsed between his Baumgarten Prize (1936) and his Kossuth Prize (1970) is some indication of both his enduring power and his roller-coaster career. However, despite his verse's power after World War II, he was out of favor with the Communist regime and was forced to work primarily as a librarian. Once the Communist reign eased, Weöres' poetry once again showed its Modernist power; *A hallgatás tornya* (*The Tower of Silence*, 1956) takes on both Communism and the extreme avant-garde, often by drawing on myth. A great technician and ironist, traveler and translator, Weöres is an important post-war Hungarian poet.

Selected works: *Selected Poems* (trans. MUIR, 1970); *Eternal Moment* (1988).

[MW]

White, Kenneth (Scotland, b. 1936) White was born in Glasgow and studied French and German at Glasgow University, graduating in 1959 and settling in France in 1967. He held lecturing posts at the universities of Bordeaux and Paris VII, interspersed with world travel, until 1983 when he became Professor of Twentieth-Century Poetics at the Sorbonne. He is largely published in France where he is well known as a poet, critic, and translator; he was awarded the Prix Médicis Étranger and the Grand Prix de Rayonnement. Travel, literal and spiritual, pervades his meditative poems, influenced by Chinese and Indian philosophy.

Selected works: *The Cold Wind of Dawn* (1966); *The Most Difficult Area* (1968); *The Bird Path: Collected Longer Poems* (1989); *Handbook for the Diamond Country: Collected Shorter Poems 1960–1990* (1990).

[LKMF]

Wilbur, Richard (United States, b. 1921) Wilbur was born in New York and educated at Amherst and Harvard (M.A., 1947). He served in the Army during World War II, a confrontation with 'the threat of Chaos' which he says prompted him to begin writing poetry. Also a noted translator, Wilbur has won many awards, including two Pulitzer and two Bollingen Prizes. He has taught at Wellesley, Wesleyan, and Smith Colleges, and he served as the second Poet Laureate of the United States.

Wilbur is known for his decorous, meditative lyrics that exude dazzling formal mastery; unlike many poets of his generation, he has almost never departed from the strict meter, rhyme, and stanzaic forms of his earliest work, a determined path that has earned him both praise and criticism. With his air of sophistication and elegance, his playful, ironic wit, and his stubbornly optimistic outlook on the possibilities of transcendence and spirituality in human experience, Wilbur remains highly regarded while standing apart from many of his contemporaries. Poems, for Wilbur, are 'conflicts with disorder', and he resolutely believes that poets can and must create order with their imagination and their metaphors, even if only provisionally. While his poetry shrewdly observes the 'things of this world', and remains deeply connected with sensuous experience, it frequently reaches after visionary truths that lie beyond the physical realm.

Selected works: *The Beautiful Changes* (1946); *Things of this World* (1956); *The Mind-Reader* (1976); *New and Collected Poems* (1988).

[AE]

Williams, C. K. (United States, b. 1936) Since *With Ignorance* (1977), Charles Kenneth Williams has written almost exclusively in long, unrhymed lines that allow him to transcend his topics by affording each detail its own philosophic complexity. In the title poem of *Tar* (1983), he moves from describing the roofing of a house to a consideration of the nearby Three Mile Island disaster, by way of a discussion of heat. Winner of a National Book Critics' Circle Award and the 2000 Pulitzer Prize for *Repair* (1999), Williams teaches one semester each year at George Mason University, and divides his time between the United States and Paris.

[CV]

Williams, Hugo (England, b. 1942) Williams was born in Berkshire and attended Eton College. He was influential in the literary establishment in the late 1960s and early 1970s. In addition to his poetry, Williams is known for his travel journals, *All Over the World* (1966) and *No Particular Place to Go* (1981).

Williams' best-known poetry is influenced and inspired by his world travels and is characterized by a sense of mystery and sentiment. This sentiment sets Williams' work apart from much contemporary English poetry. Williams' early work is rather minimalist; his poems tend to be imagistic and short, utilizing simple and direct language. Williams' later works are longer and more personal in nature. He won the Faber Memorial Prize for *Love-Life* (1979) and in 1980 he won the second prize in the National Poetry Competition for 'Tangerine'.

Selected works: *Symptoms of Loss* (1965); *Sugar Daddy* (1970); *Writing Home* (1985); *Selected Poems* (1989); *Dock Leaves* (1994).

[BB]

Williams, Waldo (Wales, 1904–71) Considered by many to be the twentieth century's most original Welsh poet, Williams was born into an English-speaking home in Haverfordwest, only learning Welsh at the age of seven when his family moved north. His upbringing was radical (his parents were pacifists in World War I) and religious. He experienced mystical revelations in adolescence and these had a profound effect on his work, which can be characterized as Blakean: epiphanic, pantheistic, patriotic but anti-militaristic (Williams was imprisoned twice in the 1960s for withholding income tax in protest against the Korean War). After an extended apprenticeship publishing light verse, Williams' mature style blossomed in a single influential volume, *Dail Pren* (*The Leaves of the Tree*, 1956). *The Peacemakers*, a bilingual selection by Tony Conran, appeared in 1997.

[BS]

Williams, William Carlos (United States, 1883–1963) A medical doctor, Williams has emerged as one of the most influential modern American poets. His work is always written in the idiom of the United States, the conversational speech of that country, without becoming slang; his short lines depict the vigor and energy of American life. At an early age he freed himself from the influence of EZRA POUND, the Imagists, and especially from T. S. ELIOT, with whom Williams' pared-down free verse is in great contrast.

'Emotion', said Williams, 'clusters about common things, the pathetic often stimulates the imagination to new patterns – but the job of the poet is to use language effectively, his own language, the only language which is to him authentic. In my own work, it always sufficed that the object of my attention be presented without further comment.' He also proclaimed, 'No ideas but in things', and in a short, simple poem such as 'The Red Wheel Barrow', in sixteen words he managed to convey a still life, energy momentarily at rest. That poem is also constructed with a painterly attention to detail, each two-line stanza shaped like a wheelbarrow.

Not all Williams' poems are as deceptively simple. His five-volume magnum opus, *Paterson*, is a Modernist fugue of lyrics, newspaper articles, history, and a life in disintegration. Louis Untermeyer spoke of the work as bringing American life into focus 'by his juxtaposition of the exquisite and the crass'.

Williams was born on September 17, 1883 in Rutherford, New Jersey, where he lived all his adult life. His father was born in Birmingham, England, his mother in Mayaguaz, Puerto Rico. Williams went to the Horace Mann High School in New York City; Chateau de Lac near Geneva, Switzerland; and to the University of Pennsylvania, where he took a medical degree in 1906. It was there he first met Pound and H.D. He interned for two years in Manhattan, then took a year of graduate study in pediatrics in Leipzig. His first book, *Poems*, appeared in 1909 when he was twenty-three.

Williams set up private practice in Rutherford and eventually became head pediatrician of the General Hospital in neighboring Paterson. He produced a steady flow of poems, essays, short stories, plays, novels, autobiography, and criticism. *Paterson*, originally published in five separate books between 1946 and 1958, his personal testament, also included excerpts from his correspondence with the young poet ALLEN GINSBERG. Originally, Williams considered *Paterson* to be finished in 1951 – but in 1958 he published a fifth book. Toward the end of 1960 and early in 1961 he was planning a sixth installment, but ill health prevented him from completing the project. He was awarded the Pulitzer Prize posthumously for *Pictures from Brueghel and Other Poems* (1962).

Selected works: *The Collected Poems of William Carlos Williams* (1986); *Paterson* (1963); *In the American Grain* (prose, 1925); *Autobiography* (1951).

[RP]

Wilner, Eleanor (United States, b. 1937) Wilner was born in Cleveland, Ohio, and educated at Goucher College and Johns Hopkins University. The recipient of a MacArthur fellowship, she teaches in the M.F.A. Program for Writers at Warren Wilson College.

A longtime peace and civil rights activist, Wilner seeks to challenge our memory of the past and acceptance of inherited traditions. Integrating lyric and narrative, her poems rewrite myth and history and offer themselves as a lens through which to view the psyche; a similar strategy conflates a particular myth with an event such as the Gulf War's Operation Desert Shield.

Selected works: *Maya* (1979); *Shekhinah* (1984); *Sarah's Choice* (1989); *Otherwise* (1993); *Reversing the Spell* (1998).

[JT]

Wingfield, Sheila (England, 1906–92) Sheila Beddington was born in Hampshire, and received a minimal amount of formal education in Brighton. She married Mervyn Wingfield, ninth Viscount Powerscourt (she sometimes wrote under the pseudonym Sheila Powerscourt), with whom she had three children.

While her work earned her favorable reviews, Wingfield wrote in secret, keeping her work from an uninterested father, and later, a disapproving husband. Upon Mervyn's death in 1973, Wingfield became involved with the literary community, although her new-found connections did not significantly alter her work, which maintained its common themes of history and the folklore of the English and Irish countryside.

Selected works: *Beat Drum, Beat Heart* (1946); *Real People* (1952); *A Kite's Dinner: Poems, 1938–1954* (1954); *Sun Too Fast* (1974); *Admissions: Poems, 1974–77* (1977).

[SG]

Winters, Yvor (United States, 1900–68) Born in Chicago, Winters grew up in Eagle Rock, California. He attended the University of Chicago, but upon contracting tuberculosis, moved to a sanitarium in Santa Fe – after completing only two years of his undergraduate degree. Winters finished his undergraduate degree and earned an M.A. from the University of Colorado in 1925. He pursued further graduate studies and became an influential professor at Stanford, where he taught until he retired in 1966.

Winters' early poems, such as those in his collections *The Bare Hills* (1927) and *The Proof* (1930), express a Modernist's idea of a Transcendental surrender to nature. And yet, during this period Winters' style and focus changed, and he began to espouse traditional rhyme and meters. Often, these works seem uncomfortably moralistic.

Despite numerous awards for poetry, including the 1961 Bollingen Prize for his *Collected Poems* (1952; revised edition, 1960), Winters is best known as a critic and teacher.

[CP]

Wojahn, David (United States, b. 1953) Wojahn's poetry blends the past and the present to achieve a dreamlike relationship with time and a vertical understanding of place. His first book, *Icehouse Lights*, won the Yale Younger Poets Prize in 1982. His most recent, *In the Falling Hour* (1997), is haunted by the loss of his wife, the poet Lynda Hull; the elegies he writes for her and for others focus on the minute – parts of a body, a random statement, background music. Thus Wojahn's almost random details give memory room to improvise against the backdrop of grief.

[CV]

Wondratschek, Wolf (Germany, b. 1943) Influenced by the counterculture movement of the 1960s, Wondratschek emerged as the rock'n'roll poet of the 1970s in two ways. First, from syntax to diction, his poems' linguistic directness is colloquial and terse; some poems are written to be performed as rock songs. Second, similar to commercial rock music, Wondratschek's poetry was a critical and popular success. The publication of a one-volume edition of his previous four collections of poetry, *Chuck's Room: All Poems and Songs* (1981), was advertised with a reminder that these four volumes had already sold a total of over 100,000 copies.

The poetry of the 1970s, in collections such as *Chuck's Room* (1974) and *Her Quiet Laughter in Another Man's Ear* (1976), presented male gender roles and the difficulty of meaningful love relationships in a tone displaying both aggression and feelings of resignation. Beginning in the 1980s, Wondratschek moved to a more traditional evocation of the male macho in collections such as *The Loneliness of Men* (1983).

[IRS]

Wright, Charles (United States, b. 1935) Charles Wright was born in Pickwick Dam, Tennessee, and educated at Davidson College, the University of Iowa, and as a Fulbright fellow at the University of Rome. He teaches at the University of Virginia.

Wright's poetry is distinctive for the luminosity of its images and incantatory lines. Both seem to rise not just organically but inevitably from the poems' content, with its evocation of place and preoccupation with the two-sided phenomenon of recollection and forgetting. His interest in Eastern philosophy has seemed to deepen with each new book. Profoundly influenced by EZRA POUND, Wright has been able to achieve his own relationship with Eastern ideas apart from the Orientalized misconceptions put forth by the Modernists.

Wright has received numerous awards, including the Pulitzer and National Book Critics' Circle Prizes. His critical reputation continues to grow.

Selected works: *Hard Freight* (1973); *Bloodlines* (1975); *The Southern Cross* (1981); *Country Music* (1982); *The Other Side of the River* (1984); *Zone Journals* (1988); *The World of the Ten Thousand Things* (1990); *Chickamauga* (1995).

[JT]

Wright, James (United States, 1927–80) Wright was born in the industrial city of Martins Ferry, Ohio, and grew up in a working-class family. He attended Kenyon College, where he studied with JOHN CROWE RANSOME, and the University of Washington, where he earned a Ph. D. and studied with THEODORE ROETHKE. He taught at the University of Minnesota, and then at Hunter College in New York for many years.

His early work is heavily influenced by THOMAS HARDY, ROBERT FROST, and E.A. ROBINSON, and by the prevailing academic mode of the 1950s; it features an impersonal voice speaking in formal, rhymed, and metered stanzas, expressing tender sympathy for any form of suffering, and identifying with the poor, defeated, and alienated. While Wright grew dissatisfied with this decorous style, his friendship with ROBERT BLY and his experience translating Spanish-American and German poetry sparked a famous stylistic transformation. By combining Surrealistic imagery with a tough, American vernacular voice and free verse form, Wright created an influential new style (often referred to as 'deep image' poetry). This new poetry is more open, personal, and imagistic; still concerned with loneliness and suffering, Wright plumbed the unconscious for strange metaphors, startling juxtapositions, and lyrical epiphanies. Some of Wright's most memorable poems use stark images to convey an isolated speaker's momentary union with a mysterious, beautiful natural world from which he stands estranged.

Selected works: *Saint Judas* (1959); *The Branch Will not Break* (1963); *Above the River: The Complete Poems* (1992).

[AE]

Wright, Jay (United States, b. 1935) Wright was born in Albuquerque, New Mexico, and educated at the University of New Mexico, Berkeley, Rutgers, and Union Theological Seminary.

An African-American who grew up in a culture produced by the co-mingling of Mexican, Native American, and European cultures, Wright is fascinated by ritual and myth-making. Much of his work has dealt with the trans-oceanic ties between cultures, including the U.S., West Africa, and Mexico. Wright is also known for the directness and lyricism of his poetic voice.

Selected works: *The Homecoming Singer* (1971); *Soothsayers and Omens* (1976); *Dimensions of History* (1976); *Explications/Interpretations* (1984); *Boleros* (1991).

[JT]

Wright, Judith (Australia, 1915–2000) Wright is among Australia's most distinguished and popular poets, earning recognition and esteem both for the quality of her poetry and for her conservation work in her native country. Wright's poetry, which now spans a fifty-year literary career, reflects her concern with nature and attempts to bridge the separation between people and the natural world.

Born and raised on a ranch in Armidale, New South Wales, Wright attended the University of Sydney, spent a year in Europe, and later worked as a part-time lecturer in Australian literature at numerous Australian universities. She founded and served as president of the Wildlife Preservation Society of Queensland from 1962 to 1974, and was a member of the Aboriginal Treaty Committee in 1978–83. Although she has received honorary doctorates from numerous Australian universities, Wright chose to remain a countrywoman rather than pursue a professorship. A prolific author, Wright's work includes juvenile books, novels, criticism, and short stories, in addition to the many books of poetry for which she is best known.

Wright's poetry contains a strong sense of time and place, confronting contemporary issues in her native country, particularly white Australians' treatment of Aboriginals and their land. In her later work, Wright expresses growing anger at exploitive abuses of her homeland and its indigenous people, abuses that she believes will be catastrophic for the perpetrators as well as their victims. Wright's poetry, though thought-provoking, is not propaganda. Her lush poems are filled with vivid imagery that relates the natural cycle of creation and rebirth, exploring the human connection to nature and the manner in which that connection is challenged by 'development'.

Wright, who was awarded the Queen's Medal for Poetry in 1992, is technically capable of a variety of forms. Her poems move fluidly from personal to social issues and from nature to politics. *Birds* (1962) is a lightweight book in which Wright expresses her love of nature. *The Other Half* (1966) marks a change in tone, as Wright grows increasingly displeased with the ruination of her native land. *The Coral Battleground* (1977), one of her most political works, is a passionate argument for defense of Queensland's Great Barrier Reef from oil and mining companies. More recent works continue to push for conservation, while also focusing on subjects such as the complexities of human relationships.

Selected works: *The Moving Image* (1946); *Woman to Man* (1949); *The Two Fires* (1955); *Birds* (1962); *Five Senses: Selected Poems* (1963); *The Other Half* (1966); *Collected Poems* (1971); *The Double Tree: Selected Poems* (1978); *Phantom Dwelling* (1985); *A Human Pattern* (1992); *The Flame Tree* (1994); *Collected Poems, 1942–1985* (1994).

[LK]

Wylie, Elinor (United States, 1885–1928) Born in Somerville, New Jersey, Wylie grew up in Washington, D.C., where her father served as Solicitor-General of the U.S. When she was seventeen she went to Europe to study art until 1915, living primarily in England, where her first collection of verse, *Incidental Numbers* (1912), was privately published. Her second collection, *Nets to Catch the Wind*, appeared in 1921 and demonstrated a significant advance from her often sentimental earlier work.

Intensely emotional yet highly controlled, Wylie's work has received little critical attention since her death. Her strongest work, such as the sequence of love sonnets 'One Person', is both lyric and concise, but much of her poetry seems dated and conventional to modern readers.

Selected works: *The Orphan Angel* (novel, 1926; U.K. title *Mortal Image*, 1927); *Collected Poems* (1932); *Collected Prose* (1933); *Last Poems* (1942).

[JDS]

X

Xu Zhimo (China, 1897–1937) Xu, poet and essayist, was born into an affluent family of bankers in Haining, Zhejing. In his short life, Xu was spared the financial problems which his contemporary Chinese writers often experienced. In 1918, his father sent him to the United States to study banking, but he soon developed a strong interest in poetry, and an even stronger interest in the patriotic enthusiasm demonstrated by the Chinese youth during the May Fourth Movement. He discontinued his studies and returned to China in 1919. In the spring of 1921, his father sent him to Cambridge University to study economics, but nineteenth-century British poetry occupied all his time and energy. Xu began to write poems during his stay in Britain, and began to publish poems and essays in 1922 upon his return to China. They instantly won him fame.

Xu's early lyrics are short, emotionally powerful, usually enhanced by a haunting rhythm, and enforced by a witty syntax and burning enthusiasm. *The Tiger*, his first collection of poems, brilliantly expresses his romantic sensitivity, untamed passions, and youthful idealism. It was not long before his poetry changed dramatically: his unconstrained idealism was replaced by a strong sense of loss, frustration, and grief. Meanwhile, he wrote a number of essays, commenting on the social, political, and literary issues in a unique rhetoric rarely surpassed in modern Chinese writing. Pompous, ironical, emotional, and pungent, these essays were controversial in his day but enjoy great popularity with readers now.

Xu, as he admitted, was an 'unteachable individual', who lived by nothing but his own ideals. He divorced the wife his parents had arranged for him but kept in close touch with her, while having a tempestuous affair with the wife of a high-ranking army officer, a situation really unconventional in his day. He taught in a number of universities, including Beijing University. He died in a plane crash on November 19, 1937. His tragic death was mourned nationwide.

[LG]

Y

Yang Lian (China, b. 1955) One of the leading contemporary poets, Yang was born in Beijing. After graduation from high school, he was sent to settle in the countryside for a few years. He later returned to Beijing and now works in the Writing Workshop as a professional writer in the Art Ensemble of the Central Broadcasting Company. Yang began to publish poems in the later 1970s. His well-known poems include 'The New Sun Each Day', 'Tibet', 'The Soul of Rituals', 'The Dead', and the multi-sectioned 'Dunhuang'. Yang figures as a prominent Chinese Western poet, who successfully represents the unique Western wilderness not only through a fresh, bold, and typical Western imagery highly charged with cultural undertones, but also through a modernist perspective which moves the Chinese verse tradition toward a new height. His most successful endeavor in this regard is seen in his masterpiece *Nuorilong* (1986), a poem which, in its dense and radical imagistic representation of Tibetan Buddhism, stirred the usually quiet Chinese literary arena almost to a boil.

[GL]

Yeats, William Butler (Ireland, 1865–1939) Yeats is one of the finest, most influential poets of the twentieth century, a towering figure in both Irish and world poetry. His work, spanning six decades and straddling Romanticism and Modernism, evolves and matures but remains rooted in well-defined themes: Ireland, spirituality, and aesthetics.

The son of painter John Butler Yeats, W.B. Yeats spent his childhood in Dublin and London, with family holidays in County Sligo, Ireland, where he developed a passion for the Irish landscape and an interest in Irish mythology and legend. Settling in Dublin in the 1890s, Yeats became a founding member of the Irish Literary Renaissance, which set out to define 'Irishness'. With Lady Gregory, John Synge, AE, and George Moore, Yeats used Celtic myth, folklore, and landscape to create a literature separate and distinct from the British tradition. Yeats evokes this Celtic mysticism and myth in such early volumes as *The Wind among the Reeds* (1899) and *In the Seven Woods* (1904). As a founder of the Abbey Theatre, Yeats also wrote many plays, including *Cathleen Ni Houlihan* (1902).

In his early twenties, Yeats fell in love with Maud Gonne, a beautiful, strong-willed Irish nationalist who encouraged his involvement in Irish politics. It is about Gonne that most of Yeats's love poems are written, notably 'Words' and 'No Second Troy' in *The Green Helmet and Other Poems* (1910). Yet, as Yeats became disillusioned with Irish politics, the Gaelic peasantry, and Gonne herself (who married patriot Sean McBride in

1903), his poetry shifted from dreamy, romantic verse to a colder, purer, and more mature style. *Responsibilities* (1914) shows this sloughing off of Celtic mythologies and the development and exploration of contemporary images and themes, including his own bitterness. In *The Wild Swans at Coole* (1919), Yeats expressed his growing admiration for the Anglo-Irish ascendency. Indeed, as Ireland was torn apart by Civil War, Yeats retreated further from his earlier nationalism, although he never abandoned his passion for Ireland. In *Michael Robartes and the Dancer* (1921), 'Easter, 1916' memorializes those executed after the Easter Rising and the 'terrible beauty' born of history's nightmare. In 1922, Yeats was elected to the Senate of the Irish Free State.

Yeats married Georgie Hyde Lees in 1917 and physically withdrew to Thoor Ballylee, an ancient stone tower, where the couple raised their two children. Having long nurtured an interest in mysticism and the occult, Yeats wrote *A Vision* (1925), an exposition of his own mythology, presenting history as a series of cycles or 'gyres', which correspond to personal or individual patterns of self. Many of Yeats' later poems utilize this complex, esoteric system, though familiarity with *A Vision* is not essential to understanding the work.

The poems in *The Tower* (1928) and *The Winding Stair* (1933) – 'Sailing to Byzantium', 'Leda and the Swan', 'Among School Children', and the Crazy Jane poems – deal with the cycles of history, myth-making, and the artist's relationship between reality and beauty and are among Yeats's finest. In later years, Yeats continued to write masterful lyrics, including 'Lapis Lazuli' and 'Under Ben Bulben', which deal with aging and look back on his earlier work with sagacious self-scrutiny.

Yeats was awarded the Nobel Prize for Literature in 1923.

[CT]

Yevtushenko, Yevgenii Aleksandrovich (Russia, b. 1933) Born in Irkutsk, Yevtushenko was raised and educated in Moscow. Unlike his contemporary VOZNESENSKY, the prolific Yevtushenko's poetic style is conventional, though popular. His reputation was particularly enhanced after the publication of 'Babi Yar' (1961) and 'Nasledniki Stalina' ('The Heirs of Stalin,' 1962), poems so critical of Soviet society and government that they were then taken out of print until the 1980s. Despite this censure, Yevtushenko became a member of the Presidium of the USSR Writers' Union in 1967. Over the next two decades he published several important collections of lyrics, including *Idet bely sneg* (*Snow is Falling*, 1969), *Ottsovskii slukh* (*Paternal Rumor*, 1975) and *Tochka opory* (*Fulcrum*, 1981). After Gorbachev's era, Yevtushenko's poetic activities decreased as his national and international involvement in other artistic activities increased.

Selected works: *Razvedchiki gryadushchego* (*Scouts of the Future*, 1952); *Tretii sneg* (*Third Snow*, 1955); *Ia sibirskoi porody* (*I am of Siberian Stock*, 1971); *Tochka opory* (*Fulcrum*, 1981).

[RN]

Yosano Akiko (Japan, 1878–1941) Yosano was born in Sakai just south of Osaka, the third daughter of a merchant. At an early age she acquired a thorough knowledge of the classics of Japanese literature and became acquainted with the new literary movement. In 1900 she submitted some of her poems in *tanka* form to *Myojo*, the literary magazine headed by Yosano Hiroshi. She later met him and the acquaintance grew into a romance; the following year she ran away from home, went to Tokyo, and married him. Around this period she was extremely active in the pages of *Myojo*, and the publication of her first collection of poems, entitled *Midaregami* (*Tangled Hair*, 1901), attracted widespread attention. In the works *Koogi*, *Dokuso*, *Koigoromo*, and *Maihime*, published from 1904 to 1906, she continued to develop and bring to maturity her own special literary talent. Romantic love and human passions were the major subjects of her poetry.

Turning her attention to fiction, she also produced modern language versions of such early classics as *The Tale of Genji*. Her social criticism, contained in both poetry and prose, was consistently humanistic. As an active critic, she involved herself particularly with questions relating to women. She also helped found a woman's college called Bunka Gakuin, which laid emphasis upon education in the arts.

The collection of poems entitled *Hakuohsu*, published posthumously, dealt with her emotional life in the years following the death of her husband in 1935. Her poetry, filled with sensual passion and vivid imagination, opened the way for the modernization of the *tanka* and her highly literary achievement signaled a new era in Meiji period romanticism.

[LY]

Young, Andrew (Scotland, 1885–1971) Young was born in Elgin, educated at Edinburgh University and the Presbyterian New College, and ordained a minister of the United Free Church in 1912. He married Janet Green in 1914; six years later he was appointed to the English Presbyterian Church at Hove, Sussex. He later joined the Anglican church and became vicar of Stonegate, Sussex, retiring in 1959 to Yapton near Chichester. As well as poems about his twin passions, nature and religion, he wrote an account of the poetry, folklore, and natural history of Britain, *The Poets and the Landscape* (1962).

Selected works: *Songs of Night* (1910); *Boaz and Ruth* (1920); *Winter Harvest* (1933); *The White Blackbird* (1935); *Speak to the Earth* (1939); *Out of the World and Back* (1958); *Quiet as Moss* (1959).

[LKMF]

Young Bear, Ray (Anthony Young Bear; United States, b. 1950) Young Bear was born in Marshalltown, Iowa, a few miles west of Tama, the location of the Mesquakie Tribal Settlement which is his family home. Educated at Claremont College, Grinnell College, the University of Iowa, Iowa State, and Northern Iowa University, Young Bear has held visiting positions at Eastern Washington University and the University of Iowa.

Young Bear's poetry, he has said, comes from his desire to transmit his Native voice as it arises from his tribal language and music. His writing in English reserves a translated quality that can create a surreal, dreamy, and evocative mix of image and syntax. At times, Young Bear puts a collective persona to use in poems, a persona that speaks to us from his ancestors. At other times, the voice is that of a Vietnam veteran trying to make real an experience that does not easily connect with tribal reality. Often anthologized and critically acclaimed, Young Bear's complex and lovely poetry is collected in two volumes, *Winter of the Salamander* (1980) and *The Invisible Musician* (1989).

[HEE]

Yu Guangzhong (Taiwan, b. 1928) Poet, essayist, and scholar, Yu, a native of Yongchun, Fujian, China, graduated from Taiwan State University in 1950. His first book of poetry, *Threnodies of Seamen* (1952), received immediate attention from critics. As a translator, editor, and professor of English, Yu has made a great contribution to the introduction of Western literature, particularly American literature, in Taiwan. Besides being a well-recognized scholar of Western literature, Yu is well-versed in Chinese classics as well. He has been visiting professor since the early 1960s at over a dozen universities in the U.S. to teach Chinese literature. As a poet, Yu has enjoyed an envious reputation in the Chinese-speaking world. He has been considered by some as one of the finest contemporary Chinese poets, who preserves the best elements of the classic Chinese tradition within a cosmopolitan context. Nevertheless, others argue against his admirable efforts in preservation, and regard him as a conservative poet, claiming that Yu's modernity is only embodied in his techniques. His major books of poetry include *The Blue Feather* (1954), *The Halloween* (1964), and *Associations of the Lotus Flower* (1967).

[LG]

Z

Zabolotsky, Nikolai Alekseevich (Russia, 1903–58) A seminal Russian modernist, Zabolotsky was a founding member of the absurdist group, OBERIU; he published his first, best book of verse, *Stolbtsy* (*Columns*, 1929) – a grotesque description of Leningrad life under the New Economic Program – one year after the group's founding. Sensing an artistic affinity, Samuel Marshak asked the OBERIU poets to write for his children's magazines, *Eizh* and *Chizh*; Zabolotsky also wrote and translated for *Detgiz*, the Publishing House for Children. His *Second Book of Verse* appeared in 1937.

Unwilling to adapt to social realism, Zabolotsky was persecuted by Soviet authorities before the *Second Book*; after it, he was deemed 'out of step with Soviet psychology' and sent to a labor camp in 1938. Released in 1946 but banned from Leningrad and Moscow, Zabolotsky settled in a small town and began to translate the medieval poem *Slovo o polku Igoreve* (*The Lay of Igor's Campaign*) and publish occasional poems of his own. Though most of his post-camp poetry appeared posthumously, he did have a coterie of international admirers. Generally underrated and frequently mocked during his lifetime, today Zabolotsky is recognized as one of the most talented and most important Russian poets of the late Modernism.

[RN]

Zach, Nathan (Israel, b. 1930) Born in Berlin in 1930, Zach and his family emmigrated to the Land of Israel in 1936. In poems and essays he led the Modernist movement in Hebrew poetry of the 1950s, challenging the dominance and poetic value of the 'state generation' of poets such as NATHAN ALTERMAN, and paving the way to poetry devoid of sentimentalism, formalized language, and excessive lyricism. Zach's poetry is direct and economical, often resorting to irony and colloquialisms, with strong emphasis on the human experience and individual meditation. Zach has a Doctoral degree from the University of Essex, and has held editorial and academic positions. He translated works of BRECHT, Dürrenmatt, and others, and was the recipient of the Bialik Prize for Literature (1989). His initial poetry collection, *First Poems*, came out in 1955, and his most recent collection, *Because I Am Around*, in 1996. Translated poems have been published in English, including 'Against Printing' (1967) and 'The Static Element' (1982); his work has also been translated into French and German.

[ER]

Zagajewski, Adam (Poland, b. 1945) Zagajewski was born in Lvov in the first year of the Soviet occupation of Poland. His family soon moved to the industrial city of Gliwice. Zagajewski studied psychology and philology at Jagiellonian University, and became the most prominent representative of the Generation of '68. With JULIAN KORNHAUSER, he published a collection of sketches, *A World Not Introduced* (1974), regarded as the manifesto of the New Wave poetic movement which opposed the official language of Communist ideology and called instead for a truthful, sanctified use of language. In a second collection of sketches, *Second Breath* (1978), he confronted the attitudes of older Polish writers – such as ZBIGNIEW HERBERT and TADEUSZ ROZEWICZ – whom the younger generation accused of ignoring the problems of contemporary Poland in favor of a more isolated, contemplative life.

Zagajewski's first two collections of poems, *Bulletin* (1972) and *Meat Market* (1975), emerge out of the generational conflict of the New Wave movement, whereas his later poetry, beginning with *Letter: Ode to Quantity* (1982), is more meditative – examining poetry's sacred origins and the threat posed to art and to our lives by totalitarian culture. The mature poet argues that the best defense against collectivism is creative individualism and meditative solitude, rather than forced solidarity and subservience to a cause. In his newest collection, *Mysticism for Beginners* (1997), the poems – increasingly lyrical and personal in tone – abound in particularly heightened moments of 'sensual and cerebral ecstasy', posited against the 'mere repetition and accumulation of experience' (Jaroslaw Anders).

Since 1982 Zagajewski has lived in Paris with his wife and daughter, and he has taught each spring since 1989 in the University of Houston Creative Writing Program.

Selected works: *Hot, Cold* (1975); *The Thin Line* (1983); *Tremor: Selected Poems* (1985); *Solidarity, Solitude* (1990); *Canvas* (1991); *Two Cities* (1995); *Mysticism for Beginners* (1997).

[RD]

Zanzotto, Andrea (Italy, b. 1921) Zanzotto was born in Pieve di Soligo, in the Veneto region where he still lives. In his first collections, Zanzotto displayed a turgid style and an intentionally rich, at times even baroque, language which soon became the mark of his unique poetry. To these features he soon added a carefully orchestrated linguistic pastiche in which the highest literary tradition clashes with the most stereotypical language borrowed from mass media and pop culture. The result is an explosive, tragic and satirical portrayal of a self incapable of establishing actual communication with the world, or even of asserting its own existence by means of words.

Selected works: *Dietro il Paesaggio* (*Behind the Landscape*, 1951); *IX Ecloghe* (*Nine Eclogues*, 1962); *Pasque* (*Easters*, 1973); *Fosfeni* (*Phosmenes*, 1983); *Fantasie di avvicinamento* (*Fantasies of the Approach*, 1991); *Meteo* (1996).

[GS]

Zaturenska, Marya Alexandrovna (United States, 1902–82) Zaturenska is one of the most exquisite lyric poets of her generation. For its formal precision and lyric intensity, her work can be compared favorably with that of EDNA ST VINCENT MILLAY, LOUISE BOGAN, and ELINOR WYLIE. Zaturenska's first book, *Threshold and Hearth*, appeared when she was thirty-two and won the Shelley Memorial Award. Her second, *Cold Morning Sky* (1937), won the Pulitzer Prize. Her last collection, *The Hidden Waterfall*, appeared in 1974, when the poet was in her seventies, and showed no flagging of ability.

Zaturenska was born in Kiev, Russia. Her maternal family was Polish, and as a young girl she learned Polish and Russian folksongs. The family moved to New York City in 1909, when she was eight. She received scholarships to Valparaiso University and graduated from the University of Wisconsin Library School in 1925. She married the poet Horace Gregory and they had two children. For decades they lived in a pre-Colonial cottage in Palisades, New York.

Selected works: *Collected Poems* (1960); *The Hidden Waterfall* (1974).

[RP]

Zephaniah, Benjamin (England, b. 1958) Benjamin Obadiah Iqbal Zephaniah was born in Birmingham, raised in Jamaica, and spent his early teens in school in England. Zephaniah began his career as a performance poet (see LINTON KWESI JOHNSON, MERLE COLLINS).

Zephaniah's poetry addresses a multitude of cultural and political issues, paying special attention to questions of racism and classism. His interests are clearly global: in a single collection his voice stretches from London to El Salvador to China, with many other stops along the way. His cultural readings range from machismo to rap music to the royal family in Britain. Much of his work is an attempt to popularize poetry and make it accessible to people of all classes.

In addition to his work as a poet, Zephaniah is an accomplished playwright; he won the BBC Young Playwrights Festival Award in 1988 for *Hurrican Dub*. Having been a writer-in-residence in Liverpool and chair of the Hackney Empire Theatre, Zephaniah has also been nominated for the prestigious Professorship of Poetry at Oxford. He currently lives and writes in London.

Selected works: *Rasta Time in Palestine* (1990); *City Psalms* (1992); *Propa Propaganda* (1996).

[BB]

Zimunya, Musaemura Bonas (Zimbabwe, b. 1949) Zimbabwe's most accomplished English-language poet, Zimunya is less well-known than his contemporaries CHENJERAI HOVE and DAMBUDZO MARECHERA, perhaps because poetry is his primary genre. Born in communal land near Mutare, Zimunya was educated at Munyarari School, Chikore Secondary School, Goromonzi High School, and the (then) University of Rhodesia. His early poetry appeared in local magazines such as *Chirimo*, *Two Tone*, and *Rhodesian Poetry*, the South African magazine *New Coin*, and Chinua Achebe's *Okike*. In 1972, he was on the editing committee of the Goromonzi school magazine, published by the country's first secondary school for Africans. Imprisoned following a student protest in 1975, he went to England to finish his degree. In 1978, the year he received his B.A., his poetry appeared in an anthology, *Zimbabwean Poetry in English*. He went on to receive advanced degrees in English literature at the University of Kent and published *Zimbabwe Ruins* (1979) while there. After Zimbabwean independence in 1980, Zimunya returned to edit *And Now the Poets Speak* (with Mudereri Kadhani, 1981), which contains thirteen of his own poems. He then published four books of poetry: *Kingfisher, Jikinya and Other Poems* (1982), *Thought-tracks* (1982), *Country Dawns and City Lights* (1985), and *Perfect Poise and Other Poems* (1993). He has become a prolific editor of African poetry anthologies, including one in Shona; most of them contain some of his own work. He is now a Senior Lecturer in English at the University of Zimbabwe.

Selected works: *Chakarira Chindunduma* (ed., *Rebellion Sounds*, 1985); *Samora! Tribute to a Revolutionary* (ed. with Chenjerai Hove and Gibson Mandishona, 1986); *Birthright: A Selection of Poems from Southern Africa* (ed., 1989); *The Fate of Vultures: New Poetry of Africa* (ed. with Kofi Anyidoho and PETER PORTER, 1989).

[KT]

Zukofsky, Louis (United States, 1904–78) The son of immigrant Russian Jews, Zukofsky was born in New York City and he remained throughout his life a New York City poet by inclination and subject.

After entering Columbia University at age sixteen, Zukofsky's poetic career blossomed when EZRA POUND asked him in

1928 to edit a special issue of *Poetry on the Objectivists* – a group of mostly New York City poets who adhered to 'direct treatment of the thing' and considered the poem an object with historical significance.

The inter-connection of poetry and history fueled Zukofsky's political consciousness, and throughout the 1930s he participated in left-wing activities and described himself as a Communist. These political ideas found their way into Zukofsky's epic poem, *A*, which is organized around Bach's 'The Passion According to St Matthew' as well as ideas from Henry Adams and Karl Marx.

In 1939, Zukofsky's poetry shifted from the political to the familial. In that year he married Celia Thaew, a musician and composer he had met in 1933, and they had a son, Paul, who became a concert violinist. The demands of the family left little time for writing, and the writing that did take place bears the stamp of domestic life.

The 1960s and 1970s brought Zukofsky some recognition as poets such as ROBERT DUNCAN and ROBERT CREELEY spoke of their admiration for him and the influential scholar Hugh Kenner began to champion Zukofsky's writing. Zukofsky's posthumous reputation has enjoyed a brief surge, perhaps related to the academic favor granted the avant-garde.

Selected works: *A* (1993); *Complete Short Poetry* (1997).

[DC]

Zwicky, Fay (Australia, b. 1933) Zwicky was born in Melbourne and lives in Perth. She began writing as a student at the University of Melbourne. She worked as a concert pianist before teaching English at the University of Western Australia from 1972 until 1987. She has written poetry, essays, and short stories, and is also well-known as a literary critic. She edited *Quarry* (1981), a selection of poems written by Western Australians, as well as *Journeys* (1982) and an anthology of poems by ROSEMARY DOBSON, GWEN HARWOOD, DOROTHY HEWETT, and JUDITH WRIGHT.

Zwicky's poetry reflects on various aspects of contemporary life. It seeks to challenge patriarchal oppression of women's voices and experiences. At home in various modes, Zwicky's poetry ranges from the satirical and parodic to the elegiac.

Selected works: *Isaac Babel's Fiddle* (1975); *Kaddish and Other Poems* (1982); *The Lyre in the Pawn-shop* (essays) (1986); *Procession* (1987); *Ask Me* (1990); *A Touch of Ginger* (1991); *Poems 1970–92* (1993); *The Gatekeeper's Wife* (1997).

[AP]